T0351819

Measuring and Accounting for Innovation in the Twenty-First Century

Studies in Income and Wealth,
Volume 78

NATIONAL BUREAU *of*
ECONOMIC RESEARCH

Measuring and Accounting for Innovation in the Twenty-First Century

Edited by   **Carol Corrado, Jonathan Haskel, Javier Miranda, and Daniel Sichel**

The University of Chicago Press

Chicago and London

The University of Chicago Press, Chicago 60637
The University of Chicago Press, Ltd., London
© 2021 by National Bureau of Economic Research
Published 2021
Printed in the United States of America

30 29 28 27 26 25 24 23 22 21   1 2 3 4 5

ISBN-13: 978-0-226-72817-9   (cloth)
ISBN-13: 978-0-226-72820-9   (e-book)
DOI: https://doi.org/10.7208/chicago/9780226728209.001.0001

Library of Congress Cataloging-in-Publication Data

Names: Corrado, Carol, editor. | Haskel, Jonathan, editor. |
    Miranda, Javier (Economist), editor. | Sichel, Daniel E., editor.
Title: Measuring and accounting for innovation in the twenty-first
    century / edited by Carol Corrado, Jonathan Haskel, Javier Miranda,
    and Daniel Sichel.
Other titles: Studies in income and wealth.
Description: Chicago : University of Chicago Press, 2021. | Series:
    NBER studies in income and wealth | "This volume contains revised
    versions of the papers presented at the Conference on Research
    in Income and Wealth entitled "Measuring and Accounting for
    Innovation in the 21st Century," held in Washington, DC, on March
    10–11, 2017"—Acknowledgments. | Includes bibliographical
    references and index.
Identifiers: LCCN 2020047087 | ISBN 9780226728179 (cloth) |
    ISBN 9780226728209 (ebook)
Subjects: LCSH: Industrial productivity—Measurement—
    Congresses. | Economics—Technological innovations—Congresses. |
    Evaluation—Congresses.
Classification: LCC HD56.25 .M4366 2021 | DDC 338/.064072—dc23
LC record available at https://lccn.loc.gov/2020047087

♾ This paper meets the requirements of ANSI/NISO Z39.48-1992
(Permanence of Paper).

Relation of the Directors to the Work and Publications of the NBER

1. The object of the NBER is to ascertain and present to the economics profession, and to the public more generally, important economic facts and their interpretation in a scientific manner without policy recommendations. The Board of Directors is charged with the responsibility of ensuring that the work of the NBER is carried on in strict conformity with this object.

2. The President shall establish an internal review process to ensure that book manuscripts proposed for publication DO NOT contain policy recommendations. This shall apply both to the proceedings of conferences and to manuscripts by a single author or by one or more co-authors but shall not apply to authors of comments at NBER conferences who are not NBER affiliates.

3. No book manuscript reporting research shall be published by the NBER until the President has sent to each member of the Board a notice that a manuscript is recommended for publication and that in the President's opinion it is suitable for publication in accordance with the above principles of the NBER. Such notification will include a table of contents and an abstract or summary of the manuscript's content, a list of contributors if applicable, and a response form for use by Directors who desire a copy of the manuscript for review. Each manuscript shall contain a summary drawing attention to the nature and treatment of the problem studied and the main conclusions reached.

4. No volume shall be published until forty-five days have elapsed from the above notification of intention to publish it. During this period a copy shall be sent to any Director requesting it, and if any Director objects to publication on the grounds that the manuscript contains policy recommendations, the objection will be presented to the author(s) or editor(s). In case of dispute, all members of the Board shall be notified, and the President shall appoint an ad hoc committee of the Board to decide the matter; thirty days additional shall be granted for this purpose.

5. The President shall present annually to the Board a report describing the internal manuscript review process, any objections made by Directors before publication or by anyone after publication, any disputes about such matters, and how they were handled.

6. Publications of the NBER issued for informational purposes concerning the work of the Bureau, or issued to inform the public of the activities at the Bureau, including but not limited to the NBER Digest and Reporter, shall be consistent with the object stated in paragraph 1. They shall contain a specific disclaimer noting that they have not passed through the review procedures required in this resolution. The Executive Committee of the Board is charged with the review of all such publications from time to time.

7. NBER working papers and manuscripts distributed on the Bureau's web site are not deemed to be publications for the purpose of this resolution, but they shall be consistent with the object stated in paragraph 1. Working papers shall contain a specific disclaimer noting that they have not passed through the review procedures required in this resolution. The NBER's web site shall contain a similar disclaimer. The President shall establish an internal review process to ensure that the working papers and the web site do not contain policy recommendations, and shall report annually to the Board on this process and any concerns raised in connection with it.

8. Unless otherwise determined by the Board or exempted by the terms of paragraphs 6 and 7, a copy of this resolution shall be printed in each NBER publication as described in paragraph 2 above.

Contents

Prefatory Note   xi

Introduction   1
Carol Corrado, Jonathan Haskel,
Javier Miranda, and Daniel Sichel

I. EXPANDING CURRENT MEASUREMENT FRAMEWORKS

1. **Expanded GDP for Welfare Measurement in
   the Twenty-First Century**   19
   Charles Hulten and Leonard I. Nakamura

2. **Measuring the Impact of Household Innovation
   Using Administrative Data**   61
   Javier Miranda and Nikolas Zolas

3. **Innovation, Productivity Dispersion, and
   Productivity Growth**   103
   Lucia Foster, Cheryl Grim, John C. Haltiwanger,
   and Zoltan Wolf

II. NEW APPROACHES AND DATA

4. **How Innovative Are Innovations?
   A Multidimensional, Survey-Based Approach**   139
   Wesley M. Cohen, You-Na Lee,
   and John P. Walsh

5. **An Anatomy of US Firms Seeking**
   Trademark Registration   183
   Emin M. Dinlersoz, Nathan Goldschlag,
   Amanda Myers, and Nikolas Zolas

6. **Research Experience as Human Capital in**
   New Business Outcomes   229
   Nathan Goldschlag, Ron Jarmin, Julia Lane,
   and Nikolas Zolas

III. Changing Structure of the Economy

7. **Measuring the Gig Economy: Current**
   Knowledge and Open Issues   257
   Katharine G. Abraham, John C. Haltiwanger,
   Kristin Sandusky, and James R. Spletzer

8. **Information and Communications Technology,**
   R&D, and Organizational Innovation:
   Exploring Complementarities in Investment
   and Production   299
   Pierre Mohnen, Michael Polder,
   and George van Leeuwen

9. **Digital Innovation and the Distribution**
   of Income   323
   Dominique Guellec

IV. Improving Current Measurement Frameworks

10. **Factor Incomes in Global Value Chains:**
    The Role of Intangibles   373
    Wen Chen, Bart Los, and Marcel P. Timmer

11. **Measuring Moore's Law: Evidence from Price,**
    Cost, and Quality Indexes   403
    Kenneth Flamm

12. **Accounting for Innovations in Consumer Digital**
    Services: IT Still Matters   471
    David Byrne and Carol Corrado

13. **The Rise of Cloud Computing: Minding Your Ps,**
    Qs, and Ks   519
    David Byrne, Carol Corrado, and Daniel Sichel

14. BEA Deflators for Information and Communications Technology Goods and Services: Historical Analysis and Future Plans   553
Erich H. Strassner and David B. Wasshausen

Contributors   573
Author Index   577
Subject Index   585

Prefactory Note

This volume contains revised versions of the papers presented at the Conference on Research in Income and Wealth entitled "Measuring and Accounting for Innovation in the 21st Century," held in Washington, DC, on March 10–11, 2017.

Support for the general activities of the Conference on Research in Income and Wealth is provided by the following agencies: the Bureau of Economic Analysis, the Bureau of Labor Statistics, the Census Bureau, the Board of Governors of the Federal Reserve System, the Statistics of Income/Internal Revenue Service, and Statistics Canada.

We thank Carol Corrado, Javier Miranda, Jonathan Haskel, and Daniel Sichel, who served as conference organizers and as editors of the volume.

Introduction

Carol Corrado, Jonathan Haskel, Javier Miranda,
and Daniel Sichel

The National Income and Product Accounts and other economic statistics—designed in an age when the structure of the economy was vastly different than that of today—do not yet fully account for the wide range of innovative activities that are plainly evident in everyday experience. This limitation of our existing measurement system significantly hinders researchers, analysts, and policy makers. Better measures of innovative activity are necessary to understand the challenges and consequences of innovation and to inform the design of policies that best promote it.

In March 2017, the Conference on Research in Income and Wealth (CRIW) of the National Bureau of Economic Research (NBER) held a conference at the McDonough School of Business at Georgetown University in Washington, DC. The purpose of this conference was to bring together academic researchers, staff from the statistical agencies, and members of the broader community studying and assessing innovation to advance the agenda of more completely and systematically accounting for innovative activity in national accounts and other economic statistics. This volume includes most of the papers presented at the conference. The papers have

Carol Corrado is senior advisor and research director in economics at the Conference Board and a senior policy scholar at the Center for Business and Public Policy, McDonough School of Business, Georgetown University.

Jonathan Haskel is professor of economics at Imperial College Business School, Imperial College London, and director of the doctoral program at the school.

Javier Miranda is a principal economist at the US Census Bureau.

Daniel Sichel is professor of economics at Wellesley College and a research associate of the National Bureau of Economic Research.

For acknowledgments, sources of research support, and disclosure of the authors' material financial relationships, if any, please see https://www.nber.org/books-and-chapters/measuring-and-accounting-innovation-21st-century/introduction-measuring-and-accounting-innovation-21st-century.

undergone review and, in some cases, substantial revision since their presentation at the conference. These revisions importantly reflect the excellent comments provided by discussants at the conference and two anonymous reviewers of the volume.

Before getting to a summary of the conference, the conference organizers and attendees would like to thank those who made the conference a success and the NBER/CRIW volume possible: the NBER and CRIW for financial support, Georgetown University's McDonough School of Business for hosting the conference, and NBER staff, especially Helena Fitz-Patrick for crucial assistance in compiling this volume and Brett Maranjian for exceptional organizational and logistical support.

I.1   Background

This conference and volume focus primarily on the challenges of how best to measure innovation, track its effects on economic activity and inflation, and understand how innovation has changed the structure of an increasingly digitized economy. At the same time, the chapters also relate to challenges of economic measurement that long have been the subject of CRIW conferences.

Measuring innovation is a challenging task, both for researchers and for national statisticians. One approach statisticians use is to conduct a survey that measures innovation, and an international consensus has developed a manual and definition of innovation for this purpose. Published as the "Oslo Manual" (OECD/Eurostat 2018), *innovation* is defined as "a product or process (or combination thereof) that differs significantly from the unit's previous products or processes and that has been made available to potential users (product) or brought into use by the unit (process)." This definition distinguishes between innovation as an outcome (an innovation) and the activities through which innovations come about (innovation activities). It is difficult to measure the value (and thus the impact) of innovation outcomes using surveys, however.[1]

Another approach is that implicit in a simple macroeconomic growth model whereby the fruits of innovation are subsumed in total factor productivity (TFP). This approach also is not entirely satisfying. Indeed, the concern about TFP growth as a measure of innovation is perhaps best captured by Moses Abramovitz's observation in a 1956 article that TFP in many ways is a "measure of ignorance" (Abramovitz 1956). Digging deeper into Abramovitz's perspective, he showed that an index of US output was 1,325 in 1944–53 relative to 100 in 1869–78 but that inputs were 381 rela-

---

1. Surveys that follow the Oslo Manual aim to capture whether or not the organization has introduced new products or brought new processes into use during a reference period (e.g., two years). While this provides a "count" of innovation outcomes for the period, it does not get at their relative value or economic importance.

tive to 100. From this, he concluded that almost all growth in US output was over and above growth of measured inputs. He wrote, "Since we know little about the causes of productivity increase, the indicated importance of this element may be taken to be some sort of measure of our ignorance about the causes of economic growth in the United States." Despite ongoing concerns sparked by Abramovitz, he actually provided what is perhaps the best response—one that has animated many CRIW conferences, including this one—in the part of his comment that is not often quoted. The full sentence is as follows: "Since we know little about the causes of productivity increase, the indicated importance of this element may be taken to be some sort of measure of our ignorance about the causes of economic growth in the United States *and some sort of indication of where we need to concentrate our attention*" (italics added).

The papers in this conference are in the spirit of the latter point made by Abramovitz—namely, the continued need to concentrate attention on sources of growth and innovation, including analyses of direct innovation outcome measures such as patents and "Oslo Manual" survey-based data. For those not familiar with work on innovation, four themes in this conference show what a very long way the innovation measurement literature has come since the time of Abramovitz's writing. First, consider that real output measures depend on both nominal output and quality-adjusted prices, and both are challenging to measure when there is innovation and structural change in an economy. Today's Census Bureau surveys cover virtually all services industries, whereas in Abramovitz's time, coverage of industry sectors outside of manufacturing was extremely limited. The development and implementation of firm-level databases based on linked waves of business registers and associated surveys have put a spotlight on the importance of new business formation and firm-level entry and exit as a channel through which productivity change occurs.[2]

Obtaining price measures that correctly adjust for quality change and the introduction of new goods remains as daunting a task as it was in Abramovitz's time, especially in sectors undergoing rapid change (e.g., digital services) and products for which defining a constant-quality unit of output is difficult (e.g., cloud services or semiconductors). But a huge literature has addressed these issues and illustrates the progress that has been made. Emphasis in recent years has been on whether changes due to digitization and whether some improvements in consumer welfare should be included in GDP, topics this conference directly addresses and advances.[3]

Second, measuring value added at the industry, firm, or establishment level (as well as measuring TFP) requires better measured flows of labor

2. See, e.g., Foster, Haltiwanger, and Krizan (2006); and Foster, Haltiwanger and Syverson (2008, 2016). For a survey, see Syverson (2011).

3. Recent reviews of these literatures include Byrne and Corrado (2017a, 2017b); Corrado et al. (2017); Dynan and Sheiner (2018); Moulton (2018); and Sichel (2019).

and capital services—including quality-adjusted input prices for purchased inputs—to better isolate the spillovers (i.e., social returns) that should be part of TFP. This task entails many of the same issues confronted in accurately capturing real output (e.g., relevant disaggregation and theory-consistent formulas for aggregation as exemplified by the seminal contributions of Jorgenson and Griliches 1967 and Diewert 1976) as well as keeping up with ongoing change in the economy. For tangible capital, a key challenge is obtaining quality-adjusted prices for capital goods undergoing rapid quality change. For purchased services and intangible capital, more fundamental definitional issues come into play as well. And for both intangible capital and some types of high-tech capital, businesses produce capital goods on their own account (rather than purchasing them in the market), and these new means of production will require new techniques of measurement. In each of these cases, much of the new activity is spurred by innovative activity, which only can be tracked fully if economic measurement can account for each of these pieces.

Third, the importance of intellectual property in market capitalization of public firms and of intangible capital in overall investment has increased dramatically in recent decades, as highlighted in Lev (2001); Corrado, Hulten, and Sichel (2009); Corrado and Hulten (2010); Lev and Gu (2016); and Haskel and Westlake (2017). Some types of intangible capital generally are captured in national accounts as both outputs and inputs, including research and development (R&D), software, mineral exploration, and artistic and literary originals. Getting accurate measures of investment and capital (both nominal and real) for these assets is essential for tracking inputs to innovation. Some types of intangible capital identified by Corrado, Hulten, and Sichel (2005, 2009)—including industrial design, organizational capital, training, and brand equity—typically are not counted as business investment in national accounts. These assets are extensively deployed by businesses and so affect economic growth, though their effect on *measured* economic growth is confounded by their omission from measures of output (not counted as business investment) and from measures of inputs (not counted as productive capital). Because intangible capital often is connected to innovative activity, improving measures of intangibles will facilitate a fuller tracking of innovation. Moreover, because of the difficulties of measuring activities related to intangibles, it is important to derive alternative measures of innovation, such as counts of trademarks and self-reported innovation in addition to patents.

Fourth, as with the asset boundary related to intangible capital, the definition of GDP implicitly considers some activities in scope while others are considered out of scope. For example, most household production is not counted in GDP because GDP largely focuses on economic activity mediated by markets. This choice can create challenges when certain activities shift from households to market-mediated activity or the other way. For example, consider a worker who becomes an Uber driver. Some of her output is unrecorded, as she drives family to school (nonmarket work). Some is recorded as output via credit card data when she drives paying riders, but her business capital input is not measured because she uses a household car. Or the output of a part-time delivery person is recorded, but due to difficulties of reporting hours and self-employment status, labor input is not recorded. Similarly, home computers, tablets, and smartphones have boosted the "domestic capital stock" and have enhanced home production by either using the devices directly (booking flights from home, writing Wikipedia entries) or enabling a marketplace to exist where none existed before (ride-sharing). These examples highlight the importance of thinking hard about the appropriate asset and activity boundaries for GDP and how appropriate boundaries may have changed over time.

This framework, while quite broad, provides context for the conference and the chapters in this volume, summarized below.

I.2   Summary

To set the stage for the conference, CRIW chair Katharine Abraham and NBER president James Poterba opened the conference with remarks in the morning. Abraham highlighted CRIW's rich history and emphasized why now, in an era of fake news and alternative facts, it is more important than ever to get right basic facts about the economy. She also highlighted key challenges in economic measurement, including declining response rates to economic surveys. Poterba developed Abraham's broad measurement theme and suggested that intense public and business interest in economic statistics creates a historic opportunity for making progress on improving measures of the economy. To seize this opportunity effectively, Poterba highlighted the importance of bringing together statistical agencies from around the world, academics, and the business community. Poterba also put a smile on the faces of CRIW members with his comment that the CRIW is a jewel in the crown of the NBER.

The papers in the conference took different approaches to investigating our ignorance surrounding innovation, and they largely relate to four broad questions. First, how should current measurement frameworks be expanded to incorporate more fully the role and consequences of innovative activity? Second, what new approaches and data would be most useful to enhance our understanding of innovation? Third, how has innovation changed the structure of the economy, including production processes, labor markets, and financial activities? Finally, what changes within the current measurement framework would improve our ability to more fully capture innovative activity?

On the first theme of how current measurement frameworks should be expanded, one question of particular interest is whether and how the asset and production boundaries used in current measurement frameworks (such as in the national accounts) need to be adjusted to more fully account for innovation-related changes in output and inputs. The issue of boundaries and definitions is taken up by the first chapter in this volume. In "Expanded GDP for Welfare Measurement in the 21st Century," Charles Hulten and Leonard I. Nakamura make a powerful argument that GDP, as a measure of production, omits much of the benefits arising from the digital revolution. They highlight that consumer choices today are informed by far more information than in the past and, with advances in communications technology, that information is free or very low cost and readily available 24/7 in almost any location. In addition, many benefits of the digital revolution directly benefit consumers without ever appearing in GDP (including the significant inputs of consumer time that are required to produce them). Thus they argue that there is a disconnect or wedge between growth in real GDP and that of consumer well-being. To capture this idea, they follow Lancaster (1966) and supplement the conventional growth accounting framework with a technology for consumer decision-making. This approach yields an expanded measure of GDP (which the authors refer to as EGDP). With this framework, the authors analyze the wedge between real GDP and consumer well-being. Based on a series of case studies, the authors make the case that this wedge likely is large enough to be consequential and too large to be ignored.

Diane Coyle's lunchtime talk at the conference covered some similar themes. She offered insightful perspectives on several key issues for GDP and welfare measurement, including production boundaries, the provision of free goods, the role of outlet substitution as new ways of buying goods and services arise, the digitization of consumer goods, the role of bundling of goods and services and cross subsidies, and cross-border issues. Coyle highlighted the need to think through the boundary between what should be counted as quality change or left as unmeasured consumer surplus and accounted for elsewhere, as in Hulten and Nakamura (above). She also argued that even in conventional national accounts, the production/ nonproduction boundaries are more fluid than often recognized: the treatment of owner-occupied housing, for example.

Chapter 2 by Javier Miranda and Nikolas Zolas ("Measuring the Impact of Household Innovation Using Administrative Data") highlights a different aspect of how activity boundaries implicit in the definition of GDP lead to the nonmeasurement of certain categories of production and innovative activity within the household sector. In particular, they focus on patents obtained by businesses without employees as a proxy for identifying household innovation given that such businesses usually represent household entrepreneurs. They find that the value of household innovations patented between 2000 and 2011 is $5 billion. This estimate may seem modest, but survey evidence suggests only a small fraction of household innovations actually is patented.[4] This topic relates directly to the very engaging dinner talk on household innovation by Eric von Hippel. He made the case that household innovation is pervasive, creates substantial value, and contributes importantly to household well-being. Chapter 2 by Miranda and Zolas, along with von Hippel's talk and his contemporaneously issued book (von Hipple 2017), highlights efforts to better understand this area of household innovation and production.

Another way in which current measurement frameworks can be expanded is by digging more deeply into the detailed dynamism underlying economic growth, and the availability of detailed microdata makes this possible. In chapter 3, "Innovation, Productivity Dispersion, and Productivity Growth," Lucia Foster, Cheryl Grim, John C. Haltiwanger, and Zoltan Wolf draw on the literature on firm dynamics to investigate how microdynamics feed through to aggregate or industry measures of productivity growth. They study the US economy using the Longitudinal Business Database (LBD), an establishment-level database founded on the Business Register and consisting of the universe of employer businesses in the nonfarm business sector of the United States (about 7 million establishments and 6 million firm observations per year for 1976–2013). The authors investigate how the dispersion of productivity at the industry level and the growth of productivity respond to a surge of entry, looking in particular at high-tech and other industries. They draw on the idea of Gort and Klepper (1982), who suggested that an initial wave of entrants, who are experimenting and learning, will subsequently be selected out into leavers and stayers. This pattern would lead to a rise and then a fall in productivity dispersion that ultimately would be followed by subsequent productivity growth. This outcome is the broad pattern the authors observe in the US data: in the late 1990s, there was an increase in the entry rate and productivity dispersion, but this was followed by falling entry and growth, and although contrary to the theory, rising dispersion.

Another set of chapters in this volume focuses on the development and utilization of new data and approaches to measuring innovative activity and its economic effects. Measuring and tracking innovation and innovative activity is increasingly difficult yet critical from a policy and managerial perspective. In chapter 4, "How Innovative Are Innovations? A Multidimensional Survey-Based Approach," Wesley M. Cohen, You-Na Lee, and John P. Walsh summarize key challenges with existing administrative and survey-based measures and propose that an expanded focus be taken when designing firm-based surveys to include richer data at the level of individual innovations. In their empirical analysis, the authors demonstrate the usefulness of this conceptual approach using their new innovation survey. They then suggest new or improved measures of innovation consistent with this

4. See Sichel and von Hippel (forthcoming).

approach that were not included in the survey. The authors show how shifting our attention from the firm as the unit of analysis to the innovation helps us assess the technological significance of an innovation, its likelihood of success, and ultimately its potential impact on the state of current knowledge. The authors argue that this complementary approach will allow policy makers and managers to make better-informed investment decisions based on an improved understanding of innovations and their markets.

Trademarking represents another unexplored source of information for tracking innovation, and in chapter 5, "An Anatomy of US Firms Seeking Trademark Registration," Emin M. Dinlersoz, Nathan Goldschlag, Amanda Myers, and Nikolas Zolas make a strong case that trademarking is a valuable indicator of innovative activity. In particular, they construct a new administrative dataset that combines data on trademark applications and registrations from the US Patent and Trademark Office Trademark Case Files Dataset (TCFD) with data on all firms from the US Census Bureau's LBD. The resulting dataset is comprehensive, covering all employing firms regardless of size, industry, or location between 1976 and 2015. It is the first effort to systematically link these data in the United States and provides a way to explore the value of the intangible associated with trademarks, such as brand awareness and product loyalty, as well as nonpatented innovations and their relation to business dynamics. In their chapter, the authors explore the relation of trademark application filing to firm employment, revenue growth, and firm innovative activity as measured by R&D and patents. The authors show trademark registration is a precursor of firm success and is tied to innovation. Firms in the United States have substantially higher employment and greater revenue in the period following first filing for a trademark relative to control firms. The chapter also finds higher average R&D expenditure and patenting by first-time trademark filers both before and after initial filing compared to control firms.

Regarding the sources of innovation, chapter 6, "Research Experience as Human Capital in New Business Outcomes," by Nathan Goldschlag, Ron Jarmin, Julia Lane, and Nikolas Zolas brings together several datasets to examine the linkages among university R&D, human capital, and business start-ups. The key underlying idea is that knowledge assets—typically not captured on a firm's balance sheet—are critical to understanding the value of a company, its ability to innovate, and ultimately its success. This chapter explores how an employee's prior work and research experience affects the outcomes of start-up firms, including growth, survival, and innovative activity. The authors draw from a rich set of administrative data sources, including payroll transaction data from the human resource files of 22 major research universities, unemployment insurance wage records underlying the Longitudinal Employer Household Dynamics (LEHD) dataset, Internal Revenue Service (IRS) form W-2, and the Longitudinal Business Database to construct new measures of workplace experience for US workers, including direct measures of research experience as well as experience in R&D labs, high-tech businesses, and universities. The authors find evidence of the importance of these forms of previous employee experience to the outcomes of start-up firms generally and high-tech firms specifically.

A third topic of the conference focused on how innovation is changing the structure of the economy, including production processes, labor markets, and financial activities. One area where innovation has had high visibility is in the rise of the "gig" economy. In chapter 7, "Measuring the Gig Economy: Current Knowledge and Open Issues," Katharine G. Abraham, John C. Haltiwanger, Kristin Sandusky, and James R. Spletzer provide a typology of work arrangements and review how different arrangements, and especially gig activity, are captured in existing data, noting that a challenge for understanding recent trends is that the monthly Current Population Survey of households and administrative data (e.g., tax data) paint a different picture, with the former showing little evidence of the growth in self-employment that would be implied by a surge in gig activity and the latter providing evidence of considerable recent growth. The authors match individual-level survey and administrative records and find that a large and growing fraction of those with self-employment activity in administrative data have no such activity recorded in household survey data. Promising avenues for improving the measurement of self-employment activity include the addition of more probing questions to household survey questionnaires and the development of integrated datasets that combine survey, administrative, and potentially, private data.

One of the key relationships that needs to be understood better in the modern economy is that between new types of tangible capital (notably information and communications technology [ICT]) and new types of organizational forms: think of the revolution in the print media industry, for example, or the effect of computerization on just-in-time-style manufacturing. In chapter 8, "Information and Communications Technology, R&D, and Organizational Innovation: Exploring Complementarities in Investment and Production," Pierre Mohnen, Michael Polder, and George van Leeuwen investigate whether ICT (hardware), R&D, and organizational change are complementary in production and how much they influence total factor productivity. Such an investigation requires combinations of datasets (another theme of this conference). Typical firm-level datasets have information on outputs (such as sales) and on inputs (such as capital and operating spending) but do not typically have information on organizational change. Surveys of innovation and organization have the latter information but typically not accounting data. Thus Mohnen, Polder, and van Leeuwen merge together the Dutch Business Register and Oslo Manual–based innovation survey data. In their merged dataset, which spans 2008–12, 45 percent of manufacturing and 35 percent of service sector firms report organizational innovation (the introduction of new business practices, knowledge management systems, methods of workplace organization, and management of external relations). They find strong complementarities between ICT investment and organization innovation. Their approach enables them to calculate rates of return, and they find the highest rate of return to be for firms investing in ICT but also organizational innovation.

Innovation and its attendant implications for organization of activity also may affect the distribution of income. This issue is explored in chapter 9, "Digital Innovation and the Distribution of Income," by Dominique Guellec. He suggests that features of the digital economy such as economies of scale might lead to market concentration and rents for "superstar firms," feeding through into high returns for "insiders" in those firms (such as top executives) and for shareholders and thus income inequality. One countervailing force is that entry might be easier with digital technologies, and thus the position of top firms might be easier to challenge. The author finds that the forces of concentration seem to have prevailed. To investigate the implications, he looks at how labor shares of GDP evolved across 27 Organisation for Economic Co-operation and Development (OECD) countries within 16 manufacturing industries over the period 1995–2011. The chapter finds that labor shares have fallen, controlling for other factors, in those country-industries with growing patenting (their preferred measure of innovation). Combining these results with other evidence suggesting that top executive pay has risen in country-industries where concentration has risen, Guellec argues that the growth of digital economy has had a tendency to lower the labor share and widen labor-income inequality.

Baruch Lev's lunchtime talk focused on how ongoing innovation (especially the rising importance of intangible capital) has affected financial accounting. Because these assets are central to firm value but only captured in limited ways on firm financial reports, Lev made the case that financial reports have become increasingly less useful indicators of company performance and that share price informativeness also has been falling. His comments highlighted the important role that could be played by business accounting in tracking innovative activity and how making progress on economic measurement will require collaboration among many different groups of stakeholders.

A final topic addressed by the chapters is how best to improve innovation-related measures of economic activity within the current conceptual frameworks for measurement. In chapter 10, "Factor Incomes in Global Value Chains: The Role of Intangibles," Wen Chen, Bart Los, and Marcel P. Timmer extend the usual approach to modeling production, arguing that studies need to look at cross-border production to complement country studies. They set out a global value chain (GVC) production function that tracks the value added in each stage of production in any country-industry and define a new residual as the difference between the value of the final good and the payments to all tangibles (capital and labor) in any stage. They focus on GVCs of manufactured goods and find the residual, which they interpret as income accruing to intangibles that are (mostly) not covered in current national accounts statistics. They find this residual—the return to intangibles in their system—to be rather large. They also document decreasing labor and increasing capital income shares over the period 2000–2014 as mainly due to increasing income for intangible assets—in particular, in GVCs of durable goods. They further suggest that this period should be seen as an exceptional period in the global economy during which multinational firms benefitted from reduced labor costs through offshoring while capitalizing on existing firm-specific intangibles, such as brand names, at little marginal cost.

Accurate measures of quality-adjusted prices can be challenging to obtain for products undergoing rapid technical advances, such as semiconductors. Getting these prices right is critical given the role that semiconductors play as one of the general-purpose technologies underlying the digital revolution. In chapter 11, "Measuring Moore's Law: Evidence from Price, Cost, and Quality Indexes," Kenneth Flamm provides a comprehensive history of the evolution of semiconductor technology in recent decades and how these developments generated the rapid price declines often summarized in Moore's law. Flamm provides evidence that since around 2000, both the pace of technical advance and the rate of price declines have slowed for high-volume semiconductors—including memory chips, microprocessors, and custom-chip designs outsourced to contract manufacturers. (This general pattern also is evident in official measures of semiconductor prices.) If Flamm's assessment is right, this slowdown bodes ill for future gains in productivity with a critical element of the digital revolution developing more slowly. However, Flamm's results (and those implicit in official price indexes) are not without controversy, and his discussant, Stephen Oliner, raised a variety of questions and pointed to other work that reaches a different conclusion.[5]

In chapter 12, "Accounting for Innovations in Consumer Digital Services: IT Still Matters," David Byrne and Carol Corrado present a framework for measuring the GDP impacts of innovations in consumer content delivery, which have been especially rapid since the advent of the 21st century, or the "mobile information age." They argue that the flow of services from consumers' connected IT capital capture what Brynjolfsson and Saunders (2009) call "free goods" and that this service flow should augment the existing measure of personal consumption in GDP. They develop a quality-adjusted price index for these services as well as the paid-for access services (already included in GDP) that are needed for content delivery via consumer-owned IT devices. Their estimates imply that accounting for these innovations in consumer content delivery matters: the innovations boost the consumer

---

5. See Byrne, Oliner, and Sichel (2018).

surplus of connected users by about $30,000 (2017 dollars) from 2004 to 2017 and contribute more than .5 percentage points per year to US real GDP growth during the last 10 years. Their accounting of innovations in consumer content delivery is (conservatively) estimated to have moderated the post-2007 GDP growth slowdown by nearly 0.3 percentage points per year. The price index for paid-for content delivery services (i.e., cellular, cable TV, and multidevice streaming services) that they develop in this chapter has a similar impact on consumer price inflation—that is, relative to official consumer prices calculated by the Bureau of Economic Analysis, Byrne and Corrado argue elsewhere that prices for consumer digital access services (alone) have had an increasing deflationary impact since 1987 (Byrne and Corrado 2020).

Cloud computing is one area where developments have leapt ahead of measurement. In chapter 13, "The Rise of Cloud Computing: Minding Your Ps, Qs, and Ks," David Byrne, Carol Corrado, and Daniel Sichel document the explosive growth of cloud computing, develop new quarterly hedonic price indexes for cloud computing services, and investigate the puzzle of why investment in IT equipment in the National Income and Product Accounts (NIPAs) has been so weak while capital expenditures for IT equipment associated with cloud infrastructure has exploded. On prices, the chapter focuses on those at Amazon Web Services and estimates that from 2009 to 2016, cloud computing prices fell rapidly, with quickening and double-digit declines after 2014. On the IT equipment puzzle, the chapter argues that cloud service providers are undertaking large amounts of own-account investment in IT equipment and that some of this investment may have been missed in the GDP accounts. (In the 2018 Comprehensive Revision of the NIPAs, the Bureau of Economic Analysis took steps to better capture this own-account investment.)

The final chapter is by Erich H. Strassner and David B. Wasshausen of the Bureau of Economic Analysis (BEA): "BEA Deflators for Information and Communications Technology Goods and Services: Historical Analysis and Future Plans." With an aim toward facilitating and encouraging further price research, the chapter first provides a historical perspective and analysis of BEA's information and communications technology (ICT) prices, including an overview of the sources and methods used to construct their quality-adjusted prices. The authors then discuss current work and future plans for continuing to ensure the accuracy of BEA's price indexes and corresponding inflation-adjusted measures and provide an update that assesses recent progress as reflected in BEA's 15th comprehensive update of the national accounts, released in 2018.

I.3   Conclusion

As in past NBER and CRIW conferences, this one stimulated a rich discussion by experts in the areas covered by the volume. Discussants' comments on the chapters provided extremely valuable insights and stimulated further conversation. For these contributions, we thank discussants Barry Bosworth, Bronwyn Hall, Shane Greenstein, Jonathan Haskel, Stephen Oliner, Mark Roberts, and Scott Stern. As noted above, we also were fortunate to have three dynamic speakers during meals provide insightful comments that dovetailed tightly with the themes of the conference. For these comments, we thank Diane Coyle, Baruch Lev, and Eric von Hippel for their important contributions to the conference.

In addition, we were fortunate to conclude the conference with a terrific panel discussion on next steps. That panel, chaired by Ernst Berndt, included Dennis Fixler, Erica Groshen, Ron Jarmin, and Scott Stern. Berndt focused on the relationship between the academic/research community and the statistical agencies. While in the past, academics have offered suggestions for how statistical agencies can improve statistics, Berndt suggested that the statistical agencies offer suggestions on research topics to academics as well as suggestions for organizational collaboration. Fixler reviewed progress on measuring innovation made by the Bureau of Economic Analysis in the past decade. He also highlighted some key areas in which further progress is needed, including ongoing efforts to improve quality adjustment, how best to incorporate private data, and how best to integrate and share data with other statistical agencies. Groshen picked up on the conference theme of the interaction between innovation and organizational structure and emphasized that the statistical system needs to be responsive to changes in organizational structures in the economy. Specifically, all data need to have identifiers so that data can be linked, aggregated, and disaggregated correctly. She also argued that statistical programs should, where possible, be reengineered to replace survey data with administrative data to engender, at least in part, increased efficiency and nimbleness in our measurement system. Like Berndt, Jarmin focused on the importance of collaboration between statistical agencies and outside researchers. Echoing Fixler, he noted the importance of thinking through how best to link in specialized data from private sources. He also highlighted the potential value of collecting different datasets in a centralized place for researchers to access as easily as possible given data security and resource constraints. Stern focused on the central question of the conference: What is innovation? He noted that economists are good at measuring inputs to innovation with a presumption that these inputs translate into output that is valued. He also highlighted the importance of better understanding innovation that occurs outside firms and more fully thinking through how we account for the benefits of innovation. As an example, he cited solar energy, which has a modest effect on GDP but is potentially very significant in reducing a negative externality.

As organizers of the conference, we believe that important progress was made on Abramovitz's charge to dig deep to better understand our ignorance about innovation. As noted, understanding the sources and implications of innovation is a vast and complex problem. Given the wide range of approaches and data presented and discussed at the conference, we believe that further progress will depend on greater collaboration between micro- and macroeconomists, between researchers and practitioners, between the business community and statistical agencies and researchers (not least because of the immense amount of data possessed by the private sector), and between those who directly study innovation and those who work on broader issues of productivity, economic growth, and economic transformation. In our view, the problem is too complex for any individual or single approach to meet the challenge. It is our hope that the conversations and ideas sparked at the conference will be the basis of continued progress and collaboration.

References

Abramovitz, Moses. 1956. "Resource and Output Trends in the United States since 1870." *American Economic Review* 46 (2): 5–23.

Brynjolfsson, Erik, and Adam Saunders. 2009. *Wired for Innovation: How Information Technology Is Reshaping the Economy*. Cambridge, MA: MIT Press.

Byrne, David, and Carol Corrado. 2017a. "ICT Asset Prices: Marshalling Evidence into New Measures." Finance and Economics Discussion Series 2017-016, February, revised October. Washington, DC: Board of Governors of the Federal Reserve System.

Byrne, David, and Carol Corrado. 2017b. "ICT Services and Their Prices: What Do They Tell Us about Productivity and Technology?" *International Productivity Monitor* 33 (December): 150–81.

Byrne, David, and Carol Corrado. 2020. "The Increasing Deflationary Influence of Consumer Digital Access Services." *Economics Letters* 196, article 109447.

Byrne, David, Stephen Oliner, and Daniel Sichel. 2018. "How Fast Are Semiconductor Prices Falling?" *Review of Income and Wealth* 64 (3): 679–702.

Corrado, C., C. Hulten, and D. Sichel. 2005. "Measuring Capital and Technology: An Expanded Framework." In *Measuring Capital in the New Economy*, edited by C. Corrado, J. Haltiwanger, and D. Sichel, 11–46. NBER Studies in Income and Wealth 65. Chicago: University of Chicago Press.

Corrado, Carol, and Charles Hulten. 2010. "How Do You Measure a 'Technological Revolution'?" *American Economic Review* 100 (5): 99–104.

Corrado, Carol, Kevin Fox, Peter Goodridge, Jonathan Haskel, Cecilia Jona-Lasinio, Daniel Sichel, and Stian Westlake. 2017. "Improving GDP: Demolishing, Repointing, or Extending?" Indigo Prize Joint 1st Place Essay, September.

Corrado, C., C. Hulten, and D. Sichel. 2009. "Intangible Capital and US Economic Growth." *Review of Income and Wealth* 55 (3): 661–85.

Diewert, W. E. 1976. "Exact and Superlative Index Numbers." *Journal of Econometrics* 4 (2): 115–45.

Dynan, Karen, and Louise Sheiner. 2018. "GDP as a Measure of Economic Well-Being." Hutchins Center Working Paper No. 43, August.

Foster, Lucia, John Haltiwanger, and C. J. Krizan. 2006. "Market Selection, Reallocation, and Restructuring in the U.S. Retail Trade Sector in the 1990s." *Review of Economics and Statistics* 88 (4): 748–58.

Foster, Lucia, John Haltiwanger, and Chad Syverson. 2008. "Reallocation, Firm

Turnover, and Efficiency: Selection on Productivity or Profitability?" *American Economic Review* 98 (1): 394–425.

Foster, Lucia, John Haltiwanger, and Chad Syverson. 2016. "The Slow Growth of New Plants: Learning about Demand?" *Economica* 83 (1): 91–129.

Gort, Michael, and Steven Klepper. 1982. "Time Paths in the Diffusion of Product Innovations." *Economic Journal* 92 (367): 630–53. https://doi.org/10.2307/2232554.

Haskel, Jonathan, and Stian Westlake. 2017. *Capitalism without Capital: The Rise of the Intangible Economy*. Princeton, NJ: Princeton University Press.

Jorgenson, Dale W., and Zvi Griliches. 1967. "The Explanation of Productivity Change." *Review of Economic Studies* 34 (3): 249–83.

Lancaster, Kelvin J. 1966. "A New Approach to Consumer Theory." *Journal of Political Economy* 74 (2): 132–57.

Lev, Baruch. 2001. *Intangibles: Management, Measurement and Reporting*. Washington, DC: Brookings Institution Press.

Lev, Baruch, and Feng Gu. 2016. *The End of Accounting and Path Forward for Investors and Managers*. Hoboken, NJ: Wiley.

Moulton, Brent R. 2018. "The Measurement of Output, Prices, and Productivity: What's Changed since the Boskin Commission?" *Brookings Institution*, July 25. https://www.brookings.edu/research/the-measurement-of-output-prices-and -productivity/.

OECD/Eurostat. 2018. *Oslo Manual 2018: Guidelines for Collecting, Reporting and Using Data on Innovation*, 4th ed. The Measurement of Scientific, Technological and Innovation Activities. Paris: OECD.

Sichel, Daniel E. 2019. "Productivity Measurement: Racing to Keep Up." *Annual Review of Economics* 11:591–614.

Sichel, Daniel, and Eric von Hippel. Forthcoming. "Household Innovation and R&D: Bigger Than You Think." *Review of Income and Wealth*, forthcoming.

Syverson, Chad. 2011. "What Determines Productivity?" *Journal of Economic Literature* 49 (2): 326–65.

von Hippel, Eric. 2017. *Free Innovation*. Cambridge, MA: MIT Press.

I

Expanding Current Measurement Frameworks

Expanded GDP for Welfare Measurement in the 21st Century

Charles Hulten and Leonard I. Nakamura

1.1 Introduction

We are in the midst of a technological revolution of tectonic proportions, centered on the rapid advances in the generation, transmission, use, and storage of information. Schmidt and Rosenberg (2014) have termed it "the Internet Age," an era in which "the Internet has made information free, copious, and ubiquitous" (10–11). However, its reach goes beyond the internet per se to include major advances in health care and higher education and structural changes in finance, banking, and indeed nearly all sectors of the economy. Moreover, it is more than just a profusion of new products. The information revolution has led to major changes in the organization of firms, the location of production, and the way goods and services are distributed. One result has been an increase in the well-being of consumers.

The question addressed in this chapter is whether the procedures currently used to measure GDP adequately capture this increase. There are

Charles Hulten is professor emeritus of economics at the University of Maryland and a research associate of the National Bureau of Economic Research.

Leonard I. Nakamura is an emeritus economist at the Federal Reserve Bank of Philadelphia.

The views expressed in this chapter are those of the authors and do not necessarily reflect those of the Federal Reserve Bank of Philadelphia or the Federal Reserve System. We thank Kyle Brown, Carol Corrado, John Fernald, David Friedman, Erica Groshen, Fatih Guvenen, Nancy Humphrey, Brent Moulton, Jon Samuels, Dan Sichel, Rachel Soloveichik, Hal Varian, and staff members at the Bureau of Labor Statistics and the Bureau of Economic Analysis for help and advice. Jeanna Kenney provided excellent research assistance. For acknowledgments, sources of research support, and disclosure of the authors' material financial relationships, if any, please see https://www.nber.org/books-and-chapters/measuring-and-accounting-innovation-21st -century/expanded-gdp-welfare-measurement-21st-century.

good reasons to think that they do not.[1] The new information goods do not always play by the same "rules" as those typically counted in GDP, which is an aggregate measure of the goods and services whose value is, for the most part, determined by market transactions. Much of the information available over the internet is not accompanied by direct transactions, in effect at a direct price of zero, so there is no monetary yardstick with which to estimate its value to the consumer. Thus while some of this information does indeed involve economic activity supported by transactions that are captured in GDP, the direct consumer welfare value of the information is not counted as GDP.

The statistical system has also struggled with the advent of new or improved goods that deliver superior outcomes per dollar of expenditure. Improvements in the effectiveness of outcomes have occurred in a wide range of goods, from transportation and electronic equipment to health and welfare services. Even before the digital revolution, the service sector posed problems for economic measurement because output is often measured in terms of inputs rather than outcomes, and as Griliches (1992, 1994) has noted, it is not even clear what actually constitutes output. The digital revolution has increased these problems with innovations like minimally invasive surgery, which brings an enormous increase in patient comfort at a relatively small increase, or even decrease, in resource cost.

The improvement in consumer welfare is the common theme that links the measurement problems associated with the "free" information and the advent of new and better goods and services. One response has been to focus on how current GDP procedures can be adapted to accommodate the range of goods involved, but this approach faces an uphill battle. The essential problem is about not just how efficiently goods and services are produced but also how effectively they are used in consumption to generate welfare. The basic hypothesis of this chapter is that the two are not the same.

Our recent research has approached this problem by bringing consumer choice into the GDP measurement framework using the standard utility maximization framework of economic theory (Hulten and Nakamura 2018), extending the "production" approach to GDP by adding a separate technology for the consumption of goods. It follows Lancaster (1966), who argued that consumer utility is derived from the characteristics of bundles of goods acquired and not from the goods themselves and that there is a *consumption technology* that transforms goods, measured at production cost, into consumption "activities" or "commodities" that provide utility. This approach allows for an explicit modeling of the wedge that may exist between the acquisition cost of the goods acquired and the resulting outcomes (as with health care), and that outcome may depend on idiosyncratic

---

1. For example, Coyle (2014) remarked that GDP was "a measure of the economy best suited to an earlier era."

factors like the existing state of health or education, on which the outcome is contingent.

Once the consumption technology wedge is introduced into the analysis, it is but a short additional step to assume that it may shift over time as the innovations introduced by the digital revolution enable consumers to make more efficient use of their incomes. We term this form of innovation *output saving*, since a given level of welfare can be achieved with fewer resources, but it could equally be called *utility augmenting*, since it allows consumers to get more "bang for their buck." In effect, this treats the consumption technology in the same conceptual way that Robert Solow (1957) adopted in his analysis of the productivity residual, which measured costless "resource-saving" shifts in the production function. The latter describes an increase in the productivity of inputs, while the output-saving innovation refers to the "productivity" of the consumption technology.

We then adapt the conventional equivalent and compensating variations of standard economic theory to measure the increase in consumer utility arising from output-saving innovation. This results in a general equilibrium dollar metric for measuring the benefits from innovations that go directly to the consumer. We add this dollar metric to conventional GDP to obtain an expanded concept of GDP. Expanded GDP (EGDP) provides a natural framework for incorporating the results of empirical research on the information economy into a broader measure of consumer well-being. It allows for the possibility that aggregate economic welfare can increase more rapidly than conventional real GDP during periods of rapid innovation.

The next two sections of this chapter set out the conceptual framework and rationale for EGDP.[2] The goal is to decompose the growth rate of EGDP into output saving, resource saving, resource using, and input accumulation. This is essentially the conventional growth accounting framework with output-saving innovation added and costless product quality change reclassified as part of the consumption technology. The material that follows is then devoted to an examination of the empirical work that supports each of the sources of growth. The final section pulls together the results to address the question of whether the implied estimate of EGDP may have grown faster than real GDP over the last three decades. Our estimates suggest that it did.

1.2   The Theory of Aggregate Output

1.2.1   Gross Domestic Product and Income

GDP in nominal prices is, with some exceptions, an estimate of the value of goods and services that flow through markets in a given year. GDP in

---

2. The technical derivations and assumption can be found in our previous paper (Hulten and Nakamura 2018) on which the current chapter builds.

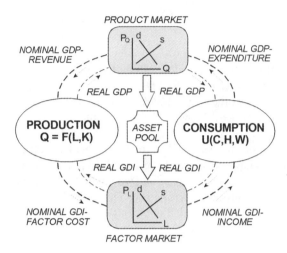

Fig. 1.1   Circular flow diagram for GDP and GDI

constant prices is a synthetic concept that pulls together the corresponding quantities of goods and services. It is not a good itself, though in growth theory it is often treated as such, but an index of aggregate output whose base year value equals nominal GDP. GDP is linked to gross domestic income (GDI) by the circular flows of inputs and output through product and factor markets.[3] The representation, shown in figure 1.1, divides an economy into two basic functions: the production of goods and services and their consumption by households, which also supply the inputs into production. The linkage between these flows is determined, in the production sector, by a production function $Q = F(L,K)$ that links the flow of output Q to the flow of inputs of labor L and capital K via the prevailing technology $F(\cdot)$; on the consumption side of the economy, the utility function $U(C,H,W)$ transforms the output C into utility and guides the decision of how much of the available time endowment to allocate to leisure H and how much to labor L as well as the decision about how much consumption should be deferred to future years by building up wealth W. The outer counterclockwise flow shows the stream of payments into and out of the two sectors as they enter and exit the markets for outputs and inputs. They indicate, in the top part of the diagram, the identity between the amount spent by consumers and the amount received by the producer, which together define nominal GDP. At the bottom, the producers' factor cost is the consumers' income, defining GDI. The balancing of supply and demand in the product and factor markets establishes the equalities of the flows. To complete the picture, the revenue that flows into the business side is equal to the factor cost that flows

3. See Patinkin (1973) for a discussion of the structure and history of the circular flow model.

out, and the income that flows to the consumer flows out as expenditure on products. The resulting GDI equals GDP, some $20 trillion in the United States as of mid-2018.

Nominal GDP is measured in the prices prevailing in each year. It sums the product of the price of each good and the corresponding quantity, just as nominal GDI sums the product of the price of each input and its quantity. An estimate of the price change is typically used to deflate the nominal value to arrive at the corresponding quantity, which is represented in figure 1.1 by the inner clockwise flow that tracks the movement of output and input quantities between producers and consumers. Prices are represented implicitly in figure 1.1 by the intersection of the supply and demand functions in the markets for inputs and outputs. They play a central role in regulating the composition of the flow of goods. They also play a key role in efforts to introduce the benefits of new and improved goods into the circular flow representation of the economy.

The aggregate nature of GDP and GDI masks a wealth of detail in the underlying input-output structure of the economy. Thus GDP is not a measure of the entire production of goods by the constituent sectors of the economy, since sectoral production also includes the intermediate goods delivered to other industries as inputs. The consumption, investment, government, and net exports components of GDP are "final demand" goods available for current or future consumption, domestic and foreign. This is a point that should not be ignored when assessing the impact of innovation on the economy, since the innovation may appear very differently when it enters a sector of the economy than when it impacts final demand (e.g., Hulten 1978). The I-O structure of the economy also implies that GDI is equal to the total value added of labor and capital and not the total cost of production across sectors, which also includes the cost of the intermediate inputs.

Household production deserves special comment given the attention it has received in the literature on the mismeasurement of GDP. One problem with accounting for household production is its conflation with goods consumption, since both occur within the home and often involve the same agents. The boundary between the production of a meal in a restaurant and the same meal produced at home by the same chef is not so much a matter of production as the method of distribution.

1.2.2 Capital Formation

GDP and GDI are snapshots of the size of the aggregate economic flows in a time period. The bulk of US GDP goes to the provision of current wants, while the investment component represents the use of current resources to satisfy future consumption. Provision for future wants is, however, not explicitly represented in the traditional circular flow framework, although this need not be the case. Figure 1.1 shows that the traditional framework can be expanded to include the flows of investment from the product markets to a separate capital account, in which there is the producers' stock of capital K on the one hand and the consumer wealth W that it implies on the other. This wealth arises from the decision by consumers to defer current consumption by saving, which diverts resources away from the production of consumption goods to the production of capital goods. This investment adds to the existing capital stock and builds the future capacity needed to produce consumption goods in the future. The result is shown in the area in the center of figure 1.1 labeled "asset pool."[4]

The pool of the productive capital contains different types of tangible capital (equipment and structures) as well as intangible capital. Intangible capital includes R&D, investments in product development and marketing, customer support, and human resources and organizational development. These investments are intended to develop new or better goods, processes, and markets on the one hand and to improve the organization and management of firms on the other. Until quite recently, expenditures for intangible capital except computer software (only added in 1999) were treated as intermediate inputs and thus ignored in the circular flow representation of the aggregate economy. This changed in 2013 with the capitalization by the Bureau of Economic Analysis (BEA) of R&D and expenditures for artistic originals. This move added 3 percent to 4 percent to US GDP that had theretofore gone uncounted, but this amount accounts for less than half of the list of intangibles advocated by Corrado, Hulten, and Sichel (2005, 2009).

1.3   GDP and Consumer Welfare

1.3.1   Diagrammatic Exposition of Innovation and GDP

The circular flow model is a descriptive framework that links the flow of goods and payments in the economy. The role of both the utility and production functions is to transform the flow of inputs and outputs that passes through their segments of the economy. They are treated symmetrically in this process. However, this is emphatically not the way they are treated in standard economic theory, where the maximization of utility is the objective of economic activity and the production technology is a constraint on the achievable outcome. A schematic representation of this optimization exercise is shown in figure 1.2, where the first three links show labor and capital being transformed by technology into output (real GDP) via the production function. The output is then transferred to the consumer through the product market, in which the volume and price of each good are determined by the interaction of supply and demand. Once the price and quantity of each good are determined, aggregate GDP follows immediately. Under the standard optimization assumptions, the resulting GDP represents the maxi-

4. This figure is based on figure 2 of Corrado and Hulten (2015).

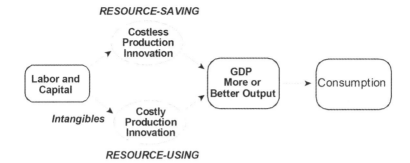

Fig. 1.2   **Resource-saving and resource-using innovation**

mum attainable utility. An increase in real output Q is assumed to increase utility, and a proportional increase in Q may result in an equal proportional increase in utility (but only if the marginal utility of real income equals one). In this case, a comprehensive measure of real GDP is a sufficient statistic for estimating the increase in well-being (in the sense of the utility function).

Innovation affects output in two ways in this setup. The production function can shift upward for a given combination of labor and capital, causing the inputs to be more productive. This is the situation envisioned by Robert Solow in his 1957 formulation of the total factor productivity (TFP) residual, in which the shift is treated as an autonomous process that is costless in terms of the need for resources (it falls as "manna from heaven"). It includes innovation due to inspiration and tinkering but mainly represents knowledge spillovers, which Nordhaus (2005) argues is the primary source of macro-innovation. It is labeled "resource-saving" in the figure due to the costless improvements in productivity it enables. The second source of innovation shown in the figure is systematic investment in innovation. This involves the intangible capital noted in the preceding section. Because it implies a systematic commitment of resources, it is labeled "resource-using" in the figure.

There is a further distinction between innovation that increases the quantity of output and innovation that increases the quality of existing goods or introduces new goods that is implicit in figure 1.2. The former is typically called "process-oriented" technical change, while the latter is "product-oriented." This is the rationale for distinguishing between more or "better" output in the GDP part of the figure, reflecting the convention that "better" is typically expressed as more output for purposes of measurement, to the extent that an adjustment is actually made.

1.3.2   GDP Expanded to Allow for Direct Consumption Benefits

Most thinking about GDP has focused on figures 1.1 and 1.2. Indeed, figure 1.2 illustrates the point at which the conventional measurement framework leaves off. However, an increase in the consumption efficiency and

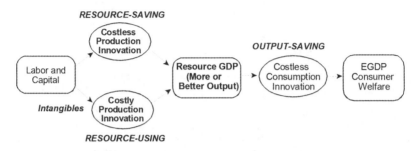

Fig. 1.3   Innovation including output-saving consumption technology

the increase in well-being it enables do not fit easily in the conventional framework. To address this problem, we have proposed expanding the figure above to include a separate technology for consuming the goods obtained from producers. It follows Lancaster's 1966 "New Approach" to consumer theory in which consumer utility is derived from the characteristics of the goods acquired and not from the goods themselves, and there is a consumption technology that transforms goods, measured at production cost, into consumption "activities" or "commodities" that provide utility.

This is relevant for the issues at hand, since once the idea of a separate technology for consumption is introduced, the distinction between output and outcomes has a natural theoretical basis.[5] Moreover, it is reasonable to expect that the technology might change over time in ways that make consumer choice more efficient, as, for example, when an increase in information allows consumers to derive more utility from the amount of money or time expended. This form of innovation is "utility-augmenting," since it enables an increase in consumer welfare for the same amount of resources, or equivalently, it is "output-saving," since the prior level of welfare can be achieved with fewer resources. As a concrete example, consider a free social media app that steers drivers away from traffic jams, enabling them to reach their destinations more swiftly with less expenditure on gasoline. The app lets consumers make better driving decisions, but there is no visible transaction. Without the expansion of GDP that we propose, the app shows up in GDP as a decline in output.

Figure 1.3 adds a consumption technology to the schema set out in figure 1.2. The concept of GDP shown in the middle of the figure is now real output measured at *resource cost*. This is the output acquired at its marginal cost of production and is the output that is transformed by the consumer into the Lancaster commodities that yield utility. Output-saving/utility-augmenting innovation operates as a link between resource output and commodity util-

---

5. The importance of the interaction between producer and consumer is also emphasized by Peter Hill (1999).

ity and is the source of the wedge between GDP growth and the increase in well-being. The size of this wedge is also affected by *costless* improvements in the quality of the resource output transferred to the consumer. The costless feature of quality change means that the marginal resource cost of a higher-quality version of a good is zero, and the benefit in terms of increased utility goes directly to the consumer as opposed to the conventional practice of treating it as simply more of the older version of the product. In other words, the conventional approach implicitly treats costless improvements in the product quality as a shift in the production function (resource-saving technical change), whereas we propose to treat it as a shift in the consumption technology (output-saving technical change).

The expansion of conventional output from figure 1.2 to figure 1.3 can be formalized as a change in the utility function from $U(Q_t)$ to $U[c(Q_t,t)]$. The consumption technology $c(Q_t,t)$ replaces Q_t, and the time-shifter t is present in the consumption technology to allow the transformation of resource-based goods into Lancaster commodities to become more efficient over time, yielding more utility per unit output. It parallels the productivity-enhancing manna-from-heaven role played by the t-shifter in the Solow production function. The consumption technology $c(Q_t,t)$ models the wedge between the two sides of the economy and introduces a conceptual richness that GDP alone cannot achieve. In addition, it can be extended to accommodate additional state variables, as in section 1.8, where we discuss state contingency in health and education.

1.3.3   The Consumption Technology and Expanded GDP

What exactly does a separate consumer technology mean for the measurement of GDP? Is there a dollar metric of the size of the output-outcome wedge? The problem is that the right-hand side of figure 1.3 links output in constant dollar prices to utility whose natural units are unobservable utils. However, this is a familiar problem in economic theory. The standard solution is to appeal to the compensating and equivalent variations (the *CV* and *EV*) associated with the utility maximization problem as monetary metrics of the distance between two indifference curves on the utility function. The *CV* and *EV* are measures of the willingness to pay for moving from a lower to a higher indifference curve, thereby converting a change in utility into a monetary value whose units are commensurable with those of GDP.[6] Figure 1.4 shows how this might work.

The production possibility frontier PPF_0 for two goods, X and Y, is shown in this figure at an initial point in time ($t = 0$). It represents the maximal combinations of X and Y that can be produced from the labor and capital

---

6. Since our objective is to obtain a dollar metric of output-saving innovation that can be incorporated into the conventional GDP framework, the question of how much happier the consumer feels is not a concern in this chapter. How much the consumer is willing to pay for the change in utility is.

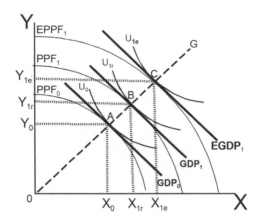

Fig. 1.4   GDP, EGDP, and the compensating variation

available in that year given the prevailing technologies for producing the goods (the first three stages of figure 1.3). U_0 is the highest attainable indifference curve of the representative consumer, and the tangency between this indifference curve and the PPF_0 constraint is located at the point A associated with the optimal X_0 and Y_0. The tangency defines the equilibrium prices, P_0^X and P_0^Y, and the line $P_0^X X_0 + P_0^Y Y_0$, defines GDP_0. The slope of the GDP line at A can therefore be interpreted as the ratio of the marginal costs of producing X and Y but also as the ratio of the marginal utilities of consuming these goods.

The growth of labor and capital, plus resource-saving and resource-using technical change, causes the PPF_0 to shift upward to PPF_1 between periods $t = 0$ and $t = 1$. An equilibrium is established at the point B on the expansion path $0G$ at a higher indifference curve U_{1r} with an amount of real $GDP_{1r} = P_0^X X_{1r} + P_0^Y Y_{1r}$. The subscript r is used here to denote that the quantities of X and Y are measured in resource units. The dollar value of the real growth occurring between the two periods equals $GDP_{1r} - GDP_{0r}$, and the rate of growth is $(GDP_{1r} - GDP_{0r})/GDP_{0r}$. The allocation of this rate among the growth in the inputs and technology can be estimated using the Solow (1957) residual method. $GDP_{1r} - GDP_{0r}$ in this diagram is also the change in the amount of real consumption expenditure.

This is where the usual "theory" of GDP leaves off, as in figure 1.3. When the utility-augmenting Lancaster consumption technology is included in the analysis, a second source of value comes into play. An increase in the amount of information freely available for consumer choice or a costless improvement in product quality causes the utility function to shift outward to U_{1e} in figure 1.4 even though output in resource units (X_{1r}, Y_{1r}) remains unchanged, as do real GDP_1 and prices (P_0^X, P_0^Y). At these prices, the tangency between U_{1e} occurs at the point C. This tangency implicitly defines a new frontier labeled $EPPF_1$ to emphasize that it is the effective-output possibility frontier associated with the production possibilities frontier PPF_1. A pair of virtual outputs (X_{1e}, Y_{1e}) are defined in which the outputs are now denominated in efficiency units (hence the subscript e). This convention transforms the units of X and Y from the cost of the resources they embody into the units of the utility they convey. If the transformation results in the same proportion θ for both goods, as in figure 1.4, the result is $X_{1e} = (1 + \theta)X_{1r}$, and $Y_{1e} = (1 + \theta)Y_{1r}$. This is the phenomenon we have called utility-augmenting (or output-saving) technical change: an increase in utility for the same amount of resource-based output (occurring in this example at the rate θ).[7]

A little algebra establishes that the shift in utility from U_{1r} at B to U_{1e} at C is related to θ in the following way: $U_{1e} = (1 + \theta)U_{1r}$, under the simplifying assumptions of figure 1.4 so that $\theta = [(U_{1e}) - U_{1r})]/U_{1r} = \Delta U/U$. In other words, the rate of change of output-saving technical change is associated with the rate of change in utility between points B and C in figure 1.4. This is hardly surprising in view of the way we have defined output-saving technical change. A more important result emerges from the fact that the line tangent to U_{1e} at C can be used to define what we have termed *expanded GDP*. $EGDP_1 = P_0^X X_{1e} + P_0^Y Y_{1e}$. It then follows that $EGDP_1 = (1 + \theta)(P_0^X X_{1r} + P_0^Y Y_{1r}) = (1 + \theta)GDP_1$. In other words, output-saving technical change leads to a grossed-up form of real GDP as conventionally defined. Here is where the CV and EV measures of the willingness to pay enter the analysis. Since relative prices are assumed not to change during the move from B to C, we denote the CV/EV by V and note that it is the monetary "distance" between the lines $EGDP_1$ and GDP_1. In other words, $V = EGDP_1 - GDP_1 = (1 + \theta)GDP_1 - GDP_1$, from which it follows that $V = \theta GDP_1$ and that $\theta = V/GDP_1$. This result is significant for the issues at hand because it shows that the unobservable rate of output-saving technical change, θ, is potentially observable through the use of consumer surplus techniques.[8]

It is also important to emphasize that the definition of V used in arriving at EGDP is a general equilibrium concept involving both X and Y and that V must be estimated accordingly. The implication of this point is not readily apparent in figure 1.4 because it is drawn with indifference curves that shift in a parallel way and because the θ is the same for both X and Y. In this

---

7. Figure 1.4 is a simplified formulation from Hulten and Nakamura (2018). It is meant to illustrate the underlying role of a utility-enhancing shift in the consumption technology in a general equilibrium context. We have adopted a utility function that embodies simplifying assumptions. The indifference curves of $U(X, Y)$ are homothetic (radial blowups of a base curve), so the shifts have a neutral effect on the consumption Y/X ratio when relative prices do not change.

8. V in these equations is defined as the *distance* between the indifference curves in two time periods, and θ refers to the *rate* at which the consumption technology shifts over the interval. The interval may refer to one year (the simple case analyzed in this section) or the cumulative effects of many years. In general, V should not be used as a direct measure of θ and therefore should not itself be added to annual GDP to arrive at EGDP unless adjusted for the time horizon involved to get at θ.

situation, the expansion path of the economy, $0G$, is a straight line, and the price ratio P^X/P^Y is constant. When there are separate rates for each good, θ_X and θ_Y, the price ratio P^X/P^Y can change, as can the expansion path. In this case, the EV and CV differ, since they reflect different ratios. This is a familiar problem, but it implies that a partial equilibrium estimate of either θ_X or θ_Y separately holding the price of the other good constant, V_X or V_Y, does not capture the full impact of the change in the θ. Moreover, the sum of the resulting partial equilibrium V_X or V_Y is not equal to the general equilibrium V except under very strong restrictions on the utility function (Varian 1992). This, too, should be kept in mind when evaluating studies that add a partial equilibrium estimate of the willingness to pay for various technology goods to annual GDP.

1.3.4   Information and Product Quality Change as Sources of Output-Saving Innovation

The rationale for output-saving innovation has thus far been presented largely in terms of the benefits of increased information for efficient consumer choice and the associated V as a monetary metric of those benefits. However, the output-saving effect is more general in its scope. Two types of the output-saving technical changes can be distinguished. The first is product-*dis*embodied innovation, μ, which includes the benefits of increased information but also includes costless improvements in outcomes in the provisions of many services (e.g., improvements in convenience, the diffusion of best-practice techniques in the service sectors). The second is product-embodied innovation in consumption goods, which itself comes in two forms: improvements in the design of existing goods (quality change) and the advent of innovative new goods that embody characteristics not seen before or not available in past years.

Quality change and new goods share the common feature that they are goods that embody desirable new features. However, they differ in the way the features affect utility. In the first, new varieties of *existing* goods enter the market with superior characteristics, and it is common to treat the superior variety as though it were equivalent to having more of the inferior variety it replaces. In terms of figure 1.4, this treats the good X_{1e} as a multiple $(1 + \beta)$ X_0, holding μ and λ constant and letting β denote the rate of quality change (also, Y_{1e} is a multiple $(1 + \beta) Y_0$). In this formulation, "better" is assumed to be equivalent to more. This approach incorporates product quality innovation at a rate β into the analysis of figure 1.4 symmetrically with μ. Both are calibrated using the equivalent increase in the bundle (X_0, Y_0). The sum of the two equals the rate of output-saving innovation—that is, $\theta = \mu + \beta$.

The compensating variation V developed in figure 1.4 provides a metric for a generic θ but could in principle be applied to μ and β separately. However, because the latter is embodied in products that are transacted in markets, there is another avenue of approach to the problem of estimating

β based on prices. It exploits the fact that, because the change in utility is assumed to be costless, the amount of money spent to purchase the quantities (X_{1r}, Y_{1r}) is the same as the amount associated with (X_{1e}, Y_{1e})—that is, that $P_0^X X_{1r} + P_0^Y Y_{1r} = P_0^{Xe} X_{1e} + Y_{1e}$. The P^{Xe} and P^{Ye} are the shadow prices of the effective outputs X_{1e} and Y_{1e} and are denominated in equivalent units (we assume here that there is no pure price inflation, so the accounting can be done in base-year prices). Since the same expenditure $P_0^X X_{1r}$ allows the consumer to acquire X_{1e}, P_0^{Xe}, $P_0^X X_{1r} = P_0^{Xe} X_{1e}$. It then follows that P_0^X / P_0^{Xe} is equal to the X_{1e}/X_{1r}, which in turn equals $(1 + \beta)$. Thus as utility increases by the factor β, the cost of acquiring this utility falls. This formulation reduces the problem of estimating β to the problem of estimating the relevant price ratio. We will revisit this approach in the sections that discuss the associated empirical procedures and problems.

One further point is important here. Because output-saving technical change means that each dollar spent on either good "buys" more utility, this increase would normally imply that more of the good subject to technical change would be demanded by consumers and that the quantity demanded would increase to the point at which the gap between the new marginal utility and acquisition price would be extinguished. However, the opportunity for this arbitrage does not exist in all cases. When a superior pharmaceutical drug arrives in the marketplace, the individual consumer does not respond by buying more of the drug until the marginal utility equals the old one but instead purchases the new standard regimen. Nor do people necessarily usually purchase more personal computers as their efficiency increases and the efficiency price falls; there may even be a shift to less-expensive tablets. There are many situations in which the market mechanism does not arbitrage the benefits of innovation, and in this case, there will be a gap between the goods measured at cost of acquisition and the corresponding benefits received, and this gap may persist, giving rise to utility-enhancing innovation.

1.3.5   Quality Change Embodied in New Goods

The treatment of quality change in its β form relies on the assumption that "better" can be measured in terms of more of an inferior good. This is a tidy solution that locates β in the theoretical framework of figure 1.4 and is useful for empirical work. But "better as more" embodies the paradox that a good that is sufficiently superior that it needs separate treatment is also essentially a multiple of the replaced good. However, it may be more accurate to regard the superior variety as a new good that offers capabilities that the previous version did not. Again, a pharmaceutical drug with a high degree of efficacy does not achieve the same outcomes as multiple doses of an earlier treatment with a low degree of efficacy.

Unfortunately, treating a significant change in the β quality as a new good leads to a host of other problems. From a theoretical standpoint, a new good Z cannot be located on the XY axis of figure 1.4. It appears on a new Z axis and becomes incorporated in GDP as $P^X X + P^Y Y + P^Z Z$. Because of the sudden appearance of the Z, there is no prior price or quantity with which to estimate the gain in consumer utility from its arrival. The Hicks-Rothbart solution is to regard quantity of Z as zero prior to its introduction because its theoretical price was too high and there was zero consumer demand. The solution posits the existence of a "reservation" price that is just low enough to attract consumers to the market for Z. The difference between the reservation price and the actual price prevailing when the good is introduced is then used as a measure of the increase in utility resulting from the arrival of Z. The empirical problem is then to estimate this reservation price.

It should also be noted that the implementation of the reservation price approach requires econometric modeling. This, in turn, requires assumptions and procedures that lie outside of the normal sphere of data measurement. It is also time consuming and must be repeated for each new good, so it is not economical for use in statistical programs that produce annual data series that must be internally consistent over time. This problem applies to the Bureau of Labor Statistics (BLS) price program, and they thus use an imputation procedure that, as we shall see, has the general effect of linking the new good to the subcategory to which it is assigned at, or near, the mean value of the other goods in the subcategory. This way of incorporating new goods into the price indexes used to compute real GDP is conceptually the same as the way it treats quality change in existing goods, except that it refers to quality change in a class of goods that may or may not be closely related. This approximation procedure may thus miss much of the value of the innovation embodied in truly new goods like the internet.

1.4   The Estimation of Innovation and EGDP

1.4.1   An Overview

The Industrial Revolution and its aftermath have resulted in a dramatic increase in income. Angus Maddison's 2007 estimates of world GDP since 1700 suggest that real-world GDP per capita increased by almost ninefold over the period 1700–1998, with most of the increase coming during the later stages of the Industrial Revolution. Moreover, the increase from 1700 to 1998 was by far the largest in the countries that led that revolution. The increase in the countries of Western Europe was nearly 18-fold, and that in the United States over the shorter 1820–1998 period was estimated to be 22-fold, leaving the rest of the world far behind. Moreover, estimates of real GDP per capita in the national accounts (table 7.1) show that real GDP per capita has increased by over 250 percent from 1950 to 2017 and by around 50 percent from the inception of the internet in the early 1990s to 2017.

The centuries since the start of the Industrial Revolution also witnessed extraordinary improvements in the well-being of individuals. The world of

1820 lacked effective medical treatments for most serious afflictions. The discovery of the germ theory of infection by Joseph Lister was a major step forward, ultimately persuading surgeons they should wash their hands prior to surgery. The development of effective forms of anesthesia was also a huge advance in medical treatment (today, it is hard to imagine surgery without it). Antibiotics in the 20th century allowed the treatment of routine infections that previously led to many deaths. Similarly, the development of vaccines brought fearsome diseases like smallpox, diphtheria, tetanus, yellow fever, and polio more or less under control, with enormous increases in human well-being. The medical revolution proceeds apace with important breakthroughs in surgery (noninvasive, robotic, and nano). Diagnostic procedures have evolved from the simple X-ray (a breakthrough in its day) to CT scans and MRIs. These innovations have had a major impact on life expectancy, which increased from 48 years to 78 years over the course of the 20th century. How much GDP would society be willing to sacrifice in order to protect these gains?

Significant increases in welfare also occurred in other areas. The first half of the 19th century was a period without electricity, flush toilets, central heating, telecommunications, and automobiles and aircraft. The growth in labor-saving home appliances, like automatic washing machines and refrigeration, brought large and direct gains in the well-being of families, as did residential air conditioning. Many advances have come since the mid-20th century. As recently as 1950, a quarter of America's homes had no flush toilet, according the US Census Bureau housing data. In 1990, only 1 percent of US homes lacked complete plumbing facilities, but in 1940, nearly half lacked complete plumbing. Improvements in sanitation were also important in increasing public health. In 1960, about one in five households had no telephone available. Wood was used as a major heating fuel in 1940 (23 percent) but virtually disappeared by 1970 (only 1.3 percent). Robert Gordon (2016) has chronicled the gains in welfare that arose from many of these innovations.

The rapid uptake of digital goods is significant in this regard. According to Census estimates, the fraction of adults with internet use at home went from one in five in 1997 to nearly three-quarters in 2012. Moreover, estimates by the Pew Research Center show that the percentage of adults who use at least one social media site increased from less than 1 in 10 in 2005 to two-thirds in 2015, and other Pew surveys found that the market penetration of smartphones more than doubled from 2011 to 2016, from 35 percent to 77 percent.[9] The rapid uptake was matched by a dramatic increase in speed and capacity. In 1988, internet speeds on dial-up modems were 9.6 Kb, while 2G cellular speeds were about the same. Now broadband speeds up to 1 gigabit are available in a few locations, and 100 Mb and higher speeds are

9. US Census Bureau (2014); Perrin (2015); Pew Research Center (2017); Anderson (2015).

widely available. And 4GLTE cellular speeds are 100 Mb, and these too are in wide use. Over a 27-year period, from 1988 to 2015, speeds have gone up some 10,000 times, or a 40 percent annual rate.

1.4.2   Sorting Out the λ, μ, and β Effects

The overview of the preceding section suggests that a high degree of innovation activity accompanied a sustained growth rate of real GDP. The question raised in this chapter is whether the gains in individual well-being are fully valued by the corresponding gains in income per capita and, if not, how much additional welfare was generated by a shift in what we have called the consumption technology. In more precise parametric terms, innovation enters the picture via the λ, μ, and β. The remaining sections of this chapter review a more detailed look at the link between the growth in real GDP per capita and the growth in consumer well-being and EGDP, with a view toward assessing their potential magnitude and the implied biases vis-à-vis current statistical practice.

The parameters λ, μ, and β and intangible capital are part of the larger framework underlying the figures. We have studied this framework in the two-sector (X, Y) case, but the problem at hand involves the impact of innovation on the growth rates of aggregate real GDP per capita and individual welfare, so it is appropriate to reformulate the problem in a one-sector form. The various components of interest come together to form the basic framework linking the growth in welfare per capita, $u - \ell$, to the growth in output per worker, $(q^r - \ell)$, and the parameters of output-saving innovation. This yields the basic economy-wide sources-of-welfare-growth equation of this chapter:

$$(1) \qquad\qquad u - \ell = \mu + \beta + (q^r - \ell).$$

This equation indicates that the representative person's welfare depends on both the amount of income they have and how well they use it. (The variable $q^r - \ell$ here represents the growth rate of output per worker measured at resource cost, not effectiveness.) The term $q^r - \ell$ can be further decomposed to yield the conventional Solow sources-of-output-growth equation:

$$(2) \qquad\qquad q^r - \ell = \lambda + v_K(k - \ell) + v_N(n - \ell).$$

This second equation indicates that the growth rate of output per worker is composed of the following elements: the growth rate of tangible capital per worker $(k - \ell)$ and the growth rate of intangible capital per worker $(n - \ell)$, each weighted by their respective income shares, v_E and v_N. These income shares are proxies for the corresponding elasticities of output in the standard Solow sources-of-growth framework. The λ measures the resource-saving technical change, while $v_N(n - \ell)$ is a measure of resource-using intangible innovation.[10]

---

10. A more detailed description of the sources-of-growth model and the role of the income shares is given in the survey by Hulten (2001).

Two elaborations of (1) and (2) are necessary for the empirical literature described in the following sections. As previously noted, the statistics on real GDP in the United States embody a correction for quality change, implying that the observed growth rate is $q^e = q^r + \beta$ if the correction for β is complete and accurate. This correction implies, in turn, that equation (1) must also be modified to account for the fact that the use of q^e as the output growth means that β is suppressed into output and does not appear explicitly in (1), with the result that

(3) $u = \mu + (q^e - \ell) = \lambda^e + v_K(k - \ell) + v_N(n - \ell).$

The q^e-based TFP residual conflates the true λ productivity, the shift in the production function, with the quality effect, with the result that $\lambda^e = \lambda + \beta$. In other words, the use of real GDP, as presented in official statistics, has the effect of concealing the true shift in the production function, unless the magnitude of β is known. However, the size of β is nowhere shown in the official statistics.

A second modification of this framework is needed because, as we shall see, the β that gets embedded in q^e and λ^e is estimated with a significant degree of bias, giving β' instead. The bias in β results in a corresponding bias in output growth, which becomes $q^{e'} = q^r + \beta'$. When this biased estimate is used in place of q^e, the growth equation becomes

(4) $u = \theta + [\beta - \beta'] + (q^{e'} - \ell) = \lambda^{e'} + v_K(k - \ell) + v_N(n\ell).$

The $q^{e'}$-based TFP residual now conflates the productivity effect and the biased quality effect, with the result that $\lambda^{e'} = \lambda + \beta'$. As before with (3), neither the biased β' nor the degree of bias $[\beta - \beta']$ is recorded in official statistics. However, there are numerous occasional studies of the bias in price statistics that can be used to get an impression of its potential magnitude.

1.5   The Supply-Side Contribution to Overall Growth

1.5.1   The Sources of Output Growth

The sources-of-growth results for the US *private business economy*, based on equation (4), are shown in table 1.1 for the period 1948 to 2007. A version of this sources-of-growth model is presented in this table, derived from studies of Corrado and Hulten (2010, 2015), where it is shown that the annual growth rate of private business efficiency output per unit of labor over the period 1948 to 2007 averaged 2.4 percent. The sources of this growth are reported in the rows of table 1.1, which correspond to the elements on the right-hand side of (2) (with the addition of a term that corrects for changes in the composition of the labor force, due largely to increased educational attainment). For the period as a whole, this decomposition reveals that the deepening of tangible capital accounted for 27 percent of the 2.4 percent output growth, of which 10 percent came from information and communications

Table 1.1   Sources of growth in US private business sector (average of annual growth rates)

	1948–2007	1948–73	1973–95	1995–2007
1. Output per hour $[q^e—\ell]$	2.41	2.99	1.56	2.76
Percentage point contribution to output per hour of:				
2. Tangible capital $[s_K(k-\ell)]$	0.65	0.76	0.52	0.67
Memo: ICT equipment	0.23	0.11	0.28	0.37
3. Intangible capital $[s_N(n-\ell)]$	0.42	0.30	0.39	0.74
Memo: R&D (NSF/BEA)	0.10	0.08	0.07	0.17
4. Labor composition	0.20	0.15	0.26	0.2
5. TFP $[\beta' + \lambda]$	1.14	1.78	0.39	1.16
Percentage of total contribution to output per hour of:				
2. Tangible capital	27%	25%	33%	24%
Memo: ICT equipment	10%	4%	18%	13%
3. Intangible capital	17%	10%	25%	27%
Memo: R&D (NSF/BEA)	4%	3%	4%	5%
4. Labor composition	8%	5%	17%	7%
5. TFP	47%	60%	25%	42%

ICT refers to information and communications technology equipment, BEA to the Bureau of Economic Analysis, NSF to the National Science Foundation, TFP to total factor productivity. The latter includes both β' and λ terms, since the hyperoutput concept, Q^e, is used in these data rather than resource-based output, Q^r. The procedures used to estimate product quality innovation are, at best, incomplete, hence the β' rather than a true β.

Source: Corrado and Hulten (2010, 2015).

technology (ICT) equipment per worker hour. Intangible capital contributed 17 percent, of which only 4 percent came from formal R&D. Changes in the composition of the workforce added 8 percent, while the TFP residual explained by the other sources made the largest contribution at 47 percent.

These estimates refer to the period as a whole. A look at the subperiods reveals some important within-period trends. It is significant for the taxonomy of innovation presented in section 1.3 that the long-term trend in TFP moved downward since the 1960s. TFP grew at an average annual rate of 1.8 percent over the period 1948 to 1965 and explained almost half of the growth rate of output per worker hour; the growth rate fell to 1.2 percent in the most recent period, 1995 to 2007, and its contribution to output growth fell from 60 percent to just over 40 percent. The declining trend in TFP is also evident in figure 1.5, which plots the time trend in the four-year moving average over the slightly longer period up to 2011 (because of the moving average, the initial year shown is 1955). The growing gap between TFP and output per worker hour indicated a declining relative contribution of TFP to the latter.

However, while the trend in TFP is downward, the contribution of intangible capital deepening, $v_N(n-\ell)$, shown in table 1.1, followed a generally

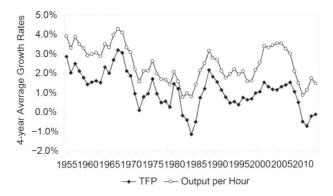

Fig. 1.5   Growth in output per hour and TFP, US NFB, 1955–2011

upward trend. An important implication of these contrasting trends is that there has been a shift away from costless resource-saving innovation (augmented by the product-quality part of what we have termed output-saving innovation) toward costly resource-using innovation, as represented by $v_N(n - \ell)$. The sum of the two has not changed all that much, but the welfare implications have. Resource-saving innovation is a "free lunch" in terms of the direct increase in welfare, while resource-using innovation represents a sacrifice in consumption. The free lunch is the better alternative from the welfare standpoint, but it is really not a choice variable. On the other hand, it is no great surprise that as technological complexity rises, innovation requires more than serendipity to be sustained, hence the increased importance of systematic and focused investments in innovation and the associated equipment and learning.

Resource-saving and resource-using technical changes are not the only factors in the innovation process. ICT equipment has been an important coinvestment of intangible capital during the digital revolution, as has the increase in the composition of the labor force toward more educated and highly skilled workers. When the growth in the contribution of human capital is combined with the ICT term and then added to the intangible capital term, the result shows a substantial change from the period 1948–73 to 1995–2007, from 0.56 percent in the earlier period (19 percent of overall growth) to 1.31 percent (a 47 percent contribution). Thus the relative contribution of TFP has declined, but innovation and its correlates have not, although the composition has changed.

1.5.2   Critique of the Growth Accounting Results

Growth accounting produces estimates that are by far the most secure results in the empirical chain linking resources and technology to EGDP in figure 1.3. They are supported by national accounting data assembled by the BLS in its official productivity estimates. They are, however, inevitably not without problems. Indeed, Abramovitz (1956) famously noted that the TFP residual is, in a sense, a "measure of our ignorance," since it sweeps together all the factors that affect output growth that cannot be measured explicitly. These include not only the effects of costless advances in technology, which are partly due to spillover externalities of technical knowledge whose property rights are hard to protect, but also nontechnological factors such as the omitted variables like infrastructure capital, nonmarket but resource-using output from household production, and chronic biases in the estimation of service-sector output. And even if the TFP residual were accurately measured, there is still the identification problem of sorting out the separate magnitudes of β and λ.

There is also a troublesome identification problem arising from the failure to account adequately for the effect of fluctuations in aggregate demand on the intensity of use of labor and capital. Capital is measured as a stock of accumulated past investment (adjusted for depreciation) rather than as a flow of actual services emanating from the stock. The stock itself does not change much during fluctuation in demand, but the flow of productive services does, and the degree of capital utilization changes over the business cycle. As a result, the gap between the stocks and flows is forced into the residual measure of TFP, causing the procyclicality of TFP seen in figure 1.5. It is for this reason that the time period covered in table 1.1 stops at 2007, the year before the Great Recession. Thereafter, TFP growth dropped significantly and, indeed, turned negative, indicating a contraction in the level of productive efficiency.

A negative growth rate of TFP is plausible during sharp downturns in economic activity, but it is hard to reconcile with its conventional interpretation as an indicator of technical change over longer periods of time. However, this is precisely what happens in some individual industries, notably those engaged in the production of services. Another part of the BLS productivity program presents growth accounting estimates for individual industries in the US economy based on a variant of (3) in which output, gross of deliveries to other industries, is decomposed into the share-weighted contribution of the inputs, now expanded to intermediate inputs obtained from other industries. The concept of λ at the industry level and the estimate of residual TFP reflect changes in the efficiency with which gross output is produced. The resulting TFP growth is found to be zero for the service sector (North American Industry Classification System [NAICS] industries 54 through 81) over the period 1987–2015. It is actually negative for the shorter period 1987–2007. Moreover, the TFP annual growth rate is negative for the entire 1987–2015 estimates for some service subsectors: Educational Services (−0.5 percent); Ambulatory Health Care (−0.4 percent); Hospitals, Nursing, and Residential Care (−0.9 percent); Management of Companies and Enterprises (−0.4 percent); and Legal Services (−0.3 percent).

It is possible that lower productivity is inherent in the production of services, and they possibly suffer from Baumol's cost disease, although this is controversial and, in any event, refers to labor productivity (output per unit labor) and does not envision negative productivity change.[11] Indeed, negative TFP growth over three decades is highly implausible, and all the more so when it is recognized that these decades span the digital revolution. To emphasize this point, if the level of TFP in education were indexed to 100 in 1987, the index would fall to 87 in 2015. For Hospitals, Nursing, and Residential Care, the index in 2015 would fall to 77. This indicates a drop in TFP in education and health care of a large magnitude that would certainly have been noticed "on the ground" had it actually occurred.

While the Baumol explanation may play a role, the dominant factor explaining a prolonged period of negative TFP is most likely output mismeasurement. The mismeasurement explanation was discussed by Zvi Griliches (1994), who observed that "the conceptual problem arises because in many services sectors it is not exactly clear what is being transacted, what is the output, and what services correspond to the payments made to their providers" (7). He thus labeled the industries we are discussing as hard-to-measure industries. A consequence is that there is no agreement as to the units of measurement that underlie output of some services, and current procedures may not even be getting the resource-based Q^r right, much less the efficiency-based Q^e. However, price deflators are also part of the problem, for, as he observed in 1992, there are a "number of service industries series . . . deflated by makeshift deflators."

The Griliches statement touches on one of the key ideas modeled in our framework: that consumer outcomes are different from produced output, and output is different from the expenditures. These measurement issues are echoed in Cutler and Berndt (2001), who point to what they have called the "output movement" in health economics, which attempts to measure the impact of medical care on health outcomes rather than the amount of resources expended. In the case of output and productivity of the education sector, Triplett and Bosworth (2004) summarized the proceedings of their April 2000 Brookings-sponsored workshop and observed that "there was very little agreement on how to develop strong quantifiable measures of either output or productivity. Particular concerns were expressed about how to adjust for variations in education quality" (286).

In defense of the BLS program, the BLS website that presents the non-

11. The Baumol disease explanation of the lower productivity was challenged by events after the first productivity slowdown. Triplett and Bosworth (2004) found the services were not that much a drag on overall output per worker growth. Looking at a longer period than Griliches, they report a speed-up in services relative to the goods-producing sectors. Labor productivity in the services rose from an average annual growth rate of 0.7 percent during the 1987–95 period to 2.6 percent in the years 1995–2001; for the goods-producing sector, the corresponding numbers were 1.8 percent and 2.3 percent, respectively. They also find that 80 percent of the increase in the overall growth in output per unit labor after 1995 was due to ICT's contribution to the service sectors, contrary to the hypothesis that services were inherently resistant to productivity change. However, Sichel (1997) argues that only a limited amount of the productivity slowdown can be attributed to the change in industrial composition per se.

manufacturing industry productivity estimates contains this disclaimer: "Output and the corresponding inputs for nonmanufacturing industries are often difficult to measure and can produce productivity measures of inconsistent quality. Customers should be cautious when interpreting the data."[12] It is hard to criticize the BLS for not fully solving the problems with service sector output measurement highlighted by Griliches.

1.5.3   Problems with Measuring Intangible Capital

We have thus far focused on problems with the estimates of TFP, but there are also problems associated with the intangible capital term in (3) and table 1.1. The intangible capital term, $v_N(n - \ell)$, is a proxy for resource-using innovation, but it too is subject to measurement error. Intangible capital tends to be produced within an enterprise on an own-account basis, and its intangible nature makes the extent of its presence hard to detect. Moreover, own-account production does not generate an explicit price and quantity from which its quantity and value can be inferred. Instead, much of our information about this kind of capital is obtained from general surveys or from imputations with a large scope for error. As previously noted, the BEA moved in 2013 to capitalize R&D and artistic originals and to add them to GDP rather than treating them as within-firm intermediate goods that do not find their way into GDP.

Software had been represented in the national accounts since 1999, but even the list of intangibles included by the BEA and presented in the BLS productivity estimates falls short by about one-half of the longer list in the taxonomy developed by Corrado, Hulten, and Sichel (2005, 2009). The estimates in table 1.1 are based on an updated version of the Corrado-Hulten-Sichel framework and thus differ from those presented in the BLS productivity tables, which include only a partial list.[13]

1.6   Estimates of Innovation on the Consumption Side of the Economy

1.6.1   An Overview of the Problems Involved

The previous section reviewed the empirical work on the two main variables of supply-side innovation: the Solow residual and the intangible capital effect. We turn now to the consumption side and the variables that shift the consumption technology, μ and β. This type of innovation is inherently

---

12. Multifactor Productivity and Related KLEMS Measures from the NIPA Industry Database, 1987 to 2016 (https://www.bls.gov/mfp/mprdload.htm).

13. One consequence of capitalized intangibles is that the relative importance of TFP as a source of growth falls from 50 percent to 39 percent when moving from the BLS TFP estimates to the fuller list (Corrado and Hulten 2014, table 3). Another consequence is that the resulting investment is added to GDP, which is thereby increased in size, but not so much in its rate of growth, which is only modest.

more difficult to measure because it involves a shift in utility, for which there are no regularly published estimates, whereas production-side innovation involves output, for which such estimates are available. Moreover, the latter is based on well-established concepts, while the factors that shift the consumption technology are new to this chapter. However, conventional statistical practice does include some of the effects of β in the adjustment of output for quality change, although the implied β is not shown explicitly and is associated with production, not consumption. Measuring the effects of μ is even more of a challenge, since it is not embodied in specific goods, though it does emanate from goods (as internet information does from computers and smartphones). This example points to another complication that arises because μ and β are linked in ways that make them hard to separate (medical care offers numerous other examples, such as the computer-based machinery that enables minimally invasive surgery).

This said, estimating μ and β can at least be approached via individual studies of their value as revealed by consumer preference. We will review some of these sources of information in the remaining sections of this chapter. We first focus on the measurement of quality change and the evidence of the potential size of β found in academic research and government programs. Much of the literature relating to β is actually about the bias with which β is estimated in official statistics, which is the rationale for the reformulation of our basic model to include the explicit bias term $[\beta - \beta']$ in (4). We postpone our discussion of the disembodied term μ in sections dealing with the internet, health care, and education.

1.6.2   Estimates of Product Quality Change

The problem of measuring product quality change is one of the most heavily studied issues of measurement statistics, with three blue-chip panels presenting assessments of the degree of product quality bias in official price indexes and recommending solutions: the 1961 Stigler Commission, the 1996 Boskin Commission, and the 2002 Schultze Commission. Major assessments of the procedures used by BLS and BEA have been published by members of those agencies (Moulton and Moses 1997; Groshen et al. 2017). There is, in addition, a large academic literature. The overall thrust of these efforts is a consensus (though perhaps a weak one) that price statistics have been, and still are, subject to a variety of measurement biases, and the main question is about the magnitude of the biases.

The fact that biases have lingered over many decades is a testament to just how difficult the problems are. Indeed, Shapiro and Wilcox (1996) called quality change "the house-to-house combat of price measurement" and argued that "there is no simple formula that one can apply to deduce a magnitude of the problem, nor any simple solution. Unfortunately, there is no substitute for the equivalent of a ground war: an eclectic case-by-case assessment of individual products" (124). This combat has, however, produced some notable victories, and the case of computers is a salient example. The BEA makes a quality adjustment to the output price of computers and peripheral equipment in personal consumption expenditures in order to reflect the advances in computing power enabled by Moore's law, with the result that the price fell at an average annual rate of -1 percent from 1960 to 1985, then by -21 percent per year from 1985 to 2000, followed by a -11 percent decline from 2000 to 2015. These declines imply a high rate of quality-induced price change P^e when compared to a baseline scenario of no change in the resource price P^r. And computers are not the only example of rapid quality change. The BEA's prepackaged computer software and accessories price deflator also includes an adjustment for quality change (Abel, Berndt, and White 2007), and it declined at an average annual rate of -17 percent over the period 1985–2000 and by -5.5 percent from 2000 to 2015.

Moore's law applies to goods directly affected by the silicon revolution, like computers, but its reach is far wider. Computer chips and software are embedded in many devices, from smartphones to vehicles and machine tools. Byrne and Corrado (2017b) provide estimates of the implied wired telecommunications services deflator based on measures of the improving quality (and rapid deflation) of telecommunications equipment developed in Byrne and Corrado (2015) and methods described in Byrne and Corrado (2017a). They do so for *nonresidential* wireless services rather than for personal consumption expenditures, and they find a rate of deflation 7 percentage points below the official measures from 2004 to 2014. This study points to the need to distinguish between the quality change in a good that accrues to consumers and that which affects the supply of goods passing through markets.

As for a broader range of goods, Bils and Klenow (2001) use the Consumer Expenditure Survey to estimate "quality Engel curves" for 66 durable goods using the idea that richer households pay more for each good. They estimate that quality growth averages 3.7 percent per year for their sample of goods, with 2.2 percent showing up as pure price inflation, and conclude that BLS procedures do not fully account for the impact of quality upgrading.

Some mention must also be made of product innovation brought to marketplace in the form of new goods. Hausman (1996) examined the introduction of a new brand of breakfast cereal and found that the treatment of new goods in official statistics missed a significant amount of the innovation that had occurred. Hausman's 1999 study of the introduction of mobile cellular telephones reached the same conclusion.

1.6.3   The BLS Price Measurement Program

The BLS is the government agency charged with the bulk of the Shapiro-Wilcox house-to-house combat in the price measurement battle. It is the source of many of the price statistics used by the BEA to derive real GDP, but its main task is to prepare a monthly report on the prices consumers pay for a sample "basket" of goods, with the general objective of determining how much the cost of living has increased due to monetary price inflation. Price inflation erodes the "bang for the buck" of each dollar of income, and the Consumer Price Index (CPI) indicates (in principle) how much additional income is required to maintain the average consumer at the previous period's level of utility if nominal income were not to change. The CPI can thus serve as a cost-of-living adjustment for wage and other contracts and government benefit programs, but it also measures the general rate of price inflation in consumer goods and the erosion in purchasing power that implies. Since an improvement in product quality provides more "bang for the buck" for each dollar spent and offsets the inflationary erosion, it must be taken into account.

One implication of product innovation is that the same basket of goods cannot be priced repeatedly over a period of time when new, and sometimes superior, goods enter the marketplace and find their way into the basket, and others are driven out of the market by innovation. The agents assigned to go out each month to price these goods in a retail outlet are often confronted with the problem of finding alternative items to price. The procedures they follow are described in chapter 17 of the BLS Handbook of Methods (US Bureau of Labor Statistics 2018).

The prescribed procedures are complicated and not easy to summarize. Fortunately, the survey by Groshen et al. (2017) gives an excellent and up-to-date overview of the program. When an item that was priced in the preceding month goes missing, the agents look for a similar item with which to replace it in the sample. This matched-model approach is the "cornerstone" of the CPI program. Groshen et al. (2017) report that for the period from December 2013 to November 2014, "matches were found for items in the Consumer Price Index 73 percent of the time. Of the remaining 27 percent of items that were not matched, 22 percent reflected temporarily missing items, such as a bathing suit in Milwaukee in December. The other 5 percent represented a permanent disappearance" (190–91). These percentages are on a monthly, not annualized, basis. They go on to say,

> When a match permanently ends in the Consumer Price Index and the same good cannot be tracked from one period to the next, then (except for housing) the Bureau of Labor Statistics initiates a quality adjustment procedure after a replacement good has been established. When the replacement has characteristics very similar to the exiting product, the price of the replacement product is used in place of the exiting product. For example, of the 5 percent of the CPI that represented permanently disappearing items during the period noted above, three-fifths of those items were replaced by a similar good. For the remaining two-fifths, where the characteristics were judged to be insufficiently close, BLS staff made a quality adjustment to the replacement product's price. (191).

The nature of the quality adjustments made to the prices of the missing two-fifths is one of the salient questions about the CPI's ability to account adequately for product innovation. According to the CPI chapter 17 in the BLS Handbook (US Bureau of Labor Statistics 2018), the adjustment involves an imputation procedure:

> Imputation is a procedure for handling missing information. The CPI uses imputation for a number of cases, including refusals, inability to collect data for some other reason (the item may be out of season), and the inability to make a satisfactory estimate of the quality change. Substitute items that can be neither directly compared nor quality adjusted are called noncomparable. For noncomparable substitutions, an estimate of constant-quality price change is made by imputation. There are two imputation methods: Cell-relative imputation and class-mean imputation. (20)

It is these last two imputations that are the source of much controversy. When a new good like the cell phone or the ATM arrives in the marketplace, it is assigned a price that reflects the average price change of the goods in the product class to which it is assigned (or the average price of a subset of goods in the class). Thus, as previously noted, the technological innovations embodied in wholly new goods are incorporated with a procedure based on the price of goods that do not embody the innovation.

This problem extends to the rotation of items into and out of the sampling frame. The BLS Handbook states, on page 12 of the CPI chapter 17, that "to enable the CPI to reflect changes in the marketplace, new item and outlet samples are selected each year, on a rotating basis, for approximately 25 percent of the item strata in each PSU [primary sampling unit]" (US Bureau of Labor Statistics 2018). This rapid substitution is a welcome feature of the price program because it allows new goods to enter the CPI sample, including those that embody innovative new technology. Overlap procedures are used in incorporating the rotated sample into the index.

The price hedonic method is another way that quality and sample composition issues are handled in the CPI.[14] Groshen et al. (2017) report that "in the Consumer Price Index, about 33% of the total expenditures in the underlying basket of goods are eligible for quality adjustment with hedonics. Housing-related expenditures account for most of this share" (192).[15] These statistics suggest that very few item categories are subject to the hedonic method, despite the recommendation of the Stigler Commission (1961) review of price measurement that specifically referred to the Griliches study

14. The basic idea of price hedonics is to regress the observed transaction price of a sample of goods on a set of characteristics to estimate the shadow price of each characteristic. The price of a bundle with more, or different, characteristics can then be estimated and, by extension, the price of a bundle that possesses more characteristics. Computers are a prime example. Here, the unit price of a new model of computer that embodies a faster processor speed, better graphics, and more memory often remains more or less the same (controlling for inflation) as the preceding inferior model.

15. The hedonic regression for housing-related expenditures estimates the rate of deterioration of rental units over time, so the reported inflation rates are higher than the rate of rental price increase to account for the worsening quality of the rental unit over time.

of hedonics in new cars. For its treatment of the price of cars, the BLS uses a measure of the resource cost of new car features rather than hedonic measures of the value of car features in both the PPI and the CPI programs. In this method, the costs of new options added to the standard light vehicle are removed from new car prices in estimating inflation. Recent decades have been a period of remarkable technological innovation in autos, often at relatively low cost per automobile, using sensors, computer power, and software to improve driving. These improvements include safety warning signals, enhanced cruise control, self-parking, and backup vision. The BLS uses the cost method primarily for autos.

The totality of the CPI program is enormous given the huge number of items in the universe of all consumer goods and services. It is all the more impressive because the process must be repeated month after month, without fail. And this is far from the only BLS program, since the bureau is also responsible for many other data collection programs. Moreover, it accomplishes its main mission: to provide a timely cost-of-living adjustment that is accepted by those affected by the outcome. This political economy aspect is perhaps its most important feature given the large transaction costs involved in bargaining and renegotiation that would need to occur in the absence of an acceptable price index (indeed, this was the genesis of the CPI). To accomplish its mission, the BLS must contend with the dynamic nature of the economy and the changing quality of goods, but again, this is not its main mission. One consequence is that the BLS does not report the amount of the quality correction it makes—its implicit estimate of β. That is embodied in its price estimates that are used for output deflation by the BEA.

1.6.4   The Bias in Quality Measurement

More attention has been given to the size of the implied bias in the price deflators (and the bias in β) than to the size of β itself. The subject has generated numerous studies, articles, and conference volumes (including some in the Conference on Research in Income and Wealth Studies in Income and Wealth series). These studies tend to produce mixed results about the size of the CPI bias. The estimates by Groshen et al. (2017) present a recent assessment of the overall bias based on past studies (including Lebow and Rudd 2003; Greenstein and McDevitt 2011). They put the downward bias in the annual growth of real GDP at −0.26 percent in 2015 due to consumer goods and at −0.15 percent due to private investment (real GDP growth was around 2.0 percent in that year). The former is particularly relevant to this chapter, since the "PC services (including internet)" component of the −0.26 percent downward bias was only –0.04 percent (the contribution of medical bias was −0.12 percent). The "raw" annual bias in PC/internet services was an annual −6.50 percent (based on Greenstein and McDevitt 2011), but the GDP share of this category was so small that the share-weighted growth bias barely moved the GDP needle.

Other studies have also found larger biases than those reported in Groshen et al. (2017). Bils (2009) concludes that "price inflation for durables has been overstated by nearly 2 percentage points per year" and found that the BLS procedures for the CPI for autos and trucks understated quality improvements by 2.6 percentage points a year over that period. Indeed, when a large part of the value of a new car is due to electronics and software, new car features have very little additional resource cost and thus are unlikely to appear as a price reduction. Thus the gradual advent of a driverless car, with a concomitant increase in leisure for the driver and reduction in accidents, is not likely to appear in measures of output. The aforementioned 2001 Bils and Klenow study of 66 durable goods also concluded that BLS procedures do not fully account for the impact of quality upgrading. Other studies are consistent with this conclusion. Based on their review of the available evidence, Shapiro and Wilcox (1996) place the midpoint (median) of their subjective probability distribution for the overall bias in the CPI at just under 1.0 percentage point per year with an 80 percent confidence interval stretching from 0.6 percentage point per year to 1.5 percentage points per year. Byrne, Fernald, and Reinsdorf (2016) provide estimates of the annual biases in investment price deflators, which range from 0.9 percent for software to 12.0 percent for computers and peripherals (the Greenstein and McDevitt [2011] estimate is in the middle of this range).

The four studies of the value of broadband evaluated by Syverson (2017) provide estimates of consumer surplus that he extrapolates to 2015 that range from a low of $17 billion to a high of $132 billion, including the Nevo, Turner, and Williams (2016) study of internet access. It might also be noted that the hedonic regression for internet broadband services used in the BLS PPI program includes a regression coefficient on download speed that suggests the 40 percent increase in speed experienced historically and would translate to a 12 percent further annual decrease in price.[16] This, in turn, would result in a decrease in the growth rate of the total PCE deflator that, if applied to both internet access and cellular phone service, would increase real output by $32 billion annually.

1.7 Information, the Internet, and Consumption Technology

1.7.1 The Nature and Value of Information

Measuring the amount of information that floods our senses every day is problematic, and in any event, it is not the volume of information in bits or bytes that matters for economic measurement. What matters is the perceived value to the recipient, and this depends on the way the information is organized, its relevance (often situational), its credibility or perceived accuracy,

16. See US Bureau of Labor and Statistics (2019).

and its timeliness. Too much unstructured or irrelevant information can have a negative effect—the noise-to-signal problem. The valuation of information is thus difficult, and it is compounded by the fact that most information flows without data-specific prices.

The information revolution has increased both signal and noise. For the purpose of this chapter, we confine our attention to the disembodied output-saving innovations in the information that provide value to consumers, where value is determined by the amount they would be willing to pay if necessary for that which is in fact provided free of direct charge. We have formulated this as the parameter μ. The magnitude of this parameter, as measured by the willingness-to-pay metric V of section 1.3, is of great consequence for the question of whether the growth rate of conventional real GDP provides a satisfactory measure of the dynamic changes in the economy over the course of the digital revolution. Addressing this question is the overarching goal of this chapter, and to this end, the rest of this section will marshal the available evidence on the size of V and μ.[17]

1.7.2 Current Treatment of Information in the Statistical System

BEA data from the US national accounts by industry show that the GDP originating in the category "Information-communications-technology-producing industries" amounted to $1.1 trillion in 2016, or about 6 percent of GDP. The scope of this category is rather broad, including the manufacturing of computer and electronic equipment, which, when removed, causes this fraction to fall to 4.5 percent. A still narrower grouping with a focus on information services includes only "Data processing, Internet publishing, and other information services" (1.5 percent) and "Computer systems design and related services" (0.6 percent). Together, these two industries account for $400 billion.

When the focus shifts to the consumer expenditures component of GDP (PCE), BEA data for the categories "Telecommunication services" and "Internet access" show that consumers spent $230 billion on the categories "Telecommunication services" and "Internet access" in 2016, or 1.8 percent of PCE and 1.2 percent of GDP. When expenditures for "Information processing equipment" and "Telephone and related communications equipment" are added to the list, the total increases to around $380 billion, or 3.0 percent of PCE and 2.0 percent of GDP. By way of comparison, Groshen et al. (2017) report a GDP share for the category "PC services (including

---

17. Any attempt to assess the role of information in promoting consumer utility should recognize its public good nature. It is nonrival (one person's use of the internet does not crowd out anyone else's use), and it is difficult and cumbersome to create markets that price individual "units" consumed. Determining the optimal amount of a public good and determining its value are classic problems in public finance. Many information goods can be classified as partial public (or "club") goods for which access fees are charged (e.g., the use of the gasoline tax to finance road systems). Some are pure public goods, as with information broadcasted over networks.

Internet)" of 0.6 percent for 2015 (the ratios we report are virtually the same for 2015 as in 2016). The larger point is that, in any case, the GDP associated with the digital economy is small using national accounting data.

If this were the final word on the subject, then the aggregate consequence of the digital revolution may be smaller than many of its enthusiasts claim. However, this is far from the last word. Many of the information goods consumed are transferred without a direct charge, and there is thus no monetary value to include in GDP. The cost to providers of producing the good is often defrayed using indirect or ancillary revenues. Google and Facebook illustrate this problem. They are firms that have as their primary functions serving consumers with search results and social networking, respectively, and, each firm's economic model is to provide its primary function at no direct cost to the consumer, supporting this economic activity with advertising. The two companies, together, in their annual reports reported annual revenues in 2016 of over $115 billion, largely from advertising, and had a total market value of roughly $1 trillion as of mid-2017. This business model implies that the flow of payments does not relate to the price or quantity of the information goods provided to consumers. The monetary flows involved appear in GDP via the prices and quantities of the goods that are advertised.

Some part of the total value of information is covered by system access fees charged for network use. These payments tend to be blanket fees that are unrelated or only loosely related to the quantity or value of the information or social interaction on which value is based. Moreover, it is also true that some of the information offered at a zero marginal cost over the internet or other media is simply free, provided *pro bono publico* by internet application developers (von Hippel 2016; Sichel and von Hippel 2019), or crowdsourced and without a measured resource cost.

The value of the information services actually recorded in GDP is in the range of $100 billion to $400 billion, depending on how broad a definition is used.[18] The question is how much this range understates the true value to consumers, as revealed by the price they would be willing to pay for the "free" information goods. This is the question to which we now turn.

1.7.3   The Measurement Literature on the Internet's Contribution to Welfare

A small but growing number of studies address the measurement issues implied by Schmidt and Rosenberg's (2014) remark that "the Internet has

---

18. It should be emphasized that the internet is scarcely the only channel through which information reaches the population. Education is an even more important channel, whether learning takes place in schools or at home or among peers. Books and other media are important, as is life experience. Much of this escapes GDP, and a full account would be a challenging task. Our goal in this chapter is limited to an analysis of how costless increases in digital sources of information can provide consumer benefits beyond those recorded in GDP and thereby present a different assessment of economic progress.

made information free, copious, and ubiquitous." They cover both the internet and the explosion in timely information it enables but also the devices needed to enable the digital revolution. The former are associated with disembodied output-saving technical change, μ, and will be the focus of the studies reviewed below.

There are several ways to measure the value of the internet's information and entertainment flows, one of which is to use econometric techniques to estimate the expenditure function or the compensating and equivalent variations associated with the utility function (V), or the system of demand equations associated with these functions. This can, in principle, get at the non-GDP contribution to consumer welfare in a framework that also includes the GDP contribution to the extent that goods are priced. This is the approach followed by Redding and Weinstein (2020).[19]

Another line of attack on the problem is to introduce time cost into the analysis of value. A search engine can be seen as creating consumer value by reducing the time cost involved in acquiring information, and Varian (2009) adopts this approach using a finding from Chen, Jeon, and Kim (2014), who had students at the University of Michigan obtain answers to questions using either a search engine or the library of the University of Michigan. The students who used the search engine were more successful, getting answers to questions posed in an average of 7 minutes compared to 22 minutes using the library. Varian calculated an implied individual consumer value of roughly $500 per year. Goolsbee and Klenow (2006) use a value-of-time approach but focus on the internet as a whole using a parametric consumption function analysis. They estimate that the value of the time spent on the internet translates into a consumer surplus of $2,500 to $3,800 per year. Syverson (2017) also conducts an exercise in which he updates the Goolsbee and Klenow estimate of the value of the internet and obtains a measure of the aggregate increase in the value of broadband of $842 billion in the post-2004 time period. Other creative approaches to the consumer surplus problem use questionnaires, surveys, and microdata. The literature includes Brynjolfsson, Hu, and Smith (2003); Aguiar and Waldfogel (2018); Quan and Williams (2016); and Dolfen et al. (2019).

Another way to deal with zero prices is with direct measures of willingness to pay. An unusual opportunity to estimate willingness to pay with a free good is discussed in Noll, Peck, and McGowan (1973). The slow diffusion of broadcast TV meant that some rural households had to pay for broadcasts that were free elsewhere. Using demand analysis, they were able to estimate that households would be willing to pay some 3 percent of income for free TV. However, such natural experiments are rare in the

---

19. The Redding-Weinstein methodology assumes that time-varying demand shifts cancel on average. This assumption may not be valid when net gains in consumer technology, such as those generated by the internet, occur.

literature. One alternative is simply to ask people about their willingness to pay for a search engine. Varian (2009) used Google consumer surveys to ask this question and found that on average, consumers were willing to pay $36 a year for search engines, a much smaller number than his back-of-the-envelope welfare calculation. However, more recent work by Brynjolfsson et al. (2018) suggests that the minimum payments consumers would accept (willingness to accept or WTA) for loss of access to search engines may be as large as $5,000 a year. This estimate suggests a value of about $1 trillion missing from GDP from search alone.

A small industry has arisen in evaluating consumer willingness to accept the price of Facebook. Brynjolfsson, Eggers, and Collis (2019) report a willingness to accept Facebook of about $506 per user, with 202 million users, or $100 billion in aggregate. They also estimate that this amount adds 0.05 to 0.11 percentage points to the growth of real GDP (in other words, the increment to μ is between 5 and 11 basis points). In another study, an auction experiment conducted by Corrigan et al. (2018) puts the value of doing without Facebook for an entire year at $1,000 to $2,000 per adult person in the United States, with an implied value of as much as $250 billion to $500 billion a year. The largest-scale experiment, Allcott et al. (2019), finds a similar value.

Finally, Nakamura, Samuels, and Soloveichik (2018) argue that even if we measure the cost of "free" information and entertainment in terms of their cost of production, the gains from marketing-supported information and entertainment are substantial. Taken from the cost side alone, total nominal value in 2015 was $103 billion from internet contributions to personal consumption expenditures. This cost estimate does not include the volunteer time invested by consumers in creating internet content, nor does it attempt to estimate any consumer surplus—just business-paid input costs in producing internet content. The authors argue that including their conservative methodology would lower the PCE deflator by roughly 0.1 percent.

In sum, the results of different approaches vary from as little as $100 billion to considerably more than $1 trillion. This range of values suggests that there is ample potential for welfare gains to the consumer beyond those that are not included in the value of personal consumption expenditures and GDP. However, it is important to recall the caveats of section 1.33 of this chapter. The studies reviewed in this section are mostly focused on individual goods like Facebook, and the results are partial equilibrium estimates of their value and thus are incomplete efforts to get at our EGDP. While doing so is a valuable step in this direction, goods with the broad scope of Facebook and the internet are bound to affect relative prices for many other goods in the economy, and the *ceteris paribus* assumption of partial equilibrium analysis is increasingly problematic as the importance of a good increases. Moreover, the important study by Brynjolfsson, Eggers, and Collis (2019) illustrates another issue raised in passing in section 1.3.3: the aggregate willingness to accept Facebook is large in dollar terms, but when expressed as an annual rate rather than a cumulative total, the contribution to GDP is found to amount to only 0.05 to 0.11 percentage point.

1.8 Health and Education: Individual Heterogeneity and the Role of State Contingency

The consumption technology as formulated in this chapter refers to the average state of health or knowledge, whereas much of the actual gain from innovation is contingent on an individual's current state of being or on changes in that state. The benefit of a health care intervention or expenditure, for example, depends on the state of health, and it is often shocks to that state that trigger the demand for the intervention. Moreover, the success of the intervention is often contingent on the severity of the shock (the same is true of some legal and financial problems). Other interventions are intended to improve the ambient state of being. The benefits of obtaining an education, for example, involve a move from one level of knowledge to another. Similarly, some health interventions are intended to improve the ambient state of health through healthier lifestyles and preventative medicine. Moreover, education and health interventions may interact in ways that strengthen each other.

A health care innovation, such as minimally invasive surgery, will generally affect a subset of the population, and perhaps only a small subset. The gains to those affected may be quite large, but they appear small when averaged into the total population. Moreover, some innovations may allow a subset of those afflicted that were previously untreatable to be helped. The innovation may improve the welfare of that subset, but if the success rate of the treatment is lower for this group than for the population as a whole, and if success rates are used as an indicator of innovation, the metric may send a false signal.

An extension of the EGDP program to allow for individual heterogeneity in contingent states is not easy, since it involves the utility of individuals and a way of aggregating their utilities. The standard way is to appeal to an explicit social welfare function (as opposed to the one implied by the use of averages). This step involves the introduction of value judgments into the measurement of GDP and EGDP. This is a major step, and since the basic thrust of this chapter is to explore the EGDP concept per se, it is a step we will defer to subsequent research.

1.8.1 Innovation in Health Care

The review of the bias in price statistics by Groshen et al. (2017) identified health care as a major source of the accuracy problem. Health care has been a hard-to-measure industry for a long time because of the problems associated with the disconnect between expenditures and outcome that forms the basis for the "output movement" described by Cutler and Berndt (2001). It has been the beneficiary of rapid innovation, much of which has improved outcomes for given levels of expenditure, which constitute our output-saving technical change. The case of minimally invasive surgery has been noted already, but there are many other examples.

Recent studies have found large potential biases in health care. For example, Dauda, Dunn, and Hall (2018) find that annual medical price inflation declined by 4.8 percent relative to aggregate inflation rates over the period 2001–14. With health care expenditures accounting for 17 percent to 20 percent of personal consumption during this period, this would add close to 1 percent to the growth rate of the total. They also report that for heart attacks, congestive heart failure, and pneumonia, 30-day risk-adjusted mortality rates fell significantly over this 13-year period (−39 percent, −25 percent, and −40 percent, respectively), while 30-day risk-adjusted expenditure rose much less rapidly (−1 percent, +20 percent, and +11 percent, respectively). In other words, outcomes have improved over the period with much less of an increase in spending, the very phenomenon our framework seeks to address.

Output-saving innovation is also present in the studies by Chernew et al. (2016), who report that disability-adjusted life years increased 1.8 years at age 65 between 1992 and 2008, of which they attribute 1.1 years to improved health treatment, particularly of heart disease and vision problems. Along the same lines, the Murphy and Topel (2006) calculation of the value of the 20th century increases in life expectancy from 48 to 72 finds a very large number, $1.2 million per person, for the representative person in 2000 in the United States. However, it should be noted that valuing human capital is a perilous enterprise, as is assigning changes in the value to factors other than medical treatment (Fogel 2012). Still, taken together, these health care studies highlight the importance of outcomes (longevity, mortality rates) as opposed to expenditures.

Another example of utility-enhancing technical change comes from the recent study by Rothwell et al. (2016), who found that taking aspirin for 12 weeks following a stroke or ministroke lowers the probability of a recurrent stroke or heart attack during that period from 4.3 percent to 1.9 percent. The cost of avoiding one stroke or heart attack is thus $40, assuming an aspirin cost of $.01 per tablet, orders of magnitude smaller than the consumer benefit, however measured.

1.8.2   The Case of Education

There have been major gains in educational attainment in the United States but also large expenditures and poor test results (see summary in Hulten and Ramey 2019). Education premia have led to rising incomes for much of the population, and increased productivity has propelled output growth. The average quality of life has doubtless risen as well, but how much more tuition college students would be willing to pay over and above the amount they already pay for this enhanced quality of life is unclear.[20] In this section, we explore another aspect of education's impact of individual welfare: the importance of initial states and individual heterogeneity in assessing the welfare benefits of education.

Formal education is an output of the schooling industry, but student learning and maturation are the relevant outcomes. Schooling is an important channel through which learning occurs, but family, peers, and personal experience all make important contributions to these outcomes. Student "inputs" of effort are also important and depend on idiosyncratic characteristics like motivation and general openness to change. As Hulten and Ramey (2019) observe, "[Poor] K-12 results cannot be attributed to the quality of schooling alone . . . Research suggests that the cognitive and noncognitive skills developed by age three have fundamental effects on the ability to learn. Thus, K-12 schools have little control over key inputs into their production functions" (8).

Improvements in the outcomes of historically underserved student populations have a large payoff to society and, importantly, to those individuals who stand to benefit. Tracking the gains to the average student will tend to understate the gains to this population not only in terms of increased personal income but also in the nonmonetary improvements in the quality of their life. Subsuming these gains in a measure based on average experience thus risks missing some of the most important welfare benefits of improved educational outcomes.[21]

1.9   Final Thoughts on the Path Ahead for EGDP Measurement

In his 1994 American Economic Association (AEA) presidential address, Griliches observed, "It is not reasonable for us to expect the government to produce statistics in areas where concepts are mushy and where there is little professional agreement on what is to be measured and how" (14). This observation applies in full force to the current measurement problems associated with the technological revolution currently underway. These problems are as much a matter of inadequate theoretical development as of inadequate statistics. Addressing the former is the rationale for our current work. To this end, we have proposed the theoretical construct of expanded GDP as a new measure of aggregate economic activity that builds on existing GDP. Our review of the empirical literature and the available data suggests that this

20. Education plays an important role in the quality of life. It exposes people to ideas and possibilities that expand consumer horizons and enhance the enjoyment of life. Put in economic terms, it allows people to get more enjoyment out of each dollar they spend, as with the shift in the consumption technology.

21. Quality-adjusted labor is considered exogenous in our discussion, but education partially endogenizes it.

effect is nonnegligible, perhaps amounting to as much as a trillion dollars or more. While it is true that the GDP share of the digital economy is relatively small, as some have noted, we have shown in our earlier paper that the effect on EGDP growth can be quite large despite this small share (Hulten and Nakamura 2018). In our previous study, we conducted a thought experiment in which the bias in price deflators noted by Groshen et al. (2017) when combined with the impact of output-saving technical change could easily be a full percentage point (100 basis points) higher. Given that the average annual top-line growth of the private business sector shown in table 1.1 of this chapter is 2.76 percent for the period 1995–2007, a 100 basis point increase is significant.

We emphasize that this hypothetical estimate is *not* intended as our best guess at the contribution of output-saving innovation to expanded economic growth, but it *is* intended to show that the consumption technology and its utility-enhancing effect are potentially too large to be ignored. We recognize that adding a consumption technology to the conventional GDP framework is by no means an easy task, and one not to be undertaken lightly. Part of the value of GDP lies in the continuity of the time record that allows for meaningful comparisons with past eras, and there is thus a tension between updating the accounts to reflect the current economy and maintaining comparability over time. One way to deal with this quandary is through the use of satellite accounts to bridge the gap. A satellite account preserves the main accounting structure of GDP while at the same time providing a home for the more speculative estimates emerging from the study of the current technical revolution.

Fortunately, the BEA has already made a start in this direction with its innovation accounting and limited capitalization of intangible assets. This innovation accounting could be expanded in several important ways. One is to extend the current list of intangible capital included in GDP to encompass a broader range of intellectual property, enterprise-specific human capital, and organizational assets. Another important step is for the BLS and the BEA to work together to improve price statistics so that they more accurately reflect and classify product innovation. Taking on the challenge posed by new goods, like the internet and mobile communication devices, is of central importance in this regard. Yet another major step within the scope of existing statistical programs is for the BLS to report separately the extent of product innovation already embodied in its quality-corrected price estimates. Finally, the research from the "outcome movement" in health care research should be accorded a high priority.[22]

The task of building a full innovation satellite account is daunting. The history of the national accounts is a history of overcoming one daunting

---

22. It must also be said that the BLS is continually working to improve the CPI and the PPI. For example, it is moving to what has been called a diagnosis or a disease-centric approach (Roehrig 2017). The BEA has also made much progress on the problem of measuring outcomes in the provision of health care services, but the path ahead is long and difficult.

challenge after another. The result of these efforts has been what Samuelson and Nordhaus have called "One of the Great Inventions of the 20th Century."[23]

References

Abel, Jaison R., Ernst R. Berndt, and Alan G. White. 2007. "Price Indexes for Microsoft's Personal Computer Software Products." In *Hard-to-Measure Goods and Services: Essays in Honor of Zvi Griliches*, edited by Ernst R. Berndt and Charles R. Hulten, 269–89. NBER Studies in Income and Wealth 67. Chicago: University of Chicago Press.

Abramovitz, Moses. 1956. "Resource and Output Trends in the United States since 1870." *American Economic Review* 46 (2): 5–23.

Aguiar, Luis, and Joel Waldfogel. 2018. "Quality Predictability and the Welfare Benefits from New Products: Evidence from the Digitization of Recorded Music." *Journal of Political Economy* 126 (2): 492–524.

Allcott, Hunt, Luca Braghieri, Sarah Eichmeyer, and Matthew Gentzkow. 2019. "The Welfare Effects of Social Media." NBER Working Paper No. 25514. Cambridge, MA: National Bureau of Economic Research.

Anderson, Monica. 2015. "Technology Device Ownership: 2015." Pew Research Center, October 29. http://www.pewInternet.org/2015/10/29/technology-device-ownership-2015.

Bils, Mark. 2009. "Do Higher Prices for New Goods Reflect Quality Growth or Inflation?" *Quarterly Journal of Economics* 124 (2): 637–75.

Bils, Mark, and Peter J. Klenow. 2001. "Quantifying Quality Growth." *American Economic Review* 91 (4): 1006–30.

Brynjolfsson, Erik, Avinash Collis, W. Erwin Diewert, Felix Eggers, and Kevin J. Fox. 2020. "Measuring the Impact of Free Goods on Real Household Consumption." *AEA Papers and Proceedings* 110 (May): 25–30.

Brynjolfsson, Erik, Avinash Collis, and Felix Eggers. 2019. "Using Massive Online Choice Experiments to Measure Changes in Well-Being." *Proceedings of National Academy of Science* 116 (15): 7250–55.

Brynjolfsson, Erik, Yu (Jerry) Hu, and Michael D. Smith. 2003. "Consumer Surplus in the Digital Economy: Estimating the Value of Increased Product Variety at Online Booksellers." *Management Science* 49 (11): 1580–96.

Byrne, David M., and Carol A. Corrado. 2015. "Prices for Communications Equipment: Rewriting the Record." Finance and Economics Discussion Series 2015-069. Washington, DC: Board of Governors of the Federal Reserve System.

Byrne, David, and Carol Corrado. 2017a. "ICT Asset Prices: Marshaling Evidence into New Measures." Finance and Economics Discussion Series 2017-016. Washington, DC: Board of Governors of the Federal Reserve System. https://www.federalreserve.gov/econres/feds/files/2017016r1pap.pdf.

Byrne, David, and Carol Corrado. 2017b. "ICT Prices and ICT Services: What Do They Tell Us about Productivity and Technology?" Finance and Economics Discussion Series 2017-015. Washington, DC: Board of Governors of the Federal Reserve System. https://doi.org/10.17016/FEDS.2017.015.

---

23. Cited by Landefeld (2000).

Byrne, David M., John G. Fernald, and Marshall B. Reinsdorf. 2016. "Does the United States Have a Productivity Slowdown or a Measurement Problem?" *Brookings Papers on Economic Activity*. Washington, DC: Brookings Institution Press.

Chen, Yan, Grace YoungJoo Jeon, and Yong-Mi Kim. 2014. "A Day without a Search Engine: An Experimental Study of Online and Offline Searches." *Experimental Economics* 17 (4): 512–36.

Chernew, Michael, David M. Cutler, Kaushik Ghosh, and Mary Beth Landrum. 2016. "Understanding the Improvement in Disability Free Life Expectancy in the U.S. Elderly Population." NBER Working Paper No. 22306. Cambridge, MA: National Bureau of Economic Research.

Corrado, Carol A., and Charles R. Hulten. 2010. "How Do You Measure a 'Technological Revolution'?" *American Economic Review* 100 (2): 99–104.

Corrado, Carol A., and Charles R. Hulten. 2014. "Innovation Accounting." In *Measuring Economic Progress and Economic Sustainability*, edited by D. W. Jorgenson, J. S. Landefeld, and P. Schreyer, 595–628. NBER Studies in Income and Wealth 72. Chicago: University of Chicago Press.

Corrado, Carol A., and Charles R. Hulten. 2015. "Financial Intermediation in the National Accounts: Asset Valuation, Intermediation, and Tobin's q." In *Measuring Wealth and Financial Intermediation and Their Links to the Real Economy*, edited by C. R. Hulten and M. B. Reinsdorf, 125–47. NBER Studies in Income and Wealth 73. Chicago: University of Chicago Press.

Corrado, Carol A., Charles R. Hulten, and Daniel E. Sichel. 2005. "Measuring Capital and Technology: An Expanded Framework." In *Measuring Capital in the New Economy*, edited by Carol Corrado, John Haltiwanger, and Daniel Sichel, 11–46. NBER Studies in Income and Wealth 65. Chicago: University of Chicago Press.

Corrado, Carol A., Charles R. Hulten, and Daniel E. Sichel. 2009. "Intangible Capital and US Economic Growth." *Review of Income and Wealth* 55 (3): 661–85.

Corrigan, Jay R., Saleem Alhabash, Matthew Rousu, and Sean B. Cash. 2018. "How Much Is Social Media Worth? Estimating the Value of Facebook by Paying Users to Stop Using It." *PLoS ONE* 13 (12). December 19. https://doi.org/10.1371/journal.pone.0207101.

Coyle, Diane. 2014. *GDP: A Brief but Affectionate History*. Princeton, NJ: Princeton University Press.

Cutler, David M., and Ernst R. Berndt. 2001. "Introduction." In *Medical Care Output and Productivity*, edited by David M. Cutler and Ernst R. Berndt, 1–12. NBER Studies in Income and Wealth 62. Chicago: University of Chicago Press.

Dauda, Seidu, Abe Dunn, and Anne Hall. 2018. "Are Medical Care Prices Still Declining? A Systematic Examination of Quality-Adjusted Price Index Alternatives for Medical Care." Working paper presented at NBER/CRIW Summer Institute.

Dolfen, Paul, Liran Einav, Peter J. Klenow, Benjamin Klopack, Jonathan D. Levin, Larry Levin, and Wayne Best. 2019. "Assessing the Gains from E-Commerce." Working paper. http://web.stanford.edu/~leinav/wp/ecommerce.pdf.

Fogel, Robert W. 2012. *Explaining Long-Term Trends in Health and Longevity*. Cambridge: Cambridge University Press.

Goolsbee, Austan, and Peter J. Klenow. 2006. "Valuing Consumer Products by the Time Spent Using Them: An Application to the Internet." *American Economic Review Papers and Proceedings* 96 (2): 108–13.

Gordon, Robert J. 2016. *The Rise and Fall of American Growth: The U.S. Standard of Living Since the Civil War*. Princeton Economic History of the Western World. Princeton, NJ: Princeton University Press.

Greenstein, Shane, and Ryan McDevitt. 2011. "Evidence of a Modest Price Decline in US Broadband Services." *Information Economics and Policy* 23 (2): 200–211.

Griliches, Zvi. 1992. Introduction to *Output Measurement in the Service Sectors*, edited by Zvi Griliches, 1–22. NBER Studies in Income and Wealth 56. Chicago: University of Chicago Press.

Griliches, Zvi. 1994. "Productivity, R&D, and the Data Constraint." *American Economic Review* 84 (1): 1–23.

Groshen, Erica L., Brian C. Moyer, Ana M. Aizcorbe, Ralph Bradley, and David Friedman. 2017. "How Government Statistics Adjust for Potential Biases from Quality Change and New Goods in an Age of Digital Technologies: A View from the Trenches." *Journal of Economic Perspectives* 31 (2): 187–210.

Hausman, Jerry. 1996. "Valuation of New Goods under Perfect and Imperfect Competition." In *The Economics of New Goods*, edited by T. Bresnahan and R. Gordon, 209–37. NBER Studies in Income and Wealth 58. Chicago: University of Chicago Press.

Hausman, Jerry. 1999. "Cellular Telephone, New Products, and the CPI." *Journal of Business and Economics Statistics* 17 (2): 188–94.

Hill, Peter. 1999. "Tangibles, Intangibles and Services: A New Taxonomy for the Classification of Output." *Canadian Journal of Economics* 32 (2): 426–46.

Hulten, Charles R. 1978. "Growth Accounting with Intermediate Inputs." *Review of Economic Studies* 45 (3): 511–18.

Hulten, Charles R. 2001. "Total Factor Productivity: A Short Biography." In *New Developments in Productivity Analysis*, edited by Charles R. Hulten, Edwin R. Dean, and Michael J. Harper, 1–47. NBER Studies in Income and Wealth 63. Chicago: University of Chicago Press.

Hulten, Charles. 2015. "Measuring the Economy of the 21st Century." *NBER Reporter* 4:1–7.

Hulten, Charles, and Leonard Nakamura. 2018. "Accounting for Growth in the Age of the Internet: The Importance of Output-Saving Technical Change." NBER Working Paper No. 23315. Cambridge, MA: National Bureau of Economic Research.

Hulten, Charles R., and Valerie A. Ramey. 2019. "Education, Skills, and Technical Change, Implications for Future U.S. GDP Growth: An Introduction and Overview." In *Education, Skills, and Technical Change: Implications for Future U.S. GDP Growth*, edited by Charles R. Hulten and Valerie A. Ramey, 1–19. NBER Studies in Income and Wealth 77. Chicago: University of Chicago Press.

Lancaster, Kelvin J. 1966. "A New Approach to Consumer Theory." *Journal of Political Economy* 74 (2): 132–57.

Landefeld, J. Steven. 2000. "GDP: One of the Great Inventions of the 20th Century." *Survey of Current Business*, January, 6–14.

Lebow, David, and Jeremy B. Rudd. 2003. "Measurement Error in the Consumer Price Index: Where Do We Stand?" *Journal of Economic Literature* 41 (1): 159–201.

Maddison, A. 2007. *Contours of the World Economy, 1–2030 AD: Essays in Macroeconomic History*. Oxford: Oxford University Press.

Moulton, Brent R., and Karin E. Moses. 1997. "Addressing the Quality Change Issue in the Consumer Price Index." *Brookings Papers on Economic Activity* 1:305–66.

Murphy, Kevin M., and Robert H. Topel. 2006. "The Value of Health and Longevity." *Journal of Political Economy* 114 (5): 871–904.

Nakamura, Leonard, Jon Samuels, and Rachel Soloveichik. 2018. "'Free' Internet Content: Web 1.0, Web 2.0, and the Sources of Economic Growth." Federal Reserve Bank of Philadelphia Working Paper 2018-17.

Nevo, Aviv, John L. Turner, and Jonathan W. Williams. 2016. "Usage Based-Pricing and Demand for Residential Broadband." *Econometrica* 84 (2): 411–43.

Noll, Roger G., Merton J. Peck, and John J. McGowan. 1973. *Economic Aspects of Television Regulation.* Washington, DC: Brookings Institution.

Nordhaus, William D. 2005. "Schumpeterian Profits and the Alchemist Fallacy Revised." Yale Working Papers on Economic Applications and Policy, Discussion Paper No. 6.

Patinkin, Don. 1973. "In Search of the 'Wheel of Wealth': On the Origins of Frank Knight's Circular-Flow Diagram." *American Economic Review* 63 (5): 1037–46.

Perrin, Andrew. 2015. "Social Media Usage: 2005–2015." Pew Research Center, October 8. http://www.pewInternet.org/2015/10/08/2015/Social-Networking -Usage-2005-2015.

Pew Research Center. 2017. "Mobile Fact Sheet." http://www.pewInternet.org/fact -sheet/mobile.

Quan, Thomas W., and Kevin Williams. 2016. "Product Variety, across Market Demand Heterogeneity, and the Value of Online Retail." Cowles Foundation Discussion Paper 2054, November.

Redding, Stephen J., and David E. Weinstein. 2020. "Measuring Aggregate Price Indexes with Taste Shocks: Theory and Evidence for CES Preferences." *Quarterly Journal of Economics* 135 (1): 503–60.

Roehrig, Charles. 2017. "A Comparison of Bureau of Economic Analysis and Bureau of Labor Statistics Disease-Price Indexes." Bureau of Economic Analysis Working Paper 2017-3. https://www.bea.gov/system/files/papers/WP2017-3.pdf.

Rothwell, Peter M., Ale Algra, Zhengming Chen, Hans-Christoph Diener, Bo Norrving, and Ziyah Mehta. 2016. "Effects of Aspirin on Risk and Severity of Early Recurrent Stroke after Transient Ischaemic Attack and Ischaemic Stroke: Time-Course Analysis of Randomised Trials." *Lancet* 388 (10042): 365–75. http://dx.doi .org/10.1016/S0140-6736(16)30468-8.

Schmidt, Eric, and Jonathan Rosenberg (with Alan Eagle). 2014. *How Google Works.* New York: Grand Central.

Shapiro, Matthew D., and David W. Wilcox. 1996. "Mismeasurement in the Consumer Price Index: An Evaluation." In *NBER Macroeconomics Annual 1996*, Vol. 11, edited by Ben S. Bernanke and Julio J. Rotemberg, 93–154. Cambridge, MA: MIT Press.

Sichel, Daniel E. 1997. "The Productivity Slowdown: Is a Growing Unmeasurable Sector the Culprit?" *Review of Economics and Statistics* 79 (3): 367–70.

Sichel, Daniel E., and Eric von Hippel. 2019. "Household Innovation, R&D, and New Measures of Intangible Capital." MIT Sloan School of Management Working Paper.

Solow, Robert M. 1957. "Technical Change and the Aggregate Production Function." *Review of Economics and Statistics* 39 (3): 312–20.

Stigler, George, ed. 1961. *The Price Statistics of the Federal Government.* Report to the Office of Statistical Standards, Bureau of the Budget. Prepared by the Price Statistics Review Committee of the NBER. Stigler Commission. New York: National Bureau of Economic Research.

Syverson, Chad. 2017. "Challenges to Mismeasurement Explanations for the US Productivity Slowdown." *Journal of Economic Perspectives* 31 (2): 165–86.

Triplett, Jack E., and Barry P. Bosworth. 2004. *Productivity in the U.S. Services Sector: New Sources of Economic Growth.* Washington, DC: Brookings Institution Press.

US Bureau of Labor Statistics. 2018. *Handbook of Methods.* Consumer Price Indexes, chapter 17. https://www.bls.gov/opub/hom/pdf/homch17.pdf.

US Bureau of Labor Statistics. 2019. "PPI Introduces Hedonic Quality Adjustment for Internet Access Indexes." Modified March 6, 2019. https://www.bls.gov/ppi/broadbandhedonicmodel.htm.

US Census Bureau. 2014. "Computer and Internet Access in the United States: 2012." February. https://www.census.gov/data/tables/2012/demo/computer-internet/computer-use-2012.html.

Varian, Hal. 1992. *Microeconomic Analysis*. 3rd ed. New York: W. W. Norton.

Varian, Hal. 2009. "Economic Value of Google." BEA Advisory Council Meeting, December. http://cdn.oreillystatic.com/en/assets/1/event/57/The%20Economic%20Impact%20of%20Google%20Presentation.pdf.

von Hippel, Eric. 2016. *Free Innovation*. Cambridge, MA: MIT Press.

Measuring the Impact of Household Innovation Using Administrative Data

Javier Miranda and Nikolas Zolas

2.1 Introduction

The study of innovation has traditionally centered on the institution where it is believed to be conducted, which has primarily consisted of the firm. The underlying assumption is that innovation is the output from an R&D production function that has the inventor at its core and where the inputs (materials and human capital) are fully accounted for. Some of the inputs may take the form of knowledge originating outside the firm, like universities, government labs, and other firms. In this regard, government and university labs have long been recognized as sources of knowledge and invention. Other firms may contribute to the R&D process through research joint ventures or may license their technologies. Increasingly, however, researchers are highlighting the importance private households play as sources of invention and innovation in this process (e.g., von Hippel, de Jong, and Flowers 2012; Arora, Cohen, and Walsh 2016). In this chapter we aim to contribute to this strand of the literature by using US Census Bureau administrative data combined with United States Patent and Trademark Office (USPTO) patents data to document household innovations. The

Javier Miranda is a principal economist at the US Census Bureau.
Nikolas Zolas is a senior economist at the US Census Bureau.
Any opinions and conclusions expressed herein are those of the authors and do not necessarily represent the views of the US Census Bureau. All results have been reviewed to ensure that no confidential information is disclosed. We thank Eric Von Hippel, Dan Sichel, Wesley Cohen, Scott Stern, Nathan Goldschlag, participants in the NBER Conference Measuring and Accounting for Innovation in the 21st Century, and two anonymous referees for helpful comments and feedback. For acknowledgments, sources of research support, and disclosure of the authors' material financial relationships, if any, please see https://www.nber.org/books-and-chapters/measuring -and-accounting-innovation-21st-century/measuring-impact-household-innovation-using -administrative-data.

use of administrative data gets around some of the problems with current studies in this area, specifically small sample sizes in household surveys, low power estimates, and low response rates that may raise questions about nonresponse bias (Deming 1990).

Use of administrative data provides a rich tapestry of the types of innovations undertaken by households and their characteristics, but it has its own limitations. We focus on the set of household innovations we can identify in administrative data—that is, those that are granted a patent by the USPTO. Admittedly, this excludes perhaps what might be the lion's share of household innovation: that which is not patented. By contrast, we focus on what might be the most valuable innovations (Arora, Cohen, and Walsh 2016), and we do so in a systematic manner. We match these patents to Census Bureau administrative files to understand the demographic characteristics of household inventors as well as the characteristics of the unincorporated businesses they start to get a sense for their impact and value.[1] Use of administrative records comes with other important limitations. Specifically, there is no way for us to determine whether these patents were developed during leisure time or as a remunerated activity. Here we make the strong assumption that if they have not been assigned to a firm, there was no direct remuneration for the development of the innovation.

When documenting the characteristics of household innovations, we describe the technology classes they fall under, their impact and novelty as captured by the analysis of backward and forward looking citations, and the breadth of their application as captured by a generality index. In addition, we document the characteristics of inventors, their age, gender, race, and origin. When looking at business formation, we examine the dynamics of unincorporated businesses that are tied to inventors and their performance relative to similar businesses without inventors, specifically their revenue and growth performance.

We find household inventors are disproportionately US-born relative to salaried inventors. They are relatively white. Household inventors are also disproportionately under 25 or over 55. Across the board we find a deficit in female and black inventors relative to the overall working-age population. Household inventors work on technology classes disproportionately tied to consumer products, such as design, mechanical and other. Patents associated with household innovation are about half as likely to be considered "radical."[2] In terms of value, household innovations accumulate approximately 27–33 percent fewer citations on average. While their citation impact is smaller, it remains remarkably high. Finally, we find that few household

---

1. Patents by independent inventors have been found to display the largest rates of transfer (Serrano 2010), so in future drafts we will explore the characteristics of patents that transition to existing firms.
2. We follow the definition in Dahlin and Behrens (2005): a radical innovation is one that is considered novel, unique, and impactful.

inventors attempt to create a business around their invention. When they do, these businesses have higher revenues on average and are more than twice as likely to transition to hire their first employee than nonemployers who do not patent. Back-of-the-envelope calculations suggest patented household innovations granted in a given year might generate revenue between $7.2 billion and $8.2 billion in 2000 dollars.

The remainder of the chapter is structured as follows. Section 2.2 provides background. We follow with a description of the data in section 2.3. We describe basic features of patented household inventions in section 2.4. Our analysis of business formation and outcomes follows in section 2.5. We conclude in section 2.6.

2.2   Background

Innovation is traditionally thought of as a process that takes place inside a firm. In this context, outside sources of knowledge and invention, including universities, government labs, and other firms, have long been recognized as important inputs to the firm's R&D function. Increasingly, however, innovation researchers are focusing on households as important sources of knowledge and innovation. The study of household innovation, however, has been hampered by data availability.

The first set of household innovation studies looked at user innovations in specific product markets. Early examples include von Hippel (1976) and Shah (2000), who look at user innovation in scientific instruments and new sporting goods, respectively. Their methodology involves a retrospective study of a selected sample of commercially successful innovations as identified by either experts in the field or direct analysis of new product features. This was followed by interviews of relevant product and industry experts. Both of these authors find that a large percentage of the innovations were in fact invented, prototyped, and tested by users of the equipment rather than the equipment manufacturer. In the case of scientific instruments, von Hippel (1976) finds existing instrument manufacturers would incorporate user innovations into their products with a focus on improved engineering. In the case of sporting goods, Shah (2000) finds users built innovative equipment for their own use. The inventors tended to be young, and they often built businesses in order to appropriate the benefits from their innovations.

Follow-up studies have tried to more broadly describe the characteristics of the innovators and the rate of user innovation. Lüthje (2004) conducts a survey of users of outdoor sporting equipment identified from the direct mail order listing of two sporting goods manufacturing firms. While response rates are relatively low at 26 percent, the author finds a large share of respondents, 37 percent, claimed at least one idea. Of these, 30 percent claimed their idea provided a solution to a problem that was not offered by the manufacturer. Reportedly, only 4 in 10 took their ideas beyond concept by developing prototypes. Franke and Shah (2003) look at innovation within four distinct communities of extreme sports enthusiasts. Communities of consumer users were identified through websites or competition rosters. With a survey response rate of 38 percent, the authors find 32 percent of community members claimed an innovation, and of these, 14.5 percent considered the innovation to be a completely new product. In their sample, 23 percent of innovators believed their innovations had been or would be commercialized by a third party. These innovators did not appear to benefit financially from their innovations. Whether results from these and other surveys of leading users and enthusiasts are representative of broader user communities remains an open question.[3]

Von Hippel, de Jong, and Flowers (2012) take a broader approach to this question by conducting a household survey to look at inventions by a representative sample of consumers in the United Kingdom. These are innovations tied to households and their unincorporated businesses. Specifically, they look at the development and modification of consumer products by product users. The types of household innovations they focus on exclude on-the-job innovations, which are already accounted for in official statistics. Instead, they focus on innovations that were developed during uncompensated leisure time. With a survey response rate of 15 percent, they find 6.2 percent of UK consumers engaged in consumer product innovation in the previous three years. When comparing against the amount of R&D investment by UK firms, they estimate the volume of household-based expenditures exceeded that of firms by a factor of 2.3 times.[4] They conclude private households are a major source of invention.

The survey of von Hippel, de Jong, and Flowers (2012) is centered on consumer product innovations. The bulk of the innovations, 98 percent, are product modifications rather than new product creations. Most of the innovations, 80 percent, are in a few product classes that are related with how people spend their time: crafts and tools, sports and hobbies, gardening, as well as child, dwelling, or pet related. Only 17 percent of the innovations are believed to be adopted by others to some degree, and only 2 percent of the innovations are protected by intellectual property rights. There are relatively few software innovations. Von Hippel, de Jong, and Flowers (2012) are the only study collecting demographic information from a representative consumer sample rather than a community of interest. They find that inventors tend to be male, educated, and either a student or over age 55. Issues with this and other representative consumer surveys that have followed include high nonresponse rates, small sample sizes, and confusion regarding the

---

3. A good survey of consumer user studies can be found in de Jong (2016).
4. Von Hippel, de Jong, and Flowers (2012) find the average customer invention requires an expenditure of £101 and 4.8 days.

definition of innovation by consumers. With these limitations, a general conclusion is the apparent low adoption rates of innovations by enterprises.

Following a different approach, Arora, Cohen, and Walsh (2016) conduct a survey of manufacturing firms to examine the extent to which US firms use external sources of invention for their innovations. Arora, Cohen, and Walsh (2016) focus on the whole manufacturing sector regardless of industry or whether firms own patents or conduct R&D. Their sample is drawn from the Dun & Bradstreet business frame but adjusted with US Census Bureau–based weights to match the population of manufacturing firms by industry, size, and age. For the analysis, they focus on product innovations (and exclude process innovations) at firms with more than 10 employees. With response rates of 30.3 percent, they find that of the 16 percent of firms that innovated (introduced a product that is new to the market), 49 percent report their most important new product originated from outside. They find customers are the most pervasive source of inventions, although not the source of the most valuable ones. The more valuable inventions are sourced from technology specialists, who include independent inventors. These inventors patent their own inventions at relatively high rates (56 percent)—higher than university, supplier and customer sourced inventions (at 36 percent, 34 percent, and 16 percent, respectively). They find independent inventors are also a more common source of inventions for small firms.

2.3 Data

We focus our analysis on patented household innovations. Our primary source of patent data is the US Patent and Trademark Office PTMT Custom Patent Data Extract. These data are produced annually from the bibliographic text (i.e., front page) of the patent documents. The source covers all granted patents by the USPTO and detailed information, including the patent number, type of patent, filing date, issue date, inventor information, assignee name at time of issue, and classification information for each.

We impose some initial restrictions on the patents we analyze—namely, keeping those that have been granted domestically while excluding government patents. Table 2.1 looks at the number of patents by assignee type in our sample. We center our analysis on patents granted between 2000 and 2011. Our sample includes a total of 1.29 million patents granted between 2000 and 2011. The bulk of these, 80 percent, are assigned to businesses. Most of the remaining patents, 19.2 percent, are unassigned. There are very few patents, 0.8 percent, assigned to individuals. While unassigned patents are assumed to belong to the inventor, it will be the case that some of these belong to firms but were not assigned at time of grant. We explore the extent of this problem by reviewing patents with large teams of inventors to get a sense for the amount of noise in the data. Our assumption is that the average

Table 2.1   US patents by assignee type and year

	Individual	Business	Unassigned	Total
2000	970	79,500	21,500	107,000
2001	980	82,900	20,100	109,000
2002	930	81,200	19,000	106,000
2003	890	82,900	18,300	107,000
2004	860	80,100	16,300	101,000
2005	790	71,400	13,500	89,000
2006	980	88,700	16,200	110,000
2007	870	81,600	14,900	101,000
2008	760	81,400	14,300	99,400
2009	850	84,700	13,400	102,000
2010	960	108,000	16,500	130,000
2011	950	110,000	15,900	130,000
Total	10,800	1,032,000	200,000	1,290,000

Source: Authors' calculations based on public USPTO data on granted patents by US entities between 2000 and 2011.

Notes: Counts are rounded to comply with disclosure requirements.

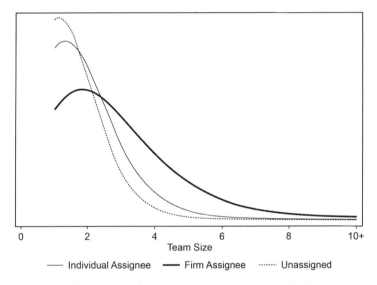

Fig. 2.1   Kernel distribution of team size by assignee type, 2000–2011
Source: Own calculations based on USPTO data on granted patents applied for between 2000 and 2011.

firm patent will be developed by larger teams of inventors. The results can be seen in figure 2.1. The team size distributions for unassigned and individual assigned patents are fairly similar and well to the left of firm-assigned patents. Unassigned patents have the larger share of single-inventor patents (nearly 80 percent of unassigned patents have a single inventor). Looking at the right tail of the distribution, we find that fewer than 1 percent of unassigned and individual-assigned patents have inventor team sizes of five or more, compared to the nearly 7 percent of firm-assigned patents.

Firm-assigned patents present a challenge to us. The patent data do not include firm identifiers or flags that might help us distinguish patents assigned to employers from those assigned to nonemployer businesses. It is not unreasonable to think, however, that independent inventors might assign their patents to their own unincorporated nonemployer business. However, we do not want to exclude these inventors from our analysis, since their patents might be particularly valuable. We rely on the US Census Bureau longitudinal patent-business database (BDS-IF) to identify and exclude from our analysis patents assigned to employer businesses while keeping those assigned to nonemployer businesses.[5] We identify patents assigned to nonemployer firms by matching all patents to the US Census Bureau's Business Register of nonemployer firms.[6] A large percentage of patents, nearly 80 percent, match to the employer universe files. The employer matches tend to be based on the assignee name and address, while the nonemployer matches mostly occur through the inventor. We remove the known employer matches from Graham et al. (2018) from our universe of matches, leaving us with approximately 200,000 raw nonemployer firm matches. Our set of initial matches requires further refining. A high-quality firm-inventor match does not guarantee the inventor is matched to its firm, particularly when the match may not be unique. Therefore, we retain only cases where the social security number of the inventor and the social security number in the nonemployer firm record line up.[7] This filtering process leaves us with a total set of approximately 125,000 patents. We remove an additional 55,000 patents by only keeping the unduplicated matches.[8] Finally, we drop patents that are associated with nonemployers that have an unusually large number of patents assigned to them.[9] This leaves us with a total of 68,000 patents

---

5. The BDS-IF identifies patents assigned to employer businesses while keeping those assigned to nonemployer businesses. See Graham et al. (2018) for details of the matching methodology. Briefly, it uses both the assignee and inventor information to form a match. The use of two independent pieces of information to identify the assignee firm provides a high level of reliability in the match.

6. All businesses that file an income tax form to the Internal Revenue Service (IRS) authorities and have no associated payroll tax form are included in the nonemployer Business Register. See appendix A for details of the matching methodology.

7. This comparison is done indirectly. The Census Bureau strips personally identifiable information from all of its internal files to protect the confidentiality of records. Specifically, the Census Bureau replaces an individual's name and address (and social security number, if present) with a protected identification key (PIK) using the PVS system. Each name-address pairing has a unique PIK in the system. The Census Bureau assigned a PIK to the patent data using the name and location information.

8. The PVS system does not guarantee an inventor in the USPTO database will receive a unique person identifier. In cases where the identifying information is not unique enough, multiple PIKs are assigned.

9. These might be holding entities with no associated employers.

Table 2.2   Percentage of patents by assignee type, type of business, and year

	Individual			Business			Unassigned		
	E	NE	U	E	NE	U	E	NE	U
2000	2.1	57.9	40	91.5	1.8	6.7	0	28.8	71.2
2001	1.4	63.8	34.7	91.6	1.9	6.5	0	29.2	70.8
2002	(D)	55.5	44.5	92	1.7	6.3	0	23.5	76.5
2003	(D)	56.9	43.1	92.4	1.7	5.9	0	23.7	76.3
2004	(D)	53.8	46.2	92.2	1.7	6.1	0	23.9	76.1
2005	1.6	55.6	42.7	91.8	1.8	6.4	0	25.3	74.7
2006	2	51.4	46.6	91.8	1.8	6.3	0	23.7	76.3
2007	1.8	52.3	45.9	92.2	1.7	6.1	0	21.5	78.5
2008	2.6	48.1	49.3	92.2	1.7	6.1	0	21.4	78.6
2009	1.4	50.5	48.1	92.3	1.7	6.1	0	21.4	78.6
2010	1.3	55.5	43.3	92	1.7	6.2	0	23.5	76.5
2011	1.7	56.3	42	90.9	1.9	7.2	0	23.9	76.1
Total	1.3	55	43.7	91.9	1.8	6.3	0	24.4	75.6

Source: Authors' calculations based on public USPTO data on granted patents applied for between 2000 and 2011.
Notes: Type of business: E = Employer, NE = Nonemployer, U = Unknown. (D) identifies suppressed values.

associated with nonemployer businesses that we are confident belong to the inventors behind the patents.

Table 2.2 shows the percentage of patents matched to employer businesses (E) and nonemployer businesses (NE) by assignee type and year. Patents that remain unmatched (U) are not associated with business activity as captured by the Business Register. Table 2.2 highlights a clear separation in the match rates by assignee type, with the vast majority of firm-assigned patents linked to employer firms. By contrast, individual-assigned patents have much lower match rates. Only about 50 percent of patents are associated with some form of business activity, with most of it tied to nonemployer firms. Finally, only 30.4 percent of unassigned patents are tied to some form of business activity.

2.4   Characteristics of Patented Household Innovations

In this section, we describe the characteristics of patents and inventors associated with what we call patented household innovations, which include patents that are either unassigned or assigned to individuals. We contrast those with patents assigned to firms. We start by describing differences in the demographic composition of the inventors associated with the patents before delving into the characteristics of the actual patents.

2.4.1   Inventor Demographics

To highlight potential differences in demographic characteristics of inventors associated with household innovations, we link demographic informa-

Table 2.3   **Inventor demographics by assignee type and type of business**

	Individual			Business			Unassigned		
	E	NE	U	E	NE	U	E	NE	U
Male	86.5	91.4	90.6	92.1	91.8	90.7	(0)	89.3	87.7
US born	72.1	82.1	80.3	66.1	67.4	63.2	(0)	82.8	81.3
Black	1.8	2.1	3.5	0.9	0.9	1	(0)	3.1	4.2
White	78.4	84.8	83.1	73.9	75.8	72.9	(0)	84.2	83.1
Other	19.8	13.1	13.4	25.2	23.3	26.1	(0)	12.6	12.8
Age < 25	1.8	1.6	3.9	0.5	1.2	0.9	(0)	2	2.3
< Age < 55	73.9	67.1	58	81	75.3	77.1	(0)	65	63.1
Age > 55	24.3	31.4	38.1	18.5	23.5	22	(0)	33	34.5
Total Inventors*	110	6,600	1,200	1,320,000	19,200	77,100	(0)	37,300	38,400
Total Patents*	60	4,700	1,100	666,000	10,800	40,400	(0)	31,100	35,100

Source: Authors' calculations based on public USPTO data on granted patents applied for between 2000 and 2011.

Notes: Type of business: E = Employer, NE = Nonemployer, U = Unknown. * Counts are rounded to comply with disclosure requirements. (D) identifies suppressed values.

tion from administrative US Census Bureau files to the inventors in the patent records. They provide basic demographic information, including gender, race, country of origin, and birth date for all people in the United States with a social security number.

Information from the demographic files is linked by use of a protected identification key (PIK) available on both sets. We are not able to uniquely identify all inventors in the patent documents in our files due to limitations of the data.[10] There are 1.48 million inventors associated with the 1.29 million patents that form our analysis. We are able to obtain demographics for inventors on 856,000 of the 1.29 million patents.[11] Overall, we find inventors tied to firm assignees are more likely to be uniquely identified than individual assignees or unassigned patents. We also find that the patents unmatched with demographic data are mostly concentrated in the sectors of "Design" and "Plants." Details of the matching procedure's results can be found in appendix B.

Table 2.3 shows demographic information for the set of inventors we were able to identify by assignee type and type of economic activity. There are some notable differences in the demographic composition of the patent types but also some similarities. The first thing to notice is that the vast majority of patents are filed by males. This is true across all assignee types and is consistent over time.[12] Innovation activity, whether household or

10. The identification would be greatly facilitated if the USPTO were able to collect either a birth date or an SSN/TIN.
11. We are able to identify demographics from 884,000 patents, but 28,000 of the patents are later classified as reassigned, which are dropped from our analysis.
12. Time series results note shown.

firm based, appears to be a male dominated activity. This is consistent with Bell et al. (2016), who find a similar deficit in female innovators. However, it should be noted that we cannot distinguish whether females (and other groups of inventors) are less likely to invent or rather less likely to patent given that they have invented. This is one of the key limitations of using patent data, which remains a proxy for innovation and does not necessarily capture all forms of innovation.

Firm-based patents disproportionately favor foreign-born inventors relative to individual-assigned patents and unassigned patents, with approximately one-third of inventors affiliated with firm-assigned patents being foreign born compared to 20 percent for other assignee types. Given this, it is perhaps not too surprising that firm-assigned patents are less likely to be associated with black or white inventors and nearly twice as likely to be associated with "other" races relative to individual-assigned and unassigned patents. The share of foreign-born inventors outweighs their relative share in the labor force at 16.7 percent of the total in 2015.[13] We find there is a deficit of black inventors across the board, again consistent with Bell et al. (2016).[14]

Finally, individual-assigned and unassigned patents disproportionately favor both older (over 55) and younger inventors (under 25). Nearly one-third of the household inventors are 55 years and older compared to the 20 percent found in firm-assigned patents. This is consistent with von Hippel, de Jong, and Flowers (2012), who find household innovations are disproportionately tied to students and men over 55.

To summarize our findings, household innovators (associated with individual assigned and unassigned patents) are more likely to be US born, white, under 25, and over 55 than firm based innovators. In the case of the latter, the proportion of household innovators above the age of 55 is more than 12 percentage points higher (31.6 versus 18.8). Across the board, we find a deficit of female and black inventors relative to the population of employed workers and an overrepresentation of foreign-born inventors.

2.4.2   Technology Class

We next focus on the types of technology classes associated with household innovations. Previous research has focused on consumer product innovations and has found innovations tended to be focused in a few product classes. Here we focus on the broader set of patented innovations. We look at the technology composition by assignee type. We also look at those that lead to direct business activity and those that do not. For our classification, we use the primary United States Patent Classification (USPC) code assigned to each patent and group them into eight broad classes consisting of the fol-

13. Shares of foreign-born in the labor force are reported in Bureau of Labor Statistics (2016).
14. Blacks and whites made up 12 percent and 79 percent, respectively, of the labor force population in 2015 (Bureau of Labor Statistics 2016).

Table 2.4   **Percent of US patents by assignee type and technology class**

	Individual	Business	Unassigned
Chemical	6.9	10.7	5
C&C	11.3	29.4	5.8
Design	19.8	9.2	27.1
D&M	10	11.4	6.4
E&E	8.6	18.2	8.1
Mechanical	16	10.6	17.5
Others	26.7	10.1	29
Plant	0.6	0.4	1.1
Total*	10,800	1,030,000	200,000

Source: Authors' calculations based on public USPTO data on granted patents applied for between 2000 and 2011.
Notes: Technology Class: C&C = Computers and Communications, D&M = Drugs and Medical, E&E = Electrical and Electronic. * Total patent counts in this row are rounded to comply with disclosure requirements.

lowing: Chemicals; Computers and Communication (C&C); Design; Drugs and Medicine (D&M); Electrical and Electronics (E&E); Mechanical; Plant Patents; and Other. The grouping by USPC class is based on Hall, Jaffe, and Trajtenberg (2001) and expanded to include new patent classes as detailed in Dreisigmeyer et al. (2014). Table 2.4 shows the breakdown by assignee type. We find firm-assigned patents are disproportionately in Chemical, C&C, and E&E relative to individual assignee and unassigned patents. By contrast, they are underrepresented in Design, Mechanical, and Other. Table 2.A12 in appendix C provides a listing of technology subcategories associated with each broad class. Among the technologies included in Mechanical and Others are Motors, Engines, and Parts; Transportation; and Miscellaneous, such as hardware and tools. Others include Amusement Devices, Apparel and Textile, and Furniture and House Fixtures, and miscellaneous, such as Robots and Aquatic Devices. All are fairly typical consumer products. Design patents provide protection to ornamental designs embodied in or applied to an article of manufacture. Analysis of the top 50 companies having been granted design patents shows that these are dominated by technology, automotive, and consumer product companies.[15]

Table 2.5 breaks down the previous table by business activity. The patterns here replicate the findings discussed regardless of business type. A few things stand out. First, the majority of Design patents are not associated with business activity and remain unmatched. This is true for both individual-assigned and unassigned patents and suggests fundamental differences, perhaps in the value of design patents vis-à-vis utility patents and maybe the

15. For details, see report from Intellectual Property Owners Association (2015).

Table 2.5   Patent technology class: Percent by assignee type and type of business

	Individual assignee			Business assignee			Unassigned		
	E	NE	U	E	NE	U	E	NE	U
Chemical	7	8.6	4.8	10.7	10	10.8	0	6.1	4.6
C&C	16.8	15.1	6.3	29.5	29.4	28.1	0	9.3	4.6
Design	14	3	41.1	9.3	6.9	9.4	0	4.8	34.3
D&M	25.9	11.6	7.6	11	13.5	16.6	0	7.8	6
E&E	15.4	10.4	6.2	18.5	13	15.2	0	9	7.8
Mechanical	11.2	18.9	12.6	10.8	9.8	8.7	0	22.5	15.8
Others	7.7	32.3	20.3	10	13.9	9.9	0	40.4	25.3
Plant	2.1	0	1.2	0.3	0.9	0.9	0	0.1	1.4
Total*	140	5,900	4,700	949,000	18,000	65,500	0	49,000	151,000

Source: Authors' calculations based on public USPTO data on granted patents applied for between 2000 and 2011.

Notes: Each column adds up to one. Technology Class: C&C = Computers and Communications, D&M = Drugs and Medical, E&E = Electrical and Electronic. Type of business: E = Employer, NE = Nonemployer, U = Unknown. * Total patent counts in this row are rounded to comply with disclosure requirements. (D) identifies suppressed values.

requirements for grants. Second, patents with a firm assignee in the Drugs and Medical class are harder to match to business databases, perhaps due to the complex structure of firms developing them.

We combine our technology classes with the individual demographics to identify compositional differences between employer patents and household innovations. Table 2.6 takes the difference in the proportion of patents by technology class and demographic characteristic between nonemployer patents and employer patents. The table highlights several key differences, most of which are significant. Design patents clearly differentiate themselves in terms of demographics. The previous sections have alluded to the fact that nonemployer patent holders are disproportionately male, US born, white, and older than employer patent holders. However, this does not seem to be the case for Design patents, where the opposite holds. It appears design patents in employer businesses are disproportionally associated with white, male, US-born inventors, where they might hold a relative advantage, signaling the very different nature of these types of patents.

2.4.3   Team Size

Evidence from surveys and product studies suggest the complexity and knowledge embodied in household innovations might not run very deep. A typical story might be that of a consumer who modifies the face of a clock to teach their kids how to tell time.[16] Consistent with this, survey data also show that the average expenditure in developing a household innovation is not very high. In this section, we explore whether this is also true of

16. This story is taken from von Hippel, de Jong, and Flowers (2012).

Table 2.6   Demographic differences by technology class: Nonemployer versus employer

	Male	US born	Black	White	Other	Age < 25	25 < Age < 55	Age > 55
Chemical	0.8*	7.1***	0.6***	5.3***	−5.9***	1.2***	−11.3***	10.2***
C&C	0.3	6.6***	0.6***	4.5***	−5***	0.5***	−9.9***	9.3***
Design	−6.1***	−0.9	4.3***	−5.8***	1.5*	1.7***	−8.7***	7***
D&M	2.1***	5***	0.7***	3.9***	−4.6***	0.7***	−11***	10.3***
E&E	0.1	8.2***	0.7***	7.4***	−8.2***	1.4***	−13.2***	11.8***
Mechanical	−0.9***	7***	0.9***	4.8***	−5.8***	1.2***	−11.6***	10.4***
Others	−5.4***	6.4***	2***	2.8***	−4.7***	1.1***	−8.9***	7.8***
Plant	1	28.8***	−0.7	−12.5**	13.2***	1.9	−12.2	10.3
Total	−1***	10.4***	1.1***	7.1***	−8.3***	1.1***	−11.8***	10.8***

Source: Authors' calculations based on public USPTO data on granted patents applied for between 2000 and 2011.

Notes: Numbers represent the difference in the proportion of patents between nonemployer and employer patents. Technology Class: C&C = Computers and Communications, D&M = Drugs and Medical, E&E = Electrical and Electronic. Type of business: E=Employer, NE = Nonemployer, U = Unknown. * $p < .05$, ** $p < .01$, *** $p < .001$.

patented household innovations. We follow Jones (2009) and use team size as a measure of the complexity and depth of knowledge associated with a particular innovation. The burden-of-knowledge hypothesis would indicate that household innovations require smaller team sizes.

Figure 2.1 plots the distribution of team sizes by assignee types and shows that firm-assigned patents tend to have significantly larger team sizes on average. The size distribution for individual assignee and unassigned patents is fairly similar and rests well to the left of firm-assigned patents. A large share of individual-assigned and unassigned patents are developed by a single inventor relative to patents assigned to firms. There are single inventors on 60.7 percent of individual-assigned patents and 83.5 percent of unassigned patents versus 30.8 percent on firm-assigned patents. Table 2.7 tabulates the mean team size by assignee type, technology class, and type of business and finds similar results across them. Team sizes for patents matched to nonemployer businesses tend to be significantly smaller on average than patents matched to employer firms, having on average nearly one fewer team member. Patents with no associated business activity have the smallest team size on average. Consistent with Jones (2009) and Kim and Marschke (2015), Drugs and Medicine and Chemicals tend to be composed of the largest inventor teams, while Design patents consist of the smallest teams.

2.4.4   Impact

Household survey data indicate that the impact and quality of household innovations might not be very high. Survey respondents often indicate they do not expect their inventions to be adopted. In this section, we explore

Table 2.7   Mean team size by technology class, assignee type, and type of business

	Individual assignee			Business assignee			Unassigned		
	E	NE	U	E	NE	U	E	NE	U
Chemical	3.1	1.93	1.38	3.06	2.47	2.86	0	1.48	1.32
C&C	2.67	1.88	1.31	2.65	2.32	2.53	0	1.47	1.27
Design	1.9	1.68	1.42	2.21	1.7	2.11	0	1.28	1.19
D&M	2.92	1.9	1.46	3.1	2.45	2.91	0	1.53	1.39
E&E	2.18	1.76	1.31	2.56	2.13	2.4	0	1.38	1.22
Mechanical	1.63	1.68	1.24	2.49	1.98	2.3	0	1.29	1.15
Others	1.73	1.67	1.27	2.44	1.98	2.28	0	1.29	1.15
Plant	2	1	1.04	1.25	1.15	1.3	0	1.68	1.31
All patents	2.38	1.8	1.36	2.65	2.24	2.49	0	1.37	1.21

Source: Authors' calculations based on public USPTO data on granted patents applied for between 2000 and 2011.

Notes: Technology Class: C&C = Computers and Communications, D&M = Drugs and Medical, E&E = Electrical and Electronic. Type of business: E = Employer, NE = Nonemployer, U = Unknown. (D) identifies suppressed values.

whether this extends to patented household innovations. In this section, we follow the literature and use citation counts as a noisy measure of the quality of a patent and its technological impact. We then use a new measure of impact that takes account of the structure of forward- and backward-looking citations to identify radical patents. Finally, we examine whether these innovations are general purpose or instead narrow in application. We ignore truncation issues in the analysis, assuming similar impacts across types of patents.

2.4.4.1   Citations

For our citation measures, we use the latest citation count (as of December 2015) collected from PatentsView and link them to our dataset. Figure 2.2 shows the distribution of citation counts by assignee type. Table 2.8 reports the means by assignee type, business type, and broad technology class. On average, individual-assigned patents have a lower mean citation count than firm-assigned patents. The mean citation for firm-assigned patents is 16.4, while the mean citation count for individual-assigned patents is 11.3 and 10.2 for unassigned patents.[17] The difference in average citation counts is driven in part by an across-the-board lower citation count across technology classes. However, some of the largest differences in mean citation counts can be found in the Design, Mechanical, and Others categories—precisely the areas where household innovations are concentrated—so composition effects contribute to the overall difference. More interesting, perhaps, is the finding that household innovations are quite heavily cited on average, and

---

17. Approximately 160,000 patents out of the 1.29 million have zero citations. The proportion of patents with zero citations by matched data and assignee type is approximately equivalent to the proportion of total patents by matched data and assignee type.

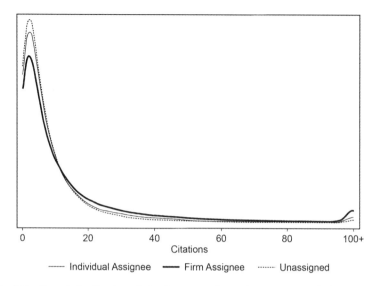

Fig. 2.2 Kernel distribution of citation counts by assignee type, 2000–2011
Source: Own calculations based on USPTO data on granted patents applied for between 2000 and 2011.

Table 2.8   **Mean citation count by technology class, assignee type, and type of business**

	Individual assignee			Business assignee			Unassigned		
	E	NE	U	E	NE	U	E	NE	U
Chemical	8.9	7.52	7.25	10.42	8.78	11.77	0	7.08	6.22
C&C	17.04	23.21	19.89	20.34	23.92	21.93	0	16.41	14.41
Design	6.65	8.58	6.18	12.32	11.38	10.7	0	8.55	7.07
D&M	18.86	23.73	17.65	25.73	22.81	21.75	0	18.66	15.32
E&E	12.09	13.1	9.61	13.84	16.26	15.14	0	10.6	8.88
Mechanical	10.88	7.81	7.78	11.79	14.88	12.64	0	8.13	6.56
Others	9	9.98	8.98	14.45	12.39	12.3	0	8.03	7.72
Plant	1.67	0.5	0.36	0.31	0.35	0.32	0	0.76	0.29
All patents	13.1	13.28	9.34	16.36	16.49	16.81	0	10.13	8.09

Source: Authors' calculations based on public USPTO data on granted patents applied for between 2000 and 2011.
Notes: We exclude patents with zero citations. Technology Class: C&C = Computers and Communications, D&M = Drugs and Medical, E&E = Electrical and Electronic. Type of business: E = Employer, NE = Nonemployer, U = Unknown. (D) identifies suppressed values.

in some areas, such as Computers and Communications and Electrical and Electronic, the difference is not very large. Looking at the citations across type of business activity, we find patents have a mean citation count of 16.4, 13.4, and 11.4, respectively, for patents associated with employer businesses, nonemployer businesses, and no business activity. Again, these differences

Table 2.9   Pseudo-maximum log likelihood regression on patent citations

Dependent variable	Citations (1)	Citations (2)
Grant year	−0.1616***	−0.1622***
	(0.00760)	(0.00757)
Team size	0.07265***	0.06831***
	(0.00426)	(0.00403)
Employer patents	0.23618***	
	(0.02269)	
Nonemployer patents	0.07342***	
	(0.01385)	
Unmatched patents	Dropped	Dropped
Firm-assigned patents		0.04132
		(0.02733)
Individual-assigned patents		−0.2460***
		(0.02746)
Unassigned patents	Dropped	Dropped
USPC fixed effects	Yes	Yes
Constant	326.192***	327.522***
	(14.7814)	(14.7207)
Observations	1,290,000	1,290,000

Standard errors are clustered at the USPC Technology Class level. * $p < .05$, ** $p < .01$, *** $p < .001$.

appear to be driven by composition effects as well as generally lower citation counts within particular technology classes.

To examine differences in citation counts after controlling for technology composition, we run a Poisson regression on citations, looking at the impact of business type after controlling for patent class (main USPC code) and grant year (table 2.9). Column 1 looks at citation impact by business type and column 2 by assignee type. Focusing on column 1, we see the difference in the logs of expected citations is 0.288 units higher for patents matched to employer firms and 0.06 units higher for patents matched to nonemployer firms relative to unmatched patents, holding everything else constant. (These values convert the above coefficients into interpretable units.) This is equivalent to a citation count that is 33.4 percent higher for employer-matched patents and 6.2 percent higher for nonemployer-matched patents, for a difference of 27 percent in citations between employer and nonemployer patents. Looking at the differences in citations by assignee type, column 2, we find a similar difference between firm-assigned patents and individual-assigned patents. The coefficient values give a difference in the logs of expected citations of 0.096 units higher for firm-assigned patents and –0.247 units lower for individual-assigned patents relative to reassigned patents. This is equivalent to a citation count that is 10 percent higher for firm-assigned patents and 22 percent lower for individual assigned patents, for a difference of 32 percent.

2.4.4.2   Radical Patents

Household innovators will be relatively resource constrained compared to firms. These innovators might choose to focus on technologies that require smaller investments and prior knowledge—they are not complex. Consistent with this idea, section 2.4.2 documented the disproportionate weight design patents have among household innovators. In this section we explore whether this might lead them also to work on innovations that represent breaks with past knowledge within specific technology fields. Also in this section, we assess the proportion of breakthrough patents among patented household innovations as defined by whether they represent a "radical" break from existing knowledge in that field. Since it is the focal point of a new technological trajectory, the patent itself must be cited.

Our measure builds on the concepts of Dahlin and Behrens (2005) but is extended to the universe of patents in the USPTO patent database (Dreisigmeyer et al. 2014). Dahlin and Behrens (2005) define the term *radical invention* as one that meets three properties: (1) it is novel, meaning it has distinctive features that are missing in previously observed inventions; (2) it is unique, meaning it is the focal point of a new technological trajectory; and (3) it must be adopted, meaning it should influence future inventions. The authors operationalize this idea by examining both forward and backward citation patterns for any given patent. Forward citations are citations to a patent made by other later patents. It is a measure of the patents impact on future inventions and its value in the market. Backward citations are defined by the prior art cited by the patent itself. Backward citations contain information about the radicalness of the innovation. The more radical a technology, the more likely it is to cite prior art outside its own patent class, since this will necessarily involve combining different elements rather than inventions from its own field.

Table 2.10 reports the number of patents (per thousand) that qualify as being radical by assignee type, business type, and technology class. In general, patents matched to employer firms are more than twice as likely to be considered radical versus patents matched to nonemployer firms and unmatched patents. This does not appear to be driven by compositional differences in the patent types, as employer-match patents and firm-assigned patents consistently have higher rates of radical patents across all technology classes. Design patents appear to have high rates of radical innovations. Many of these appear to be self-referencing and do not have much of an impact outside the patenting firm, suggesting these might be disproportionately defensive patents. While there are relatively fewer radical patents among household innovators, there is still a nontrivial number of them. We examine some of the radical patents identified. The bulk of them are found in Computers and Communications, Design, and Drugs and Medical. They include a system for providing traffic information to a plurality of mobile

Table 2.10   Proportion of radical patents (per thousand) by technology class, assignee type, and type of business

	Individual assignee			Business assignee			Unassigned		
	E	NE	U	E	NE	U	E	NE	U
Chemical	0	3.9	4.5	18.1	17.5	17.6	0	1.7	2
C&C	41.7	14.5	6.7	14.1	18.7	15.5	0	5.7	3.7
Design	0	11.2	9.8	28.4	19.8	21.9	0	9.4	12.3
D&M	0	13.1	8.4	25.6	22.8	22.3	0	3.4	3.2
E&E	0	6.5	0	13.2	15.2	14.8	0	2.3	3.1
Mechanical	0	4.5	3.4	12	17.8	16.5	0	2.8	2.3
Others	0	5.7	3.1	15.2	13	16.5	0	1.8	1.4
Plant	0	0	0	1.6	0	5.2	0	0	0.5
Total	7	7.8	6.4	16.8	17.2	17.4	0	2.9	5.7

Source: Authors' calculations based on public USPTO data on granted patents applied for between 2000 and 2011.
Notes: Technology Class: C&C = Computers and Communications, D&D = Drugs and Medical, E&E = Electrical and Electronic. Type of business: E = Employer, NE = Nonemployer, U = Unknown.

users connected to a network, a system for dynamically pushing information to a user utilizing a global positioning system, a method and apparatus for securing a suture, and a flash memory drive with a quick connector. All these technologies had broad impacts in their fields.

2.4.4.3   Generality Index

Finally, we describe the breadth of impact patented household innovations have outside of their own fields. Some technologies are more specific, with a limited application across industries, while others have a wider field of application. We use the patent classification codes to generate a measure of generality, G_i, that is close to that used by Hall and Trajtenberg (2004) as follows:

$$G_i = \sqrt{\sum_j^{n_i} s_{ij}^2},$$

where s_{ij} denotes the percentage of citations received by patent i that belong to patent class j out of n_i patent classes. This is simply the square root of the Herfindahl concentration index, and therefore if a patent is cited by subsequent patents that belong to a wide range of fields, the measure will be low and close to 0. By contrast, if the citations are concentrated in a few fields, the measure will be close to 1. Furthermore, if a patent has a single citation in the same technological field, this measure will be equal to 1 and it won't be defined when it receives no citations.[18]

18. This modified measure of generality retains important properties of metric spaces (or distance functions) that allow us to measure the distance, instead of just a similarity, between two patents.

Table 2.11   **Mean (modified) generality index by technology class, assignee type, and type of business**

	Individual assignee			Business assignee			Unassigned		
	E	NE	U	E	NE	U	E	NE	U
Chemical	0.6	0.64	0.62	0.6	0.61	0.59	0	0.63	0.65
C&C	0.58	0.59	0.6	0.63	0.62	0.63	0	0.62	0.63
Design	0.87	0.8	0.86	0.88	0.84	0.88	0	0.79	0.86
D&M	0.63	0.68	0.71	0.66	0.66	0.65	0	0.68	0.71
E&E	0.62	0.66	0.69	0.66	0.64	0.65	0	0.66	0.68
Mechanical	0.61	0.72	0.71	0.67	0.66	0.66	0	0.7	0.72
Others	0.64	0.69	0.7	0.67	0.68	0.67	0	0.69	0.7
Plant	1	1	1	0.99	1	0.99	0	1	1

Source: Authors calculations based on public USPTO data on granted patents applied for between 2000 and 2011.
Notes: Technology Class: C&C = Computers and Communications, D&D = Drugs and Medical, E&E = Electrical and Electronic. Type of business: E = Employer, NE = Nonemployer, U = Unknown.

We compute a Generality Index for patents in our sample that were granted up through 2008 to limit the impact of right censoring. Table 2.11 looks at the mean generality index by assignee type, type of business activity, and technology class. In general, firm-assigned patents find application across a broader set of technological fields. This is particularly true for Chemical, Drugs and Medical, and Mechanical. Independent inventors appear to focus on technologies that have narrower impacts. Across the board and as expected, patents in Computers and Communications and Chemical have broader applicability, receiving the highest number of citations outside their field. By contrast, Design patents have the most limited application.

2.5   Business Formation and Outcomes

Having established how patents associated with household innovations differ from traditional patents, this section looks at the types of businesses associated with household innovations—their characteristics, innovation dynamics, and outcomes. The goal is to assess whether the innovator is able to monetize their innovation through either increased business income, possibly from licensing, or the use of the patent. There are other ways the inventor might monetize their innovation that we do not observe here, such as through direct payments.[19] It should be noted that the majority of patented household innovations are not directly tied to a business that the inventor owns. Table 2.5 shows that only 19 percent of patented household innovations, those accounted for by individual assignee and unassigned pat-

19. This form of income might be observed through their income tax forms.

ents, are associated with a business. The equivalent rate for patents with a declared business assignee is 93 percent.

2.5.1   Characteristics of Patenting Firms: Industry, Age, and Size

We start by looking at the industry composition of the nonemployer firms that obtain a patent. Patenting nonemployer firms are extremely rare. Out of more than 20 million nonemployer firms in a typical year, only around 5,000 firms will seek out a patent (less than 0.03 percent). We limit our analysis to nonemployer firms that are born after 2000. We exclude existing non-employers born prior to avoid left censoring in the patents we can match.[20] Figure 2.3 shows the industry composition of patenting nonemployer firms weighted by number of patents they own (top) and that of all nonemployer firms (bottom). Figure 2.3 shows that a disproportionate share of patents originate at nonemployer firms that engage in Professional Services, followed by Finance and Real Estate and Retail. This is very different from the industry composition of nonemployer firms, which is dispersed much more evenly across industries.

Businesses associated with household innovations differ from the overall population of nonemployer businesses. We are interested in understanding whether the trigger for creating these businesses is the expectation of a patent grant and thus a means to try to capitalize on an innovation or instead if the business activity predates the patent application. We explore similar patterns for firms with employees. Figure 2.4 graphs the distribution of firm age when the firm/inventor applies for their first patent for both employer and nonemployer firms.[21] We define firm age based on the year the business first filed income taxes. We look at applications by patenting firms in 2010. We limit our analysis to firms up to age 10. If a firm first files income taxes after the application is filed, we assign a negative age equal to the difference between application year and birth year. Figure 2.4 shows that a significant share of businesses apply for their patent before they generate revenue. The mass of distribution is to the left of their second year of business activity. Approximately 43.6 percent of nonemployer firms that are granted a patent apply for the patent prior to starting their nonemployer business activity. For many other businesses, the birth of the business coincides with the patent application year. A nontrivial number of patent applications, 18 percent, are filed three or more years after starting the business activity. Compared to employer businesses, household innovators are more likely to start their businesses at the time of application, although the two distributions are centered around age 0. The tighter distribution for nonemployers can be attributed to the shortened life cycle of nonemployer firms, most of which

20. Currently we can only work with patent data starting in 2000. If we were to include incumbent nonemployers in 2000, there would be no way for us to determine which ones received a patent prior to 2000.

21. We only observe granted patents.

A. Patenting

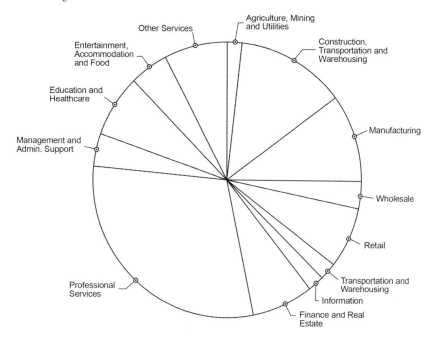

B. All

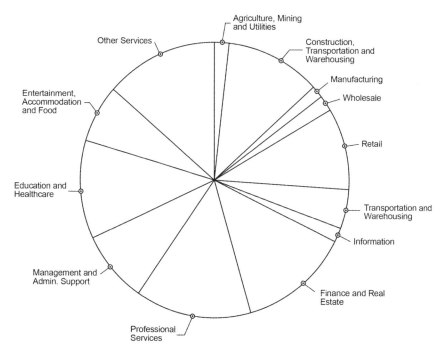

Fig. 2.3   Industry composition of nonemployer firms, 2000–2011

Source: Own calculations based on USPTO and US Census Bureau data on granted patents applied for between 2000 and 2011.

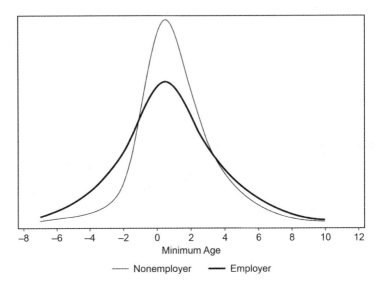

Fig. 2.4   **Kernel distribution of age of nonemployer firm for first patent, 2010**
Source: Own calculations based on USPTO and US Census Bureau data on patent-holding firms age 10 years or less in 2010.

are very short-lived with more than 50 percent of nonemployer firms exiting before year two and 70 percent of nonemployer firms exiting by year three (Fairlie and Miranda 2017).

We are interested in understanding the revenue generated by household innovations vis-à-vis innovations tied to established employer businesses. Figure 2.5 looks at the revenue distribution for firms that own patents as a function of their employer status. As before, we focus on the cross section of firms age 10 or less in 2010. Revenue follows a log-normal pattern with the distribution centered at $10,000 for household innovations.[22] Revenue for innovative employer businesses is similarly shaped but centered around much larger revenues of $1.2 million. Businesses associated with household innovations do not appear to generate much income on average at time of application. There is, however, a fairly wide distribution with a standard deviation of $97,500.

Figure 2.6 looks at income growth before and after patent grant. To avoid composition effects as a result of firm exit, we show results for a balanced panel of firms that survive for a minimum of five years. For comparison we show revenue for employer businesses. We normalize revenue to equal 100 at grant time, t, to facilitate comparison with employer businesses. Figure 2.6 shows that income growth prior to patent grant is considerable and very

22. It should be noted that firms that patent prior to starting their business (negative age firms) are not included in the distribution.

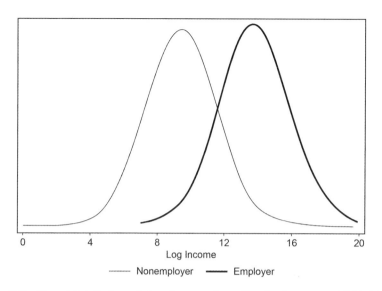

Fig. 2.5   Kernel distribution of size of nonemployer firm for first patent, 2000–2011

Source: Own calculations based on USPTO and US Census Bureau data on granted patents applied for between 2000 and 2011.

Kernel = Gaussian, Degree = 3, Bandwidth = 0.5
Sample consists of 2,400 nonemployer and 3,700 employer firms

Fig. 2.6   Total income before first patent, balanced panel

Source: Own calculations based on USPTO and US Census Bureau data on granted patents applied for between 2000 and 2011. Sample includes a balanced panel of patenting firms centered at patent grant.

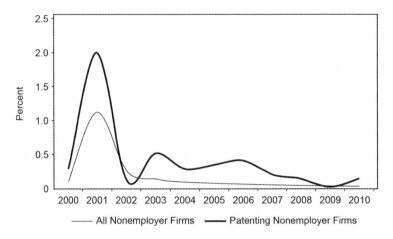

Fig. 2.7   Transition to employer firms by year, 2000 cohort
Source: Own calculations based on USPTO and US Census Bureau data; 2000 cohort of nonemployer business.

similar for both employer and nonemployer business. In the two years prior to patent grant, revenue grows by 25 percent relative to the base. Income plateaus for nonemployer businesses shortly after grant and starts declining one year after. Very few firms transition to employer status, so this pattern is not due to excluding successful exits out of nonemployment. Revenue growth by employer businesses seems to be very different after grant. These firms display an acceleration of revenue that seems to exhaust itself two years after grant. Overall, these results suggest that on average, household innovators are not as successful in capitalizing their innovations after grant.

2.5.2   Dynamics and Transition to Employer Status

Finally, we look at the probability that a nonemployer business hires employees—in particular whether patenting activity is associated with the successful growth expansion to a business that generates paid jobs for other individuals. For this exercise, we focus on the cohort of new nonemployer start-ups in 2000 and ask ourselves how many transition into employer status each year after.

We find that of the approximately 5.24 million new nonemployer entrants in 2000, around 100,000 eventually transition to employer firms over their lives, for a cumulative transition rate of approximately 2 percent. Of this cohort, 3,700 nonemployer firms hold a patent. Of these, 125 will transition to employer firms over their life cycles, for a cumulative transition rate of around 3.4 percent, or 70 percent higher than nonpatenting firms. Annual transitions are graphed in figure 2.7. As we can see, patenting firms are more than twice as likely to transition to employer firms within the first two years relative to nonpatenting firms.

2.5.3   The Value of Household Innovations

Relatively few household innovations become the foundation of a business. However, those that do give us an indication of the value of these innovations if only from the revenue they generate. Household innovations that do not directly translate into a business owned by the inventor might be expected to generate income in other ways that we do not observe in the data, such as contracts or direct payments. Many others might be monetized by incumbent companies with specific market knowledge and resources to market and profit from the innovation. Many others may simply never be pursued directly but contribute to the knowledge base that generates other innovations. Other innovations might go unnoticed, and yet others may simply have no value at all. Assigning value to these innovations is difficult if not impossible. However, a simple back-of-the-envelope calculation might give us a sense of the magnitude of their overall value. To this end, we calculate a range of potential values based on both the marginal and average direct incomes generated by businesses owned by household inventors. We focus first on innovations tied to nonemployer businesses. We calculate the average income generated by those businesses while they remain in operation. For simplicity, we ignore income generated by these businesses after they hire their first employee, since there are relatively few transitions. We base our calculation on the cohort of firms born in 2000 that own a patent. We track these firms through 2011 or until they exit.

Our starting point for identifying the economic value of these patents is to first come up with a revenue elasticity for each patent grant. In Table 2.12, we run several revenue specifications based on known factors that are seemingly unrelated to the innovation itself but can potentially impact the revenue stream of these businesses. These include technology sector and zip code–year controls, as well as demographic controls (male, US born, race, and age) across the full nonemployer sample and patenters only. In column (5), we control for selection using a Heckman selection model. The results from our specifications reveal that patents have a positive and significant impact on revenue. Across all nonemployer and patenting firms, the specifications suggest that a 10 percent increase in granted patents is associated with a 0.3 percent to 0.4 percent increase in revenue (combining the elasticities of the patent application and grant), while a 10 percent increase in citations is associated with a 0.03 percent to 0.06 percent increase in revenue. These results are consistent after controlling for selection.

In attempting to compute the economic value of these patents, we first need to tabulate the total number of household innovations as measured by patents and the number of businesses associated with these patents. Tables 2.1 and 2.2 tell us that we have approximately 93,000 matched patents to nonemployer businesses. These 93,000 patents match to 42,000 unique nonemployer businesses (2.2 patents per business). Assuming the same employer-

Table 2.12   **Regression results on nonemployer revenues**

Regression	OLS (1)	OLS (2)	OLS (3)	OLS (4)	Heckman selection (second stage) (5)
Sample	All	Patenters only	All	Patenters only	All
Citations	0.0048***	0.0060***	0.0045***	0.0056***	0.0039***
	(0.0003)	(0.0009)	(0.0003)	(0.0009)	(0.0008)
Patent applications	0.0305***	0.0260***	0.0262***	0.0175***	0.0254***
	(0.0009)	(0.0039)	(0.009)	(0.0039)	(0.0011)
Patent grants	0.0135***	0.0078***	0.0117***	0.0079***	0.0139***
	(0.0010)	(0.0023)	(0.0009)	(0.0023)	(0.0011)
Team size	−0.0019***	−0.0027***	−0.0027***	−0.0035***	−0.0026***
	(0.0003)	(0.0009)	(0.0003)	(0.0009)	(0.0004)
Demographic controls	No	No	Yes	Yes	Yes
Zip-year fixed effects	Yes	Yes	Yes	Yes	Yes
Patent-sector fixed effects	Yes	Yes	Yes	Yes	Yes
R^2	0.019	0.259	0.062	0.278	
Observations	198,110,000	41,500	198,110,000	41,500	198,110,000

Notes: Robust standard errors are clustered at the patent-sector level. Selection equation for column 5 includes demographic controls and zip-year fixed effects. The selection coefficient is –6.0557 with SE 0.0628 and is significant to the 0.1 percent. * $p < .05$, ** $p < .01$, *** $p < .001$.

to-nonemployer match ratios in table 2.2 and applying them to the set of unmatched patents gives us 184,000 unmatched nonemployer patents, which would convert to approximately 83,000 nonemployer businesses (assuming the same ratio of patents per business). We therefore need to approximate the revenue streams for the 83,000 "missing" nonemployer businesses to tabulate the full economic impact of household innovations. Nonemployer businesses with patents generate approximately $10,200 in annual revenue on average (versus $9,700 generated on average for nonemployer businesses that hold no patents). Nonemployer businesses with patents also have an average survival rate of 3.95 years (versus 2.72 years for nonemployer businesses without patents). Therefore, if we take the aggregate lifetime revenue of the 42,000 nonemployer businesses with patents, we get an economic value of approximately $1.7 billion (or $18,500 per patent). Applying the same values to the 83,000 "missing" nonemployer businesses with patents gives us a cumulative economic value of $5.0 billion for all household innovations between 2000 and 2011 in real 2000 dollars.

It is important to note that this calculation requires a number of strong assumptions that may differ greatly from reality. First, the revenue generated by businesses started by household inventors themselves is the same as the revenue generated by household innovations whose outcomes we are not able to observe, including those sold to or appropriated by existing businesses. Second, businesses started by household inventors would not generate revenue were it not for the innovation. Third, the cost of developing the innovation is negligible. Finally, we have limited our analysis to patented household innovations. While arguably the most valuable innovations, likely they represent but a small portion of all household innovations. We have made no effort to place an economic value on innovations that are not known to the patent system.

2.6   Conclusion

Households are increasingly recognized as an important source of invention and innovation. Survey data show independent inventors contribute substantially to consumer product innovations that are later incorporated into the products of incumbent firms. A challenge with survey data is the small sample sizes, which either limit what we can learn about the most valuable innovations (the right tail of the distribution) or limit the scope of the innovations we can study. In this chapter, we use administrative data from the US Patent and Trademark Office and the US Census Bureau to describe patented household innovations in a systematic way. While patented innovations arguably represent but a very small slice of household innovations, they are perhaps the most valuable one. We match these patents and their inventors to US Census Bureau demographic and business data. We explore the demographic characteristics of housed inventors vis-à-vis salaried inventors, the characteristics and impact of their innovations, and their value when these inventors monetize their innovations through their own business.

We find household inventors are disproportionately born in the United States when compared with salaried inventors, and consequently they are also relatively white. Businesses that hire inventors disproportionately hire foreign-born inventors relative to their size in the population—an indication these corporations might engage in brain gain by tapping foreign markets. Household inventors are disproportionately under 25 and over 55, consistent with the idea that household innovation is a leisure activity. Across the board, whether household or corporate inventors, we find a deficit in female and black inventors relative to the population as a whole.

Looking at the types of innovations, we find household inventors work in technology classes disproportionately tied to consumer products, such as Design, Mechanical, and Other. These patents are about half as likely to be considered "radical" when compared with corporate patents. In terms of value, household innovations accumulate approximately 27 percent to 32 percent fewer citations on average. While their citation impact is smaller, it remains remarkably high, with an average of 13.6 citations per patent (through December 2016). Finally, we find that relatively few household inventors start a business around their innovation. Only 19 percent of household innovations are tied to a business. These businesses average $10,000 in revenue at time of patent application and are more than twice as likely to transition to hire their first employee than nonemployers who do not patent.

Finally, our back-of-the-envelope calculations suggest patented household innovations granted between 2000 and 2011 may generate approximately $5.0 billion in revenue in 2000 dollars. While this might not be extraordinary when compared to the value of corporate patents, it is nontrivial, which raises important questions about R&D and innovation policy.

To conclude, patented household innovations have impact and value. Many of them are radical and represent breakthroughs in their fields. Despite efforts to understand their role in the economy, our knowledge of innovations and their inventors remains limited. Administrative data help shed light on this population and their impact. Combined with a targeted survey of household inventors and their patented inventions, this could go a long way to expand our knowledge in this area.

Appendix A

Matching Process and Data Construction

In this section, we outline the matching process between USPTO-granted patents and the full nonemployer dataset (Integrated Longitudinal Business Database, or ILBD) at Census. We start by describing the individual datasets and features of the datasets that will be matched. We then outline the matching algorithm and post a number of statistics on the match rates across different patent types.

2.A1   USPTO Patent Data

The USPTO patent database consists of all granted patents applied for between 2000 and 2011 by US entities. We use the patent class information to impose restrictions on the set of patents used in our analysis. Depending on the patent documents, patents can be assigned to firms, individuals, or governments. These can each be either domestic or foreign. In addition, the patents can be unassigned. This happens when the inventors have not granted the rights to the invention to a corporation, university, or government agency or to other individuals. In these cases, the patents are assumed to remain with the inventor, but in some cases, they can later be reassigned to firms. We exclude from the set of patents we analyze those that belong to

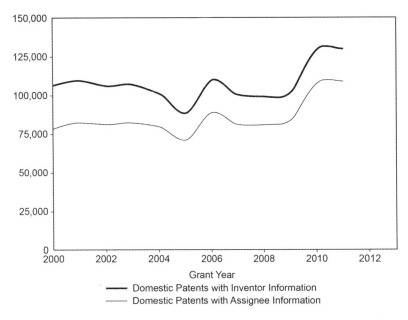

Fig. 2.A1   Mean (modified) annual patent application counts of granted US patents by application year, 2000–2013

governments and all foreign patents. We assume these are not tied to independent US-based inventors and exclude all foreign entities as well as government patents.[23] Counts of domestic patents with inventor and assignee data are plotted in figure 2.1.

Our matching algorithm attempts to create name and address matches from two distinct sources of information contained in USPTO patents: (i) the assignee, typically a firm, for whom patent ownership belongs and (ii) the inventor—persons who may or may not be affiliated with a firm that came up with the patent. In cases where no assignee is named, it is assumed that the patent's ownership belongs to the inventor and/or inventors. We are primarily interested in collecting names and any geographical data associated with the patents. We compile our matching database from two distinct sources of data from USPTO, each associated with either the assignee or the inventor.

2.A1.1   Cleaning of USPTO Assignee Data

The matching information for assignees is limited to the firm name, city, and state. We use city and state as our blocking variables and allow for fuzzy

---

23. We only keep patents of assignee type "02—US Company and/or Corporation" and type "04—US Individual," as well as patents with missing assignee information that originate in the United States and contain US inventor data.

Table 2.A1   Assignee counts from USPTO data on granted patents by US entities, 2000–2011

	All patents	Domestic patents with assignees	Unique assignee-geographic pairs	Unique assignees
2000	107,000	79,500	20,800	18,800
2001	109,000	82,900	21,000	18,900
2002	106,000	81,200	19,600	17,800
2003	107,000	82,900	19,200	17,700
2004	101,000	80,100	18,600	17,200
2005	89,000	71,400	17,100	15,900
2006	110,000	88,700	19,900	18,300
2007	101,000	81,600	18,300	17,000
2008	99,400	81,400	17,900	16,700
2009	102,000	84,700	17,900	16,700
2010	130,000	108,000	21,200	19,800
2011	130,000	110,000	21,700	20,200
Total	1,290,000	1,030,000	123,000	102,000

Source: Authors' calculations on public USPTO data on granted patents applied for by US entities between 2000 and 2011.

Notes: Counts are rounded to comply with disclosure requirements.

matching based on name. We start with approximately 1.29 million patent observations across all years and drop around 260,000 patents that do not have an assignee name to match against, leaving us with 1.03 million patents to match assignee information against. Nearly all of the 1.03 million patents have geographic information, including city and state, to match against.

In each year, there are on average 18,000 unique assignee names to match against and slightly more geographic pairs, indicating that a small subset of assignees applies for patents from multiple locations. The total number of unique assignees between 2000 and 2011 is approximately 102,000 and provides potential matches for 1.03 million patents (80 percent of possible matches).

2.A1.2   Cleaning of USPTO Inventor Data

Inventors are listed separately from the assignees and are considered wholly different, as they are typically employees of the assignee firms. Inventor data contains a separate identifier for each inventor and also contains city- and state-level geographic data. Multiple inventors can work on each patent. The number of inventors greatly exceeds the number of assignees. Because the ILBD mainly consists of person-level identifiers, inventors will serve as a primary matching criterion.

In each year, there are around 160,000 unique inventor names on average to match the ILBD against and nearly 1 million unique individuals associated with patents granted between 2000 and 2011. Nearly all of the data

Table 2.A2   **Inventor counts from USPTO data on granted patents by US entities, 2000–2011**

	All patents	Domestic patents with inventors	Unique inventor-geographic pairs	Unique inventors
2000	107,000	107,000	161,000	153,000
2001	109,000	109,000	166,000	158,000
2002	106,000	106,000	165,000	157,000
2003	107,000	107,000	169,000	160,000
2004	101,000	101,000	164,000	156,000
2005	89,000	88,900	149,000	142,000
2006	110,000	110,000	177,000	167,000
2007	101,000	101,000	166,000	157,000
2008	99,400	99,300	166,000	157,000
2009	102,000	102,000	175,000	165,000
2010	130,000	130,000	220,000	205,000
2011	130,000	130,000	222,000	207,000
Total	1,290,000	1,290,000	1,200,000	990,000

Source: Authors' calculations on public USPTO data on granted patents by US entities between 2000 and 2011.

Notes: Counts are rounded to comply with disclosure requirements.

contains geographic information of some form, including city and/or state, with a small proportion of inventors applying for patents across multiple locations. Combining these data with the assignee data gives us the full matching criteria to perform our name and address match. To summarize our matching frame, we have approximately 180,000 unique inventors and assignees to match the ILBD against in every year. These 180,000 inventors and assignees represent around 110,000 patents in each year for 1.29 million total patents.

2.A2   Integrated Longitudinal Business Database Cleanup

On the nonemployer side of the data, we start by combining all the individual cross sections of the ILBD from 2000 to 2011. The ILBD consists of both nonemployer businesses (identified with an Employer Identification Number, or EIN) and sole proprietorships (identified by a PIK). The breakdown and counts of businesses of each type are as follows.

The identifying information used to link to the patents consists of a name, city, and state, along with a unique identifier that is able to link nonemployer businesses over time. Names are given by two separate name variables. We separate the two name variables and stack them with their unique identifier in order to obtain every name combination in the database. In addition, approximately 55 percent of the names consist of two individuals separated by an ampersand, such as "John & Jane Doe." We separate out each of these

Table 2.A3   Nonemployer businesses counts by type

Year	Nonemployer businesses	Nonemployer EIN	Nonemployer PIK
2000	16,530,000	2,120,000	14,410,000
2001	16,980,000	2,230,000	14,750,000
2002	17,650,000	2,270,000	15,380,000
2003	18,650,000	2,420,000	16,230,000
2004	19,520,000	2,530,000	16,990,000
2005	20,390,000	2,670,000	17,720,000
2006	20,770,000	2,590,000	18,180,000
2007	21,710,000	2,620,000	19,090,000
2008	21,350,000	2,540,000	18,810,000
2009	21,700,000	3,000,000	18,700,000
2010	22,110,000	3,000,000	19,110,000
2011	22,490,000	3,050,000	19,440,000
Total	239,850,000	31,040,000	208,810,000

Source: Nonemployer statistics.

Notes: Counts are rounded to comply with disclosure requirements. PIK, protected identification key; EIN, employer identification number.

observations into two observations (e.g., "John Doe" and "Jane Doe"). All together, these combinations give us more than 297 million unique observations for the 183 million nonemployer businesses to match against.

2.A3   Matching Algorithm

Once the two matching datasets have been completed, we run the following name and address matching algorithm in order of best possible match to worst possible match: (a) Name, City, and State: Only the inventor dataset of the USPTO contains CITY data; (b) Name and State: Includes both inventor and assignee data and consists of the largest possible match; and (c) Name Only: Worst possible match set, but we can keep unique matches.

We use the SAS PROC DQMATCH algorithm to run the match. After each step, we only keep the residual nonmatched patents so that each patent can only be matched according to one of the criteria sets above. Table 2.A4 provides summary statistics on the full match rates by step. These consist of the raw matches (prior to any cleaning).

We are able to match approximately 80 percent of the 1.29 million patents that we start out with. More than two-thirds of the matches occur at the highest quality, where the patent's assignee/inventor's name, city, and state matched a nonemployer business' name, city, and state. Approximately one-fifth of the matches occur at the "name and state" resolution, with the remaining matches occurring at the "name" resolution. Each of these matches can occur through an inventor match, an assignee match, or for some patents, both. The breakdown of match by identifier is as follows.

Table 2.A4   **Number of patent matches by match criteria, 2000–2011**

	Number of matches	Total matches (%)
Match Criteria 1—Name, City, and State	713,000	69
Match Criteria 2—Name and State	207,000	20
Match Criteria 3—Name Only	117,000	11
Total	1,037,000	

Source: Authors' calculations using ILBD data.
Notes: Counts are rounded to comply with disclosure requirements.

Table 2.A5   **Breakdown of matches by identifier, 2000–2011**

	Matched patents	Inventor only	Assignee only	Both
Match Criteria 1—Name, City and State	713,000	500,000	102,000	112,000
Match Criteria 2—Name and State	207,000	130,000	53,000	24,000
Match Criteria 3—Name Only	117,000	78,000	26,000	13,000
Total Patents	1,037,000	708,000	181,000	149,000

Source: Authors' calculations using ILBD Data.
Notes: Counts are rounded to comply with disclosure requirements.

Nearly 70 percent of the matches occur through the inventor, which is expected, since nearly 90 percent of the patent-matching criteria are through the inventor. About 14 percent of patents are matched through both the inventor and the assignee, with the remaining being matched through the assignee. The next step in the matching process is to filter out the patents that are actually linked with employer firms, keep patents that have identified inventors in the Person Identification Validation System (PVS) process, drop duplicate matches (e.g., more than one identifier for a patent-name combination), and finally augment our data using unique PVSed patents.

2.A4   Cleaning the Set of Matches

Starting with our set of 103 million matches, the first step in the cleaning process is to remove all the patents associated with employer firms using an existing Census firm-level crosswalk (see Graham et al. 2018). These patents may have matched to the nonemployer data either through the inventor who is employed by an employer firm that is the assignee or if the name of the nonemployer business is very similar or identical to the name of an employer business. The existing Census firm-level crosswalk exists from 2000 to 2011 and covers more than 1.5 million patents, of which 958,000 originate in the United States, with the remaining belonging to foreign assignees with US subsidiaries. This crosswalk was created using a triangulation of name-address matching of assignee data merged with linked employee-employer inventor data. The crosswalk covers around 90 percent of all domestic patents with firm assignees. Filtering out the employer patents will remove approximately 80 percent of the patents matched to the nonemployer data (838,000 patents were removed). This suggests that a large percentage of inventors at employer firms also have nonemployer businesses. Not all of the patents from these inventors are removed from the final dataset—only the patents that are identified as being assigned to an employer firm.

The next step in the cleaning of the matches involves filtering out the matches that have not been linked to Census data using the Census Bureau's PVS. The PVS process assigns an anonymous, unique person identifier (PIK) to individuals using name and address information and matching it against the Social Security Administration's numerical identification file (Numident). The matching process is probabilistic, and it is possible for an individual to receive multiple identifiers (PIKs), especially if they provided only partial information. The USPTO patent data underwent the full PVS process for the original Census firm-level crosswalk, generating PIKs for all the inventors identified in patents, based on names and a zip code. Because the information used to generate these matches is rather coarse (only name and zip), approximately 30 percent of the patent-inventor combinations have a unique identifier (PIK), while 75 percent have fewer than five identifiers. The zip code is the unique characteristic here that we miss in our nonemployer matching process and hence can be used to validate our existing matches. Our filter involves directly linking all the PIKs assigned to each patent from the PVS process and merging them with the PIKs generated in the nonemployer matches. We drop patents that were matched to the nonemployer through the inventor name but are not identified in the PVS process. This removes nearly 40 percent of the existing matches.

The third step in the filter process drops duplicate matches by patent identifier and name. These are patents that cannot be assigned to a specific person or business because of multiple matches. There are several instances where patents match to multiple nonemployer identifiers after the name and address match and after the filters have been applied. Think of an inventor named David Smith in Washington, DC, and a company named David Smith also located in Washington, DC. First, there are possibly many unincorporated entities named David Smith, so the match might not be unique. Even if the match is unique, we do not know whether the owner is the inventor (i.e., there are many David Smiths). Since there is no way to distinguish between these nonemployer matches, we elect to drop them. This removes 45 percent of existing matches.

The next step in the filter process involves "winsorizing" our existing matches by the assignee code. In this case, we count the number of patents by assignee code-year and drop the patents for the assignee code-year com-

Table 2.A6   Filtering out employer patents, 2000–2011

Grant year	Original match	Removal of employer patents	Keep PVS	Drop duplicate	Winsorize and augment with PVS
2000	83,800	19,700	14,400	10,500	10,200
2001	86,000	19,000	14,100	10,500	10,100
2002	84,100	18,000	11,300	8,700	8,300
2003	85,100	17,300	10,900	8,500	8,200
2004	80,900	15,900	9,900	7,600	7,400
2005	71,800	13,700	8,500	6,800	6,500
2006	88,500	16,500	9,900	8,000	7,700
2007	81,300	14,700	8,500	6,800	6,500
2008	80,600	14,300	8,000	6,400	6,100
2009	83,200	14,000	8,000	6,400	6,000
2010	106,000	18,200	10,700	8,700	8,200
2011	106,000	18,300	10,400	8,300	7,900
Total	1,037,000	200,000	125,000	97,000	93,000

Source: Authors' calculations using LBD Data.
Notes: Counts are rounded to comply with disclosure requirements.

binations that are in the top 0.5 percent. This number ranges between 20 and 50 patents per year. Our assumption is that due to size constraints, the number of patents a nonemployer business can produce in a year is limited, and these observations are likely to have been missed by the existing Census firm-level crosswalk or are "unique" for entirely different reasons. This removes a further 7.5 percent of matches.

Finally, we augment our matches using the unique inventor identifiers from the PVS process. As mentioned earlier, approximately 30 percent of the patent-inventor combinations have a unique identifier (PIK). We keep the ones with the unique identifier and merge them with the full nonemployer database to identify nonemployer businesses that our matching methodology may have missed. We then augment our existing matches with this database. This increases the number of matches by approximately 5 percent for a total of 68,400 matched patents. Table 2.A6 summarizes the full effect of each matching stage.

This completes the matching process for the nonemployer data. Starting from 1.29 million patents, we are able to successfully match 68,400 patents to the nonemployer data. The full breakdown of matches by dataset is below.

We denote the "unmatched" as unknown, since a fairly large proportion of these patents were initially matched to the nonemployer dataset but were dropped either because the inventor's personal identifier was not listed in the PVS process or because the invention-name combination had more than one individual listed (dropped out during deduplication process). A breakdown of the "Unknown" matches is given in table 2.A8.

Table 2.A7   Total matches by type, 2000–2011

Grant year	Total	Employer	Nonemployer	Unknown
2000	107,000	72,700	10,200	24,400
2001	109,000	75,900	10,100	23,200
2002	106,000	74,700	8,300	23,000
2003	107,000	76,600	8,200	22,100
2004	101,000	73,800	7,400	20,200
2005	88,900	65,500	6,500	16,900
2006	110,000	81,500	7,700	20,600
2007	101,000	75,300	6,500	18,800
2008	99,300	75,100	6,100	18,200
2009	102,000	78,200	6,000	17,800
2010	130,000	99,500	8,200	22,000
2011	130,000	99,900	7,900	22,100
Total	1,290,000	949,000	93,000	249,000

Source: Authors' calculations using LBD Data.
Notes: Counts are rounded to comply with disclosure requirements.

Table 2.A8   Breakdown of unknown matches, 2000–2011

Grant year	Total unknown	Unmatched	Matched	Drop in PVS process	Duplicates/ winsorized
2000	24,400	14,800	9,600	6,400	3,200
2001	23,200	14,200	9,000	6,000	3,000
2002	23,000	13,300	9,700	7,700	2,000
2003	22,100	13,000	9,100	7,400	1,700
2004	20,200	11,600	8,600	7,000	1,500
2005	16,900	9,600	7,300	6,100	1,100
2006	20,600	11,700	9,000	7,900	1,100
2007	18,800	10,500	8,300	7,400	900
2008	18,200	10,000	8,300	7,400	800
2009	17,800	9,700	8,100	7,200	900
2010	22,000	11,900	10,200	8,900	1,200
2011	22,100	11,600	10,500	9,500	1,100
Total	249,000	142,000	108,000	89,000	18,600

Source: Authors' calculations using LBD data.
Notes: Counts are rounded to comply with disclosure requirements.

Table 2.A8 tells us that approximately 141,000 of the 273,000 unknown patents were unmatched across all Census datasets, which implies that around 132,000 patents were linked to the nonemployer. Of these, approximately 67 percent were dropped, as they were not listed in the PVS process, with the remainder dropping due to being either duplicates or "winsorized."

Appendix B
Matching Demographics to Patent Data

Matching the patent data to the demographic data is a relatively straightforward process of merging multiple files and dropping duplicate matches allocated in the PVS process. We start with the original patents that have undergone the PVS process. Of our starting point of 1.29 million patents, 989,000 have undergone the PVS process (76.7 percent). These 989,000 PVSed patents have 2.28 million inventor names associated with the patents (average team size of approximately 2.3) and 9.98 million inventor PIKs associated with them, indicating that each inventor name has on average around 4 PIKs. We start by keeping the PIK with the highest PVS score by patent-inventor combination. This removes 3.76 million of the 9.98 million starting inventor PIKs. We want to unduplicate the remainder of these PIKs and only keep the inventors with a unique PIK. Removing all the duplicate PIKs associated with each inventor name leaves us with 1.79 million unique inventor PIKs associated with nearly 884,000 patents from the 989,000 patents that underwent the PVS process. A yearly breakout of the counts is below.

If we break out the counts by assignee type, we find differences in the ratio of the patents that undergo the PVS process by assignee type, along with differences in the ratio of inventors with unique PIKs by assignee type. Firm assignees are most likely to have undergone the PVS process (82 percent), followed by individual assignees (75 percent), while fewer than 50 percent of

Table 2.A9   **Breakdown of PVS process for inventors, 2000–2011**

Grant year	Patents	PVS patents	Inventor names	Inventor PIKs	Inventor PIKs (highest PVS)	Unique Inventor PIKs	Patents with unique inventor PIKs
2000	107,000	82,700	165,000	748,000	418,000	128,000	71,800
2001	109,000	88,400	183,000	802,000	468,000	143,000	77,600
2002	106,000	79,100	172,000	760,000	442,000	136,000	70,100
2003	107,000	80,900	180,000	787,000	470,000	143,000	72,200
2004	101,000	77,900	175,000	754,000	453,000	139,000	69,600
2005	89,000	69,700	159,000	693,000	422,000	126,000	62,500
2006	110,000	83,800	196,000	853,000	531,000	155,000	75,300
2007	101,000	74,300	177,000	773,000	496,000	139,000	66,900
2008	99,400	72,700	176,000	750,000	486,000	138,000	65,500
2009	102,000	77,000	190,000	833,000	546,000	149,000	69,500
2010	130,000	101,000	252,000	1,110,000	731,000	198,000	91,500
2011	130,000	102,000	255,000	1,130,000	755,000	199,000	91,800
Total	1,290,000	989,000	2,280,000	9,980,000	6,220,000	1,790,000	884,000

Source: Authors' calculations.

Notes: Counts are rounded to comply with disclosure requirements. PIK, protected identification key.

Table 2.A10   Breakdown of PVS process for inventors by assignee type, 2000–2011

	Individual assignee			Business assignee			Unassigned		
Grant year	Patents	PVS patents	Patents with unique inventor	Patents	PVS patents	Patents with unique inventor	Patents	PVS patents	Patents with unique inventor
2000	970	810	650	79,500	65,100	58,300	21,500	13,400	10,200
2001	980	870	710	82,900	71,500	64,500	20,100	12,500	9,500
2002	930	660	560	81,200	66,200	60,100	19,000	8,900	6,700
2003	890	670	560	82,900	68,400	62,400	18,300	8,500	6,500
2004	860	640	550	80,100	66,600	60,700	16,300	7,700	5,900
2005	790	600	490	71,400	60,000	54,800	13,500	6,800	5,200
2006	980	700	600	88,700	72,800	66,500	16,200	7,500	5,900
2007	870	620	510	81,600	65,000	59,600	14,900	6,400	4,900
2008	760	490	430	81,400	64,100	58,700	14,300	6,000	4,600
2009	850	590	470	84,700	68,500	62,800	13,400	5,800	4,400
2010	960	720	590	108,000	89,700	82,400	16,500	7,800	6,000
2011	950	730	610	110,000	90,800	83,300	15,900	7,800	6,000
Total	10,790	8,090	6,720	1,032,000	849,000	774,000	200,000	98,900	75,800

Source: Authors' calculations.
Notes: Counts are rounded to comply with disclosure requirements.

Table 2.A11   Breakdown of demographic match rate by sector, 2000–2011

Sector	Individual assignee	Firm assignee	Unassigned
Chemical	75.1	82.2	47.1
C&C	73.9	81	52.1
Design	11	11.4	9
D&M	75	83	50.7
E&E	75.4	82.2	43.6
Mechanical	75.6	82.1	47.4
Others	75.7	80.9	51.8
Plant	11.9	10.1	5
Total proportion	62.1	75	38

Source: Authors' calculations using LBD data.
Notes: Counts are rounded to comply with disclosure requirements.

unassigned patents undergo the PVS process. Looking at the proportion of inventors that have unique PIKs by assignee type, we find that nearly 91 percent of inventors in firm-assigned patents have a unique PIK associated with their name. This is higher than the ratio found in individual-assigned patents (83 percent) and the ratio in unassigned patents (76.7 percent). The full breakdown by assignee type is below.

Starting from the nearly 884,000 patents with unique inventor PIKs, we then merge it with the Census Numident file, which contains the demographic information we are interested in. The Numident match rate is around 100 percent, thus completing the full demographic matching process for each patent. Turning back to the unmatched patents, we break down the match rate by sector. We show that the patents without unique PIKs and no demographic data are mainly concentrated in the "Design" and "Plant" patent sector, as shown in table 2.A11.

Appendix C
Technology Classes

Table 2.A12   Technological categories as defined in Hall et al. (2001) plus additions in bold

Category code	Category name	Subcategory code	Subcategory name	Patent classes
1	Chemical	11	Agriculture, Food, Textiles	8, 19, 71, 127, 442, 504
		12	Coating	106,118, 401, 427
		13	Gas	48, 55, 95, 96
		14	Organic Compounds	532, 534, 536, 540, 544, 546, 548, 549, 552, 554, 556, 558, 560, 562, 564, 568, 570, 987
		15	Resins	520, 521, 522, 523, 524, 525, 526, 527, 528, 530
		19	Miscellaneous-chemical	23, 34, 44, 102, 117, 149, 156, 159, 162, 196, 201, 202, 203, 204, 205, 208, 210, 216, 222, 252, 260, 261,349, 366, 416, 422, 423, 430, 436, 494, 501, 502, 506, 510, 512, 516, 518, 585, 588
2	Computers and Communications	21	Communications	178, 333, 340, 342, 343, 358, 367, 370, 375, 379, 385, 398, 455, 725
		22	Computer Hardware and Software	341, 380, 382, 395, 700, 701, 702, 704, 705, 706, 707, 708, 709, 710, 712, 713, 714, 902
		23	Computer Peripherals	345, 347, 726
		24	Information Storage	360, 365, 369, 711, 720, G9B
		25	Data Processing	715, 717, 718, 719
3	Drugs and Medical	31	Drugs	424, 514
		32	Surgery and Medical Instruments	128, 600, 601, 602, 604, 606, 607
		33	Biotechnology	435, 800, 930
		39	Miscellaneous—Drug and Med.	351, 433, 623
4	Electrical and Electronic	41	Electrical Devices	174, 200, 327, 329, 330, 331, 332, 334, 335, 336, 337, 338, 392, 439
		42	Electrical Lighting	313, 314, 315, 362, 372, 445

5 Mechanical	43	Measuring and Testing	73, 324, 356, 374, 850
	44	Nuclear and X-rays	250, 376, 378, 976
	45	Power Systems	60, 136, 290, 310, 318, 320, 322, 323, 361, 363, 388, 429
	46	Semiconductor Devices	257, 326, 438, 505
	49	Miscellaneous—Elec.	191, 218, 219, 307, 346, 348, 377, 381, 386, 703, 716
	51	Materials Processing and Handling	65, 82, 83, 125, 141, 142, 144, 173, 209, 221, 225, 226, 234, 241, 242, 264, 271, 407, 408, 409, 414, 425, 451, 493
	52	Metal Working	29, 72, 75, 76, 140, 147, 148, 163, 164, 228, 266, 270, 413, 419, 420
	53	Motors, Engines, and Parts	91, 92, 123, 185, 188, 192, 251, 303, 415, 417, 418, 464, 474, 475, 476, 477
	54	Optics	352, 353, 355, 359, 396, 399
	55	Transportation	104, 105, 114, 152, 180, 187, 213, 238, 244, 246, 258, 280, 293, 295, 296, 298, 301, 305, 410, 440
	59	Miscellaneous—Mechanical	7, 16, 42, 49, 51, 74, 81, 86, 89, 100, 124, 157, 184, 193, 194, 198, 212, 227, 235, 239, 254, 267, 291, 294, 384, 400, 402, 406, 411, 453, 454, 470, 482, 483, 492, 508, 968
6 Others	61	Agriculture, Husbandry, Food	43, 47, 56, 99, 111, 119, 131, 426, 449, 452, 460
	62	Amusement Devices	273, 446, 463, 472, 473
	63	Apparel and Textile	2, 12, 24, 26, 28, 36, 38, 57, 66, 68, 69, 79, 87, 112, 139, 223, 450
	64	Earth Working and Wells	37, 166, 171, 172, 175, 299, 405, 507
	65	Furniture, House Fixtures	4, 5, 30, 70, 132, 182, 211, 256, 297, 312
	66	Heating	110, 122, 126, 165, 237, 373, 431, 432
	67	Pipes and Joints	138, 277, 285, 403
	68	Receptacles	53, 206, 215, 217, 220, 224, 229, 232, 383
	69	Miscellaneous—Others	1, 14, 15, 27, 33, 40, 52, 54, 59, 62, 63, 84, 101, 108, 109, 116, 134, 135, 137, 150, 160, 168, 169, 177, 181, 186, 190, 199, 231, 236, 245, 248, 249, 269, 276, 278, 279, 281, 292, 300, 368, 404, 412, 428, 283, 289, 434, 441, 462, 503, 901, 903, 977, 984
Design	79	Design patents	Dxx
Plant	89	Plant patents	PLT

Source: Hall, Jaffe, and Trajtenberg (2001) plus own additions based on new technology codes.

References

Arora, Ashish, Wesley M. Cohen, and John P. Walsh. 2016. "The Acquisition and Commercialization of Invention in American Manufacturing: Incidence and Impact." *Research Policy* 45 (6): 1113–28.
Bell, A., R. Chetty, X. Jaravel, N. Petkova, and J. Van Reenen. 2016. "The Lifecycle of Inventors." Working paper, June 5, 2016.
Bureau of Labor Statistics. 2016. "Foreign Born Workers: Labor Force Characteristics 2015." Press Release. Published May 19, 2016. Accessed February 18, 2017. https://www.bls.gov/news.release/pdf/forbrn.pdf.
Dahlin, Kristina B., and Dean M. Behrens. 2005. "When Is an Invention Really Radical? Defining and Measuring Technological Radicalness." *Research Policy* 34 (5): 717–37.
de Jong, J. P. 2016. "Surveying Innovation in Samples of Individual End Consumers." *European Journal of Innovation Management* 19 (3): 406–23.
Deming, W. Edwards. 1990. *Sample Design in Business Research*, vol. 23. New York: John Wiley.
Dreisigmeyer, David, Stuart Graham, Cheryl Grim, Tariqul Islam, Alan Marco, and Javier Miranda. 2014. "A Patent Classification System for the Business Dynamics Statistics." Discussion paper, mimeo.
Fairlie, Robert W., and Javier Miranda. 2017. "Taking the Leap: The Determinants of Entrepreneurs Hiring Their First Employee." *Journal of Economics and Management Strategy* 26 (1): 3–34.
Franke, Nikolaus, and Sonali Shah. 2003. "How Communities Support Innovative Activities: An Exploration of Assistance and Sharing among End-users." *Research Policy* 32 (1): 157–78.
Graham, Stuart J. H., Cheryl Grim, Tariqul Islam, Alan C. Marco, and Javier Miranda. 2018. "Business Dynamics of Innovating Firms: Linking US Patents with Administrative Data on Workers and Firms." *Journal of Economics and Management Strategy* 27 (3): 372–402.
Hall, Bronwyn H., Adam B. Jaffe, and Manuel Trajtenberg. 2001. "The NBER Patent Citation Data File: Lessons, Insights and Methodological Tools." Technical report. Cambridge, MA: National Bureau of Economic Research.
Hall, Bronwyn H., and Manuel Trajtenberg. 2004. "Uncovering GPTs with Patent Data." Technical report. Cambridge, MA: National Bureau of Economic Research.
Jones, Benjamin F. 2009. "The Burden of Knowledge and the Death of the Renaissance Man: Is Innovation Getting Harder?" *Review of Economic Studies* 76 (1): 283–317.
Kim, Jinyoung, and Gerald Marschke. 2015. "Teams in R&D: Evidence from US Inventor Data."
Lüthje, Christian. 2004. "Characteristics of Innovating Users in a Consumer Goods Field: An Empirical Study of Sport-Related Product Consumers." *Technovation* 24 (9): 683–95.
Serrano, Carlos J. 2010. "The Dynamics of the Transfer and Renewal of Patents." *RAND Journal of Economics* 41 (4): 686–708.
Shah, Sonali. 2000. "Sources and Patterns of Innovation in a Consumer Products Field: Innovations in Sporting Equipment." WP-4105. Cambridge, MA: Sloan School of Management, Massachusetts Institute of Technology.
von Hippel, Eric. 1976. "The Dominant Role of Users in the Scientific Instrument Innovation Process." *Research Policy* 5 (3): 212–39.
von Hippel, Eric, Jeroen P. J. de Jong, and Stephen Flowers. 2012. "Comparing Business and Household Sector Innovation in Consumer Products: Findings from a Representative Study in the United Kingdom." *Management Science* 58 (9): 1669–81.

Innovation, Productivity Dispersion, and Productivity Growth

Lucia Foster, Cheryl Grim, John C. Haltiwanger, and Zoltan Wolf

3.1 Introduction

We explore the dynamic relationship among business entry, productivity dispersion, and productivity growth in order to develop an *indirect* indicator for recent innovation in an industry. We hypothesize that periods of rapid innovation are accompanied by high rates of entry, significant experimentation, and as a result, a high degree of within-industry productivity dispersion. Following this experimentation phase, successful innovators and adopters grow, while unsuccessful innovators contract and exit yielding productivity growth. Thus patterns in the dynamic relationship among entry, productivity dispersion, and productivity growth may help direct our attention to areas of the economy where innovation has likely occurred. We examine these patterns using a new economy-wide dataset tracking entry, productivity dispersion, and productivity growth at the firm level.

Lucia Foster is chief of the Center for Economic Studies at the US Census Bureau.

Cheryl Grim is assistant center chief for interdisciplinary research at the Center for Economic Studies at the US Census Bureau.

John C. Haltiwanger is Distinguished University Professor of Economics at the University of Maryland and a research associate of the National Bureau of Economic Research. He was a part-time Schedule A employee of the Census Bureau when this chapter was written.

Zoltan Wolf is an economist at Westat.

This is a revised version of a chapter presented at the NBER Conference on Research in Income and Wealth (CRIW) conference Measuring and Accounting for Innovation in the 21st Century, held in Washington, DC, in March 2017. We thank Nick Bloom, Jonathan Haskel, Ron Jarmin, Jim Spletzer, and CRIW conference attendees for helpful comments on an earlier draft. Any opinions and conclusions expressed herein are those of the authors and do not necessarily represent the views of the US Census Bureau. All results have been reviewed to ensure that no confidential information is disclosed. For acknowledgments, sources of research support, and disclosure of the authors' material financial relationships, if any, please see https://www.nber .org/books-and-chapters/measuring-and-accounting-innovation-21st-century/innovation -productivity-dispersion-and-productivity-growth.

We pursue an indirect approach to measuring innovation in order to overcome the challenges of directly measuring innovation. Much of the innovation literature measures *inputs* to innovation (such as R&D expenditures) or proxies for the *output* of innovation (such as patents), but it is likely that such direct measures capture only a small fraction of firm innovative activity. We attempt to identify innovation through its impact on more easily measured concepts (entry and productivity). This is analogous to the approach in astronomy of measuring black holes through the characteristics of nearby visible stars whose properties act according to laws of nature. While social science does not have laws of nature as such, economics has organizing principles about the behavior of economic agents that help direct our attention to areas of the economy where innovation is likely to have occurred. Our objective is to explore this indirect approach with some novel empirical analysis and in turn to discuss questions that can be addressed with these and related data.

We do this by weaving together the literature on productivity dispersion and growth and the literature on innovation and firm dynamics. Starting with the former, the large within-industry productivity *dispersion* commonly found in the firm-level productivity literature (Syverson 2011) may reflect many factors and mechanisms: idiosyncratic productivity shocks, managerial ability and practices, frictions, distortions, degree of competition, economies of scope, and product differentiation. In healthy economies, reallocation of resources away from low-productivity to high-productivity firms acts to reduce this dispersion and yields productivity growth. We explore a related but distinct hypothesis relating within-industry productivity dispersion and productivity growth in the context of innovation dynamics within industries.

For the second strand of the literature, we build on Gort and Klepper (1982), who hypothesize stages of firm dynamics in response to technological innovations. While they focus on product innovations, their insights apply to process innovations as well. An insight key for our purposes is that periods of rapid innovation yield a surge in entry and a period of significant experimentation followed by a shakeout period when successful developers and implementers grow while unsuccessful firms contract and exit. This is relevant for productivity dispersion because the success or failure of entrepreneurs in the process of experimentation can contribute to dispersion, the subsequent reallocation of resources, and eventually, economic growth.

A large literature has developed models of innovation via creative destruction with some of these features.[1] Related theoretical models that highlight the role of entrants and young firms for innovation in models of creative destruction include Acemoglu et al. (2017). These creative destruction mod-

---

1. For example, Jovanovic (1982); Klette and Kortum (2004); and Lentz and Mortensen (2008).

els of innovation are related to the empirical literature that finds that the reallocation of resources is an important determinant of aggregate productivity growth.[2] Also related to these ideas are the now well-known findings that young businesses, particularly those in rapidly growing sectors, exhibit substantial dispersion and skewness in the growth rate distribution.[3]

The evolution of the productivity distribution within the context of innovation dynamics is an underexplored area of empirical research due, in part, to data limitations. Gort and Klepper (1982) investigated their hypotheses primarily using firm-level registers that permitted tracking entry, exit, and continuers in industries but not outcomes like productivity growth and dispersion. While there has been an explosion of research using firm-level data since then, much of what we know about productivity dispersion and dynamics is about the manufacturing sector (Syverson 2011). We overcome these data limitations by exploiting a newly developed *economy-wide* firm-level database on productivity (Haltiwanger et al. 2017).

Using this database, we investigate these issues focusing on the nature of the relationship between industry productivity growth and within-industry productivity dispersion. We also look at the relationship between firm dynamics and the evolution of the firm-level productivity dispersion in industries undergoing rapid productivity growth. Our investigation takes place in the context of the surge in US productivity in the 1990s to early 2000s and the subsequent productivity slowdown.[4] Some have hypothesized that this reflects a slowdown in the pace and implementation of innovation and technological change, especially in the IT-intensive sectors (Gordon 2016; Byrne, Oliner, and Sichel 2013). Others have argued that there is an increase in frictions and distortions slowing down productivity-enhancing reallocation dynamics (e.g., Decker et al. 2018) or the diffusion in productivity (Andrews, Criscuolo, and Gal 2016).

We first report broad patterns in aggregate and microdata that provide additional motivation for our analysis. We show that the period prior to 2000 has rising entry, increased within-industry productivity dispersion, and high productivity growth in the high-tech sectors of the US economy. In contrast, the period following 2000 has falling entry, increased within-industry productivity dispersion, and low productivity growth in the high-tech sectors. We also find within-industry dispersion in productivity is much greater for young compared to mature firms. These findings are not novel to this chapter (see Decker et al. 2016, 2018) but serve as a useful backdrop for our analysis.

To help understand these broad-based patterns, we use firm-level data

---

2. See Griliches and Regev (1992); Baily, Hulten, and Campbell (1992); Baily, Bartelsman, and Haltiwanger (2001); Petrin, White, and Reiter (2011); and Foster et al. (2017).
3. See Dunne, Roberts, and Samuelson (1989); Davis, Haltiwanger, and Schuh (1996); Haltiwanger, Jarmin, and Miranda (2013); and Decker et al. (2016).
4. See Fernald (2014); Byrne, Sichel, and Reinsdorf (2016); and Andrews, Criscuolo, and Gal (2016).

for the US private sector to construct measures of firm entry, within-industry productivity dispersion, and industry-level productivity growth at a detailed industry level. We use low-frequency variation to abstract from high-frequency cyclical dynamics and a difference-in-difference specification that controls for time and industry effects. We find that a surge in entry in an industry is followed by a rise in within-industry productivity dispersion and a short-lived slowdown in industry-level productivity growth. Following this, there is a decline in productivity dispersion but an increase in productivity growth. These findings are larger quantitatively for industries in the high-tech sectors of the US economy.

We also explore the contribution of reallocation dynamics to productivity growth to better understand the role innovation plays in the reallocation of resources between firms. We find there is a high contribution from increased within-industry covariance between market share and productivity underlying the productivity surge in the high-tech sectors in the late 1990s. The productivity slowdown in the post-2000 period in high-tech is due to both a decrease in within-firm productivity growth and also a decrease in this covariance.

Our findings are broadly consistent with the Gort and Klepper (1982) hypotheses that a period of innovation yields a period of entry and experimentation followed by a shakeout period with successful firms growing and unsuccessful firms contracting and exiting. In this respect, some aspects of our results provide microlevel evidence for the hypothesis that the productivity slowdown is due to a decreased pace of innovation and technological change. However, we are reluctant to make that inference for at least two reasons. First, our investigation does not include direct measures of innovation. Second, the patterns in the post-2000 period are not consistent with a slowdown in innovation as the primary source for the post-2000 productivity slowdown. With that hypothesis, we would have expected to observe a decline in productivity dispersion; instead, the findings in Decker et al. (2018) show dispersion rises even though the fraction of activity accounted for by young firms falls dramatically in the post-2000 period.[5]

We view the results from our empirical exercises as suggestive, highlighting the potential measurement benefits of studying the joint dynamics of entry, productivity dispersion, and productivity growth. In the second half of the chapter, we discuss open questions and next steps suggested by our analysis with a focus on the measurement and analysis of innovation.

The rest of the chapter proceeds as follows. We next provide discussion on the conceptual underpinnings of our empirical analyses and interpretations.

---

5. There are additional reasons to be cautious in this inference. Decker et al. (2018) find that there has been a decrease in responsiveness of growth and exit to productivity growth. The latter is consistent with an increase in adjustment frictions. We discuss these issues further below.

We describe the data and measurement issues in section 3.3. Our empirical exercises examining patterns of entry, productivity dispersion, and productivity growth and reallocation dynamics are in section 3.4. In section 3.5, we discuss open questions, measurement challenges, and areas for future research suggested by our analysis. Section 3.6 presents concluding remarks.

3.2 Conceptual Underpinnings

We begin by reviewing the sources of measured productivity dispersion within industries. For this purpose, it is critical to distinguish between underlying sources of technical efficiency and measured productivity across firms in the same sector. In empirical applications, the latter is typically some measure of "revenue productivity," which sometimes is a multifactor measure of input and other times is revenue per unit of labor. In either case, revenue productivity measures are inherently endogenous to many different mechanisms and factors. For ease of discussion, we follow the recent literature in referring to measures of technical efficiency as TFPQ, revenue measures of total factor productivity as TFPR, and revenue-based measures of labor productivity as LPR.

As noted in the introduction, measured productivity differences between firms may be attributed to a variety of factors. The link that connects innovative activity and dispersion is experimentation following an innovation that generates heterogeneity in the factors that cause dispersion. Many models of firm heterogeneity start with the premise that there is some source of exogenous as well as endogenous differences in TFPQ across firms. In some models, this is due to inherent characteristics of the firm reflecting permanent differences in the technology distribution (e.g., Lucas 1978; Jovanovic 1982) that may in turn stem from many factors, such as managerial ability. In other models, the firms are subject to new, and typically persistent, draws. of TFPQ each period (Hopenhayn 1992; Hopenhayn and Rogerson 1993; Ericson and Pakes 1995). Endogenous differences in TFPQ may stem from differences in adoption of management practices (e.g., Bloom et al. 2019) or differences in realizations of endogenous innovations in investment (e.g., Acemoglu et al. 2017).[6] A variety of reasons have been put forth to justify how high- and low-TFPQ firms can coexist (i.e., why the most productive firms do not take over the market); these range from economies of scope

---

6. Even in these cases with endogenous adoption of management practices or investment in innovation, there still is typically an underlying exogenous source of heterogeneity that induces heterogeneous adoption/investment and/or there are stochastic returns from such adoption/ investment. These potentially endogenous factors play an important role. For example, using data from the Management and Organizational Practices Survey, Bloom et al. (2018) find large differences in management practices across plants, and these differences explain about one-fifth of the difference between the 90th and 10th productivity percentiles.

(Lucas 1978), to product differentiation (Melitz 2003), to adjustment frictions (Hopenhayn and Rogerson 1993; Cooper and Haltiwanger 2006), and all of these factors likely play some role empirically.

These factors, together with the ample evidence that there is price heterogeneity within sectors (Syverson 2004; Foster, Haltiwanger, and Syverson 2008; Hottman, Redding, and Weinstein 2016), imply that revenue productivity (TFPR and LPR) dispersion will also be present within sectors and revenue productivity measures will be correlated with TFPQ at the firm level (Haltiwanger 2016; Haltiwanger, Kulick, and Syverson 2018).[7] Thus one source of variation in measured revenue productivity across sectors and time is variation in dispersion in TFPQ as well as other idiosyncratic shocks to fundamentals such as demand shocks. Another factor that impacts within-industry revenue productivity dispersion is the business climate, as broadly defined to include distortions in output and input markets that impede growth at more-productive firms and contraction and exit at less-productive firms. This has been the theme of the recent misallocation literature (Restuccia and Rogerson 2008; Hsieh and Klenow 2009; Bartelsman, Haltiwanger, and Scarpetta 2013). An economy or industry that experiences a deterioration in the business climate should, from this perspective, exhibit a decline in productivity along with a rise in dispersion in revenue productivity. The intuition is that rising frictions and distortions reduce the tendency for marginal revenue products to be equalized, implying in turn a rise in revenue productivity dispersion. A detailed discussion on how these factors affect dispersion in revenue-based productivity measures can be found in Foster et al. (2016).

As another example, Hurst and Pugsley (2011, 2017) emphasize that nonpecuniary benefits play an important role in the occupational decision to become an entrepreneur. Their insight is that the potentially different incentives underlying entrepreneurial behavior will be reflected by measured differences in productivity as well as firm size and growth. They argue that there are large differences across sectors in terms of attractiveness for entrepreneurs with high nonpecuniary benefits. This might be yet another factor that helps account for dispersion in TFPQ within some industries, but this is likely less important in innovation-intensive industries. Such sectoral heterogeneity is one of the (many) reasons we control for detailed industry fixed effects in our empirical analysis.

How do innovation and firm dynamics associated with innovation relate

---

7. There is a knife-edge case emphasized by Hsieh and Klenow (2009): with constant returns to scale and isoelastic demand without adjustment costs or other factors (like overhead labor), revenue productivity should have zero dispersion in equilibrium even if there is dispersion in TFPQ. The reason is the elasticity of firm-level prices with respect to TFPQ is equal to exactly -1 in this knife-edge case (see Haltiwanger, Kulick, and Syverson 2018). This knife-edge case is interesting theoretically to help fix ideas but is not very useful empirically, since there is much evidence that factors such as adjustment costs make this knife-edge case irrelevant in practice.

to heterogeneity in measured productivity? The basic idea in Gort and Klepper (1982) is that a period of intensive transformative innovation within an industry is accompanied by (and/or induces) entry. This period is characterized by entrants engaging in substantial experimentation and learning. Since experimentation and learning involve trials and errors, which yield different outcomes, there is likely to be an increase in dispersion in TFPQ accompanied by increases in dispersion in TFPR and LPR. In addition, if increased innovation and entry beget a higher share of young businesses and they are more likely to face more frictions, uncertainty, and distortions, then dispersion in TFPR and LPR will rise further.[8] As the experimentation phase identifies successful innovators and adopters of new products and processes, these firms are likely to grow, while their unsuccessful competitors will contract and exit. This process leads to a period of productivity growth from both within-firm productivity growth (at successful innovators) and productivity-enhancing reallocation dynamics. The latter should reduce productivity dispersion through both selection and also the maturing of the more successful firms.

With the above considerations in mind, we hypothesize that the innovation dynamics described in Gort and Klepper (1982) imply the following about entry, productivity dispersion, and productivity growth dynamics. Following a surge in entry accompanying innovation, we should observe a period of rising dispersion in LPR within industries that will in turn be followed by increased industry-level productivity growth. The latter will reflect both within-firm productivity growth of the successful developers and adopters and the reallocation of resources to such firms.

The impact of innovation dynamics on productivity dispersion hypothesized by Gort and Klepper (1982) is consistent with the many different sources of productivity dispersion discussed above. Instead, we view the Gort and Klepper hypothesis as providing insights into potentially important driving forces for low-frequency within-industry variation in the dynamic relationship among innovation, entry, productivity dispersion, and productivity growth. The empirical analysis that follows focuses on these low-frequency within-industry dynamics.

3.3   Data and Measurement

Our main dataset in this chapter is a newly developed extension to the Longitudinal Business Database (LBD). The LBD is an economy-wide,

---

8. We use the term *frictions* for factors that the social planner cannot overcome, such as adjustment costs that are part of the technology of adjustment. In contrast, we use the term *distortions* for market failures, policies, or institutions that impede firms adjusting to their optimal size. Jovanovic (1982) provides motivation for greater information frictions faced by young firms. Hsieh and Klenow (2009) provide motivation for why young firms are likely to face higher distortions due, for example, to imperfect capital markets.

establishment-level database primarily derived from the Census Bureau's Business Register and augmented by other survey and administrative data (see Jarmin and Miranda 2002). It covers the universe of employer businesses in the nonfarm business sector of the United States: about 7 million establishments and 6 million firm observations per year for 1976–2013. It contains establishment-level information on detailed industry, geography, employment, and parent firm affiliation. The LBD has robust links for businesses over time, making this dataset particularly well suited for the measurement of business dynamics such as job creation and destruction, establishment entry and exit, and firm start-ups and shutdowns. These links make it possible to aggregate the establishment-level data to the firm level, where firm growth dynamics abstract from mergers and acquisitions and other ownership activity.

A firm start-up is defined as a new firm entity with all new establishments; a firm exit is defined as a firm entity that ceases to exist, with all of its establishments shutting down; and firm growth is measured as the employment-weighted average of the establishments owned by the firm (for details see Haltiwanger, Jarmin, and Miranda 2013). These features also make it feasible to define firm age in a manner that abstracts from mergers and acquisitions and ownership change activity. A firm's age is determined by its longest-lived establishment at the time of the firm's founding and then progresses one additional year over calendar time. Firm-level industry is measured as the modal industry for the firm based on its employment shares across six-digit or four-digit North American Industry Classification System (NAICS) industries. In this analysis, we focus on four-digit NAICS industries.[9]

We do not use direct measures of innovation in our empirical analysis; instead, we use a surge of entry and young firm activity as an indirect proxy for innovative activity. Gort and Klepper (1982) suggest that stage 1 of a period of increased within-industry transformative innovation is followed by a surge of entry (stage 2). To shed further light on this process, we group industries into high-tech and other industries (which we call nontech). For high-tech, we adopt the strategy of Decker et al. (2018), who follow Hecker (2005) in defining high-tech industries as the science, technology, engineering, and math (STEM)-intensive industries. In practice, high-tech industries include all of the standard information and communications technology (ICT) industries as well as biotech industries.

---

9. One concern is that this definition of industry is a potential source of measurement error for large, complex multiunits, especially since much of our analysis exploits within-industry variation in productivity dispersion and growth. The use of four-digit as opposed to six-digit industry effects mitigates this concern somewhat. Decker et al. (2018) have explored this issue using a more sophisticated approach to controlling for industry-year effects (based on taking into account the full distribution of employment shares for each firm) and found that the patterns of dispersion and growth within industries are largely robust to this concern.

Our productivity measure relies on the recently developed firm-level measures of nominal revenue in the LBD developed by Haltiwanger et al. (2017). Haltiwanger et al. (2017) use nominal revenue data at the tax reporting or employer identification number (EIN) level from the Business Register (the underlying source for the LBD) to create measures of nominal revenue for over 80 percent of firms in the LBD for their sample period. To mitigate issues of selection due to missingness, they develop inverse propensity score weights so that the revenue sample is representative of the full LBD. We use the Haltiwanger et al. (2017) revenue-enhanced LBD in our analysis, including the propensity score weights. Following Decker et al. (2018), we convert nominal revenue to real measures using Bureau of Economic Analysis (BEA) price deflators at the industry level (this involves using four-digit deflators when available and three- or even two-digit deflators otherwise). Our firm-level measure of labor productivity (hereafter "productivity") is the log of the ratio of real revenue to employment. A key limitation of this measure is that the output concept is a gross concept rather than value added, so it is not readily comparable across industries (see Haltiwanger et al. 2017). Following Haltiwanger et al. (2017) and Decker et al. (2018), we focus on patterns controlling for detailed (four-digit) industry and year effects.[10] We provide further details about this in our empirical exercises below.

Our econometric analyses are based on industry/year-specific moments of firm-level productivity. We construct within-industry measures of productivity dispersion and within-industry measures of productivity growth and supplement these with industry-level information on start-up rates from the full LBD. We tabulate measures such as the share of employment accounted for by young firms ("young" is less than five years old) and the share of employment accounted for by start-ups (firm age equal to zero). The version of the LBD we use covers 1976–2013 so that we can construct these measures for years prior to the available revenue data (available 1996–2013). This facilitates some of the dynamic specifications that use lagged entry rates in our analysis below.

Our dispersion measure throughout this chapter is the interquartile range (IQR) within an industry in a given year. We focus on the IQR because it is less sensitive to outliers than the standard deviation (see Cunningham et al. 2017). Our measure of within-industry productivity growth aggregates real revenue and employment data to the four-digit industry level, and then we compute the log first difference at the industry level. In our exercises using the Dynamic Olley-Pakes decomposition developed by Melitz and Polanec

---

10. Haltiwanger et al. (2017) and Decker et al. (2018) use six-digit NAICS as compared to our use of four-digit NAICS. We use the latter for two reasons. First, this mitigates the measurement problems of using modal industry. Second, the focus of our analysis is industry-level regressions using moments computed from the firm-level data. The six-digit NAICS data are quite noisy for industry-level analysis, particularly analysis that is not activity weighted.

(2015), we exploit firm-level changes in labor productivity as well as the other terms in that decomposition.

Finally, the focus of this chapter is on the longer-term relationship among these three important concepts of entry, productivity dispersion, and productivity growth. We have two strategies to attempt to abstract away from business-cycle variation. In some exercises, we use Hodrick-Prescott (HP) filtering to ameliorate the impact of business cycles; in other exercises, we use three-year nonoverlapping periods to conduct our analysis.

3.4   Empirical Evidence

We examine the relationship among innovation, entry, productivity dispersion, and productivity growth motivated by the hypotheses in Gort and Klepper (1982), discussed in section 3.2. Assuming that the businesses in high-tech industries are more innovative than those in other sectors, these hypothesized Gort and Klepper (1982) dynamics should be more likely to occur in these industries. We explore whether this is the case in our data by examining whether the nature of the dynamics differs between high-tech and nontech industries. We start our empirical analysis by providing some basic facts about the patterns of entry, productivity dispersion, and productivity growth for industries grouped into the high-tech and nontech sectors. These basic facts are already reasonably well known in the literature, but they provide helpful motivating evidence for our subsequent analysis.

3.4.1   Basic Facts

We start with the key industry-level indicator concerning start-ups and the share of activity accounted for by young firms. In figure 3.1, we plot the employment shares for high-tech (solid line) and nontech (dashed line) industries for both start-ups (PANEL A) and young firms (panel B). There are noticeable differences in the start-up patterns for high-tech as compared to nontech in panel A. While nontech shows a gradual decline over time in employment shares, high-tech shows a humped-shape pattern culminating in the three-year period between 1999 and 2001. This difference is even more dramatic for young firms, as is shown in panel B of figure 3.1. Together these panels highlight the surge in entry and young firm activity in high-tech in the 1990s.[11]

We next turn to the second key moment of interest: within-industry productivity dispersion. We start by simply examining the within-industry dispersion of productivity for firms based on their age (young versus mature) and whether they are in high-tech or nontech. Again, dispersion is measured by the interquartile range within an industry in a specific year. We

---

11. The patterns in figure 3.1 are already well known (see, e.g., Haltiwanger, Hathaway, and Miranda 2014; and Decker et al. 2016).

A. Startups

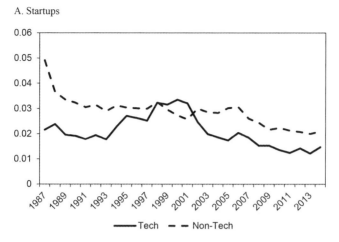

B. Young Firms (Age < 5)

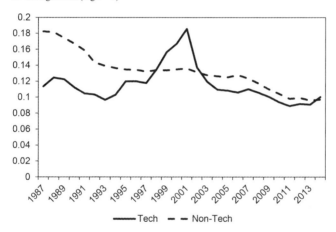

Fig. 3.1   Share of employment at high-tech and nontech industries
Source: Tabulations from the LBD.

use the same time-invariant industry employment weights to aggregate the industry-level patterns to high-tech and nontech industries. Figure 3.2 plots dispersion for young (solid lines) and mature (dashed and dotted lines) and high-tech (heavier line and dashes) and nontech.[12]

As expected, young firms (regardless of their tech status) have more dis-

12. Note that this figure is similar to analysis conducted in Decker et al. (2018). See their figure 7. The latter controls for six-digit industry effects. Also, Decker et al. (2018) use a more sophisticated manner of controlling for such effects for multiunit establishment firms that have activity in more than one six-digit industry. The patterns we show in figure 3.2 are consistent with these alternatives, suggesting our use of four-digit industry effects is not distorting the patterns.

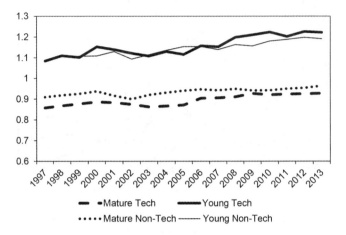

Fig. 3.2   Within-industry dispersion in labor productivity

Source: Tabulations from the LBD. Dispersion is the interquartile range of within-industry log revenue per worker. Industry defined at the four-digit NAICS level.

persion within industries than do mature firms (solid lines are well above the dashed and dotted lines). The differences between high-tech and nontech vary over the two firm age groups. For young firms, high-tech generally has greater dispersion than nontech; for mature firms, nontech has greater dispersion than high-tech. This difference is a reminder that there are many things driving dispersion, and nontech is a heterogeneous group. Moreover, within firm age groups, dispersion is rising throughout the whole sample period. This is consistent with the Gort and Klepper (1982) hypotheses of more experimentation; however, it is also consistent with potentially rising frictions for young firms leading to greater dispersion in productivity.[13]

Finally, we examine labor productivity growth at the aggregate (broad sector) level from official Bureau of Labor Statistics (BLS) statistics and aggregates using our microlevel data. We start by focusing on BLS data. Panel A of figure 3.3 plots BLS labor productivity growth rates for the high-tech and nontech broad sectors measured as employment-weighted within-industry (four-digit) labor productivity growth based on gross output per worker. For employment weights, we use time-invariant employment shares so that the depicted patterns hold industry composition constant. We present four measures in this panel: the annual BLS labor productivity growth (dashed and dotted lines) and the smoothed HP filtered version of this growth (solid lines) for high-tech (heavier lines) and nontech industries. It is evident from the annual versions of the plots (dashed and dotted lines)

---

13. Decker et al. (2018) explore the hypothesis of whether rising dispersion is due to rising frictions/distortions and focus on declining responsiveness to shocks as one potential explanation. We return to discussing this issue further below.

A. BLS Data Annual and HP Filter

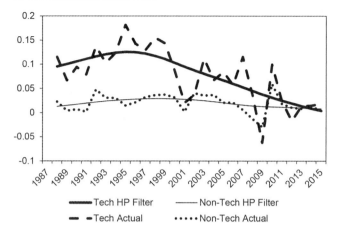

B. BLS Aggregate Data and Census Micro Data (HP Filtered)

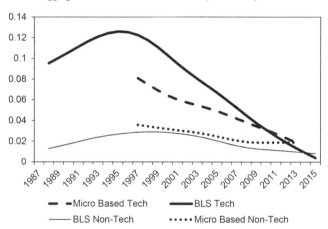

Fig. 3.3   Labor productivity growth for high-tech and nontech industries
Source: BLS and tabulations from the dataset described in Haltiwanger et al. (2017).

that there is substantial cyclicality. Turning to the HP filtered (solid) lines, we see productivity growth rising in high-tech and then falling sharply post 2000, confirming earlier studies. Nontech has much more muted patterns but rises slightly in the 1990s and falls post-2000.

Next we look at the aggregates constructed from the firm-level data and compare them to the BLS data. The microaggregates are based on employment-weighted within-industry labor productivity growth measured by log real gross output per worker. That is, using the firm-level data, we first construct industry-level labor productivity growth and then use the same type of time-invariant industry employment weights to aggregate to high-tech and nontech sectors. Panel B of figure 3.3 plots the HP filtered labor productivity growth rates for BLS aggregate data (solid lines, repeating those from panel A) and Census microdata (dashed and dotted lines) for high-tech (heavier lines) and nontech. We find that micro-based aggregates track BLS productivity patterns reasonably well.

3.4.2   Dynamic Relationship between Entry and Productivity

To explore the dynamic relationship among entry, productivity dispersion, and productivity growth, we use a panel regression specification exploiting industry-level data (from microlevel data) over time using a standard difference-in-difference approach. The hypotheses from Gort and Klepper (1982) are that a surge of within-industry entry will yield an increase in dispersion followed by an increase in productivity. To investigate these hypotheses, we estimate the following specification:

$$(1) \quad Y_{is} = \lambda_s + \lambda_i + \sum_{k=1}^{2}[\beta_k \, Tech * Entry_{is-k} + \delta_k NonTech * Entry_{is-k}] + \varepsilon_{is},$$

where Y_{is} denotes either within-industry/year productivity dispersion or within-industry productivity growth. Since we are primarily interested in low-frequency variation, we calculate productivity growth as the three-year average for subperiods in our sample (1997–99, . . . , 2009–2011, 2012–13; note that the last period is only two years). We use a standard difference-in-difference specification with period effects (λ_s) and industry effects (λ_i). The *tech* dummy is equal to 1 if industry is in high-tech and is 0 otherwise; the *nontech* dummy is equal to 1 if industry is nontech and is 0 otherwise. *Entry* is the start-up rates from the full LBD. In order to examine the role of lags, we take advantage of the fact that we can measure start-ups for earlier periods, so we compute start-ups for the additional three-year periods: 1991–93, 1994–96. We let the impact of entry have a distributed lag form over two three-year subperiods encompassing a total of six years. We view this analysis as exploratory, and it would be of interest to consider even richer dynamic specifications that potentially allow for the type of long and variable lags that Gort and Klepper (1982) suggest are potentially important.

The results of the specification on productivity dispersion are shown in table 3.1. We find that an increase in entry in one subperiod (three-year period) leads to a significant increase in productivity dispersion in the next subperiod. Moreover, this effect is larger in the high-tech sector. The fact that the coefficients on the second lag are not significant suggests that this effect at least diminishes over time. We interpret this to mean that following an innovation (as proxied by the entry rate), there is an increase in productivity dispersion shortly thereafter representing the experimentation and differential success in the development and adoption of innovations.

The analogous results from the productivity growth specification are shown in table 3.2. Here there is a different pattern in the timing. An increase

Table 3.1   **Productivity *dispersion* and entry**

Lag 1 Entry * Tech	0.929**
	(0.458)
Lag 1 Entry * Nontech	0.563***
	(0.190)
Lag 2 Entry * Tech	−0.791
	(0.491)
Lag 2 Entry * Nontech	−0.082
	(0.174)
Industry effects	Yes
Period effects	Yes
R^2	0.93
Number of observations	1,541

Source: Panel regression estimated from industry by year moments computed from the revenue enhanced LBD.

Table 3.2   **Productivity *growth* and entry**

Lag 1 Entry * Tech	−0.516
	(0.367)
Lag 1 Entry * Nontech	−0.791***
	(0.152)
Lag 2 Entry * Tech	1.136***
	(0.393)
Lag 2 Entry * Nontech	0.871***
	(0.139)
Industry effects	Yes
Period effects	Yes
R^2	0.38
Number of observations	1,541

Source: Panel regression estimated from industry by year moments computed from the revenue enhanced LBD.

in the start-up rate results in a decrease in productivity growth in the next subperiod, although this effect is only statistically significant in nontech. This suggests there is some evidence that the period of experimentation and dispersion can yield an initial drag on productivity. It is only in the subsequent periods that we see an increase in productivity growth. The productivity growth impact is larger for firms in high-tech industries as compared to firms in nontech industries.

The dynamic responses for both productivity dispersion and productivity growth are depicted in figure 3.4. While the patterns are more pronounced for high-tech, they are also present for nontech. The finding that the entry-to-dispersion-to-growth dynamics are present for industries outside of high-tech suggests that the Gort and Klepper (1982) hypothesized dynamics may be more pervasive across a broad range of industries. Further investigation

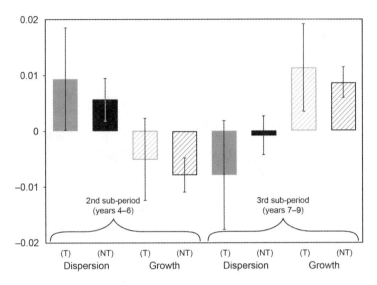

Fig. 3.4   Changes in productivity dispersion and growth from a 1 percent (one-time) increase in entry rate

Source: Authors tabulations from estimated coefficients; see tables 3.1 and 3.2. The left side of the chart represents one subperiod after entry (years 4–6); the right side represents two subperiods after entry (years 7–9). High-tech (T) results are in gray; Nontech (NT) results are in black. Solid bars show results for productivity dispersion; hashed bars show results for productivity growth. The black "whiskers" show approximate 95 percent confidence intervals. Thus the first gray bar shows the change in three-year-average productivity dispersion after a 1 percentage point increase in the three-year-average entry rate for high-tech. All other bars are analogous.

of these issues and the differences in the patterns across industries is an important area for future research.

Given these results, an interesting and open question is whether these dynamics help account for the aggregate patterns of productivity growth and dispersion. Even though more research is needed, we think that the Gort and Klepper (1982) dynamics are not sufficient to understand the patterns in figures 3.1–3.3 for high-tech, particularly in the post-2000 period. In high-tech, we observe a rise in entry (figure 3.1), a rise in productivity dispersion (figure 3.2), and a rise in productivity (figure 3.3) in the 1990s. While the timing is not exactly consistent with figure 3.4, these 1990s patterns are broadly consistent with Gort and Klepper (1982) hypothesized dynamics. However, in the post-2000 period, we observe a decline in entry and productivity but a continued and even sharper rise in within-industry productivity dispersion. From the Gort and Klepper (1982) perspective, we should have observed a decline in productivity dispersion.

What factors might account for the rising within productivity dispersion in the post-2000 period? Decker et al. (2018) find that there has been declining responsiveness of firms to shocks. They find that high-productivity firms are less likely to grow, and low-productivity firms are less likely to shrink and exit in the post-2000 period relative to earlier periods. They argue that this is consistent with a rise in frictions and distortions and helps explain the decline in productivity and the pace of reallocation in the post-2000 period. They also note that a rise in frictions is consistent with a rise in dispersion in revenue labor productivity, as the increase in frictions will slow the pace at which marginal revenue products are equalized. It may also be the case that the same increase in frictions helps account for the decline in entry in the post-2000 period.

For current purposes, this discussion is a reminder that many factors other than innovation dynamics underlie the joint dynamics of entry, productivity dispersion, and productivity growth. In the next section, we explore some of these issues by examining the nature of the contribution of allocative efficiency to productivity growth in high-tech.

3.4.3   Dynamic Micro-Macro Productivity Decomposition

In principle, the rise in productivity growth following the experimental phase in the Gort and Klepper (1982) framework should be due to both within-firm productivity growth of the successful innovators and the reallocation of resources toward such successful innovators. To investigate these issues, we use the Dynamic Olley-Pakes (DOP) decomposition developed by Melitz and Polanec (2015).

Melitz and Polanec (2015) extend the Olley-Pakes (OP) method to include entry and exit in a manner that allows for careful tracking of within-firm changes. Similar to Olley-Pakes, their decomposition of an index of industry-level productivity growth includes terms for changes in average productivity growth and a covariance term, but they split these components out to distinguish between firms that continuously operate and firms that enter and exit. Their decomposition is shown in equation (2):

$$(2) \quad \Delta P_{it} = \Delta \bar{p}_{it,C} + \Delta \mathrm{cov}_C(\theta_{ft}, p_{ft}) + \theta_{Nt}(P_{Nt} - P_{Ct}) + \theta_{Xt-1}(P_{Ct-1} - P_{Xt-1}),$$

where Δ indicates year-over-year log difference; P_{it} is the index of industry-level productivity in industry i in period t defined as the weighted average of firm-level productivity using firm-level employment weights θ_{ft} (the share of employment of firm f in total industry employment); P_{it} is the unweighted average of (log) firm-level productivity for the firms in industry i; C denotes continuer firms (those with employment in both $t-1$ and t) so that and C_{t-1} and C_t denote continuers in periods $t-1$ and t, respectively; N_t denotes entrants from $t-1$ to t; and X_{t-1} denotes firms that exit from $t-1$ to t. The first term in the expression, $\Delta \bar{p}_{it,C}$, represents average (unweighted) within-firm productivity growth for continuing firms; the second term, $\mathrm{cov}_C(\theta_{ft}, p_{ft})$, represents the change in covariance among continuing firms; the third term captures the contribution of entry; and the fourth term captures the contribution of exit.

Using the weighted average of firm-level productivity as an index of industry-level productivity is common in the literature but must be used with appropriate caution. As Decker et al. (2018) show, applying this approach with total factor productivity (TFP) yields traditional industry-level TFP measures (industry output per composite input) only under constant returns to scale and perfect competition. In the absence of the latter, variations in this index will exhibit greater volatility than traditional measures of TFP, as the curvature in the revenue function will yield lower reallocation than is implicit in using this index. Still, this index for industry-level labor productivity tracks traditional measures of output per worker relatively well in practice (see figure 3.3). Moreover, appendix B of Decker et al. (2018) shows that the OP decomposition theoretically tracks aggregate labor productivity more closely than aggregate TFP measures over the empirically relevant range of adjustment costs. We use the DOP decomposition using labor productivity with appropriate caution about interpretation.

In the DOP framework, the changing covariance terms depend critically on (1) there being dispersion in productivity across firms, (2) the covariance between productivity and employment share being nonzero within industries, and (3) the covariance changing over time. We first calculate the components in equation (2) for each industry in each year and then aggregate the annual components to the high-tech level using time-invariant industry employment weights in order to keep industry composition constant (as we have done in figures 3.1–3.3). Focusing on the contribution of the within-industry dynamics in the high-tech sector in this manner helps us understand the role of dispersion for this critical innovative set of industries.

Figure 3.5 reports the annual DOP decomposition, where all components are smoothed by the HP filter. We find declining DOP within and covariance terms indicating smaller contributions by both firm-level productivity growth and between-firm reallocation. We find only a modest role for net entry, but this should be interpreted with caution, since this is the average annual net entry contribution reflecting the contribution of entrants in their first year. The contribution of entry arguably takes time, and our evidence from table 3.2 suggests that this is the case.[14]

We draw several inferences from our related exercises in this section. First, the late 1990s were a period of rapid productivity growth, intensive entry, high young-firm activity, rising productivity dispersion (for young firms in particular), and a large contribution of reallocation activity. Second, the industry level difference-in-difference regressions imply complex timing: entry yields rising productivity dispersion almost shortly after but impacts

14. It might seem surprising that the change in the DOP within is so low and then turns negative. Decker et al. (2017) conduct related analysis of the DOP decomposition for the entire private sector. They emphasize that the weighted within term of decompositions such as the Foster, Haltiwanger, and Krizan (2001; FHK) decomposition is larger than the DOP within term. They note that the DOP within is based on unweighted changes in productivity dominated by small firms. For the purposes of the current chapter, this is not a critical issue. In unreported results, we have found that the weighted FHK within is larger than the DOP within and always remains positive. However, it declines in the same fashion as the DOP within for high-tech.

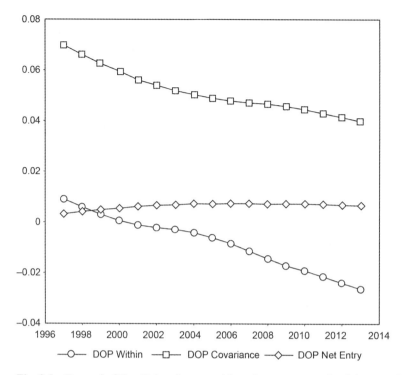

Fig. 3.5   Dynamic Olley-Pakes decomposition of aggregate productivity growth and weighted within-plant growth in high-tech industries

Source: Tabulations from the LBD. Decompositions at the four-digit level for industries in the high-tech sector. Four-digit decomposition averaged across industries using time invariant employment weights.

productivity growth with a significant lag. Third, during the productivity slowdown, entry declined, contributions from within-firm productivity growth were smaller, and reallocation activity declined. Fourth, productivity dispersion kept rising during this period. This last piece of evidence does not mesh well with the Gort and Klepper (1982) dynamics, suggesting that rising dispersion after the 2000s appears to be outside the scope of this model. As we have noted above, one possible explanation for the latter is rising frictions and distortions.

3.5   Conceptual and Measurement Challenges

Our empirical analyses in section 3.4 are intended to be exploratory. Our results suggest that there are systematic patterns in the joint dynamics of entry, within-industry productivity dispersion, and within-industry productivity growth that shed light on innovation dynamics. However, there are many open conceptual and measurement questions about using this indirect approach to capturing innovation, especially with respect to direct approaches to measuring innovation. In this section, we describe those open questions in light of ongoing and potential measurement and research efforts to understand innovative activity. We do not attempt to provide a survey of the voluminous literature on measuring innovation. Instead, we highlight recent and current efforts with a focus on US statistical agencies in general and the US Census Bureau in particular. As background, the work from two large related research projects at the US Census Bureau lies behind much of the indirect approach taken in this chapter. The first of these, the LBD project, seeks to improve measures of firm dynamics. The second of these, the Collaborative Micro Productivity (CMP) project, seeks to prove the usefulness of producing higher moment statistics from microlevel data (using productivity as the pilot statistic; see Cunningham et al. 2017).

In the remainder of this section, we discuss four areas of interest for the measurement of innovation and productivity: direct measures of innovation, linking firm entry and innovation, intangible capital measures, and high-frequency versus low-frequency analysis. We view this section of the chapter as relating ongoing efforts to improve measurement in this area to the indirect approach we have taken in the analysis above.

3.5.1 Direct Measures of Innovation: R&D Expenditures and Patents

Direct measurement of innovation is a challenge. In this subsection, we highlight a few approaches to this challenge that are particularly relevant and feasible. Some of these activities are part of ongoing research projects underway at Census. One common approach is to measure *inputs* to innovative activity, such as R&D expenditures. The Census Bureau conducts the Business Research and Development and Innovation Survey (BRDIS) in accordance with an interagency agreement with the National Science Foundation (NSF). The BRDIS (or its predecessor, the Survey of Industrial Research and Development, or SIRD) has collected firm-level information on R&D expenditures since 1953. Griliches (1980) was one of the first users of this microdata from the SIRD (combining it with other Census datasets). Since then, the survey has expanded in scope from its original focus on large manufacturing companies. However, there remain many challenges with using R&D expenditures to proxy innovation activities (see Foster, Grim, and Zolas 2016), and we focus on a few of the more relevant challenges. First, measurement quality may vary over sectors of the economy because measuring R&D expenditures is more complicated in some sectors (e.g., the service and retail sector; see Brown, Plewes, and Gerstein 2005). Second, measurement quality may vary over types of firms because activities that constitute R&D and innovation activity are easier to capture in large, mature firms with dedicated R&D divisions or establishments. Start-ups and young businesses are inherently engaged in developing products, processes, and customer base, but it is likely difficult for such firms to break out separate expenditures. Third, more generally, traditional R&D activity is a narrower concept of innovative activity compared to the broader perspective discussed below on intangible capital accumulation.

Measuring innovative activities using patents is another commonly used alternative approach. Using patents and patent citations as indicators of innovation has a long history (see the survey by Griliches 1990). Patents and patent citations as indicators suffer from many of the same limitations as R&D expenditures. They are more informative in some sectors and technologies compared to others. Pavitt (1988) argues that they offer differential protection across sectors and technologies. This also leads to differential propensities across firms to patent their innovative activity. Like R&D expenditures, this means that patents may miss important innovative activity. On the flip side, patenting activity can also provide false positives for innovation when they are used as a defensive measure. Interestingly, Gort and Klepper (1982) use patents as one of their three measures of innovation in their empirical exercises but conclude "that patents are not a good measure of the rate of technological change" (650).

There have been research efforts to integrate the R&D and patent data into the LBD. For example, the research by Acemoglu et al. (2017) takes advantage of such integration in a manner closely related to the issues we address in this chapter. Specifically, they find that in the innovation-intensive industries (essentially industries with sufficient R&D and patent activity), young firms are the most innovation intensive as measured by innovation to sales ratios. Their analysis shows the potential promise of such data integration.[15] However, Acemoglu et al. (2017) focus on only about 5 percent of all US firms.

Another example is the ongoing Census Bureau project integrating measures of innovation into the LBD to enhance both the Business Dynamics Statistics and the data infrastructure available to the research community (through the Federal Statistical Research Data Center network). The strategy is to produce an indicator for innovation based on a multidimensional concept that can encompass measures such as R&D expenditures and patents (as well as indicators such as being part of a high-tech industry; see Goldschlag and Miranda 2016). One of the first steps in this research project is building a firm-level indicator of patenting activity.

Building on the experience of earlier researchers linking patent activity to the LBD, Graham et al. (2015) supplement this with linked employee-employer data from the Longitudinal Employer Household Dynamics (LEHD) infrastructure.[16] This allows them to link not only on the business

15. This research predates the development of the revenue-enhanced LBD, which is what we use in the empirical part of this chapter.

16. The LEHD program has worker-level information matched to businesses for much of the private employers in the United States. The core of LEHD data are wage records from State Unemployment Insurance programs linked to establishment data from the Quarterly Census of Employment and Wages (QCEW). The number of records in LEHD data has increased over time as states have joined the voluntary partnership; in the most recent year, the LEHD data tracks more than 130 million worker records each quarter.

assignee name but also on inventor names listed, increasing their match rate to about 90 percent—an improvement over other earlier efforts of about 70 percent to 80 percent. Improvements in the matching and imputation methodologies to create an integrated data infrastructure are currently areas of active research; future research may delve into some measure of patent quality.

An ongoing challenge for any attempt to measure innovation is sparsity. In any dataset, such rare behavior shows up as possibly long gaps in incumbent innovator activity. Alternatively, it also implies that most business start-ups do not engage in traditionally defined innovative activity. Hurst and Pugsley (2011) find that "most surviving small businesses do not innovate along any observable margin. Very few report spending resources on research and development, getting a patent, or even obtaining copyright or trademark protection for something related to the business" (74). This finding that many start-ups are not inclined toward being innovative but are instead "lifestyle" entrepreneurs, is not inconsistent with the literature that finds that start-ups are an important source of innovation. As Acemoglu et al. (2017) note, start-ups and young firms are more innovative than older firms, but this is conditional on the start-ups and young firms being in innovation-intensive industries. Similarly, Graham et al. (2015) find that patenting is a relatively rare event for small firms but that most patenting firms are small. It also points to the importance of taking into account innovative activity not well captured by traditional measures.

Recognizing the potential importance of these innovative activities for start-ups and young businesses, the Annual Survey of Entrepreneurs (ASE) included an innovation module for 2014 and adjusted the sample to try to capture innovative firms (see Foster and Norman 2017).[17] The ASE module on innovation is based on parts of NSF's Microbusiness Innovation Science and Technology (MIST) Survey. The ASE innovation module has eight questions combining questions on inputs to innovation and direct measures of innovation. For the former, information is collected on the types of R&D activities, their cost and funding, and the associated number of employees engaged in R&D. Direct measures of innovation are in questions concerning process and product innovations, where innovations are broadly defined to include products or processes new to the market and those new to the firm. Process innovation questions focus on the nature of the innovation, such as whether it is a new way to make purchases or a new way to deliver goods or services. Furthermore, in recognition of the importance of these small firms in innovation, the Census Bureau fielded in 2017 a version of the BRDIS that targets microbusinesses (Business R&D and Innovation for Microbusinesses

17. The ASE will produce annual data on economic and demographic characteristics of employer businesses and their owners by gender, ethnicity, race, and veteran status for reference years 2014–16. The ASE represents a partnership between the Census Bureau, the Ewing Marion Kauffman Foundation, and the Minority Business Development Agency (MBDA).

Survey). Our analysis suggests that integrating the ASE with the revenue-enhanced LBD has considerable promise.

Starting with reference year 2017, the ASE will be subsumed into the Annual Business Survey (ABS). In partnership with NSF, the Census Bureau intends to conduct the ABS for reference years 2017–21. This firm-level survey will also replace the Survey of Business Owners and Business R&D and Innovation for Microbusinesses Survey (however, the Business R&D and Innovation Survey will continue to collect R&D activities for firms with 10 or more employees). Thus the ABS will bring together four areas of inquiry: business characteristics (including financing); owner characteristics (including gender, ethnicity, race, and veteran status); research and development activity and costs (for small firms only); and innovation activities. The ABS is also planned to have a modular component for topical questions. Approximately 850,000 employer firms will be sampled in the baseline reference year of 2017 and 300,000 in the remaining years (see Foster and Norman 2017).

With fully integrated data, the type of analysis conducted in this chapter could be greatly enhanced. Such analysis would permit direct measures of innovation that would be useful for either hypothesis testing or external validity checks. Direct measures integrated with other elements of the data infrastructure would be very useful also for exploring possible heterogeneity in the type of dynamics we have discussed.

In addition, our findings suggest that tracking the joint dynamics of entry, productivity dispersion, and productivity growth offers a potentially useful cross check for traditional measures of innovation. Suppose, for example, that we observe Gort and Klepper (1982) dynamics in an industry where the traditional measures of R&D and patents do not capture innovation; this could suggest that this is an industry where these traditional measures are less informative about innovation dynamics. We regard combining the indirect and direct approaches to measuring innovative activity as a high priority for future research.

3.5.2 Linking Entry and Innovation

Our analysis suggests a tight link between surges in innovation and entry; however, there are open "chicken and egg" questions about their respective timing and interactions. For example, a surge of innovation may occur first at incumbent firms, and this could induce entry. Alternatively, the surge of innovation may occur jointly with the surge in entry because innovators create new firms to engage in innovative activity. The Gort and Klepper (1982) model distinguishes between these two sources and their impacts: innovations from incumbent firms tend to produce incremental changes, and innovations from sources outside the set of current producers tend to produce transformational changes and thus induce entry. While some evidence and models suggest the latter is important (see Acemoglu et al. 2017), it is possible that the dynamics are more subtle, so this remains an open area of measurement and research.

One way to investigate this would be to track the career paths of individual innovators and their links to firms. Using the LEHD infrastructure to link the individual innovators into the revenue-enhanced LBD would enable exploring the inherent chicken-egg issues about innovation and entry. That is, one could examine whether transformational innovations arise from employees of incumbent firms who then go on to spin off new firms. If this is the case, it may appear that the innovation occurred outside the incumbent firm when, in fact, it was incubated at the incumbent firm.

A challenge here is that innovators may go from being employees of incumbent firms to being business owners of new firms and ultimately become employees of the new firm if and when the firm incorporates. This implies that tracking the career history of innovators will also involve tracking business owners. Administrative and survey data on business owners will thus need to be integrated into the data infrastructure. A team at Census is exploring the use of person-level business owner identifiers in the administrative data for this purpose.[18] Our analysis highlights the substantial payoffs from such data integration, as this has the potential to greatly enhance our understanding of the connection between entrepreneurship and innovation, as well as the subsequent productivity and job growth gains from such activity.

A related challenge here is that, as discussed above, there are a host of factors that impact the incentives for entry into entrepreneurship that may yield surges or declines in the pace of entry within a country or industry. Recall that the Hurst and Pugsley (2011, 2017) hypothesis is that nonpecuniary benefits are the primary driver of many entrepreneurs and that entrepreneurs entering for such motives are concentrated in specific industries. A surge or decline in entry in such sectors may have little to do with innovation and productivity growth. Sorting the relative importance of the factors influencing entrepreneurship is an important area of research. The ASE includes some questions concerning the motivations and aspirations of entrepreneurs (see Foster and Norman 2017, for a discussion). One question concerns reasons for owning the business and includes checkboxes for responses such as "Wanted to be my own boss" and "Best avenue for my ideas/goods services." A second question asks about aspirations for the business over the next five years and includes checkboxes for responses such as "Larger in terms of sales or profits" and "About the same amount of sales or profits." Tracking the career history of entrepreneurs as well as incorporating information

---

18. A recent example of the application of integrated data is Bell et al. (2017). Using data on patents, tax records, and test scores from New York school districts, they show that family income and exposure to innovation during childhood significantly increases the propensity to become inventors.

about the activities and incentives of entrepreneurs as discussed in this section should help in this effort.

3.5.3   Intangible Capital

Another interesting area of inquiry is to relate the innovative activities associated with entrants and young firms to the growing literature on measuring and understanding the growth of intangible capital. One interpretation of our work in this chapter is that we use entry as a proxy for innovation. It might be fruitful to think about the time and resources associated with entry and young-firm activity as a measure of intangible capital investment. This perspective is consistent with the broad view of intangible capital of Corrado, Hulten, and Sichel (2005, 2009) and Corrado et al. (2013), who define intangible capital expenditures as any current-period expenditures by firms intended to enhance future production or sales. Other studies apply narrower definitions of innovation and intangible investment, focusing on the effects of spending on specific categories of intangible assets, such as employer-funded training, software, R&D, branding and design, and process improvement (see Awano et al. 2010 for more details). A recent example of estimating the contribution of innovation and intangible investment to growth can be found in Haskel, Goodridge, and Wallis (2014). Exploring such issues within the context of the joint dynamics of entry, dispersion, and growth would be of considerable interest.

We think a strong case can be made that entrants and young firms are inherently engaged in intangible capital investment. Likewise, young firms are engaged in activities to develop products and processes and to break into markets (such as developing a customer base; see Foster, Haltiwanger, and Syverson 2016). The experimentation phase we have discussed, and provided some evidence in support of, is another form of investment in activity. Kerr, Nanda, and Rhodes-Kropf (2014) make a related point in arguing that "entrepreneurship is fundamentally about experimentation" (25).

Exploring how to measure and track the indirect approach we have advocated in this chapter within the context of the measurement and contribution of intangible capital would be of considerable interest. Haltiwanger, Haskel, and Robb (2010) discuss and consider some promising possibilities for tracking intangible capital investment by new and young firms. For example, they find that young firms appear to be actively investing in various forms of intangible capital (using tabulations from the Kauffman Firm Survey that queries firms about their activities). Even though they find supporting evidence, they highlight the difficulties of obtaining such measures from entrants and young firms. The founders and employees of new firms are engaged in many tasks, so probing questions are needed to elicit the time and resources that should be considered as intangible capital investment.

Overall, our view is that the conceptual approach of intangible capital investment advocated by Corrado, Hulten, and Sichel (2005, 2009) has the greatest potential for direct measurement of investment in innovative activities. This approach takes the appropriate broad-based perspective on innovative investment activities and advocates capitalizing expenditures on these activities in the same manner as for physical capital expenditures. The challenge here is developing measurement instruments that can capture such intangible investment activities for all sectors and all firms, including young and small firms. We regard our indirect approach as complementary to the intangible capital approach. Combined with suitable measures of the latter, our approach could be used to study the stochastic and uncertain payoffs of investments in intangible capital. In addition, as with direct approaches to measuring innovation, our indirect approach could be used for external validity or cross validation of intangible capital measurement.

3.5.4   High- versus Low-Frequency Variation

Understanding high- versus low-frequency productivity dispersion and productivity growth dynamics would be another useful area of inquiry. The empirical results in section 3.4 suggest that an increase in industry-specific entry rates leads to increases first in productivity dispersion and then in productivity growth. As emphasized above, we estimated these relationships using low-frequency variation with the express intent of abstracting from cyclical dynamics. Since the contribution of innovation may materialize with potentially long and variable lags (see Griliches 1984) and may even arrive in multiple waves (Syverson 2013), long-run variation seems more appropriate for estimation purposes.

On the other hand, the appropriate horizon at which other factors affect dispersion is less clear a priori. Some of the results in the literature on frictions and distortions are based on annual average indicators (see, e.g., Hsieh and Klenow 2009; Foster et al. 2017). In addition, other evidence indicates that the effect of changing frictions may also be detected at higher frequencies. A recent example is Brown, Dinlersoz, and Earle (2016), who find that yearly dispersion measures increase during and after periods of deregulation.

While it may be of interest to abstract from short-run variation for certain research questions, it may be that cyclical dynamics are present and interact with lower-frequency dynamics. For example, Kehrig (2015) and Bloom (2009) document that within-industry productivity dispersion varies negatively with the cycle: it is greater in recessions than in booms. In addition, there is evidence that periods of Schumpeterian creative destruction coincide with recessions—although the extent to which this holds varies over cycles (see, e.g., Foster, Grim, and Haltiwanger 2016).

To help illustrate the effects of these complicating factors, we have estimated simple two-variable panel vector autoregression specifications (VAR) using annual time series on productivity dispersion, entry, and productivity growth by pooling high-tech industries (four-digit NAICS) between 1997 and 2013. One can think of these VARs as high-frequency analogues of the analysis in section 3.4. We show these high-frequency results to illustrate that developing a way to think about low- and high-frequency dynamics in an integrated manner would be of interest.

All the results reported below are derived from stable first-order VARs, where the underlying coefficients and standard errors are generalized method of moments (GMM) based and the lag order of the VAR is implied by standard information criteria.[19] The first impulse response function is estimated using changes in entry and dispersion, with this Cholesky ordering. Results are shown in panel A of figure 3.6: dispersion increases significantly in the wake of a positive change in entry, and the effect lasts two to three years. This finding is broadly consistent with our findings in section 3.4.[20]

However, investigation of other high-frequency dynamics reminds us of the many different factors in the joint distribution of entry, productivity dispersion, and productivity growth. Using a two-variable VAR relating productivity dispersion and productivity growth, we find (in unreported results) evidence of Granger causality from productivity growth to productivity dispersion. Panel B of figure 3.6 shows that a positive (high-frequency) productivity shock has a short-lived negative response on within-industry productivity dispersion. The short-lived negative response may be consistent with a number of theories. First, it may reflect the effect of cyclical variation in uncertainty (see Bloom 2009). Alternatively, a negative response may be related to demand-driven fluctuations in the price of fixed inputs that lead to positive selection among more productive firms (see Kehrig 2015 for more details). There are other possibilities as well, as there might be some interaction between these high-frequency dynamics and the lower-frequency dynamics that have been the focus of much of our discussion in this chapter.

A potentially useful approach would be to investigate the empirical performance of cointegrating relationships. The main advantage of the concept of cointegration would be its straightforward use in decomposing time series variation into high- and low-frequency dynamics, especially if it is reasonable to assume that different forces generate variation at different

19. We use the Stata module documented in Abrigo and Love (2016). The module integrates all the necessary steps of the empirical implementation: parameter estimation, hypothesis testing, lag order selection, and impulse response estimation.
20. The two variables in this VAR are the industry entry rate and the change in the within-industry productivity dispersion. The panel VAR has industry effects but no year effects. This is different from our low-frequency panel regressions in section 3.4, which relate entry to the level of within industry dispersion controlling for both industry and time effects. We used forward orthogonal deviations to remove industry effects from the VARs because this transformation tends to outperform the first-difference transformation when using GMM; see Hayakawa (2009).

A. Positive Entry Shock. Dashed lines show simulated 95% confidence bands.

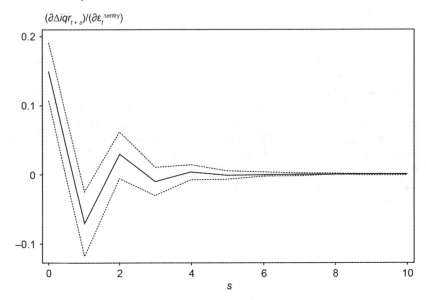

B. Positive Productivity Shock. Dashed lines show simulated 95% confidence bands

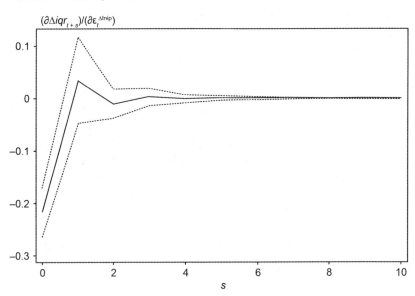

Fig. 3.6   Impulse response functions of dispersion for high-tech sector

frequencies—for example, when the long-run dynamics of entry and dispersion are related because of innovative activity and short-run variation is associated with business cycle fluctuations.

In short, this discussion of high- versus low-frequency variation highlights some of the challenges and limitations of the indirect approach we are advocating in this chapter. While we think much can be learned from our indirect approach, many other factors impact the joint dynamics of entry, dispersion, and productivity growth that need to be considered and controlled for in trying to draw inferences about innovative activity.

3.6 Concluding Remarks

Our findings suggest that there are rich joint dynamics of firm entry, within-industry productivity dispersion across firms, and within-industry productivity growth that help shed light on innovation dynamics. The patterns are broadly consistent with models of innovation where periods of rapid innovation are accompanied by a surge of entry. Such a surge in entry induces a rise in productivity dispersion and productivity growth within industries. Productivity growth stems from within-firm productivity growth by, and reallocation of resources toward, successful innovators.

Our analysis is intended to be exploratory. Our objective is to discuss the conceptual and measurement challenges, exploring these joint dynamics that appear to be important for understanding the complex nature of innovation. Part of the conceptual challenge is that alternative factors may influence the joint dynamics of entry, productivity dispersion, and productivity growth. For example, changes in frictions and distortions yield a distinct pattern of comovement, as emphasized by the recent literature. Second, moment shocks to the distribution of idiosyncratic productivity and profitability at cyclical or other frequencies are also likely important.

In terms of measuring innovation, there are efforts underway (and already interesting research based on such efforts) to integrate traditional measures such as patents, R&D expenditures, and the indicators of firm and industry dynamics that are a focus of our analysis. We think there will be substantial payoff from such efforts at further data integration. We also emphasize that even as this effort becomes increasingly realized, some open questions will remain. For example, if we can detect the presence of an innovative period in an industry as suggested by the results of this chapter, then it will be interesting to cross check the joint dynamics of entry, productivity dispersion, and productivity growth against traditional innovation measures.

We also think that the indirect approach suggested in this chapter can be fruitfully combined with the ongoing efforts to measure innovative activity by capitalizing intangible capital expenditures. Combining these efforts would serve as a useful cross check but also provide the ability to investigate the stochastic and heterogeneous returns to investment in intangible capital expenditures. Combining these efforts would also help overcome the known challenge that traditional indicators such as R&D expenditures and patents may not capture the full extent of young firms' innovative activity. Capturing intangible investment by entrants and young firms is especially challenging, since the founders and workers at young firms are inherently engaged in multitasking as they try to survive and ramp up production and their customer base for the future.

It is our view that overcoming these conceptual and measurement challenges will involve a multidimensional approach. First is continuing and expanding the integration of both person-level and business-level data. Currently, these include both survey and administrative sources, but they could also include commercial data. Second is continuing efforts to link these data longitudinally and to improve these links. Third is using a more focused approach to survey content and to use special modules like those in the Annual Survey of Entrepreneurs (or the forthcoming Annual Business Survey) to ask deeper questions about hard-to-measure concepts such as intent to innovate. Fourth is using economic relationships between relatively easy-to-measure concepts (such as entry and productivity dispersion) to help direct our measurement efforts toward areas of the economy where innovation is taking place. The payoff from these efforts could be substantial. It will only be through such efforts that we can understand the complex and noisy process through which innovation leads to productivity and job growth.

References

Abrigo, Michael R. M., and Inessa Love. 2016. "Estimation of Panel Vector Autoregression in Stata: A Package of Programs." Working Paper No. 201602. Honolulu: Department of Economics, University of Hawai'i at Manoa.
Acemoglu, Daron, Ufuk Akcigit, Harun Alp, Nicholas Bloom, and William R. Kerr. 2017. "Innovation, Reallocation, and Growth." NBER Working Paper No. 18993. Cambridge, MA: National Bureau of Economic Research.
Andrews, Dan, Chiara Criscuolo, and Peter N. Gal. 2016. "Frontier Firms, Technology Diffusion and Public Policy: Micro Evidence from OECD Countries." The Future of Productivity: Main Background Papers. Paris: OECD.
Awano, Gaganan, Mark Franklin, Jonathan Haskel, and Zafeira Kastrinaki. 2010. "Measuring Investment in Intangible Assets in the UK: Results from a New Survey." Economic and Labour Market Review 4 (7): 66–71.
Bartelsman, Eric, John Haltiwanger, and Stefano Scarpetta. 2013. "Cross-country Differences in Productivity: The Role of Allocation and Selection." American Economic Review 103 (1): 305–34.
Baily, Martin N., Eric J. Bartelsman, and John Haltiwanger. 2001. "Labor Productivity: Structural Change and Cyclical Dynamics." Review of Economics and Statistics 83 (3): 420–33.
Baily, Martin N., Charles Hulten, and David Campbell. 1992. "Productivity Dynam-

ics in Manufacturing Plants." *Brookings Papers on Economic Activity*, Microeconomics: 187–267.

Bell, M. Alexander, Raj Chetty, Xavier L. Jaravel, Neviana Petkova, John Van Reenen. 2017. "Who Becomes an Inventor in America? The Importance of Exposure to Innovation." NBER Working Paper No. 24042. Cambridge, MA: National Bureau of Economic Research.

Bloom, Nicholas. 2009. "The Impact of Uncertainty Shocks." *Econometrica* 77 (3): 623–85.

Bloom, Nicholas, Erik Brynjolfsson, Lucia Foster, Ron Jarmin, Megha Patnaik, Itay Saporta-Eksten, and John Van Reenen. 2019. "What Drives Differences in Management Practices?" *American Economic Review* 109 (5): 1648–83.

Brown, J. David, Emin Dinlersoz, and John S. Earle. 2016. "Does Higher Productivity Dispersion Imply Greater Misallocation? A Theoretical and Empirical Analysis." CES Working Paper No. 16-42.

Brown, Lawrence, Thomas Plewes, and Marisa Gerstein. 2005. *Measuring Research and Development Expenditures in the U.S. Economy*. Washington, DC: National Academy of Sciences Press.

Byrne, David, Stephen Oliner, and Dan Sichel. 2013. "Is the Information Technology Revolution Over?" *International Productivity Monitor* 25 (Spring): 20–36.

Byrne, David, Dan Sichel, and Marshall Reinsdorf. 2016. "Does the United States Have a Productivity Slowdown or a Measurement Problem?" *Brookings Papers on Economic Activity*, Conference Draft, March.

Cooper, Russell W., and John C. Haltiwanger. 2006. "On the Nature of Capital Adjustment Costs." *Review of Economic Studies* 73 (3): 611–33.

Corrado, Carol, Charles Hulten, and Dan Sichel. 2005. "Measuring Capital and Technology: An Expanded Framework." In *Measuring Capital in the New Economy*, edited by Carol Corrado, John Haltiwanger, and Dan Sichel, 11–46. NBER Studies in Income and Wealth 65. Chicago: University of Chicago Press.

Corrado, Carol, Jonathan Haskel, Cecilia Jona-Lasinio, and Massimiliano Iommi. 2013. "Innovation and Intangible Investment in Europe, Japan and the United States." *Oxford Review of Economic Policy* 29 (2): 261–86.

Corrado, Carol, Charles Hulten, and Dan Sichel. 2009. "Intangible Capital and US Economic Growth." *Review of Income and Wealth* 55 (3): 661–85.

Cunningham, Cindy, Lucia Foster, Cheryl Grim, John Haltiwanger, Sabrina Wulff Pabilonia, Jay Stewart, and Zoltan Wolf. 2017. "Dispersion in Dispersion: Measuring Establishment-Level Differences in Productivity." Unpublished paper.

Davis, Steven J., John C. Haltiwanger, and Scott Schuh. 1996. *Job Creation and Destruction*. Cambridge MA: MIT Press.

Decker, Ryan, John Haltiwanger, Ron S. Jarmin, and Javier Miranda. 2016. "The Decline of High Growth Young Firms in the U.S.: Where Has All the Skewness Gone?" *European Economic Review* 86:4–13.

Decker, Ryan, John Haltiwanger, Ron S. Jarmin, and Javier Miranda. 2017. "Declining Dynamism, Allocative Efficiency, and the Productivity Slowdown." *American Economic Review Papers and Proceedings* 107 (5): 322–26.

Decker, Ryan, John Haltiwanger, Ron S. Jarmin, and Javier Miranda. 2018. "Changing Business Dynamism: Shocks vs. Responsiveness." NBER Working Paper No. 24236. Cambridge, MA: National Bureau of Economic Research.

Dunne, Timothy, Mark J. Roberts, and Larry Samuelson. 1989. "The Growth and Failure of US Manufacturing Plants." *Quarterly Journal of Economics* 104 (4): 671–98.

Ericson, Richard, and Ariel Pakes. 1995. "Markov-Perfect Industry Dynamics: A Framework for Empirical Work." *Review of Economic Studies* 62 (1): 53–82.

Fernald, John. 2014. "Productivity and Potential Output before, during, and after the Great Recession." *NBER Macroeconomics Annual 2014*, vol. 29, edited by Jonathan A. Parker and Michael Woodford, 1–51.

Foster, Lucia, and Patrice Norman. 2017. "The Annual Survey of Entrepreneurs." *Journal of Economic and Social Measurement*, nos. 3–4:199–224.

Foster, Lucia, Cheryl Grim, and John Haltiwanger. 2016. "Reallocation in the Great Recession: Cleansing or Not?" *Journal of Labor Economics* 34 (S1), Part 2: 293–331.

Foster, Lucia, Cheryl Grim, and Nick Zolas. 2016. "A Portrait of Firms That Invest in R&D." CES Working Paper No. 16-41.

Foster, Lucia, Cheryl Grim, John Haltiwanger, and Zoltan Wolf. 2016. "Firm-Level Dispersion in Productivity: Is the Devil in the Details?" *American Economic Review Papers and Proceedings* 106 (5): 95–98.

Foster, Lucia, Cheryl Grim, John Haltiwanger, and Zoltan Wolf. 2017. "Macro and Micro Dynamics of Productivity: From Devilish Details to Insights." NBER Working Paper No. 23666. Cambridge, MA: National Bureau of Economic Research.

Foster, Lucia, John Haltiwanger, and Chad Syverson. 2008. "Reallocation, Firm Turnover, and Efficiency: Selection on Productivity or Profitability?" *American Economic Review* 98 (1): 394–425.

Foster, Lucia, John Haltiwanger, and Chad Syverson. 2016. "The Slow Growth of New Plants: Learning about Demand?" *Economica* 83 (329): 91–129.

Foster, Lucia, John Haltiwanger, and C. J. Krizan. 2001. "Aggregate Productivity Growth: Lessons from Microeconomic Evidence." In *New Developments in Productivity Analysis*, edited by Edward Dean, Michael Harper, and Charles Hulten, 303–72. NBER Studies in Income and Wealth 63. Chicago: University of Chicago Press.

Goldschlag, Nathan, and Javier Miranda. 2016. "Business Dynamics Statistics of High Tech Industries." CES Working Paper No. 16-55.

Gordon, Robert J. 2016. *The Rise and Fall of American Growth: The U.S. Standard of Living since the Civil War*. Princeton, NJ: Princeton University Press.

Gort, Michael, and Steven Klepper. 1982. "Time Paths in the Diffusion of Product Innovations." *Economic Journal* 92 (367): 630–53.

Graham, Stuart, Cheryl Grim, Tariqul Islam, Alan Marco, and Javier Miranda. 2015. "Business Dynamics of Innovating Firms: Linking U.S. Patents with Administrative Data on Workers and Firms." CES Working Paper No. 15-19.

Griliches, Zvi. 1980. "Returns to Research and Development Expenditures in the Private Sector." In *New Developments in Productivity Measurement*, edited by John W. Kendrick and Beatrice N. Vaccara, 419–62. Chicago: University of Chicago Press.

Griliches, Zvi. 1984. Introduction to *R&D, Patents, and Productivity*, edited by Zvi Griliches, 1–20. Chicago: University of Chicago Press.

Griliches, Zvi. 1990. "Patent Statistics as Economic Indicators: A Survey." *Journal of Economic Literature* 28:1661–1707.

Griliches, Zvi, and Haim Regev. 1992. "Productivity and Firm Turnover in Israeli Industry: 1979–1988." NBER Working Paper No. 4059. Cambridge, MA: National Bureau of Economic Research.

Haltiwanger, John. 2016. "Firm Dynamics and Productivity: TFPQ, TFPR and Demand Side Factors." *Economia* 17 (1): 3–26.

Haltiwanger, John, Ian Hathaway, and Javier Miranda. 2014. "Declining Business Dynamism in the U.S. High-Technology Sector." Kauffman Foundation.

Haltiwanger, John, Jonathan Haskel, and Alicia Robb. 2010. "Extending Firm Surveys to Measure Intangibles: Evidence from the United Kingdom and United States." Unpublished paper.

Haltiwanger, John, Robert Kulick, and Chad Syverson. 2018. "Misallocation Measures: The Distortion That Ate the Residual." NBER Working Paper No. 24199. Cambridge, MA: National Bureau of Economic Research.

Haltiwanger, John, Ron S. Jarmin, Robert Kulick, and Javier Miranda. 2017. "High Growth Young Firms: Contributions to Job, Output and Productivity Growth." In *Measuring Entrepreneurial Businesses: Current Knowledge and Challenges*, edited by John Haltiwanger, Erik Hurst, Javier Miranda, and Antoinette Schoar, 11–62. NBER Studies in Income and Wealth 75. Chicago: University of Chicago Press.

Haltiwanger, John, Ron S. Jarmin, and Javier Miranda. 2013. "Who Creates Jobs? Small vs. Large vs. Young." *Review of Economics and Statistics* 95 (2): 347–61.

Haskel, Jonathan, Peter Goodridge, and Gavin Wallis. 2014. "UK Investment in Intangible Assets: Report for NESTA." Working Paper No. 12846. London: Imperial College Business School.

Hayakawa, Kazuhiko. 2009. "First Difference or Forward Orthogonal Deviation—Which Transformation Should Be Used in Dynamic Panel Data Models? A Simulation Study." *Economics Bulletin* 29 (3): 2008–17.

Hecker, Daniel E. 2005. "High-Technology Employment: A NAICS-Based Update." *Monthly Labor Review* 128:57.

Hopenhayn, Hugo. 1992. "Entry, Exit, and Firm Dynamics in Long Run Equilibrium." *Econometrica* 60 (5): 1127–50.

Hopenhayn, Hugo, and Richard Rogerson. 1993. "Job Turnover and Policy Evaluation: A General Equilibrium Analysis." *Journal of Political Economy* 101 (5): 915–38.

Hottman, Colin J., Stephen J. Redding, and David E. Weinstein. 2016. "Quantifying the Sources of Firm Heterogeneity." *Quarterly Journal of Economics* 131 (3): 1291–1364.

Hsieh, Chang-Tai, and Peter J. Klenow. 2009. "Misallocation and Manufacturing TFP in China and India." *Quarterly Journal of Economics* 124 (4): 1403–48.

Hurst, Erik, and Benjamin Pugsley. 2011. "What Do Small Businesses Do?" *Brookings Papers on Economic Activity* 43 (2): 73–142.

Hurst, Erik G., and Benjamin Pugsley. 2017. "Wealth, Tastes, and Entrepreneurial Choice." In *Measuring Entrepreneurial Businesses: Current Knowledge and Challenges*, edited by John Haltiwanger, Erik Hurst, Javier Miranda, and Antoinette Schoar, 111–51. NBER Studies in Income and Wealth 75. Chicago: University of Chicago Press.

Jarmin, Ron S., and Javier Miranda. 2002. "The Longitudinal Business Database." CES Working Paper No. 02-17.

Jovanovic, Boyan. 1982. "Selection and the Evolution of Industry." *Econometrica* 50 (May): 649–70.

Kehrig, Matthias. 2015. "The Cyclicality of Productivity Dispersion." CES Working Paper No. 11-15 Revised 2015.

Kerr, William R., Ramana Nanda, and Matthew Rhodes-Kropf. 2014. "Entrepreneurship as Experimentation." *Journal of Economic Perspectives* 28 (3): 25–48.

Klette, Tor, and Samuel Kortum. 2004. "Innovating Firms and Aggregate Innovation." *Journal of Political Economy* 112 (5): 986–1018.

Lentz, Rasmus, and Dale T. Mortensen. 2008. "An Empirical Model of Growth through Product Innovation." *Econometrica* 76 (6): 1317–73.

Lucas, Robert E., Jr. 1978. "On the Size Distribution of Business Firms." *Bell Journal of Economics* 9 (2): 508–23.

Melitz, Marc J. 2003. "The Impact of Trade on Intra-industry Reallocations and Aggregate Industry Productivity." *Econometrica* 71 (6): 1695–1725.
Melitz, Marc J., and Sašo Polanec. 2015. "Dynamic Olley-Pakes Productivity Decomposition with Entry and Exit." *RAND Journal of Economics* 46 (2): 362–75.
Pavitt, Kevin. 1988. "Uses and Abuses of Patent Statistics." In *Handbook of Quantitative Studies of Science and Technology*, edited by A. F. J. van Raan, 509–36. Amsterdam: Elsevier.
Petrin, Amil, T. Kirk White, and Jerome Reiter. 2011. "The Impact of Plant-Level Resource Reallocations and Technical Progress on U.S. Macroeconomic Growth." *Review of Economic Dynamics* 14 (1): 3–26.
Restuccia, Diego, and Richard Rogerson. 2008. "Policy Distortions and Aggregate Productivity with Heterogeneous Plants." *Review of Economic Dynamics* 11 (4): 707–20.
Syverson, Chad. 2004. "Market Structure and Productivity: A Concrete Example." *Journal of Political Economy* 112 (6): 1181–1222.
Syverson, Chad. 2011. "What Determines Productivity?" *Journal of Economic Literature* 49 (2): 326–65.
Syverson, Chad. 2013. "Will History Repeat Itself? Comments on 'Is the Information Technology Revolution Over?'" *International Productivity Monitor* 25:37–40.

II

New Approaches and Data

4

How Innovative Are Innovations?
A Multidimensional,
Survey-Based Approach

Wesley M. Cohen, You-Na Lee, and John P. Walsh

4.1 Introduction

Policy makers, scholars and managers have a keen interest in tracking innovative activity. Measuring innovation has, however, proven difficult. For example, in the last couple of years, the Organisation for Economic Co-operation and Development (OECD) revised the Oslo Manual, the basic handbook for survey-based measures of innovation, reflected particularly in the Community Innovation Survey (CIS) administered across Europe. In the United States, the National Science Foundation (NSF) has sponsored two workshops on innovation indicators, and following earlier work in Europe

Wesley M. Cohen is the Snow Family Professor of Business Administration and a professor of economics, management, and law at Duke University and a research associate of the National Bureau of Economic Research.

You-Na Lee is assistant professor at the Lee Kuan Yew School of Public Policy, National University of Singapore.

John P. Walsh is professor of public policy and affiliated professor of strategic management at the Georgia Institute of Technology.

This research was funded by grants from the National Science Foundation (#0830349; #1262418; #1646689) and the Kauffman Foundation (#20085262) and a Startup Grant from Lee Kuan Yew School of Public Policy, National University of Singapore (#R-603-000-261-133). Additional support was provided by the Fuqua School of Business, Duke University; the School of Public Policy, Georgia Institute of Technology; and the National Institutes of Health (Award Number P50HG003391). We appreciate the helpful comments from participants in conferences and seminars at the OECD Blue Sky conference (Ghent), the NBER Conference on Research in Income and Wealth (CRIW) conference Measuring and Accounting for Innovation in the 21st Century, the NCSES/CNSTAT Workshop on Advancing Concepts and Models of Innovative Activity and STI Indicator Systems (Washington), FEDEA (Madrid), and National Institute of Science and Technology Policy (Tokyo). Finally, we thank Javier Miranda and Mark Roberts for helpful comments. For acknowledgments, sources of research support, and disclosure of the authors' material financial relationships, if any, please see https://www.nber.org/books -and-chapters/measuring-and-accounting-innovation-21st-century/how-innovative-are -innovations-multidimensional-survey-based-approach.

and elsewhere, NSF has begun to track self-reported innovation in its Business R&D and Innovation Survey (BRDIS). One challenge with existing innovation surveys (e.g., BRDIS, CIS) is that it is not clear what respondents mean when they report that they have introduced to the market a product or process that is new or significantly improved. Underlying this question of interpretation is the concern about whether reported innovations are "important." For example, does a reported innovation reflect simply a new flavor of toothpaste, or is it the first 3D printer? In this chapter, we suggest that the question of what respondents mean by "innovation" and the related question of its importance are fundamental ones that should be addressed conceptually and that this conceptualization should precede and guide measurement.

We start with Schumpeter's distinction between invention and innovation (Schumpeter, 1934). *Invention* refers to a discovery or the creation of a novel tangible (or virtual) artifact. *Innovation* refers to the commercialization of an invention—that is, the introduction of an invention to the market—and all that entails. Accordingly, we accept the definition of an innovation as a good, service, or process that is new to the market.[1] We suggest, however, that simply defining an innovation as being "new or significantly improved" is insufficient. Without knowing more, we cannot assess how innovative or important the innovation is. In this chapter, we propose moving beyond a categorical judgment of an innovation that focuses exclusively on novelty (e.g., "first to market") to consider the question of what features of an innovation potentially affect social welfare or, indeed, the likelihood of the invention being discovered and commercialized to begin with. In this chapter, we first propose what the relevant features may be. We then empirically illustrate the usefulness of such a multidimensional characterization using recently collected survey data for the US manufacturing sector and selected service sector industries. Finally, we provide some suggestions for new attribute-based innovation measures and conclude the chapter.

Figure 4.1 helps clarify the distinctions we are trying to highlight. The figure shows the innovation process, from the inputs (such as R&D) and its various determinants (such as technical information and information on market needs), to ideas (some of which are observable through patent data), to innovation (the new or significantly improved good, process, or service), to the social welfare impacts. This figure is used to organize the conceptual discussion rather than being an attempt to impose a "linear model" on the innovation process. For simplicity, the many external influences and feedback loops are excluded. A key distinction in this schematic is between the

---

1. In this chapter, we are not analyzing organizational or marketing innovations, which have also begun to be incorporated into innovation surveys. In addition, while we are discussing innovations by firms, much of what we discuss would also apply to public or nonprofit sector innovations, where one might use the phrase "implementation of the invention" rather than "introduction to the market."

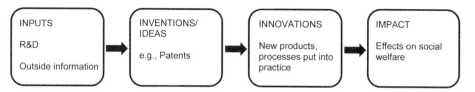

Fig. 4.1   The innovation process

characteristics of the innovation and its impact. We argue that it is important to measure how "innovative" an innovation is, separate from its impacts, in order to understand the relationships between inputs and innovations and between innovations and their impacts (Dahlin and Behrens 2005).

A fair question is, Why collect data on the characteristics of innovations per se? Why not just focus exclusively on their social welfare impacts, including their impacts on, say, productivity growth, lives affected, and so on? The reason is that, from both a managerial and policy perspective, it is useful to know, first, what kinds of innovations are worthy of private or public investment. Should they be innovations that are technologically significant in the sense that they represent a large inventive step? How about the prospective utility of the investment—reflecting the acuteness or the pervasiveness of a social need? At a first order, managers and policy makers make decisions that target specific features of an innovation, typically assuming some relationship between those features and an innovation's impact, either on profit, sales, and growth for managers or on social welfare for policy makers.

Correspondence between features of an innovation and their impact is not, however, straightforward. As a consequence, we need measures characterizing those features to better understand what features impact social welfare, including how and under what conditions, as well as to better understand the drivers of the different features of innovation. To illustrate, what we may call technological significance is not necessarily predictive of impact. For example, consider the discovery of high-temperature superconducting materials. This was a Nobel Prize–winning discovery that was expected to be transformative for the cost of electricity transmission and numerous other applications. That has not come to pass, at least not yet, largely due to the inability to manufacture such materials at commercial scale. Or consider the introduction of the Segway, a technically challenging achievement that was initially also thought to be transformative—at least by its inventor, Dean Kamen—for human-level transportation. Segways are indeed now commercialized and in use, but they are far from transformative. At the same time, there are numerous instances of innovations that are technologically incremental that have had enormous economic impacts. Consider, for example, the introduction of self-service grocery stores (and the follow-on innovation of the shopping cart) or the commercialization of containerized shipping. Neither of these innovations reflected large inventive steps technologically, but their impacts on productivity and economic growth have been substantial. Thus we suggest that it would be helpful for policy makers and managers to understand, for example, the circumstances under which more or less substantial technological leaps may pay off, particularly if those leaps come at considerable expense. Such understanding requires, however, measures of the relevant characteristics of an innovation—and that those characteristics be identifiable independent of their ultimate commercial or social impacts.

In this chapter, we are also arguing that we need surveys to collect data on critical features of innovations. But why? Why not rely exclusively on existing administrative patent data or R&D survey data to characterize innovations? Why go to the additional expense and effort of designing and administering surveys to characterize innovation? First, we would suggest it is not a question of using either administrative data or innovation surveys. Indeed, these approaches can complement one another, by allowing us both to use one modality to address questions that cannot be addressed by the other and also, where both approaches can be used, to compare findings to illuminate the virtues and limitations of each. For example, by comparing survey-based and patent-based measures of knowledge flows from public research institutions, Roach and Cohen (2013) showed that the patent citation data systematically underestimate the knowledge flows from public research to industrial R&D—by as much as 50 percent. At the same time, this comparative exercise suggested that as a measure of knowledge flows from public research, patent references to the nonpatent literature were a superior measure to using references only to other patents.

One possible advantage of innovation surveys over patent and existing R&D data is that large-scale innovation surveys offer a more flexible vehicle for collecting data than either the R&D or patent data, at least currently. With innovation survey data, at least when one is in a position to guide the formulation of questions, one is not restricted to the construction of measures from preexisting administrative data or from long-standing standardized surveys constructed for other purposes, including the R&D data collected through financial reporting systems or national statistical agencies. At the same time, survey data come with their own limitations, with pitfalls that may afflict sample construction as well as survey design and administration. Hence we begin below with a summary assessment of the advantages and limitations of R&D and patent data as measures of innovation. The purpose is to make an argument for supplementing these conventionally employed data sources with surveys that collect data on specific attributes of innovations that allow one to assess their importance.

In section 4.2 of the chapter, we briefly review several current approaches to measuring innovation, including R&D surveys, patent data, and innovation surveys. In section 4.3 we discuss the multiple dimensions of innovation that innovation surveys can be designed to capture. In section 4.4 we make an initial effort to empirically operationalize those dimensions. In section

4.5, we conduct a number of exploratory, empirical analyses to illustrate the utility of this multidimensional characterization. Section 4.6 suggests alternative measures of these dimensions of innovation. Section 4.7 presents our conclusions.

4.2   Current Approaches to the Measurement of Innovation

Social scientists, from different disciplines and often with different scholarly objectives, have used different data sources in their statistical studies of innovation. The three major data sources employed to study innovation are government data on R&D expenditures, patent-based measures, and survey-based measures.[2]

4.2.1   R&D Expenditures

R&D expenditures reflect an input into the innovative process, with research expenditures typically thought to be associated with invention and development associated with the prototyping and other activities designed to prepare an invention for market introduction. Innovation scholars, particularly economists, have typically used R&D data either as a dependent variable in studies of the factors driving firms' investments in innovative activities or as a factor of production—R&D or knowledge capital—in analyses of productivity growth. An advantage of R&D expenditure data is their availability, at least for public companies in the United States. Data on nonpublic companies are accessible via confidential NSF data, which also provide limited data on R&D composition across the categories of basic, applied, and development activity and, more recently, R&D dedicated to product versus process innovation.

It has been widely recognized since Mansfield (1968), however, that, while R&D is a key input into both invention and innovation, it is not the only one. Mansfield estimated that R&D expenditures reflect only about 50 percent of the investment required to bring an innovation to market, with additional investments in marketing, distribution, and manufacturing required for commercialization. We also know from a survey of the inventors of patented inventions that not all the patented inventions of firms originate from the firms' R&D operations, although most do (Lee and Walsh 2016). In addition, other sources of innovation within firms escape any recognition by either R&D or patenting activity, and these can be important, as shown by the literature on learning by doing (Thompson 2012; cf. Hollander 1965 for Dupont's rayon manufacturing processes).

There is perhaps an even more significant challenge to thinking that R&D expenditures are a reliable index of firms' innovative activities. On the basis

2. See section 2 of Cohen and Levin (1989) for an early critical discussion of R&D and patents as measures of innovation.

of the survey data used for the present study, Arora, Cohen, and Walsh (2016) indicate that for the US manufacturing sector, 49 percent of innovating firms report that the invention underlying their most important product innovation in the 2007–9 period was acquired from an outside source. Moreover, this percentage varies substantially across industries and across firms within industries. Hence for a significant (and varied) share of innovations, the R&D (or other inventive activity) that produced the underlying invention did not occur in the innovating firm, weakening the link between a firm's own R&D and its innovations.

There are other well-known concerns with R&D data. Griliches (1979) long ago argued that a proper measure of innovative input should reflect not the knowledge generated by R&D in any one period but the services of an accumulated stock of knowledge. Such an exercise, however, runs into challenges tied to the specification of lags, the determination of an appropriate depreciation rate, and the impact of spillovers from other firms (Cohen and Levin 1989).

4.2.2   Patent Measures

In addition to R&D data, patent data are also often used in studies of innovation. An important virtue of patents as a data source is that patent applications are vetted and curated by examiners. In addition, recent efforts by scholars such as Hall, Jaffe, and Trajtenberg (2001) and Li et al. (2014) have added value to these administrative data by cleaning the data, constructing useful measures based on the data, and making the data more accessible, creating an important data resource for innovation scholars. Another virtue of such data is that patents and linked documentation offer a wealth of information that lends itself to creative use and measure construction. Indeed, scholars have employed patent data to construct analogs to a number of the characteristics of innovations considered below, as well as other features, including, for example, measures of originality, generality, novelty, and economic value (Jaffe and De Rassenfosse 2017).

Notwithstanding these considerable virtues, patents reflect an intermediate outcome of the innovative process—invention—and thus do not constitute a measure of innovation (i.e., newly commercialized product/process) per se. Underscoring this limitation, only a fraction of patented inventions are ever commercialized (Griliches 1998; Svensson 2015; Walsh, Lee, and Jung 2016). Moreover, for those patents that are commercialized, the correspondence between patents and commercialized products varies substantially. In what are called discrete product industries, such as chemicals and pharmaceuticals, a new product may comprise relatively few patented elements. In contrast, in complex product industries such as computers, telecommunications equipment, and others, there may be hundreds of patents or more tied to a given product (Cohen, Nelson, and Walsh 2000; Nagaoka and Walsh 2009).

Even as a measure of invention, patents are also limited. First, not all inventions are patented, and patent propensity (measured as the percentage of innovations associated with at least one patent) varies considerably across industries. For example, according to Arora, Cohen, and Walsh (2016), patent propensities in the manufacturing sector range from 11 percent in the furniture industry to 72 percent in the medical equipment industry, with an average product patent propensity of about 50 percent.

4.2.3 Surveys

Numerous survey efforts have addressed innovation, and we will only briefly identify a handful here. Surveys dealing with innovation may be divided into three groups: (1) surveys focusing on R&D and its correlates, including the "Yale Survey" (Klevorick et al. 1995; Levin et al. 1987) and the "Carnegie Mellon Survey" (Cohen, Nelson, and Walsh 2000, 2002); (2) surveys of inventors of patented inventions (Giuri et al. 2007; Nagaoka and Walsh 2009); and (3) surveys tracking innovation itself. In this chapter, we are only concerned with the latter, the most prominent of which is the CIS, which was first administered in 1992 and is now administered widely in Europe, with equivalent surveys administered across the globe. While surveys also have a variety of limitations and concerns (as documented in the Oslo Manual), including cost, sampling issues, response biases, and difficulties with questionnaire design, here our main concern with innovation surveys as currently designed is the problem of interpretation. What do respondents mean when they report "new to the market" innovations, and are these reported innovations important? If so, in what sense? Is there an impact on sales, profits, growth, and so on? What about industry-wide impacts?

4.3 Toward a Multidimensional Perspective

In this chapter, we are proposing that some portion of innovation surveys employs the innovation as the unit of analysis and focuses on selected attributes of identified innovations as a basis for constructing measures of those attributes. By adopting this perspective, we are departing from the standard approach of the CIS and almost all innovation surveys in current use. Taking the firm as the exclusive unit of analysis, the CIS asks respondents to address questions regarding a firm's innovations considered collectively. For example, the CIS commonly asks what percentage of sales are accounted for by all products that are new to the market.[3] The approach described here, in

---

3. The CIS questions, following the harmonized July 2014 version of the CIS questionnaire, ask for the prior three years, 2012–14, whether the respondents introduced any "new or significantly improved goods" that were (1) "New to your market"; (2) "Only new to your enterprise"; or (3) "A 'first' in your country, Europe or the world?" The survey then asks what share of total turnover comes from each of these categories.

contrast, is most effectively implemented if questions are framed in terms of a specific innovation. The proposed approach, however, is not a substitute but a complement to current practice. While firm-level analyses can answer some questions about innovation, innovation-level analyses can answer others, and as a practical matter, both types of questions can be implemented in the same instrument. The impossibility of using surveys to collect data on the population of all innovations, however, requires careful attention to sampling strategies.

We begin with a basic definition of an innovation that is consistent with that employed in CIS surveys. We define an innovation as a new or significantly improved offering (i.e., a good, service, or process) that is "new" relative to the *status quo ex ante* in a given market. As argued above, however, we suggest that characterizing an offering as "new or significantly improved" is not very helpful if we ultimately want to understand how and to what degree a new offering impacts social welfare. Going beyond a categorical judgment of novelty, we suggest five features of an innovation to be *potentially* relevant for an assessment of its potential social welfare impact. We are not claiming that this is a definitive list but simply hope to initiate a dialogue around the idea that for the purpose of assessing the impacts of innovation, it is useful for innovation surveys to characterize different dimensions of innovation.

4.3.1   Features of Innovations

In this section, we identify features of an innovation that are potentially tied to its social welfare impact. These particular features are drawn from writings on innovation in a range of fields, including economics, history, organizational theory, and sociology.[4] These attributes do not characterize innovations in any absolute sense (e.g., the absolute gain in efficiency of an algorithm) but characterize innovations in relation to a context such as the state of technical knowledge, market acceptance, the capabilities of a firm to bring an innovation to market, or even the capacity of the broader market environment to support a new product's commercialization. Some of these attributes, such as technological significance, bear on the invention(s) underlying an innovation, while others, such as utility, characterize the commercialized product or process.

Technological Significance. The technological significance of an innovation may be characterized in terms of either its novelty or its impact on technical performance. Regarding novelty, one would want to know the extent to which the technical characteristics of an innovation differ from existing products or processes. *How* novel or technologically different is an identified innovation as compared to existing goods, processes, or services? To what

---

4. We do not claim that our focus on the features of identified innovations is novel. As noted above, scholars working with patent data have long been constructing measures of different features of inventions.

extent does an innovation reflect an advance in the underlying knowledge? This notion of technological novelty resembles what a patent examiner tries to assess by judging both an invention's absolute novelty against prior art and whether an invention is nonobvious (where nonobviousness may be more critical for our purposes). In Europe, examiners assess the "inventive step," which is closer to the concept of this dimension of technological significance. Several different patent-based measures have been constructed and employed in the past to evaluate degree of novelty.[5] The correspondence between degree of novelty and ultimate social impact is, however, not straightforward, as suggested by the observation that the preponderance of patents is never commercialized. However, without some independent metric of technological significance (i.e., one not based on impact), we are unable to answer the question of when or how technological novelty leads to greater or lesser impact and what aspects of the innovation process produce more or less novel technologies.

A second way to characterize the technological significance of an innovation is the degree to which an innovation improves the technical performance of a process or a product as compared to prior generations of similar processes or products. For example, we might track the degree of improvement in the clock speed of a microprocessor, the conversion rate of a solar cell, or the improvement in fuel efficiency of a new automobile engine. For a process innovation, technological performance improvement would be reflected in the cost savings per unit of output. For products and processes, one complication with this characterization is that the relevant performance dimensions of a new or improved product can be complex, and the assessment of performance improvements may also be challenging where such improvements are only realizable when a product is implemented with other technologies or in different organizational settings (see below). Moreover, there may well be improvements in performance unrelated to the technology of a product or process. Finally, an open question is the strength of the relationship between the first way of characterizing technological significance—that is, the novelty of an advance—and the degree to which the associated innovation affects the technological performance of a product or process.

Utility. Utility may be characterized in terms of the pervasiveness or acuteness of the need addressed by the innovation. Although firms and others have expectations regarding the utility of a new or improved product at the moment of introduction, it is difficult to assess utility without evidence

---

5. For example, Fleming (2001) and Strumsky and Lobo (2015) classify inventions as novel if the associated patent reflects "combinatorial novelty" either by being the first instance of a (new) technology (United States Patent and Trademark Office [USPTO] subclass) on a patent or if it is the first instance of a particular pairwise combination of existing technologies on patents. Shane (2001) assessed the novelty of an invention simply on the basis of the number of backward citations. Text-analysis methods have been used to check for the technological distance between new patents and existing patents (Yoon and Kim 2012).

of actual impact on use. Pragmatically assessing utility could entail gathering data on the sales of a new product over time, though such data are also limited as a measure of demand for an innovation, since they reflect the interaction of supply and demand and also reflect related decisions, such as those around marketing and distribution. Nonetheless, detailed data on price and volumes would be helpful. And more helpful still would be sales data on any prior generations of a new product, allowing one to begin to assess the incremental benefit.

One problem, however, with market-based measures of utility is the possibility that for some products and in some settings, there may be numerous individuals who could benefit from a new product but lack the means to pay for it. Consider, for example, the utility of a malaria vaccine in sub-Saharan Africa. The need for such a vaccine is obvious, suggesting a different, nonmarket-based measure of utility, such as lives saved or improved.

We might also examine utility of an invention or innovation in terms of its potential for increasing firms' abilities to achieve future innovations, possibly spawning a wide variety of subsequent technologies and applications. One may think of two ways in which an innovation may significantly contribute to subsequent innovation. First is the use of the technology as an input to the research process for other innovations (i.e., research tools). Some innovations in biotechnology might be of this sort. CRISPR is a recent example; recombinant DNA is an earlier example. Second are general-purpose technologies (GPTs) that can generate a wide variety of applications across numerous industries (Bresnahan and Trajtenberg 1995). The microprocessor, the computer, and the internet are prominent examples.

Distance or "Implementation Gap." The management literatures on corporate strategy and organizations (e.g., Adner 2006; Teece 1986) and the economics literature on diffusion (e.g., David 1990; Rosenberg 1976) highlight a third attribute of innovations related to both their probability of being implemented and their impact. These literatures suggest that the commercialization of innovations may be affected by (1) the innovating firm's internal capabilities, including the expertise and capabilities it possesses or can readily acquire, as well as the way the firm is managed or organized; (2) the organizational capabilities of prospective consumers or users of the innovation; (3) the availability of essential complementary technical components required for the development of the innovation; and (4) the external availability of complementary goods, services, and technologies that support the sale of the innovation. What we are calling "distance" or an "implementation gap" may thus be due to factors internal or external to the innovating firm. Whether internal to the firm or not, implementation gaps can affect the success with which a firm commercializes an invention or, indeed, whether an invention is commercialized at all. The premise for considering what we are calling "distance" is that innovations are not implemented in isolation;

their implementation typically depends on the availability of other artifacts, capabilities, and forms of organization within and across firms—both internal and external to the innovating firm.

Implementation gaps internal to the firm may be the consequence of constraints on existing capabilities, including manufacturing, marketing, and sales capabilities. The inventor of a new tennis racket, for example, may not be able to commercialize the product due to limited access to marketing capabilities or distribution channels. On the other hand, if the requisite capabilities are easily developed or are readily available via market transactions, then the implementation gap is less. Consider, for example, clinical testing of drugs. Over the past three decades, such capabilities have become readily available as a service. As a consequence, they represent less of a constraint on, say, a biotech firm's efforts to develop a drug and get it through the FDA approval process, assuming that the biotech firm has sufficient financial resources. Marketing and sales capabilities in the pharmaceutical industry are, however, more difficult to access or develop internally.

An external implementation gap that has constrained the commercialization of electric automobiles is the absence of a well-developed network of charging stations. Another instance of distance imposed by the environment external to the innovating firm is when customers do not possess the skills and processes that would enable adoption of a new product or it would take a substantial reorganization of their capabilities to implement the innovation. For example, Kubota, Aoshima, and Koh (2011) describe two rival chemical innovations (resists) for semiconductor production where one was readily incorporated into existing semiconductor manufacturing practices while the other, although higher in technological significance, required major readjustments in the existing production processes of the users. In this case, the resist with lower technological significance but lower distance and, in turn, lower cost of adoption dominated over the more technologically significant but higher distance resist.

Uniqueness. For uniqueness, the issue is whether anyone else could have independently commercialized a similar offering at about the same time, in which case an innovation would be judged as less unique. The argument here is analogous to Merton's (1973) arguments about simultaneous discovery in science (calculus, for example). Simultaneity may occur because two or more firms are working on developing the same innovation or because two or more firms have access, perhaps via licensing, to the same invention that would become an input to their innovative activity. Or as Marshall (1890) argued when discussing agglomeration benefits, low uniqueness may result because the ideas are "in the air," available to all to build on. In contrast, there may be cases where particular firms or inventors have special capabilities or distinctive insights that are not broadly shared, and hence the observed innovation would be unlikely to have developed had not that innovator developed them. These may include cases where the components of the idea lay fallow for a long time before somebody was able to incorporate them into the innovation. One could argue that Merck's development and introduction of statins was such a case of high uniqueness, as many firms had the chemical in their hands while failing to develop the innovation (cf. Baba and Walsh 2010). In contrast, the business model innovation of self-service grocery stores appears to have been independently invented in various parts of the country at about the same time (Zimmerman 1955). The social welfare implication of less uniqueness is that society may still reap the benefits of an innovation even if a specific innovating firm failed to pursue development of the innovation or ceased production or delivery.

Imitability. The question is how easy it is for another firm to copy an innovation once the idea of the innovation is known or introduced to the market. To the extent that an innovation is imitable, the prospects for its diffusion increase, potentially affecting a broader swath of society. As Teece (1986) highlights, imitability is a function of replicability and the strength of intellectual property protection. To the extent that patents, for example, are more easily invented around, patents constitute less of a barrier to imitation and the diffusion of the innovation. Replicability refers to others' ability to copy, notwithstanding intellectual property protection, and is likely to be a function of both the distribution of capabilities across prospective imitators and the particular characteristics of the technology, such as the complexity and observability to outside firms of the innovation or the process that produced it. An example of both the importance of others' capabilities and observability is the Toyota Production System, a process innovation. Toyota freely gave tours of its factories because it was confident that others could not readily reproduce the whole of its production process even if they saw it in action, due to its complexity and the considerable tacit and other knowledge that underpins it (Spear and Bowen 1999). An example of the role of complexity and low visibility is hybrid corn. Because the corn was a double hybrid and the parent stocks were kept secret, one could not readily tell from the final product how to copy the innovation, although with significant experimentation, one could develop rival hybrids. In contrast, once one sees a self-service grocery store, one can readily replicate the innovation absent barriers to entry or other impediments to imitation.

Also affecting replicability is the degree to which the knowledge is "sticky," meaning that it is more likely that only some firms or other entities have the requisite skills to commercialize an invention because those skills are either learned in-house through their development of the technology or developed from significant experience in the industry (von Hippel 1994). Some surgical innovations may be of this form and hence may be less imitable, at least until a new cohort of surgeons can be trained in the new methods. In contrast, other surgical innovations may involve standard skills of the profession applied in a new way and hence can be readily imitated once the new technique is publicized. Industries also may differ systematically in how practice-based versus science-based knowledge is (Jensen et al. 2007). Arora and Gambardella (1994) and von Hippel (1994) both argue that more science-based knowledge regimes are likely to provide more widespread access to relevant knowledge and hence greater imitability.

4.3.2   Further Considerations

These different attributes of an innovation do not operate independently of one another. And indeed, it is typically interactions across these attributes that would assist efforts to characterize and ultimately understand the impact of an innovation. Consider, for example, a technologically significant innovation that is deployed in an environment lacking essential complementary infrastructure: a malaria vaccine. Although technologically significant and addressing a need that is both pervasive and acute, the vaccine's administration in sub-Saharan Africa may be quite limited in the face of an implementation gap tied to a need for constant refrigeration and skilled personnel for its administration. A counterexample is provided by the technologically significant discovery (awarded the Nobel Prize in medicine) that ulcers are caused by bacteria. Utility could be quickly realized because the distance tied to the implementation of this discovery was virtually nil; physicians in industrialized nations were already employing the appropriate antibiotic for a range of other ailments. An example of an innovation, no component of which was high on technological significance at the time of its introduction but that yielded widespread utility and, in turn, impact was iTunes. The key to iTunes' success was a set of existing complementary components and capabilities, including a well-designed physical device, the iPod; easy-to-use software; and the availability of a range of digital rights agreements that enabled an extensive song catalog.

The example of iTunes raises another challenge for using surveys to assess the importance of a given innovation—time. The iTunes innovation would never have succeeded had not other innovations preceded it, from the microprocessor to the internet, the MP3 player, and so on. Surveys capture data, however, at a point in time. And many innovations may yield utility, but as suggested above, only once other foundational inventions and necessary complements and organizational changes have been realized. David's (1990) comparison of the diffusion of the dynamo to that of the computer provides a clear illustration of the point as it applies to GPTs. Similarly, it took many years to fully realize the utility of the networked computer, and hence the payoff from the various attributes of the innovation was not realized until long after its initial commercialization. Moreover, many pioneering innovations are subject over time to subsequent improvements that affect their diffusion (Rosenberg 1976). And of course, the attributes of an innovation will condition incentives that in turn affect the likelihood that an invention will be commercialized to begin with (see the middle part of figure 4.1). The implication is that survey-based measures that capture the different features of an innovation at a point in time may not be predictive of long-run impact.

Given measures of the characteristics of innovations, managers, policy makers, and economists are obviously interested in assessing their impacts on firms, industries, consumers, and so on. It is obviously the case, however, that those impacts depend on numerous other factors. A clearer understanding of these attributes and the factors conditioning their impacts, however, are key to understanding not only the *ex-post* impacts (the last arrow in figure 4.1) but also the *ex-ante* drivers of innovation (e.g., incentives to engage in R&D or to convert ideas into innovations—the first two arrows in figure 4.1). For example, if we take the case of the battery-powered electric car, we can imagine problems related to "distance" at each arrow in our diagram. To begin, there is the problem of going from R&D to ideas, which may be related to the absorptive capacity of auto firms for the knowledge necessary for electric car production (see Cohen and Levinthal 1990, and Henderson and Clark 1990). Then there is the problem of going from ideas to innovation, which may be related to automakers' capabilities related to batteries and electric motors, an aspect of the "distance" considered in this chapter. Finally, there is also the "distance" due to *ex-ante* consumer practices related to driving habits, the range of electric cars, and the availability and costs of complementary services, such as charging stations. More generally, a full understanding of the attributes of an innovation and their impacts on various aspects of social welfare depends heavily on contextual factors, including firm capabilities, appropriability conditions, market structures, the common practices of buyers, and other variables—long studied—that will interact with the different attributes of an innovation in affecting outcomes, as reflected in the last arrow in figure 4.1.

4.4   Data and Measures

The purpose of the empirical analyses below is to illustrate the usefulness of developing survey-based measures of the different dimensions of innovations for (1) increasing the interpretability of survey-based innovation measures, (2) providing new insights into the correlates and possible impacts of innovation, and (3) stimulating further empirical and theoretical work. The analysis does suffer from an important limitation: the data were not collected for the purpose at hand.[6] As a consequence, they provide a limited

---

6. The objective of the original project was to characterize the "division of innovative labor"—that is, the degree to which innovating firms acquired their major innovations from outside sources, the sources used, and the channels through which inventions are acquired. Our findings on the division of innovative labor for the US manufacturing sector are provided in Arora et al. (2016).

basis—but a basis nonetheless—for making our argument. In this section, we describe our data and the measures employed.

4.4.1   Data: Survey Design

Our data are from a phone survey of firms in US manufacturing and selected service sector industries (see Arora et al. 2016 for more details on the sample).[7] Our sampling frame was the Dun & Bradstreet (D&B) Selectory database. Note that we not sampling on being innovators nor on being R&D performers (in contrast to the survey efforts of Levin et al. 1987 and Cohen, Nelson, and Walsh 2000).[8]

To obtain a substantial number of innovators from each industry, we stratified our sample along multiple dimensions. To begin, we selected all the D&B cases in our population of industries.[9] The sample was stratified into 28 industries at the three- or four-digit North American Industry Classification System (NAICS) code level. Furthermore, the sampling frame was divided by size (Fortune 500; over 1,000 employees but not Fortune 500; 500 to 1,000 employees; 100 to 499 employees; 10 to 99 employees; and 1 to 9 employees) and by whether the respondent is a start-up, defined as a single-product firm that is less than five years old.

We oversampled large firms, notably firms over 1,000 employees, with Fortune 500 firms sampled with certainty across all business units.[10] We also oversampled (1) start-up firms; (2) firms from more innovative industries, using CIS data from Europe to estimate innovation rates for each industry; (3) those in NAICS code industry 533 (lessors of intellectual property) as a primary or secondary industry; and (4) less-populated industries to ensure minimum sample sizes for industry-level estimates. Other categories were undersampled. While we used the D&B industry classifications for sampling, the D&B industry classifications of respondents' industries were confirmed and, if necessary, updated based on survey responses. We use these updated industry classifications for our analyses. Furthermore, we use a postsample weighting procedure (described below) to make the data representative of

7. NORC, at the University of Chicago, administered our survey.

8. This sampling strategy is analogous to that employed by the Community Innovation Survey (CIS) in Europe and the US National Science Foundation (NSF) Business R&D and Innovation Survey (BRDIS).

9. Because all cases stay in the sample, errors in the D&B data used for stratification only affect the efficiency of the sampling, not its representativeness (Kalton 1983).

10. For the Fortune 500 firms in our sample, we collected information on the parent firm and all its subsidiaries listed in D&B in our population industries, even if those were not the main industry of the parent firm. The parent firm and its subsidiaries were grouped into business units, defined as a firm's activities within a given NAICS industry, with the parent firm and each subsidiary grouped by its primary NAICS code. The sampling unit for the Fortune 500 firms is a business unit, defined as the firm's activity in a NAICS industry. Thus a diversified Fortune 500 firm may appear multiple times in the sample. All firms other than Fortune 500 firms were assigned a single sampling unit based on their primary NAICS code, implying that we are treating these as single-industry firms.

the US firm population in manufacturing and our selected business service industries.

The survey design included cognitive testing of the questionnaire with potential respondents, pretesting of the instrument and protocol, and multiple rounds of follow-up contacts to increase response rate. We designed the survey instrument with a branching logic so that noninnovative firms received only a brief questionnaire, and firms that innovated were asked more details about their innovation process and outcomes. The sample consisted of 28,709 cases. An initial screening eliminated many cases (e.g., bakeries that are in retail, not manufacturing), leaving a final sample of 22,034. The interview protocol started with a D&B contact name—ideally the marketing manager, product manager, or for smaller firms, the business manager. We then worked through the receptionist or other contacts to find an appropriate respondent.[11]

The survey was in the field from May to October 2010. In the end, we received 6,685 responses, yielding an adjusted 30.3 percent response rate. Nonresponse bias tests comparing D&B data for respondents and nonrespondents show that the sample represents the population on firm age, being multiproduct, region, and its likelihood to export. With a 20 percent response rate, units of Fortune 500 firms were somewhat less likely to respond. Similarly, large firms, multiunit firms, and public firms were somewhat less likely to respond. With regard to industry-level response rates, pharmaceuticals had a low response rate, but still over 20 percent. A recoding of industry assignments to reflect survey responses rather than initial D&B categorizations identified another 179 out-of-population respondents.

We reweighted the sample with postsample weights based on US Census data on the population of firms in our industries, size strata, and age strata. We constructed a matrix of these three dimensions of stratification from a custom report provided by the US Bureau of the Census[12] and then constructed a set of weights for our 5,871 responses in the relevant industry and size categories that reflect the population distribution of this three-dimensional matrix. After applying these weights, our sample should represent the underlying population in terms of the industry-size / start-up distribution (Kalton 1983). These weights are used in all our empirical analyses.

For the purposes of this chapter, we exclude the very smallest establishments (less than 10 employees). The result is a sample of 5,157 cases for the manufacturing sector and 714 observations for the service sector, weighted to reflect the underlying Census-derived distribution on industry-size / start-up.

---

11. According to the interview script, an appropriate respondent would be "the marketing manager or another person in your company familiar with the firm's products and services." This flexibility in finding an appropriate contact person was a key rationale for using a phone survey rather than post mail or email surveys.

12. We thank Ron Jarmin and his team at the US Bureau of the Census for providing this report.

Table 4.1   **Examples of innovations in sampled manufacturing industries**

Industry	Innovation
Food	Antioxidant chocolates
Food	Live active cheddar cheese with probiotics
Beverage	Vitamin-enhanced flavored spring water
Textile	Heat-resistant yarn
Textile	New varieties of garments
Paper	Low-surface-energy light tapes resistant to air, water, detergents, moisture, UV light, and dust
Paper	Hanging folder with easy slide tab
Petroleum	Nondetergent motor oil
Chemicals	BioSolvents—water-based emulsion technology
Pharmaceutical	Oral gallium to prevent bone decay
Pharmaceutical	Inhalation anesthetics
Plastics	Styrene-based floor underlayment
Minerals	Multiwall polycarbonate recyclable panels
Minerals	Solar glass and coating technologies for solar modules
Metals	Solder system and nanofoils
Metals	New water faucets and bath products
Electronics	USB-to-GPIB interface adapter
Electronics	20-h IPS alpha LCD panel
Semiconductors	Linear voltage regulators
Semiconductors	Phase change memory
Transport equipment	Improved alcohol sensing system

Notes: Reprint of table 1 in Arora, Cohen, and Walsh (2016).

4.4.2   Descriptive Statistics

In this study, we focus exclusively on product, rather than process, innovations. Following prior innovation surveys, we asked the respondent if the firm had earned any revenue in 2009 from a new or significantly improved good or service introduced between 2007 and 2009. For those that said yes, we asked whether their most significant innovation (defined as that product innovation accounting for the plurality of 2009 sales in the respondent's market) was new to the market—that is, introduced "in this industry before any other company."[13] We do not specify a geographical boundary to the "industry" and are thus not limiting responses to a local or domestic market.[14] Table 4.1 provides illustrative examples of innovations introduced by firms in the manufacturing sector. For the purpose of this chapter, we will

13. Our new-to-the-market (NTM) figure may underestimate the percentage of firms introducing NTM innovations. For example, a firm's most significant (i.e., highest-selling) innovation may not be NTM, but it's second most significant innovation may be, implying that the firm is incorrectly classified as not being an NTM innovator. However, any bias is likely to be small because a sizable fraction of firms introduces only one innovation during the sample period (see Arora et al. 2016).

14. We also did not count as innovators firms that either reported that they introduced their "most significant innovation" outside of the 2007–9 time window or reported zero 2009 sales revenue due to this innovation.

Table 4.2a   Manufacturing: Descriptive statistics

Manufacturing Industries (N)	NTF Inno (N)	NTF Rate (%)	Innovator (N)	Inno Rate (%)	Imit Rate (%)
Food (302)	138	39	54	13	25
Beverage and Tobacco (60)	28	43	10	18	23
Textile Mills (39)	20	49	8	26	22
Textile Product Mills (76)	28	36	12	16	16
Apparel and Leather (97)	35	33	14	12	18
Wood Product (75)	19	21	5	7	12
Paper (125)	50	31	30	16	14
Printing and Related Support (187)	85	42	18	7	33
Petroleum and Coal Products (47)	14	30	6	20	8
Chemical (except Pharma) (318)	183	52	97	25	25
Pharmaceutical and Medicine (128)	80	62	34	31	25
Plastics and Rubber (340)	185	47	74	17	26
Nonmetallic Mineral (324)	102	29	36	9	18
Primary Metal (325)	132	38	44	9	26
Fabricated Metal (426)	183	38	63	10	26
Machinery (389)	197	45	103	21	22
Computers/Electronics (except Semiconductor) (287)	202	67	108	36	29
Semiconductor and Other (302)	199	60	93	28	28
Electrical Equipment (315)	189	56	93	28	24
Transportation Equipment (344)	192	50	102	27	21
Furniture and Related Product (263)	117	41	41	14	24
Medical Equipment (136)	83	55	37	21	33
Miscellaneous (except Medical) (252)	144	55	68	26	26
Manufacturing all (5157)	2,605	42	1,150	16	24
Large (1267)	829	65	465	39	23
Medium (946)	533	54	229	23	29
Small (2944)	1,243	39	456	13	23

Notes: NTF Inno (N): Number of new-to-the-firm innovators; NTF Rate (%): Share of new-to-the-firm innovators; Innovator (N): Number of innovators (i.e., those having a new-to-the-market innovation); INNO_RATE (%): Share of innovators (i.e., those having a new-to-the-market innovation); Imit Rate (%): Share of imitators: If the respondent reports a new-to-the-firm innovation but not a new-to-the-market innovation, then it is an imitator (note that due to missing data on one or the other item, it is possible for the aggregate percentages of Innovator and Imitator to not sum to percentage of NTF).

call firms that introduce a new or significantly improved product that is new to the industry "innovators" and firms that introduce new or improved products that are only new to the firm, but not new to the industry, "imitators."

Tables 4.2a and 4.2b present summary statistics for the rates of innovation and imitation overall and by industry, where we aggregate our observations of firms into 23 manufacturing industry groups and 7 service sector industry groups, defined largely at the three-digit NAICS code level. The figures in

Table 4.2b   **Selected service sector industries: Descriptive statistics**

Service industries (N)	NTF Inno (N)	NTF Rate (%)	Innovator (N)	Inno Rate (%)	Imit Rate (%)
Software Publishers (87)	63	74	30	36	36
Motion Picture and Sound (47)	28	58	8	17	40
Telecommunications (101)	64	59	20	15	42
Data Processing (83)	48	51	17	15	35
Professional, Scientific, and Tech Svc (162)	79	42	34	17	23
Engineering Svc (130)	54	35	23	13	21
Computer Systems Design (104)	63	56	23	25	28
Service all (714)	399	47	155	18	27
Large (145)	99	69	51	38	30
Medium (98)	68	64	21	20	41
Small (471)	232	44	83	17	25

Notes: NTF Inno (N): Number of new-to-the-firm innovators; NTF Rate (%): Share of new-to-the-firm innovators; Innovator (N): Number of innovators (i.e., those having a new-to-the-market innovation); INNO_RATE (%): Share of innovators (i.e., those having a new-to-the-market innovation); Imit Rate (%): Share of imitators: If the respondent reports a new-to-the-firm innovation but not a new-to-the-market innovation, then it is an imitator (note that due to missing data on one or the other item, it is possible for the aggregate percentages of Innovator and Imitator to not sum to percentage of NTF).

tables 4.2a and 4.2b and all subsequent tables are weighted to be representative of firm size and industry distributions.

Tables 4.2a and 4.2b show that 42 percent and 47 percent of firms in the manufacturing and service sectors, respectively, report introducing a new-to-the-firm (not necessarily new-to-the-market) or significantly improved products in the prior three years in manufacturing. There are significant differences in the rates of new or improved product introduction across industries. For example, at least 60 percent of firms in computers, pharmaceuticals, semiconductors and software publishing introduced a new-to-the-firm (NTF) product, while less than 30 percent of firms in wood or mineral products did so. If we limit product innovations to the introduction of something new to the market (NTM), qualifying a respondent as an innovator, we find that 16 percent of manufacturing firms and 18 percent of our service sector firms report having introduced such an innovation, with rates of 30 percent or higher in computers, pharmaceuticals, and software publishing, while wood, printing, mineral products, and metals have rates below 10 percent. As noted, in what follows, the term *innovation* refers to products that are new to the market.

Tables 4.2a and 4.2b also show that larger firms are more likely to innovate and more likely to introduce new products. In manufacturing, we find that 39 percent of small firms but 65 percent of large firms report introducing new products (i.e., new to them). For innovations (i.e., new to the market), the rates in manufacturing were 13 percent and 39 percent for small and large firms, respectively—and the rates were similar in the service sector. Thus larger firms are more likely to have at least one innovation, which is expected in light of the relationship between firm size and R&D (cf. Cohen and Klepper 1996). Interpreting the difference between an industry's rate of NTF product introductions (which include NTM and NTF) and NTM product introductions as measuring imitation (Imit Rate in tables 4.2a and 4.2b), we find that the imitation rate is relatively stable across industries in manufacturing but much less so in the service sector. It also appears to be nonmonotonically related to size in both the manufacturing and service sectors, with the medium-sized firms characterized by the highest imitation rates.

To assess the validity of our survey, we compare our manufacturing sector findings regarding innovation rates with those from other innovation surveys. The rank-order correlations between our survey-based NTM innovation rates at the industry level and other innovation-related measures, such as the percentage of firms that conduct R&D or patent, are high, above 0.7.[15] For the cross-national comparisons, one might expect differences across otherwise comparable national economies simply due to differences in the distribution of respondents across firm size classes and industries and the fact that innovation rates differ across these dimensions. Nonetheless, as compared to 42 percent of our respondents that earned revenue in 2009 from NTF products introduced since 2007, the CIS in the United Kingdom reports that about 34 percent of manufacturing respondents had introduced such a new product between 2006 and 2008. For Germany, 49 percent of manufacturing respondents report introducing an NTF product. Turning to innovation, about 38 percent of the NTF respondents in our survey had introduced a product that was NTM as well. The comparable figure for the United Kingdom is 51 percent, and that for Germany is 45 percent. Thus despite differences across the three countries in the rate at which manufacturing firms introduce new products, the share of those products that are NTM is similar. Moreover, the overall rates of product innovation are also similar to our estimate of 16 percent, ranging from about 17 percent for the United Kingdom to 22 percent for Germany. Thus our data appear to benchmark reasonably well with CIS data from Germany and the United Kingdom, which is reassuring since the question we employ to initially identify "NTM" innovators resembles the question employed in the CIS.[16] Moreover, our

15. Our patent data were obtained from PATSTAT, from which we estimated the percent of firms in each industry that had a patent application.

16. Note, however, that the means from our survey, and from the CIS, are much higher than those from the US BRDIS or Japan's National Innovation Survey. And yet the correlations are quite high between the BRDIS industry percentages and our industry percentages for the same indicators.

measure of innovation corresponds sensibly with other innovation-related measures (see Lee 2015 for a detailed analysis).

4.4.3   Measure Construction

The key questions that motivate this chapter are as follows: What do respondents mean by "innovation," and how important are those innovations? Our approach to designing our survey allows us to begin to address these issues. Rather than asking about a firm's innovations overall, as does the CIS (e.g., the percentage of sales accounted for by the firm's innovations), we ask the respondent to answer follow-on questions with respect to a specific innovation—their most important innovation—in an identified line of business, where "most important" is defined as that new or significantly improved product accounting for a plurality of their sales in the line of business.

Below we describe measures corresponding to the innovation characteristics highlighted in the prior section. It is important to recall that the survey providing the data for this analysis was not designed to develop the kind of multidimensional assessment of innovation that we are proposing. As a consequence, the attributes identified above are only partially represented and are subject to the limitations discussed below.

The measures are constructed as follows:

1. *Technological significance.* We will measure only one aspect of technological significance, novelty and nonobviousness, on the basis of whether an invention underlying the innovation had a patent associated with it—a patent filed by either the innovating firm or an outside entity such as another firm or a university if the innovation was acquired from that entity (PATENT). A patent will primarily reflect whether an examiner judged the invention to be novel and nonobvious. This measure suffers from several limitations. First, as suggested above, this measure does not reflect the second dimension of technological significance—the product performance improvement tied to the product. Second, the measure is categorical rather than continuous. Third, it is subject to the points raised above regarding patent data—that not all inventions are patented, and the propensity to patent varies across industries and firms. Fourth, the measure is tied to a patent, and in complex product industries such as computers, the technological significance of a new product transcends that of any one patentable element given that the commercialized product may embody numerous patented and unpatented elements.

2. *Utility.* We measure utility by the percentage of the respondent's sales in a line of business accounted for by their most important innovation (INNO_SALES). This measure should reflect the revenue impact of their most important innovation and thus, at least in a relative sense, the prevalence of the need that the innovation addresses. This figure, however,

depends on not only the utility buyers derive from the product but also the pricing, marketing, and other decisions made by the firm and, more generally, reflects the interaction of demand and supply conditions. Moreover, this measure only reflects the short-run market impact of the innovation, and many new products take some time before their market potential is more fully realized.

3. *Distance.* We measure only internal distance, not the external distance characterizing the external market environment discussed above. To assess distance from the respondent's existing capabilities, we use responses to two survey questions. We asked innovating firms whether, in order to commercialize the innovation, they developed new sales and distribution channels (New_Mktg) and, in a separate question, whether they had invested in new types of equipment or hired employees with distinct skills (New_EqSk). Below, we will occasionally use these measures separately. The form of this measure that we will feature, however, is whether the innovator both acquired new equipment and personnel with distinct skills *and* developed new distribution channels (NEW_CAPAB). The undertaking of either or both of these activities suggests that the innovation is substantially new to the firm in the sense that to commercialize the innovation, the firm had to acquire assets, capabilities, or relationships that they did not previously possess. A limitation of this measure is that it reflects investment decisions on the part of the firm and thus reflects not only distance but also whether the firm expected the new product in question to be valuable enough to justify the investment in these new capabilities, potentially conflating measures of distance with the other dimensions of the innovation that may condition the expected value of the innovation, such as utility or technological significance.

4. *Imitability/uniqueness.* Our survey data do not permit us to distinguish between these two related concepts. Moreover, the only survey measure that comes close to imitability is respondents' judgment of the number of firms that "have introduced or are likely to introduce" a competing innovation (INNO_RIVALS). A limitation of this measure is that it conflates two concepts: technological competition and imitability. What the measure directly reflects is the former, though presumably intensity of technological competition faced by a firm should be related to the latter.

As noted above, none of these measures are "clean" in the sense of only measuring the innovation attribute in question, and they may be conflated with other factors. For example, PATENT and NEW_CAPAB conflate what we would like to measure with the expected economic value of an innovation. At the same time, such shortcomings might be viewed more favorably: the incorporation of the expected economic value of the innovation into the firm's decision to invest in patents or capabilities might thereby make these indicators more accurate reflections of the importance of the innovation.

Despite these limitations, we argue that our measures nonetheless reflect to some degree the different dimensions of innovation identified above and provide a basis for addressing the question of how important a respondent's "most important" innovation is and in what sense.

4.4.4   Interpreting the Measures

4.4.4.1   *Are the "New or Significantly Improved" Innovations Important?*

Using the measures of the different dimensions, one can estimate innovation rates for which there is some confidence that the innovations in question are significant beyond the simple assessment of whether a product is simply new to the market. In this section, we build on our findings reported above that 16 percent of firms are innovators (i.e., with new-to-the-market innovations) in the manufacturing sector and 18 percent in the service sector, as shown in tables 4.2a and 4.2b. How does the innovation rate change if we focus, say, on just those innovations that garner more than 10 percent, or even 50 percent, of an innovator's sales? The rates drop markedly, to 8 percent and 5 percent, respectively, for the manufacturing sector and 11 percent and 8 percent for the service sector industries, suggesting that a sizable fraction—about half for manufacturing—that report a new-to-the-market innovation are realizing 10 percent or less of their business unit sales revenue from that new product. One qualification to this particular criterion for establishing significance is that, given that it is based on the share of a firm's own sales in a market, the percentage of sales for a new product will be affected by the size of the firm. For example, the same new product that may account for 10 percent of a large firm's sales may represent a much larger share of sales for a small firm. The consequence is that, in using this particular measure for assessing the utility of a given innovation, one typically needs to control for firm size, as we do in analyses below.

Another possible filter for assessing importance is the percentage of innovations that are sufficiently different from what firms produced or delivered previously that they had to purchase new types of equipment or hire personnel with different skills (New_EqSk) to bring the innovation to market. As noted above, this variable not only reflects distance but, given that it is a realization, also reflects a judgment of the expected value of an innovation. From table 4.3a, we see that 47 percent of innovating respondents in the manufacturing sector reported this to be the case, implying that only about 8 percent of our respondents in the manufacturing sector (i.e., 16 percent * 47 percent) introduced an innovation that required such investments. What about innovating firms having to develop new sales and distribution channels (New_Mktg)? Only 6 percent of respondents (i.e., 16 percent * 39 percent) in the manufacturing sector introduced an innovation requiring such activity. Finally, what is the rate at which firms undertook both of these activities to commercialize their innovations—that is, develop new distri-

Table 4.3a   Summary statistics for innovation indicators for manufacturing sector

Manufacturing industries (N)	Inno Rate (%)	Inno Sales (%)	Patent Rate (%)	INNO RIVALS (N)	NEW CAPAB (%)	New Mktg (%)	New EqSk (%)
Food (302)	13	17	32	2.0	25	38	49
Beverage and Tobacco (60)	18	32	59	2.5	70	80	70
Textile Mills (39)	26	5	66	2.7	41	52	52
Textile Product Mills (76)	16	12	40	1.5	28	28	30
Apparel and Leather (97)	12	18	72	1.6	28	72	38
Wood Product (75)	7	15	3	2.7	52	76	76
Paper (125)	16	12	37	1.6	31	43	36
Printing and Related Support (187)	7	19	38	2.8	43	57	76
Petroleum and Coal Products (47)	20	11	71	4.0	24	48	29
Chemical (except Pharma) (318)	25	14	46	2.1	16	36	30
Pharmaceutical and Medicine (128)	31	31	66	2.4	7	21	42
Plastics and Rubber (340)	17	16	57	2.3	18	34	44
Nonmetallic Mineral (324)	9	13	45	2.0	12	29	25
Primary Metal (325)	9	9	36	2.0	20	31	52
Fabricated Metal (426)	10	17	41	2.0	15	22	52
Machinery (389)	21	19	58	2.1	19	35	44
Computers/Electronics (except Semiconductor) (287)	36	24	62	2.3	27	41	49
Semiconductor and Other (302)	28	23	65	2.4	30	41	56
Electrical Equipment (315)	28	20	62	2.4	15	34	34
Transportation Equipment (344)	27	26	46	1.9	23	32	47
Furniture and Related Product (263)	14	20	44	2.6	10	35	36
Medical Equipment (136)	21	27	77	2.5	42	59	67
Miscellaneous (except Medical) (252)	26	19	51	2.3	35	58	47
Manufacturing all (5157)	16	19	50	2.2	24	39	47
Large (1267)	39	12	72	2.5	16	30	45
Medium (946)	23	14	53	2.5	22	35	48
Small (2944)	13	21	46	2.1	26	42	47

Notes: INNO_RATE (%): Share of innovators (i.e., those having a new-to-the-market innovation); Inno_Sales (%): Mean % of total sales from new-to-the-market innovations; Patent Rate (%): Share of innovators that patented any part of their new-to-the-market innovation or have a patented externally sourced innovation; INNO_RIVALS (N): Mean number of rivals capable of introducing competing innovation; NEW_CAPAB (%): Share of innovators that developed new sales/distribution channels *and* bought new types of equipment or hired employees with new skills; New_Mktg (%): Share of innovators that developed new sales/distribution channels; New_EqSk (%): Share of innovators that bought new types of equipment or hired employees with new skills.

bution channels *and* acquire new types of equipment or hire personnel with different skills (NEW_CAPAB)? In the manufacturing sector, only 4 percent (i.e., 16 percent ∗ 24 percent) of respondents meet this standard for firms' most important innovations. In the service sector, table 4.3b shows that 60 percent of innovating respondents reported that they had to purchase new types of equipment or hire personnel with different skills, implying that 11 percent of respondents introduced an innovation requiring such invest-

Table 4.3b   **Summary statistics for innovation indicators for selected service sector industries**

Service industries	Inno Rate (%)	Inno Sales (%)	Patent Rate (%)	INNO RIVALS (N)	NEW CAPAB (%)	New Mktg (%)	New EqSk (%)
Software Publishers (87)	36	25	56	2.9	41	67	42
Motion Picture and Sound (47)	17	28	84	2.7	59	59	75
Telecommunications (101)	15	28	56	2.5	45	48	76
Data Processing (83)	15	44	21	2.5	68	93	70
Professional, Scientific, and Tech Svc (162)	17	26	58	2.3	45	56	56
Engineering Svc (130)	13	15	37	2.6	19	19	55
Computer Systems Design (104)	25	34	38	3.4	35	49	67
Service all (714)	18	27	47	2.8	40	51	60
Large (145)	38	26	74	3.0	46	60	54
Medium (98)	20	13	49	2.7	28	47	43
Small (471)	17	29	43	2.7	40	50	64

Notes: INNO_RATE (%): Share of innovators (i.e., those having a new-to-the-market innovation); Inno_Sales (%): Mean % of total sales from new-to-the-market innovations; Patent Rate (%): Share of innovators that patented any part of their new-to-the-market innovation or have a patented externally sourced innovation; INNO_RIVALS (N): Mean number of rivals capable of introducing competing innovation; NEW_CAPAB (%): Share of innovators that developed new sales/distribution channels *and* bought new types of equipment or hired employees with new skills; New_Mktg (%): Share of innovators that developed new sales/distribution channels; New_EqSk (%): Share of innovators that bought new types of equipment or hired employees with new skills.

ments (i.e., 18 percent * 60 percent). Similarly, 51 percent of innovators had to develop new sales and distribution channels, implying that 9 percent of respondents had an innovation requiring such activity (i.e., 18 percent * 51 percent). Only 7 percent (i.e., 18 percent * 40 percent) of respondents had an innovation that required both kinds of new capabilities. This exercise distinguishes between the larger share of firms that have reported innovation per the simple "new-to-the-market" criterion from innovations that likely differ from what the firms have commercialized before and are of much greater value given that the measure signals investment in new equipment, personnel, and sales capabilities.

Thus we suggest that using criteria based either on percentage of sales or on significant investments tied to commercialization can inform judgments about the relative importance of respondents' innovations. We are also able to flexibly apply such measures as screens to refine those judgments.

4.4.4.2 Are the Dimensions Distinct?

We have suggested that while in theory our measures should reflect distinct features of an innovation, the measures as constructed are also likely related for reasons outlined above. To assess how distinct they are from one another, we calculated the correlations among these measures, computed

Table 4.4   Correlations (for manufacturing industries having 10 or more innovators)

	Inno Rate	Imit Rate	Inno Sales	Patent Rate	INNO RIVALS	NEW CAPAB	New Mktg
Inno Rate	1.00						
Imit Rate	0.13	1.00					
Inno Sales	0.22	0.17	1.00				
Patent Rate	**0.43**	0.11	**0.39**	1.00			
INNO_RIVALS	0.15	**0.70**	0.22	0.08	1.00		
NEW_CAPAB	−0.15	0.14	**0.38**	0.27	−0.10	1.00	
New Mktg	−0.12	0.04	0.12	**0.45**	−0.18	**0.79**	1.00
New EqSk	−0.04	0.11	**0.51**	**0.36**	0.00	**0.79**	**0.56**

Notes: N = 32 disaggregated manufacturing industries. INNO_RATE (%): Share of innova-tors (i.e., those having a new-to-the-market innovation); Inno_Sales (%): Mean % of total sales from new-to-the-market innovations; Patent Rate (%): Share of innovators that patented any part of their new-to-the-market innovation or have a patented externally sourced innova-tion; INNO_RIVALS (N): Mean number of rivals capable of introducing competing innova-tion; NEW_CAPAB (%): Share of innovators that developed new sales/distribution channels *and* bought new types of equipment or hired employees with new skills; New_Mktg (%): Share of innovators that developed new sales/distribution channels; New_EqSk (%): Share of in-novators that bought new types of equipment or hired employees with new skills. Bold means $p < .05$.

at the industry level, as shown in table 4.4. For the purpose of this exercise, we define our industries at a relatively disaggregated level, at the three- or four-digit NAICs code level, and apply a cutoff of at least 10 innovator observations per industry. This breakdown yields 32 manufacturing indus-tries.[17] This analysis could not be conducted for our selected service sector industries due to too few industries that meet the 10 observation cutoff. For the manufacturing sector, we observe that while a number of these vari-ables are correlated, it would appear that they do reflect distinct dimensions. Using our main indicators (INNO_SALES, PATENT, INNO_RIVALS, and NEW_CAPAB), we find that none of the correlations exceed 0.4, and relatively few are significant at conventional levels. We also find that each is correlated with the rate of innovation but none with a correlation coef-ficient above 0.5. We also observe that some of these dimensions are more closely related than others. For example, INNO_SALES, the average share of sales due to the innovation, is correlated with NEW_CAPAB, the per-centage of innovating firms' investment in new types of equipment, per-sonnel, and the development of distribution channels (r = 0.38), sensibly suggesting a link between investment in innovation commercialization and demand conditions. We also observe that our measure of the technologi-cal significance of the innovation—namely, the percentage of innovations

17. We started with 41 disaggregated manufacturing industries. After excluding manufactur-ing industries with fewer than 10 innovators, we ended up with a total of 32 manufacturing industries.

within an industry that are linked to a patent (PATENT)—is also correlated with INNO_SALES (r = 0.39). Although PATENT is a rather imprecise measure of technological significance given the low bar for patentability, the relationship is consistent with a link between the incentive to patent an innovation and its economic value. PATENT is also sensibly correlated with the percentage of firms within industries that claim to be innovators (r=0.43). In our correlation matrix, we also include the variable IMITATORS, which is the percentage of firms that report that they introduced a product new to the firm but not to the industry. We see that this measure is strongly and sensibly related to our measure of imitability, INNO_RIVALS (r = 0.70), our measure of the number of firms that "have introduced or are likely to introduce" a competing innovation.

4.4.4.3   Selected Cross-Industry Differences and Similarities in the Nature of Innovation

Table 4.5 ranks 24 industries on our measures of the different attributes of innovations (based on disaggregated industries spanning manufacturing and business services, again dropping industries with fewer than 10 innovators, and then aggregating to the displayed industry categories) and thus highlights important similarities and differences in the character of innovation across industries. In the table, we have highlighted the top third and bottom third of industries on each measure to illustrate the variation in innovation characteristics across industries. Some examples may help illustrate the multidimensionality of innovation and how this varies across industries. To start with some typical examples, we observe that medical devices—typically thought of as a highly innovative industry—ranks highly on most dimensions of innovativeness, particularly share of sales, the patent rate, and investments in new capabilities for commercializing their innovations, although it is only average in terms of the innovation rate (INNO_RATE). Computers and semiconductors also rank either high or average on several dimensions. On the low-innovation end, we have industries such as mineral products and metal products, which have low rates of innovation and relatively low values on several of our dimensions of innovativeness (sales, patenting, and new capabilities). We see a similar pattern in engineering services (with low rates of innovation, sales from innovation, patenting, and investment in capabilities) even though this might be seen as a technology-based industry. Hence these industries largely follow the patterns we expect, although medical equipment is more imitator dominated than many might expect. On the other hand, when we compare chemicals and plastics with pharmaceuticals, we see some telling differences. We find all three of these chemistry-based industries at or above the median for innovation, with pharmaceuticals the highest and all at or above the median on patenting, again with pharmaceuticals the highest. Pharmaceuticals stands out in terms of the share of sales from the innovation, with its 31 percent well above the

Table 4.5   Industry "innovativeness" rankings

Industry (no. of innovators)	INNO RATE	Inno Sales	Patent Rate	NEW CAPAB
Food (54)	*13*	*17*	*32*	25
Beverage and Tobacco (10)	18	**32**	**59**	**70**
Textile Product Mills (12)	16	*12*	*40*	28
Apparel and Leather (14)	*12*	18	**72**	28
Paper (30)	16	*12*	*37*	**31**
Printing and Related Support (18)	*7*	19	*38*	**43**
Chemical (except Pharma) (88)	**25**	*14*	45	*15*
Pharmaceutical and Medicine (34)	**31**	**31**	**66**	*7*
Plastics and Rubber (74)	17	*16*	**57**	*18*
Nonmetallic Mineral (36)	*9*	*13*	45	*12*
Primary Metal (37)	*13*	*10*	*41*	23
Fabricated Metal (51)	16	19	43	*16*
Machinery (86)	22	19	52	22
Computers/Electronics (except Semiconductor) (108)	**36**	24	**62**	27
Semiconductor and Other (93)	**28**	23	**65**	30
Electrical Equipment (93)	**28**	20	**62**	*15*
Transportation Equipment (102)	27	26	46	23
Furniture and Related Product (41)	*14*	20	44	*10*
Medical Equipment (37)	21	**27**	**77**	**42**
Software Publishers (30)	**36**	25	56	**41**
Data Processing (17)	*15*	**44**	*21*	**68**
Professional, Scientific, and Technical Svc (28)	16	25	55	**53**
Engineering Svc (23)	*13*	*15*	*37*	*19*
Computer Systems Design (15)	24	24	*35*	**40**
Mean	20	21	50	29
Median	17	19	46	26

Notes: Based on 37 disaggregated industries spanning manufacturing (N = 32) and business services (N = 5), again dropping industries with fewer than 10 innovators and then aggregating to the displayed industry categories, excluding Miscellaneous Manufacturing industries. Bold reflects the top tercile on a given dimension; italics indicate the bottom tercile. INNO_RATE (%): Share of innovators (i.e., those having a new-to-the-market innovation); Inno_Sales (%): Mean % of total sales from new-to-the-market innovations; Patent Rate (%): Share of innovators that patented any part of their new-to-the-market innovation or have a patented externally sourced innovation; NEW_CAPAB (%): Share of innovators that developed new sales/distribution channels *and* bought new types of equipment or hired employees with new skills.

mean, while chemicals and plastics are well below the mean at 14 percent and 16 percent, respectively. Recalling that this share-of-sales figure reflects the share of business unit sales for the innovation that accounts for a plurality of the respondent's revenue, these results suggest that drug companies are much more focused on single blockbuster innovations as compared to other chemicals industries that appear to be focused on a larger number of innovations with more modest market impacts. Also, all three show low rates of investment in new capabilities, but with pharmaceuticals the lowest by far. Hence while the innovations in chemicals, especially pharmaceuticals, are ranked highly on market impact and technical significance, they also tend to be low on our measure for distance, even compared to medical devices. These figures suggest clear differences in the nature of innovation across industries and suggest differences in innovation strategies. For example, firms in some industries tend to hew closely to existing capabilities or focus more on blockbusters.

**4.5   Illustrating the Utility of Measuring the Characteristics
of Innovations**

4.5.1   Differences across Sectors and Industries

With these measures, we can also compare empirical patterns across sectors and industries that further reflect differences in both the nature of innovation and its impact. For example, above we saw the baseline innovation rate between the manufacturing and service sectors to be close: 16 percent versus 18 percent, respectively (See tables 4.2a and 4.2b). Once we consider impacts and "significant" innovation rates, the story changes. For example, we see that the average percent of business unit sales accounted for by the firm's most important innovations (INNO_SALES) is substantially higher in the service sector, at 27 percent, versus 19 percent for the manufacturing sector (see tables 4.3a and 4.3b). We also observed in section 4.4 that a higher proportion of respondents in services—7 percent (i.e., 18 percent ∗ 40 percent)—invested in new types of equipment and personnel and developed new distribution channels relative to the 4 percent observed in the manufacturing sector. We probe what may lie behind this pattern by comparing the sales revenue distributions of innovations in manufacturing versus software.

4.5.2   Software versus Manufacturing

In figure 4.2, we present a frequency distribution of the percentage of respondents in, respectively, the manufacturing sector and software industries, ordered by the contribution of their most important product innovation to business unit sales. For this analysis, we define software broadly to include software publishers, data processing, and computer systems design (cf. tables 4.2b and 4.3b). What we observe for the manufacturing sector is expected—namely, that the share of respondents largely declines as the reported share of business unit sales accounted for by their most important innovation increases. In other words, it is relatively rare for a recently introduced innovation (i.e., a new-to-the-market product)—even that which accounts for a plurality of a firm's sales in a market—to account for more than 50 percent of business unit sales. We find the opposite pattern, however, for software, where the percentage of respondents increases with the reported share of business unit sales accounted for by their most important innovation. Indeed, it is common for software firms' most important innova-

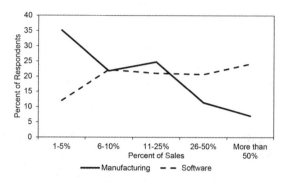

Fig. 4.2   Share of sales from innovation, manufacturing vs. software

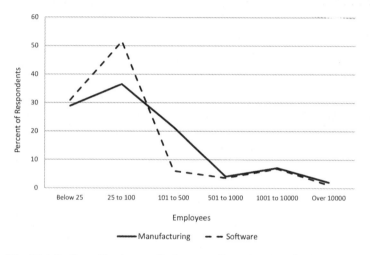

Fig. 4.3   Distribution of business unit size, manufacturing vs. software

tion to account for more than half of the business unit sales.[18] To see whether these differences are driven by differences in the size distribution between manufacturing and software, we examine the business unit size distributions. Figure 4.3 shows that the size distributions are very similar between those two sectors, with a large percentage of small firms in each, suggesting that the differences in business unit sales in figure 4.2 may not be driven by differences in the size distribution. We confirmed this by using a linear probability model, regressing a dummy variable indicating whether an innovation accounted for more than a 50 percent share of business unit sales against a dummy variable representing software (versus manufacturing), as well as

18. One qualification is that we have compared software with all manufacturing. However, when we compare software with only those manufacturing industries that may be considered high innovation intensity industries, identified as those with above-the-median industry share of sales from products that are new to the firm, we find similar differences in the frequency distributions.

the log of business unit employees, and find that software innovations are significantly more likely to account for more than 50 percent of sales, even controlling for business unit size. We find the same result if we use more than a 25 percent share as the dependent variable.

To understand the different frequency distributions in figure 4.2, we might consider that a new software product can reach a larger market more quickly and at lower cost than a new product in the manufacturing sector due to digitization and the low cost of distribution via the web. In contrast, the investment and associated adjustment costs and time lags for expanding capacity and distributing goods are much higher in manufacturing. This would suggest that in software, the cost of expansion tied to a successful product will be lower and the returns to investment in the production and distribution of a product higher than in manufacturing, consistent with the notion that greater scale can be achieved with a lower fixed cost investment in software.[19]

While the greater returns to fixed investment in product and sales capabilities may explain more rapid growth in software sales tied to a firm's highest-selling new product, it alone cannot, however, explain our figure 4.2 results showing that very high sales shares associated with this highest-selling innovation are more common in software than in manufacturing. What could provide an explanation is the possibility that software firms' most important new products are more likely to replace a prior leading product in software as compared to manufacturing; that is, software firms' leading products are more likely to cannibalize prior generations of a leading product. If this were true, we should see little change in software firms' market share tied to new product introductions. To consider this possibility, in table 4.6 we present the results of a simple ordinary least squares (OLS) probability model regressing the direction of the change in market share on INNO_SALES and log of business unit (BU) size. We code whether a respondent's market share declines (coded as "−1"), stays the same (coded as "0"), or grows ("+1"). Consistent with our conjecture, we observe no relationship between market share change and INNO_SALES in software. In contrast, in manufacturing, we see a significant positive relationship between direction of change in market share and INNO_SALES.[20]

19. If the returns to investment in production and distribution tied to innovation in software exceed those in manufacturing, we might expect to see a stronger link between the share of own-business unit sales tied to firms' most important new products (INNO_SALES) and their investment in new equipment, personnel, and distribution channels (NEW_CAPAB), as well as between INNO_SALES and a component of NEW_CAPAB—namely, whether the firm developed new marketing and distribution channels to commercialize the innovation (New_Mktg). Indeed, the correlation between INNO_SALES and NEW_CAPAB for software ($r = 0.30$) exceeds that for manufacturing ($r = 0.15$), and the correlation between INNO_SALES and New_Mktg ($r = 0.43$) reflects a much tighter link between investment in the development of new sales and distribution channels and revenues in the software industry than that observed for the manufacturing sector ($r = 0.12$).

20. Due to the large standard error on the estimate of the coefficient for INNO_SALES for software firms ($N = 54$), we cannot, however, reject the null hypothesis that the coefficients for manufacturing and software are equal ($F = 1.06$, $p = 0.3$). The results are qualitatively identical when we use an ordered logit model.

Table 4.6   Regression of market share change on innovation sales share, for manufacturing and software

	MS change (manufacturing)			MS change (software)		
Parameter	Estimate (SE)	Estimate (SE)	Estimate (SE)	Estimate (SE)	Estimate (SE)	Estimate (SE)
INNO_SALES		0.006*** (0.001)	0.005*** (0.001)		0.002 (0.005)	0.000 (0.005)
ln(BU Size)	−0.033** (0.015)		−0.022 (0.015)	−0.162** (0.062)		−0.161** (0.062)
Intercept	0.651*** (0.074)	0.398*** (0.041)	0.500*** (0.085)	1.263*** (0.223)	0.553*** (0.201)	1.251*** (0.261)
N	899	899	899	54	54	54
R^2	0.008	0.032	0.035	0.109	0.003	0.109

Notes: OLS regression coefficients displayed with *at .10; ** at .05; *** at .01. Standard errors in parentheses.

4.5.3   Competition and Innovation

In this section, we consider whether we can use our measures of innovation and its attributes to shed light on one of the long-standing preoccupations of the literature on innovation: the link between market competition and the innovative performance of industries.[21] Using the measures constructed above, we explore a conjecture—that the link between competition and innovation may differ markedly depending on the nature of competition within industries. For this analysis, we propose dividing industries into two types—one where product innovation is central to competition and another where product innovation matters less for competition—where firms compete, for example, mainly via price or advertising. Using the same sample of manufacturing industries employed in section 4.4, we divide these industries into two groups. We will use our measure of the percentage of sales due to products that are new to the firm—but not necessarily new to the market—to coarsely distinguish between industries where competition features innovation versus industries where it does not. We again apply a cutoff of 10 observations of innovators per industry and divide the industries at the median value of this measure (i.e., the percentage of sales due to products that are new to the firm) and simply characterize the 16 industries that are above the median as innovation intensive and the other 16 industries as not.

Table 4.7 shows the means for our featured variables between the two industry groups. As shown in table 4.7, almost all the innovation indicators in the innovation-intensive industries exceed their corresponding values in the less-innovation-intensive industries. What is surprising is the relationship

---

21. See Cohen (2010) for a review of this vast literature.

Table 4.7   **Innovation indicators for low and high innovation intensity industries**

	Manufacturing		
		NTF sales	
	All (4,590)	Low (2,286)	High (2,304)
INNO RATE (%)	18	16	20
Imit Rate (%)	25	24	25
INNO SALES (%)	20	17	22
NTF Sales (%)	24	20	27
Patent Rate (%)	51	45	55
NEW_CAPAB (%)	24	21	26
New Mktg (%)	39	36	42
New EqSk (%)	46	41	51
INNO_RIVALS (N)	2.2	2.1	2.3

Notes: For industries having 10 or more innovators. Low/high based on below or equal to / above median of industry means of the percentage of sales due to new-to-the-firm innovations. INNO_RATE (%): Share of innovators (i.e., those having a new-to-the-market innovation); Imit Rate (%): Share of imitators; INNO_SALES (%): Mean % of total sales from new-to-the-market innovationsl NTF Sales (%): Mean % of total sales from new-to-the-firm innovations; Patent Rate (%): Share of innovators that patented any part of their new-to-the-market innovation or have a patented externally sourced innovation; NEW_CAPAB (%): Share of innovators that developed new sales/distribution channels *and* bought new types of equipment or hired employees with new skills; New_Mktg (%): Share of innovators that developed new sales/distribution channels; New_EqSk (%): Share of innovators that bought new types of equipment or hired employees with new skills; INNO_RIVALS (N): Mean number of rivals capable of introducing a competing innovation.

between technological competition and industry innovation rates. For this exercise, we employ our measure, INNO_RIVALS—the number of firms that "have introduced or are likely to introduce" a competing innovation—as a measure of the intensity of competition based on product innovation rather than as a measure of imitability. Comparing more- and less-innovation-intensive industries, we observe a clear difference in the relationship between the percentage of firms that are innovators (not imitators) within industries (INNO_RATE) and INNO_RIVALS. In the innovation-intensive industries, the correlation is 0.47. In the less-innovation-intensive industries, in contrast, the correlation is –0.10 and statistically insignificant.[22] This difference is consistent with the idea that in more innovation-intensive industries, competition stimulates product innovation—approximating what Aghion et al. (2005) have called "neck and neck" competition—while in less-innovative industries, where competition may largely take other forms (e.g., price), there is little relationship between the share of innovating (new-

22. We also find a sharp qualitative difference in the relationship between the percentage of firms that are innovators within industries (NTM) and the percentage of firms that are imitators (IMITATOR). In the innovation-intensive industries, the correlation is 0.46, while in the less innovation-intensive industries, the correlation is −0.30.

to-the-market) firms and firms subject to more-intense competition around product innovation. Consistent with this observation is the possibility that in innovation-intensive industries, there is greater pressure to develop and commercialize more-significant product innovations to "escape from competition" (per Aghion et al. 2005). To probe this, we examine the relationship between the average share of business unit sales attributed to the firm's most important innovation, INNO_SALES, and investment in new capabilities to commercialize the innovation, NEW_CAPAB. Across the more innovation-intensive industries, the correlation is 0.47, as compared to −0.12 in the less innovative industries. This suggests that in the innovation-intensive industries, where technological competition is more severe, firms are introducing more "distant"—and likely more valuable—innovations requiring more investment in new capabilities, while in the less-innovation-based industries, there is little relationship between the sales share attributable to new products and the need for new capabilities, suggesting that the innovations introduced in such industries are more incremental and more closely tied to existing capabilities. A substantive implication of this argument is that for models tying R&D to the intensity of competition, it may be useful to recognize that the forms of competition differ across industries, and innovation of a more substantive, perhaps more technical, sort is simply not an important means of competing in many industries.

4.5.4   Innovation-Level Indicators of Value and Outside Sources of Invention

Analyzing innovators' acquisitions of inventions from outside sources using the same data as employed here, Arora, Cohen, and Walsh (2016) also illustrate the value of our innovation-specific attributes. For the present purpose, we will build on one of the questions addressed in Arora, Cohen, and Walsh (2016): For firms that acquire their key inventions from an outside source, how does the value of those inventions vary by source? For example, how does the value of inventions acquired from customers compare with that from other sources—say, internally generated suppliers, or what Arora, Cohen, and Walsh call "technology specialists," which include universities, independent inventors, and contractors.

The extent to which a firm's innovation draws on a particular source should reflect the net surplus—the value of the invention from that source minus the cost of acquiring and commercializing it. Arora, Cohen, and Walsh (2016) report that customers are the most pervasive outside source of inventions in the manufacturing sector. A further analysis showed, however, that inventions sourced from technology specialists are of higher value and that the high share of customer-sourced inventions is associated with a relatively low cost of acquisition. Arora, Cohen, and Walsh (2016) did not, however, go further than interpreting all their measures as simply different indicators of

Table 4.8   **Different dimensions of innovativeness of innovations by source**

	Econ. val.	Distance		Tech. sig.
	Sales >50%	New_EqSk	New_Mktg	Patent
Customer	−0.06***	−0.04	0.00	−0.08**
	(0.02)	(0.04)	(0.04)	(0.03)
Supplier	0.06**	−0.19***	0.01	−0.11**
	(0.03)	(0.05)	(0.05)	(0.05)
Tech special	0.07***	0.14**	0.10**	0.28***
	(0.03)	(0.05)	(0.04)	(0.04)
Other firm	−0.03	0.00	0.02	−0.08
	(0.03)	(0.06)	(0.06)	(0.06)
Controls (R&D, size, industry dummies, parent size, age)	Yes	Yes	Yes	Yes
Obs	927	1,012	1,017	1,019
R^2	0.15	0.14	0.16	0.26

Selected results from Arora, Cohen, and Walsh (2016).

Notes: Excluded category is Internal. OLS regression coefficients displayed with *at .10; ** at .05; *** at .01. Standard errors in parentheses.

the economic value of innovation. They did not consider what particular features of innovation each of those different measures might also reflect. Reinterpreting these measures as reflecting distinct features of innovation, we relate the likelihood of scoring high on these different dimensions to the origin of these innovations—that is, whether they originate from suppliers, customers, technology specialists (universities, engineering firms, or R&D service contractors), other firms in the industry, or internally. In our framework, the different dimensions of innovations include (1) utility, measured as whether the associated sales accounts for more than 50 percent of business unit sales; (2) distance, measured as whether the innovator invests in new equipment or hires personnel with distinct skills (New_EqSk) to commercialize the innovation (distance) or develops new sales and distribution channels (New_Mktg); and (3) technological significance, measured as whether there is a patent on the innovation. Table 4.8 presents the results.[23] Since all the dependent variables in table 4.8 are expressed as dummy variables, we can compare coefficients across the specifications. We see that the impacts of particular sources vary across the different dimensions of innovation. Specifically, inventions originating from technology specialists have an especially strong association with technological significance compared to their impact on the distance or utility measures, which is consistent with the notion that innovations sourced from technology specialists are best characterized by

23. These are based on tables 5a and 5b in Arora, Cohen, and Walsh (2016).

their technological significance. On the other hand, we find a clear negative relationship between suppliers as a source and the likelihood that the innovating firm invests in new types of equipment—that is, distance as compared to its relationship with utility or technological significance. This is consistent with the notion that existing equipment suppliers in particular are unlikely to offer innovation ideas that will require their customers—that is, the innovating firms—to purchase types of equipment that are very different from what they are already employing. In other words, supplier-sourced innovations tend to be characterized by relatively low distance. This analysis suggests that our dimensions can be used to understand not just the relative value of different sources, as Arora, Cohen, and Walsh (2016) do, but also the nature of the innovations derived from different sources (e.g., their technical significance or distance). Furthermore, these analyses again show a benefit of focusing on a single innovation when asking about sources of innovation, as this is what allows comparisons of the character of innovation across the different sources of the underlying invention.

4.6   Suggestions for New Attribute-Based Innovation Measures

As noted, the survey providing the basis for our empirical analyses above was not originally designed for developing measures of all the attributes of innovation considered in our conceptual discussion. In this section, building on both our conceptual discussion and empirical analyses, we offer suggestions for other measures of the different attributes of innovation featured in our conceptual discussion. Recall that these measures should focus on a specific innovation. We will again confine our discussion to product innovations and survey-based measures.

Technological Significance. Our current measure of *technological significance* is a dichotomous measure of whether an invention underlying the innovation had a patent associated with it. As suggested above, this measure is limited. First, the technical standards for patentability are low, and second, a large fraction of inventions are not patented. To overcome the limitations of this measure, one suggestion is to ask respondents to assign scores for the invention underlying the innovations, asking respondents for their judgments regarding technological significance (No and Walsh 2010; Walsh, Lee, and Nagaoka 2016). For example, adapting language from the survey of American and Japanese inventors of patented inventions (Nagaoka and Walsh 2009), one might simply ask respondents, "Compared to other technical developments in your field during the year the focal innovation was commercialized, how would you rate the technical significance of your invention?" with the corresponding categories: *Top 10 percent, Top 25 percent but not top 10 percent, Top half but not top 25 percent, Bottom half,* and *Don't know.* Although this measure may not be free from potential reporting biases, it represents an expert assessment of relative technological significance.[24] This question is also targeted to technological significance apart from the innovation's economic value or impact. One may also pose a prior question to assess whether the innovation—that is, the firm's new or significantly improved product—reflects any technological advance at all and to what extent. One approach would be to ask whether the product is based on the firm's own R&D or if it embodies purchased (e.g., licensed) technology. A complementary line of questioning might assess whether the technology embodied in the new product differs markedly from competing firms' products. One would then, of course, define what "markedly" may mean—for example, employing new technological approaches to solving technical problems.[25]

To assess whether the innovation actually reflects a technological advance affecting product performance, one could inquire if the innovation was functionally superior on any performance dimension to existing products or whether it was simply different but not functionally superior (e.g., a different flavor of toothpaste or a new clothing design). To the extent that there are well-established performance metrics (e.g., clock speed for chips, conversion rate for solar cells, miles per gallon, or miles per charge), one might elicit estimates of performance improvements over existing products.

Another aspect of technological significance is whether the innovation in question provides a basis for subsequent advance. We would again suggest a question based on observable behavior or outcomes. For example, one may inquire whether the firm has a follow-on R&D project dedicated to improving the product or has contracted with another firm to do so.

Utility. Our main measure employed in our empirical analysis reflected the share of own sales linked to a new product. This measure, as noted above, is limited given that it reflects not only some measure of utility on the part of buyers but also the pricing, marketing, and other decisions made by the firm. There are, however, any number of other questions that one might ask to elicit information about utility. For example, respondents may have a sense of both the addressable market—that is, the potential market size—and the

24. Prior work suggests this may be a useful ordinal measure of technological significance. Walsh, Lee, and Nagaoka (2016) report that among patents granted in the United States and also filed in Japan and Europe (triadic patents), 15 percent of US inventors rated their patents in the top 10 percent in technical significance, and 34 percent reported being in the bottom 50 percent. Since we would expect an overrepresentation of inventions of high technical significance in a sample of triadic patents (compared to all patented and unpatented inventions), these figures suggest that inventors were reasonably accurate in their assessments of the relative technological significance of their patents. This self-reported measure has also been shown to be correlated with commercialization of the invention, project size (the number of person-months dedicated to the project), patent scope (the number of IPC classes the patent spans), and forward citations, all of which we might expect to be correlated with technological significance (No and Walsh 2010; Walsh, Lee, and Nagaoka 2016).

25. One caution in implementing these questions is that marketing or similar personnel may not be able to assess the technical contributions of their or others' innovations, requiring use of a different-respondents-for-different-questions approach, as in the NSF Business R&D and Innovation Survey.

share of the addressable market that their product reached. Presumably the size of the addressable market will relate to the product's expected growth in sales over time. Such information again, however, reflects outcomes of pricing and other decisions on the part of the firm and its rivals. We would also want to ask whether the new product is sold mainly to existing customers, new buyers in a market that the firm currently serves, or buyers in a new market. The answer to these questions would also be useful in our consideration of the dimension of "distance" discussed below. Potentially bearing on both utility and technological significance, one could also inquire whether the innovation reflects an improvement on an existing product or an altogether new product.

Other questions addressing utility would consider whose utility. For example, one could ask whether it is end consumers or firms that buy the firm's new products. Per the discussion above on whether a firm's innovation provides the basis for subsequent advance, it would also be useful to know whether the firm's innovation is employed by firms in either its industry or other industries in follow-on R&D leading to new products or technologies, which would be the case, for example, with general-purpose technologies.

Another important limitation of market-based measures of utility, as noted above, is that there are innovations for which most prospective users of a new product may not be able to afford the product (e.g., a malaria vaccine in Africa). Thus in lieu of market-based metrics, it would be useful to ask, for example, how many lives may be affected or even saved by the provision of the product. In some industries (e.g., hospitals or medicine), one could also elicit measures of improvements in patient outcomes (e.g., time until recovery, reductions in mortality or morbidity, changes in life expectancy).

Distance. As discussed above, we think of distance or the implementation gap as reflecting the degree to which either the firm's own capabilities or the external environment—particularly the absence of complementary goods or services—may constrain the firm's ability to commercialize a new invention. We suggest that our two measures employed in our empirical analysis—whether the firm needed to acquire new equipment or personnel with new skills, on the one hand, or acquire new sales or distribution channels, on the other—represent useful measures. One necessary change, however, is to separate the question of hiring new personnel from that of acquiring equipment.

Another question regarding the internal constraints on commercialization would be to inquire if the firm needed to reorganize its operations in any way to commercialize the innovation.[26] Similarly, one might consider if commercialization of the product required entirely new organizational units

---

26. To make this more concrete, one might ask if, in the course of commercializing the innovation, the firm had to modify any business objectives, the way decision rights are allocated in the firm, the way product or personnel performance is evaluated, or reporting structures or incentive systems or if new alliances and partnerships with other firms in previously unrelated downstream or upstream industries had to be developed.

or capabilities to produce and/or deliver the product. An example is the iPod, which required a new platform, iTunes, to deliver music and challenged an assumption that music should be sold in a physical album and that online music file sharing should be free.

To the extent that the inventions underlying an innovation originate from other industries or reflect technologies that are not typically employed by the firm, this may limit the ease with which the firm's own capabilities and practices will support the innovation or even its acquisition. Therefore, we can measure *distance* by asking the respondent if the concept for the new product originates from their own industry or from a different industry or employs technologies with which the firm has no experience.[27] We could also ask whether developing the invention required expertise from outside the firm.[28]

There is also that aspect of distance concerned with the external constraints on commercialization. Specifically, it would be useful to know if commercialization of the product required complementary products or services offered by other firms and whether the lack of such complements impeded either the quality or the availability of the firm's new product. For example, Walsh, Lee, and Jung (2016) asked if the reasons for not commercializing an invention included delays in the availability of complementary technologies or the absence of application technologies.

Replicability/Uniqueness. Currently, our measure, based on the number of firms that "have introduced or are likely to introduce" a competing innovation, not only conflates imitability with technological competition; it also does not clearly distinguish the concept of *replicability* from that of *uniqueness.* To address uniqueness, future surveys could ask if the innovating firm was aware of other firms developing similar products at the time of product introduction. For another indicator of uniqueness, one could ask firms what share of their innovation projects overlap with those of their rivals, where high overlap suggests less uniqueness.[29]

To probe replicability, one could ask if another firm introduced a competing alternative and, if so, how long it was after the innovating firm's product introduction (i.e., replicability), which is adapted from the Carnegie Mellon Survey administered by Cohen et al. (2000). Furthermore, one can also ask imitators the same question: How long was it until they introduced a competing alternative to the innovator's product innovation? Asking these questions of both innovators and imitators would provide a validity check at the industry level. One could also measure replicability at the industry level by asking about the use of reverse engineering as a source of information about competitors' products.[30] Also, for those who externally sourced their

---

27. Such measures resemble bibliometric measures that use information on the technological distance between the focal invention's technology class and the technology classes documented in the patent's prior art references.

28. A similar question was asked in the Carnegie Mellon Survey (Cohen et al. 2000).

29. A version of this question was asked in the Carnegie Mellon Survey (Cohen et al. 2000).

30. A version of this question was asked in the Carnegie Mellon Survey (Cohen et al. 2000).

innovation, one could also ask whether the focal firm could have acquired a similar innovation elsewhere, as was done in the Arora, Cohen, and Walsh (2016) survey. One could use this as a measure of uniqueness, especially if the measure was used at the industry level since it suggests whether innovations are available from multiple sources.

While the bulk of our discussion has been about product innovation (in part reflecting the dominance of questions about product innovation in the Arora, Cohen, and Walsh 2016 survey), one could also measure various dimensions of process innovation. *Technological significance* could be measured using similar items, asking for a ranking comparing the process innovation to others in the industry (see the discussion above for a sample item). One could also measure performance improvements, such as time or cost per unit reductions, as measures of technological significance (as is regularly modeled in the learning by doing literature). *Distance* could be measured by indicators relating to the need to purchase new equipment or hire personnel with new skills in order to implement the process innovation. Similarly, measures of engineering hours expended implementing the process innovation might be another measure of the distance from existing practices. *Uniqueness* could be measured with items similar to those used for product innovation. For example: "Could this process innovation have been sourced from another engineering firm from the one used? Could a different plant of the same firm have developed this process innovation?" One might also ask if the process innovation depended on the existence of unique equipment or unique skills among the workforce. The Fosbury flop in high-jump is one example of a significant process innovation, in terms of performance, with low uniqueness (and also high replicability). *Replicability* might be measured by the importance of secrecy for protecting the process innovation (similar to the items in the Carnegie Mellon Survey asking about the importance of secrecy for appropriating the returns to process and to product innovations, respectively). As noted above, the Toyota Production System is seen as having low replicability and hence little need for secrecy. Process innovations in the food and chemicals industries that depend on customized bacteria might be another example of low replicability. *Utility* may be measured by the share of a firm's products that benefited from the process innovation, or by the share of the firms in an industry that adopted the process innovation. Statistical quality control or lean manufacturing processes might be examples with very high utility.

* * *

In addition to the above suggestions for guiding future innovation surveys' assessments of selected attributes of innovation, we would make one additional suggestion related to survey design more generally. We would encourage surveys to address these detailed questions not only to the innovators within an industry but to the imitators as well. Many questions about the social welfare impacts of innovation turn on the degree to which firms can and do imitate others' products.

4.7　Conclusion

We suggest that with proper design, innovation surveys can provide valuable data on innovation rates that inform judgments about whether the reported innovations are important, and in what sense, and thus are more interpretable than claims that such innovations are simply "new to the market." There are several keys to doing this. First, we recommend asking respondents questions about a specific innovation in an identified line of business. In our case, the questions focused respondents on their business unit's most important innovation, defined as that which accounted for a plurality of revenue in a line of business.[31] To advance our understanding of the impact of innovation, we also recommend conceptualizing innovation as having different dimensions. We proposed five that are potentially linked to the social welfare impacts of innovation: technological significance, utility, distance (or implementation gap), uniqueness, and imitability.

The chapter also illustrates the utility of our approach, using newly collected data from an innovation survey of the US manufacturing sector and selected service sector industries to construct measures corresponding, however roughly, to the proposed dimensions of innovation. Using these data, we showed how the measured characteristics could inform judgments about the importance of innovations in different industries. By recognizing the distinct features of innovations, we also showed how these features, when combined in novel and distinct ways in selected industries, can provide a more nuanced view of innovation and its complexity. Finally, we used our constructed measures to provide some simple, illustrative insights into the nature of innovation and its impact and how that may differ across industries distinguished by sector or by the intensity of innovation competition. More importantly, in these exercises employing our measures of the different dimensions of innovation, we established empirical relationships and patterns that raise questions for future research. Future work could also test the implications of these dimensions for firm or macroeconomic outcomes—for example, incorporating our dimensions into Crepon, Duguet, and Mairesse's (1998) models. In addition, complementary qualitative studies of the development and commercialization of specific innovations may help unpack the dimensions more clearly and develop our understandings of how the various dimensions of innovations relate to firm and industry conditions, outcomes, and social welfare impacts.

---

31. One could instead ask respondents to focus, for example, on their most recent new product to reduce the biases that come from focusing on "most important" innovations.

References

Adner, R. 2006. "Match Your Innovation Strategy to Your Innovation Ecosystem." *Harvard Business Review* 84:98–107.

Aghion, P., N. Bloom, R. Blundell, R. Griffith, and P. Howitt. 2005. "Competition and Innovation: An Inverted-U Relationship." *Quarterly Journal of Economics* 120:701–28.

Arora, A., W. M. Cohen, and J. P. Walsh. 2016. "The Acquisition and Commercialization of Invention in American Manufacturing: Incidence and Impact." *Research Policy* 45 (6): 1113–28.

Arora, A., and A. Gambardella. 1994. "The Changing Technology of Technological Change: General and Abstract Knowledge and the Division of Innovative Labour." *Research Policy* 23:523–32.

Baba, Y., and J. P. Walsh. 2010. "Embeddedness, Social Epistemology and Breakthrough Innovation: The Case of the Development of Statins." *Research Policy* 39:511–22.

Bresnahan, T. F., and M. Trajtenberg. 1995. "General Purpose Technologies 'Engines of Growth'?" *Journal of Econometrics* 65:83–108.

Cohen, W. M. 2010. "Fifty Years of Empirical Studies of Innovative Activity and Performance." In *Handbook of the Economics of Innovation*, edited by Bronwyn H. Hall and Nathan Rosenberg, 129–213. Amsterdam: Elsevier.

Cohen, W. M., and S. Klepper. 1996. "A Reprise of Size and R&D." *Economic Journal* 106 (437): 925–51.

Cohen, W. M., and R. C. Levin. 1989. "Empirical Studies of Innovation and Market Structure." *Handbook of Industrial Organization* 2:1059–1107.

Cohen, W. M., and D. A. Levinthal. 1990. "Absorptive Capacity: A New Perspective on Learning and Innovation." *Administrative Science Quarterly* 35:128–52.

Cohen, W. M., R. R. Nelson, and J. P. Walsh. 2000. "Protecting Their Intellectual Assets: Appropriability Conditions and Why US Manufacturing Firms Patent (or Not)." NBER Working Paper No. 7552. Cambridge, MA: National Bureau of Economic Research.

Cohen, W. M., R. R. Nelson, and J. P. Walsh. 2002. "Links and Impacts: The Influence of Public Research on Industrial R&D." *Management Science* 48:1–23.

Crépon, B., E. Duguet, and J. Mairesse. 1998. "Research, Innovation and Productivity: An Econometric Analysis at the Firm Level." *Economics of Innovation and New Technology* 7:115–58.

Dahlin, K. B., and D. M. Behrens. 2005. "When Is an Invention Really Radical? Defining and Measuring Technological Radicalness." *Research Policy* 34 (5): 717–37.

David, P. 1990. "The Dynamo and the Computer: An Historical Perspective on the Modern Productivity Paradox." *American Economic Review* 80:355–61.

Fleming, L. 2001. "Recombinant Uncertainty in Technological Search." *Management Science* 47:117–32.

Giuri, P., M. Mariani, S. Brusoni, G. Crespi, D. Francoz, A. Gambardella, W. Garcia-Fontes, A. Geuna, R. Gonzales, and D. Harhoff. 2007. "Inventors and Invention Processes in Europe: Results from the PatVal-EU Survey." *Research Policy* 36:1107–27.

Griliches, Z. 1979. "Issues in Assessing the Contribution of Research and Development to Productivity Growth." *Bell Journal of Economics* 10 (1): 92–116.

Griliches, Z. 1998. "Patent Statistics as Economic Indicators: A Survey." In *R&D and Productivity: The Econometric Evidence*, edited by Zvi Griliches, 287–343. Chicago: University of Chicago Press.

Hall, B. H., A. B. Jaffe, and M. Trajtenberg. 2001. "The NBER Patent Citation Data File: Lessons, Insights and Methodological Tools." Cambridge, MA: National Bureau of Economic Research.

Henderson, R. M., and K. B. Clark. 1990. "Architectural Innovation: The Reconfiguration of Existing Product Technologies and the Failure of Established Firms." *Administrative Science Quarterly* 35 (1): 9–30.

Hollander, S. 1965. *The Sources of Increased Efficiency: A Study of DuPont Rayon Plants.* Cambridge, MA: MIT Press.

Jaffe, A. B., and G. De Rassenfosse. 2017. "Patent Citation Data in Social Science Research: Overview and Best Practices." *Journal of the Association for Information Science and Technology* 68:1360–74.

Jensen, M. B., B. Johnson, E. Lorenz, and B. Å. Lundvall. 2007. "Forms of Knowledge and Modes of Innovation." In *The Learning Economy and the Economics of Hope,* edited byBengt-Åke Lundvall, 155–82. London: Anthem.

Kalton, G. 1983. *Introduction to Survey Sampling.* Thousand Oaks, CA: Sage.

Klevorick, A. K., R. C. Levin, R. R. Nelson, and S. G. Winter. 1995. "On the Sources and Significance of Interindustry Differences in Technological Opportunities." *Research Policy* 24:185–205.

Kubota, T., Y. Aoshima, and Y. Koh. 2011. "Influence That Distance from the Divisional Environment Has on the Innovation Process: A Comparative Analysis of ArF Resist Materials Development." IIR Working Paper. Tokyo: Hitotsubashi University Institute of Innovation Research.

Lee, Y.-N. 2015. "Evaluating and Extending Innovation Indicators for Innovation Policy." *Research Evaluation* 24:471–88.

Lee, Y.-N., and J. P. Walsh. 2016. "Inventing While You Work: Knowledge, Non-R&D Learning and Innovation." *Research Policy* 45:345–59.

Levin, R. C., A. K. Klevorick, R. R. Nelson, S. G. Winter, R. Gilbert, and Z. Griliches. 1987. "Appropriating the Returns from Industrial Research and Development." *Brookings Papers on Economic Activity* 3:783–831.

Li, G.-C., R. Lai, A. D'Amour, D. M. Doolin, Y. Sun, V. I. Torvik, Z. Y. Amy, and L. Fleming. 2014. "Disambiguation and Co-authorship Networks of the US Patent Inventor Database (1975–2010)." *Research Policy* 43:941–55.

Mansfield, E. 1968. *Industrial Research and Technological Innovation: An Econometric Analysis.* London: Longmans, Green.

Marshall, A. 1890. *Principles of Economics.* London: Macmillan.

Merton, R. K. 1973. *The Sociology of Science: Theoretical and Empirical Investigations.* Chicago: University of Chicago Press.

Nagaoka, S., and J. P. Walsh. 2009. "Commercialization and Other Uses of Patents in Japan and the US: Major Findings from the RIETI-Georgia Tech Inventor Survey." Research Institute of Economy, Trade and Industry (RIETI).

No, Y., and J. P. Walsh. 2010. "The Importance of Foreign-Born Talent for US Innovation." *Nature Biotechnology* 28:289–91.

Roach, M., and W. M. Cohen. 2013. "Lens or Prism? Patent Citations as a Measure of Knowledge Flows from Public Research." *Management Science* 59:504–25.

Rosenberg, N. 1976. "Factors Affecting the Diffusion of Technology." In *Perspectives on Technology,* edited by N. Rosenberg, 189–210. London: Cambridge University Press.

Schumpeter, J. 1934. *Capitalism, Socialism, and Democracy.* New York: Harper & Row.

Shane, S. 2001. "Technological Opportunities and New Firm Creation." *Management Science* 47:205–20.

Spear, S., and H. K. Bowen. 1999. "Decoding the DNA of the Toyota Production System." *Harvard Business Review* 77:96–108.

Strumsky, D., and J. Lobo. 2015. "Identifying the Sources of Technological Novelty in the Process of Invention." *Research Policy* 44:1445–61.

Svensson, R. 2015. "Measuring Innovation Using Patent Data." IFN Working Paper.

Teece, D. J. 1986. "Profiting from Technological Innovation: Implications for Integrations, Collaboration, Licensing and Public Policy." *Research Policy* 15:285–305.

Thompson, P. 2012. "The Relationship between Unit Cost and Cumulative Quantity and the Evidence for Organizational Learning-by-doing." *Journal of Economic Perspectives* 26:203–24.

Von Hippel, E. 1994. "'Sticky Information' and the Locus of Problem Solving: Implications for Innovation." *Management Science* 40:429–39.

Walsh, J. P., Y.-N. Lee, and T. Jung. 2016. "Win, Lose or Draw? The Fate of Patented Inventions." *Research Policy* 45:1362–73.

Walsh, J. P., Y.-N. Lee, and S. Nagaoka. 2016. "Openness and Innovation in the US: Collaboration Form, Idea Generation and Implementation." *Research Policy* 45:1660–71.

Yoon, J., and K. Kim. 2012. "Detecting Signals of New Technological Opportunities Using Semantic Patent Analysis and Outlier Detection." *Scientometrics* 90:45–61.

Zimmerman, M. M. 1955. *The Super Market: A Revolution in Distribution.* New York: McGraw-Hill.

5

An Anatomy of US Firms Seeking Trademark Registration

Emin M. Dinlersoz, Nathan Goldschlag,
Amanda Myers, and Nikolas Zolas

5.1 Introduction

Attracting consumers and retaining them as loyal customers are critical for a firm's survival and growth. Among the many ways of building and protecting a loyal customer base, trademarks are unique. By protecting a firm's intangible assets, trademarks can reduce consumer search and switching costs, lower the expense of introducing and marketing new products, and generate brand awareness and loyalty. While trademarks generally facilitate establishing and enhancing goodwill, they may not always be directly linked to a particular attribute of the firm. Goodwill can be generated through investment in consistent quality, exceptional customer service, a distinctive portfolio of products, or a unique service or innovation that makes a firm stand out. The fact that not all firms file to register trademarks, despite the

Emin M. Dinlersoz is a principal economist at the Center for Economic Studies at the US Census Bureau.

Nathan Goldschlag is a senior economist at the Center for Economic Studies at the US Census Bureau.

Amanda Myers is an economist at the United States Patent and Trademark Office.

Nikolas Zolas is a senior economist at the Center for Economic Studies at the US Census Bureau.

Any opinions and conclusions expressed herein are those of the authors and do not necessarily represent the views of the US Census Bureau and the US Patent and Trademark Office. All results have been reviewed to ensure that no confidential data are disclosed. The authors would like to thank Carol Corrado, Jonathan Haskel, Daniel Sichel, and Javier Miranda—the organizers of the 2017 Conference on Research in Income and Wealth (CRIW) conference Measuring and Accounting for Innovation in the 21st Century, conference participants, and especially the discussant, Mark Roberts, for helpful comments and suggestions. Veronika Penciakova provided expert research assistance. For acknowledgments, sources of research support, and disclosure of the authors' material financial relationships, if any, please see https://www.nber.org/books-and-chapters/measuring-and-accounting-innovation-21st-century/anatomy-us-firms-seeking-trademark-registration.

relatively low cost of doing so, suggests that certain firms stand to benefit more from trademark registration than others.[1]

Theory contends that firms use trademarks to appropriate the returns from investments in goodwill. Firms are therefore more likely to select into trademark registration when the returns to reputation, product quality, and scale and scope expansion are high.[2] Likewise, when innovative activity complements goodwill by enhancing product or service quality and inducing customer loyalty, firms have more motivation to protect accumulated and anticipated goodwill with a trademark registration. The benefits derived from using a trademark can, in turn, affect firm performance and productivity. When firms successfully leverage trademarks to differentiate goods or services and insulate themselves from copying and competition by registering trademarks, they can achieve faster growth. At the same time, the price elasticity of demand for firms with trademarks can be lower, leading to higher markups. Maintaining higher markups, in turn, may intensify firms' advertising and marketing activities or foster further investment in quality enhancement and process or product innovation. Consequently, protection of trademarks through registration can have long-term consequences for a firm's competitive position in the market as well as the industry concentration.

While theory suggests trademarks can play a critical role in firm dynamics and innovation, empirical research regarding which firms in the United States use trademarks and the benefits they thereby derive is relatively sparse, especially when compared to other intellectual property such as patenting. The small but growing body of empirical literature on trademarks relies primarily on application and registration data from other countries, particularly the United Kingdom, Australia, and France. Such firm-level studies generally find trademark filing and/or registration to be correlated with product differentiation, marketing, and innovation, though results vary by industry. The prior literature also finds a positive relationship between trademark registration and firm market value, productivity, and survival, indicating that the private value of trademarks to firm is positive, though there is yet no clear conclusion regarding their social value. Still, most firm-level research to date relies on datasets of large, publicly traded firms, which casts doubt on the applicability of results to the population of firms that seek trademark registration.

One major obstacle to empirical analysis of trademark use by firms in

---

1. One rationale for why not all firms file to register trademarks is provided by Landes and Posner (1988, 271–72): If trademarks signal consistent quality, quality may be costly to maintain and can be verified by consumers after purchase. Hence only the firms that can afford to provide such consistent quality will tend to seek trademark registration.

2. See, e.g., Landes and Posner (1987, 1988) and Economides (1988) for theoretical arguments on the connection between trademarks and consumer behavior. For recent models of firm dynamics under costly and gradual customer acquisition, see Dinlersoz and Yorukoglu (2012) and Gourio and Rudanko (2014).

the United States is the lack of comprehensive data on firm-level trademark activity. Recently, however, there has been substantial progress on this front. The United States Patent and Trademark Office (USPTO) has made available trademark data that covers nearly 7 million trademark applications for the period 1870–2015. The USPTO Trademark Case Files Dataset (TCFD) is a remarkable synthesis of various trademark activity by firms.[3] It contains detailed information on applications for trademark registration as well as the commercial use, renewal, assignment, and cancelation of registered trademarks. It identifies the date an application is filed with the USPTO and proceeds to registration and what product categories or classes of goods and services are covered by a registration. However, the TCFD has little to contribute regarding the characteristics of the firms that seek trademark registration and when exactly in their life cycle they do so. It is, therefore, not possible to uncover how trademark filing is related to firm characteristics and dynamics with the TCFD alone.

This chapter reports on the construction of a new dataset that combines the TCFD with firm-level microdata at the US Census Bureau. The dataset fills a void in the literature by linking trademark activity with firm characteristics, performance, and dynamics in the United States. It provides information on the incidence and timing of trademark filing and registration over the life cycle of a firm and thus opens several research possibilities. The trademark-firm linked data can be used to explore not only what kind of firms seek to register trademarks but also when they do so and how trademark filing is related to firm dynamics, such as entry, survival, employment and revenue growth, and R&D and patenting intensity. This chapter provides a first look at the connection between trademark filing and broader measures of firm outcomes based on the constructed data. An objective of this initial analysis is to explore some of the selection and treatment effects associated with seeking federal trademark registration in terms of firm growth and innovation.

Key events early in the life cycle of firms may signal the emergence of high-growth firms and generate skewness in firm outcomes. There is a growing interest in identifying precursors of successful businesses. Recent research indicates that having a patent or a trademark application is highly correlated with the ultimate success of an early entrepreneurship activity, as measured by rare events such as an IPO or a high-value acquisition.[4] Analysis of the constructed data likewise indicates that trademark filing is correlated with employment and revenue growth. There appears to be strong selection into trademark registration based on firm size and age, though size is a more critical correlate. Firms that do not apply for trademark registration

---

3. See Graham et al. (2016) for details on the construction and features of the USPTO Trademark Case Files Dataset.
4. See, for instance, Fazio et al. (2016).

in their initial years are unlikely to do so unless they experience employment growth. Difference-in-difference analysis suggests sizable treatment effects, with firms seeking trademark registration having substantially higher employment and greater revenue in the period following first filing relative to similar control firms.

Among the least studied aspects of trademarks is their ability to capture firm innovation. Trademarks can be used to capture the value of firm innovative outputs that are not covered by patents, such as innovations in retail, services, customer relations, and knowledge-intensive products. Little is known, however, about this function of trademarks. More evidence is needed on firms' use of trademarks to appropriate returns from innovation and the relationship between trademark activity and more traditional measures of innovative activity. Firm-level analysis of the constructed data indicates that firms with R&D and patent activity are very likely to apply to register trademarks. Further, the relatively high copresence of trademark applications and R&D activity in firms without patents suggests that, for at least some firms, trademarks may capture innovative outputs of R&D investment not accounted for by patents. Difference-in-difference analysis also supports a complementarity between applying to register trademarks and innovative activity, showing higher average R&D expenditure and patenting by first-time trademark filers both before and after initial filing compared to similar control firms. These initial results warrant further investigation. Still, they provide preliminary evidence that trademark filings are correlated with firm innovation and that trademark-based metrics may serve to improve measurement of innovation in the economy.

The chapter is organized as follows. The next section gives a brief overview of the prior literature leveraging firm and trademark application data predominantly from countries other than the United States. Section 5.3 provides the theoretical motivation for analyzing the connection among trademarks; applications for trademark registration; and firm characteristics, dynamics, and innovation. Section 5.4 discusses the data inputs and the algorithm used to match the trademark data with data on firm characteristics. The analysis in section 5.5 documents the characteristics of firms that seek trademark registration and provides a first look at how trademark filing is correlated with firm growth and innovation. Section 5.6 concludes with a discussion of the streams of future research made possible by the trademark-firm linked data.

5.2   Prior Literature

There is a small but growing body of empirical work concerning trademarks. Much of the recent work examining trademark data at the firm level is limited to the European and Australian context. For the United States, most research leverages datasets of publicly traded firms, such as Compustat, which cover a fraction of those firms seeking trademark registration. The lack of comprehensive data on trademark filing by private firms and small to medium-sized enterprises has been a major impediment to empirical research regarding the use of trademarks and the relationship among trademark filing and firm characteristics, dynamics, and innovative activity in the United States.

Schautschick and Greenhalgh (2016) provide a comprehensive survey of the empirical research on trademarks. Several conclusions emerge from the survey. First, there has been considerable growth in trademark application demand since the mid-1970s in Australia, the United Kingdom, and the United States, with qualitatively similar trends in trademark-filing growth across these countries between 1975 and 2002.[5] The services sector, as well as deregulated and restructured industries, exhibit the highest rates of growth in trademark-filing growth during this period. Interestingly, the surge in trademark applications appears to lead a similar surge in patent filings in developed countries by about 10 years. Still, there is no formal econometric analysis that establishes the connection between the timing of patents and trademarks at the firm-level, and whether firm trademark filing leads or lags patent applications is an open question. Second, at the country level, increased demand for product variety and quality appears to drive growth in trademark applications compared to the expansion of output. In general, the studies surveyed indicate that trademark filing is correlated with product differentiation, marketing, and innovation. However, the degree of this correlation depends on the industries investigated. Finally, firm-level studies indicate that firms use trademarks to protect identity and reputation and that the private value of trademarks to firms is generally positive, but there is no clear conclusion on the social value of trademarks. The latter depends on the trade-off between market efficiency–improving and procompetitive effects of trademarks and the potential for firms to make inefficient investments to protect reputation and leverage reputational assets to erect barriers to entry. Further research is needed to assess the relative magnitudes of these different effects.

At the macro level, Baroncelli, Fink, and Javorcik (2005) also document a number of regularities in trademark registrations across countries. Using World Intellectual Property Organization data for a panel of countries over the period 1994–98, they find evidence that higher development is correlated with a dominance of domestic brands at home and a stronger presence of these brands in foreign markets, as indicated by foreign residents' share of trademark registrations. However, they also note growth in foreign trademark registrations held by entities in developing countries, potentially reflecting increased exports to markets in more developed countries and the resulting need to protect growing brands. At the sector and industry level,

---

5. See figure 2 in Schautschick and Greenhalgh (2013).

Baroncelli, Fink, and Javorcik (2005) observe that most trademark registrations occur in industries characterized as R&D intensive, particularly scientific equipment and pharmaceutical sectors, and advertising intensive, such as clothing, footwear, and food products. Business services also exhibit higher trademark registration intensity—a finding echoed by Millot (2011) for Germany and France.

Multiple studies document the relatively rapid growth in service marks between 1980s and 2000s in developed countries—Greenhalgh, Longland, and Bosworth (2003) for the United Kingdom; Jensen and Webster (2004) for Australia; and Graham et al. (2013) for the United States. In particular, the latter study finds that service marks filings grew by nearly 50 percent between 1998 and 2000 in the United States, potentially as a result of the dot-com boom of the late 1990s.[6] These patterns reflect the growing importance of the service sector in developed economies and potentially denote a rise in service-related innovations. the value of which is captured through trademarks.

A handful of studies leverage firm-trademark matched datasets to examine the connection between firm characteristics and trademark filing or registration activity. Greenhalgh, Longland, and Bosworth (2003) use panel data on medium and large manufacturing firms in the United Kingdom and find an inverse relationship between trademark-filing intensity and firm size. Smaller firms, as measured by either employment or sales, exhibit higher trademark-filing intensity. However, the panel consists mainly of large, publicly listed firms with many subsidiaries, which calls into question the applicability of results to the broader population of firms relying on trademarks.

Greenhalgh and Rogers (2008) use data on both manufacturing and service firms in the United Kingdom to investigate the role of firm characteristics on activities related to intellectual property, including trademark filing. They find that while intellectual property assets are not always monotonically related to firm growth, size is nevertheless a strong predictor of whether a firm applies for a patent and/or seeks trademark registration. Their study also indicates diminishing returns to firm size in terms of such activity. In both services and manufacturing, patent and trademark-filing intensity declines as firms get larger. The results of both Greenhalgh, Longland, and Bosworth (2003) and Greenhalgh and Rogers (2008) denote the significant relationship between trademark-filing intensity and firm size in the United Kingdom, a finding replicated by Jensen and Webster (2006) for Australian firms.

Sandner (2009) provides a detailed investigation of companies' trademark portfolios using the world's largest publicly traded companies—those included in the Reuters and Compustat financial databases. The study identifies 4,085 companies that satisfy the selection criterion in their latest income

6. See figure 16 in Graham et al. (2016).

statement.[7] Results indicate that companies build trademark portfolios to deliberately protect the company brand. Using trademark applications to infer brand management decisions, the study finds that product introductions prompt varied decisions regarding whether to extend existing trademarks or devise novel trademarks to cover new products. Thus trademark filings can reflect both the creation of new brands and the expansion of existing brands to encompass new products.

Sandner and Block (2011) use data from various countries, including the United States, to assess the market value of trademarks. They find a positive effect of trademark registrations on firm value, controlling for patenting and R&D activity. However, their study is limited to Community Trademarks registered by the Office for Harmonization in the Internal Market (now the European Intellectual Property Office, or EUIPO) and publicly traded firms from Compustat. The final dataset consists of a relatively small set of 1,216 large, publicly traded firms, and the results, like those of most prior studies at the firm level, provide little information on trademark registrations held by private firms.

A few studies have focused specifically on trademark filings by small to medium-sized firms. Greenhalgh and Rogers (2007) build a database that spans the entire set of UK firms for the period 2001–5. The database contains millions of small to medium-sized firms matched with trademark applications and substantially expands on the scope of the studies discussed earlier, even though the time period covered is relatively short. One main conclusion that emerges from this study is that smaller firms are more intellectual property intensive, tending to have higher volumes of patent and trademark applications relative to their assets, compared to larger firms.

To examine such firms' motivation to seek federal US trademark registration, Block et al. (2015) use an online survey of 600 small and medium trademark applicants in internet and technology sectors selected from CrunchBase (formerly TechCrunch), a crowdsourced database of US firms. They use factor analysis to establish three distinct motivations for seeking trademark registration—protection, marketing, and exchange. They then use cluster analysis to build a typology of firms based on trademark motivations, resulting in four clusters—trademark skeptics, marketing-focused trademark users, marketing plus protection-focused trademark users, and trademark advocates.[8] This study demonstrates that there may be significant heterogeneity in firm motivations for seeking trademark registration. In a related paper using a comparably sized sample of small and medium firms in Belgium, Flikkema, De Man, and Castaldi (2014) investigate how

---

7. Companies with revenues of 400 million Euros or more (as of the time of the analysis).
8. Trademark advocates value all trademark motives highly, while the marketing-focus group values trademarks for marketing purposes but does not report protection or exchange as motivation for filing. The marketing plus protection-focused group is the largest, comprising one-third of the firms, and ranks both marketing and protection motives highly.

companies use and interpret trademarks. Their analysis reveals that 60 percent of recently registered trademarks indicate innovative activity, mainly in the form of product or service innovation. These results encourage further scrutiny into trademark filings by small and medium firms, especially in the United States, where research has been largely limited to large, publicly traded firms.

Recent work has also utilized the USPTO Case Files Dataset in conjunction with other datasets in the United States to study incentives to use and protect trademarks and assess the value of trademarks for firms. Aurora, Bei, and Cohen (2016) explore the incentives to use and protect trademarks for firms in the United States by bringing together survey data from the Division of Innovative Labor on firms' new product development activities and industry-level data from the NETS (National Establishment Time-Series) database to understand the connection among trademarks, competition, and first-mover advantages. Heath and Mace (2017) offer evidence, using the Federal Trademark Dilution Act and its subsequent revision, that trademark protection through registration has economically significant effects in the case of publicly traded firms in Compustat. These studies, nevertheless, do not provide a comprehensive analysis of trademark-filing propensity for all firms in the United States.

The existing literature summarized so far highlights the need for comprehensive longitudinally linked firm-level trademark data in the United States, especially for privately held firms. The rest of the chapter describes how this type of dataset is constructed by combining trademark-related information from the USPTO Case Files Dataset with data on firms, public and private, available at the US Census Bureau. It then demonstrates how the new dataset can be used to better understand the connection between trademark filing and firm attributes, dynamics, and innovation.

5.3   Theoretical Motivation

The theoretical literature sets forth a variety of ways trademarks can be related to firm outcomes and performance.[9] A fundamental function of trademarks highlighted in theory is that of an information signal to promote market efficiency and reduce consumer search costs, especially for experience goods. As source-identifying devices, trademarks convey information regarding the unobserved attributes of a firm and its products (e.g., quality) and therefore reduce information asymmetry and consumer search costs, particularly in markets where the attributes of goods or services are not readily discernible. Firms are incentivized to invest in goodwill to reap rewards from the reputational value exemplified by the trademark. Thus trademarks

---

9. See, e.g., Landes and Posner (1987, 1988, 2003) and Economides (1988) for reviews and assessment of the theory of trademarks.

with positive reputational value can facilitate customer acquisition, generate customer loyalty, and facilitate scale and scope expansion. As a result, trademarks can reduce the price elasticity of demand, allow firms to maintain higher prices, and facilitate investment into not only further reputation-building activities but also R&D and innovation. Additionally, by protecting a firm's intangible assets and stock of goodwill, trademarks insulate firms from competition and infringement of their products or services.

In view of the various theoretical roles of trademarks summarized above, one expects both strong selection and treatment effects associated with application for trademark registration. Firms for which reputational assets would yield higher returns are more likely to select into trademark registration. A more productive firm with better growth prospects, a firm that can commit to high quality, or a firm with a large customer base stands to gain more from trademark registration because the benefits accrue from a larger current and future stock of goodwill. Thus firms that seek to register a trademark for the first time may be those that are larger, more productive, have better product quality, and experience faster growth. In particular, young firms with an innovative product or service expected to yield a large future profit stream may seek trademark registration with a higher propensity.

Trademarks can also induce potentially large treatment effects. Trademarks can contribute to the firm's ability to expand into other product types and new markets based on the established brand name, goodwill, and loyalty. Trademarks can also prevent the infringement of a firm's brand and the erosion of its stock of goodwill. In markets with relatively homogeneous goods, trademarks can serve a role akin to product differentiation based on quality and reduce the intensity of price competition. This reduction can lead to higher markups and growth for firms that can successfully differentiate themselves using trademarks. All of these effects suggest that the posttrademark-filing dynamics of a firm can differ from both the pretrademark-filing dynamics and the dynamics of firms that do not seek to register trademarks at all.

The innovative activity of firms is likely to have a significant impact on both selection and treatment effects associated with trademarks. Firms that engage in R&D and patenting may be more likely to seek trademark registration ex post to appropriate greater returns from their innovations. For instance, a firm that invests in product and process R&D is more likely to generate higher-quality products, sustain lower costs, or induce more demand and customer loyalty and hence build a larger stock of goodwill. Such firms have a greater incentive to protect accumulated and anticipated goodwill with a trademark registration. Therefore, when innovating firms select into trademark use, an application for trademark registration would follow R&D and patenting as a lagging indicator of innovative activity.

Trademark filing may also directly reflect innovative activity not captured by R&D or patents. Many service innovations, or innovations in information- and knowledge-intensive industries, may be better protected by trademarks rather than patents. More generally, where innovations are not patent-eligible subject matter or were developed with informal protection mechanisms, firms may be more likely to seek trademark registration to protect against imitation and secure the firm's current and future stock of goodwill. To the extent that trademark applications reflect such innovations and their associated goodwill, the knowledge of which firms apply for trademarks can enable more accurate identification of the broader population of firms engaging in innovative activity.

Trademarks may also enhance firms' innovation activity. A large stock of goodwill, accumulated and protected by trademarks, can increase a firm's incentives for innovation. A firm with many loyal customers can benefit more from cost-reducing R&D, since reductions would spread over a larger customer base. Similarly, product introductions can be more valuable and involve less risk of imitation for firms with a trademark, as new products can readily enjoy the existing protection and established goodwill of the firm's trademark. Furthermore, where strong goodwill enhances market power, firms with trademarks may be more likely to invest in exploratory R&D. These considerations suggest that firms may engage in R&D and patenting more intensely after they secure a trademark registration. In this sense, trademark filings may also be leading indicators of innovative activity.

In summary, theory suggests that there may be strong selection and treatment effects associated with a trademark application. Both the pre- and posttrademark evolution of firms with a trademark application may differ significantly from that of firms that do not seek trademark registration. Furthermore, innovative activity captured by R&D and patenting can be strongly correlated with trademark filing. These two types of activities can complement each other, leading to high firm-level correlation among trademark application, R&D, and patenting. The relative timing of innovation and trademark filing over the firm life cycle may be informative in understanding whether trademark applications can serve as precursors to innovation. Empirical analysis in the following sections will explore some of the selection and treatment effects associated with trademark filings suggested by the theory of trademarks. It will also examine the connection between trademark filings and innovative activity, as measured by R&D and patents, at the firm level.

5.4   Data

This section describes the datasets used to link trademark application filing information with longitudinal firm data. It provides an outline of the methodology for matching trademark data to firms. Because the trademark data consist of many separate files and a large number of variables, it is important to develop a strategy for using all the relevant information from trademark applications by firms to facilitate the matching process.

5.4.1   Data on Trademarks

The data on trademarks comes from the USPTO TCFD. This dataset was constructed by economists at the USPTO from trademark case files made available by the USPTO on the Data.gov website. The case files were organized and streamlined to form several electronic files that can be readily used by researchers to conduct large-scale analysis. The accompanying paper, Graham et al. (2013), provides an excellent account of how the TCFD was constructed and a first look at some of the patterns of trademark-filing activity that emerge from the data. The TCFD contains detailed information on USPTO trademark applications and registrations for the period 1870–2015. The information on trademarks includes, but is not limited to, ownership, assignment, prosecution events, classification, and renewal history.

In the United States, trademark registrations are subject to a use requirement, which obligates the owner to use the mark on goods or in connection with services in order to establish and maintain trademark rights. The use requirement derives from American common law and subsequent codification in federal statutes.[10] An entity establishes and can enforce common law trademark rights solely by using a mark in commerce. A federal US trademark Principal Register registration confers benefits beyond common law, specifically national-scope rights, prima facie evidence of ownership, and recordation with US Customs and Border Protection for preventing the importation of infringing goods.

The TCFD captures only information on entities that seek a federal US trademark registration. It does not capture the population of firms that relies solely on common-law trademark rights. This is an important distinction because the selection and treatment effects considered here are limited to those associated with filing for federal trademark registration at the USPTO. Results may not be applicable to the broader set of firms with only common-law trademark rights.

To file a US trademark application, an applicant must specify the goods and services on and for which she uses or intends to use the trademark. The identified goods and services define the scope of trademark protection covered by the registration and generally cannot be overly broad.[11] Still,

---

10. Under American common law, a trademark owner has the exclusive right to prevent unauthorized third parties from using the same or similar mark on goods and services where such use would likely cause confusion among consumers as to the source of the goods and services offered under the mark. An entity may establish trademark rights solely by using a distinctive mark on the goods or in connection with the services. Registration at the state or federal level provides additional benefits but is not necessary for an entity to create and enforce common-law trademark rights. The Lanham Act of 1946 ("Trademark Act") established the modern US federal trademark registration system, providing for the protection of trademarks used in commerce and registered with the USPTO (15 U.S.C. § 1051 et seq.).

11. The US adopted the International Classification of Goods and Services under the Nice Agreement (the so-called "Nice Classification") on September 1, 1973. Prior to that date, the USPTO used a US trademark classification system. Our match is restricted to trademarks registered under the Nice Classification system.

even within the same class, there can be considerable variation in the specificity of the goods and services listed and thereby the breadth of trademark protection.

An applicant can apply to register a trademark already in commercial use or for which she has a bona fide intent to use the trademark on the identified goods or in connection with the identified services.[12] However, such "intent-to-use applications" can only be registered after the owner uses the trademark in the ordinary course of trade in commerce and provides a declaration and evidence supporting such use to the USPTO.[13] Filing for a US trademark registration costs a relatively small fee per class.[14] During substantive examination, the USPTO determines whether the applied-for trademark is legally protectable and there is no "likelihood of confusion" with a previously registered trademark owned by another party.[15] If the examining attorney determines the applied-for mark is registrable, the USPTO publishes the trademark for a limited opposition period, during which time third parties may file a formal opposition to the registration. Oppositions are fairly rare, instituted in less than 3 percent of published applications (Graham et al. 2013). Unopposed applications for trademarks already in use are issued a US trademark registration. Allowed intent-to-use applications must first establish commercial use before the applied-for mark can be registered.

A trademark owner can renew a US trademark registration indefinitely so long as the trademark is used on the listed goods or in connection with the listed services. The owner must provide proof of continued use and pay prescribed fees to the USPTO 6 years after registration and at each 10-year renewal event.[16] Failure to do so results in the registration being canceled.

---

12. To file based on use in commerce under Trademark Act §1(a), the owner must submit a declaration stating that the mark is used in the ordinary course of trade in commerce that Congress can regulate—that is, interstate commerce or commerce between the United States and foreign nations, as of the filing date. See TMEP §901.03. To file based on intent to use under §1(b), the applicant must have a bona fide intention to use the mark in commerce on the goods and services listed in the application in the near future. See TMEP §1101.

13. Intent-to-use applications became available to applicants in November 1989 as a result of the Trademark Law Revision Act of 1988. A small but growing minority of applications are filed with the USPTO based on a foreign application or registration for the same trademark or an extension of an international registration to the United States. Authorized by international treaties, such applications can be registered prior to the trademark being used in US commerce; however, generally only applicants with a foreign "country of origin" can obtain such US trademark registration. Owners with foreign addresses are excluded from the match with US firm data.

14. For most of the time period covered by the matched data, the per-class filing fee ranged from $175 to $375 for a paper filing and $325 to $335 for an electronic filing.

15. An applied-for trademark can be refused as not registrable if, among other possible grounds, it is generic or merely descriptive; geographic; a surname; deceptive; a municipal, state, national, or foreign flag or insignia; or the name, likeness, or signature of a living person used without their consent (15 U.S.C. §1052). See TMEP §1200. Examining attorneys search existing registrations and pending applications for similar trademarks and assesses whether the use of the applicant's trademark on the identified goods or in connection with the identified services is likely to cause confusion among consumers (15 U.S. C. §1052(d)). See TMEP §1207.

16. In the sixth year after the registration date, the trademark owner must maintain the registration by filing an affidavit or declaration of continued use and provide specimen(s) depict-

Data coverage in the TCFD varies over time. Graham et al. (2013) indicate that there is little coverage of classification, prosecution events, and owner records for trademark registrations issued before 1962.[17] The coverage improves for registrations issued during the period 1962–77, and there is substantial improvement in coverage for filings and registrations after 1977. Coverage becomes nearly 100 percent after 1982. Key data items are populated at a rate of 89 percent or more for the period 1977–2015. Firm-level longitudinal micro data are available in the US Census Bureau starting in 1976. Much of the well-covered 1977–2015 period in the TCFD coincides with the coverage of the data on firm characteristics. However, left censoring of the firm data in 1976 and relatively lower coverage of the trademark data before 1977 implies that firms born before 1976 may not match with any trademark data, even if they applied for or registered a trademark before 1977. Likewise, for firms born before 1977, there is no way to assess whether a matched trademark filing reflects the firm's first trademark application—a key trademark-related event in the life cycle of firms. Therefore, the primary focus of the empirical analysis will be on firms born in or after 1977.

5.4.2   Data on Firms

The trademark data are matched with the US Census Bureau's Business Register (BR), which contains administrative data for the universe of non-farm businesses in the United States. The BR is also the sampling frame for the Census Bureau's economic surveys. It contains information on a firm's employment, payroll, and revenues, as well as geography and industry classification of their associated establishments. Analysis of firm trademark activity requires longitudinal data to track firms over time and identify when in their life cycle such activity occurs. The Longitudinal Business Database (LBD) provides a longitudinally linked version of the BR at the establishment level for the period 1976–2014. The LBD also enables identification of entry and exit of firms and establishments. Since the LBD coverage starts in 1976, there is no age information for firms established in that year. The empirical analysis is restricted to firms born in or after 1977 to avoid this censoring in age and ensure accurate identification of the first occurrence of a trademark filing in a firm's life cycle.

The primary measures of firm size used in this chapter are employment and revenue. Prior work, detailed in Haltiwanger et al. (2017), has linked observations in the BR to construct a longitudinal firm revenue database.

---

ing use in US commerce for the listed goods and services and pay prescribed fees (15 U.S.C. §§1058(a)(1)). See TMEP §1604. Ten-year renewal terms were instituted for registrations issued on or after November 16, 1989. Registrations issued prior to that date had 20-year terms until the first renewal event following that date. Thus all live registrations are subject to 10-year terms as of November 16, 2009. Registrants must pay separate maintenance and renewal fees for each class in the registration. For most of the time period covered by the matched data, the fee for (paper or electronic) filing an affidavit or declaration of use is $100 per class, and the fee for (paper or electronic) filing a renewal application ranged from $300 to $400 per class.

17. See table 1 in Graham et al. (2016).

The analysis here uses this database to examine the connection between firm revenue growth and trademark filing.

In addition to the BR, the matching process utilizes the Integrated Longitudinal Business Database (ILBD). Even after matching to the BR, there are many trademark applications in the TCFD that do not match to an employer firm. Many of these trademarks may be owned by nonemployer businesses that do not appear in the BR. The ILBD contains individuals' income tax records, including Schedule C earnings from an individually operated business or sole proprietorship.[18] The ILBD nonemployer universe is used to identify matches for those trademark applications that were not matched to the employer universe in the BR. These nonemployer trademark links are used primarily to better understand the accuracy of the matching process. Future work will leverage these links to examine the dynamics of nonemployer firms seeking federal trademark registration.

5.4.3   Matching Process

In the absence of disambiguated identifiers, such as an Employer Identification Number (EIN), shared between the TCFD and the BR, name and address matching techniques must be applied to combine the two datasets.[19] The TCFD contains over 7.2 million trademark applications and 17.4 million ownership records.[20] The universe of TCFD records is filtered to include only the applications filed in or after 1976 (the beginning of the BR data) and excludes foreign businesses, federal and state government entities, and all individuals. After imposing these restrictions, there are over 5 million unique trademark records that have the potential to match to the BR and LBD.

The first step of the matching strategy to link the TCFD and BR is to extract all unique combinations of name and address information from the TCFD. Matching algorithms then clean and standardize the name and address fields in both the TCFD and the BR.[21] Once standardized, an initial subset of potentially matching records is identified based on weak match criteria applied to names only. From this subset, matches of different quality are extracted using various combinations of fuzzy and exact name and address matching. A string comparator that captures the similarity of text across fields is used to further refine and subset matches. More than 80 percent of matches rely on the business name and three address (street, city, and state) fields—relatively strict criteria that tend to yield higher-quality

---

18. See Davis et al. (2007) and Haltiwanger and Jarmin (2007) for details on the construction of the ILBD.

19. For a detailed description of the matching methodology, see the appendix.

20. Ownership records are captured in the TCFD at key points in the trademark's life cycle (e.g., filing, publication, registration) even if there is no change in ownership. This inflates the number of ownership records in the TCFD beyond the number of unique trademark application-owner pairs.

21. Common strings, such as "LLC" and "LTD," and punctuation, such as "." and "@," are removed.

matches. Results from the BR match are then integrated with the LBD. Information from the LBD is leveraged to further refine matches.

A trademark application filing can predate a firm's entry to the BR, as some firms may apply for a trademark registration even before they become employers (pay their first wage or hire their first employee). Thus trademark applications that do not match to the BR are matched to the ILBD, the universe of nonemployer businesses. For this study, matches to nonemployer businesses are used primarily to better understand the quality of matches to the employer universe. Future work will investigate the growth and transition dynamics of nonemployer businesses seeking trademark registration.

Ultimately, 83 percent of trademark records match to the LBD and 2.4 percent to the ILBD. The LBD match rate declines over time, falling from 89 percent in the 1980–89 registration year period to 73 percent for the 2010–14 period. However, the matches become less ambiguous over time. The share of unique matches rises from 59 percent in the 1980–89 registration year period to 88 percent for 2010–14. The declining match rate is primarily driven by businesses identified as Limited Liability Companies (LLCs) in the TCFD. LLCs are one of the fastest growing business types in the trademark applicant universe and in the general population of firms. To explore the declining match rate, several hypotheses are investigated, including deteriorating string quality, a compositional shift in trademark filings toward nonemployers, and the growth of informal business. As detailed in the appendix, there is no obvious culprit that can explain why a declining share of trademark owner records in the TCFD match to the LBD. A random sample of matches is classified by clerical review as either true or false positives. These classifications are then used to calculate the precision of the TCFD-LBD matches. The precision of matches is over 90 percent and remains stable over time aside from a slight decline to 87 percent in the 2010–14 period.

5.5   Analysis

This section provides a first look at the characteristics of firms seeking federal trademark registration in the United States based on the constructed data. For the purposes of this chapter, a "trademark-filing firm" is defined as one that has filed an application for a trademark at some point in its life cycle. In view of the theoretical motivation, the main goal of the empirical analysis is to understand both selection and treatment effects—how trademark-filing firms differ from those that do not file trademark applications both before and after their first trademark filing. At the firm level, first trademark application is identified by the first-ever filing of an application to register a trademark with the USPTO. The analysis therefore focuses on selection and treatment effects of trademark-filing activity via the federal trademark system, and nontrademark-filing firms comprise firms without any trademark applications, regardless of whether they do or do not own trademarks under common law. While it would be ideal to separate nontrademark applicants into two subsets—those that own common-law trademarks and those that do not—the lack of comprehensive data on common-law trademark rights-holders prevents such differentiation. However, since the dynamics of firms with common-law trademark rights would tend to be more like those of formal trademark-filing firms, the inclusion of the former in the nontrademark-filing group would tend to reduce, rather than inflate, selection and treatment effect estimates.

It should also be noted that not all trademark applications mature to registration. Applications can be abandoned during substantive examination or following allowance for failure to establish commercial use of the applied-for mark or as a result of third-party opposition proceedings. The analysis presented here focuses on trademark application filing because it is the first indication of a firm's intent to register a trademark. It endeavors to fill a gap in the prior literature regarding which firms seek trademark registration and when in their life cycle they enter into this activity. However, because legal benefits accrue from trademark registration, not application filing, treatment effects would tend to be larger for firms whose applications mature to registration. Thus including all trademark-filing firms, regardless of whether an application proceeds to registration, would yield more conservative estimated treatment effects. Subsequent research will also consider the treatment effects of registration alone.

For the empirical analysis, only firms born in or after 1976 are considered. As discussed before, this restriction ensures that left-censoring of firm age does not affect results, but it also renders the age distribution of firms to be heavily skewed toward young firms in the earlier part of the sample period. The age distribution gradually evolves to be more representative over time. In particular, in 1977, the only firms in the sample will be new firms born in that year. However, for any given year $t > 1977$, firm age will range from zero (firms born in year t) to $t - 1977$ years (firms that were born in 1977 and survived until at least year t). Some of the empirical analysis considers only the later years of the sample period, when the firm age distribution is more representative. Specifically, the results for $t + 1997$ are presented whenever the analysis demands a representative firm age distribution.

The analysis focuses on the first-ever filing to register a trademark by a firm, regardless of whether the trademark is eventually registered or not. This critical event denotes when in their life cycle firms select into the population of firms that apply to register a trademark. In principle, one can use the filing date variable in the TCFD associated with each trademark application to identify the timing of the firm's first trademark activity. However, the process is a bit more complicated, because there can be several applications for the same trademark corresponding to use in different classes or on different products within the same class. For instance, a firm may initially apply to

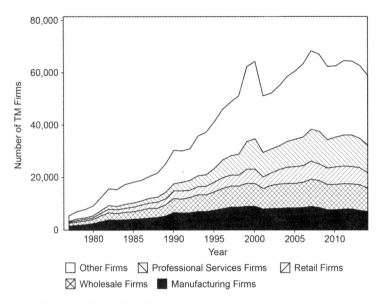

☐ Other Firms   ◣ Professional Services Firms   ▨ Retail Firms
☒ Wholesale Firms   ■ Manufacturing Firms

Fig. 5.1   Number of firms filing for a trademark for the first time, by sector over time

register a trademark for computer hardware services but may later extend the same trademark to another product offering, such as customized computer software. For cases where there is more than one application for a trademark or multiple trademarks, the minimum filing date across the firm's portfolio of trademark applications is used to identify the first-ever trademark filing.

5.5.1   Trends in Trademark Filing by Broad Sectors of the Economy

To paint a broad picture of trademark-filing activity in the United States, consider first some general patterns of trademark applications across sectors of the economy. Figure 5.1 shows the distribution of firms that file to register a trademark for the first time by sector based on their NAICS sector. (Vintage consistent industry classifications developed by Fort & Klimek [2018] are used to classify firms by industry in which they have the largest total employment.) Note that the number of first-time trademark-filing firms grows initially for all sectors starting with the beginning of the sample through the 1990s. This trend is, in part, driven by the fact that only new and relatively young firms are present in the sample for the earlier years, as discussed earlier. Since younger firms may have more incentive to apply for trademark registration relative to older counterparts, the number of first-time trademark filers increases as the stock of young firms initially expands and dominates the sample age composition. Later in the sample period, the distribution of firm age approaches a more representative one, and the number of first-time trademark-filing firms becomes relatively more stable in many sectors.

There is a notable expansion of first-time trademark filing by professional services firms starting with the 1990s, when the firm age distribution becomes relatively more representative, and extending through the mid-2000s. Similar growth in first-time filing is evident for wholesale firms and, to a limited extent, retail firms. In contrast, first-time trademark filing by manufacturing firms has somewhat declined during the same period, likely reflecting the decline of manufacturing in the United States that has accelerated especially in the 2000s. Surprisingly, there is more entry into trademark filing by wholesale firms compared to retail firms over the sample period, possibly indicating the greater importance of goodwill in business-to-business transactions. Throughout the sample period, first-time trademark filers in the "Other Firms" category are both the largest and fastest growing, which is expected given that this category lumps together industries that are likely to be trademark intensive, such as information, education and health care, entertainment, accommodation, and food and other services.[22]

The dot-com era spike in trademark applications is also clearly visible before 2000, mainly for professional services firms and "Other Firms."[23] This spike is potentially related to the proliferation of internet-based commerce and a need to identify and protect brands in cyberspace. As the 2001 recession hits, first-time trademark filing declines sharply. Thereafter, entry by new trademark filers increases across sectors, except manufacturing, until the Great Recession in 2007. Overall, first-time trademark filing appears to be procyclical, at least in recent decades. By the end of the sample in 2013, the largest number of first-time filers are in the "Other Firms" category, followed by professional services, wholesale, and manufacturing. Among all sectors, retail has the fewest number of first-time trademark filers as of 2013.

5.5.2   Who Trademarks, When, and How Much?

This section examines the patterns of trademark filing by firm size and age, the two key conditioning variables frequently used in the firm dynamics literature. The number of employees and the age of firms when they first file a trademark application are important in understanding the potential selection effects of trademarks. This section also explores the intensity of trademark filing, as measured by the number of trademark applications per firm, and firm size and age.

5.5.2.1   Firm Size, Age, and Trademark Activity

Table 5.1 presents, by year, the average size (employment) and age of firms that filed for a trademark registration for the first time during the period 1997–2013 (labeled as "Firms with first TM filing"). It also contains, for

22. The "Other Firms" category includes the firms classified in the industries outside of manufacturing, retail, wholesale, and professional services. See table 5.2 for a list of all industries.
23. These trends are also seen in high-tech industries, where young firm activity surged in the 1990s and then collapsed after 2001. See Goldschlag and Miranda (2015) for details.

Table 5.1   **Firm size (employment) and age for trademarking and nontrademarking firms**

Year	Firms with a TM filing		Firms with current-year TM filing		Firms with first TM filing		Firms with no TM filing		Average number of TMs per firm
	Mean size	Mean age	Mean size	Mean age	Mean size	Mean age	Mean size	Mean age	
1997	100.1	7.8	190.5	6.2	75.9	4.0	9.5	6.5	2.3
1999	102.0	8.3	180.2	6.2	50.2	4.0	9.7	7.0	2.4
2001	101.3	8.9	214.3	7.2	54.9	4.6	10.0	7.6	2.3
2003	93.5	9.7	200.5	7.8	50.9	4.8	9.6	7.9	2.2
2005	89.6	10.3	196.7	8.1	47.8	4.9	9.5	8.2	2.3
2007	89.8	10.7	186.5	8.4	52.7	5.2	9.7	8.7	2.2
2009	84.5	11.5	188.9	9.3	48.0	5.9	9.5	9.6	2.1
2011	81.5	12.2	186.5	9.6	46.6	5.7	9.4	10.2	2.2
2013	83.9	13.8	200.8	11.6	57.5	8.3	9.7	10.8	2.2

comparison, the same statistics for firms that have not filed to register a trademark as of the specified year (labeled as "Firms with no TM filing"), have at least one trademark filing up to that year (labeled as "Firms with a TM filing"), and have filed for a new trademark registration in that year (labeled as "Firms with current-year TM filing").

The main message from table 5.1 is that first-time trademark-filing firms are young but also large relative to firms that do not seek trademark registration. The average firm age at the time of the first trademark filing ranges from four to six for most years included in table 5.1, indicating that many firms that seek trademark registration for the first time do so relatively early in their life cycles. The average age of first-time trademark-filing firms increases over time. However, this pattern is evident in each category in table 5.1, reflecting, in part, the overall aging of the US firm population as a result of the persistent decline in new firm entry—a trend extensively documented in recent research.[24] The rise in mean age over time is also driven by the fact that firms in the analysis get older as one moves further away from the initial year of the sample (1997).

The first-time trademark filers are also relatively large. For instance, in 1997, firms that first filed to register a trademark had an average of roughly 76 employees, nearly eight times the average employment of firms that had no trademark applications. This gap narrows in subsequent years, mainly because the average size of first-time trademark-filing firms declines, while that of nontrademark-filing firms is largely constant. Still, in 2013, the average employment of first-time trademark filers was roughly 58, about six times that of firms with no trademark filings.

24. See, e.g., Decker et al. (2016).

Table 5.2   Firm size (employment) and age for trademarking and nontrademarking firms: Sectoral differences

Industry	Firms with a TM filing		Firms with a current year TM filing		Firms with first TM filing		Firms with no TM filing	
	Mean size	Mean age	Mean size	Mean age	Mean size	Mean age	Mean size	Mean age
Agriculture, Mining, and Utilities	203.5	14.4	536.7	11.0	181.3	8.0	11.3	11.3
Construction, Transportation, and Warehousing	92.8	14.4	238.7	12.2	81.6	10.2	7.4	10.7
Manufacturing	113.9	16.7	282.2	14.4	53.3	8.8	17.5	13.4
Wholesale	43.6	15.0	99.4	12.8	38.1	8.5	8.5	12.1
Retail	68.3	12.5	201.1	9.9	19.4	7.4	7.9	10.5
Information	76.6	13.0	256.6	10.9	61.5	6.5	8.6	9.4
Finance and Real Estate	88.5	14.0	233.8	12.3	64.4	9.5	5.2	10.7
Professional Services	39.3	12.1	84.5	9.3	43.5	7.0	5.5	10.3
Management and Admin. Support	153.8	14.1	345.9	12.0	116.9	9.0	15.8	9.9
Education and Health Care	210.4	14.3	487.9	12.2	126.8	9.4	15.7	11.6
Entertainment, Accommodation, and Food	94.0	12.2	212.3	9.9	44.8	7.6	15.5	8.5
Other Services	32.6	14.7	68.1	12.8	25.3	9.5	5.7	13.0

Table 5.1 also shows that firms that have filed for at least one trademark ("Firms with a TM filing") are larger and older than the firms that do not apply for trademark registration. Likewise, firms that apply to register additional trademarks in any given year ("Firms with current-year TM filing") are much larger than nontrademark-filing firms but also tend to outsize firms that have at least one trademark application. Interestingly, these firms that continue to build their trademark portfolios tend to be younger than firms with some trademark-filing activity. One interpretation of this result is that firms that continue to seek trademark registration are mostly large and successful companies that expand their scale and scope by introducing new products and services under the brand name and goodwill already established.

The patterns in table 5.1 are also apparent by sector. Table 5.2 presents the average firm size and age for the panel of trademark and nontrademark-filing firms across all years in the 1997–2013 period. In each sector, firms that apply to register a trademark for the first time are, on average, much larger than firms that do not seek trademark registration. The difference in average size is the largest in agriculture, mining, and utilities, where first-time trademark-filing firms maintain 16 times more employees on average. The smallest difference is in retail, where the average employment of first-time filers is more than double that of nontrademark-filing firms. Sector-level differences in average firm age also mirror the pattern found for the general

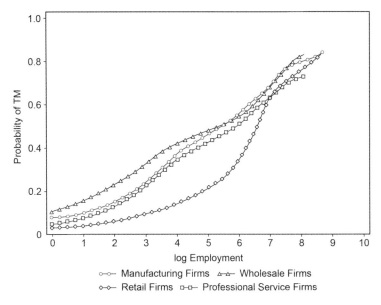

Fig. 5.2   Probability that a firm has a trademark filing, by firm size and sector

population of firms in table 5.1. Across sectors, first-time trademark-filing firms are, on average, 2.5 years younger than the firms without trademark applications. The largest age disparity is in manufacturing, where first-time filers are nearly 5 years younger, on average, than firms that do not apply for trademark registration. In construction, transportation, and warehousing, however, the difference in average age between first-time filers and nontrademark-filing firms is only 0.5 years.

Across sectors, firms that have at least one trademark application and those that apply to register additional trademarks are, on average, 10 and 25 times larger, respectively, than firms that do not seek trademark registration. Again, the largest differences in average employment are in agriculture, mining, and utilities, as well as finance and real estate.

Figure 5.2 plots the relationship between the propensity of a firm having applied to register a trademark and its size measured by employment. The likelihood of a trademark filing increases with size for all sectors, though the patterns of growth differ. The probability of having a trademark filing increases much faster with employment for smaller firms in wholesale, manufacturing, and professional services. For example, the probability that a firm with roughly 20 employees (≈ 3 in log scale) in one of these sectors files to register a trademark is 0.20 to 0.30. This probability increases to around 0.40 at 55 employees (≈ 4 in log scale). For retail, on the other hand, the likelihood of a trademark filing is relatively low until approximately 150 employees (≈ 5 in log scale), after which it grows sharply and catches up to

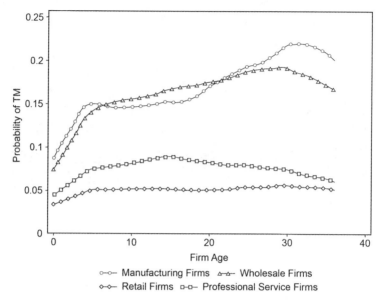

Fig. 5.3   **Probability that a firm has a trademark filing, by firm age and sector**

the other sectors. For any given firm size, the probability of a trademark filing is generally highest in manufacturing and wholesale sectors, though professional services is a close third, and retail is roughly equivalent for very large firms. In general, figure 5.2 reinforces the results in tables 5.1 and 5.2 and indicates there is a strong connection between firm size and trademark filing.

The relationship between firm age and propensity to apply to register a trademark, plotted in figure 5.3, is not as strong. While the probability that a firm has a trademark filing increases with age in general, the rate of growth is much less pronounced compared to size. In addition, the relationship is not necessarily monotonic.

Across sectors, the steepest increase in the probability of filing to register a trademark generally occurs between age 0 (new firms) and age 5. As firms age, there is little to no, or even negative, growth in the probability of trademark filing. The most sustained growth is in manufacturing, where the probability rises from roughly 0.08 to 0.20 between age 0 and age 36 (the oldest firms in the sample). Combined with figure 5.2, the patterns in figure 5.3 suggest that firm size is a more critical correlate of trademark application than firm age and that firms who do not seek trademark registration in the early years of their life cycle are unlikely to do so unless they experience employment growth. Thus the relationship between firm growth and trademark filing transcends mere firm experience and survival, hinting that

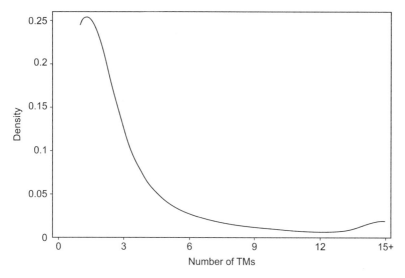

Fig. 5.4   Distribution of firm trademark intensity (number of trademark filings by a firm)

the decision to apply for a trademark registration is a strategic one made by the firm.

The analysis so far indicates that first-time trademark filing is concentrated in young and large firms. There appears to be strong selection into trademark filing, at least based on two key observable firm characteristics: size and age. This finding is consistent with the theoretical view that firms that are successful and grow in size early in their life cycles have a greater incentive to formally protect their goodwill through registered trademarks. In addition, the fact that trademark filers are much larger and older than nontrademark-filing firms suggest that trademark-filing firms continue to perform better after initial trademark application, pointing to potential treatment effects of trademarks that will be explored further in subsequent sections.

5.5.2.2   Firm Trademark Intensity

The analysis thus far has focused on the characteristics of trademark-filing firms without considering how intensely those firms rely on trademark registrations to protect their goodwill. One measure of trademark intensity is the number of trademark applications filed by a firm, akin to the number of patent applications or products per firm. Figure 5.4 shows the kernel density plot of the count of trademark applications per firm during the sample period. The distribution exhibits the typical features of firm-level discrete outcomes: it is highly positively skewed and has a long right tail. Most firms have a small number of trademark filings (fewer than 3), but there are also many firms with large trademark application portfolios in the right tail of the distribution—some with at least 15 trademark filings. Such large trademark portfolios may result from firms expanding into related and unrelated business lines to take advantage of established goodwill but can also reflect rebranding or other marketing activities. It is important to note that the skewness in firm trademark application intensity is different than that in patent intensity. Patent applications are highly concentrated among a small number of top patenting firms, whereas trademark filings are much more dispersed, and the top applicants hold relatively smaller portfolios.

How much has trademark-filing intensity changed over time? Do firms own increasingly larger application portfolios on average? Table 5.1 documents the average number of trademark filings per firm by year over the period 1997–2013. For the years covered in the table, the average is around two trademark applications per firm. While the average is somewhat higher in the earlier years, it appears to be relatively stable, suggesting little change in overall trademark-filing intensity over time.

5.5.3   Trademarks and Firm Growth

Both theory and the prior descriptive analysis suggest that there are strong selection and treatment effects associated with trademark application filing. This section focuses on the evolution of firms before and after their first trademark filing, without any attempt to identify a causal link between trademark application and firm evolution. The goal is to determine whether trademark-filing firms differ from nontrademark-filing firms in key outcome measures both before and after the initial filing. To do so, the analysis first considers the growth trajectory of newly formed firms that apply to register a trademark in their first year compared to those that do not. It then uses nearest-neighbor propensity score matching to identify a more precise control group for all treated firms (the ones that apply for a trademark registration for the first time) and more closely examines the treatment effects associated with first-time trademark filing. It should be noted, however, that the matching estimator does not eliminate concerns due to unobserved characteristics of treated firms.

5.5.3.1   Firm Growth before and after Trademark Filing: New Firms

Figure 5.5 presents the firm size-age profile for all new firms (age zero firms) that apply to register a trademark in their first year versus those that do not seek trademark registration at all. The figure suggests that firms that file in their first year of existence tend to have a very different growth trajectory compared to nontrademark-filing firms. Trademark-filing new firms also tend to be larger, even in their first year, compared to nontrademark-filing counterparts. This result suggests a strong selection into trademark filing at firm birth based on size. Average employment for first-year trademark filers is higher for any given age, and the employment gap between the two

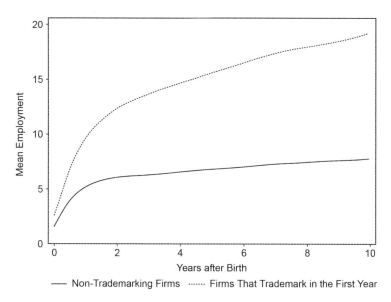

Fig. 5.5 **Average employment of new firms over time, by trademark filing status in the year of birth**

groups widens as firms age. Firms that file for a trademark registration upon birth tend to experience a steeper increase in employment in their first year. Average employment more than triples from roughly 2.5 employees in year zero to nearly 10 employees by year one. While both types of firms tend to grow with age, average employment grows much faster for the firms with a trademark application filing compared to those without one.[25]

Note that these trends are not conditional on industry, year of birth, or any other observables for new firms. The size-age profile of new firms, both trademark filing and nontrademark filing, is likely to vary based on such factors. Likewise, selection into a trademark filing is likely to be correlated with various firm characteristics other than size. To more carefully consider the relationship between trademarks and growth, the next section introduces a propensity score matching method used to control for the effects of some observables at the firm level.

5.5.3.2   Firm Growth before and after Trademark Filing: Propensity Score Matching

To form a control group for all first-time trademark-filing firms (not just the new firms) based on their observable characteristics, a propensity score matching methodology is implemented. The indicator of first-time

---

25. Note also that figure 5.5 is not conditional on survival, so it does reflect the differences in failure rates for firms that apply for a trademark registration versus those that do not.

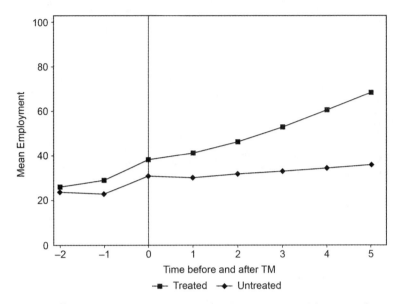

Fig. 5.6   Average employment before and after first trademark filing, treated vs. control group

trademark filing in any given year is modeled as a function of firm size (employment), age, average payroll (payroll per employee), multiunit status, industry fixed effects, and prior-year size in a logit framework. The model is estimated for each year separately. The predicted probabilities from the estimated model are then used to attach a propensity score to all firm-year combinations—treated and nontreated. For each treated firm, a matching firm is selected through propensity score nearest-neighbor matching. The control group is further restricted to matching firms of the same age as the treated firm in the year of first trademark filing. In some cases, this process yields more than one match for each treated firm. The analysis proceeds with weights, when needed, to account for multiple matches.

Figure 5.6 plots average employment before and after the first trademark filing for firms that apply to register a trademark (treated) and the matching control firms (untreated).[26] The year of the first trademark filing is normalized to $t = 0$ and is indicated by a vertical line in figure 5.6. For the two years prior to trademark filing ($t = -1, -2$), the average employment for treated and control firms is relatively similar. Nevertheless, treated firms are somewhat larger on average, including at the year of the trademark filing. Average employment grows for both treated and control firms before filing. However,

26. For the control group, the mean for any firm outcome measure is calculated using weights, which are equal to the inverse of the number of control firms corresponding to a given treated firm.

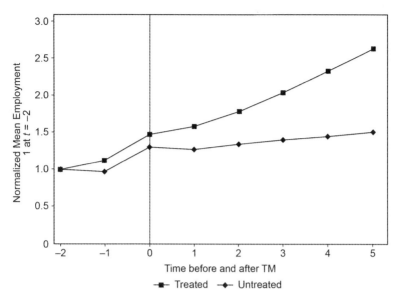

Fig. 5.7   **Normalized average employment before and after first trademark filing, treated vs. control group**

while average employment increases substantially for the treated firms after filing, there is a much smaller increase for the control group. As a result, the gap in average size between treated and control groups grows considerably. Five years after first filing ($t = 5$), the average employment of the trademark-filing firms is nearly twice that of the control group.

For better visual comparison of the trends, in figure 5.7, mean employment levels are normalized to one for both groups at $t = -2$ two years before the first trademark filing. The difference in mean employment between the two groups is statistically significant for each period t.[27] Figure 5.7 makes it clear that average employment is increasing in the year prior to filing for both treated and control groups. After filing, however, there is continuing growth in average employment for treated firms but much less expansion for the control group. In particular, average employment for the treated firms five years after the first trademark filing ($t = 5$) is about 80 percent higher than at the time of filing. For the control group, mean employment exhibits little growth in the five years following filing.

Figure 5.8 repeats the exercise in figure 5.7 with firm revenue for treated and control firms. Prefiling revenue trends are similar for the two groups but diverge at the year of first filing. The average revenue gap between treated and

27. Confidence intervals are not shown because the large number of firms in the sample generates very precise averages with tight confidence intervals. Therefore, the differences are statistically significant for each t.

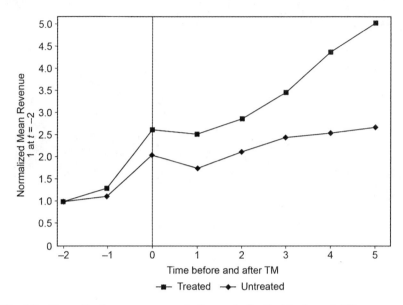

Fig. 5.8   Normalized average revenue before and after first trademark filing, treated vs. control group

control groups is fairly constant through two years after filing but expands considerably thereafter. For treated firms, revenue increases by about 100 percent five years after trademark filing. The control group exhibits a much more modest growth of about 35 percent over the same horizon. As in the case of employment, these patterns suggest the presence of potentially large benefits to trademark-filing firms in terms of revenue.

Taken together, figures 5.6–5.8 show considerable differences in the growth of employment and revenue for trademark-filing firms compared to their matched controls for both pre- and postfiling periods. Prefiling patterns suggest the potential presence of selection based on unobservables not accounted for in propensity score matching, as treated firms tend to be somewhat larger on average than the controls—though the difference is not substantial. Postfiling patterns also indicate the likely presence of trademark treatment effects. Treated and control firms diverge substantially in terms of average employment and revenue after first trademark filing. The gap in mean employment and revenue between the two groups expands noticeably two years postfiling. This pattern may simply reflect application pendency at USPTO or suggest that some effects of trademark filing are more gradual and take time to emerge.[28]

28. The average total pendency at USPTO for trademark applications is 8 to 12.5 months depending on the method of filing. See https://www.uspto.gov/dashboards/trademarks/main.dashxml.

Table 5.3   **Regression analysis of the relation between various firm outcomes and the first trademark filing**

Independent variables	Dependent variable			
	Employment	Revenue	R&D exp.	Patents
$FILE_i$	0.143***	0.323***	0.406***	0.011***
	[0.015]	[0.023]	[0.121]	[0.002]
$POST\_FILE_{it}$	0.997***	0.197***	0.191*	0.001
	[0.018]	[0.011]	[0.075]	[0.001]
$FILE_i \times POST\_FILE_{it}$	0.297***	0.195***	0.783***	0.013***
	[0.008]	[0.013]	[0.133]	[0.001]
$CONSTANT$	6.459***	7.376***	5.108***	−0.011**
	[0.032]	[0.018]	[0.069]	[0.003]
R^2	0.24	0.18	0.41	0.05
N	9.5M	5M	80K	10M

Notes: All regressions include industry (four-digit NAICS) and year fixed effects. All dependent variables are transformed using hyperbolic sine transformation. Standard errors clustered by industry are in parentheses. *, **, *** indicate significance at 10, 5, and 1 percent, respectively. N is rounded to avoid disclosure. Each control firm is weighted by the total number of control firms for the corresponding treated firm.

To understand the connection among firm growth, innovation, and trademark application filing further, the following difference-in-difference regression framework is considered for the treated firms and their matched controls:

$$(1) \quad \tilde{Y}_{it} = \alpha + \beta_F FILE_i + \beta_P POST\_FILE_{it} + \beta_{FP} FILE_i \times POST\_FILE_{it}$$
$$+ YEAR_t + INDUSTRY_i + \varepsilon_{it},$$

where the treatment status of firm i is indicated by $FILE_i$, and the time period t after treatment by $POST\_FILE_{it}$. The dependent variable $\tilde{Y}_{it}$ is the inverse hyperbolic sine transformation of the four dependent variables considered:

$$\tilde{Y}_{it} = \ln\left(Y_{it} + \sqrt{Y_{it}^2 + 1}\right).$$

This transformation is useful, in particular because there are several cases of no patenting or R&D expenditure in both treated and control groups. The coefficients β_F and β_{FP} measure, respectively, the effects of being in the treated group (trademark-filing firms) prior to treatment and being in the treated group *and* in the treatment period (years after first filing for trademark-filing firms).

Table 5.3 presents the results from the estimation of (1). The first two columns show the estimates for employment and revenue as the dependent variables that measure size. Note two key overall results in table 5.3. First, estimates of the β_F coefficient indicate that treated firms are, on average, larger in terms of both employment and revenue than the control group in the period before trademark filing. This finding indicates the likely presence of unobserved characteristics, not controlled for via propensity score matching, that are correlated with trademark filing. Second, estimates for the β_{FP} coefficient indicate sizable treatment effects. In the period following the first trademark filing, treated firms have, on average, approximately 34 percent higher employment and 24 percent greater revenue compared to the control group.[29] Overall, the results of the regression analysis for employment and revenue suggest that there are significant selection and treatment effects associated with first trademark filing. These effects will be investigated in further detail in future work.[30]

5.5.4   Trademarks and Innovative Activity

Next, consider the firm-level connection between different types of innovative activity and trademark applications. The theoretical motivation in section 5.3 suggests that investments in goodwill accumulation and innovation can be complements. An implication is that measures of these two types of investments should be correlated to some degree at the firm level. The next section explores the copresence of trademark applications and innovative investment, as measured by R&D, and innovative output, as measured by patents. It also examines the timing of the first trademark filing relative to that of R&D expenditures and patenting.

The patent data are derived from patent-firm linked data from the US Census Bureau, which combines the Longitudinal Business Database with the USPTO's patent database.[31] The firm-level R&D data are sourced from the Standard Industrial Research and Development Survey (SIRD) and Business R&D and Innovation Survey (BRDIS), conducted by the US Census Bureau for the National Science Foundation.[32] While the patent and trademark data pertain to the entire set of firms observed in the LBD, R&D expenditure data are only available for firms sampled in the SIRD and BRDIS. To analyze the trademark-filing and patent application activity by R&D-performing firms, the sample is therefore restricted to those firms that reported some or no R&D activity in the SIRD and BRDIS. While

---

29. Note that (1) implies that the percent change in $\left(Y_{it} + \sqrt{Y_{it}^2 + 1} \right)$ for the treated group in the treatment period can be estimated as $100[\exp(\hat{\beta}_{FP}) - 1]$. For Y_{it} not too small, the last estimate also approximates the percent change in Y_{it} due to a change in $FILE_i \times POST\_FILE_{it}$ from 0 to 1, because $Y_{it} + \sqrt{Y_{it}^2 + 1} \approx 2Y_{it}$ for Y_{it} not too small.

30. In particular, more stringent matching processes will be explored to understand whether the control group can match the treatment group better during the pretreatment period. This exercise will further clarify whether the differences in the pretreatment period between the treated and control groups are due to unobserved characteristics of the treated firms or can be eliminated with further refinement of the matching process.

31. See Graham et al. (2015) describing the "triangulation" process linking USPTO patents with the Census LBD. Their work has been extended to include patenting activity by firms from 2011 onward.

32. See Foster, Grim, and Zolas (2016) for more details on this survey and the characteristics of R&D-performing firms.

Table 5.4   **Patent application and R&D activity for all firms versus firms with trademark filing**

		All US firms		
Year	Firms	% of firms with patents	% of firms with R&D	% of firms with patents and R&D
1997	4,700,000	0.40	0.17	0.10
1999	4,900,000	0.46	0.18	0.11
2001	4,900,000	0.51	0.19	0.12
2003	5,200,000	0.53	0.23	0.14
2005	5,500,000	0.53	0.29	0.16
2007	5,600,000	0.54	0.32	0.17
2009	5,300,000	0.58	0.42	0.22
2011	5,300,000	0.60	0.47	0.24
		Firms with trademark filing		
Year	Firms	% of firms with patents	% of firms with R&D	% of firms with patents and R&D
1997	126,000	8.33	3.33	1.98
1999	154,000	8.44	3.31	1.95
2001	169,000	9.17	3.43	2.07
2003	182,000	9.34	4.07	2.42
2005	202,000	9.41	4.85	2.87
2007	227,000	9.03	5.07	2.91
2009	241,000	9.13	5.81	3.32
2011	254,000	9.06	6.69	3.66

Notes: The figures provide fractions of firms that have ever applied for a patent or performed R&D. Patent data comes from USPTO and R&D data from the BRDIS. Figures are rounded for disclosure purposes.

the survey, combined with the survey weights, is intended to be nationally representative, the raw (unweighted) firm counts, which tend to skew heavily toward R&D-performing firms, are used.

5.5.4.1   *Firm-Level Correlation and Relative Timing of R&D, Patents, and Trademark Filings*

Table 5.4 presents information on the copresence of innovative activity among trademark-filing firms. It shows the fraction of firms with patent applications and R&D activity for firms that have filed for a trademark registration and all firms in the United States. The share of trademark filers with patenting and/or R&D activity remains relatively small (between 8 percent and 9 percent of trademark-filing firms own at least 1 patent application and 3 percent to 7 percent perform R&D). However, table 5.4 indicates that trademark-filing firms are 15 to 20 times more likely to file for a patent or perform R&D compared to a typical US firm. From the perspective of better measuring firm innovation, this result is encouraging. To the extent that

Table 5.5   Copresence of trademark filing, patent applications, and R&D activity

		Firms with patent applications		
Year	Firms	% of firms with trademarks	% of firms with R&D	% of firms with trademarks and R&D
1997	19,000	55.26	25.79	13.16
1999	22,500	57.78	24.44	13.33
2001	25,000	62.00	23.20	14.00
2003	27,500	61.82	25.82	16.00
2005	29,000	65.52	30.34	20.00
2007	30,500	67.21	31.80	21.64
2009	31,000	70.97	37.10	25.81
2011	32,000	71.88	39.06	29.06

		R&D-performing firms		
Year	Firms	% of firms with trademarks	% of firms with patents	% of Firms with trademarks and patents
1997	8,000	52.50	61.25	31.25
1999	8,800	57.95	62.50	34.09
2001	9,200	63.04	63.04	38.04
2003	12,000	61.67	59.17	36.67
2005	16,000	61.25	55.00	36.25
2007	18,000	63.89	53.89	36.67
2009	22,000	63.64	52.27	36.36
2011	25,000	68.00	50.00	37.20

Notes: The figures provide fractions of firms that have ever applied for a patent or trademark, or performed R&D. Patent data comes from USPTO and R&D data from the BRDIS. Figures are rounded for disclosure purposes.

trademark data capture forms of innovation not typically accounted for by patents, this finding suggests that broadening the definition of innovating firms to include trademark-filing firms can enhance the identification of the innovative segment of the firm population. On the other hand, if most trademarks are used merely to differentiate largely homogeneous products rather than introduce true product or process innovations, trademark-filing firms may contribute little to the understanding of innovative activity by firms.

The picture is very different when considering the copresence of trademark filings among patent applicants and R&D active firms. Among the firms that have filed for a patent or performed R&D, table 5.5 suggests that the majority have applied for at least one trademark registration, with the rate steadily rising over time. Among patent-filing firms, 55 percent had applied for at least one trademark registration in 1997, with this figure rising to nearly 72 percent in 2011. Among R&D-performing firms, 52 percent had filed for at least one trademark registration in 1997, and as many as 68 percent had done so in 2011. More interesting, however, is the change in

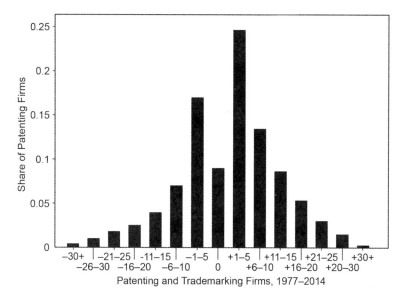

Fig. 5.9 **Timing of first patenting application relative to first trademark filing for firms that do both**

the proportion of R&D-performing firms seeking patents versus trademark registrations. In 1997, more than 61 percent of R&D-performing firms filed for at least one patent (versus the 52 percent that applied for at least one trademark registration). By 2011, the balance of innovative output changed, where only 50 percent of R&D-performing firms filed for at least one patent (versus the 68 percent that applied for at least one trademark registration). From an innovation measurement perspective, this reversal in output among R&D-performing firms supports the notion that for at least a subset of firms, trademarks may capture innovative outputs of R&D investment not accounted for by patents.

Combined, tables 5.4 and 5.5 hint that trademark filing may be a precursor to innovative activity in the form of patenting or R&D, with trademark registration growing in importance among innovative firms. This lends some support to the theoretical argument that firms that engage in patent and R&D activity also invest in protecting the gains from innovation—potentially in the form of a higher-quality product, better reputation, or larger customer base.

Figure 5.9 shows the distribution of firms based on the timing of patent activity relative to the first trademark application filing. Each bar indicates the proportion of patent and trademark filers as a function of the date of their first patent filing relative to the date of the first trademark filing. The timing of patent activity relative to the timing of trademark activity is grouped into five-year bins before and after time zero—the reference point that indicates the firm filed for its first patent in the same year it filed for its first trademark registration. Nearly 10 percent of patent and trademark filers filed for their first patent and trademark registration in the same year. Approximately 25 percent of patent and trademark filers filed for their first patent one to five years after their first trademark filing, and around 17 percent filed for their first patent in the one to five years prior to their first trademark application. In fact, almost 50 percent of firms with both patent and trademark applications filed for their first patents and trademark registrations within a five-year window, which strongly supports the notion that the two activities are intertwined. With respect to the overall timing of the two activities, in the majority of cases (59 percent), the first trademark application filing leads to or coincides with the first patent filing. This result lends some support to the theoretical argument that firms that trademark also invest the returns from accumulated goodwill into product and process innovation.

5.5.4.2   *Patenting and R&D Spending before and after Trademark Filing*

This section analyzes further the link between trademarks and innovation by examining issued patents and R&D expenditures by trademark-filing firms before and after their first trademark filing compared to a control group. It utilizes the same control group of nontrademark-filing firms identified via propensity score matching as in the analysis of employment and revenue above.

Figure 5.10 plots the average number of patents before and after the first trademark filing for firms that apply to register trademarks (treated) and the matching control firms (untreated). Mean patenting counts are again normalized to one for both groups at $t = -2$ two years before the first trademark filing. Trends in average patenting leading up to trademark filing are somewhat different. Average patenting increases for both groups in the year prior to filing. However, while the treated group exhibits a large increase in the year of filing, the control group's average patenting declines. After filing, average patenting grows at a similar rate for both treated and control firms, though the gap does expand two years postfiling. Between $t = 2$ and $t = 5$ growth in the average number of patents is about 30 percent for the treated firms compared to only about 15 percent for the control group.

The difference-in-difference model specified in (1) is used to analyze innovative activity for treated and control groups before and after the first trademark application. The last two columns of table 5.3 report the estimation results for R&D expenditures and the number of issued patents as the dependent variables. For both the R&D expenditures and the number of patents, the treatment group has higher values for the prefiling period, as indicated by the estimated value of β_F. As in the case of employment and revenue, this finding suggests the likely presence of unobserved factors that result in higher patent and R&D activity for treated firms prior to trademark

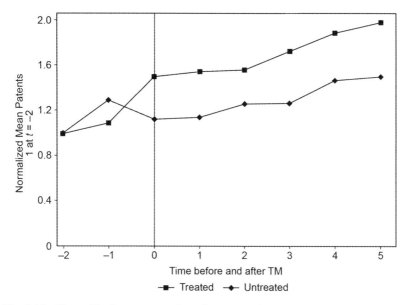

Fig. 5.10   **Normalized average number of patents before and after the first trademark filing, treated vs. control group**

filing. In the postfiling period, average R&D expenditure and patenting by treated firms are higher than those of control firms, as the estimated values of β_{FP} suggest.

Overall, the results suggest that both selection and treatment effects associated with trademark filing are relevant for understanding firm-level innovative activity, as the theory suggests. Further investigation of both of these effects with a more stringent matching process to obtain a control group is left for future work.

5.6   Conclusion

The progress of empirical research on trademark activity by US firms has been largely hampered by the lack of comprehensive firm-trademark linked data. This chapter reports on the construction of a new firm-level longitudinal dataset that allows for the tracking of trademark-filing activity over the life cycle of a firm. The dataset brings together the USPTO's Trademark Case Files Dataset and the US Census Bureau's Business Register and the Longitudinal Business Database for the period 1976–2014. Using the linked dataset, it is possible to identify if, and when, a firm first applies for a trademark. This key event is then tied to firm characteristics and dynamics to understand the nature of selection associated with trademark filing as well as the treatment effects related to a trademark application.

The data are used to examine how firm employment, revenue, R&D expenditures, and patenting change after a firm's first trademark filing compared to their prefiling levels. The analysis suggests the potential presence of strong selection and treatment effects associated with trademarks. Compared to the general population of firms, first-time trademark filers tend to be younger and larger firms. In addition, an initial analysis using a propensity score matching exercise indicates that average firm employment and revenue tend to be higher for firms after they file for their first trademark compared to a control group. For first-time trademark-filing firms, both patenting and R&D activity are also higher after the filing, again, compared to a control group.

The results also indicate that while most of the firms that have applied for trademark registration do not engage in innovative activity as measured by patent filings or grants, the proportion of trademark-filing firms with a patent application is significantly higher than that of all firms. To the extent that trademarks capture firm-level innovative activity not accounted for by patents, the relatively small presence of patents in trademark-filing firms and the copresence of trademark applications and R&D expenditure without any patenting are encouraging in terms of broadening the definition of the innovative segment of firms in the economy beyond simply those that have patents. Nevertheless, a sizable fraction of firms with patents and R&D activity also tend to have trademark applications. This finding may indicate that trademark registrations are used by innovative firms to protect potential gains from innovation. However, the reverse may also be true. Where trademark filing proceeds patent and R&D activity, firms may be investing the gains from accumulated goodwill into product and process innovation.

The trademark-firm linked dataset opens up several possibilities for future research. For instance, there is a large body of work in the marketing literature for which the dataset is highly relevant. The theoretical literature emphasizes a connection between trademarks and customer acquisition and loyalty-building by firms. Various models focus on the role of trademarks in reducing consumer search and switching costs, establishing brand loyalty and goodwill, and signaling quality.[33] In general, by protecting a firm's investments in marketing and reputation-building, trademarks can lead to a higher intensity of advertising and marketing expenditures, as trademark registrants can better appropriate the benefits from such expenditures. The new dataset can be instrumental in testing some of these theoretical implications.

There is also more to explore regarding the connection between trademarks and firm scale and scope. In particular, the role of trademark registra-

33. See, e.g., Landes and Posner (1987, 1988) and Economides (1988) for theoretical arguments on the connection between trademarks and consumer behavior. For recent models of firm dynamics under costly and gradual customer acquisition, see Dinlersoz and Yorukoglu (2012) and Gourio and Rudanko (2014).

tion in new product introductions and changes in a firm's product portfolio can be examined. For instance, using changes in the narrowly defined industry classifications for a firm's products before and after trademark filing, one can investigate whether trademark registrations facilitate scope expansion into products that are not closely related to a firm's core product portfolio.

Another avenue of research that can benefit from the new dataset is the valuation of trademarks. The dataset allows for the observation of first trademark registration by a firm, as well as its subsequent trademark registrations, and trademark reassignments. Reputation indicated by a trademark is a valuable asset that needs to be protected.[34] A reputable name or mark can also be traded.[35] The information contained in the trademark applications and assignments can be used, in conjunction with measures of firm value, to attach valuations to trademarks. In addition, the oppositions placed against a trademark filing and the resulting procedural outcomes observed in the dataset can be used to measure the inherent value of certain trademarks, as oppositions would be unlikely if the trademark was of little value.

Appendix

Data Construction

Given the lack of disambiguated identifiers, such as an EIN, that are shared between the TCFD and the BR, the two datasets have to be brought together using name and address matching techniques. The current matching effort is focused on matching domestic businesses observed in the trademark ownership database to the employer firm universe. Future work will incorporate businesses found in the trademark assignments database, which captures the transfer of trademarks between businesses, foreign trademark-filing firms with domestic establishments, and nonemployer trademark-filing firms. The final output of the matching methodology will be firm-level links between Census Bureau data and records in the TCFD.

The input frame for the matching process is the ownership databases in the TCFD. Several conditions are used to subset the raw owner file records that will be considered for matching to the BR. First, the filing, registration, and publication dates are used to exclude all trademarks for which the maximum year is less than 1976, the earliest year of the BR. Second, the country field is used to identify domestic trademark owners. Finally, the owner data file also contains certain types of businesses that are unlikely to be covered in the BR. These include entities representing federal and state governments as well as

---

34. See Cabral (2005) for a review of the theoretical literature on the economics of reputation. See also Cabral and Hortacsu (2010) and Cabral (2012) for studies of reputation on the internet.
35. See Tadelis (1999) for a theoretical analysis of reputation as a tradeable asset.

Table 5.A1   Input frame

Input frame	Trademarks (thousands)	Ownership records (thousands)
Owner file	7,214	17,381
Excluding pre-1976	6,907	16,937
Excluding foreign	5,939	14,407
Excluding federal, state, individual	5,048	12,289

Source: USPTO Trademarks Casefile Database, author's calculations.
Notes: Counts in thousands.

individuals. The owner entity type code is used to exclude these cases from the match to the BR. Table 5.A1 shows the count of unique trademarks and owner records after applying each restriction to the sample.[36] The owner file initially contains more than 7 million trademarks and 17 million owner records. This reduces to almost 5 million trademarks and 12 million owner records after excluding foreign, federal, state, and individuals and those before 1976.

The first step in the matching process is the extraction of all unique name and address combinations from the owner data file. The owner data file contains an observation for each owner recorded for each trademark application, registration, and publication from 1870 to 2014.[37] Name and address information are collected at different times during a trademark's life cycle, often for the same business entity. Not only are there multiple instances of the name and address information for one or more businesses associated with a trademark; there are also different types of business names. For example, each record in the TCFD may include "former," "doing business as," and "composed of" business names. Each owner record also includes two street address variables, which correspond to the first and second lines of the owner's street address. In many cases, the owner's full street address is split across these fields. It is not always the case, however, that line 1 should precede line 2. For example, line 1 might include the suite number, while line 2 contains the street address or vice versa. In order to maximize the chances of identifying a match for each business in the TCFD, each unique name (across all name types) is combined with combinations of line 1 and line 2 of the street address (i.e., line 1, line 2, line 1 concatenated with line 2, and line 2 concatenated with line 1). This process produces one or more name and address combinations that have the potential to match to the BR for each owner record.

The next step in matching the TCFD data to the BR is the cleaning and preparation of both datasets. First, common strings that provide little identifying information for matching are removed from both datasets. These include symbols and punctuation (e.g., "&," "," "@"), common words

36. Each trademark has one or more "owner records," or records in the ownership database. Each record captures a different stage of the application, review, and registration process.
37. As noted above, we exclude records filed, registered, and published prior to 1976.

(e.g., "and," "the"), and abbreviations or designations (e.g., "Co.," "LLC," "LTD"). Additional standardization procedures are used to standardize the name, street, and city fields.[38] Values in the state field are cleaned and standardized, and the zip code field is subset to five digits. These cleaning algorithms are applied to the name and addresses from both the TCFD and the BR. Once cleaned, the name and addresses from both datasets are matched using fuzzy string techniques combined with a blocking methodology.

The matching of the TCFD to the BR proceeds in several steps. First, an initial subset of potential matches is identified based on a relatively loose name-only match criterion between all unique name and addresses extracted from the TCFD and all establishments in the BR.[39] All matches not meeting this very loose criterion are excluded. Matches of different quality from this initial match set are extracted based on combinations of name and address fields. These match categories are based on whether the match is on the name in conjunction with different address fields (street, city, state, and zip code). Next, a string comparator is used to further clean and subset the matches. The Jaro-Winkler (JW) string comparator, which takes values ranging from zero to one as a function of how similar two strings are, is calculated for the TCFD and BR name and city pairs. Additionally, a composite JW score is calculated across all three fields. Name-only matches, which tend to be of the lowest quality, and matches made using only the name and a single address variable are kept only if the JW score between the name fields is greater than 0.85.[40] Across all match passes, only the highest-quality pass is kept for each TCFD name and address. Among the remaining matches, the composite JW score is used to select only the highest-quality matches.

The next step of the matching aggregates the establishment-level results from the BR match described above to the target firm-level match and integrates those matches with the LBD. From the LBD, the first and last year of observation for each firm ID are extracted. All unique combinations of TCFD name and address and firm ID are kept. The first and last firm years, in combination with the minimum and maximum trademark-filing years associated with each TCFD name and address, are used to clean firm-level matches. Since trademark filing can plausibly occur well before a firm enters the employer universe, all matches that occur within a three-year window before and after the firm's first and last year observed in the LBD are kept.

The final stage of the cleaning algorithm involves additional disambiguation of business names in the TCFD in order to increase the number of unique firm-TCFD matches. First, additional name standardization is performed to group matched and unmatched cases. Information from the LBD

---

38. These standardization procedures include algorithms found in the SAS Data Quality suite.

39. This and other fuzzy name matches are done using SAS Data Quality algorithms. Where noted, we use the Jaro-Winkler string comparator to clean matches.

40. This and other cutoff values were reached by visual inspection of the matches and JW scores. The score of 0.90 balanced Type I and Type II errors.

Table 5.A2   Match quality distribution

Match pass	Share of matches
Name, Street, City, State	81.3
Name, State, Zip Code	4.8
Name, Zip Code	0.0
Name, State	5.1
Name Only	8.7

Source: USPTO Trademarks Casefile Database, Business Register, author's calculations.
Notes: Match passes listed in order of decreasing quality.

is then leveraged to further reduce multiple matches. In eliminating certain duplicate matches, matched firms are required to have positive employment, and cases where a firm has more than 10 trademarks *and at the same time* the number of trademarks exceed the number of employees are also dropped. Table 5.A2 shows the match quality distribution for the resulting linked data. The majority (81 percent) of matches use a combination of name, street, city, and state. Note also that less than 10 percent of the matches rely on name only, which is a relatively weak criterion that will tend to generate more false positives compared to matches with address blocking.

In order to better understand why TCFD name and addresses do not receive a firm match, unmatched cases are matched to the nonemployer business register (ILBD). The ILBD is based on administrative data on income tax returns (Form 1040 with attached Schedule C[s]). In the ILBD, some of the observations include individual's names, while others pertain to firm names. To carry out the match, an algorithm is applied to determine whether an observation likely represents an individual's name. Steps generally similar to the match to the BR are then followed to match the unmatched trademarks to the names and addresses appearing in the ILBD. For this study, these matches are used primarily to better understand the quality of matches to the employer universe. Future work will investigate matches to nonemployer businesses and their growth and transition dynamics.

Table 5.A3 shows the match rates between trademarks in the TCFD owner file and the LBD and ILBD by decade. This table also reports the percent of employer matches that are unique. The overall match rate to the LBD is over 83 percent and 2.4 percent to the ILBD. The first point to note is that the number of trademarks filed each year has grown substantially over time. The match rate to the employer universe has fallen about 16 points between the 1980s and the 2010s. The percent of matches that are unique is increasing over time, rising from 59 percent in the 1980s to 88 percent in the 2010s. The match rate to the nonemployer universe, in contrast to the employer match, has been growing since 1990.

Analysis of the underlying matched and unmatched records reveals sev-

Table 5.A3   **Match rates by decade**

		LBD		ILBD
Years	Trademarks	match rate	Percent unique	Match rate
1980–89	363,000	88.8	59.0	
1990–99	582,000	88.8	64.6	1.4
2000–2009	1,058,000	83.9	75.2	2.7
2010–14	649,000	73.3	87.7	3.8

Source: Observation counts rounded. USPTO Trademarks Casefile Database, LBD, author's calculations.

Notes: Decades are defined by trademark registration year. Percent unique is the share of matches that are to a single firm id. The range of the BR and LBD is 1976 to 2014 and the range of the ILBD is 1993 to 2014.

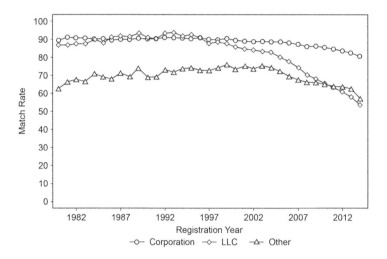

Fig. 5.A1   LBD match rate by legal form of organization
Source: USPTO Trademarks Casefile Database, LBD, author's calculations.
Notes: Only registered trademarks included. Corporations and LLCs are identified using the legal entity type code found in the TCFD.

eral patterns.[41] First, the decline in match rates begins in the late 1990s and speeds up around 2010. As shown in figure 5.A1, the decline is most pronounced among records identified as "Limited Liability Company" (LLC) in the TCFD. The match rate for LLCs falls from about 91 percent in the early 1990s to less than 45 percent in 2014. In addition, LLCs are the fastest

41. For this analysis, only the registered trademarks are considered rather than applications for trademarks, since registered trademarks require demonstration of commercial use and thus may be better associated with employer businesses in BR and LBD.

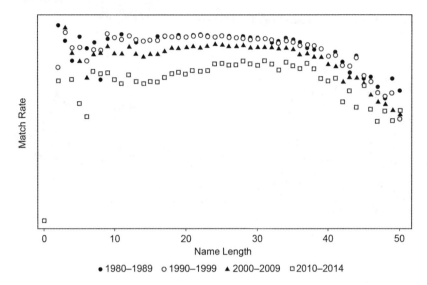

Fig. 5.A2   Match rate and string length
Source: USPTO Trademarks Casefile Database, LBD, author's calculations.
Notes: Match rates on the *y* axis suppressed to avoid the disclosure of sensitive information.

growing entity type in the TCFD over this period, rising from about 2,000 filings in 1990 to almost 100,000 filings in 2014. The fraction of LLCs has also been growing over this period in the general population of firms.

To investigate the declining match rate between the TCFD and the LBD, several hypotheses for the decline are explored, including deteriorating string quality, a compositional shift toward nonemployers, and the growth of informal businesses. First, if the quality of the string variables in the TCFD (e.g., name and address fields) declines over time, this could adversely affect the match rate to the LBD. To explore this hypothesis, measures of mean string length are constructed over time for both names and addresses. The average name length and match rate exhibit very similar time series patterns with a simple correlation of 0.96. Moreover, the average string length of the name variable falls from almost 24.5 characters to fewer than 22.5, which could represent an 8 percent loss of information over the period. Figure 5.A2 shows the relationship between string length and match rate over time. Both relatively short and long string names have lower match rates. Importantly, the match rate declines over time for all string lengths. This implies that the decreasing information in the TCFD name field is unlikely to account for the declining match rate to the LBD.

Another potential explanation for the decline in match rates would be a compositional shift toward nonemployers among businesses filing for trademarks. As shown in Table 5.A3, the match rate to the ILBD does increase over time. However, the increased matches to the nonemployer universe are not enough to make up for the decline in the LBD match rate. Assuming all TCFD businesses not found in the LBD were true nonemployers, the ILBD match rate would need to be at least five times larger to fill the gap in the falling employer match rate.[42] It is also the case that the vast majority of records in the ILBD are person records derived from tax filings for sole proprietorships. These records often have the individual filer's name as the name of record in the ILBD. Manual inspection of the unmatched cases later in the time series suggests that the vast majority of unmatched cases include business names rather than person names.

If a growing share of trademark application filings are associated with informal or not-yet-implemented business ideas, one would expect the match rate to employer firms to fall over time. A number of the unmatched cases filed in recent years appear to have a web presence on platforms such as Etsy or Facebook. It could be the case that either these types of businesses do not earn enough revenue to file a Schedule C or the businesses were operated only sporadically. According to the 2017 Internal Revenue Service (IRS) instructions for form 1040, self-employed individuals who had net earnings of less than $400 were not required to file a Schedule C and would therefore not appear in the ILBD. Additionally, the 2017 IRS instructions for form Schedule C clarify that a "sporadic activity or a hobby does not qualify as a business." With trademark application fees as low as $275 for electronic applications, it is possible that some individuals file for trademarks in order to protect the potential exploitation of a business idea that otherwise remains a hobby.[43] As with a compositional shift toward nonemployer businesses, a growing share of informal businesses in the TCFD would prove the declining match rate to the BR to be innocuous.

Finally, the quality of the matches is analyzed. A random sample of over 350 matches is classified as either a true or false positive by clerical review. Once classified, the precision of the matching methodology can be measured. The precision measure, commonly used to evaluate the quality of information retrieval algorithms, captures the proportion of matches that are true matches. The match turns out to be fairly precise, with an overall precision score of 94 percent, meaning that 94 percent of the matches represent true matches based on the sample analyzed. The precision of matches is relatively stable over time, falling slightly by the end of the period.

Name and address matching techniques result in robust linkages between the information in the TCFD and Census Bureau information on businesses

---

42. As an additional validation we compare the share of nonemployers specifically among LLCs in the BR from 2007 to 2014, years for which we are able to distinguish LLCs. The share of nonemployers among LLCs is actually falling in the BR over time, a finding inconsistent with a compositional shift toward nonemployers among the universe of LLCs driving the decline in match rates.

43. Trademark applications may be filed as "use in commerce" or "intent to use in commerce." In either case, in order for an application to obtain registration, the USPTO requires proof that a trademark is used in commerce. See Graham et al. (2013) for details.

in the BR and LBD. The TCFD is relatively large, containing over 5 million trademarks. Over the period, about 83 percent of these trademarks are matched to at least one firm ID. While the match rate somewhat declines over time, the ambiguity of those matches—that is, how many TCFD records end up being linked to multiple firm IDs—also declines. The decline in match rate is concentrated among records flagged as LLCs in the TCFD. Several potential explanations for the decline in the employer match rate are explored, but none are able to entirely explain the patterns observed in the data. Ultimately, matches prove to be of high quality, with a precision score of over 90 percent.

References

Arora, Ashish, Xiaoshu Bei, and Wesley M. Cohen. 2016. "Why Firms Trademark (or Not): Evidence from the U.S. Trademark Data." Working paper, Duke University.

Baroncelli, Eugenia, Carsten Fink, and Beata S. Javorcik. 2005. "The Global Distribution of Trademarks: Some Stylized Facts." *World Economy* 28:765–82.

Block, Jorn, Christian Fisch, Alexander Hahn, and Philipp Sandner. 2015. "Why Do SMEs File Trademarks? Insights from Firms in Innovative Industries." *Research Policy* 44:1915–30. http://dx.doi.org/10.1016/j.respol.2015.06.007.

Cabral, Luis. 2005. "The Economics of Trust and Reputation: A Primer." Monograph in progress, New York University. http://pages.stern.nyu.edu/126lcabral/reputation/Reputation_June05.pdf.

Cabral, Luis. 2012. "Reputation on the Internet." In *The Oxford Handbook of the Digital Economy*, edited by M. Peitz and J. Waldfogel, 343–54. Oxford: Oxford University Press.

Cabral, Luis, and Ali Hortacsu. 2010. "The Dynamics of Seller Reputation: Evidence from eBay." *Journal of Industrial Economics* 58:54–78.

Decker, Ryan, John Haltiwanger, Ron S. Jarmin, and Javier Miranda. 2016. "Where Has All the Skewness Gone? The Decline in High-Growth (Young) Firms in the U.S." *European Economic Review* 86:4–23.

Davis, Steven, John Haltiwanger, Ron Jarmin, C. J. Krizan, Javier Miranda, Al Nucci, and Kristen Sandusky. 2007. "Measuring the Dynamics of Young and Small Businesses: Integrating the Employer and Nonemployer Universes Firms." NBER Working Paper No. 13226. Cambridge, MA: National Bureau of Economic Research.

Dinlersoz, Emin, and Mehmet Yorukoglu. 2012. "Information and Industry Dynamics." *American Economic Review* 102:884–913.

Economides, Nicolas. 1988. "The Economics of Trademarks." *The Trademark Reporter* 78:523–39.

Flikkema, Meindart, Ard-Pieter De Man, and Carolina Castaldi. 2014. "Are Trademark Counts a Valid Indicator of Innovation? Results of an In-Depth Study of New Benelux Trademarks Filed by SMEs." *Industry and Innovation* 21: 310–31.

Foster, Lucia, Cheryl Grim, and Nikolas Zolas. 2016. "A Portrait of Firms That

Invest in R&D." US Census Bureau Center for Economic Studies Paper No. CES-WP-16-41.

Goldschlag, Nathan, and Javier Miranda. 2016. "Business Dynamics Statistics of High Tech Industries." US Census Bureau Center for Economic Studies Paper No. CES-WP-16-55.

Gourio, François, and Leena Rudanko. 2014. "Customer Capital." *Review of Economic Studies* 81 (3): 1102–36.

Graham, S., G. Hancock, A. C. Marco, and A. F. Myers. 2013. "The USPTO Trademark Case Files Dataset: Descriptions, Lessons, and Insights." *Journal of Economics and Management Strategy* 22 (4): 669–705.

Graham, Stuart, Cheryl Grim, Tariq Islam, Alan Marco, and Javier Miranda. 2018. "Business Dynamics of Innovating Firms: Linking U.S. Patent Data with Administrative Data on Workers and Firms." *Journal of Economics & Management Strategy* 27 (3): 372–402.

Greenhalgh, C., M. Longland, and D. Bosworth. 2003. "Trends and Distribution of Intellectual Property: U.K. and European Patents and U.K. Trade and Service Marks, 1986–2000." Report for the U.K. Intellectual Property Office.

Greenhalgh, C., and M. Rogers. 2007. "Trade Marks and Performance in UK Firms: Evidence of Schumpeterian Competition through Innovation." Economics Series Working Papers 300, University of Oxford, Department of Economics.

Greenhalgh, C., and M. Rogers. 2008. "Intellectual Property Activity by Service Sector and Manufacturing Firms in the U.K., 1996–2000." In *The Evolution of Business Knowledge*, edited by Harry Scarbrough, 295–314. Oxford: Oxford University Press.

Haltiwanger, John, and Ron Jarmin. 2007. "Integrated Longitudinal Business Database: Data Overview." 2007 Kauffman Symposium on Entrepreneurship and Innovation Data, November 2.

Haltiwanger, John, Ron Jarmin, Robert Kulick, and Javi Miranda. 2017. "High Growth Young Firms: Contributions to Job, Output, and Productivity Growth." In *Measuring Entreprenurial Businesses: Current Knowledge and Challenges*, edited by John Haltiwanger, Erik Hurst, Javier Miranda, and Antoinette Schoar, 11–62. NBER Studies in Income and Wealth. Chicago: University of Chicago Press.

Heath, Davidson, and Christopher Mace. 2017. "What's a Brand Worth? Trademark Protection, Profits and Product Quality." Working paper, University of Utah.

Jensen, P. H., and E. Webster. 2004. "Patterns of Trademarking Activity in Australia." *Australian Intellectual Property Journal* 15:112–26.

Jensen, P. H., and E. Webster. 2006. "Firm Size and the Use of Intellectual Property Rights." *Economic Record* 82:44–55.

Landes, William, and Richard Posner. 1987. "Trademark Law: An Economic Perspective." *Journal of Law and Economics* 30:265–309.

Landes, William, and Richard Posner. 1988. "The Economics of Trademark Law." *The Trademark Reporter* 78:267–306.

Landes, William, and Richard Posner. 2003. *The Economic Structure of Intellectual Property Law*. Cambridge, MA: Harvard University Press.

Millot, Valentina. 2011. "Firms' Intangible Assets: Who Relies on Trademarks? Analysis of French and German Firms' Trademarking Behaviour." DRUID working paper. http://druid8.sit.aau.dk/acc_papers/mrfhruoxl97gjekxq4ajhh8ln9o2.pdf.

Sandner, Philipp. 2009. "The Identification of Trademark Filing Strategies: Creating, Hedging, Modernizing, and Extending Brands." *The Trademark Reporter* 99:1257–98.

Sandner, Philipp, and Joern Block. 2011. "The Market Value of R&D, Patents, and Trademarks." *Research Policy* 40:969–85.
Schautschick, Philipp, and Christine Greenhalgh. 2016. "Empirical Studies of Trade Marks: The Existing Economic Literature." *Economics of Innovation and New Technology* 25 (4): 358–90.
Tadelis, Steve. 1999. "What's in a Name? Reputation as a Tradeable Asset." *American Economic Review* 89:548–63.

Research Experience as Human Capital in New Business Outcomes

Nathan Goldschlag, Ron Jarmin, Julia Lane, and Nikolas Zolas

6.1 Introduction

Start-ups and entrepreneurial firms contribute disproportionately to job creation and productivity growth (Decker et al. 2014; Acemoglu et al. 2018). The workforce composition of young firms plays an equally important role in shaping dispersion in start-up outcomes (Audretsch, Keilbach, and Lehmann 2006; McGuirk, Lenihan, and Hart 2015). Human capital, whether acquired through experience (Glaeser, Kerr, and Ponzetto 2010), on-the-job training (Lazear and Shaw 2007; Bender et al. 2016; Bloom et al. 2014), or university-based research experience, is an important determinant

Nathan Goldschlag is a senior economist at the Center for Economic Studies at the US Census Bureau.

Ron Jarmin is deputy director and chief operating officer of the US Census Bureau.

Julia Lane is professor in the Wagner School of Public Policy at New York University and Provostial Fellow in Innovation Analytics and professor at the Center for Urban Science and Progress.

Nikolas Zolas is is a senior economist at the Center for Economic Studies at the US Census Bureau.

This research was supported by the National Center for Science and Engineering Statistics NSF SciSIP Awards 1064220 and 1262447; NSF Education and Human Resources DGE Awards 1348691, 1547507, 1348701, 1535399, 1535370; NSF NCSES award 1423706; NIHP01AG039347; and the Ewing Marion Kaufman and Alfred P. Sloan Foundations. Lane was supported through an Intergovernmental Personnel Act assignment to the US Census Bureau. We thank Scott Stern, participants at the Measuring and Accounting for Innovation in the 21st Century conference, and anonymous reviewers for helpful comments. The research agenda draws on work with many coauthors, but particularly Bruce Weinberg and Jason Owen Smith. Any opinions and conclusions expressed herein are those of the authors and do not necessarily represent the views of the US Census Bureau. All results have been reviewed to ensure that no confidential information is disclosed. For acknowledgments, sources of research support, and disclosure of the authors' material financial relationships, if any, please see https://www.nber.org/books-and-chapters/measuring-and-accounting-innovation-21st-century/research-experience-human-capital-new-business-outcomes.

of growth and survival for young firms. Moreover, this relationship may be particularly salient for innovative, R&D-intensive, and high-tech firms, who increasingly demand a highly trained workforce. This chapter contributes to this literature by developing new measures of workplace experience, particularly within R&D-intensive and high-tech firms. We also make use of an entirely new data source that directly measures research experience. We examine the relationship between those measures and start-up survival, growth, and innovative activities such as patenting and trademarking.

We describe the construction of four new human capital measures derived from two different sources. The first is a direct measure of research experience derived from a new dataset drawn from the human resource files of a set of research-intensive universities. The data capture all payroll transactions for all individuals—including undergraduate students, graduate students, and postdoctoral fellows—employed on funded scientific projects at 22 major universities (Lane et al. 2015). These data are the first to directly measure the human capital developed through project-level investments in university science. The second, third, and fourth measures are indirect in nature. They are drawn from LEHD (Longitudinal Employee-Household Dynamics) and W-2 data and create new worker-level measures of human capital based on whether each worker has worked in R&D labs, high-tech businesses, or universities.

We also describe the construction of two new datasets on start-ups. The first of these is a Startup Firm History File drawn from the Longitudinal Business Database (LBD), supplemented with additional information from the Census Bureau's Business Register. In addition, we create a Startup Worker History File derived from worker-level data on jobs and earnings. These new files provide a national frame of start-ups, their survival, and their growth between the years 2005 and 2015, as well as a national frame of all workers affiliated with these start-ups.

Our results suggest that a one-worker increase in the number of high-human-capital employees in a start-up firm's workforce is associated with a lower probability of survival to the next period by 0.74 to 4.8 percentage points, depending on the experience type. However, for start-ups that do survive to the first period, the hiring of one of these workers in the founding year is associated with a 1.3 to 4 percentage point increase in employment growth and a 2.2 to 5 percentage point increase in revenue in the following year. This is suggestive evidence that high-human-capital employees elect to go to more high-risk start-ups that exhibit "up or out" dynamics—either exiting or growing quickly. On the innovation side, the addition of one high-human-capital individual is positively related to patent and trademark outcomes in the next period, with patent filings increasing by 0.5 to 9.2 percentage points and trademark filings increasing by 1.5 to 7.5 percentage points in the following year. Our measures of human capital also explain a significant amount of the variation in innovation outcomes, where the inclusion of our basic measures of human capital help explain an additional 40 percent of variation in patenting outcomes and 11 percent of variation in trademarking outcomes.

The direction of causality may be complex in this setting. Start-ups with inherently risky ideas or production technologies may exhibit higher demand for high-human-capital workers. Moreover, there may be several important channels through which high-human-capital workers impact young firms. First, high-human-capital workers may simply represent an important input to the firm's production technology. Alternatively, there may be important interaction effects between high-human-capital workers and the tacit knowledge they bring to the firm. Regardless of the mechanism, the results presented in this chapter are consistent with the view that there is a positive and significant relationship between workforce experience and business start-up outcomes.

6.2 Background

Our focus on start-ups is informed by literature that suggests that young entrepreneurial businesses are important for introducing and diffusing innovations in the economy. Several authors have shown indirect linkages between formal investments in research and innovation and entrepreneurship and economic growth (Bania, Eberts, and Fogarty 1993; Lowe and Gonzalez-Brambila 2007; Hausman 2012). In particular, the work of Akcigit and Kerr (2018) shows that the relative rate of major inventions is higher in small firms and new-entrant firms. Guzman and Stern (2016) note that the early-stage choices of start-ups—their "digital signatures"—are particularly important in predicting their future success.

There is a growing literature linking human capital to the survival and growth of such new businesses (Audretsch, Keilbach, and Lehmann 2006; McGuirk, Lenihan, and Hart 2015). In particular, the decision to start a business and its subsequent productivity and success are associated with having an entrepreneurial workforce (Glaeser, Kerr, and Ponzetto 2010; Syverson 2010). Related work also suggests that highly innovative individuals make "exceptional" contributions to economic growth (Kerr et al. 2016). Indeed, the personnel economics and management literatures draw on extensive studies of businesses and human resource practices, which suggest that many productive businesses either invest in job-based training or seek to hire well-trained individuals (Lazear and Shaw 2007; Bender et al. 2016; Bloom et al. 2014). A related literature links external R&D investment and the success of the R&D efforts of individual firms (Tambe 2014). In-depth studies of the components of intangible assets in contributing to firm productivity and success invariably mention the importance of training (Corrado, Hulten, and Sichel 2005). In addition to affecting innovative outcomes, human capital measures such as on-the-job training have also been linked to firm productivity (Black and Lynch 1996; Bartel et al. 2014).

For our purposes of measuring the relationship between human capital and start-up outcomes, we draw on two sets of literature. The first has studied human capital acquisition through learning by doing and experience. The second addresses the transmission of new knowledge through the flows of individuals from one business to another.

The role of experience in terms of learning how to perform complex new tasks through trial and error has been extensively discussed in the endogenous technical change literature (Romer 1990). There is also a great deal of evidence to support the notion that past experience imparts valuable business skills (Lafontaine and Shaw 2016) and that firm growth can be significantly affected by workers with experience in R&D activities (Jones 2002; Acemoglu et al. 2013).

The role of university research training specifically on innovative activity and business start-ups is supported by compelling anecdotal evidence. This includes linking the growth of Silicon Valley to the presence of Stanford, the success of Boston to the excellent set of universities in the area, and the arising of the Research Triangle to the research activity of Duke University, the University of North Carolina, and North Carolina State. An extensive literature ties regional economic development clusters to the presence of active research universities, suggesting that research-trained individuals flow into innovative new businesses (Hausman 2012; Glaeser, Kerr, and Ponzetto 2010; Kantor and Whalley 2013, 2014). To this end, Corrado and Lane note that the data needed to determine the economic and social value created by innovation in organizations should include "detailed data on workers— their skills, their responsibilities, and their knowledge—including their flows across companies were desired for transformative research on the combined process of entrepreneurship and innovation" (Corrado and Lane 2009).

Taken together, these various literatures are consistent with the notion that hiring workers with experience is a way firms gain tacit knowledge, particularly when ideas are complex (Duranton and Puga 2004; Gertler 2003). The work of Lee Fleming and coauthors, for example, suggests that if there are impediments to research-experienced workers moving from one firm to another, less innovation occurs (Fleming, King, and Juda 2007; Marx, Singh, and Fleming 2015). Our own work suggests that research-trained workers are more likely to work at firms with characteristics closely linked to productivity (Zolas et al. 2015).

However, there has been little work done in terms of measuring the experience of workers at different types of firms. The Annual Survey of Manufactures provides counts of production and nonproduction workers; most other business data sources simply provide counts of employees. In principle, a particularly useful source of evidence in this context is economy-wide linked employer-employee data, such as the LEHD data (Abowd, Haltiwanger, and Lane 2004). Abowd, Haltiwanger, and Lane (2005) have used linked data to compute person-specific measures of human capital but do not directly compute measures of research experience. While some work has shown that there are returns to experience at R&D-performing firms (Barth, Davis, and Freeman 2016), there has been no study to our knowledge that directly measures experience in high-tech firms, R&D labs, universities, or scientific projects and ties it to start-up outcomes. In this chapter, we analyze the link between these types of experience and among workers at start-ups and the outcomes of those start-ups, including survival, growth, and innovative activity.

6.3   Framework, Data, and Measurement

We follow much of the literature (Lazear and Shaw 2007; Bender et al. 2016; Bloom et al. 2014) in adopting a simple reduced-form framework to examine outcomes for start-ups in terms of their survival, employment and revenue growth, and innovative activities, such as being granted patents and registering trademarks. Conceptually, outcomes (Y) for start-up firm f at time t are driven by the quantity and quality of human capital (HK) it employs as well as standard controls such as capital (K), technology (A), and external factors (X) such as macroeconomic conditions and industry factors:

$$(1) \qquad Y_{ft} = F(A_{ft}, K_{ft}, HK_{ft}, X_{ft}).$$

There is some evidence that the effect of human capital will be important for businesses whose production processes involve performing complex tasks (Ichniowski, Shaw, and Prennushi 1997). As a result, the analysis that follows provides separate analyses for high-tech businesses; the scale of the data permits such detailed analyses. The rest of this section describes how such businesses are identified, how the human capital measures are constructed, and how start-up outcomes are measured.

6.3.1   Identifying and Classifying Start-Ups

The Startup History file is constructed as an unbalanced panel dataset. The primary frame for the data is the LBD, supplemented with additional information from the Census Bureau's Business Register, upon which the LBD is based. We utilize this file to identify start-ups as age-zero firms. Once the start-ups have been identified, we supplement the data with geocodes (state- and county-level FIPS, along with Census Tract information if available) and Employer Identification Numbers (EINs) taken from the Business Register. These variables are used to subsequently characterize the workforce associated with each start-up gathered from both LEHD and W-2 records. The full file contains data on employment, payroll, industry, geography, firm type, and birth/death of the firm.

For the purpose of characterizing worker experience, firms are classified as R&D labs, high-tech, or universities. The R&D lab measure is created by identifying R&D laboratories within R&D-performing firms. First, we identify R&D-performing firms using the Business R&D and Innovation Survey (BRDIS) and the Survey of Industrial Research and Development (SIRD).[1] A firm is classified as an R&D-performing firm if it has positive R&D expenditures during the year the employee was affiliated with the firm. R&D laboratories are identified by establishment-level industry codes, specifically North American Industry Classification System (NAICS) 5417, which is defined as "Scientific Research and Development Services." The high-tech definition is based on the relative concentration of science, technology, engineering, and math (STEM) employment by industry as in Hecker (2005) and Goldschlag and Miranda (2020). We use the high-tech classification to both subset the universe of start-ups within a year and to characterize worker experience, identifying individuals with prior experience in high-tech industries. The university measure is derived from Integrated Postsecondary Education Data System (IPEDS) and Carnegie Institute data, which provide a frame of universities in the United States. We use the national university research outlays collected by the National Center for Science and Engineering Statistics at the National Science Foundation to subset our sample of universities to the top 130 research universities, which account for 90 percent of total federally funded university-based R&D expenditures.

While capital, financing, management, and macroeconomic conditions are not directly measured in the data, because the data are longitudinal, we can include firm and time/industry/geography fixed effects.

6.3.2 Human Capital Measures

The first three human capital measures are derived from a new dataset called the Startup Worker History File, which characterizes the workforce associated with each start-up in its first year. It is created from the universe worker-level data on jobs derived from administrative records in both the LEHD and W-2 records and covers the period 2005–15.

The frame covers each paid job for each worker from 2005 to 2015 as reported at both the EIN level via Internal Revenue Service (IRS) form W-2 and state-level unemployment insurance wage records. The latter underlie the core LEHD infrastructure (Abowd, Haltiwanger, and Lane 2004) used to generate the Quarterly Workforce Indicators (QWI) and are necessary to identify the establishment for the bulk of multiunit firms (Abowd et al. 2009). The combined data includes more than 3 billion person-EIN-year observations (approximately 70 percent match across the W-2 and LEHD universes, 20 percent are found only in the W-2 records, and 10 percent are only found in LEHD). These data are enhanced with the LEHD Individual Characteristics File (ICF), which includes demographic data on

---

1. We use the SIRD to identify R&D firms between 2005 and 2007 and BRDIS for 2008–14. Firms with positive expenditure in R&D in a given year are classified as R&D performing.

persons, including sex, age, race, and place of birth. We are able to link 43 million of the 3 billion person-EIN-year observations to start-ups in their birth year, giving us an average of nearly 4.5 million person-start-up observations each year.[2]

The first three measures of human capital are indirect in nature, since they do not directly measure research experience. They are derived from an individual's work history in the years prior to being employed at a given start-up in its first year and capture employment experience in R&D labs, high-tech businesses, and universities. In the case of R&D labs, we include all workers employed in an R&D-performing firm in an R&D lab (2007 NAICS code 5417). We classify workers as having high-tech experience if they have worked in a high-tech industry and their earnings in those positions fall within the top half of the earnings distribution within that industry for a given year. This earnings condition minimizes the likelihood of classifying workers in support or administrative roles as having high-tech experience. We use a similar approach to classify workers with experience at national research universities.

The fourth, more direct measure is derived from UMETRICS data (Lane et al. 2015), which include, at the time of writing, 22 universities accounting for about 26 percent of all federally funded research.[3] The data are derived from universe personnel and financial records of participating universities. Although four files are provided by each university, the key file of interest in this project is the employee file. These individuals will compose a subset of the university experienced workers described previously. For each funded research project, both federal and nonfederal, the file contains all payroll charges for all pay periods (identified by period start date and period end date). This includes links to both the federal award ID (unique award number) and the internal university identification number (recipient account number). In addition to first name, last name, and date of birth, the data include the employee's internal deidentified employee number and the job title (which we map into broad occupational categories). The Catalog of Federal Domestic Assistance (CFDA), which is included in each award identifier, allows us to classify projects by the funding agency. The years covered by each university's data vary, as each university provided data as far back as their record keeping allowed.

6.3.3   The Start-Up Worker History File

The start-up worker history file, from which our human capital measures are derived, is constructed in three steps. The first step involves identifying

---

2. This figure differs from the reported Business Dynamics Statistics (BDS), which calculate employment at start-ups at a specific point in time (March 12). Our figures are higher, reflecting employee-employer transitions (i.e., workers who work briefly for a start-up and then move to a different job). The 48 million observations represent 37.8 million unique individuals.

3. UMETRICS stands for Universities: Measuring the Impacts of Research on Innovation, Competitiveness and Science.

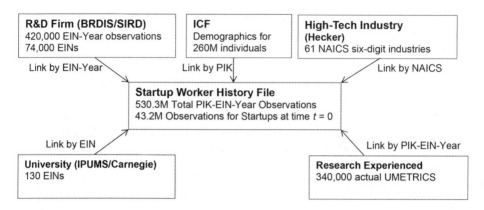

Fig. 6.1   Start-up worker history file

person and firm characteristics in the years prior to start-up. The LEHD and W-2 data provide worker histories for 260 million individuals for each employer (at the EIN level) for each year in the period 2005–15. Their individual characteristics are captured by matching to the ICF, which provides information on date of birth, foreign-born status, and sex.

The EIN of their employers is then matched to the BRDIS/SIRD data to determine whether the employer is an R&D-performing firm. There are 74,000 of those EINs and 420,000 resulting EIN-year observations. A subset of these records will be associated with the R&D lab NAICS industry. The EIN is also matched to firms in 61 six-digit high-tech industries. Employment on a grant is determined by a match to UMETRICS data; there are 340,000 research-experienced individuals between 2005 and 2015.

Start-ups are identified as firms of age zero. The total worker history file thus has 530.3 million protected identification key (PIK)-EIN-year start-up observations. Of those, 43.2 million observations are associated with start-ups in year zero.

Figure 6.1 provides a graphical illustration of the process.

The second step involves measuring human capital at the start-up level. There are 4.9 million EINs associated with age-zero firms in the data, of which about 35,000 have hired individuals with work experience in R&D-performing labs—the number of such employees totals 67,000. About 371,000 EINs have hired at least one individual with high-tech experience—the number of these employees totals 806,000. About 442,000 EINs have hired at least one university-experienced employee; the number of these totals 882,000. There are about 11,000 start-ups that have hired a total of 13,000 individuals with research experience at the UMETRICS universities. The process is described graphically in figure 6.2.

The third and final step involves merging the start-up EIN file with the

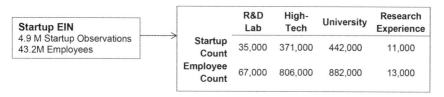

		R&D Lab	High-Tech	University	Research Experience
Startup EIN 4.9 M Startup Observations 43.2M Employees	**Startup Count**	35,000	371,000	442,000	11,000
	Employee Count	67,000	806,000	882,000	13,000

Fig. 6.2   Creating start-up file

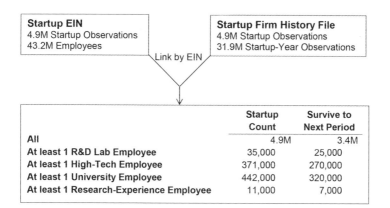

	Startup Count	Survive to Next Period
All	4.9M	3.4M
At least 1 R&D Lab Employee	35,000	25,000
At least 1 High-Tech Employee	371,000	270,000
At least 1 University Employee	442,000	320,000
At least 1 Research-Experience Employee	11,000	7,000

Fig. 6.3   Start-up history file

Start-Up Firm History File, classifying start-up types and outcomes at time $t = 0$ and calculating how many survive to the year subsequent to their birth. That information is graphically presented in figure 6.3. Of the 4.9 million start-ups we observe, 3.4 million survive to the next period, or about 69 percent. This compares to 71 percent for start-ups with at least one employee with R&D lab experience, 72 percent for high-tech and university experience, and 64 percent for research experience.

6.3.3   Start-Up Outcomes

While a wide variety of outcome measures can be generated, here we focus on survival to period $t + 1$, employment growth between t and $t + 1$, revenue growth between t and $t + 1$, patenting in $t + 1$, and trademarking in $t + 1$.[4] Survival is a binary indicator for start-ups that have positive employment in $t + 1$. Employment growth and revenue growth are calculated as the log difference of employment between t and $t + 1$, which can be interpreted as a percentage change. Patenting and trademarking in $t + 1$ is measured

---

4. We track outcomes only to $t + 1$ due to limitations on how far back in time each UMET-RICS institution's data goes. Outcomes measured further in the future would limit the sample of start-ups and individuals under consideration.

as applying for a patent in $t + 1$ that is eventually granted and filing for a trademark in $t + 1$ that is eventually registered.

Start-ups are linked to patent grants and trademark filings through existing crosswalks between United States Patent and Trademark Office (USPTO) and Census data. Patent linkages are based on a triangulation methodology first described in Graham et al. (2018). Their linkage methodology simultaneously leverages information on both patent inventors and assignees in combination with job-level information from the LEHD to distinguish between true and false matches. By using more information than traditional patent-linkage efforts (e.g., fuzzy business name and geography), the triangulation match produces more and higher-quality linkages. Trademarks are matched to start-ups using the match described in chapter 5 of this volume (Dinlersoz et al.). The business name and address information found in the USPTO's Trademark Case File Database are used to create firm-trademark linkages. To measure innovative outcomes of start-ups, we identify whether a start-up applied for a patent in the year after its birth ($t + 1$) that was eventually granted. Similarly, we identify whether each start-up filed for a trademark in $t + 1$ that was eventually registered.

6.4   Basic Facts

This section establishes some basic facts on the human capital composition of start-ups and their outcomes.

6.4.1   Start-Up Facts

We begin by highlighting some facts regarding start-ups and their outcomes. Between 2005 and 2015, one-year survival rates typically hover around 68 percent but are higher for high-tech start-ups in every year. As is well known, the number of start-ups dropped in 2007 by 25 percent (relative to 2005) and by 33 percent the following year—by 2013, the start-up count was still at the same level. High-tech start-up employment follows a similar pattern: the total number of employees at $t = 0$ declined by more than 30 percent between 2005 and 2014.

It is rare for start-ups to have high-human-capital workers as employees in their first year.[5] Approximately 0.25 percent of employees at start-ups have experience working in an R&D laboratory, around 2.5 percent have experience working at a high-tech firm, and 2 percent have been linked through their earnings with a research university. The proportion of start-ups that have individuals formerly paid on research grants is even smaller, with fewer

---

5. It is important to keep in mind that the results are left-censored, as the LEHD has somewhat limited coverage prior to 2000.

Table 6.1   **Start-up statistics at year 0**

All start-ups	Mean	Fuzzy median	Standard deviation
Employment	5.6	2.0	16.5
Payroll per employee (thousands)	29.6	17.7	84.0
Revenue (thousands)	540.2	232.5	958.7
Patents	0.02	—	3.1
Trademarks	0.06	—	0.7

High-Tech Start-ups	Mean	Fuzzy median	Standard deviation
Employment	4.0	1.5	14.4
Payroll per employee (thousands)	54.4	39.8	64.8
Revenue (thousands)	428.9	181.2	824.4
Patents	0.11	—	10.2
Trademarks	0.20	—	1.2

Notes: Statistics calculated pooling 2005–15 start-ups in the LBD and tabulating the first-year statistics. Because employment figures are captured at a stationary point in time (March 12), if a firm is shown to have zero employment in their birth year, then the following year's employment is taken as the employment at $t = 0$. Fuzzy medians are calculated by taking the mean of firms between the 45th and 55th percentile levels. Real revenue is in 2009 dollars.

than 0.05 percent of employees being linked to a research grant from one of the 22 UMETRICS universities.

Table 6.1 provides some information about the characteristics of start-ups in their initial year of existence. The vast majority of start-ups, across all start-up types, start off very small in their first year: 75 percent of all start-ups have fewer than 5 employees at time $t = 0$; more than 50 percent of start-ups have 2 or fewer employees. Fewer than 5 percent of start-ups have more than 20 employees in the initial period. While the average revenue for start-ups exceeds half a million dollars per year, this measure is somewhat skewed, as the median start-up generates less than a quarter million dollars in its first year, with the median revenue being even smaller in high-tech firms. While these size characteristics are mostly consistent across firm types, the payroll per employee and innovation measures are quite different. High-tech firms offer the highest mean payroll per employee, paying nearly twice as much as a typical start-up, and have innovation rates (as measured by patents and trademarks) that are three to five times higher than the typical start-up.

The dataset also enables us to describe the human capital composition of the start-up workforce. Table 6.2 documents the employment composition of all start-ups in the left-hand panel and high-tech start-ups in the right-hand panel. Individuals in start-ups that have at least one high-tech-experienced employee are younger, less likely to be female or black, more likely to be foreign born, and more likely to be Asian than other start-ups. Individuals in start-ups that have at least one university- or research-experienced employee

Table 6.2 Start-up employee mean demographic characteristics at time 0

| | All start-ups | | | | | High-tech | | | | |
| | Start-ups with at least one worker with experience in: | | | | | Start-ups with at least one worker with experience in: | | | | |
	Total	R&D	High-tech	University	Research	Total	R&D	High-tech	University	Research
Count	**43.2M**	67,000	806,000	882,000	13,000	**1M**	21,000	416,000	48,000	1,000
Birth year	**1974**	1969	1970	1980	1982	**1971**	1965	1969	1980	1979
Female	**45%**	44%	32%	54%	54%	**30%**	36%	27%	31%	26%
Foreign	**21%**	24%	24%	14%	18%	**25%**	24%	28%	25%	29%
White	**73%**	75%	75%	75%	70%	**74%**	80%	74%	72%	69%
Black	**12%**	7%	7%	12%	8%	**6%**	3%	5%	5%	2%
Hispanic	**16%**	10%	9%	8%	6%	**9%**	13%	8%	7%	4%
Asian	**6%**	13%	13%	8%	13%	**12%**	13%	15%	17%	19%
Other	**7%**	4%	4%	4%	8%	**7%**	2%	5%	5%	8%
duration		4.73	5.29	2.46	1.85		5.93	6.05	2.42	2.20

Source: LBD combined with Individual Characteristics File (ICF)

Notes: Statistics calculated pooling 2005–15 start-ups in the LBD and tabulating the first-year demographic statistics. Figures have been rounded for disclosure purposes. (D) indicates that the number has been suppressed for disclosure. Note that counts in this and subsequent tables are rounded for disclosure limitation reasons.

Table 6.3 **Distribution of start-ups hiring research experienced workers by funding source**

	NIH	NSF	DOD	DOE	Other federal	Nonfederal
Number of start-ups hiring UMETRICS workers	3,500	1,900	700	400	5,400	3,000
Proportion of start-ups in high-tech (%)	7.2	16.8	21.0	17.4	6.4	9.4
Ratio relative to proportion of all start-ups in high-tech (4.4%)	1.64	3.82	4.77	3.95	1.45	2.14

Notes: Statistics calculated pooling 2005–15 start-ups in the LBD and tabulating the funding sources for each of the UMETRICS experienced workers. UMETRICS workers can be funded through multiple agencies and start-ups can hire multiple UMETRICS experienced workers, so that the counts are not mutually exclusive. Figures have been rounded for disclosure purposes. (D) indicates that the number has been suppressed for disclosure.

are even younger but are more likely to be female; research-experienced start-ups are more likely to be Asian and less likely to be black.

The demographic differences are even starker among start-ups in high-tech industries. Overall, employees in these start-ups are less likely to be female, more likely to be foreign born, much less likely to be black, and much more likely to be Asian. These patterns are even stronger for those with university and research experience.

The literature suggests that high levels of human capital should be disproportionately valued by firms with complex production processes (Abowd et al. 2005). That is borne out by our data. Even though high-tech start-ups account for only 4.4 percent of all start-ups in the United States, they account for 17 percent of start-ups hiring at least one R&D-experienced worker, 36 percent of start-ups hiring high-tech workers, 6 percent of start-ups hiring university-experienced workers, and 8 percent of start-ups hiring research-experienced workers.

Of course, the first three human capital measures, while extremely valuable in measuring potential research experience (in the same spirit, but in more detail, than older measures such as employment tenure and labor market experience), include a variety of workers.

The direct measures offered by UMETRICS enable us to tease out the relationships in more detail. Table 6.3 shows the subset of start-ups who hired workers employed on research grants in the 22 UMETRICS universities by funding source. In all cases, start-ups that hired funded researchers were more likely to be high-tech—the ratio is particularly high for those hiring individuals who worked on grants funded by the National Science Foundation, the Department of Defense, and the Department of Energy.

The detail included in the UMETRICS data allows us to similarly char-

Table 6.4   Distribution of start-ups hiring research-experienced workers by occupation

	Faculty	Graduate student	Postgraduate	Undergraduate	Other
Number of start-ups	3,500	1,900	700	400	5,400
Proportion of start-ups in high-tech (%)	12.0	15.2	9.8	6.0	8.3
Ratio relative to proportion of all start-ups in high-tech (4.4%)	2.73	3.45	2.23	1.36	1.89

Source: LBD combined with UMETRICS worker file.

Notes: Statistics calculated pooling 2005–15 start-ups in the LBD and tabulating the funding sources for each of the UMETRICS experienced workers. Start-ups can hire multiple UMETRICS experienced workers so that the counts are not mutually exclusive. Figures have been rounded for disclosure purposes. (D) indicates that the number has been suppressed for disclosure.

acterize the propensity to be in high-tech industries by the skill level of researchers, as reported in table 6.4. Start-ups hiring graduate students and faculty are much more likely to be high-tech than other start-ups; the pattern for undergraduate hiring is much more similar to the start-up distribution as a whole.

Finally, the data enable us to drill down into the more detailed industry distribution of start-ups. Table 6.5 shows vast compositional differences in the worker types of high-tech start-ups within narrowly defined industries. More than 85 percent of all high-tech start-ups are in the fields of computer design (NAICS 5415), engineering (NAICS 5413), or R&D laboratories (NAICS 5417). More than half of high-tech start-ups are in computer design. While there is some variation in the shares of each worker type across these industries, more than 80 percent of each of the worker types are affiliated with a start-up in one of those three industries. Although only 5 percent of high-tech start-ups are R&D labs, almost two-thirds of start-ups who hired workers with R&D experience and over one-third of start-ups hiring workers with research experience are R&D labs.

6.4.3   Start-Up Outcomes and Human Capital Composition

This section provides some initial descriptive results about the link between workforce experience and start-up outcomes (survival to period $t + 1$, employment growth to $t + 1$, Revenue growth to $t + 1$, patent in $t + 1$, and trademark in $t + 1$). We start by first exploring the proportion of start-ups that experiences each type of outcome considered.

Figure 6.4 provides some useful initial insights about start-up outcomes. Although, by and large, start-ups that hire workers with R&D, high-tech, and university experience are more likely to survive than those that do not, start-ups that hire UMETRICS-experienced individuals show about the same survival rate as the typical start-up. Moreover, in the analyses

Table 6.5			Industry sector of high-tech start-ups at year 0			
	All start-ups		Start-ups hiring workers with			
Start-up sector	Counts	Distribution (%)	R&D experience (%)	High-tech experience (%)	University experience (%)	Research experience (%)
AERO MANU	700	0.30	0.18	0.36	0.34	(D)
COMM MANU	700	0.30	0.27	0.36	0.34	(D)
COMP DESIGN	128,100	54.28	14.64	53.80	46.21	40.83
COMP MANU	800	0.34	0.27	0.29	0.34	(D)
DATA PROCESS	6,700	2.84	1.00	2.99	4.14	4.17
ENGINEER	61,500	26.06	6.36	28.47	20.69	14.17
INFO SERVICE	8,800	3.73	0.91	1.82	5.86	5.00
INSTRUM MANU	1,800	0.76	0.91	1.02	1.03	1.67
INTERNET	1,300	0.55	0.18	0.58	0.69	(D)
ISP	2,600	1.10	0.18	1.09	0.69	(D)
OIL GAS	4,500	1.91	0.18	2.04	1.03	(D)
PHARMA	1,100	0.47	1.64	0.58	1.03	1.67
RD LAB	12,900	5.47	67.82	3.80	14.14	28.33
SEMI MANU	1,600	0.68	0.91	0.88	1.03	1.67
SOFTWARE	3,500	1.48	0.82	1.75	2.76	4.17
Total	236,000		11,000	137,000	29,000	1,200

Notes: Statistics calculated pooling 2005–15 start-ups in the LBD. Figures have been rounded for disclosure purposes. (D) indicates that the number has been suppressed for disclosure.

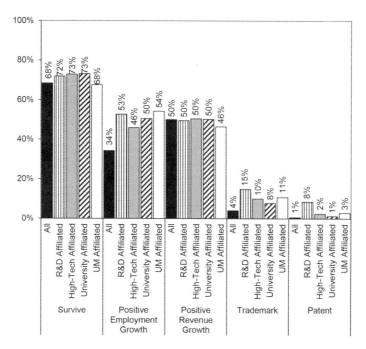

Fig. 6.4   Outcomes of all start-ups, *t* + 1

Notes: Figure shows the share of each start-up sample that experiences each outcome.

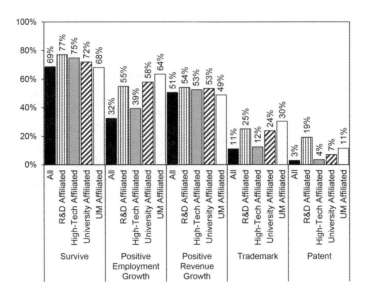

Fig. 6.5   Outcomes of high-tech start-ups, *t* + 1

Notes: Figure shows the share of each start-up sample within high-tech industries that experiences each outcome.

that follow, we find that the higher survival rates for firms that hire high-human-capital workers are primarily a compositional effect. Controlling for other characteristics of the start-up, such as industry and size, these firms are generally less likely to survive. Consistent with an "up or out" dynamic, start-ups hiring high-human-capital individuals are more likely to see employment growth than those in the economy at large, and this is particularly true for UMETRICS start-ups. The picture is a little different for revenue growth—UMETRICS start-ups have lower revenue growth. Patent and trademark activity are consistently substantially higher for all start-ups hiring experienced workers—and UMETRICS start-ups are second only to start-ups that hire R&D-experienced workers in both of these dimensions of innovation. As figure 6.5 shows, an almost identical pattern holds true, albeit at different levels, for high-tech start-ups.

For high-tech start-ups, we see a greater proportion of firms patenting and trademarking, especially among start-ups with high-human-capital workers. The "up-or-out" dynamic is even clearer for start-ups with research-trained workers in high-tech industries, which are less likely to survive, more likely to hire additional employees, and more likely to trademark.

6.5   Analysis

In this section, we expand on the framework provided in equation (1) and formalize our model to control for a number of nonhuman capital characteristics. We assume that the functional form of equation (1) is a linear combination of exponential functions, allowing us to use a log-linear estimation and calculate multiple outcome measures for each start-up (survival, employment growth, revenue growth, patenting, and trademarking) one year after the birth of the firm. We regress these outcomes against the start-up's workforce and other characteristics in the year of firm birth ($t = 0$). Our main empirical specification is as follows:

$$(2) \quad Y_f = \alpha + \beta_1 \ln EARN_{f0} + \sum_{k=1}^{9} \delta_k SIZE_{kf0} + \beta_2 \ln \overline{AGE_{f0}} + \beta_3 \ln FEMALE_{f0}$$

$$+ \beta_4 \ln FOREIGN_{f0} + \beta_5 \ln RD_{f0} + \beta_6 \ln HT_{f0} + \beta_7 \ln UNI_{f0}$$

$$+ \beta_8 \ln Research\ Experience_{f0} + \varepsilon.$$

The key measures of interest are the workforce human capital measures—the number of workers who have worked in R&D-performing firms, high-tech firms, and universities—as well as the number who have direct research experience. As noted above, survival is a binary measure capturing whether a start-up had positive employment in $t + 1$, employment and revenue growth is calculated as the log differences in the values between t and $t + 1$, and patenting and trademarking is a binary measure capturing whether the start-up applied for a patent that was eventually granted or filed for a trademark that was eventually registered. The earnings variable is the inverse hyperbolic sine transformation of the start-up worker's earnings (collected from the W-2 or LEHD).[6] The size categories consist of six separate groupings: 1 employee, 2–5 employees, 6–9 employees, 10–19 employees, 19–49 employees, and 50 or more employees. For worker types, we take the inverse hyperbolic sine transformation of the number of each type of worker at the start-up at time $t = 0$. Other controls include zip code-year fixed effects and industry fixed effects.

The richness of the data permits the introduction of many controls. In particular, we can include mean earnings of the firm workforce as well as firm employment size categories. We interact demographics with each of the R&D worker types to identify potential nonlinearities of being a certain type of worker (e.g., female university worker).[7]

Since the Census Bureau data does not have direct measures of technology, we control for industry, detailed geography, and year using fixed effects. External macroeconomic conditions are proxied by zip code-year fixed effects and industry fixed effects.

---

6. We use the inverse hyperbolic sine transformation to address the fact that many start-ups have zero high-human-capital workers.

7. Note that these interaction terms are the result of multiplying continuous counts of employees falling into each group and that any given employee may belong to any number of designated groups.

6.5.1   Baseline Results

We begin by simply describing the contribution of each factor to start-up outcomes. Table 6.6 describes the explanatory power of a group of covariates to the start-up outcomes of survival, employment growth, revenue growth, patenting, and trademarking in the next period. Table 6.6 shows that just controlling for location and industry fixed effects can explain a small share of the variance in outcomes. Including initial firm characteristics, such as employment size and mean earnings at $t = 0$, contributes significantly to the share of variance explained in all the outcomes. Including demographic controls—such as the mean age of the employees, number of female employees, foreign-born status, and race—increases the explanatory power for future employment growth but has little effect on revenue, survival, and innovation. Including our basic human capital measures leads to an insignificant increase in the explanatory power of the model in survival and employment growth across all firms but does have significant power in our model for revenue growth, patenting, and trademarking. In particular, the human capital elements contribute an additional 40 percent in explanatory power for patenting outcomes in the following period and an additional 10 percent in explanatory power for trademarking. These patterns continue to hold for high-tech start-ups, with human capital contributing an additional 25 percent in explanatory power for patents and an additional 4.5 percent in revenue and 4.7 percent in trademarking. Table 6.6 highlights the explanatory power of human capital in relation to start-up growth and innovative outcomes.

Table 6.7 provides the key results associated with the full regression. Briefly, the relationship between the different measures of human capital and start-up survival and growth (in terms of both employment and revenue) is measurable and quite large. Start-ups that employ workers with experience working in R&D labs, high-tech, and universities are less likely to survive. Our human capital measures are clearly associated with positive employment and revenue growth. Using the fully controlled specification, our results suggest that employing one additional R&D worker is associated with a 1.4 percentage point increase in employment growth (conditional on survival).[8] This figure increases to 4 percentage points for one additional high-tech worker and 3.6 percentage points for a former university employee.[9] We see similar patterns in revenue growth. For all start-ups, the hiring of one additional high-human-capital worker is associated with a 1.4 to 4 percentage point increase in employment growth and a 2.3 to

8. Note that the coefficient interpretation is based on adding a single worker of a given type to the mean number of workers of that type at time $t = 0$ across all start-ups.

9. Again, it is important to note that we are not making claims about the direction of causality. Start-ups with more volatile ideas or production technologies may be more likely to hire high-human-capital workers.

Table 6.6   Explanatory power (R^2) of start-up covariates

All start-ups	Survival, $t+1$	Employment growth, $t+1$	Revenue growth, $t+1$	Patent, $t+1$	TM, $t+1$
Geography-year and industry dummies only	0.230	0.019	0.026	0.014	0.041
Geography-year and industry dummies + initial firm characteristics	0.342	0.184	0.027	0.016	0.049
Geography-year and industry dummies + initial firm characteristics + Demographics	0.344	0.303	0.031	0.017	0.050
Geography-year and industry dummies + initial firm characteristics + Demographics + human capital	0.344	0.303	0.032	0.029	0.056
Share of explained variance explained by human capital	**0.1%**	**0.3%**	**3.1%**	**41.4%**	**10.7%**

High-tech start-ups	Survival, $t+1$	Employment Growth, $t+1$	Revenue Growth, $t+1$	Patent, $t+1$	TM, $t+1$
Geography-year and industry dummies only	0.248	0.071	0.067	0.058	0.084
Geography-Year and industry dummies + initial firm characteristics	0.354	0.218	0.07	0.072	0.113
Geography-year and industry dummies + initial firm characteristics + demographics	0.355	0.371	0.085	0.078	0.123
Geography-year and industry dummies + initial firm characteristics + demographics + human capital	0.358	0.377	0.089	0.104	0.129
Share of explained variance explained by human capital	**0.8%**	**1.6%**	**4.5%**	**25.0%**	**4.7%**

Notes: Table reports changes in R^2 using different sets of covariates. The first specification regresses outcomes on geography, year, and industry dummies. Each subsequent specification adds additional covariates such as firm characteristics, worker demographics, and finally our human capital measures.

Table 6.7   OLS on all start-up outcomes, 2005–15

	Survival, $t+1$	Employment growth, $t+1$	Revenue growth, $t+1$	Patent, $t+1$	TM, $t+1$
ln RD_{f0}	-0.0481***	0.0156*	0.0456***	0.105***	0.0849***
	(0.00407)	(0.00717)	(0.0127)	(0.0136)	(0.0134)
ln HT_{f0}	-0.0268***	0.0474***	0.0596***	0.0121***	0.0488***
	(0.00333)	(0.00415)	(0.00384)	(0.000772)	(0.00311)
ln UNI_{f0}	-0.0177***	0.0431***	0.0282***	0.00541***	0.0299***
	(0.00215)	(0.00416)	(0.00536)	(0.000915)	(0.00319)
Observations	4,930,000	3,370,000	1,910,000	4,930,000	4,930,000
R^2	0.344	0.303	0.032	0.029	0.056
Start-ups that hired UMETRIC university employees:					
Overall					
ln $RESEARCH_{f0}$	-0.00902*	0.0204*	0.0272+	0.0139***	0.0180***
	(0.00357)	(0.00858)	(0.0161)	(0.00175)	(0.00396)
Observations	68,000	45,000	17,000	68,000	68,000
R^2	.567	.397	.148	.109	.146
Start-ups that hire UMETRIC university employees:					
Decomposed by funding source					
NIH	-0.00662	0.0440**	-0.00850	0.0141***	0.0210**
	(0.00612)	(0.0144)	(0.0262)	(0.00299)	(0.00679)
NSF	-0.00852	0.0432*	0.0506	0.0259***	0.0313**
	(0.00864)	(0.0204)	(0.0381)	(0.00420)	(0.00954)
DOD	-0.00217	-0.0158	0.0615	0.0528***	0.0235
	(0.0134)	(0.0313)	(0.0551)	(0.00649)	(0.0147)
DOE	-0.0127	-0.0222	0.174*	0.0452***	-0.0432*

(0.0177)	(0.0415)	(0.0787)	(0.00865)	(0.0196)
Other federal funding				
−0.00594	0.0192+	−0.0109	−0.00605*	−0.00507
(0.00486)	(0.0115)	(0.0212)	(0.00237)	(0.00538)
Nonfederal funding				
0.000349	0.0108	0.0558+	0.00217	0.0225**
(0.00670)	(0.0161)	(0.0309)	(0.00326)	(0.00740)
R^2 .567	.397	.148	.109	.146

Start-ups that hire UMETRIC university employees:
Decomposed by occupation

Faculty				
−0.0143	−0.0926**	−0.0151	0.0566***	0.00230
(0.0146)	(0.0338)	(0.0586)	(0.00708)	(0.0161)
Graduate student				
−0.0204*	0.0225	0.0578	0.0416***	0.0289**
(0.00921)	(0.0223)	(0.0429)	(0.00449)	(0.0102)
Postgrads				
−0.00804	−0.127***	−0.0297	0.0430***	−0.00418
(0.0164)	(0.0383)	(0.0692)	(0.00800)	(0.0182)
Undergraduate				
−0.00713	0.0784***	0.0461+	0.00192	0.00889
(0.00525)	(0.0126)	(0.0241)	(0.00257)	(0.00583)
Other (admin, technician)				
−0.00605	0.0251*	0.0237	0.00658**	0.0242***
(0.00499)	(0.0118)	(0.0213)	(0.00244)	(0.00554)
R^2 .567	.397	.148	.109	.146

Notes: Observations are start-up-year combinations. Clustered robust standard errors in parentheses (by four-digit industry-year). $+ p < .10$, $*p < .05$, $**p < .01$, $***p < .001$; controls included for size and average earnings, proportion of workforce that is female, foreign born, and interactions of female, foreign born with all the different types of research experience (e.g., foreign female R&D lab workers). In order to account for zeros in our logged counts of high-human-capital workers, we implement an inverse hyperbolic sine transformation. Interpretation of coefficients is based on the addition of one worker of a given type to the mean of that type of worker across all start-ups at time $t = 0$. The mean number of R&D workers, high-tech workers, and university workers at time $t = 0$ is 0.0114, 0.1534, and 0.1686, respectively. Observations have been rounded for disclosure purposes.

5 percentage point increase in revenue growth (conditional on survival). We see fairly large coefficients on the patenting and trademarking outcomes for R&D lab workers, with the addition of one R&D lab worker contributing a 9.2 percentage point increase in patent filing and a 7.5 percentage point increase in trademark filing.

The second panel of table 6.7 reports the results for the subset of start-ups that hired employees from the 22 institutions that provided UMETRICS data. The interpretation of the coefficient is thus relative to the effects of hiring an individual trained on a research grant over and above those who simply have experience working in one of these 22 universities. The results are consistent. Start-ups that hired research-trained individuals were more likely to fail than those who only hired university-experienced individuals (which are in turn more likely to fail than other start-ups, as established in the first panel). However, those that survive are more likely to create jobs, have higher revenue, and file more patents and trademarks. However, those that survive have higher revenue and file more patents and trademarks relative to start-ups that hired university-experienced workers.

The third and fourth panel of table 6.7 delves more deeply into the types of projects and skill embodied within our direct measure of human capital. Start-ups that hire workers funded by Department of Defense (DOD) and Department of Energy (DOE) grants are much more likely to patent, again relative to start-ups that hire nonresearch-trained workers at these universities. Start-ups that hire workers trained on National Institutes of Health (NIH)- and National Science Foundation (NSF)-funded grants see greater employment growth. Interestingly, faculty, graduate students, and postgrads contribute more to patenting and trademark activity, while undergraduates are associated with greater employment growth.

Table 6.8 reports estimates similar to the top panel of table 6.7 (with the full set of controls) but for start-ups in high-tech industries. The results are substantively unchanged. The magnitude of the coefficients is also significantly larger than the coefficients in the previous table, which confirms our hypothesis that the relationship with measures of human capital is more sensitive among high-tech start-ups. In the case of employment growth, increasing the number of high-human-capital workers by 10 percent is associated with a 0.29 to 0.93 percentage point increase in employment growth and a 0.63 to 0.88 percentage point increase in revenue growth for high-tech firms. The same increase in R&D-lab-experienced workers is associated with a 1.82 percentage point increase in patenting and a 1.14 percentage point increase in trademarking.[10]

In addition to these tables, we have estimated the same specification over different-size groups of start-ups and find that the results are robust and do

10. Disclosure limitation protocols preclude us from doing a deeper dive using UMETRICS-only data.

Table 6.8   OLS on high-tech start-up outcomes, 2005–15

	Survival, $t + 1$	Employment growth, $t + 1$	Revenue growth, $t + 1$	Patent, $t + 1$	TM, $t + 1$
ln RD_{f0}	−0.0515***	0.0287	0.0632*	0.182***	0.114***
	(0.00706)	(0.0146)	(0.0305)	(0.0211)	(0.0239)
ln HT_{f0}	0.0423***	0.0823***	0.0865***	−0.00551*	0.00308
	(0.00549)	(0.00366)	(0.00638)	(0.00234)	(0.00417)
ln UNI_{f0}	−0.00633	0.0933***	0.0879***	0.0142*	0.0711***
	(0.00429)	(0.00748)	(0.0127)	(0.00648)	(0.0137)
Other controls	Yes	Yes	Yes	Yes	Yes
Observations	210,000	140,000	95,000	210,000	210,000
R^2	0.358	0.377	0.089	0.104	0.129

Notes: Observations are start-up-year combinations. Robust standard errors in parentheses. *p <.05, **p <.01, ***p < .001; controls included for size and average earnings, proportion of workforce that is female, foreign born, and interactions of female, foreign born with research experience.

not differ greatly. To summarize our empirical findings, with the exception of survival, we find mostly positive and significant associations between R&D experience, high-tech experience, university experience, and research-trained experience and start-up performance. These human capital measures are associated with much riskier outcomes: survival of such start-ups is significantly less likely. However, conditional on survival, these basic measures of human capital have positive and significant effects on employment growth and revenue growth for the following period. The explanatory power of these measures is surprisingly high, contributing more than 15 percent to the cumulative explanatory power of high-tech start-up employment growth.

6.6   Conclusion

This chapter leverages new data about workforce human capital that can be used to provide more insights into the survival, growth, and innovative activity of new businesses. Our human capital measures have a negative impact on survival but a significant and positive association with employment growth and revenue growth conditional on survival. These results are consistent with the view that there is a relationship between workforce experience and business start-up outcomes. While it is important to note that the cumulative magnitude of the effects of these human capital measures on start-up outcomes is relatively small, it is also important to consider that these are very basic measures of human capital (binary and extensive margin type measures).

Overall, these findings point to the important role human capital plays in the outcomes of young businesses. While we neglect to say that the relationship is causal, there are multiple mechanisms that may suggest this is the case. One mechanism by which these human capital measures might affect start-up outcomes is through knowledge diffusion. A worker's experience in university-based research activities and the experience individuals gain by working in different types of environments (R&D laboratories, high-tech industries, and/or universities) might transmit tacit knowledge that is valuable to firms. Moreover, the importance of tacit knowledge may vary by the types of tasks workers perform, which is consistent with the evidence that our human capital measures are relatively more important in high-tech industries. A firm's investment in technology may also affect the value of human capital, making some types of knowledge more valuable through complementarities and others less valuable through substitutability. These types of interactions provide scope for future research using these data.

As always, there is much more to be done with these data, particularly as the time series grows. It should be possible to include more information about the project level factors identified by Corrado and Lane as important, such as "the roles of: organizational practices (employment and management); organizational characteristics (employee knowledge and skills, business model, IT use); environmental and cultural factors (location and networks); entrepreneurial factors (firm age and origin)" (Corrado and Lane 2009). In future work, we will do just that. We will expand the analysis of research experience to capture network effects as well as the effects of intensive exposure to research-intensive environments. We will also examine a broader set of outcome measures, including for start-ups that went public or became exceptionally large. It is always difficult to identify causal relationships, but we have begun to investigate the effects of sharp changes in funding, such as the 2009 American Recovery and Reinvestment Act (ARRA), as well as changes in funding to different research areas.

References

Abowd, J. M., J. Haltiwanger, R. Jarmin, J. Lane, P. Lengermann, K. McCue, K. McKinney, and K. Sandusky. 2005. "The Relation among Human Capital, Productivity, and Market Value: Building Up from Micro Evidence." In *Measuring Capital in the New Economy*, edited by Carol Corrado, John Haltiwanger, and Daniel Sichel, 153–204. NBER Studies in Income and Wealth 65. Chicago: University of Chicago Press.

Abowd, J. M., J. Haltiwanger, and J. Lane. 2004. "Integrated Longitudinal Employer-Employee Data for the United States." *American Economic Review* 94:224–29.

Abowd, J. M., B. E. Stephens, L. Vilhuber, F. Andersson, K. L. McKinney, M. Roemer, and S. Woodcock. 2009. "The LEHD Infrastructure Files and the Creation of the Quarterly Workforce Indicators." In *Producer Dynamics: New Evidence from Micro Data*, edited by Timothy Dunne, J. Bradford Jensen, and

Mark J. Roberts, 149–230. NBER Studies in Income and Wealth 68. Chicago: University of Chicago Press.

Acemoglu, D., U. Akcigit, N. Bloom, and W. Kerr. 2013. "Innovation, Reallocation and Growth." Cambridge, MA: National Bureau of Economic Research.

Acemoglu, D., U. Akcigit, N. Bloom, and W. Kerr. 2018. "Innovation, Reallocation and Growth." *American Economic Review* 108:3450–91.

Akcigit, U., and W. R. Kerr. 2018. "Growth through Heterogeneous Innovations." *Journal of Political Economy* 126 (4): 1374–1443.

Audretsch, D. B., M. C. Keilbach, and E. E. Lehmann. 2006. *Entrepreneurship and Economic Growth*. Oxford: Oxford University Press.

Bania, N., R. W. Eberts, and M. S. Fogarty. 1993. "Universities and the Startup of New Companies: Can We Generalize from Route 128 and Silicon Valley?" *Review of Economics and Statistics*: 761–66.

Bartel, A. P., N. D. Beaulieu, C. S. Phibbs, and P. W. Stone. 2014. "Human Capital and Productivity in a Team Environment: Evidence from the Healthcare Sector." *American Economic Journal: Applied Economics* 6 (2): 231–59.

Barth, E., J. Davis, and R. B. Freeman. 2016. "Augmenting the Human Capital Earnings Equation with Measures of Where People Work." NBER Working Paper No. 22512. Cambridge, MA: National Bureau of Economic Research. https://doi .org/10.3386/w22512.

Bender, S., N. Bloom, D. Card, J. Van Reenen, and S. Wolter. 2016. "Management Practices, Workforce Selection and Productivity." Cambridge, MA: National Bureau of Economic Research.

Black, S. E., and L. M. Lynch. 1996. "Human-Capital Investments and Productivity." *American Economic Review* 86:263–67.

Bloom, N., R. Lemos, R. Sadun, D. Scur, and J. Van Reenen. 2014. "JEEA-FBBVA Lecture 2013: The New Empirical Economics of Management." *Journal of the European Economic Association* 12:835–76.

Corrado, C., C. Hulten, and D. Sichel. 2005. "Measuring Capital and Technology: An Expanded Framework." In *Measuring Capital in the New Economy*, edited by Carol Corrado, John Haltiwanger, and Daniel Sichel, 11–46. NBER Studies in Income and Wealth 65. Chicago: University of Chicago Press.

Corrado, C., and J. Lane. 2009. "Using Cyber-enabled Transaction Data to Study Productivity and Innovation in Organizations." Global COE Hi-Stat Discussion Paper Series 099. The Conference Board.

Decker, R., J. Haltiwanger, R. Jarmin, and J. Miranda. 2014. "The Role of Entrepreneurship in US Job Creation and Economic Dynamism." *Journal of Economic Perspectives* 28 (3): 3–24.

Duranton, G., D. Puga. 2004. "Micro-foundations of Urban Agglomeration Economies." *Handbook of Regional and Urban Economics* 4:2063–2117.

Fleming, L., I. I. I. Charles King, and A. Juda. 2007. "Small Worlds and Regional Innovation." *Organization Science* 18:938–54.

Gertler, M. S. 2003. "Tacit Knowledge and the Economic Geography of Context, or the Undefinable Tacitness of Being (There)." *Journal of Economic Geography* 3:75–99.

Glaeser, E. L., W. R. Kerr, and G. A. M. Ponzetto. 2010. "Clusters of Entrepreneurship." *Journal of Urban Economics* 67:150–68.

Goldschlag, N., and J. Miranda. 2020. "Business Dynamics Statistics of High Tech Industries." *Journal of Economics & Management Strategy* 29 (1): 3–30.

Graham, S. J., C. Grim, T. Islam, A. C. Marco, and J. Miranda. 2018. "Business Dynamics of Innovating Firms: Linking US Patents with Administrative Data on Workers and Firms." *Journal of Economics & Management Strategy* 27 (3): 372–402.

Guzman, J., and S. Stern. 2016. "The State of American Entrepreneurship: New Estimates of the Quantity and Quality of Entrepreneurship for 15 US States, 1988–2014." Cambridge, MA: National Bureau of Economic Research.

Hausman, N. 2012. "University Innovation, Local Economic Growth, and Entrepreneurship." http://ideas.repec.org/p/cen/wpaper/12-10.html.

Hecker, D. E. 2005. "High Technology Employment: A NAICS-Based Update." *Monthly Labor Review* 128:57.

Ichniowski, C., K. Shaw, and G. Prennushi. 1997. "The Effects of Human Resource Management Practices on Productivity: A Study of Steel Finishing Lines." *American Economic Review* 87:291–313.

Jones, C. I. 2002. "Sources of US Economic Growth in a World of Ideas." *American Economic Review* 92:220–39.

Kantor, S., and A. Whalley. 2013. "Knowledge Spillovers from Research Universities: Evidence from Endowment Value Shocks." *Review of Economics and Statistics* 96:171–88.

Kantor, S., and A. Whalley. 2014. "Research Proximity and Productivity: Long-Term Evidence from Agriculture." *Review of Economics and Statistics* 96 (1): 171–88.

Kerr, S. P., W. Kerr, Ç. Özden, C. Parsons. 2016. "Global Talent Flows." *Journal of Economic Perspectives* 30:83–106.

Lafontaine, F., and K. Shaw. 2016. "Serial Entrepreneurship: Learning by Doing?" *Journal of Labor Economics* 34:S217–S254.

Lane, J. I., J. Owen-Smith, R. F. Rosen, and B. A. Weinberg. 2015. "New Linked Data on Research Investments: Scientific Workforce, Productivity, and Public Value." *Research Policy* 44 (9): 1659–71. https://doi.org/10.1016/j.respol.2014.12.013.

Lazear, E. P., and K. L. Shaw. 2007. "Personnel Economics: The Economist's View of Human Resources." *Journal of Economic Perspectives* 21:91–114.

Lowe, R. A., and C. Gonzalez-Brambila. 2007. "Faculty Entrepreneurs and Research Productivity." *Journal of Technology Transfer* 32:173–94.

Marx, M., J. Singh, and L. Fleming. 2015. "Regional Disadvantage? Employee Noncompete Agreements and Brain Drain." *Research Policy*. 44:394–404.

McGuirk, H., H. Lenihan, and M. Hart. 2015. "Measuring the Impact of Innovative Human Capital on Small Firms' Propensity to Innovate." *Research Policy*. 44:965–76.

Romer, P. M. 1990. "Endogenous Technological Change." *Journal of Political Economy* 98:S71–S102.

Syverson, C. 2010. "What Determines Productivity?" Cambridge, MA: National Bureau of Economic Research.

Tambe, P. 2014. "Big Data Investment, Skills, and Firm Value." *Management Science* 60:1452–69.

Zolas, N., N. Goldschlag, R. Jarmin, P. Stephan, J. Owen-Smith, R. F. Rosen, B. M. Allen, B. A. Weinberg, and J. I. Lane. 2015. "Wrapping It Up in a Person: Examining Employment and Earnings Outcomes for Ph.D. Recipients." *Science* 350 (6266): 1367–71.

III

Changing Structure of the Economy

7

Measuring the Gig Economy
Current Knowledge and Open Issues

Katharine G. Abraham, John C. Haltiwanger,
Kristin Sandusky, and James R. Spletzer

7.1 Introduction

In recent years, the popular press has been full of stories premised on the idea that the share of US jobs that do not involve a formal employer-employee relationship is large and growing. Both media sources and scholars have adopted the term *gig economy* to refer broadly to these less-structured work arrangements as well as more narrowly to the subset of flexible jobs mediated through various online platforms. The latter have been viewed as yielding an increasingly "on-demand" economy where goods and services can be acquired through apps on smartphones and other web-based applications. The current discussion regarding alternative work arrangements echoes an earlier discussion that arose in the late 1980s and 1990s (e.g., Abraham 1988, 1990; Barker and Christensen 1998). Then as now, there was talk of dramatic growth in the number of people working in contingent

Katharine G. Abraham is professor of economics and survey methodology at the University of Maryland and a research associate of the National Bureau of Economic Research.

John C. Haltiwanger is Distinguished University Professor of Economics at the University of Maryland and a research associate of the National Bureau of Economic Research. He was a part-time Schedule A employee of the US Census Bureau when this chapter was written.

Kristin Sandusky is an economist at the US Census Bureau.

James R. Spletzer is a principal economist at the US Census Bureau.

Any opinions and conclusions expressed herein are those of the authors and do not necessarily represent the views of the US Census Bureau. All results have been reviewed to ensure that no confidential information is disclosed. We thank Joseph Altonji, Barry Bosworth, Carol Corrado, Susan Houseman, Ron Jarmin, Kristin McCue, and participants in the Conference on Research in Income and Wealth (CRIW) conference Measuring and Accounting for Innovation in the 21st Century for helpful comments and suggestions on earlier drafts. For acknowledgments, sources of research support, and disclosure of the authors' material financial relationships, if any, please see https://www.nber.org/books-and-chapters/measuring-and-accounting -innovation-21st-century/measuring-gig-economy-current-knowledge-and-open-issues.

or precarious jobs—positions in which workers had no long-term connection to a particular business but were employed to complete a specific task or for a defined period of time—or under other nonstandard employment arrangements. The recent resurgence of interest in nontraditional work arrangements reflects the perception that new technology, along with the restructuring of business enterprises made possible by this technology, is producing an accelerated pace of change in the organization of work that is having important effects on both workers and firms.

While there has been considerable discussion about the changing nature of work and its broader implications for workers and firms, different sources of data send conflicting messages regarding the prevalence of nonemployee work generally and gig employment specifically. Individuals performing nonemployee work should be classified as self-employed. In the Current Population Survey (CPS) and other household surveys, the percentage of the workforce that is self-employed has shown no upward trend and in fact has been drifting downward since at least the mid-1990s. In contrast, administrative data derived from tax filings provide stronger support for the popular perception that nonemployee work arrangements are a growing phenomenon (see, e.g., Katz and Krueger 2019a). More definitive evidence regarding trends in nonemployee work is essential for understanding how changing work arrangements may be affecting workers and their families, as well as for investigating the implications of ongoing changes in the structure of work for firm performance, productivity, and growth. Better information about the features of nonemployee work—who is doing it, what types of tasks they are performing, how households are combining income from nonemployee work with income from other sources, and why firms choose to use gig and other nonemployee workers in place of traditional employees—also is needed. In this chapter, we show how administrative and other data can be used in conjunction with household survey data to improve our understanding of the gig economy and the broader implications of changing work arrangements.

Much of the discussion of the gig economy, as well as the broader discussion of nonemployee work arrangements, has focused on the implications of growth in these arrangements for workers and their families. On the one hand, gig work may appeal to individuals for whom it provides the flexibility to better match their skills to work projects. Making a similar point, Hurst and Pugsley (2011), for example, argue that self-employed workers enjoy substantial nonpecuniary benefits in the form of being their own boss, being able to set their own schedule, and so on. On the other hand, some performing gig work are not doing so by choice. Similar to others who are not employees of the firms for which they are providing labor services, gig workers do not enjoy the legal rights and protections afforded under the unemployment insurance system, the workers compensation system, the Fair Labor Standards Act, and other laws and regulations written with more traditional employment arrangements in mind (Harris and Krueger 2015). Further, those who rely primarily or exclusively on self-employment are markedly less likely to have health insurance or a retirement plan (Jackson, Looney, and Ramnath 2017) and may have hours and earnings that are substantially more variable and less predictable.

Advances in technology resting on digitization and the interconnectivity of the internet have made it increasingly attractive for firms to reorganize their activities to have more work performed by individuals who are not employees of the firm. These new technologies make it more feasible to organize work on a project-specific basis, utilizing a changing cast of workers with the mix of skills that is appropriate for each project (National Academies Press 2017). Similar to the motivations that have been posited for other sorts of contracting out (Abraham and Taylor 1996; Dube and Kaplan 2010; Goldschmidt and Schmieder 2017), utilizing nonemployees as they are needed rather than hiring traditional employees may be a means of reducing wage and benefit costs as well as positioning the firm to respond quickly to shifts in demand. These same technological advances have facilitated the segmentation of the various aspects of firms' production processes more generally (see, e.g., Fort 2017). On the other hand, while offering some clear advantages to firms, increased reliance on outsourcing generally and nonemployees specifically also implies less accumulation of firm-specific human capital. Even within narrowly defined sectors, there is enormous heterogeneity in the productivity and profitability of individual firms (see, e.g., Foster, Haltiwanger, and Krizan 2001). Differences in the ability to attract, train, and retain high-quality workers, especially those performing functions that are core to the firm, seem likely to be an important part of the explanation for this heterogeneity in firm-level outcomes.

Growth in nonemployee work also matters for the measurement of economic activity. The current system of economic measurement is designed for a world in which workers have a traditional employment relationship or operate a formal business. Nonemployee work may not be fully captured in existing data sources. Each month, for example, the CPS collects information from households about work that household members have done for pay or profit. Similar to the questions asked on other household surveys, the CPS employment questions may not always cue respondents to report work outside of a conventional job or business and are not designed to probe regarding the nature of the arrangements under which work occurs. Further, they focus primarily on the main job a person holds, with a more limited set of questions asked about additional work activity. Other surveys collect information from businesses on the number of people they employ and the hours those employees work but do not attempt to measure the labor input of people who are not on those businesses' payrolls.

To the extent that an increasing share of the work embodied in firms' products is supplied by nonemployees whose hours are not well captured by existing data collections, measures of labor productivity growth may be distorted. Labor productivity is defined as output per hour worked. The Bureau of Labor Statistics (BLS) major-sector productivity program uses CPS data to measure the hours of the self-employed. If there have been increases in nonemployee work that are not well captured by the CPS, the growth in labor hours may have been understated and the growth in labor productivity correspondingly overstated. Further, if different sectors have made more- or less-intensive use of nonemployee labor input, the pattern of growth in productivity may have been distorted as well.

In principle, measures of multifactor productivity should take into account firms' use of purchased services. Multifactor productivity is defined as output relative to an index of inputs to production, weighted according to their shares of production costs. So long as purchased services are well measured, changes in the amount of nonemployee labor embedded in those services will be reflected in measured multifactor productivity. In practice, limited data on purchased services are collected, and estimates of how the use of these services is allocated across industries may not be especially accurate. Houseman (2007), for example, cites evidence suggesting that estimates from the input-output tables used in the construction of industry productivity statistics significantly understated the growth in the use of staffing services in manufacturing during the 1990s. Similar problems may exist with respect to the measurement and allocation of labor services provided by nonemployee workers.

A somewhat different measurement problem may arise if nonemployee workers sell services directly to consumers or produce tangible or intangible capital. In principle, one would like this output to be included in gross domestic product and incorporated into the measurement of productivity. Information on output is collected primarily through surveys and censuses of the employer businesses that account for the lion's share of production. In constructing its estimates of total output, the Bureau of Economic Analysis adjusts the figures for employer businesses using information on the revenues of nonemployer businesses (Bureau of Economic Analysis 2017). Still, any failure of the existing measurement system to fully capture output for final demand that is produced by nonemployee workers could be an additional source of distortion in measured trends in output and productivity.

In this chapter, we seek to clarify what different sources of data can tell us about changes in the prevalence and nature of both gig employment and nonemployee work arrangements more generally over time. We begin with a discussion in section 7.2 of the heterogeneity of nonemployee work and the challenges this heterogeneity poses to its measurement and assessment. Section 7.3 considers the two main types of data that have been used to study past trends in nonemployee work—surveys of households and administrative data. The discrepancy between the flat or declining trend in self-employment shown by measures based on household surveys and the long-term growth in similar measures based on administrative data is a significant puzzle. To reconcile these conflicting trends, we turn to analysis of a newly created linked data file that contains household survey data from the Annual Social and Economic (ASEC) supplement to the CPS and administrative information based on tax records for the same individuals. Preliminary findings based on this linked file are reported in section 7.4. Although there is some CPS-ASEC self-employment for which we can find no corresponding tax records, the amount of such undocumented self-employment has been relatively stable; in contrast, there has been a notable increase in the volume of self-employment activity reported to the Internal Revenue Service (IRS) that is not reported on the CPS-ASEC. Looking to the future, section 7.5 considers ways in which household survey data on nontraditional employment might be improved, and section 7.6 evaluates how employer survey data, tax data, and naturally occurring private-sector data might be used more effectively to improve our understanding of gig employment specifically and nonemployee work more generally. Finally, section 7.7 offers some initial thoughts about a path forward. Recognizing the limitations of each of the individual available sources of data, efforts to develop linked datasets that combine household survey data, tax data, employer survey data, and potentially, naturally occurring private-sector data are likely to have a high payoff, permitting greater insight into the changing nature of work than is possible using any single data source.

7.2   Typology of Work Arrangements

Although there has been a great deal of interest in the growth in non-traditional work arrangements in the US labor market, discussion of these arrangements has not always fully recognized their considerable heterogeneity. Combining arrangements with very different characteristics and then attempting to generalize about them runs the risk of being quite misleading. Table 7.1 lays out a typology that attempts to clarify similarities and differences across a variety of ways of organizing work, separated broadly into employee and self-employment arrangements. The table also identifies where these arrangements might be captured in household survey and administrative data, as well as where gig employment specifically might be counted.

7.2.1   Work Arrangements and Their Characteristics

One challenge in characterizing the evolution of work arrangements is that there are many different ways to organize work. The first column of table 7.1 lists a number of work arrangements that have been discussed in the literature. The categories listed in the table are not necessarily mutually exclusive, and in some cases, a job might fall into more than one category. In

Table 7.1   Work arrangement types and characteristics

Work arrangement type	Work arrangement characteristic						How work arrangement reported		
	Paid wage or salary	Expectation of continuing relationship	Predictable work schedule	Predictable earnings when working	Work supervised by firm paying salary	Classified as self-employed in HH surveys	Information return on which payer may report earnings [1]	Tax schedules attached to Form 1040 for reporting earnings to IRS [2]	Gig worker?
Employee									
Traditional employee	Yes	Most	Yes	Yes	Yes	No	W-2	—	No
On-call/varying schedule worker	Yes	Some	No	Yes	Yes	No	W-2	—	No
Direct-hire temporary worker	Yes	No	Yes	Yes	Yes	No	W-2	—	No
Contract company workers									
Temporary help agency worker	Yes	Some	Yes	Yes	No	No	W-2	—	No
PEO worker	Yes	Some	Yes	Yes	No	No	W-2	—	No
Other contract company worker	Yes	Some	Yes	Yes	No	No	W-2	—	No
Self-employed									
Business owners									
Incorporated business owner	Some	Most	Yes	Some	—	Inc. SE	W-2, K1 or 1099	Sched E	No
Partner in a partnership	No	Most	Yes	Some	—	Uninc. SE	K1	Sched E, SE	No
Unincorporated sole proprietor	No	Most	Yes	Some	—	Uninc. SE	1099	Sched C, SE	No
Independent contractor/freelancer	No	No	No	No	—	Uninc. SE	1099	Sched C, SE	Yes
Day laborer	No	No	No	No	—	Uninc. SE	1099	Sched C, SE	Yes
On-demand/platform worker	No	No	No	No	—	Uninc. SE	1099	Sched C, SE	Yes

[1] Information returns are required to be filed with the IRS only by certain types of payers and only for payments that exceed certain thresholds. Depending on the arrangements under which they work, those receiving nonemployee compensation could receive a 1099-MISC or, since 2011, possibly a 1099-K.

[2] Schedule E is used to report S-Corporation profits and distributions of partnership income. Some of the latter may be subject to self-employment tax. Unincorporated farm operators are required to file a Schedule F rather than a Schedule C. Individuals with incomes that are sufficiently low may not be required to file an income tax return.

addition, any given person may have multiple jobs and work under multiple arrangements. The next five columns of the table identify some key dimensions along which the listed work arrangements may differ.

Despite ongoing changes in the organization of work, traditional employment still accounts for the largest share of work in the US labor market. These are jobs on which a worker is paid a wage or salary, generally has some expectation of job security, may be full-time or part-time but has reasonably predictable hours and earnings, and is supervised by the same firm that pays her wage or salary. On-call workers and other direct-hire workers with varying schedules also appear on the payroll of the firm where they are employed, but their hours change depending on the needs of the firm, and there may be periods when they do not work at all. A direct-hire temporary worker is someone who is employed for a limited term. Direct-hire temporaries include seasonal employees such as lifeguards hired for the summer or sales clerks hired for the busy winter holiday season.[1]

An alternative to using workers hired directly onto a firm's own payroll is to use contract company workers on either a short-term or long-term basis. Temporary help agencies supply labor to businesses with intermittent, seasonal, or other temporary demands for labor; professional employer organizations (PEOs) provide workers or services on a more permanent basis; and other contract firms may provide specific services on either a short-term or a long-term basis. Individuals in these arrangements are employees, but the firm on whose behalf work is being performed (the client) is a different entity than the firm writing the worker's paycheck (the agency, PEO, or other contract firm).

As among employee arrangements, there is considerable diversity among the various categories of self-employment. The self-employed include business owners who may have a well-established clientele and a relatively predictable flow of work. These businesses may be incorporated, organized as partnerships, or operated as unincorporated sole proprietorships. The self-employed also include independent contractors or freelancers who earn money by performing one-off tasks for which they are paid an agreed sum. Such workers may not be able to count on steady work, and their hours and earnings may be volatile.[2] A day laborer is a person who gets work by waiting at a place where employers pick up people to help with short-term tasks. In some communities, for example, individuals seeking work may be known to wait in a convenience store parking lot or similar location. On-demand or platform workers can be thought of as the modern version of day laborers, but with work obtained by claiming tasks listed through an

---

1. Interestingly, the share of jobs that are seasonal has dropped significantly in recent decades (Hyatt and Spletzer 2017).

2. Independent contractors and freelancers could be folded into the unincorporated sole proprietor category, but some of those who would describe themselves as independent contractors or freelancers may not think of themselves as operating businesses.

online intermediary rather than by waiting for work at a physical location. Examples of the increasing number of online platforms that facilitate the matching of workers to those requiring services include Uber, TaskRabbit, Mechanical Turk, and Upwork.

The first characteristic we have identified as relevant to distinguishing among the various work arrangements is simply whether the person is paid a wage or salary. This can be thought of as shorthand for whether those working under the arrangement are likely to be covered by unemployment insurance, workers compensation, the Fair Labor Standards Act, and other labor market laws and regulations that are applicable to employees but generally not to those who are self-employed.[3]

A second important characteristic of a work arrangement is whether the work relationship can be expected to continue. This construct has been used by the BLS as the basis of its definition of contingent work (Polivka 1996a). Under that definition, a contingent worker is anyone who does not expect their job to last or reports that their job is temporary. Most traditional employees would not view their employment as contingent, but for consistency with how the BLS has applied this concept, we have allowed for the possibility that someone in such a position might consider their job to be at risk because they expect the business where they work to close or their position to be eliminated. Accordingly, we have entered "most" rather than "yes" for traditional employees in the column summarizing whether a continuing work arrangement exists. Someone who works only when called in or who has a varying schedule may nonetheless have an ongoing relationship with the firm at which they work. Workers supplied by a temporary help agency or other contract firm may have only a short-term relationship with the different firms that make use of their services but a continuing relationship with the temporary help agency or contract firm. In contrast, we would not expect direct-hire temporary workers to have an expectation of continuity in their work relationship. Among the self-employed, business owners seem likely to expect that their work arrangement will continue. Some independent contractors and freelancers also may have an expectation of continuity, but to the extent that they work on a task basis, this is less likely to be the case, and we have entered "no" for them in the column capturing this characteristic. Day laborers and on-demand or platform workers are unlikely to anticipate a continuing work relationship.

The third and fourth work characteristic columns pertain to whether the person in the listed work arrangement has a predictable work schedule and whether their earnings when working are predictable. Predictable hours and earnings are part of what defines a traditional employee arrangement.

---

3. The application of these laws and regulations to the owners of incorporated businesses who pay themselves a wage or salary is complicated, but in many states, business owners are permitted to opt in to coverage under the unemployment insurance and workers compensation systems.

During the term of her employment, a direct-hire temporary worker is likely to have relatively predictable hours and earnings, and the same is likely to be true of most contract company workers. An on-call worker will have unpredictable hours, but her pay while working is likely to be relatively predictable. Among the self-employed, a business owner's schedule may not be entirely predictable, but we would expect there to be a fair amount of regularity in her work hours and have entered "yes" in the relevant rows of the column capturing the predictability of hours; the earnings from time devoted to a business, however, may be less predictable. Both hours and earnings are apt to be unpredictable for independent contractors or freelancers, day laborers, and on-demand or platform workers.

A final work characteristic identified in the table, applicable only to those who are paid a wage or salary, captures whether on-the-job supervision is provided by the same firm that pays the worker's salary. This would be the case for traditional employees, on-call workers, and direct-hire temporary workers, all of whom are hired onto the payroll of the firm requiring their services. It would not be the case, however, for the employees of temporary help agencies or other contract firms who perform tasks under the supervision of the client firm but are paid by a different firm. This characteristic is associated with the so-called fissuring in the labor market that has been identified by some scholars as having weakened the opportunities and protections for workers who previously would have been employed directly by the firm for which they provide services but now are employed by a different company (Weil 2014).

7.2.2   Capturing Different Work Arrangements in Household Survey and Administrative Data

The next three columns of table 7.1 indicate where the different work arrangements might appear in household survey or tax data. Household surveys such as the CPS, the American Community Survey (ACS), and others commonly distinguish among wage and salary workers, the incorporated self-employed, and the unincorporated self-employed. In addition to traditional employees, on-call workers, direct hire temporaries, temporary help agency workers, PEO workers, and other contract company workers generally should be categorized as wage and salary workers in these data. The incorporated self-employed also typically are treated as wage and salary workers in published household survey statistics, though if a different breakout is desired, it often is possible to identify them separately. Work arrangements for which the table's first column indicated not being paid a wage or salary generally should be categorized as unincorporated self-employment in the household survey data; this includes partnerships, sole proprietorships, most independent contractors and freelancers, day laborers, and on-demand or platform workers.

Turning to tax data, wage and salary earnings produce information returns that are provided to the employee and submitted to the IRS. A Form W-2 is required for any job on which an individual earns $600 or more in wages or salary during a year. Wages or salaries that owners of incorporated businesses pay themselves are reported on the same form. Incorporated business owners also may receive distributions of business profits reported on a Schedule K-1 or payments of dividends reported on a Form 1099-DIV. Proceeds flowing from a partnership business to the individual partners are reported on a Schedule K-1. In contrast, sole proprietors and others doing nonemployee work may earn income for which there is no associated information return. If there is an information return, it is likely to be a Form 1099-MISC (for payments of nonemployee compensation of $600 or more by a business to any individual during year) or, since 2011, possibly a Form 1099-K (for settlement of payment card transactions or transactions conducted through third-party networks such as PayPal that exceed certain thresholds).

Anyone who receives self-employment income for services provided totaling $433 or more over the course of a year is required to file a Schedule SE, the form that is used to calculate self-employed individuals' Social Security and Medicare tax liability. This applies to anyone who receives distributions of partnership income or has other earnings from unincorporated self-employment activity. For the purpose of calculating personal income tax liability, individual tax filers use Schedule E to report receipt of S-corporation profits or partnership income and Schedule C to report income from an unincorporated sole proprietorship or other self-employment activity. The requirement to include a Schedule C with a self-employed tax filer's return applies even if the individual received no information returns in connection with their taxable earnings and even if business expenses fully offset the gross payments received.

The final column of table 7.1 indicates where we should expect gig employment to appear in household survey and administrative data. We first need to define what we mean by a gig worker. The term *gig* originated in the music industry, where musicians go into the studio to record one song or play in a band for one performance. The musicians with such gigs have no expectation of recording at the same studio the following day or playing with the same band the following night. Borrowing from the music industry, we define *gig employment* as one-off jobs on which workers are paid for a particular task or for a defined period of time. In terms of the work arrangement characteristics examined in table 7.1, a gig worker is not paid a wage or salary, does not expect a continuing work relationship, and does not have a predictable work schedule or predictable earnings when working. Applying this definition to the characteristics we have assigned to the various work arrangements, independent contractors and freelancers, day laborers, and on-demand or platform workers should be considered gig workers.

In household survey data, gig workers should be included among the unincorporated self-employed, but that group also includes people who are not gig workers. Another limitation of many household surveys is that because they focus on main jobs, the resulting data do not capture gig work that is supplemental to a person's primary employment. In tax data, some gig workers may receive a Form 1099-MISC, but the same form also may be used to report payments to other self-employed individuals who are not gig workers. The same is true of payments reported on a Form 1099-K. We would need to know more about the reason a payment was received—specifically, whether it was a payment to an unincorporated self-employed worker performing a one-off job—to determine whether the recipient should be considered a gig worker. Further, not all gig work generates either a Form 1099-MISC or Form 1099-K. All gig workers who are required to file a tax return should report their gross earnings and expenses from their gig work on a Schedule C. In addition, so long as their earnings exceed a minimum threshold, they should report their net earnings from gig work on a Schedule SE. While gig workers generally should be filing these schedules, not all Schedule C or Schedule SE filers are gig workers.

To the extent that household survey data or tax data allow us to identify everyone with either primary or secondary employment as an unincorporated self-employed worker, in principle, that information should provide an upper bound on the number of gig workers. Trends in unincorporated self-employment, which can be constructed using publicly available data from multiple sources, thus are a first place to look for suggestive evidence of whether gig employment has been growing over time.

7.3   Historical Data on Nonemployee Work Arrangements

Several household surveys conducted by the US Census Bureau produce regular data on the prevalence of self-employment among working Americans. The monthly CPS, conducted by the Census Bureau for the Bureau of Labor Statistics, is the source of official statistics about the US labor market. The CPS is an interviewer-administered household survey that includes questions about labor market activity during a specific reference week. CPS data can be used to identify household members whose main job during the survey reference week was in self-employment. More limited information is collected about second jobs. Each spring, the CPS-ASEC collects information about income and employment over the prior calendar year, including information on the longest job and on calendar-year self-employment earnings. Finally, since 2005, the ACS, a large mixed-mode survey conducted on a rolling basis throughout the year, has been another source of published self-employment estimates. These refer to the main job during the survey's reference week (described to the respondent as "last week").

More recently, analysts have turned to tax records in an effort to learn about the prevalence and nature of nonemployee work. As already noted, sole proprietors and general partners who have net earnings at or above just $433 (a threshold set in 1994) are required to file a Schedule SE, Self-Employment Tax. The Master Earnings File (MEF) database maintained by the Social Security Administration incorporates information on self-employment income from the Schedule SE together with information on any wage earnings reported on a Form W-2 that a person may have received during the year. The Census Bureau receives an extract (called the Detailed Earnings Record, or DER) that includes MEF records for each CPS respondent for whom a protected identification key (PIK), an encrypted Social Security Number, is available. This extract can be used to estimate the number of people filing a Schedule SE each year. In addition, any tax filer with gross nonfarm self-employment income earned as an unincorporated sole proprietor (including income earned as an independent contractor or freelancer, day laborer, or on-demand or platform worker) is required to file a Schedule C. The Schedule C information is a key ingredient in the construction of the master list of nonemployer businesses maintained by the Census Bureau.[4]

Whereas both Schedule SE and Schedule C are filed by individuals receiving self-employment income, Form 1099-MISC is filed by businesses that make payments of nonemployee income of $600 or more to any entity or individual during the calendar year. Tracking entities or people who received one or more Form 1099-MISC reporting nonemployee compensation during a calendar year offers another perspective on trends in self-employment. The fact that a Form 1099-MISC with a checked nonemployee compensation box may be reporting a payment to a business rather than an individual complicates the interpretation of the Form 1099-MISC data. In addition, a considerable amount of self-employment income has no associated Form 1099-MISC.[5] Since 2011, Form 1099-K has been used to report settlement of payment card transactions or settlement of third-party network transactions in excess of $20,000 or 200 transactions per year. Some self-employed individuals may receive a Form 1099-K, but this is relatively unusual, and most Form 1099-Ks are not issued to unincorporated self-employed individuals.

Figure 7.1 shows the trends in a number of different measures of the self-employment rate (the number self-employed under different definitions as

4. Businesses are included on the list if they report $1,000 or more in gross revenue (or in construction, $1 or more in gross revenue). In addition to information about unincorporated sole proprietors derived from Schedule C filings, the master list of nonemployer businesses also incorporates tax return information about C-corporations, S-corporations, and partnership businesses that do not have employees.
5. The data appendix provides additional details about the various household survey and administrative data sources just described. Although occasional supplements to the monthly CPS have asked more probing questions about the nature of individuals' employment arrangements, these questions have not been asked routinely, and consideration of the data generated by these occasional supplements is deferred to later in the chapter.

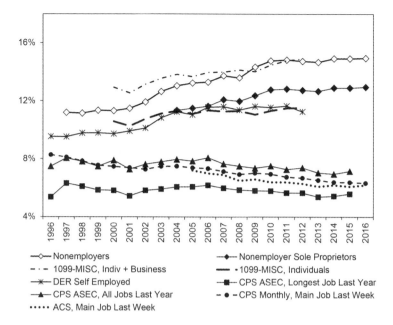

Fig. 7.1   Household survey and administrative data self-employment rates, 1996–2016

Sources: Nonemployers and Nonemployer Sole Proprietors downloaded from US Census Bureau website. 1099-MISC, Individual plus Business, and 1099-MISC, Individuals from US Department of the Treasury (2015). DER Self-Employed from authors' tabulations of linked CPS-ASEC and DER data. CPS ASEC, Longest Job Last Year and CPS ASEC, All Jobs Last Year from authors' tabulations of public-use CPS-ASEC files. CPS Monthly, Main Job Last Week downloaded from BLS website. ACS, Main Job Last Week downloaded from US Census Bureau website.

Note: Plotted estimates are self-employment as a percent of employment. For most series, employment is number of people with earned income during the calendar year from either the DER (for series based on tax data) or the CPS-ASEC (for two CPS-ASEC series). For the CPS and ACS Main Job Last Week series, employment is people employed during the survey reference week.

a percent of the corresponding total employment measure). The four series at the bottom of figure 7.1 all derive from household survey data. The series based on the monthly CPS captures the percent of employed people who are unincorporated self-employed on the main job held during the survey reference week, averaged across the 12 months of the year. This series has trended steadily downward, falling from 8.3 percent in 1996 to 6.3 percent in 2016. The main job series based on ACS data is conceptually comparable to the monthly CPS series and, although slightly lower in level, shows a similar downward trend over the years for which it is available. There are two household survey measures derived from the annual CPS-ASEC. The first shows the percent of people with any employment during the year whose longest job was in unincorporated self-employment and who had positive self-employment earnings. The second adds people whose longest job was not unincorporated self-employment but who had positive self-employment income from work outside of their longest job. These series have fluctuated somewhat but exhibit no clear trend. By construction, the first three of these series do not capture self-employment that is supplemental to a primary job. In principle, however, the more inclusive CPS-ASEC series should pick up both primary and secondary self-employment activity, and that measure behaves similarly to the others.

Five self-employment series based on administrative data series appear in the upper part of figure 7.1. These series are most comparable in concept to the more inclusive CPS-ASEC series that captures earnings during the calendar year from both primary and secondary self-employment. In each case, the numerator is some measure of the number of people or entities with self-employment earnings during the year, and the denominator is the number of individuals with earnings from any source in the DER. The share of people with earnings in the DER who have self-employment earnings has trended upward, rising from 9.5 percent in 1996 to 11.3 percent in 2012 (the last year for which we currently have these data).[6] Census counts of nonemployers are available from 1997 through 2016; published data identify sole-proprietor nonemployers separately beginning in 2004. Both have trended upward as a percent of the number of earners and, over the period from 2004 through 2016, when both are available, the upward trend in the series for sole-proprietor nonemployers has tracked the upward trend in the series for nonemployers overall.[7] Finally, the number of entities receiving nonemployee compensation reported on a Form 1099-MISC, taking individuals and businesses together, and the number of individuals for whom such compensation was reported are currently available for the period 2000–2012. These measures also have grown relative to the number of people with earnings.

Figure 7.1 makes clear that different data sources provide quite different answers to the simple question, What is the level and trend of self-employment in the US economy? Others have noted divergences between specific series; Katz and Krueger (2019a), for example, show the divergent trends in estimates of self-employment based on monthly CPS data and IRS Schedule C filings. Figure 7.1 shows that this divergence is quite general. Household surveys consistently show lower levels of self-employment than tax data and a relatively flat or declining long-term trend in self-employment as contrasted with the upward trend that is evident in tax data.

---

6. The DER estimates are based on a data file containing linked individual records from the CPS-ASEC and the DER that is discussed in the next section of the chapter.

7. For 2013–16, we do not have the DER estimate of the number of people with earnings during the year needed to construct the self-employment rates based on the Census nonemployer data. We have extrapolated the 2012 DER employment estimate forward using information on the change in employment from the Current Employment Statistics survey. See the data appendix for further details.

It would be nice to be able to say that one or the other type of measure—estimates based on household survey data or estimates based on tax data—accurately represents the prevalence and evolution of self-employment over time. In truth, however, measures of both types suffer from potential weaknesses. On the one hand, constraints on the length of the monthly CPS and ACS questionnaires mean that neither survey instrument probes deeply about household members' work arrangements. This may contribute to a variety of reporting errors. For example, a household survey respondent might fail to mention informal work that they do not think of as a job, something that further probing might uncover. To take another example, a household member who is doing work for a business may be reported as an employee of that business, even in cases where further probing might reveal that the person is in fact an independent contractor or freelancer. To the extent that nontraditional work arrangements are of growing importance, these problems could have become more serious over time.

On the other hand, administrative data capture only the information that is reported to the tax authorities on tax or information returns. Nonreporting or underreporting of income to the tax authorities is an acknowledged issue, especially with regard to self-employment income and other types of income that do not generate an information return that is submitted to the IRS. As already noted, anyone who makes payments of wage or salary income of $600 or more to an employee over the course of the year is required to file a Form W-2 with the IRS to document that payment. Businesses that make payments of $600 or more to a self-employed individual for services rendered are required to report those payments on a Form 1099-MISC. In 2011, business tax forms were modified so that business owners now must certify when they file their tax returns that all required Form 1099-MISCs have been completed and submitted. Also taking effect in 2011 was a requirement that payment settlement entities that process electronic payments to businesses report those payments to the IRS on a Form 1099-K if they exceed certain thresholds. There is no requirement, however, for households that pay for services to file a 1099-MISC. Despite efforts by the Congress to tighten the requirements for information reporting, a great deal of self-employment income generates no associated information return (Government Accountability Office 2007; Slemrod et al. 2017). Further, information returns capture only gross payments. To determine self-employment earnings, it is equally important to be able to gauge the expenses incurred in connection with this gross income, but these expenses generally are not subject to required information reporting (Government Accountability Office 2007; Slemrod et al. 2017). Not surprisingly, tax audit studies have shown that virtually all wage and salary income is reported on individual tax returns, but a notably smaller share of net nonfarm proprietor income and net farm income is reported (Slemrod and Bakija 2008).

One question is whether changes in information reporting requirements, such as those introduced in 2011, could have affected the reported prevalence and amounts of self-employment income. Research to date has not identified discontinuities in the administrative self-employment time series associated with changes in reporting requirements. With respect specifically to the changes introduced in 2011, this may be because the relatively minor increases in reported gross self-employment income that the changes appear to have induced were offset by the reporting of increased expenses (Slemrod et al. 2017).

Another potential issue to flag is that in the household survey data we have examined, our attention has been focused on the unincorporated self-employed, the group that is conceptually most comparable to the self-employment for which we have information in the DER. If the self-employed have become more likely over time to incorporate, the trend in a series that included the incorporated self-employed might be more meaningful (Hipple and Hammond 2016). We have recomputed both the monthly CPS and the ACS self-employment series with the incorporated self-employed included. Including them in the series does not change the conclusion that self-employment as measured in the household survey data has been steady or declining rather than increasing as in the tax-based administrative data.

7.4   Reconciling Household Survey and Administrative Estimates of Nonemployee Work

The most straightforward approach to understanding the discrepancies between household survey and administrative data estimates of self-employment is to compare information from the two sources for the same set of people. Using an internal Census Bureau identifier—the PIK—we have linked records from the CPS-ASEC to administrative records from the DER for the years 1996 through 2012 (the latest year for which we currently have data from the DER). The PIK is missing for approximately 20 percent to 30 percent of CPS-ASEC records, depending on the year. As described in the data appendix, we have reweighted the records with a PIK based on their characteristics to represent the population age 16 and older as a whole. In both of the datasets incorporated into the linked file, we identify unincorporated self-employment based on reports of self-employment earnings during the calendar year. To be more specific, in the CPS-ASEC, a person is defined as self-employed if they have a longest job during the year that is unincorporated self-employed and positive self-employment earnings or, if the longest job was not unincorporated self-employed, if they have positive self-employment income from some other job.[8] In the DER, a person is defined as self-employed if they had self-employment earnings reported on a Schedule SE.

8. In the CPS-ASEC, we do not know whether self-employment earnings other than from the longest job are from incorporated or unincorporated self-employment, though we expect most self-employment outside of the longest job to be unincorporated self-employment. See the data appendix for further discussion.

Table 7.2   Cross tabulation of self-employment status in linked CPS-ASEC and
                 DER data, 1996–2012

	DER not self-employed	DER self-employed	Total
CPS-ASEC not self-employed			
Number	202,311,037	10,459,170	212,770,208
Row Share	95.1%	4.9%	100.0%
Column Share	97.2%	65.4%	95.0%
CPS-ASEC self-employed			
Number	5,776,887	5,531,764	11,308,651
Row Share	51.1%	48.9%	100.0%
Column Share	2.8%	34.6%	5.0%
Total			
Number	208,087,924	15,990,935	224,078,859
Row Share	92.9%	7.1%	100.0%
Column share	100.0%	100.0%	100.0%

Source: Authors' tabulations of linked CPS-ASEC and DER data.

Notes: Numbers reported are for population age 16 plus. Data annual averages for years 1996–2012 pooled. Tabulations are weighted.

We have used these data to ask how well the CPS-ASEC and the DER agree with respect to the classification of individuals as self-employed. Table 7.2 displays a weighted cross-tabulation of self-employment status in the CPS-ASEC with self-employment status in the DER, using data that are pooled across the years 1996–2012. Although the two data sources should be measuring essentially the same thing, there is substantial disagreement between them regarding individuals' self-employment status. On average, over the 17 years for which we have data, 65.4 percent of those with self-employment income in the DER do not report any self-employment income in the CPS. Conversely, 51.1 percent of those with self-employment income in the CPS-ASEC do not report any self-employment income in the DER.

The fact that there is disagreement between the household survey and administrative data employment measures is not surprising. In earlier research, we found that on average over the period 1996–2003, about 6 percent of individuals who had unemployment insurance (UI) earnings during the first quarter of the year reported no CPS wage-and-salary employment in a UI-covered sector during the year's first three months. Conversely, about 18 percent of individuals reporting CPS wage-and-salary employment in a UI-covered sector during the first three months of the year had no first-quarter UI earnings (Abraham et al. 2013). Similarly, in weighted tabulations using the linked data file that we are using to explore the sources of discrepancy in alternative self-employment series, 9.3 percent of those with DER wage-and-salary income had no reported CPS-ASEC wage-and-salary income for the same year. Conversely, 12.4 percent of those with reported

CPS-ASEC wage-and-salary income for a year had no DER wage-and-salary income for that same year.

What is surprising, however, is the size of the off-diagonal cells in the tabulations shown in table 7.1. Whether taking the DER self-employed or the CPS-ASEC self-employed as the base, a majority of those who are categorized as self-employed in the dataset in question are not categorized as such in the other dataset. At least to some extent, this reflects the wide variety of arrangements under which self-employment activity may occur. Neither the household survey data nor the administrative data may be ideally suited to pick up all of that activity.[9]

We also are interested in how the discrepancy between the CPS-ASEC and the DER measures of self-employment has changed over time. Figure 7.2a displays the number of self-employed people as measured in the CPS-ASEC annual earnings data and the corresponding measure based on earnings data from the DER. While self-employment based on the DER grew markedly between 1996 and the mid-2000s, the corresponding CPS-ASEC measure was lower to start with and has been stagnant. Figure 7.2b shows the off-diagonals associated with cross-tabulating the CPS-ASEC and DER data on a year-by-year basis—that is, it plots the number of people who are self-employed in the DER but not the CPS-ASEC and, separately, the number who are self-employed in the CPS-ASEC but not the DER. It is apparent that virtually all of the growth in DER self-employment relative to CPS-ASEC self-employment can be attributed to growth in the number of people who are self-employed in the DER but not in the CPS-ASEC.

To further explore the discrepancy between the two measures of self-employment, we have looked a bit more closely at these off-diagonals, grouping those who are self-employed in the DER but not the CPS-ASEC into three mutually exclusive categories:

1. *No CPS-ASEC employment.* No wage-and-salary or self-employment income in the CPS-ASEC; self-employment income in the DER.[10]

2. *Self-employment second job not reported in CPS-ASEC.* Only wage-and-salary income in the CPS-ASEC; both wage-and-salary income and self-employment income in the DER.

3. *CPS-ASEC job wage and salary, classification issue.* Only wage-and-salary income in the CPS-ASEC; only self-employment income in the DER.

---

9. Some of the information used to categorize individuals as self-employed in the CPS-ASEC is imputed rather than directly reported. We chose to retain CPS-ASEC records with imputed information because that makes the data we analyze more consistent with the data used in the production of published statistics. Usable information on which values are imputed is available from 1997 forward. In calculations for the 1997–2012 period based on a sample restricted to cases with directly reported information and reweighted accordingly, we estimate that 63.4 percent of those with DER self-employment have no CPS-ASEC self-employment, and 44.3 percent of those with CPS-ASEC self-employment have no DER self-employment.

10. Individuals in this category may have only self-employment income or both wage-and-salary and self-employment income in the DER.

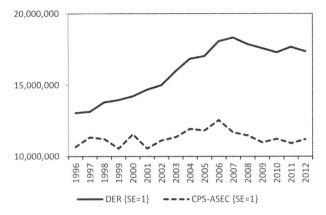

Fig. 7.2a   CPS-ASEC and DER self-employment

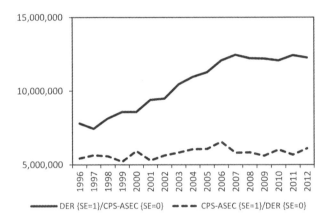

Fig. 7.2b   CPS-ASEC vs. DER Self-employment off-diagonals

Source: Authors' tabulations of linked CPS-ASEC and DER data.

Note: In fig. 7.2a, solid line is number of people with positive self-employment income in the DER and dashed line is number of people with positive self-employment income in the CPS-ASEC. In fig. 7.2b, solid line is number of people with positive self-employment income in the DER but no self-employment income in the CPS-ASEC and dashed line is number of people with positive self-employment income in the CPS-ASEC but no self-employment income in the DER. Tabulations are weighted.

Those in the first two groups may be people performing self-employment work who do not think to report it (or for whom the CPS respondent in their household does not think to report it), whether because the activity in question generated only a small amount of earnings or for some other reason. The third group may be capturing those who think of themselves as employees and may in fact be employees according to the relevant legal criteria but are paid as nonemployees and classified that way in the tax data. Given the growing concerns about worker misclassification (see, e.g., Leberstein 2012), for some purposes this group may be the most interesting.

We also have grouped those who are self-employed in the CPS-ASEC but not in the DER into three mutually exclusive categories:

4. *No DER employment.* No wage-and-salary or self-employment income in the DER; self-employment income in the CPS-ASEC.[11]

5. *Self-employment second job not recorded in the DER.* Only wage-and-salary income in the DER; both wage-and-salary income and self-employment income in the CPS-ASEC.

6. *DER job wage and salary, classification issue.* Only wage-and-salary income in the DER; only self-employment income in the CPS-ASEC.

The fourth and fifth categories capture self-employment income that is reported in the CPS-ASEC but does not appear in the tax data, either work generating too little income to trigger tax-reporting requirements or off-the-books work. Category six may be capturing individuals who are indeed self-employed but operate an incorporated business, meaning that they should not have been counted in the CPS-ASEC measure of unincorporated self-employment and would appear in the tax data as having wage and salary income but not self-employment income.

Figure 7.3a shows the evolution of the three groups within the DER{SE=1}/CPS-ASEC{SE=0} category; figure 7.3b shows the evolution of the three groups within the CPS-ASEC{SE=1}/DER{SE=0} category. Whereas there has been growth in all three of the DER{SE=1}/CPS-ASEC{SE=0} groups, employment in the three CPS-ASEC{SE=1}/DER{SE=0} groups has changed very little.

One way to summarize the information presented in these figures is to calculate the shares of the growing discrepancy between the number of people with self-employment income according to the DER and the number of self-employed people according to the CPS-ASEC accounted for by each of the different groups. For this purpose, we have averaged the numbers for the two starting years and the two ending years in our data series and then calculated the overall change in the discrepancy between those averaged endpoints. Note that either *increases* in the size of the DER{SE=1}/CPS-ASEC{SE=0} groups or *decreases* in the size of the CPS-ASEC{SE=1}/DER{SE=0} groups could have contributed to the overall discrepancy.

The percentages of the growth in the overall discrepancy accounted for by each of the six groups described above are shown in table 7.3. As was apparent from figure 7.2, the growing discrepancy between the DER and CPS-ASEC estimates of self-employment is accounted for entirely by the growing number of people identified as self-employed in the DER who are not so identified in the CPS-ASEC. This growth is split roughly evenly among the three DER{SE=1}/CPS-ASEC{SE=0} groups. The net effect of

---

11. Individuals in this category may have only self-employment income or both wage-and-salary and self-employment income in the CPS-ASEC.

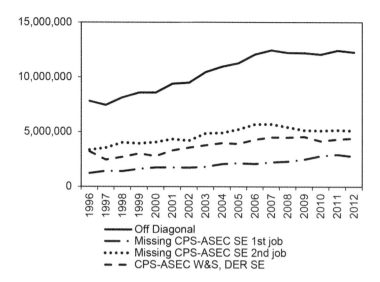

Fig. 7.3a   Decomposing DER {SE = 1}/CPS-ASEC {SE = 0} off-diagonal

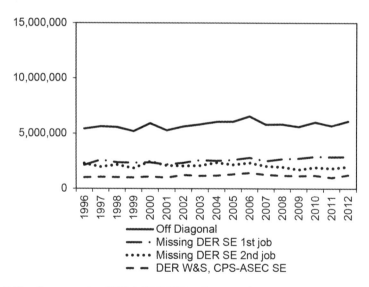

Fig. 7.3b   Decomposing CPS-ASEC {SE = 1}/DER {SE = 0} off-diagonal
Source: Authors' tabulations of linked CPS-ASEC and DER data.
Note: In each panel, off-diagonal shown as solid line is sum of three labeled subcomponents.
SE is self-employed; W&S is wage and salary. Tabulations are weighted.

Table 7.3   Accounting for growth in discrepancy between DER and CPS-ASEC self-employment estimates, 1996–97 to 2011–12

Off-diagonal category	Percent of growth in discrepancy explained
DER {SE = 1}/CPS-ASEC {SE = 0}	
1. Missing CPS-ASEC SE 1st job	34.5%
2. Missing CPS-ASEC SE 2nd job	38.4%
3. CPS-ASEC W&S job, DER SE job	35.2%
CPS-ASEC {SE=1}/DER {SE=0}	
4. Missing DER SE 1st job	−11.6%
5. Missing DER SE 2nd job	5.2%
6. DER W&S job, CPS-ASEC SE job	−1.8%

Source: Authors' tabulations of linked CPS-ASEC and DER data.
Notes: SE is self-employed; W&S is wage and salary. Tabulations are weighted.

changes in the size of the CPS-ASEC{SE=1}/DER{SE=0} off-diagonals is small and works in the direction of slightly offsetting the growing size of the DER{SE=1}/CPS-ASEC{SE=0} off-diagonals. In other words, the main issue is that there are an increasing number of people who are earning self-employment income and reporting that income to the tax authorities but for whom that income is not being reported in the CPS-ASEC.[12]

A possible explanation for the increasing number of people with self-employment activity that is captured in the DER but not reported in the CPS-ASEC might be that more of them are doing self-employment work that generates only a small amount of income. We note, however, that the average self-employment earnings of those with self-employment captured in the DER but not the CPS-ASEC are relatively substantial, averaging about $14,400 in 2012 dollars over the years 1996 through 2012 covered by our sample, and further, this average earnings level has not trended downward over time.[13]

7.5   Improving Household Survey Measures of Nonemployee Work

The preceding discussion has documented that the CPS-ASEC information on calendar-year earnings is missing a significant and increasing amount

12. In the reweighted sample that excludes cases with imputed information, which can be constructed for the period from 1997 through 2012, it is also the case that each of the three groups with DER self-employment but no CPS-ASEC self-employment accounts for roughly a third of the discrepancy in growth between the DER and CPS-ASEC series.

13. The earnings figures reported are averages of the 17 annual values. Among those who have self-employment earnings in the DER but not in the CPS-ASEC, DER earnings are largest for those with only wage and salary earnings in the CPS-ASEC and only self-employment earnings in the DER, averaging about $24,300 in 2012 dollars over the 1996–2012 period. DER self-employment earnings averaged about $11,500 for the group with no CPS-ASEC employment and about $7,900 for those who are missing a self-employment second job in the CPS-ASEC. There was no downward trend in DER self-employment earnings over our sample period for any of the three groups.

Table 7.4   **Estimates of the prevalence of selected work arrangements on main job (percent of all workers)**

Source	Independent contractors	On-call workers	Temporary help service workers	Contract firm employees
Contingent Worker Supplement, Current Population Survey, BLS estimates				
1995	6.7	1.7	1.0	0.5
1997	6.7	1.6	1.0	0.6
1999	6.3	1.5	0.9	0.6
2001	6.4	1.6	0.9	0.5
2005	7.4	1.8	0.9	0.6
2017	6.9	1.7	0.9	0.6
Quality of Worklife Survey, General Social Survey[a]				
2002	13.9	2.1	0.7	2.5
2006	13.7	2.6	1.0	3.7
2010	13.3	3.7	1.4	3.1
2014	14.1	3.1	0.5	2.7

Source: Bureau of Labor Statistics press releases reporting Contingent Worker Supplement (CWS) findings and authors' tabulations of General Social Survey data.

Notes: CWS work arrangements defined in Cohany (1996). Quality of Worklife Survey estimates based on answers to question about work arrangements. First response option is "work as an independent contractor, consultant or freelance worker"; second is "on call, and work only when called to work"; third is "paid by a temporary agency"; and fourth is "work for a contractor who provides workers and services to others under contract."

of self-employment activity. Because this series has behaved so similarly to other series based on household survey data, there is reason to suspect that the same is true of other household survey measures of self-employment.

One way to improve existing household survey measures of self-employment and alternative work arrangements more generally would be to add survey questions that probe more directly regarding these arrangements, either as part of the core survey or (perhaps more plausibly) on periodic supplements. The Contingent Worker Supplement (CWS) to the CPS, fielded on several occasions between 1995 and 2017, has included questions both about whether the individual expects his or her employment to continue and about whether the person's main job was as an independent contractor, on-call worker, temporary agency worker, or worker at a contract firm (see Cohany 1996; Polivka 1996a, 1996b). The smaller Quality of Worklife (QWL) supplement to the General Social Survey also has produced estimates on the prevalence of the same four alternative work arrangements on the main job.

Estimates of the prevalence of alternative work arrangements based on the CWS for six years between 1995 and 2017 are shown in the top panel of table 7.4; estimates from the QWL supplement to the General Social Survey (GSS) for four years between 2002 and 2014 are shown in the table's bottom panel. Although the estimates from the two surveys differ with regard to the estimated prevalence of some types of work—in particular, work as an independent contractor—they agree that the prevalence of the different alternative work arrangements has not trended upward over time. It is important to note, however, that these questions were asked only about people who had already been identified as employed in response to the surveys' standard employment questions and only about their main jobs. Both of these features mean that there is likely to be work under alternative arrangements that, in part by design, the two surveys do not capture.

In October and November 2015, before the fielding of the 2017 CWS, Lawrence Katz and Alan Krueger arranged for the core CWS questions to be collected on the Rand-Princeton Contingent Work Survey (RPCWS) administered as part of the Rand Corporation's online American Life Panel (ALP; Katz and Krueger 2019a). The intention was that the RPCWS would produce estimates for 2015 that could be compared to the CWS estimates for earlier years. In contrast to the 2017 CWS, the 2015 RPCWS produced substantially higher prevalence rates for all four types of alternative work than had been estimated in the 2005 CWS—results that were interpreted as evidence of substantial growth in the prevalence of these arrangements on individuals' main jobs. Given these findings, many people were surprised when the 2017 CWS estimates turned out to be so similar to the 2005 CWS estimates. There are several reasons, however, to have suspected that the RPCWS estimates might not be directly comparable to the earlier CWS estimates.

First, the RPCWS data were collected through an online survey panel, the ALP, whose members are assembled from a variety of sources with an unknown response rate.[14] Given the way in which it was assembled, the RPCWS sample may be less representative of the population than the CWS sample in ways that reweighting based on observables cannot fully correct. More specifically, the concern is that, even holding their demographic characteristics constant, people who are willing to participate in an online survey panel also might be more likely than others to work under nonstandard arrangements. Second, whereas the CWS asks respondents to provide information for all members of their households, the RPCWS asks respondents to report only for themselves. To the extent that respondents are able to report more fully about their own experiences than about the experiences of others in their household, this could mean that relying only on self-reports will produce more accurate information than accepting both self and proxy reports but by the same token may undermine the comparability of the RPCWS to the CWS. Third, the RPCWS and the CWS collected information for different times of the year, with the CWS asking about

14. See Pollard and Baird (2017) for a description of the methods used to create the ALP panel.

work during a mid-February reference week and the RPCWS asking about work during an October or November reference week. It is possible that the reliance on alternative work arrangements fell between 2015 and 2017 as the labor market tightened, but this seems unlikely to explain the large difference in the estimates from the 2015 RPCWS and the 2017 CWS. We view the different findings obtained in the two surveys as a cautionary tale about the importance of consistency in measurement for assessing trends in work arrangements.[15]

While the CWS, GSS, and RPCWS gather information about work arrangements that is not normally collected, they are not designed to identify nonemployee work done by people the standard questions do not identify as employed or for whom self-employment is not a primary job. As discussed in the previous section of the chapter, there are a significant number of people with no self-employment income during the year in the CPS-ASEC who do have self-employment income in the DER. On average over the 1996–2012 period, 19.3 percent of these people had no income from employment in the CPS-ASEC. Another 44.9 percent had only wage and salary income in the CPS-ASEC but wage and salary income plus self-employment income in the DER, suggesting that the CPS-ASEC may have missed a self-employment second job.[16] These numbers refer to self-employment at any point during the year rather than to self-employment at a point in time. Nonetheless, they suggest that there may be a significant amount of nonemployee work that would not be uncovered by probing only about an already-reported main job.

Several other recent surveys have contained questions designed specifically to learn about the prevalence of informal work activity. The Enterprising and Informal Work Activities (EIWA) survey (Robles and McGee 2016) was administered as an online survey to the GfK KnowledgePanel in October and November 2015. It contained a battery of items asking respondents about informal income-generating activities over the prior six months, including providing in-person services such as child care, housecleaning, or landscaping; selling new or used items at garage sales or flea markets; and selling services, selling items or renting property online. The EIWA estimates indicate that 36 percent of the adult US population engaged in at least one of these activities during the six-month reference period. Although there might be debate about whether renting or selling items should count as work activity, the survey estimates show that 27 percent of the adult population earned income by housecleaning, house sitting, yard work, or other property maintenance tasks and that 17 percent earned income by babysitting or providing child care services.

---

15. Katz and Krueger (2019b) revisits the results reported in Katz and Krueger (2019a) and comes to much the same conclusion.

16. In the previously mentioned dataset that drops imputed observations, the corresponding percentages for the period 1997–2012 are 19.5 percent and 45.0 percent.

The 2015 Survey of Household Economics and Decisionmaking (SHED), also administered via the GfK KnowledgePanel, contained a single question about whether a respondent was currently engaged in informal work activity. Among adults who were not students and not retired, about 20 percent of those under age 30, 15 percent of those age 30 to 44, and 11 percent of those age 45 and older said they were engaged in informal work (Board of Governors 2016). The 2016 SHED adopted the more detailed set of questions about informal work activity developed for the EIWA and a one-month reference period; the 2017 SHED collected similar information (Board of Governors 2017, 2018). In the SHED data, over those two years, an estimated 28.1 percent of all adults reported having earned money from informal work activities during the previous month (Abraham and Houseman 2019). A final recent survey, the Survey of Informal Work Participation (SIWP), also finds high rates of participation in informal work activities. Among household heads surveyed in the two waves of the survey conducted in January and December 2015, an estimated 32.5 percent were currently engaged in paid informal work, not including survey work, and 18.5 percent were engaged in informal work after also excluding work related to renting and selling (Bracha and Burke 2019).

One caveat regarding the three surveys just discussed—the EIWA, the SHED, and the SIWP—is that all were administered via online survey panels. Although each was weighted to match the demographic characteristics of the target population, as with the RCPWS, the concern is that the survey samples may in certain respects be unrepresentative. More specifically, one might fear that people who are willing to participate in an online survey panel also may be more likely than otherwise similar individuals to participate in informal work. Taking into account losses during the course of panel recruitment, the response rates to the EIWA and the SHED are just 4 percent to 5 percent; the response rate for the SIWP is not reported but is likely to be similar. Although there is no one-to-one relationship between response rates and nonresponse bias (Groves and Peytcheva 2008), the surveys' low response rates reinforce concern that those participating may be atypical. As discussed by Abraham and Houseman (2019), it is at least somewhat reassuring that the estimated share of people in the 2017 SHED who earned money within the past month by driving using a ridesharing app is of the same order of magnitude as estimates for the same time period from other sources. Unfortunately, comparable benchmarks for other types of informal work are lacking.[17]

---

17. In addition to the EIWA, SHED, and SIWP, the Survey of Income and Program Participation includes a category for reported work on a person's main job that cannot easily be classified as either work for an employee or self-employment. The utility of these data is limited by the fact that they do not allow different arrangements within the "other" category to be distinguished. The McKinsey Global Institute (MGI) independent work survey (Manyika et al. 2016) also attempted to capture all informal or independent work, whether it represented

A recent survey experiment described in Abraham and Amaya (2019) provides some additional evidence about how different approaches to probing for informal employment might affect the share of people for whom employment activity is reported (the employment rate) and the share of those with employment for whom more than one job is reported (the multiple job-holding rate). The experiment was embedded in a survey carried out for the 2016 Joint Program in Survey Methodology (JPSM) practicum. Subjects for the survey were recruited using Mechanical Turk, Amazon's crowdsourcing platform, and the specific estimates thus cannot be generalized, but the qualitative findings shed useful light on some of the factors that may affect household survey responses to questions about work activity.

The survey collected information on the characteristics of the members of respondents' households. It also asked questions to identify each household member's employment status and, for those who were employed, whether they held more than one job. With the exception of some special questions concerning sexual orientation and gender identity included for testing, all the questions about household members' characteristics and employment status were taken directly from the CPS questionnaire. Additional questions about informal work activity were asked about one randomly selected member of each survey respondent's household. In one version, randomly assigned to half of the cases, respondents were asked a global yes/no question about whether there had been any such work activity during the reference week (the *global* question). In the second version, respondents were asked about each of six different possible types of informal work activity, with examples provided for each of them, and to indicate whether any other type of informal work activity had been performed (the *detailed* question).[18] In cases where employment had already been reported for the person to whom the added probe applied, the respondent was asked to indicate whether any reported informal work activity had been included in the responses to the standard CPS employment questions. Employment rates and multiple job-holding rates were computed based on the responses to the CPS questions and then recomputed to incorporate the additional work activity uncovered by probing.

The first row in the upper panel of table 7.5, summarizing selected results from Abraham and Amaya (2019), displays the employment rate that is estimated based on the standard CPS questions; the second row displays the augmented employment rate that incorporates the additional information provided in response to the informal employment probe; and the third

a person's primary work or was supplemental to a primary job. The independent work concept applied in the MGI survey, however, is not comparable to that applied in other research.

18. The six types of activity in addition to the "other" category were services to other people; services to a self-employed individual or business; performing as an actor, musician, or entertainer; driving for a ride-sharing service; assisting with medical, marketing, or other research; or posting videos, blogs, or other content online. A list of examples was given for each category.

Table 7.5   Employment and multiple job-holding rates with and without probes for informal employment

Estimate	Response for self			Response for other household member		
	Global informal employment question	Detailed informal employment question	Detailed minus global difference	Global informal employment question	Detailed informal employment question	Detailed minus global difference
Employment rate (percent)						
CPS questions only	94.7	94.7	0.1	69.8	69.7	0.0
CPS plus additional questions	96.9	98.1	1.2*	73.5	76.4	2.9
Difference	2.3**	3.4**	1.2	3.7**	6.7**	3.0**
Sample size	1,364	1,340	—	1,128	1,107	—
Multiple job-holding rate among CPS employed (percent)						
CPS questions only	32.0	31.8	−0.2	10.6	10.0	−0.6
CPS plus additional questions	55.9	56.5	0.6	13.5	21.2	7.8**
Difference	23.9**	24.7**	0.7	2.9**	11.3**	8.4**
Sample size	1,291	1,269	—	787	772	—

* Significant at 0.05 level. ** Significant at 0.01 level.
Source: Abraham and Amaya (2019)

row shows the difference between the two estimates. The employment rate is defined as the percent of the sample categorized as employed during the survey reference week. The second panel of the table reports similar information on the multiple job-holding rate for those categorized as employed based on the standard CPS questions. The multiple job-holding rate is the percent of this group who had more than one job during the survey reference week. Estimates are shown separately for respondents asked to report for themselves and those asked to report for another member of their household, in each case differentiated by whether the respondent received the global probe or the more detailed probe.

Probing to ask about informal work activity produced notably higher estimated employment and multiple job-holding rates whether respondents were reporting for themselves or for another member of their household and whether the respondent received the global or the detailed probe. As already noted, the sample of Mechanical Turkers used in the study is not representative of the population as a whole, and the magnitude of the changes in these estimated rates likely would have been different in a more representative sample. Still, the fact that probing has such a consistent effect on the estimates suggests that learning about informal work activity is likely to require asking more than the standard employment questions.

In addition, the estimates suggest that asking the global question versus the more detailed question about informal work may make a larger difference when the respondent is answering questions about someone else. For those reporting about their own work activity, the two forms of the question have very comparable impacts, and the differences between the effects of the two question treatments are not statistically significant. In contrast, when the respondent is reporting for another household member, asking the detailed probe rather than the global probe produces a larger increase in both the estimated employment rate and the estimated multiple job-holding rate. Given the nature of the survey sample, the magnitudes of the differences between the estimates for respondents and those for others in the household are unlikely to generalize, but it is informative that detailed probing makes a larger difference compared to using a global probe when respondents are being asked about others in the household rather than about themselves.

Other recent research also has produced results suggesting that the standard CPS questions may not fully capture informal work activity. The 2015 SIWP surveys included employment questions similar to those on the CPS together with additional questions about informal work. Assuming that anyone who was currently engaged in informal work activity should have been counted as employed, accounting for that work would have raised the point estimate of the overall employment rate for household heads from 65.1 percent to 69.6 percent, a 4.5 percentage point increase, though the survey sample was relatively small and this increase was not statistically significant

(Bracha and Burke 2019). In a 2015 survey of Mechanical Turk respondents conducted by Lawrence Katz and Alan Krueger, taking into account small jobs or gigs beyond the main job that were not reported in response to the CPS employment questions almost doubles the multiple job-holding rate, raising it from 39 percent to 77 percent (Katz and Krueger 2019b). Taken as a whole, these findings suggest that standard household survey questions may miss some individuals' primary work activities, perhaps because the survey respondent does not think of them as a job, and that there is a sizable risk they will fail to uncover secondary work activity. Devising an appropriate set of more probing questions that could be asked at regular intervals on ongoing household surveys would allow trends in work activity and work arrangements to be gauged more accurately.

7.6   Other Sources of Information on Nonemployee Work

In addition to household survey data and the earnings information derived from Schedule SE that we have already discussed, useful information about nonemployee work could be gleaned from employer surveys, other tax records and associated data repositories, and information held by private firms. We discuss each of these potential data sources briefly in turn. A central theme of this discussion will be that the integration of survey, administrative, and private data has the potential to add important new insights to our understanding of the changing nature of work.

7.6.1   Employer Surveys

A natural approach to learning about alternative work arrangements would be to ask employers. Employer-provided information is unlikely to be especially helpful for learning about how alternative work arrangements fit into workers' careers but could be quite helpful for learning about the scale of such activity and thus for productivity measurement. Capturing firms' use of contract workers is an issue that has been of particular concern to the federal statistical agencies. More specifically, the agencies have recognized that for the purpose of measuring sectoral productivity, the employees of professional employer organization (PEO) and temporary help service (THS) firms should be assigned to the industry in which they are actually working rather than to staffing services. Dey, Houseman, and Polivka (2012) used data from the Occupational Employment Survey on the occupational distribution of staffing services employees together with information from the Contingent Worker Supplement on the industries in which staffing firms place workers to estimate the industry distribution of placements by PEO and THS firms. Over the 1989 to 2004 period studied in their paper, accounting for such placements had a noteworthy impact not only on trends in the input of labor to manufacturing but also on measures of manufacturing labor productivity.

While recognizing that this issue needs to be addressed, both BLS and Census have faced challenges in fully capturing and allocating THS and PEO activity. For a number of cycles, the Economic Census has included questions for PEO firms about the industries in which leased workers are placed (Lombardi and Ono 2010), but similar questions are not asked of temporary help service firms, nor is it clear that they would be able to answer them. BLS carried out a study in 2005 to assess the feasibility of collecting information from THS and PEO firms in the Current Employment Statistics (CES) survey on where they placed workers. The conclusion was that many THS and PEO firms do not have records concerning the industry of their clients, and a substantial minority would be unable or unwilling to provide this information on the CES (Bureau of Labor Statistics 2005). Both the Census and the BLS efforts just described sought to be able to allocate the employees of the PEO and THS firms across industries, an important but limited objective. Obtaining this information would still leave unanswered important questions about firms' use of the services of self-employed individuals working on their own account.

In principle, both the services provided by contract company workers and the services provided by sole proprietors, independent contractors, and so on should be captured in the Business Expenses Survey (BES) conducted by the Census Bureau as a part of the Economic Census and its program of annual economic surveys. Rather than asking service suppliers to provide information about their customers, the BES asks the firms that are customers to report on their spending for these services. The information obtained through the BES is an important ingredient in the construction of the Input-Output tables. The categories of expenses for which firms are asked to report vary somewhat depending on the industry but include a category for temporary staff and leased employees obtained through THS or PEO firms, a category for purchased professional and technical services, and categories for other types of purchased services. The data are collected annually for manufacturing and services but only once every five years for other industries, and they are denominated in dollars rather than in the amount of labor used to produce the service in question. Perhaps more important for our purposes, the payments in any category that a firm makes to individuals working as independent contractors or freelancers are aggregated with the payments made to more traditional businesses and cannot be separately identified.

Another interesting effort to collect information from the users of labor supplied under various arrangements was the addition of a module on this topic to the 2015 Annual Survey of Entrepreneurs (ASE).[19] The module included questions on whether the firm used different types of workers—

19. The ASE is a survey of approximately 290,000 employer firms, of which just under half are less than 10 years old. See Foster and Norman (2016) for further details about the ASE.

full time; part time; day laborer; temporary help service employee; leased employee; or contractors, subcontractors, independent contractors, or outside consultants—as well as questions regarding what share of the total number of workers were of each type and the types of tasks each type of worker performed. The approach developed for the 2015 ASE is interesting in part because it offers the possibility of insights into the use of nonemployee workers by young businesses that may be more innovative in their workforce organizational structure.

Brown, Earle, and Lee (2019) have begun to look at the data from the ASE module. Their initial estimate is that 30 percent of US firms make at least some use of contract workers, with those workers accounting for 14 percent of full-time-equivalent work effort overall. Relative to full-time employees, they find contract workers are most likely to be involved in operations, product development, and technology development activities and least likely to be involved in management and human resources activities. They also observe that new businesses are more likely than established businesses to use contract workers. There is certainly more to be gleaned from a careful examination of the data from the new ASE module, including insights about how well the module questions on the use of workers under alternative arrangements have performed and whether they might be adapted for use in other settings.

7.6.2   Tax Data

The analysis described earlier in the chapter based on CPS data integrated with records from the DER demonstrates the value of administrative data for studying the evolution of employment arrangements. That analysis made use of information on annual earnings reported on Schedule SE. That schedule does not contain information about the individuals or firms for which self-employment work is performed. Form 1099-MISC, used to report business payments of nonemployee compensation to contract workers, contains a tax identifier for both the payee and the payer. This means that access to 1099-MISC data in principle allows researchers to match individuals to the firms for which they are performing work (see, e.g., Collins et al. 2019). Some individuals may have long-standing self-employment relationships with a single firm; these should be reflected in the individual receiving a 1099-MISC from only one employer identification number (EIN) for many years consecutively. Other individuals may receive multiple 1099-MISC forms from multiple EINs with considerable turnover in the latter. These two patterns would imply quite different work arrangements from the perspective of both the individual and the firm.

Integration of other sorts of tax data also has the potential to yield new insights. As an example, in other recent work, we have created a data file containing information on self-employed sole proprietors derived from the microdata that underlie the Census Bureau nonemployer statistics, the unemployment insurance wage records contained in the Longitudinal Employer Household Dynamics (LEHD) infrastructure, and personal characteristics from the Census Bureau's Individual Characteristics File. We are using these data to study changes in the Taxi and Limousine Services industry during the period of explosive growth it has experienced following the introduction of online apps for matching workers to customers, looking at both new entrants and incumbents in the industry (Abraham et al. 2018). This is just one example of the sorts of analyses that can be carried out using this data infrastructure.

7.6.3   Financial Data

Anonymized individual-level financial records are another potential source of information about certain forms of nonemployee work. In an interesting stream of research, Farrell and Greig (2016a, 2016b) and Farrell, Greig, and Hamoudi (2018) use transaction-level data from customers with JP Morgan Chase banking and credit card accounts to examine flows of income that originate from a set of online platforms identified by the research team. Their findings suggest that online platform workers reflect a small but rapidly growing sector of the workforce. The findings also suggest, however, that such work is a secondary source of income for most households, reinforcing the importance of looking beyond the main job to develop a complete understanding of the role of nonemployee work.

Taking a somewhat different approach, Koustas (2018) analyzes transaction-level data for the users of one company's online personal financial management software. In a sample of individuals identified as receiving regular biweekly paychecks, he finds that work as an Uber driver mitigates fluctuations in pay and makes a significant contribution to allowing drivers to smooth their consumption when earnings from a main job fluctuate.

7.6.4   Private-Sector Company Data

A final source of information that has been used by researchers interested specifically in the rise of the online platform economy has been person-level data from companies in the online platform sector. Hall and Krueger (2018), for example, analyze administrative data on Uber's "drivers/partners" derived from the company's records. In addition, to enhance the administrative data, they also carried out a survey of these drivers/partners. To help provide perspective on their findings, they compare patterns of activity of drivers/partners to information from the American Community Survey on taxi drivers and chauffeurs. They find, for example, that Uber drivers/partners work fewer hours per week than taxi drivers and chauffeurs.

While the findings from these various studies are fascinating, the properties of many of the new private data sources are not yet fully understood. The JP Morgan Chase Institute has taken significant steps to facilitate access by outside researchers to their data, and other organizations also have developed collaborative relationships with outside researchers. The involvement of outside researchers undoubtedly will be helpful for learning about the strengths and weaknesses of these new types of data. Greater access by the research community to such data more generally and, ultimately, integration of these data in an appropriately secure environment with the survey and administrative records discussed above seem like worthy longer-term goals.

7.7   Conclusion and a Path Forward

The widely perceived rise of the gig economy is as yet not well measured or well understood. Gig economy workers should be classified as self-employed, but data from the core traditional household surveys do not show an increase in self-employment activity. There is more evidence in the administrative data of growth in the number of individuals receiving income from self-employment, though much of the growth observed in these data occurred between the mid-1990s and the mid-2000s, prior to the emergence of the app-based gig activity that has captured the popular imagination. If available data on self-employment are failing to capture ongoing growth in nonemployee work activity, estimates of growth in labor inputs may be too low, estimates of aggregate productivity growth may be too high, and the pattern of estimated productivity growth may have been distorted.

A challenge in understanding and measuring the rise of the gig economy is being able to document where such activity fits into the full range of nonemployee work. Identifying the key attributes that characterize different forms of nonemployee work may help us close in on the traits of jobs that are most appropriately characterized as gig work. In the framework we have developed, gig workers are a subset of the unincorporated self-employed as identified in multiple data sources. We have discussed the challenges to quantifying the prevalence of gig employment using either existing household survey data or administrative records on their own.

Our analysis highlights the potential payoff from improvements in economic measurement along two key dimensions. First, there is a high potential payoff to modules conducted at regular intervals on ongoing household surveys that would probe more deeply about nonemployee work activities. This should not be surprising, since gig employment is often a secondary activity that existing household surveys are not well designed to capture. Such activity may not be mentioned by respondents in cases where gig work is not a person's primary activity and where the standard household survey employment questions do not cue adequately that it should be reported. To the extent that job attributes define the various types of nonemployee work arrangements, probes about employment usefully could be supplemented with questions about job attributes.

A second improvement in economic measurement would be to develop estimates based on survey and administrative data that have been integrated at the individual level. Such integration offers great potential for understanding the changing nature of work, particularly for nontraditional work activities that are inherently difficult to define and measure. Measures derived from tax data show an increasing amount of self-employment that is being missed in household surveys, yet the tax data by themselves are not informative about who these workers are and may be missing "off-the-books" work. Linking tax data with household survey data gives us not only the worker's demographic characteristics but also the worker's family characteristics— something that is crucially important for understanding how gig employment is related to family income and health insurance coverage. In addition, to the extent that household surveys capture "off-the-books" work that is not reported to the tax authorities, the two sources together may provide a more complete picture than either source alone.

A key missing piece of the puzzle is to understand where nonemployee work fits into the career paths of workers. The limited evidence that is currently available suggests that much of the online platform / on-demand nonemployee work to date has been supplemental in nature rather than something that participants have undertaken as a primary activity. There is, however, much more to be done to better understand how individuals are combining traditional employment and nonemployee work. Longitudinal matched employer-employee data that also fully integrate nonemployee work activity will be invaluable for addressing these questions. Developing this data infrastructure will be challenging but is something we believe can be accomplished by building on the work we already have done to integrate the CPS-ASEC, DER, LEHD, and nonemployer business data infrastructures. Being able to add Form 1099-MISC data, including identifiers for both the recipients and the providers of reported payments of nonemployee compensation, would greatly enhance the value of the integrated data infrastructure. More generally, we envision making use of survey and administrative data to measure and analyze the full taxonomy of nonemployee work in the context of the career paths of workers over their life cycles.

Data Appendix

Household Survey Data on Self-Employment. The CPS is a monthly household survey with a sample that represents the civilian population of the United States. The basic monthly CPS questionnaire collects relatively rich information on the characteristics of all members of selected households age 16 and older, including their age, sex, race, ethnicity, nativity, disability status, and education. The monthly instrument also contains questions to determine whether household members were employed during the survey reference week (normally the week that includes the 12th of the month) and, if so, whether each person had more than one job during that week. For those categorized as employed, the CPS asks about the occupation and industry of the main job, hours on the main job, and combined hours on any other jobs. Additional questions are asked that allow a person's status on their main job to be categorized as wage and salary, self-employed with an incorporated business, self-employed with an unincorporated business, or unpaid family worker. In published BLS statistical series on self-employment based on the monthly data, individuals who operate an incorporated business are categorized as wage and salary workers rather than as self-employed, but both the incorporated and the unincorporated self-employed can be identified in the underlying microdata. Information on the industry, occupation, and type of employment for any reported *second* jobs is collected for a quarter of the sample—those in the so-called outgoing rotation groups—and is not collected at all for any additional jobs. Finally, for the quarter of the sample in the outgoing rotation groups, the monthly CPS collects information on earnings on the main job. Except for the information on disability status, which has been collected since June 2008, all of these data are available on a consistent basis beginning in 1994, the year of the most recent major CPS redesign.

The ASEC supplement administered each spring to CPS households collects information for the preceding calendar year. Respondents are asked about the number of weeks during the year worked by each member of the CPS household, the number of jobs each household member held during the year, and the industry, occupation, and type of the longest job.[20] These data allow the longest job held during the year to be categorized as wage and salary, self-employed incorporated, self-employed unincorporated, or unpaid. In addition, the CPS-ASEC supplement contains questions about wage and salary income and business income received during the year, whether from the longest job or from other jobs. The data on business income from employment other than the longest job combine income from incorporated and unincorporated self-employment. We use the responses to these questions to construct a self-employment indicator that equals one if a person is classified as self-employed unincorporated on their longest job and has positive self-employment earnings or, if the longest job was not unincorporated self-employment, has positive self-employment income on a job other than the longest job. Data from the CPS-ASEC supplement are available beginning in 1962.

Although we do not know whether self-employment earnings on a job other than the longest job are from incorporated or unincorporated self-employment, we expect most self-employment outside of the longest job to be unincorporated self-employment. We cannot look at this directly but

---

20. Individuals who hold two jobs simultaneously rather than in sequence are instructed to report holding just one job.

have looked at data from the monthly CPS that, for those in the outgoing rotation group, capture class of worker both for the main job and for any second job. Using these data, we identified people who were self-employed unincorporated on their main job or were either self-employed incorporated or self-employed unincorporated on a second job. Consistent with our prior that secondary incorporated self-employment is relatively rare, only about 2 percent to 3 percent of those categorized as self-employed according to this definition were so classified only because of a second job that was reported to be incorporated self-employment.

The ACS is a Census Bureau survey with a very large sample that represents the US civilian population. For each household member age 15 years or older, the ACS asks whether the person worked for pay during the prior seven days ("last week"). For those who are reported to have worked, additional questions collect information about the main job held during the reference week—the industry and occupation of the work and whether the person was a wage and salary worker, self-employed with an incorporated business, self-employed with an unincorporated business, or an unpaid family worker. The ACS also requests the total amounts of employee compensation and self-employment income earned by each household member over the prior 12 months. These data could in principle be used to construct an earnings-based measure of self-employment activity. Because the questions on the ACS do not ask separately about income from the longest job versus income from other jobs, however, the resulting measure would encompass everyone reporting income from either incorporated or unincorporated self-employment. ACS estimates of self-employment on the main job last week are available from 2005 through the present. Although some ACS data were collected beginning in 2001, the survey was not fully implemented until 2005, and that is the first year for which published estimates are available.

Tax Data on Self-Employment. The Master Earnings File (MEF), maintained by the Social Security Administration, is one source of administrative data on self-employment earnings. The MEF includes information on each W-2 a person received for calendar years from 1978 onward, including the earnings reported on the W-2 and the employer from whom those earnings were received, and on the total self-employment earnings in each of the same years reported on a Schedule SE filed by the taxpayer. A Schedule SE is required of sole proprietors, general partners, and farmers with gross self-employment earnings above a defined threshold that effectively has been set at $433 over the period covered by our analysis. More than 85 percent of Schedule SE filers are sole proprietors (Jackson, Looney, and Ramnath 2017). The MEF records are not public, but an extract called the Detailed Earnings Record (DER) covering all linked CPS-ASEC and Survey of Income and Program Participation (SIPP) respondents for whom there is a PIK has been provided to the Census Bureau for specified statistical uses. The extract delivered to the Census Bureau for the CPS-ASEC sample used in our analysis contains information on MEF earnings for 1978 through 2012 for individuals in the 1997 through 2013 CPS-ASEC samples, from whom survey information referencing the years 1996 through 2012 was collected.

The Census Bureau's Business Register (BR) is the master business list that the Census Bureau maintains for use as a sample frame for all of its business surveys as well as a source that is tabulated directly to produce a variety of business statistics. The BR is based primarily on administrative data from business income and payroll tax returns. It includes records for both employer and nonemployer businesses. Each record on the file is assigned a detailed industry code. Employer businesses are those with positive payroll in a year, while nonemployer businesses are those with qualifying business revenue but no paid employment. As stated on the Census Bureau's website, "Most nonemployers are self-employed individuals operating unincorporated businesses (known as sole proprietorships), which may or may not be the owner's principal source of income." To be included in the nonemployer universe for tabulation, other than in construction, a business must have at least $1,000 in gross revenue (in construction, the threshold is at least $1 in gross revenue). Businesses with more than some maximum amount of annual revenue are excluded from the nonemployer universe on the grounds that businesses with revenues over the threshold amount are likely to have employees and thus to appear on the list of employer businesses. The upper revenue threshold is determined based on the business's legal form of organization (sole proprietorship, partnership, or corporation) and industry. Information about payroll and other business costs also is recorded in the BR. Published data on nonemployers are available beginning in 1997, and statistics broken out by legal form of organization have been produced since 2004.

Form 1099-MISC also contains information relevant to assessing trends in self-employment income. This is the tax form used by businesses to report payments of nonemployee compensation. Applicable regulations require that a Form 1099-MISC be filed by business payers when nonemployee compensation paid to any source equals or exceeds $600 over the course of a year; applicable amounts are recorded in Box 7 of the form. One complication is that a Form 1099-MISC may be issued either to an individual (using a Social Security Number [SSN]) or to a business (using an EIN). Further, the dollar amounts reported on Form 1099-MISC are gross payments rather than the net amounts earned by the recipient after expenses. Individuals or businesses performing work for an individual rather than for a business will not receive a Form 1099-MISC. Staff at the Department of the Treasury have compiled counts of the number of individuals and the number of businesses receiving Form 1099-MISCs that had positive amounts reported in Box 7, Nonemployee Compensation, for each year from 2000 through 2012. These counts are available from the US Department of the Treasury (2015).

To calculate a self-employment rate—the share of workers who are self-employed—a measure of the total number of workers is needed to serve as the denominator. The denominators for the monthly CPS and the ACS measures are estimates of the number of people employed during the survey reference week based on the same survey. For the two CPS-ASEC measures, the denominator is the estimated number of people with any work activity during the year in question, again based on the same survey. The denominator for all the measures based on administrative data is the estimated number of people with any employment during the year based on the earnings captured in the DER.

We do not have DER data for 2013–16. For those years, we projected the 2012 DER employment estimate forward using the ratio of annual average employment from the Bureau of Labor Statistics monthly payroll survey (formally, the Current Employment Statistics survey) for the year in question to 2012 annual average payroll survey employment. Over the years from 1996 through 2012, the annual percent change in employment estimated using the DER and the percent change in annual average payroll survey employment have a correlation of 0.89, and the two series also had a similar mean annual growth rate (0.72 percent for the payroll survey and 0.76 percent for the estimate of employment based on the DER). The similarity in the two series' behavior over the 1996–2012 period gives us reasonable confidence that the DER employment values we project for 2013 through 2016 should be approximately correct.

Linked Household Survey-Administrative Data File. Individuals in our linked household survey-administrative sample were members of a household for which a CPS-ASEC interview was conducted in at least one year between 1997 and 2013. In each case, the reference period for these interviews was the prior calendar year, meaning that information was obtained for calendar years 1996 through 2012. These CPS-ASEC individuals were linked to W-2 and Schedule SE earnings information provided to the Census Bureau by the Social Security Administration in the form of the DER, the previously mentioned extract from the MEF. This linking was performed using the PIK, which is a replacement for the SSN.

The PIK is missing for 20 percent to 30 percent of ASEC respondents, depending on the year. We used propensity score methods to reweight the sample of people for whom we have a PIK so that they represent the population as a whole. For each year, we estimated a regression model in which an indicator for having a PIK was regressed on indicators for age group, gender, race, education, marital status, foreign-born status, state of residence, and whether the person reported being employed in the relevant CPS-ASEC. We used the coefficients from this model to calculate each individual's probability of having a PIK and applied a weight adjustment factor equal to the inverse of this probability to the CPS-ASEC estimation weight. Individuals with a PIK were retained in our sample regardless of whether we were able to locate any W-2 or Schedule SE earnings for them in the DER.

The presence of imputed values for self-employment status in the CPS-ASEC creates another complication. These values are imputed for individuals representing approximately 20 percent of the population. We have replicated our analysis with all these cases dropped from the linked sample and the data reweighted using propensity score methods to account for the loss of observations that lack directly reported information on self-employment. Restricting our attention to individuals with directly reported self-employment status had little effect on the conclusions to be drawn from our analysis.

References

Abraham, Katharine G. 1988. "Flexible Staffing Arrangements and Employers' Short-term Adjustment Strategies." In *Employment, Unemployment and Labour Utilization*, edited by R. A. Hart, 288–311. London: Unwin Hyman.

Abraham, Katharine G. 1990. "Restructuring the Employment Relationship: The Growth of Market-Mediated Work Arrangements." In *New Developments in the Labor Market: Toward a New Institutional Paradigm*, edited by K. G. Abraham and R. B. McKersie, 85–119. Cambridge, MA: MIT Press.

Abraham, Katharine G., and Ashley Amaya. 2019. "Probing for Informal Work Activity." *Journal of Official Statistics* 35 (3): 487–508.

Abraham, Katharine G., John Haltiwanger, Kristin Sandusky, and James R. Spletzer. 2013. "Exploring Differences in Employment between Household and Establishment Data." *Journal of Labor Economics* 31 (2): S129–S172.

Abraham, Katharine G., John Haltiwanger, Kristin Sandusky, and James R. Spletzer. 2018. "Driving the Gig Economy." Unpublished working paper.

Abraham, Katharine G., and Susan N. Houseman. 2019. "Making Ends Meet: The Role of Informal Work in Supplementing Americans' Income." *RSF: The Russell Sage Foundation Journal of the Social Sciences* 5 (5): 110–31.

Abraham, Katharine G., and Susan K. Taylor. 1996. "Firms' Use of Outside Contractors: Theory and Evidence." *Journal of Labor Economics* 14 (3): 394–424.

Barker, Kathleen, and Kathleen Christensen. 1998. *Contingent Work: American Employment Relations in Transition*. Ithaca, NY: Cornell University Press.

Board of Governors of the Federal Reserve System. 2016. *Report on the Economic Well-Being of U.S. Households in 2015*. Washington, DC: Board of Governors of the Federal Reserve System.

Board of Governors of the Federal Reserve System. 2017. *Report on the Economic Well-Being of U.S. Households in 2016*. Washington, DC: Board of Governors of the Federal Reserve System.

Board of Governors of the Federal Reserve System. 2018. *Report on the Economic Well-Being of U.S. Households in 2017*. Washington, DC: Board of Governors of the Federal Reserve System.

Bracha, Anat, and Mary A. Burke. 2019. "How Big Is the Gig? The Extensive Margin, The Intensive Margin, and The Hidden Margin." Unpublished working paper.

Brown, J. David, John S. Earle, and Kyung Min Lee. 2019. "Who Hires Non-standard Labor? Evidence from Employers." Presentation at the 3rd Annual IZA Conference on Labor Statistics, Kalamazoo, Michigan. July.

Bureau of Economic Analysis. 2017. *Concepts and Methods of the U.S. National Income and Product Accounts*. Washington, DC: Bureau of Economic Analysis.

Bureau of Labor Statistics. 2005. "CES Supplemental Survey Temporary Help and Professional Employer Organization Industries Cognitive Testing Results." Unpublished report. March.

Cohany, Sharon R. 1996. "Workers in Alternative Employment Arrangements." *Monthly Labor Review*, October, 31–45.

Collins, Brett, Andrew Garin, Emilie Jackson, Dmitri Koustas, and Mark Payne. 2019. "Is Gig Work Replacing Traditional Employment? Evidence from Two Decades of Tax Reforms." Internal Revenue Service Statistics of Income Working Paper.

Dey, Matthew, Susan Houseman, and Anne Polivka. 2012. "Manufacturers' Outsourcing to Staffing Services." *Industrial and Labor Relations Review* 65 (3): 533–59.

Dube, Arindrajit, and Ethan Kaplan. 2010. "Does Outsourcing Reduce Wages in the Low-Wage Service Occupations? Evidence from Janitors and Guards." *Industrial and Labor Relations Review* 63 (2): 287–306.

Farrell, Diana, and Fiona Greig. 2016a. *The Online Platform Economy: Has Growth Peaked?* JPMorgan Chase Institute Report. November.

Farrell, Diana, and Fiona Greig. 2016b. *Paychecks, Paydays, and the Online Platform Economy*. JPMorgan Chase Institute Report. February.

Farrell, Diana, Fiona Greig, and Amar Hamoudi. 2018. *The Online Platform Economy in 2018: Drivers, Workers, Sellers and Lessors*. JPMorgan Chase Institute Report. September.

Foster, Lucia, John C. Haltiwanger, and C. J. Krizan. 2001. "Aggregate Productivity Growth: Lessons from Microeconomic Evidence." In *New Developments in Productivity Analysis*, edited by C. R. Hulten, E. R. Dean, and M. J. Harper, 303–72. NBER Studies in Income and Wealth 63. Chicago: University of Chicago Press.

Foster, Lucia, and Patrice Norman. 2016. "The Annual Survey of Entrepreneurs: An Introduction." CES Working Paper No. 15-40R. May. Accessed January 31, 2017. ftp://ftp2.census.gov/ces/wp/2015/CES-WP-15-40R.pdf.

Fort, Teresa. 2017. "Technology and Production Fragmentation: Domestic versus Foreign Sourcing." *Review of Economic Studies* 84:650–87.

Government Accountability Office. 2007. *A Strategy for Reducing the Gap Should Include Options for Addressing Sole Proprietor Noncompliance*. GAO-07-1014, Report to the Committee on Finance, US Senate.

Goldschmidt, Deborah, and Johannes F. Schmieder. 2017. "The Rise of Domestic Outsourcing and the Evolution of the German Wage Structure." *Quarterly Journal of Economics* 132 (3): 1165–1217.

Groves, Robert M., and Emilia Peytcheva. 2008. "The Impact of Nonresponse Rates on Nonresponse Bias: A Meta-analysis." *Public Opinion Quarterly* 72 (2): 167–89.

Hall, Jonathan, and Alan Krueger. 2018. "An Analysis of the Labor Market for Uber's Driver-Partners in the United States." *ILR Review* 71 (3): 705–32.

Harris, Seth D., and Alan B. Krueger. 2015. "A Proposal for Modernizing Labor Laws for Twenty-First-Century Work: The 'Independent Worker.'" Hamilton Project Discussion Paper 2015-10, December.

Hipple, Steven F., and Laurel A. Hammond. 2016. "Self-Employment in the United States." Bureau of Labor Statistics, Spotlight on Statistics. March. Accessed January 31, 2017. https://www.bls.gov/spotlight/2016/self-employment-in-the-united -states/home.htm.

Houseman, Susan. 2007. "Outsourcing, Offshoring and Productivity Measurement in United States Manufacturing." *International Labour Review* 146 (1–2): 61–80.

Hurst, Erik, and Benjamin Wild Pugsley. 2011. "What Do Small Businesses Do?" *Brookings Papers on Economic Activity*, Fall 2011, 73–118.

Hyatt, Henry R., and James R. Spletzer. 2017. "The Recent Decline in Single Quarter Jobs." *Labour Economics* 46 (1): 166–76.

Jackson, Emilie, Adam Looney, and Shanthi Ramnath. 2017. "The Rise of Alternative Work Arrangements: Evidence and Implications for Tax Filing and Benefit Coverage." Office of Tax Analysis Working Paper 114. January.

Katz, Lawrence F., and Alan B. Krueger. 2019a. "The Rise and Nature of Alternative Work Arrangements in the United States, 1995–2015." *ILR Review* 72 (2): 382–416.

Katz, Lawrence F., and Alan B. Krueger. 2019b. "Understanding Trends in Alternative Work Arrangements in the United States." *RSF: The Russell Sage Foundation Journal of the Social Sciences* 5 (5): 132–46.

Koustas, Dmitri. 2018. "Consumption Insurance and Multiple Jobs: Evidence from Rideshare Drivers." Unpublished working paper.

Leberstein, Sarah. 2012. "Independent Contractor Misclassification Imposes Huge Costs on Workers and Federal and State Treasuries." National Employment Law Project. August.

Lombardi, Britton, and Yukako Ono. 2010. "Professional Employer Organizations: Who Are They, Who Uses Them, and Why Should We Care?" Center for Economic Studies Working Paper CES 10-22.

Manyika, James, Susan Lund, Jacques Bughin, Kelsey Robinson, Jan Mischke, and Deepa Mahajan. 2016. "Independent Work: Choice, Necessity, and the Gig Economy." McKinsey Global Institute. October. Accessed January 31, 2017. http://www.mckinsey.com/global-themes/employment-and-growth/independent-work-choice-necessity-and-the-gig-economy.

National Academies Press. 2017. *Information Technology and the Workforce: Automation, Augmentation and Transformation.* Washington, DC: National Academies Press.

Polivka, Anne E. 1996a. "Contingent and Alternative Work Arrangements, Defined." *Monthly Labor Review*, October, 3–9.

Polivka, Anne E. 1996b. "A Profile of Contingent Workers." *Monthly Labor Review*, October, 10–21.

Pollard, Michael, and Matthew D. Baird. 2017. *The RAND American Life Panel: Technical Description.* Rand Corporation Report.

Robles, Barbara, and Marysol McGee. 2016. "Exploring Online and Offline Informal Work: Findings from the Enterprising and Informal Work Activities (EIWA) Survey." Finance and Economics Discussion Series 2016-089. Washington, DC: Board of Governors of the Federal Reserve System.

Slemrod, Joel, and Jon Bakija. 2008. *Taxing Ourselves: A Citizen's Guide to the Debate over Taxes, Fourth Edition.* Cambridge, MA: MIT Press.

Slemrod, Joel, Brett Collins, Jeffrey Hoopes, Daniel Reck, and Michael Sebastiani. 2017. "Does Credit-Card Information Reporting Improve Small-Business Tax Compliance?" *Journal of Public Economics* 149:1–19.

US Department of the Treasury. 2015. Letter from Anne Wall, Assistant Secretary for Legislative Affairs, to Senator Mark Warner. October 27. Published in Tax Notes Today: Treasury Tax Correspondence, November 18, 2015.

Weil, David. 2014. *The Fissured Workplace.* Cambridge MA: Harvard University Press.

8

Information and Communications Technology, R&D, and Organizational Innovation
Exploring Complementarities in Investment and Production

Pierre Mohnen, Michael Polder,
and George van Leeuwen

8.1 Introduction

In the eyes of most historians of science and technology, information and communications technology (ICT) can be classified among general purpose technologies (GPT) such as the wheel, steam power, the combustion engine, and electricity (Lipsey, Carlaw, and Bekhar 2005; Jovanovic and Rousseau 2005; Brynjolfsson and McAfee 2014). It took some time before ICT showed up in the productivity statistics, but by now it is common to distinguish between ICT and non-ICT capital in productivity analysis, and a great deal of economic and labor productivity growth in the last 30 years has been ascribed to ICT capital deepening (Jorgenson, Ho, and Stiroh 2008). Even skeptics have acknowledged the transformational power of digital technology, although some claim that the economic benefits are short-lived and that the impact of ICT does not stand up to that of earlier GPTs (e.g., Gordon 2016).

Another channel through which ICT affects labor productivity growth is through its potential impact on total factor productivity (TFP). One explana-

Pierre Mohnen is professor of microeconometrics of technical change at Maastricht University.

Michael Polder is an economist at Statistics Netherlands.

George van Leeuwen is an economist at Statistics Netherlands.

The views expressed in this chapter are those of the authors and do not reflect any policy stance by Statistics Netherlands. We thank for their comments Eric Bartelsman, Emmanuel Duguet, Bronwyn Hall, Jonathan Haskel, Jacques Mairesse, Stéphane Robin, Nicolas van Zeebroeck, and the participants at various workshops. Errors are our own. For acknowledgments, sources of research support, and disclosure of the authors' material financial relationships, if any, please see https://www.nber.org/books-and-chapters/measuring-and-accounting-innovation-21st -century/ict-rd-and-organizational-innovation-exploring-complementarities-investment-and -production.

tion for the differential success of ICT capital in fostering productivity has been the argument of complementarity between ICT investment and investment in intangible assets, such as organizational capital (Brynjolfsson and Saunders 2010; Bresnahan, Brynjolfsson, and Hitt 2002). Firms need to reorganize their way of operating to benefit from digital technology and vice versa.[1]

Beyond its contribution to TFP via organizational change, ICT can also increase the returns to R&D, generating a string of new technological innovations. It can also make R&D more effective in the sense that it facilitates the gathering, documenting, and sharing of knowledge and information. Finally, besides the potential to improve research effectiveness, these characteristics of ICT can also improve the possibility and quality of collaboration between researchers.

In this chapter, we look at the triangle between ICT, technological, and nontechnological innovation. In particular, we look at R&D as an instance of technological innovation and organizational change as a nontechnological innovation. Parts of this triangle and its relation to productivity have been covered extensively in the literature. Putting the pieces together in one framework is a novelty of our analysis. We shall reassess the contribution of ICT to TFP growth and reexamine the hypothesis of complementarity between organizational innovation and ICT. In addition, we shall explore whether the returns to ICT and R&D are mutually reinforcing, in the sense that innovation is ICT facilitated and, vice versa, that the returns from ICT stem in part from the generation of knowledge.

The chapter is structured as follows. In section 8.2, we briefly review the literature on the role of ICT and R&D for productivity, on the complementarity between ICT and organizational innovation, and on the GPT aspects of ICT. Section 8.3 is devoted to modeling aspects. In section 8.4, we describe the data and the main variables. In section 8.5, we present the estimation results, and in section 8.6, we conclude.

8.2   The Literature

A vast literature has documented evidence of different determinants of productivity both at the macro- and at the microlevel (see Syverson 2011). Among the determinants, investment in ICT and the generation of knowledge feature prominently.

One strand of the literature has estimated the returns (private and social) to R&D and the contribution of R&D to TFP or economic growth following the seminal work by Griliches (1979) and with some recent advances by Doraszelski and Jaumandreu (2013); see, e.g., Hall, Mairesse, and Mohnen (2010) for a review of the literature. Another branch has related R&D to innovation and innovation to productivity, the workhorse model being the

---

1. At the aggregate level, network and spillover effects can arise, and digital technology may improve the allocation of resources (Syverson 2011).

CDM model as proposed by Crépon, Duguet, and Mairesse (1998); see Mairesse and Mohnen (2010) for an overview. Neither line of research has considered the complementarity with ICT, although recently Polder et al. (2010) and Hall, Lotti, and Mairesse (2013) have modeled R&D and ICT investment as inputs into innovation, defined as product, process, and organizational innovation.

In parallel, many studies have investigated the effect of the adoption of ICT equipment on economic performance (see, e.g., Stiroh 2010) without an explicit role for R&D. Some studies have used aggregate or sectoral data; others have used firm data. The studies that use macro or sectoral data have mainly analyzed the effect of ICT or R&D on productivity within a growth accounting framework (see Draca, Sadun, and van Reenen 2007, and Biagi 2013 for reviews of the literature) but not so much the complementarity between ICT and R&D in raising productivity.

A substantial effort has been made to measure the stocks of intangibles—including R&D but also software, databases, and organizational capital—and to assess their importance in (intangible-adjusted) cross-country GDP growth (Corrado, Hulten, and Sichel 2009; Corrado et al. 2013). These industry-level data are beginning to be used to explore complementarities between different types of assets. Chen, Niebel, and Saam (2014) and Corrado, Haskel, and Jona-Lasinio (2017) find evidence of a positive direct effect of ICT on TFP, as well as a significant indirect effect through its interaction with intangibles. Using EU KLEMS data, Pieri, Vecchi, and Venturini (2017) explore complementarities between ICT and R&D in reducing technical inefficiencies.

By contrast, the empirical studies that have been conducted on the hypothesis of complementarity between ICT and organizational change are mainly based on microdata (Bresnahan, Brynjolfsson, and Hitt 2002; Black and Lynch, 2001; Caroli and Van Reenen, 2001; Crespi, Criscuolo, and Haskel 2007; Van Reenen et al. 2010; Riley and Vahterv 2013). The available econometric evidence shows that a combination of investment in ICT and changes in organization and work practices facilitated by these technologies contributes to firms' productivity growth. Case studies reveal that the introduction of information technology is combined with a transformation of the firm, including investment in intangible assets, and a change in the relation with suppliers and customers. Electronic procurement, for instance, increases control over inventories and decreases costs of coordinating with suppliers. In addition, ICT offers the possibility for flexible production, such as just-in-time inventory management, and enterprise resource planning.

Whereas there is a lot of empirical backing at the firm level for the complementarity between ICT and organizational innovation, there is less evidence of a complementarity between R&D and ICT or between ICT and technological innovations in the form of new products or processes. Hall, Lotti, and Mairesse (2013) on Italian data; Rybalka (2015) on Norwegian data;

and Aboal and Tacsir (2018) on Uruguayan data find no conclusive evidence in favor of either a complementarity or a substitutability between R&D and ICT. Many studies have investigated the role of ICT in fostering R&D or innovation, however. For German firm data, Cerquera and Klein (2008) find that ICT is associated with an increase in the variation of productivity across firms and that this process of creative destruction gives incentives for firms to invest in R&D. Also for Germany, Engelstätter (2012) finds that different types of software have a positive effect on product and process innovation and moreover that there is complementarity between software and organizational practices in their effect on innovative performance. Polder et al. (2010) find that ICT investment is important for all types of innovation in services, while it plays a limited role in manufacturing, and Kleis et al. (2012) find that investments in information technology increase innovation output as measured by the number of patents. Van Leeuwen and Farooqui (2008) show that e-sales and broadband use affect productivity significantly through their effect on innovation output. Finally, Forman and van Zeebroeck (2012) find that internet connections increase collaborative research but not the productivity of lone researchers or of researchers located close to each other. In contrast, Spiezia (2011) concludes from an Organisation for Economic Co-operation and Development (OECD)-led international comparison study on firm data that ICT usage does not increase the probability of coming up with a new innovation developed in-house.

Finally, a related line of research looks at complementarities between different types of innovation or different types of ICT. Miravete and Pernías (2006) and Martínez-Ros and Labeaga (2009), for instance, find complementarity between product and process innovation by looking at the adoption decision. This result is confirmed in Polder et al. (2010), who look at complementarity in the production function. This latter study also finds that product and organizational innovation are complements, while process and organizational innovation are found to be substitutes. For ICT, following an approach methodologically close to ours in the current chapter, Kretschmer, Miravete, and Pernías (2012) find that different types of software are substitutes in production. The results of Bartelsman, van Leeuwen, and Polder (2017), however, point to complementarity as well as substitutability, depending on the types of software considered.

In our chapter we will address the triangle of complementarity between ICT (hardware), R&D, and organizational change by looking at the joint firm-level binary investment decisions together with their productivity effects.

8.3   Model

While it is true that ICT and R&D can be considered as inputs in the innovation process, ICT and even R&D play a direct role in the production function besides affecting innovation. Therefore, in contrast to Polder et al. (2010); Hall, Lotti, and Mairesse (2012); and Rybalka (2015), we do not resort to a CDM type of model (Crépon, Duguet, and Mairesse 1998), with innovation inputs only affecting productivity through a knowledge production function. Instead, we shall model ICT, R&D, and organizational innovation as binary choices with simultaneous feedback effects—that is, when two strategies are complements in the sense that doing one increases the returns of doing the other (Milgrom and Roberts 1990), the returns from adoption (and therefore the adoption decisions) are mutually dependent.

In our model, firms choose combinations of investments (i.e., "investment profiles") based on their (ex-ante) expected returns in terms of productivity growth. When multiple investments are involved, there is a "complementarity bonus" (or "substitutability penalty") added to the return on the individual investment. Given the simultaneous modeling of the productivity equation, the ex-post effects of the investments on productivity growth will be consistent with the ex-ante expected returns that prompted the choice for that specific combination of investments.[2] We thus model complementarities in terms of an objective function where the strategy choices (or investments) are themselves endogenous, as in Kretschmer, Miravete, and Pernías (2012), who combined the adoption and production approach recommended by Athey and Stern (1998).

Modeling the direct effect of ICT and R&D on productivity also brings our analysis closer to the literature on intangibles and growth accounting using industry-level data (Corrado, Hulten, and Sichel 2009), where R&D and ICT are considered separate types of capital. Also in conformity with the introduction of stocks of intangibles in the production function as in Corrado, Hulten, and Sichel (2009), we consider it more appropriate that investment affects the growth rather than the level of total factor productivity. The productivity levels depend on the stocks of knowledge, organizational capital, and ICT capital. The productivity growth rates instead depend on the increases in these stocks. We do not model the choice of the investment levels, only the binary choices as to whether investments in ICT, R&D, and organizational innovations are made.

8.3.1   Investment Stage

In order to test for the presence of complementarity between innovation strategies (in particular, between investing in ICT, R&D, and organizational innovation), we first consider the adoption approach—that is, the detection of joint use of strategies for reasons other than correlations in unobserved determinants (Milgrom and Roberts 1990; Athey and Stern 1998).

---

2. It could be argued that the strategy choices are made on the basis of another objective function than total factor productivity growth and that therefore, as well as for reasons of limited managerial foresight or unforeseen developments, there may be a difference between ex-ante and ex-post complementarity.

This approach is close to that of Miravete and Pernías (2006) and was also applied by Bartelsman, van Leeuwen, and Polder (2017) and Van Leeuwen and Mohnen (2017).

Consider an objective function that depends on the realization of the combination of strategies, or states. The contribution to the objective function O_{it}^j achieved by the adoption of each individual strategy, $y_{it}^j \in \{0,1\}$, where j denotes ICT, R&D, and organizational innovation, is given by the following expression:

(1)
$$O_{it}^j = \left(\beta_j' x_{it}^j + \sum_{k \neq j}(\alpha_{jk}/2)y_{it}^k + \varepsilon_{it}^j\right)y_{it}^j.$$

For reasons of identification, $\alpha_{jk} = \alpha_{kj}$. The "return" from the adoption of strategy j depends on exogenous variables x_{it}^j, which may be strategy specific, the adoption of the other strategies y_{it}^k, and a random error term ε_{it}^j. The error terms are assumed to be jointly normally distributed with unitary variances (for reasons of identification) but nonzero covariances. The dependence on the adoption of other strategies makes this a simultaneous model, in which the choice of strategies is endogenously determined. This allows us to test for potential complementarity at the investment stage in the sense that firms adopt a combination of strategies that they think will be beneficial.

The total level of the objective, which will be left unspecified for now but modeled in section 3.2 as the contribution to TFP growth, is given by

(2)
$$TO_{it} = \sum_j O_{it}^j.$$

As shown by Lewbel (2007), this way of writing the objective function avoids any incoherency and incompleteness problem—that is, it guarantees the existence and uniqueness of the endogenous dummy variables for any given realization of the exogenous variables.

Let us illustrate the model by working with two strategies, denoted as $y^j \in \{0,1\}$, $j = 1, 2$. For example, if state $(1,1)$ is chosen, where the first position refers to strategy y^1 and the second position to strategy y^2, then the contribution to TFP growth is given by[3]

(3)
$$TO_{it}(1,1) = \beta_1' x_{it}^1 + \alpha_{12} + \beta_2' x_{it}^2 + \varepsilon_{it}^1 + \varepsilon_{it}^2.$$

The coefficient α_{12} captures the complementarity (if positive) or substitutability (if negative) between the pair of strategies. For every combination of strategies, we can compute the value of the objective function. To estimate the parameters of the model, we write down the probability of every possible state. For instance, the probability that strategy 1 and strategy 2 are chosen, denoted as state $(1,1)$, is derived from the upper and lower bounds of the

---

3. Notice that for notational convenience, $\alpha_{12} = \alpha_{21}$ in equation (3) corresponds to $\alpha_{12}/2 + \alpha_{21}/2$ in equation (1).

distribution of the error terms given that the value of the objective function under (1,1) must be higher than under any pair of strategies:

(4.1) $\qquad TO_{it}(1,1) > TO_{it}(0,0) \Rightarrow \beta_1' x_{it}^1 + \alpha_{12} + \beta_2' x_{it}^2 + \varepsilon_{it}^1 + \varepsilon_{it}^2 > 0$

(4.2) $\qquad TO_{it}(1,1) > TO_{it}(1,0) \Rightarrow \beta_2' x_{it}^2 + \alpha_{12} + \varepsilon_{it}^2 > 0$

(4.3) $\qquad TO_{it}(1,1) > TO_{it}(0,1) \Rightarrow \beta_1' x_{it}^1 + \alpha_{12} + \varepsilon_{it}^1 > 0.$

State (1,1) is therefore associated to the following area of the distribution of the error terms:

(5.1) $\qquad \varepsilon_{it}^1 > -(\beta_1' x_{it}^1 + \alpha_{12})$

(5.2) $\qquad \varepsilon_{it}^2 > \max[-(\beta_2' x_{it}^2 + \alpha_{12}), -(\beta_1' x_{it}^1 + \alpha_{12} + \beta_2' x_{it}^2 + \varepsilon_{it}^1)],$

where (5.1) follows directly from (4.3) and (5.2) follows from combining (4.1) and (4.2) while conditioning on ε_{it}^1. The same reasoning can be applied to derive the adoptions for the other states.

State (1,0) is adopted when

(6.1) $\qquad TO_{it}(1,0) > TO_{it}(0,0) \Rightarrow \beta_1' x_{it}^1 + \varepsilon_{it}^1 > 0$

(6.2) $\qquad TO_{it}(1,0) > TO_{it}(0,1) \Rightarrow \beta_1' x_{it}^1 + \varepsilon_{it}^1 > \beta_2' x_{it}^2 + \varepsilon_{it}^2$

(6.3) $\qquad TO_{it}(1,0) > TO_{it}(1,1) \Rightarrow \beta_2' x_{it}^2 + \alpha_{12} + \varepsilon_{it}^2 < 0.$

(7.1) $\qquad$ In other words, when $\varepsilon_{it}^1 > -\beta_1' x_{it}^1$ and

(7.2) $\qquad \varepsilon_{it}^2 < \min[-(\beta_2' x_{it}^2 + \alpha_{12}), (\beta_1' x_{it}^1 - \beta_2' x_{it}^2 + \varepsilon_{it}^1)].$

State (0,1) is adopted when

(8.1) $\qquad TO_{it}(0,1) > TO_{it}(0,0) \Rightarrow \beta_2' x_{it}^2 + \varepsilon_{it}^2 > 0$

(8.2) $\qquad TO_{it}(0,1) > TO_{it}(1,0) \Rightarrow \beta_2' x_{it}^2 + \varepsilon_{it}^2 > \beta_1' x_{it}^1 + \varepsilon_{it}^1$

(8.3) $\qquad TO_{it}(0,1) > TO_{it}(1,1) \Rightarrow \beta_1' x_{it}^1 + \alpha_{12} + \varepsilon_{it}^1 < 0.$

(9.1) $\qquad$ In other words, when $\varepsilon_{it}^1 < -(\beta_1' x_{it}^1 + \alpha_{12})$ and

(9.2) $\qquad \varepsilon_{it}^2 > \max[-(\beta_2' x_{it}^2), \beta_1' x_{it}^1 - \beta_2' x_{it}^2 + \varepsilon_{it}^1].$

State (0,0) is adopted when

(10.1) $\qquad TO_{it}(0,0) > TO_{it}(1,0) \Rightarrow \beta_1' x_{it}^1 + \varepsilon_{it}^1 < 0$

(10.2) $\qquad TO_{it}(0,0) > TO_{it}(0,1) \Rightarrow \beta_2' x_{it}^2 + \varepsilon_{it}^2 < 0$

(10.3) $\qquad TO_{it}(0,0) > TO_{it}(1,1) \Rightarrow \beta_1' x_{it}^1 + \beta_2' x_{it}^2 + \alpha_{12} + \varepsilon_{it}^1 + \varepsilon_{it}^2 < 0.$

(11.1) $\qquad$ In other words, when $\varepsilon_{it}^1 < -\beta_1' x_{it}^1$ and

(11.2) $\qquad \varepsilon_{it}^2 < \min[-\beta_2' x_{it}^2, -(\beta_1' x_{it}^1 + \beta_2' x_{it}^2 + \alpha_{12} + \varepsilon_{it}^1)].$

As shown in Miravete and Pernías (2006), when $\alpha_{12} = 0$, the subdivision of the space of $(\varepsilon_{it}^1, \varepsilon_{it}^2)$ is the same as for the bivariate probit. When $\alpha_{12} > 0$, the states (1,1) and (0,0) are defined over a larger region of that error space, and if $\alpha_{12} < 0$, the states (1,0) and (0,1) are defined over a smaller region of that error space.

8.3.2   Productivity Growth Equation

Going one step further, the return from each investment profile can be measured in terms of productivity growth. The objective, which was left unspecified in equation (2), is then explicitly specified. In this way we integrate the strategy adoption equations with the productivity growth equation. This is what Kretschmer, Miravete, and Pernías (2012) have done in combining the "adoption approach" and the "productivity approach" of complementarity in the words of Athey and Stern (1998). Like them, we distinguish between observed and unobserved determinants of innovation; hence firms may adopt different strategies even if the observed determinants are the same. We differ from Kretschmer, Miravete, and Pernías (2012) in that we use not economic profits but productivity growth rates. Instead of combining dichotomous data on two types of software innovation with continuous variables on scale and profit, which depend on the innovation choices, we combine three dichotomous innovation indicators (ICT, R&D, and organizational innovation) with productivity growth rates that depend on the choice of investments. Another difference is that instead of maximizing a likelihood function with analytical conditional distributions, an expression that becomes more tedious to derive as the number of equations increases, we work with simulated conditional likelihoods.

To that effect, we shall estimate a total factor productivity growth equation, which depends on the chosen investment profiles. TFP growth is the portion of output growth that is not explained by the growth rates in the traditional inputs, labor and capital. In the case of two strategies, TFP growth would be given by the following expression:

$$(12) \quad TFP_{it} = \gamma_t + TO_{it} = \gamma_t + (\beta_1'x_{it}^1 + \varepsilon_{it}^1)y_{it}^1 + (\beta_2'x_{it}^2 + \varepsilon_{it}^2)y_{it}^2 + \alpha_{12}y_{it}^1y_{it}^2 + \varepsilon_{it}^3,$$

where γ_t represents disembodied technical change and ε_{it}^3 represents unobservable determinants of TFP growth.

TFP_{it} can take four values depending on the realizations of the error terms ε_{it}^1 and ε_{it}^2:

- State (1,1): $\gamma_t + \beta_1'x_{it}^1 + \alpha_{12} + \beta_2'x_{it}^2 + \varepsilon_{it}^1 + \varepsilon_{it}^2 + \varepsilon_{it}^3$ in the region defined by (5.1) and (5.2).
- State (1,0): $\gamma_t + \beta_1'x_{it}^1 + \varepsilon_{it}^1 + \varepsilon_{it}^3$ in the region defined by (7.1) and (7.2).
- State (0,1): $\gamma_t + \beta_2'x_{it}^2 + \varepsilon_{it}^2 + \varepsilon_{it}^3$ in the region defined by (9.1) and (9.2).
- State (0,0): $\gamma_t + \varepsilon_{it}^3$ in the region defined by (11.1) and (11.2).

If we assume the random vector $[\varepsilon_{it}^1, \varepsilon_{it}^2, \varepsilon_{it}^3]'$ to be normally distributed with mean 0 and variance-covariance matrix Ω, then the likelihood function associated with the observed choices of strategies and the observed values of TFP growth is given by

$$(13) \quad \mathcal{L} = \prod_{i,t} f_1\{T\dot{F}P_{it} - [\gamma_t + (\beta_1' x_{it}^1 + \varepsilon_{it}^1) y_{it}^1 + (\beta_2' x_{it}^2 + \varepsilon_{it}^2) y_{it}^2 + \alpha_{12} y_{it}^1 y_{it}^2] \mid \varepsilon_{it}^1, \varepsilon_{it}^2\}$$

$$\times F_2(\varepsilon_{it}^1, \varepsilon_{it}^2)$$

where $f_1(\,.\mid \varepsilon_{it}^1, \varepsilon_{it}^2)$ is the (conditional) univariate normal density function of ε_{it}^3 conditional on values of ε_{it}^1 and ε_{it}^2, and $F_2(\varepsilon_{it}^1, \varepsilon_{it}^2)$ is the bivariate normal distribution of ε_{it}^1 and ε_{it}^2. If we define the four regions of $(\varepsilon_{it}^1, \varepsilon_{it}^2)$ as R(1,1), R(1,0), R(0,1), and R(0,0), respectively, and the corresponding truncated distributions as $F_2(\varepsilon_{it}^1, \varepsilon_{it}^2) \mid R(1,1)$ and so on, then the likelihood function can also be written as

$$(14) \quad \mathcal{L} = \prod_{i,t} f_1[T\dot{F}P_{it} - (\gamma_t + \beta_1' x_{it}^1 + \alpha_{12} + \beta_2' x_{it}^2 + \varepsilon_{it}^1 + \varepsilon_{it}^2) \mid R(1,1)]$$

$$\times F_2[\varepsilon_{it}^1, \varepsilon_{it}^2 \mid R(1,1)] f_1[T\dot{F}P_{it} - (\gamma_t + \beta_1' x_{it}^1 + \varepsilon_{it}^1) \mid R(1,0)]$$

$$\times F_2[\varepsilon_{it}^1, \varepsilon_{it}^2 \mid R(1,0)] f_1[T\dot{F}P_{it} - (\gamma_t + \beta_2' x_{it}^2 + \varepsilon_{it}^2) \mid R(0,1)]$$

$$\times F_2[\varepsilon_{it}^1, \varepsilon_{it}^2 \mid R(0,1)] f_1[T\dot{F}P_{it} - \gamma_t \mid R(0,0)] F_2[\varepsilon_{it}^1, \varepsilon_{it}^2 \mid R(0,0)]$$

In practice, the variance-covariance matrix must be imposed to be positive definite. This can be done by using a Cholesky factorization of Ω. In the appendix, we indicate the various steps taken to calculate the maximum simulated likelihood using the Geweke-Hajivassiliou-Keane (GHK) procedure (see Train 2003; Cappellari and Jenkins 2006).

We measure TFP growth using the index approach—that is, we assume constant returns to scale, equilibrium factor holdings, and perfectly competitive markets such that the output elasticities can be measured by the observed factor shares, which we allow to vary over time and to be industry-specific. We are interested in differences in the contributions to TFP growth for firms adopting different investment profiles: (0,0), (1,0), (0,1), and (1,1). These differences can be estimated by drawing values for ε_{it}^1 and ε_{it}^2 from their respective domains of definition and then averaging over the different draws. We are also interested in finding out whether those different investments reinforce each other. This indication of complementarity (or substitutability) is given by the sign of coefficient α_{12}.

The model we have just presented can be generalized to more than two strategies. In the remainder of the chapter, we shall work with three strategies: investment in ICT, R&D, and organizational innovation. To determine the optimal investment profile—that is, the combination of strategies—each combination needs to be compared with seven other combinations. We shall estimate pairwise complementarities and returns from investing in ICT only,

R&D only, organizational innovation only, pairs of investments, all three of them, or none at all.

8.4 Data

The data used in this exercise are sourced from the Business Register and different surveys at Statistics Netherlands, which are linked at the firm level. The sample includes firms in the manufacturing sector (NACE Rev. 2 10 to 33) as well as the services sector (NACE Rev. 2 50 to 93).[4] Production data (value added, capital depreciation costs, and employment) are taken from the Production Statistics (PS). Capital services are proxied by depreciation costs (observed at the firm level). Value added and depreciation cost are deflated using industry-level price information from the Dutch National Accounts. Information on the age of a firm and whether it is foreign-owned are derived from the Business Register.

Information on R&D and organizational innovation, as well as the export status, is sourced from the Community Innovation Survey (CIS). Organizational innovations include the introduction of new business practices, knowledge management systems, methods of workplace organization (i.e., system of decision-making), and management of external relations. The CIS provides information on whether a firm is stated to have performed such an innovation in the three-year period ending in the year preceding the survey (e.g., the CIS 2010 is carried out in 2011 and concerns innovation in the period 2008–10). R&D investment is the sum of internal and external R&D and, unlike organizational innovation, refers only to the last year of the survey.

Information on ICT investment comes from the investment survey and concerns hardware only.[5] We have decided to treat the three investment types in the same way, and therefore we work with binary data for ICT and R&D, which is the only type of information we have for organizational innovation. In our analysis, a firm classifies as investing in ICT and R&D when the investment is positive, but the investment should also have some substance. This is to improve the identification of any effects of investment on TFP, where really small investments can be expected not to make any difference, and we need to distinguish between those and more substantial investment efforts. By way of threshold, we therefore exploited industry-specific data on depreciation cost by type of investment. The investment dummies then

4. The commercial R&D sector, NACE Rev 2 code 72, is excluded from the analysis, as well as oil and petroleum, NACE Rev 2 code 19.
5. From 2012 onward, the Dutch Investment Survey includes information on investment in software. We therefore focus on hardware, as including software would have substantially reduced the number of observations in our analysis.

Table 8.1   **Summary statistics for the estimation sample (2008–12, even years)**

		Manufacturing		Services		Total	
		Mean	SD	Mean	SD	Mean	SD
ICT investment	share of firms	0.42	0.49	0.40	0.49	0.41	0.49
R&D investment	share of firms	0.27	0.44	0.19	0.39	0.22	0.41
organizational innovation*	share of firms	0.45	0.50	0.35	0.48	0.39	0.49
TFP growth**	%	−0.05	0.31	−0.04	0.29	−0.04	0.30
Employment	Fte	257.31	436.03	241.01	526.86	247.21	494.33
Age	Years	24.31	15.18	20.13	15.05	21.72	15.24
Export status	share of firms	0.82	0.39	0.56	0.50	0.66	0.47
Foreign owned	share of firms	0.34	0.47	0.26	0.44	0.29	0.46

* Organizational innovation refers to the period $t - 2$ to t.
** TFP growth refers to growth from t to $t + 1$.

equal 1 when the ratio of the firm's investment to its value added exceeds the share of the depreciation cost for that capital good in value added in the firm's industry. Table 8.A1 reports the annual average of these thresholds by industry. Thus the investment dummies can be loosely interpreted as capturing whether a firm has expansionary investments or not over and above the average industry replacement rate.

Our data span the period from 2008 to 2012. We assume that R&D and ICT in period t and ORG (organizational innovation) in period $t - 2$ to t affect TFP growth between year t and year $t + 1$. Because CIS only covers even years, the eventual estimation sample refers to 2008, 2010, and 2012, where TFP growth concerns growth from 2008 to 2009 and so on. A sensitivity analysis, where the timing of the ICT and R&D investment dummies refers to $t - 2$ rather than t, gave more or less similar results as those reported in the results section of this chapter.

Table 8.1 gives the summary statistics by sector for the key variables used in the estimation separately for manufacturing and services. Firms in both sectors are on average of a similar size, whereas manufacturing firms are slightly older than their counterparts in services. Moreover, manufacturing firms are more often foreign-owned and are more likely to export. Overall, the share of exporting firms is relatively high, which is probably due to the fact that we observe mainly larger firms.

Average TFP growth is negative in both sectors, with a similar magnitude of, respectively, minus 5 percent in manufacturing and minus 4 percent in services. The fact that our data period includes the financial crisis of 2008/2009 explains these substantial negative growth figures, where average (median) TFP growth was minus 10 (minus 5) percent in these years. In the other years, the crisis aftermath, TFP growth is roughly around 0. Table 8.2 also shows that for

Table 8.2   Combinations of investment strategies (estimation sample, 2008–12, even years)

Profile	Manufacturing		TFP growth*			
	N	%	Mean	Median	Q1	Q3
000	802	0.29	−0.067	−0.029	−0.186	0.095
001	430	0.15	−0.062	−0.014	−0.170	0.094
010	123	0.04	−0.062	−0.009	−0.224	0.081
011	266	0.09	−0.023	−0.014	−0.146	0.097
100	484	0.17	−0.039	−0.018	−0.158	0.092
101	335	0.12	−0.054	−0.039	−0.192	0.106
110	140	0.05	−0.088	−0.021	−0.211	0.127
111	227	0.08	−0.008	0.018	−0.124	0.128
	2,807					

Profile	Services		TFP growth*			
	N	%	Mean	Median	Q1	Q3
000	1,665	0.36	−0.048	−0.020	−0.159	0.094
001	659	0.14	−0.059	−0.018	−0.156	0.077
010	181	0.04	−0.024	0.020	−0.158	0.112
011	259	0.06	−0.041	0.001	−0.149	0.097
100	948	0.21	−0.038	−0.014	−0.147	0.094
101	450	0.10	−0.030	−0.006	−0.130	0.105
110	162	0.04	−0.019	−0.008	−0.156	0.138
111	252	0.06	0.001	0.006	−0.126	0.128
	4,576					

Notes: Q1 and Q3 are the first and third quartile of the distribution. Combinations of ICT, R&D, and organizational innovation, where 0 = no investment and 1 = positive (net) investment. Organizational innovation refers to the period $t − 2$ to t. * TFP growth refers to growth from t to $t + 1$.

each investment profile, there are firms reporting negative as well as positive growth and that the third quartile of the TFP growth distribution is always positive. Interestingly, the distribution of TFP growth seems to roughly move to the right with the number of investments—that is, average and median TFP growth, as well as the first and third quartile of the distribution, are larger for those profiles where multiple investments are combined. This is an indication of complementarity between these investments, which will be tested more formally in our econometric model. Nevertheless, firms do not often combine these investments; witness the frequency distribution of the profiles. In manufacturing, about two-thirds of the observations concern cases where a firm does not invest at all or in a single strategy only. In services, this share is even higher, with about three-quarters of the sample.

Table 8.3 reports the summary statistics of the variables that are input to the TFP growth calculation. Using a Laspeyres index, TFP-growth was calculated as the ratio of the volume changes in value added and the total

Table 8.3   **Summary statistics for the production variables (by industry, estimation sample, 2008–12, even years)**

	Industry variables *Averages across years*		Firm variables *averages across industry and years*			
	Capital share	Labor share	Value added	Employment	Capital services	TFP growth
Manufacturing						
10–12 Food and beverages	0.35	0.65	22,468	265	3,400	−0.050
13–15 Textile, leather products	0.27	0.73	9,898	115	741	0.017
16–18 Wood and paper, printing	0.32	0.68	13,527	162	2,092	0.012
20 Chemicals	0.50	0.50	42,740	195	6,386	−0.092
21 Pharmaceuticals	0.52	0.48	69,118	433	5,176	0.283
22–23 Plastics, construction products	0.28	0.72	12,611	192	1,943	0.037
24–25 Basic metals and –products	0.24	0.76	11,222	144	1,113	−0.002
26 Electronic products	0.40	0.60	23,626	239	1,497	0.137
27 Electric equipment	0.50	0.50	31,100	410	4,059	−0.047
28 Machinery n.e.c.	0.28	0.72	22,889	233	2,486	−0.025
29–30 Transport equipment	0.33	0.67	37,808	398	4,730	0.039
31–33 Other manufacturing, repair	0.15	0.85	19,807	482	1,069	−0.005
Services						
58–60 Publishing, movie, radio and TV	0.16	0.84	22,784	247	4,405	−0.040
61 Telecommunications	0.62	0.38	57,741	275	25,460	0.073
62–63 IT and information services	0.12	0.88	15,288	170	1,497	0.036
69–71 Management, tech. consultancy	0.10	0.90	20,151	253	1,100	−0.032
73–75 Advertising, design and other	0.11	0.88	8,622	126	627	0.023
G Wholesale and retail trade	0.20	0.80	15,598	218	1,460	−0.023
H Transportation and storage	0.32	0.68	25,648	309	3,430	−0.006
I Accommodation and food serving	0.17	0.83	10,424	213	1,894	−0.030

Notes: Value added and depreciation cost in prices of 2008. Employment in full-time equivalents.

of inputs, where the capital and labor changes have been weighted by their lagged factor shares at the industry level. This approach takes into account differences in the nature of the production process between industries. Clearly, the average TFP growth differs across industries, with the pharmaceutical industry being a clear outlier.

8.5   Results

In this section, we report the estimation results of the integrated model with three types of investment, the returns for each investment profile, and

Table 8.4   Estimation results of the investment plus productivity equations (based on maximum simulated likelihood)

		Manufacturing (N = 2,807)			Services (N = 4,576)		
		Coeff.	SE	p-value	Coeff.	SE	p-value
ICT	log employment	−0.079***	0.017	0.000	0.060***	0.013	0.000
	export status	−0.121***	0.045	0.008	−0.014	0.029	0.637
	log age	0.012	0.016	0.452	0.000	0.012	0.996
	foreign ownership	−0.086**	0.038	0.024	−0.091**	0.033	0.006
R&D	log employment	−0.005	0.024	0.838	−0.068***	0.016	0.000
	export status	0.524***	0.074	0.000	0.289***	0.041	0.000
	log age	−0.004	0.027	0.869	−0.002	0.019	0.930
	foreign ownership	0.019	0.050	0.704	−0.104**	0.044	0.019
ORG	log employment	0.147***	0.021	0.000	0.108***	0.015	0.000
	export status	−0.004	0.054	0.942	−0.044	0.034	0.195
	log age	0.011	0.021	0.605	0.008	0.015	0.574
	foreign ownership	0.116**	0.044	0.008	0.070*	0.038	0.064
TFP growth	Year 2010	0.164***	0.018	0.000	0.101***	0.014	0.000
	Year 2012	0.118***	0.023	0.000	0.071***	0.017	0.000
	intercept	−0.653***	0.021	0.000	−0.498***	0.014	0.000
complementarities	ICT-R&D	0.251***	0.027	0.000	0.175***	0.025	0.000
	ICT-ORG	−0.044	0.038	0.245	0.046**	0.019	0.018
	R&D-ORG	1.279***	0.072	0.000	1.129***	0.020	0.000
Correlations	ρ_{12}	−0.229***	0.034	0.000	0.173***	0.024	0.000
	ρ_{13}	0.166***	0.044	0.000	0.045**	0.019	0.018
	ρ_{14}	−0.742***	0.021	0.000	0.811***	0.007	0.000
	ρ_{23}	−0.771***	0.036	0.000	−0.061*	0.035	0.079
	ρ_{24}	0.254***	0.049	0.000	0.011	0.032	0.733
	ρ_{34}	−0.517***	0.028	0.000	−0.695***	0.015	0.000
	σ_4	0.553***	0.015	0.000	0.503***	0.010	0.000
	Log-likelihood	−6,561.12			−9,912.21		

Notes: Significance at 10 percent (*); 5 percent (**); 1 percent (***). Intercepts in the probit equations and sector dummies for services are not reported. ρ_{ij} is the correlation between the error terms of equations i and j. The equations are numbered as follows: 1 = ICT, 2 = R&D, 3 = ORG, 4 = TFP growth.

the individual returns of each investment, both on average and as a contribution to the return of each investment profile. Anticipating that the patterns differ across industries, we present the estimation results separately for manufacturing and services.

8.5.1   Complementarities

In table 8.4, we report the results for the integrated model with simultaneous discrete-choice investment equations for ICT, R&D, and organizational innovation, mutual dependence among the three types of investment, and controlling for firm size, export status, age, and foreign ownership and for four industry subsectors in services.[6] Firm size can be seen to be positively associated with investing in our sample, except for investments in ICT for firms in manufacturing and in R&D for firms in services. Exporting firms are more frequently observed to invest in R&D and less frequently in ICT and are found to be not particularly different from nonexporting firms in terms of the frequency of organizational innovation.[7] Age is not found to be significant in any of the three equations. Foreign ownership is positively correlated to organizational innovation and negatively, whenever significant, to ICT and R&D investments. As already mentioned before, aggregate TFP growth in the Netherlands was negative just after the crisis of 2008 but then recovered in the following years, which is reflected in the year dummy pattern. The correlations between the error terms are significant, attesting to the existence of unobservables that are correlated in the adoption and the productivity equations, which justifies our estimation approach.

The three types of investment turn out to be complementary in the sense that they reinforce each other in increasing TFP growth and hence that the probability of investing in one increases the probability of investing in the other one. It is only for ICT and organizational innovation that we do not obtain a positive and significant interaction term. In the logic of our model, two investments are carried out simultaneously if they yield a larger contribution to TFP growth than if they are carried out separately or not at all. Three investments are carried out simultaneously if together they increase TFP growth by more than any pair of investments, individual investment, or no investment at all. The coefficient for the combination of ICT and organizational innovation is significantly smaller than the other α coefficients in both sectors. This is surprising because given the existing evidence in the literature, one would expect this relation to be relatively strong. A possible explanation for this finding is that we consider investment in hardware only, while the complementarity with organizational innovation could lie more in the use of software and specific types of telecommunication equipment.

By contrast, the R&D and organizational innovation combination is significant and has the highest coefficient in both sectors. This suggests that firms that invest in R&D benefit from a simultaneous organizational change. Such a complementarity could be related to the introduction of knowledge management systems or the management of external relations (such as information flows or coordination of collaborative innovation efforts), which are seen as an organizational innovation and clearly could improve the effectiveness of R&D. To our knowledge, there is not much evidence in the literature on this relation, and our finding suggests that it could be explored

6. We report in table 8.4 the estimated coefficients and not the marginal effects. However, the qualitative conclusions about patterns of significance remain the same.

7. Clearly, the causality can run both ways. Including export status is meant to control for the degree of international activities here.

Table 8.5   Average returns of individual investments depending on the investment profile

Profile		Manufacturing					Services				
		Obs	Mean	St. dev	Min	Max	Obs	Mean	St. dev	Min	Max
(0,0,1)	*ORG only*	*430*	*0.107*	*0.035*	*0.033*	*0.238*	*659*	*0.090*	*0.025*	*0.039*	*0.205*
	ORG		0.107	0.035	0.033	0.238	659	0.090	0.025	0.039	0.205
(0,1,0)	*R&D only*	*123*	*0.034*	*0.009*	*0.010*	*0.053*	*181*	*0.024*	*0.009*	*0.006*	*0.047*
	R&D		0.034	0.009	0.010	0.053	181	0.024	0.009	0.006	0.047
(0,1,1)	*R&D and ORG*	*266*	*0.057*	*0.031*	*0.003*	*0.195*	*259*	*0.033*	*0.011*	*0.010*	*0.061*
	R&D		0.021	0.012	−0.001	0.088	259	0.012	0.006	−0.001	0.030
	ORG		0.036	0.025	0.002	0.159	259	0.021	0.008	0.007	0.041
(1,0,0)	*ICT only*	*484*	*0.145*	*0.052*	*0.035*	*0.335*	*948*	*0.143*	*0.027*	*0.071*	*0.231*
	ICT		0.145	0.052	0.035	0.335	948	0.143	0.027	0.071	0.231
(1,0,1)	*ICT and ORG*	*335*	*0.164*	*0.027*	*0.105*	*0.266*	*450*	*0.121*	*0.036*	*0.053*	*0.298*
	ICT		0.083	0.016	0.052	0.140	450	0.062	0.019	0.027	0.159
	ORG		0.081	0.016	0.039	0.129	450	0.058	0.019	0.024	0.146
(1,1,0)	*ICT and R&D*	*140*	*0.044*	*0.014*	*0.012*	*0.075*	*162*	*0.037*	*0.013*	*0.012*	*0.082*
	ICT		0.025	0.008	0.006	0.044	162	0.021	0.007	0.007	0.043
	R&D		0.020	0.007	0.004	0.039	162	0.016	0.006	0.005	0.038
(1,1,1)	*all investments*	*227*	*0.102*	*0.023*	*0.017*	*0.174*	*252*	*0.064*	*0.024*	*0.023*	*0.165*
	ICT		0.059	0.011	0.013	0.082	252	0.036	0.013	0.014	0.091
	R&D		0.004	0.007	−0.019	0.023	252	0.008	0.006	−0.003	0.028
	ORG		0.039	0.014	0.005	0.091	252	0.020	0.009	0.005	0.062

in further detail. While the magnitude of the coefficient seems quite large here, our analysis of the implied average returns in the next section shows that these are plausible.

Finally, investing in ICT and investing in R&D are found to be complementary decisions, in the sense that investing in one increases the productivity of investing in the other one. This lends supports to the idea that ICT is a general-purpose technology that facilitates innovation and increases the output and productivity of R&D (Jovanovic and Rousseau 2005). Vice versa, investing in R&D increases the returns to ICT by generating knowledge that can be shared and diffused through new technology.

In sum, our results suggest that firms consider investment in ICT, R&D, and organizational innovation simultaneously and that they believe that simultaneous investment can be beneficial. In the next section, we shall examine the implied average returns of investing in certain profiles and from individual investments.

8.5.2   Returns on Investments

In our model, the expected return from a given investment profile is the same as the ex-post return in terms of TFP growth. If a certain profile is chosen, it is because its realized return is higher than the return on any other investment profile. In table 8.5, we present the average and the standard deviation of the returns earned on the seven investment profiles in manufacturing and in services.[8] In the example of two strategies given above, the return to adopting investment profile (1,1) would be given by

$$[(\beta_1' x_{it}^1 + \alpha_{12} + \beta_2' x_{it}^2 + \varepsilon_{it}^1 + \varepsilon_{it}^2) \mid R(1,1)] F_2[\varepsilon_{it}^1, \varepsilon_{it}^2 \mid R(1,1)],$$

where $R(1,1)$ are all values of ε_{it}^1 and ε_{it}^2 defined by restrictions (5.1) and (5.2).

These returns are to be understood as above-normal rates of return, since R&D and ICT are not subtracted from the traditional inputs (labor and capital) in the calculation of TFP growth. In part, these returns are random in the sense that they depend on unobservables that lie in a truncated part of their distribution, which is determined by the observed investment profile, and are to be understood as the returns conditional on having chosen that investment profile multiplied by the probability of choosing that investment profile. They are calculated via simulation using the same draws as in the estimation procedure. They are also conditional on the values taken by the vector of explanatory variables x_{it}^1 and x_{it}^2. According to our model, for each observation, the alternative investment profiles yield a return lower than the observed profile. In the case of pairs or triplets of investment, the joint returns are subdivided in the table into the return contributions made by the individual investments.

It is remarkable that the ranking of the returns per investment profile and even the magnitudes of those returns are very similar for firms in manufacturing and in services. The highest average return is earned by firms that invest at the same time in ICT and organizational innovation followed by firms that invest in ICT only. While this may seem surprising recalling the result of no complementarity for this combination, as reported above, it should be noted that we are not comparing the same firms under alternative investment profiles. The differences in return could be due to different characteristics of the firms, such as size, age, or export status. Likewise, the returns for firms that invest in all three strategies are smaller than the returns for firms that invest only in ORG, only in ICT, or in both ORG and ICT, whereas according to the complementarities, we would expect the highest returns for firms that invest in all strategies. That would only be true when comparing the same firm under different scenarios, while in our case, the composition of the sample of firms choosing any of the profiles differs.[9]

Finally, table 8.6 presents the average returns to each individual investment conditional on the firms' characteristics. These returns are calculated as follows. The average rate of return on R&D, for instance, is the return a firm gets if it belongs to the set of investment profiles (0,1,0), (1,1,0), (0,1,1),

---

8. Note that the returns in the (0,0,0) case, where no investment takes place, is 0 by definition and is not reported.

9. In most cases, the alternative (counterfactual) returns (not shown) are negative, although they only need to be lower than the returns earned on the chosen investment profile.

Table 8.6   Average returns to individual investments conditional on firms' characteristics

	Obs	Mean	Std. dev.	Min	Max
Manufacturing					
ICT	1,186	0.097	0.055	0.006	0.335
R&D	756	0.018	0.014	−0.019	0.088
ORG	1,258	0.073	0.040	0.002	0.238
Services					
ICT	1,812	0.097	0.054	0.007	0.231
R&D	854	0.014	0.009	−0.003	0.047
ORG	1,620	0.059	0.035	0.005	0.205

and $(1,1,1)$ multiplied by the respective probabilities of choosing each of those profiles. Since a firm can be in eight zones of the space spanned by $(\varepsilon_{it}^1, \varepsilon_{it}^2, \varepsilon_{it}^3)$, which are themselves determined by the firm's characteristics, and since it makes a positive return on a particular investment only if it actually invests in it, the average rate of return is a weighted average of the returns in the four profiles in which it is active regarding that investment.

It is interesting to notice that the returns are again very similar in manufacturing and in services. Investing in ICT yields on average an implied rate of return close to 10 percent, which can go as high as 33.5 percent in manufacturing and 23.1 percent in services. R&D earns on average only 1.8 percent in manufacturing and 1.4 percent in services, with at most 8.8 percent in manufacturing and 4.7 percent in services. This is definitely lower than the average rates of return on R&D reported in Hall, Mairesse, and Mohnen (2010) and those reported for the Netherlands by Bartelsman et al. (1989). The implied rate of return on organizational innovation lies in between the rate on R&D and ICT, with an average of 7.3 percent in manufacturing and 5.9 percent in services and a maximum that exceeds 20 percent.

8.6   Conclusions and Further Research

This chapter has investigated the relation between investments in ICT, R&D, and organizational innovation and the contributions of different investment profiles on TFP growth at the firm level in Dutch manufacturing and services. We find that, overall, the investment decisions are complementary in the sense that investing in one strategy increases the probability of investing in another because joint investments lead to higher TFP growth than do individual investments. We find a relatively strong complementarity between R&D and organizational innovation, which could be related to new ways of managing knowledge systems and external relations improving the productivity of R&D. To our knowledge, this relation has not been explored intensively in the literature. The fact that the magnitude of the complementarity between ICT and organizational innovation is lower than the other complementarities also merits some further investigation, in particular considering software investments in addition to those in hardware only. There is clear evidence that ICT and R&D complement each other. This implies that R&D policies could stimulate investments in ICT, and conversely, policies designed to stimulate ICT also increase the demand for R&D. Our results imply that ICT earns on average a rate of return of 9.7 percent, followed by 6 percent to 7 percent on organizational innovation and a modest 1.4 percent to 1.8 percent on R&D.

The research could be extended in a number of directions. First, information on the separate types of organizational innovation available in our data could be exploited (business practices, knowledge systems, and external relations), as those types could relate differently to ICT and R&D. Second, as mentioned above, it will be good to consider software investment next to hardware investment, even though for the Netherlands, we only have data from 2012 onward for this type of asset. Third, we could estimate the elasticities of labor and capital simultaneously with the returns to ICT, R&D, and organizational innovation. A fourth extension would be to use the intensities of R&D and ICT in the productivity growth equation instead of, or in addition to, just the binary information.

Appendix

Calculation of the Maximum Simulated Likelihood

This part is based on Train (2003) and Cappellari and Jenkins (2006). For simplicity, we take the case of two strategies and one performance equation. The example can easily be generalized to three strategies and one performance equation. We start by using a Cholesky factorization of Ω:

$$
\begin{bmatrix} \varepsilon_{1\tau}^1 \\ \varepsilon_{1\tau}^2 \\ \varepsilon_{1\tau}^3 \end{bmatrix} = C \begin{bmatrix} \eta_{it}^1 \\ \eta_{it}^2 \\ \eta_{it}^3 \end{bmatrix} = \begin{bmatrix} c_{11} & 0 & 0 \\ c_{21} & c_{22} & 0 \\ c_{31} & c_{32} & c_{33} \end{bmatrix} \begin{bmatrix} \eta_{it}^1 \\ \eta_{it}^2 \\ \eta_{it}^3 \end{bmatrix}
$$

with

$$
\Omega = C * C' = \begin{bmatrix} 1 & \rho_{21} & \rho_{31}\sigma_3 \\ \rho_{21} & 1 & \rho_{32}\sigma_3 \\ \rho_{31}\sigma_3 & \rho_{32}\sigma_3 & \sigma_3^2 \end{bmatrix},
$$

and each $\eta_{it}^j (j = 1,2,3)$ follows a standard normal distribution. We set the variances of ε_{it}^1 and ε_{it}^2 equal to 1 for reasons of identification. In order to have this Ω matrix, elements of C are as follows: $c_{11} = 1$, $c_{21} = \rho_{21}$, $c_{31} = \rho_{31}\sigma_3$, $c_{22} = \sqrt{(1 - c_{21}^2)}$, $c_{32} = (\rho_{32}\sigma_3 - c_{31} * c_{21})/c_{22}$, $c_{33} = \sqrt{(\sigma_3^2 - c_{31}^2 - c_{32}^2)}$. The ρ_{ij} coefficients are imposed to stay between -1 and 1 by using the following reparameterization:

$$\rho_{ij} = \frac{\exp(2\widetilde{\rho_{ij}}) - 1}{\exp(2\widetilde{\rho_{ij}}) + 1}.$$

We can rewrite
$$\begin{bmatrix} \varepsilon_{it}^1 \\ \varepsilon_{it}^2 \\ \varepsilon_{it}^3 \end{bmatrix} = \begin{bmatrix} c_{11}\eta_{it}^1 \\ c_{21}\eta_{it}^1 + c_{22}\eta_{it}^2 \\ c_{31}\eta_{it}^1 + c_{32}\eta_{it}^2 + c_{33}\eta_{it}^3 \end{bmatrix}.$$

Inequalities (5.1), (7.1), (9.1), and (11.1) can be rewritten as

(5.1') $$\eta_{it}^1 > -(\beta_1' x_{it}^1 + \alpha_{12})$$

(7.1') $$\eta_{it}^1 > -(\beta_1' x_{it}^1)$$

(9.1') $$\eta_{it}^1 < -(\beta_1' x_{it}^1 + \alpha_{12})$$

(11.1') $$\eta_{it}^1 < -\beta_1' x_{it}^1.$$

The first step of the maximum simulated likelihood algorithm consists in drawing for each alternative a value from the corresponding truncated standard normal distribution of η_{it}^1 using initial values of the parameters. Let us denote this value as d_{it}^1.

Inequalities (5.2), (7.2), (9.2), and (11.2) can be rewritten as

(5.2') $$\eta_{it}^2 > \max[-(a_{2it} + \alpha_{12})/c_{22}, -(a_{1it} + a_{2it} + \alpha_{12})/c_{22}]$$

(7.2') $$\eta_{it}^2 < \min[-(a_{2it} + \alpha_{12})/c_{22}, (a_{1it} - a_{2it})/c_{22}]$$

(9.2') $$\eta_{it}^2 > \max(-a_{2it}/c_{22}, (a_{1it} - a_{2it})/c_{22})$$

(11.2') $$\eta_{it}^2 < \min(-a_{2it}/c_{22}, -(a_{1it} + a_{2it} + \alpha_{12})/c_{22})$$

where $a_{1it} = \beta_1' x_{it}^1 + d_{it}^1$, $a_{2it} = \beta_2' x_{it}^2 + c_{21} d_{it}^1$.

The second step consists in drawing for each alternative a value from the corresponding truncated standard normal distribution of η_{it}^2 using initial values of the parameters. Let us denote this value as d_{it}^2.

The third step consists in changing from ε_{it}^3 to η_{it}^3 so that the final likelihood function becomes

(14')
$$\mathcal{L} = \prod_{i,t} \left(\frac{1}{c_{33}}\right) \varphi\left((T\dot{F}P_{it} - [\gamma_t + \beta_1' x_{it}^1 + \alpha_{12} + \beta_2' x_{it}^2 + (1 + c_{21})d_{it}^1 \right.$$

$$+ c_{22}d_{it}^2) - c_{31}d_{it}^1 - c_{32}d_{it}^2(/c_{33})\Phi_2(d_{it}^1, d_{it}^2)|R(1,1)$$

$$\times \left(\frac{1}{c_{33}}\right) \varphi\left((T\dot{F}P_{it} - (\gamma_t + \beta_1' x_{it}^1 + d_{it}^1) - c_{31}d_{it}^1 - c_{32}d_{it}^2)/c_{33})\Phi_2(d_{it}^1, d_{it}^2)|R(1,0)\right.$$

$$\times \left(\frac{1}{c_{33}}\right) \varphi\left((T\dot{F}P_{it} - (\gamma_t + \beta_2' x_{it}^2 + c_{21}d_{it}^1 + c_{22}d_{it}^2) - c_{31}d_{it}^1 - c_{32}d_{it}^2)/c_{33})\right.$$

$$\times \Phi_2(d_{it}^1, d_{it}^2)|R(0,1) \times \left(\frac{1}{c_{33}}\right) \varphi\left((T\dot{F}P_{it} - \gamma_t - c_{31}d_{it}^1 - c_{32}d_{it}^2)/c_{33})\right.$$

$$\times \Phi_2(d_{it}^1, d_{it}^2)|R(0,0),$$

Table 8.A1   **Depreciation shares in value added by industry (average across years)**

	ICT	R&D
10–12 Food and beverages	0.002	0.018
13–15 Textile, leather products	0.003	0.008
16–18 Wood and paper, printing	0.004	0.006
20 Chemicals	0.002	0.091
21 Pharmaceuticals	0.002	0.195
22–23 Plastics, construction products	0.002	0.027
24–25 Basic metals and –products	0.002	0.017
26 Electronic products	0.002	0.182
27 Electric equipment	0.003	0.211
28 Machinery n.e.c.	0.004	0.085
29–30 Transport equipment	0.002	0.073
31–33 Other manufacturing, repair	0.003	0.016
58–60 Publishing, movie, radio and TV	0.007	0.004
61 Telecommunications	0.016	0.005
62–63 IT and information services	0.016	0.023
69–71 Management, tech. consultancy	0.007	0.011
73–75 Advertising, design and other	0.008	0.010
G Wholesale and retail trade	0.005	0.005
H Transportation and storage	0.006	0.006
I Accommodation and food serving	0.002	0.002

Source: Statistics Netherlands, Growth accounts.

where d_{it}^1 and d_{it}^2 are draws from each of the truncated bivariate normal distributions $\Phi_2(d_{it}^1, d_{it}^2)\,|\,R(.)$ defined over the region $R(.)$, itself defined by the boundaries of η_{it}^1 and η_{it}^2, and where $\varphi(.)$ is the univariate standard normal density function and Φ_2 the bivariate normal cumulative distribution function. It is important here to account for the Jacobian of the variable transformation $(1/c_{33})$.

In our application, the model has four equations, and a step is added between the second and third step above. The logic is the same, but there are eight inequalities to take into account and eight elements in the likelihood function. The steps are repeated 50 times, and then an average is taken of the corresponding values of the likelihood function.[10] The parameters of the likelihood function are then estimated using a numerical maximization algorithm at each iteration repeating the simulation-based computation of the likelihood function starting from the updated values of the estimated parameters.

---

10. Experiments with up to 200 draws did not produce very different results.

References

Aboal, D., and E. Tacsir. 2018. "Innovation and Productivity in Services and Manufacturing: The Role of ICT." *Industrial and Corporate Change* 27 (2): 221–41.

Athey, S., and S. Stern. 1998. "An Empirical Framework for Testing Theories about Complementarity in Organizational Design." NBER Working Paper No. 6600. Cambridge, MA: National Bureau of Economic Research.

Bartelsman, E., G. van Leeuwen, H. Nieuwenhuijsen, and K. Zeelenberg. 1996. "R&D and Productivity Growth: Evidence from Firm-level Data in the Netherlands." *Netherlands Official Statistics* 11 (Autumn): 52–69.

Bartelsman, E., G. van Leeuwen, and M. Polder. 2017. "CDM Using a Cross Country Micro Moments Database." *Economics of Innovation and New Technology* 26 (1/2): 168–82.

Biagi, F. 2013. "ICT and Productivity: A Review of the Literature." JRC Technical Reports, Institute for Prospective Technological Studies, Digital Economy working paper 2013/09.

Black, S. E., and L. M. Lynch. 2001. "How to Compete: The Impact of Workplace Practices and Information Technology on Productivity." *Review of Economics and Statistics* 83 (3): 434–45.

Bresnahan, T. F., E. Brynjolfsson, and L. M. Hitt. 2002. "Information Technology, Workplace Organization, and the Demand for Skilled Labor: Firm-level Evidence." *Quarterly Journal of Economics* 117 (1): 339–76.

Brynjolfsson, E., and A. McAfee. 2014. *The Second Machine Age*. Cambridge, MA: MIT Press.

Brynjolfsson, E., and A. Saunders. 2010. *Wired for Innovation: How Information Technology Is Reshaping the Economy*. Cambridge, MA: MIT Press.

Cappellari, L., and S. P. Jenkins. 2006. "Calculation of Multivariate Normal Probabilities by Simulation, with Applications to Maximum Simulated Likelihood Estimation." *Stata Journal* 6 (2): 156–89.

Caroli, E., and J. Van Reenen. 2001. "Organization, Skills and Technology: Evidence from a Panel of British and French Establishments." *Quarterly Journal of Economics* 116 (4): 1449–92.

Cerquera, D., and G. J. Klein. 2008. "Endogenous Firm Heterogeneity, ICT and R&D Incentives." ZEW discussion paper No. 08-126.

Chen, W., T. Niebel, and M. Saam. 2014. "Are Intangibles More Productive in ICT-intensive Industries? Evidence from EU Countries." ZEW discussion paper 14-070.

Corrado, C., J. Haskel, and C. Jona-Lasinio. 2017. "Knowledge Spillovers, ICT and Productivity Growth." *Oxford Bulletin of Economics and Statistics*, https://doi.org/10.1111/obes.12171.

Corrado, C., J. Haskel, C. Jona-Lasinio, and M. Iommi. 2013. "Innovation and Intangible Investment in Europe, Japan, and the United States." *Oxford Review of Economic Policy* 29:261–86.

Corrado, C. A., C. R. Hulten, and D. E. Sichel. 2009. "Intangible Capital and U.S. Economic Growth." *Review of Income and Wealth* 5 (3): 661–85.

Crépon, B., E. Duguet, and J. Mairesse. 1998. "Research, Innovation and Productivity: An Econometric Analysis at the Firm Level." *Economics of Innovation and New Technology* 7:115–58.

Crespi, G., C. Criscuolo, and J. Haskel. 2007. "Information Technology, Organizational Change and Productivity Growth: Evidence from UK firms." CEP Discussion Paper No. 783.

Doraszelski, U., and J. Jaumandreu. 2013. "R&D and Productivity: Estimating Endogenous Productivity." *Review of Economic Studies* 80 (4): 1338–83.

Draca, M., R. Sadun, and J. van Reenen. 2007. "Productivity and ICTs: A Review of the Evidence." In *The Oxford Handbook of Information and Communication Technologies*, edited by R. Mansell, C. Avgerou, D. Quah, and R. Silverstone, 100–147. Oxford: Oxford University Press.

Engelstätter, B. 2012. "It Is Not All about Performance Gains: Enterprise Software and Innovations." *Economics of Innovation and New Technology* 21 (3): 223–45.

Forman, C. C., and N. van Zeebroeck. 2012. "From Wires to Partners: How the Internet Has Fostered R&D Collaborations within Firms." *Management Science* 58 (8): 1549–68.

Gordon, R. 2016. *The Rise and Fall of American Growth: The U.S. Standard of Living since the Civil War*. Princeton, NJ: Princeton University Press.

Griliches, Z. 1979. "Issues in Assessing the Contribution of Research and Development to Productivity Growth." *Bell Journal of Economics* 10 (1): 92–116.

Hall, B., F. Lotti, and J. Mairesse. 2012. "Evidence on the Impact of R&D and ICT Investment on Innovation and Productivity in Italian Firms." NBER Working Paper No. 18053. Cambridge, MA: National Bureau of Economic Research.

Hall, B., F. Lotti, and J. Mairesse. 2013. "Evidence on the Impact of R&D and ICT Investments on Innovation and Productivity in Italian Firms." *Economics of Innovation and New Technology* 22 (3): 300–328.

Hall, B., J. Mairesse, and P. Mohnen. 2010. "Measuring the Returns to R&D." In the *Handbook of the Economics of Innovation*, edited by B. H. Hall and N. Rosenberg, 1034–82. Amsterdam: Elsevier.

Jorgenson, D. W., M. S. Ho, and K. J. Stiroh. 2008. "A Retrospective Look at the U.S. Productivity Growth Resurgence." *Journal of Economic Perspectives* 22 (1): 3–24.

Jovanovic, B., and P. L. Rousseau. 2005. "General Purpose Technologies." In *Handbook of Economic Growth*, vol. 1, edited by P. Aghion and S. Durlauf, 1181–1224. Amsterdam: Elsevier.

Kleis, L., P. Chwelos, R. V. Ramirez, and I. Cockburn. 2012. "Information Technology and Intangible Output: The Impact of IT Investment on Innovation Productivity." *Information Systems Research* 23 (1): 42–59.

Kretschmer, T., E. Miravete, and J. Pernías. 2012. "Competitive Pressure and the Adoption of Complementary Innovations." *American Economic Review* 102 (4): 1540–70.

Lewbel, A. 2007. "Coherency and Completeness of Structural Models Containing a Dummy Endogenous Variable." *International Economic Review* 48 (4): 1379–92.

Lipsey, R., K. I. Carlaw, and C. T. Bekhar. 2005. *Economic Transformations: General Purpose Technologies and Long Term Economic Growth*. Oxford: Oxford University Press.

Mairesse, J., and P. Mohnen. 2010. "Using Innovation Surveys for Econometric Analysis." In *Handbook of the Economics of Innovation*, edited by B. H. Hall and N. Rosenberg, 1130–55. Amsterdam: Elsevier.

Martínez-Ros, E., and J. Labeaga. 2009. "Product and Process Innovation: Persistence and Complementarities." *European Management Review* 6:64–75.

Milgrom, P., and J. Roberts. 1990. "The Economics of Modern Manufacturing, Technology, Strategy and Organizations." *American Economic Review* 80:511–28.

Miravete, E., and J. Pernías. 2006. "Innovation Complementarity and Scale of Production." *Journal of Industrial Economics* 54:1–29.

Pieri, F., M. Vecchi, and F. Venturini. 2017. "Modelling the Joint Impact of R&D and ICT on Productivity: A Frontier Analysis Approach." Working paper, Universita' degli Studi di Trento.

Polder, M. 2015. "Determinants of Economic Growth and Productivity." In *ICT and Economic Growth*. The Hague: CBS, Statistics Netherlands.

Polder, M., G. van Leeuwen, P. Mohnen, and W. Raymond. 2009. "Productivity Effects of Innovation Modes." Statistics Netherlands, working paper 09033.

Polder, M., G. van Leeuwen, P. Mohnen, and W. Raymond. 2010. "Product, Process and Organizational Innovation: Drivers, Complementarity and Productivity Effects." UNU-MERIT working paper 2010-035.

Riley, R., and P. Vahter. 2013. "Innovation and Productivity in Services: The Role of Organizational Capital and IT." Mimeo.

Rybalka, M. 2015. "The Innovative Input Mix. Assessing the Importance of ICT and R&D Investments for Firm Performance in Manufacturing and Services." Discussion paper 801, Statistics Norway.

Spiezia, V. 2011. "Are ICT Users More Innovative? An Analysis of ICT-enabled Innovation in OECD Firms." *OECD Journal: Economic Studies* 2011 (1). https:// doi.org/10.1787/19952856.

Stiroh, K. J. 2010. "Reassessing the Impact of Information Technology in the Production Function: A Meta Analysis and Sensitivity Tests." *Contributions in Memory of Zvi Griliches, Annales d'Économie et de Statistique*, edited by J. Mairesse and M. Trajtenberg, July–December 2005, 79–80.

Syverson, C. 2011. "What Determines Productivity?" *Journal of Economic Literature* 49 (2): 326–65.

Train, K. 2003. *Discrete Choice Methods with Simulations*. Cambridge: Cambridge University Press.

Van Leeuwen, G., and S. Farooqui. 2008. "ICT, Innovation and Productivity." *Information Society: ICT Impact Assessment by Linking Data from Different Sources*. Eurostat report, 222–39.

Van Leeuwen, G., and P. Mohnen. 2017. "Revisiting the Porter Hypothesis: An Empirical Analysis of Green Innovation in the Netherlands." *Economics of Innovation and New Technology* 26 (1/2): 63–77.

Van Reenen J., N. Bloom, M. Draca, T. Kretschmer, R. Sadun, H. Overman, and M. Schankerman. 2010. "The Economic Impact of ICT." Final Report for the European Commission.

Digital Innovation and the Distribution of Income

Dominique Guellec

9.1 Introduction

Income inequalities have increased in most Organisation for Economic Co-operation and Development (OECD) countries over the past three decades (OECD 2015a). In the United States, the income share of the top 1 percent has soared, rising from earning on average 27 times more than the bottom 1 percent in 1980 to 81 times more in 2014. The top 1 percent income share is now almost twice as large as the bottom 50 percent share. There has been close to zero growth for working-age adults in the bottom 50 percent of the distribution since 1980 (Piketty, Saez, and Zucman 2016).

In this chapter, we argue that the increasing importance of digital innovation (which are new products and processes based on or embodied in software code and data in and beyond IT industries) is magnifying innovation-

Dominique Guellec is scientific adviser at the Observatory of Science and Technology in Paris.

Caroline Paunov co-authored the Working Paper (NBER Working Paper 23987) which captures most of the research and ideas presented in this chapter. Stefano Baruffaldi and Akira Tachibana provided valuable research support. The authors would like to thank Jonathan Haskel and participants of the NBER Conference on Research in Income and Wealth (CRIW) conference Measuring and Accounting for Innovation in the 21st Century, the Innovation and Inclusive Growth in Germany and Disruptive Innovations, Disruptive Times? Technological Innovation, Inequality and Inclusive Growth workshops of the Bertelsmann Foundation, the Symposium on Technology, Innovation and Inclusive Growth: Future Perspectives, the Conference on the Economics of Digital Change, Vienna, Austria (2016), 13th World Conference on Intellectual Capital for Communities and seminars at the Internet Policy Research Initiative, MIT (2017), the Inter-American Development Bank (2017), the Washington Centre for Equitable Growth (2017). The support of the advisory group of the Innovation for Inclusive Growth Project is also gratefully acknowledged. For acknowledgments, sources of research support, and disclosure of the author's or authors' material financial relationships, if any, please see https://www.nber.org/books-and-chapters/measuring-and-accounting-innovation-21st-century/digital-innovation-and-distribution-income.

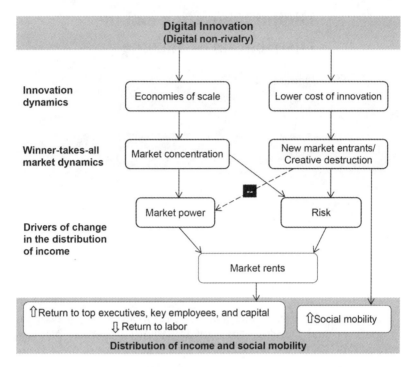

Fig. 9.1   Impacts of digital innovation on market structures and the distribution of income

based rents that contribute to increasing the income share of the top groups. Specifically, the chapter focuses on inequality coming from market rents accruing to top executives, key employees, and shareholders but little to the average employee. Figure 9.1 summarizes the mechanisms at work in my framework.

Digital innovation has received surprisingly little attention in spite of the increase in market rents—the return on productive resources, notably capital, in excess of what is needed for resources to be deployed in production—and in spite of the fact that in recent years, the evolution of top incomes owes much to increased returns to capital (CEA 2016; Piketty, Saez, and Zucman 2016). This explanation adds to others that point to globalization, the financialization of the economy, unskilled-labor-displacing technologies, and the weakening of trade unions as causes of growing income inequalities. These other changes also have to do with digitalization, which has been an enabler or a driver for globalization, financialization, and skills-biased technical change.

Viewed from the perspective of digital innovation, the increase in top income inequality partly results from the nonrival character of these intangible products, referred to as digital nonrivalry (DNR) in the remainder of the chapter. This, however, does not imply that restraining innovation would improve the well-being of the low- and medium-income categories: innovation is a major driver of economic growth and also a source of benefits to all groups in society, including the most disadvantaged.

The impact of digital innovation on income distribution is reflective of the well-known effects of innovation on market structures. It has been recognized since Schumpeter (1911) that innovation requires and generates market rents. Successful innovation endows innovators with a temporary market exclusivity based on first-mover advantage, intellectual property rights (IPR) protection, brand reputation, network externalities, and entry barriers. This exclusivity allows innovators to set prices above the marginal cost and gain rents. The nonrivalrous nature of knowledge means that the costs of new ideas come mainly from their development—typically through R&D, design, and market research—while costs of implementing and diffusing them are much lower or even nil. This gives rise to large returns to scale; the more an idea is applied, the lower the average cost. Increasing returns to scale favor large firms and concentrated market structures.

The effects of nonrivalry are magnified by intangible (digital) products that have constituted an increasing share of the US economy over the past decades (Corrado, Hulten, and Sichel 2005, 2009). With wider use of information technology (IT), software, and data, the marginal cost of production is essentially nil, and the intangible component makes most of the value of products. This applies particularly to fully intangible products such as software, as increasing returns to scale are tied essentially to the intangible component of a product. The tangible components might generate economies of scale, but not to the same extent as the intangible ones, because their variable costs are not zero (with materials, labor, and other input needed to produce additional units). Effects apply beyond the IT sector because software code and data are increasingly important across all fields of the economy.

As a consequence of digital nonrivalry, a growing number of industries are subject to "winner-take-all" dynamics—that is, markets akin to tournaments in which the best offer wins the race and captures most (if not all) of the market (Rosen 1981). Such market concentration allows winners to extract a rent by raising the price of output and/or lowering the price of inputs. Moreover, globalization has allowed successful firms to dominate not only their national market but also the larger global one, hence increasing the size of the corresponding market rent.

Digital innovation also lowers the costs of innovation, raising opportunities for "creative destruction"—the process by which new products replace current products, sometimes involving the exit of incumbent producers and entry of new ones—as it reduces barriers to entry on many markets. The capital requirement for programming software, the core of digital innovation, is much lower than for other types of innovative activities, such as those requiring special facilities to develop innovations (e.g., laboratories and experimental settings in pharmaceuticals). The intangible nature of knowledge and the opportunities for rapid scale-up facilitate creative destruction. This is exemplified by the "app economy"; individual innovators and small companies offer their products on the internet at no direct cost.

Where opportunities for creative destruction and market entry arise, the level of risk is higher than in the past: while in traditional markets, new, superior products may reduce the market share of incumbents, in a winner-take-all market, new, (even slightly) superior products can result in new firms taking over the entire market. Incumbents in such winner-take-all markets have higher market shares than firms in other markets. However, firms and investors run the risk of losing it all, as more creative destruction generates more instability in market shares and hence in income.

Higher risk leads investors to demand a risk premium, in turn increasing the average return to capital. These dynamics are most visible in the venture capital market, but they extend to other types of investment as well. This increase in risk explains in part why the average return on capital and its dispersion between firms have increased over the past two decades as digitalization was progressing (Furman and Orszag 2015).

From the perspective of innovation dynamics, market entry and creative destruction may reduce market concentration arising from the scale economies digital innovation allows for. Which of the two opposite forces dominates depends on the technology, business strategies, and of course, policy (including antitrust, entrepreneurship, and IPR). In terms of technology, radical changes in the basic technologies (e.g., the PC replacing the mainframe) reduce the advantage of incumbents and therefore favor newcomers and competition; by contrast, technology stability favors incumbents and concentrated market structures.[1]

In terms of business strategies, incumbents can identify and implement new, more powerful ways to protect their market position in the digital economy, hence mitigating the level of risk they are faced with. First are network effects—the more customers a product has, the more valuable it is to each of them—complemented by limited portability (customers cannot easily change from one product to a competitor). Technical standards are another related effect: large players encourage standards that increase entry cost and reduce customer's mobility. Third is blocking competitors from access to data. In the digital economy, data are the primary input for many innovations and services. This is reinforced in more recent technologies like artificial intelligence. Fourth, large firms can play the role of "integrators" by acquiring start-ups that have been successful in promoting new products

---

1. This is not systematic, however, as one can see from the example of artificial intelligence. The main players are the same as with the internet, because some of the key competitive factors are the same in both cases (notably access to large amounts of data).

and integrating them into their own offer. This has the twofold advantage of enriching their product portfolio and preempting potential competition.

Empirical evidence provided in this chapter shows that the forces tending toward more market concentration have prevailed over competition-enhancing forces of digital innovation, resulting in winner-take-all markets that are characterized by higher market concentration and more creative destruction. Market power and creative destruction are not in contradiction with each other. Competition in digital innovation is not about prices—in which case, the threat of new entry would discipline the incumbents—but about innovation, as new products are so innovative that they take over the market no matter the price charged by current incumbents.

How do the rents from digital innovation affect income distribution? They are mainly shared among shareholders and investors, top executives, and key employees of the winning firms, who are already in the top tier of the income distribution (as they own capital and skills and hold managerial and leading positions in firms), hence contributing to increased income inequalities. Shareholders have benefitted from a steady increase in dividends and share prices over the past decades. This has come with an increased dispersion in profits across firms (that many investors accommodate by pursuing portfolio diversification strategies). As a result, the share of capital (vs. labor) in national income has increased in the United States and most other OECD countries, particularly in innovation-intensive economic activities. Top executives have benefitted from increased compensation with the expansion of high-powered incentive schemes (like stock options and bonuses), which are aimed at monitoring their decisions in the riskier environment of winner-take-all dynamics (Hall and Liebman 1998).

Labor has not gained as much from rents, with the exception of the top categories. Indeed, top employees of successful firms have benefitted to a certain extent, as shown by the importance of cross-firm wage inequality in total income inequality (Song et al. 2015). Average employees, however, have been less successful in gaining from the rents for a number of reasons. They face more competition in the labor market and are increasingly employed in temporary work arrangements. Workers employed under alternative work arrangements (such as temporary help agency workers, on-call workers, contract workers, and freelancers), which represent the bulk of job creation in the United States for 2005–15 (Katz and Krueger 2016), are in a weak negotiating position when it comes to sharing rents. These effects of digital innovation and, more broadly, intangibles on labor add to the impacts that arise from how different worker occupations and skills profiles complement or substitute to these new technologies (see, e.g., Autor and Dorn 2013; Haskel and Westlake 2017).

Lower entry barriers that facilitate creative destruction also enable increased social mobility, as newcomers can displace incumbents. Turnover

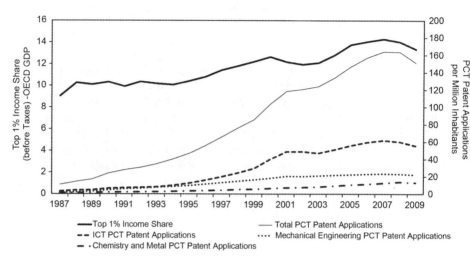

Fig. 9.2   Top 1 percent income share and PCT patent applications for selected OECD countries, 1987–2009

Source: The World Top Incomes Database, http://topincomes.g-mond.parisschoolofeconomics.eu/ (accessed July 15, 2015) for the 1 percent income share data; OECD Patents Statistics for PCT patent applications.

Note: The statistics are based on a GDP-weighted average for the following 13 OECD countries: Australia, Canada, Denmark, France, Germany, Japan, Netherlands, New Zealand, Norway, Sweden, Switzerland, the United Kingdom, and the United States. The selection is based on data availability over the 1987–2009 data period. The data appendix provides further information.

in the top income categories has increased in recent decades and is positively related to the intensity of innovation activity (as, e.g., across US states in Aghion et al. 2015).

The remainder of this chapter is structured as follows: section 9.1 describes global trends in innovation and the distribution of income. Section 9.2 defines DNR and explains why it is increasingly important. Sections 9.3 and 9.4 analyze the impacts of digital innovation on economies of scale and market concentration and on the costs of innovation and creative destruction. Section 9.5 discusses implications of these changing market trends on the distribution of income, while section 9.6 lists open research questions.

9.2   Digital Innovation and the Distribution of Income: Global Trends

Many OECD economies have seen an increase in income inequality. In particular, the top categories of income distribution increased their share in total income. This trend coincides with the growing importance of digital innovation. Figure 9.2 plots Patent Cooperation Treaty (PCT) applications and the income share of the top 1 percent for a group of OECD countries.

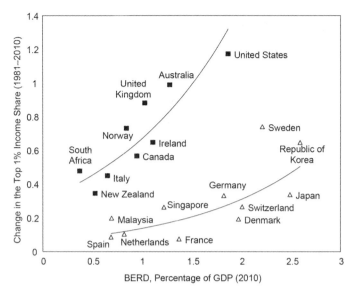

Fig. 9.3   Changes in the top 1 percent income share over 1981–2010 relative to business R&D spending as percentage of GDP in 2010

Source: The World Top Incomes Database, http://topincomes.g-mond.parisschoolofeconomics.eu (accessed July 15, 2015), for the 1 percent income share data; OECD Science and Technology Indicators for business expenditure on research and development (BERD) as percentage of GDP. The data appendix provides further information.

Note: The two lines are exponential trends for the two groups of countries.

Both series show an initially modest upward trend, followed by acceleration in the mid-1990s. Interestingly, information and communications technology (ICT) patents show the strongest upward trend of all, highlighting the growing importance of ICT in innovation.

Comparing business R&D spending (as a proxy for digital innovation) with trends in the top 1 percent income share gives a more mixed picture (figure 9.3). In a group of countries that includes the United States (jointly with Norway, the United Kingdom, and Australia), the share of the top 1 percent income owners increased more substantially than the intensity of R&D investments. In another group of countries (including Denmark, Germany, Japan, and Switzerland), strong business R&D investments coincided with positive but modest increases in the top 1 percent income shares over the past two decades. These differences may result from diverse country policy approaches to income inequality as well as from diverse industry dynamics and structures. Differences may also be driven by how economies are engaged in digital innovation and consequently in the degree to which digital innovation activities affect market structures and the distribution of income.

9.3 Digital Nonrivalry and Its Growing Importance

9.3.1 Digital Nonrivalry

Digital innovation gives knowledge (design, IPR, software code or data) a more prominent role in the value share of new products and processes than does "traditional" innovation, which is only partly intangible as the knowledge component of tangible products. Digital innovation is fully intangible and consequently allows for what we refer to here as digital non-rivalry (DNR). Hal Varian referred to the key components of digital innovations as essentially ideas, standards specifications, protocols, programming languages, and software rather than "physical devices"—consequently as innovations without physical constraints (Varian 2003).

Economists have long been familiar with the concept of nonrivalry when it comes to knowledge: one piece of knowledge can be used simultaneously by any number of users, at any scale, at low or even zero marginal cost. For instance, once assembled or designed, inventions can serve any number of users at no additional cost. This property contrasts with tangible (or physical) goods: two people can discuss fully the same idea, but they cannot eat the same apple. Nonrivalry favors "fluidity" or "ubiquity," ideas spreading instantaneously and everywhere at zero marginal cost. By contrast, the cost of producing the intangible product itself (referred to as "original" in national accounting) is sunk—that is, it is not incurred again with every additional use of the product.

The impact of nonrivalry on the real world economy has been limited until recently because ideas needed a physical carrier; they had to be embodied in a tangible good to be stored, disseminated, or commercialized: it could be a book, a new car (embodying an invention), and so on. Physical embodiment means significant production and transportation costs and favors inertia, as it requires time and resources to make the physical carrier of the idea. To diffuse the idea, you need to print and physically distribute the book and access the idea embodied in it; you need to buy the book. The price of an individual copy of the book will not reflect the total cost of producing the idea, which (in equilibrium) is shared among all copies. And this price will also include the cost of producing and diffusing physical copies of the book. The same holds with a new object—say, a car. You need to produce the new car and distribute it physically, and customers need to go to the shop and buy it. The cost of inventing the new car is split between all copies sold. Hence *when ideas are embodied in physical goods, nonrivalry is only partial, and the real-world economics of ideas is a mix of nonrival and traditional physical goods economics.*

With computers and the internet, the need for a physical carrier disappears. Ideas, once encoded in electronic bits, can be disseminated instantaneously everywhere. They really become ubiquitous and accessible at a quasi-zero

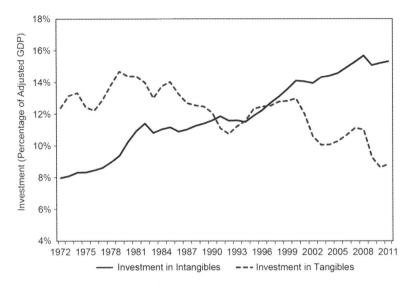

Fig. 9.4   Business investment in intangible and tangible capital, United States, 1972–2011 (percentage of adjusted GDP)

Source: OECD, based on unpublished update on C. A. Corrado and C. R. Hulten, "How Do You Measure a 'Technological Revolution?,'" *American Economic Review: Papers and Proceedings* 100 (May 2010): 99–104.

Note: Estimates are for private industries excluding real estate, health, and education.

marginal cost: we move from partial nonrivalry to total nonrivalry, which we refer to here as DNR in order to differentiate from broader-based nonrivalry and stress that its realization is tied to digitalization. With DNR, there are no more limits and delays on the diffusion of ideas: it suffices to access the site where they are presented, possibly to download a file.

9.3.2   The Growing Importance of Digital Nonrivalry

The effects of DNR have become increasingly important because of the growing importance of intangible investments over tangibles. In the United States, business investment in intangibles has risen almost continuously for the past 40 years, starting with the electronics revolution of the 1970s and increasing its pace over the past decades (Nakamura 2001). In the 2000s, intangible investments have become relatively more important than tangibles (figure 9.4). Among intangibles, computer software—a component of intangible investments—has been among the most dynamically increasing parts (Corrado, Hulten, and Sichel 2005, 2009). Until recently, official statistics have not accounted well for the large changes; Corrado, Hulten, and Sichel (2009) estimated that the omission of such investments from published macroeconomic data has consequently led to underestimates of USD 800 billion (as of 2003), excluding more than USD 3 trillion of business intangible capital stock.

A. IT-related industries

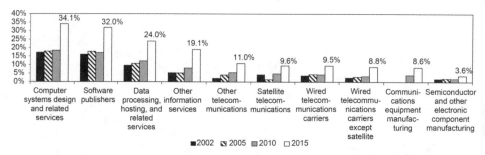

B. Other industries, 2015

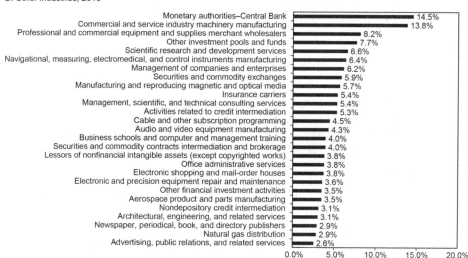

Fig. 9.5   Share of employment in software-related occupations within industries in the United States, 2002, 2005, 2010, and 2015

Source: US Bureau of Labor Statistics (2016), Occupational Employment Statistics (OES) Survey, Department of Labor.

Note: Panel B reports the share of employment in software for industries in which the share is higher than 2 percent of total employment. Industries are provided at the four-digit NAICS 2012. The data appendix describes the occupations included as software related.

The effects of DNR are also widespread across the economy because digital innovation is increasingly relevant across many other industries. Branstetter, Drev, and Kwon (2015), for instance, show that between 1981 and 2005, IT assets have become increasingly critical in production in "traditional" sectors such as automobiles, aerospace and defense, medical devices, and pharmaceuticals. Spending on software increased substantially over time, and software engineers represent an increasingly important share in employment not only in telecommunications, software, and hardware industries but also in other industries, such as finance, business services, machinery manufacturing, and other information-provider services (figure 9.5).

9.4   Impacts of Digital Innovation on the Economies of Scale and Market Concentration

9.4.1   Implications of Digital Nonrivalry for Market Concentration on Global Markets

DNR allows for massive economies of scale that favor market concentration, because with DNR, the marginal cost of diffusion is also zero for the producers: the more products sold, the lower the average cost. Once the idea has been produced and formatted, there is no need to print copies or assemble embodying objects; it is enough to upload the idea to a website, and it becomes accessible to all with a computer and an internet connection. The marginal cost of delivering it to customers is null; hence the unit cost declines linearly with the quantity sold. If a digital product succeeds on the market, the production volume can quickly adapt to demand, and sales can increase while unit costs decrease. Producers will aim to supply the entire market. Such phenomena have been observed in many industries under various names, such as "blockbusters" (pharmaceuticals, movies, aeronautics) or "superstars" (sports). In such conditions, companies with a large pool of customers have an advantage in cost over competitors, which can result in natural monopolies.

Mass production in manufacturing as developed in the Fordist model of production lowered marginal cost compared to specialized production in the previous, craftsmanship-based model. However, the marginal cost was still positive. By contrast, the marginal cost of producing knowledge-intensive products (beyond the first unit) is essentially zero. A corollary of this idea is that investments are largely used to produce "originals"—that is, to innovate, not to produce more copies of the same template. This amounts to the pure fixed costs and zero marginal costs textbook case that is an absolute exception for most production processes—except for information goods, for which it is the baseline case (Varian 2003).

On the process side, IT has lowered communication costs, hence raising the efficient size of firms whatever their industry. It is possible with IT to coordinate highly segmented and dispersed value chains of very large size. This factor is pushing toward higher market concentration in all industries. Evidence collected by Mueller, Simintzi, and Ouimet (2015) shows that the average size of the largest firms has increased significantly in 14 of the 15 countries they studied between the mid-1980s or mid-1990s and 2010. The average size of the top 50 (100) firms in the United States grew by 55.8 percent (53.0 percent) between 1986 and 2010.

Hence IT coupled with globalization have transformed both product markets and production processes in the direction of favoring large size and concentration. Brynjolfsson et al. (2007) show evidence of higher market concentration for more IT intensive industries for 1996–2006 compared to the previous period of 1987–95 (figure 9.6).

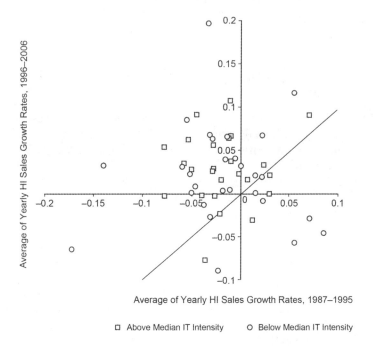

Fig. 9.6   Growth in market concentration of more and less IT-intensive industries, 1996–2006 and 1987–95

Source: Brynjolfsson et al. (2007) based on Compustat.

Note: HI refers to the Herfindahl index of firms' sales.

In markets for digital innovation, economies of scale are reinforced by several factors that foster market concentration and opportunities for smaller-scale producers to challenge incumbents: first-mover advantage, reputation effects, IPR, network effects, and product bundling, whereby different products are sold jointly, as the marginal cost is negligible. There are also opportunities for smaller-scale producers, as discussed in the next section. The expression "scale without mass" (Brynjolfsson et al. 2007) captures a closely connected idea, that it takes little time and investment for a small company (in terms of the number of employees) to become a global behemoth (in terms of turnover), as digital goods can be reproduced at the cost of a click.

A consequence of such economies of scale is the emergence of winner-take-all market structures—that is, markets with highly asymmetric market shares (Rosen 1981). The market dynamics are akin to tournaments, in which the best offer wins the race and captures most (if not all) of the market. The winner's product may only be marginally better than the alternatives, but a market with no substantial distribution costs and where up-scaling is nearly instantaneous (for instance, by distributing services on the internet) gives the winning innovation the opportunity to gain most of the market quickly. The Economic Census shows high rates of concentration for some of the markets closely associated with the digital economy and the economies of scale it allows for. For instance, among business-to-business electronic market providers, the top four providers held 34 percent of the sales 2012 (North American Industry Classification System [NAICS] code 42511). By contrast, the average share of the top four businesses in the wholesale business (NAICS code 42) was 5.6 percent.

Winner-take-all market effects are a well-known phenomenon in innovation-intensive markets. The value distribution of innovations has been shown to be very skewed. Only a few innovations are of high value, while most provide little gain: this has been measured, for instance, using the monetary evaluation given by patent holders to their titles (Harhoff, Scherer, and Vopel 2003) and in terms of the number of citations and other measures of patent quality (see, e.g., OECD 2015b). This results from a few firms dominating markets for those innovations. This tendency is accentuated by digital innovation.

Concurrent with digital innovation, globalization favors market concentration, as lower barriers to operating across borders allow for the emergence of a few global leaders (instead of a multiplicity of national ones) that benefit from the larger scale offered by global markets. This is illustrated by IT sectors with global leaders such as Google and Amazon but also across other more traditional industries in which digital innovation has become increasingly important (in product or in processes), such as pharmaceuticals, automobiles, or chemicals.

Assessing the market shares of these global actors is challenging, as national-level data only capture resident firms but not all market competitors. As an imperfect proxy, figure 9.7 computes the shares of the top 1 and 5 global companies among the 2,500 top R&D companies across different sectors; the evidence shows strong levels of concentration in some of the very dynamic sectors that are highly associated with digital innovation—notably software and computer services, financial services, and electronic and electrical equipment. Figure 9.8 plots the market shares of software and computer services against those of heavy industries.

9.4.2   Rents in Global Knowledge-Intensive Markets

Digital innovations generate higher rents than other innovations. The fact that successful innovators raise rents is not new; it was conceptualized in 1911 by Schumpeter. It is a necessary condition for innovation to occur. What is new is the scale at which this is happening, as reflected in large profit margins in sectors where digital innovation is important. Health technology, technology services, and electronic services were first, third, and fourth in the Forbes 2015 ranking of most profitable sectors, with profit margins of 20.9 percent, 16.1 percent, and 13.2 percent, respectively (finance was in second position, with margins of 17.3 percent; Forbes 2015). Aggregate

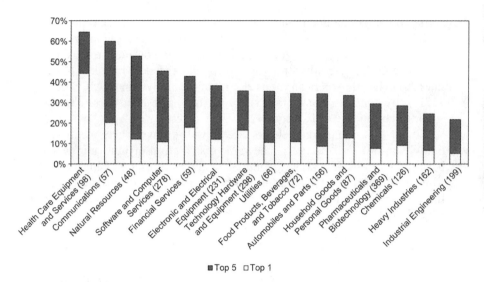

■ Top 5　□ Top 1

Fig. 9.7　Share of the top 1 and 5 companies in total sales of leading R&D firms in 2015

Source: EU (2016), EU R&D Scoreboard 2016. The shares are computed as the sales share of the top 1 and 5 firms within the total number of firms of the 2,500 R&D most-intensive firms of the EU R&D Scoreboard. The number of firms included in the total for each sector is included in brackets.

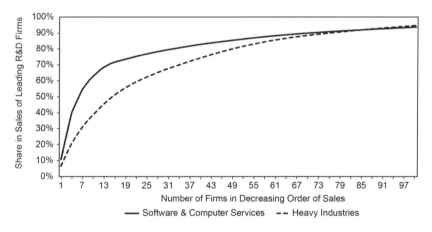

Fig. 9.8　Distribution of the 100 largest firms in terms of sales among the top R&D firms within the software and computer services and heavy industries sectors in 2015

Source: EU (2016), EU R&D Scoreboard 2016.

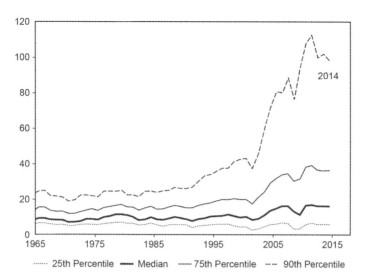

Fig. 9.9   Return on invested capital excluding goodwill, US publicly traded nonfinancial firms

Source: Furman and Orszag (2015) based on Koller, Goedhart, and Wessels (2015).

statistics also show that in the United States, the share of corporate profits in income increased (see figure 9.13 in section 9.5).

The evolution of firm profits is also consistent with increasingly winner-take-all market structures: the top percentiles of firms ranked by return on invested capital (ROIC) have grown most significantly, from less than 30 percent in the early 1990s to 100 percent in 2014 (figure 9.9). The lowest percentiles (25th) had a constant ROIC, and the median increased slightly. Data collected by McKinsey suggest that "two thirds of the non-financial firms with an average ROIC of 45% or higher between 2010 and 2014 were in either the health care or the IT sectors" (Furman and Orszag 2015). Other suggestive evidence of more winner-take-all dynamics is the rise in the share of nominal GDP of the Fortune 100 biggest American companies from 33 percent in 1994 to 46 percent in 2013 (*The Economist* 2016). Players closely associated with the digital economy have gained in importance in this ranking. Those in traditional industries in which digital innovation has become more important also rank highly.

Several supply- and demand-side characteristics favor incumbents' rents. On the supply side, economies of scale in knowledge-intensive products feed efficiency and consequently firms' market shares. One reason is that it is often not straightforward for followers to imitate a successful product immediately. Also, the advance over competitors allows first movers to hire the most skilled and creative workers (who in turn benefit from interacting with equally productive peers). Moreover, in various markets, economies of scope strengthen incumbents' market positions, as in the extreme case of platforms (e.g., Amazon, Apple, Facebook, or Google). These are best placed to launch new products or to profitably scale up existing ones (possibly invented by other firms that platforms will acquire and integrate), as they have a large consumer base that competitors cannot easily match. Owing to standards and reputation effects, products do not travel easily across platforms, and entry for competitors is restrained. Hence while technically newcomers might scale at little cost, they may not get the rewards unless they access leading platforms. These supply side conditions shape the extent to which new entrants can challenge incumbents.

On the demand side, a firm's or product's reputation often influences consumer choice in favor of incumbents; these constraints reduce entrants' opportunities to successfully penetrate markets in spite of the low product scaling costs. The market success of a product can stimulate further sales by incumbent producers, hence reducing opportunities for new entrants. Also, the technical complexity of certain knowledge products magnifies incumbents' advantage, because greater complexity increases the information asymmetry between consumers and producers; consumers prefer to buy from sellers with a specific brand with high reputations as a guarantee that the product is of good quality. Moreover, network effects—that is, product value for each user increasing with the number of users—matter in core sectors of the digital economy. Examples include software programs (the number of users of the software and its interoperability), social networks (the number of friends/colleagues/partners to communicate with), online auctions (the number of bidders and sellers), and internet search engines.[2] Ownership of big data is also an increasingly important source advantage for incumbents, as competitors can only obtain the same quality of data with difficulty. The advantage of data ownership is increasing as, for instance, machine-learning algorithms become more intelligent with larger access to data, reinforcing the advantage of incumbents with access to such data.

Regulatory and policy conditions, including with IPR and standards, are also critical. In allowing firms to protect their digital innovations, they create barriers for competition. There is, consequently, much scope for policy to influence market concentration. Standards, which may restrict entry at the same time as they may enable innovation, also apply more where production processes make intense use of digital innovations.

Certain factors may limit market concentration. One factor is the diversity

---

2. In the case of internet search engines, the network effects are indirect—that is, one group of users benefits from larger uptake by another group of users. Internet search engines offer users access to information to attract advertising revenues from firms, which they use to develop their services to attract the largest possible number of users. Pricing and other strategies are strongly affected by indirect network effects. For example, profit-maximizing prices may entail below-marginal cost pricing to one set of customers over the long run. In fact, many two-sided platforms charge one side prices that are below cost and sometimes even negative. Thus rents are not observed directly, as would be the case for single-client markets.

of consumers' tastes, which can lead to fragmented markets and monopolistic competition "à la Chamberlin" instead of large winner-take-all markets. However, digital innovation may make product differentiation less costly, allowing companies to extend their control beyond small niche markets by supplying different market segments, chasing potential competitors from their respective domains. Another and more important factor that limits market concentration comes from new entry and creative destruction that arises with lower costs of digital innovation, as discussed next.

9.5   Impacts of Digital Innovation on the Costs of Innovation, Market Entry, and Creative Destruction

This section discusses how digital innovation's effect on the costs of innovating may trigger a more rapid displacement of existing products, increasing the risk for firms to lose market revenue. Creative destruction and market entry may also reduce the market concentration DNR has facilitated.

9.5.1   Lower Entry Costs for Digital Innovations Allow for More Creative Destruction

The costs of innovating have been reduced in a number of ways with digital innovation. First, IT has lowered entry costs compared to many markets, including the costs of producing, managing, and communicating new knowledge (see, e.g., Paunov and Rollo 2016 for evidence of the use of the internet on firm innovation in developing countries). For instance, the emergence of "the cloud" has done away with large upfront investment, giving access to computing power at a low price. Second, the downstream costs of innovating—that is, the costs of producing and disseminating digital innovations—are reduced or even disappear with DNR. Using digital means for advertising and distributing a product (e.g., opening a web page on Amazon) also allows producers of physical goods to reduce marketing costs; they can reach the global market without having to incur large, sunk investment in branding and so on. This is even more the case for some of the most dynamic digital knowledge products, such as software and online services, which can be distributed directly on the internet (no transportation cost). Third, scaling costs are also lower for digital innovations, as they are immediately scalable and can reach an unlimited number of customers. Opportunities to "scale without mass" (i.e., the production of goods and services that require many fewer labor and capital inputs relative to traditional "tangible" products, as a large share of the product is intangible) extend beyond pure digital products (such as software or pure online services).

The lower cost of commercializing innovations allows for more market entry and creative destruction at a more rapid pace, increasing incumbents' risk to lose most if not all market revenue. Even where new products provide only minor improvements relative to existing ones, they may challenge

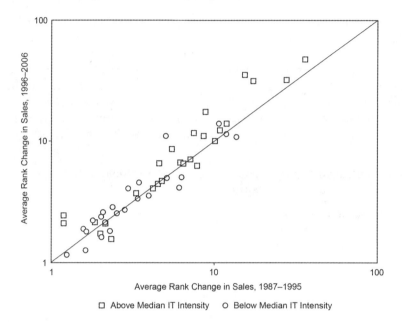

Fig. 9.10   Creative destruction in high- and low-IT-intensive sectors, 1996–2006 and 1987–95
Source: Brynjolfsson et al. (2008) based on Compustat.

incumbents. In the traditional industrial economy, even minor changes to a product would mean incurring significant costs to reach customers (retooling, marketing, etc.). With the digital economy, the main cost of introducing a new product is the cost of invention, as production and marketing costs are low or even nil. Invention costs themselves may also be low in the case of weak differentiation (technical similarity). Yet businesses facing low downstream production costs may launch marginally improved products on the market as in winner-take-all contexts; even innovations with only a marginal advantage over competing products may gain all the market. This reinforces the impact of the reduction in cost on the incentive to launch new innovations. Technical change, however, may not be more rapid overall, as it depends on total research effort. Appendix A provides a simple model of the impacts of cost reductions for digital innovations on the sequencing of innovation.

There is evidence that digital innovation has indeed increased risk that firms face in markets. Brynjolfsson et al. (2007) show that "creative destruction" (i.e., changes in firms' rank of sales in their respective industries) was more important in more IT-intensive industries following the mid-1990s (figure 9.10). Statistics on the volatility of stock market valuations of traded US companies show a similar increase over the 1990s and continued high levels from then onward (figure 9.11).

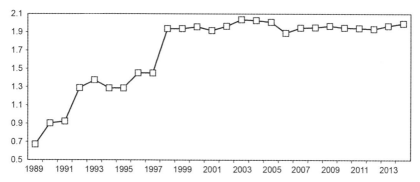

Fig. 9.11   Stock market volatility of traded US-based companies, 1989–2014
Source: Bas, Paunov, and Rodriguez-Montemayor (2017) based on Compustat.
Note: The figure plots the median standard deviation of the annual stock market price of US-based traded firms.

Volatility measures of financial investments also point to higher risk in more innovation-intensive sectors: betas (that estimate investment volatility) are higher than 1 (indicating greater risk compared to the entire market) in the biotechnology, internet, computer, and electrical equipment industries, while less knowledge-intensive industries, such as food processing and tobacco, display betas lower than 1 (figure 9.12). Also, Faurel et al. (2015) show that US firms registering more new trademarks faced higher volatility of stock market return and earnings for the 1993–2011 period.

9.5.2   Impacts of Market Entry and Creative Destruction on Market Concentration

Market concentration and creative destruction are not in contradiction with each other in markets where competition is based on digital innovation. In such markets, competition is not about prices—in which case, the threat from new entry would discipline the incumbents—but about radical product innovation, as successful new products fully displace existing ones, taking over the market no matter the price charged by incumbents. This also means that until the next innovation comes, incumbents keep their market position and do not have to bother about competition. The massive scale economies combined with business strategies that allow retention of market power allow winners to reap rents until they are replaced by successful challengers.

While the evidence shows that market concentration has increased with digital innovation—that is, that the current context is one where market concentration and creative destruction coexist—the threat of market entry and creative destruction may also reduce market concentration. The extent to which market concentration is reduced depends on technology, business strategies, and policy. Where technology brings radical change, newcomers can challenge incumbents more than where incumbents can rely on master-

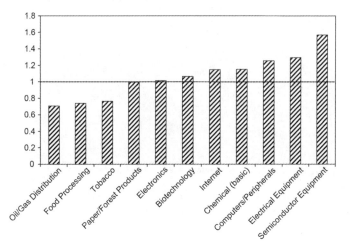

Fig. 9.12   Estimates of selected sectors' betas relative to the entire financial market for US firms in 2008–12

Source: Damodaran (2015) based on data from Bloomberg, Morningstar, Capital IQ, and Compustat.

Note: The beta of a sector is a measure of the volatility, or systematic risk, of a financial investment in a sector in comparison to the financial market as a whole. The betas are estimated by regressing weekly returns on stock of companies within a sector against a benchmark index representative of the financial market, which is the NYSE composite index. Regressions are based on data within a time window of five years previous to the reference year. The beta is unlevered by the market value debt-to-equity ratio for the sector making use of the following formula: Unlevered Beta = Beta / (1 + (1 – tax rate) (Debt/Equity Ratio)). The unlevered beta is the beta that would be obtained if the investment was on a company without any debt. The risk of an investment is, in general, higher when the ratio between debt and equity within a sector is higher. In this way, the focus is on the level of risk, which is only driven by the characteristics of the sector other than the financial structure of companies within the sector. Further details can be found at http://pages.stern.nyu.edu/~adamodar/.

ing the technology. For instance, traditional car manufacturers find themselves confronted with new business models such as the one implemented by Uber, which provides car sharing as an alternative to car ownership. Also, where incumbents have fewer opportunities to exploit network effects, platform dominance, leading technical standards, and data access,[3] more competitive market conditions may result. The latter critically depends on policy (including antitrust, entrepreneurship, and IPR).

Creative destruction may be challenged on winner-take-all markets because winning comes with advantages that allow incumbents to retain rents for at least a period of time. Particularly large market players benefit from economies of scale and scope and often from network economies. These provide them with the capital and networks needed to capitalize on

---

3. In the digital economy, data are the primary input for many innovations and services. This is reinforced in more recent technologies like artificial intelligence.

and upscale innovations. This includes the advantages large incumbents can reap from big data with better tools to make use of them. These may contribute to the marginalization of small players by a feedback loop, whereby better data allow better services, further enhancing their advantage. Moreover, in consolidated markets, incumbents have succeeded in establishing their products as essentials (as, for instance, is the case for different digital platforms). In this context, challengers develop new, more radical innovations but do not immediately replace winners. Anecdotal evidence shows that most of the many new entrants are quickly pushed out of the market (see, e.g., Decker et al. 2014 for evidence on the United States).

While start-up failure is not surprising in itself—as new business ideas usually have higher failure rates—the issue is that among the successful ones, most are taken over by incumbents. Examples include YouTube (acquired by Google) or Instagram and WhatsApp (both acquired by Facebook). This is also the case in other industries like biotechnology, where most successful start-ups are taken over by big pharmaceutical firms that increasingly act like platforms, which possess unique marketing and financial infrastructures and can externalize the most exploratory innovation to start-ups that they acquire when successful. While these acquisitions reduce competition and creative destruction, they may contribute to increasing the efficiency of industry ecosystems, as good radical innovations developed in small firms can create more value once deployed at larger scale.

9.6   How Do Rents Generated by Higher Market Concentration and Greater Risk Affect the Distribution of Income?

This section discusses how changes in market structures and risk brought by digital innovation have affected the distribution of income. It describes the mechanisms accounting for higher returns to the top of the income distribution—resulting in higher returns to capital, top executives, and top employees but less to average workers. The mechanisms explain aggregate findings by Forbes (2000) on the correlation between higher growth across US states and higher levels of income inequality and returns to the top 1 percent and 10 percent and by Aghion et al. (2015) on differences in innovation intensities and higher returns to the top 1 percent.

9.6.1   Effects of Digital Innovation on the Distribution of Income

The impact channel of digital innovation on the distribution of income that has been discussed in the literature is about complementary or substitutability to different types of labor. The debate, which dates back to the industrial revolution, has aimed at identifying whether technological change is skill-biased or not (see Haskel et al. 2012). More related to digital innovation, several studies have investigated the substitution effects of automation, specifically with regards to routinized operations that machines can easily execute (see Goos and Manning 2007; Autor and Dorn 2013; Michaels, Natraj, and Van Reenen 2014). Also, Acemoglu and Restrepo (2016) show a robust negative effect of the adoption of robots on employment and wages. As to effects on pay of top income groups, Haskel and Westlake (2017) discuss how the rise of intangibles in the economy—closely related to an increase in digital innovation—may also result in superstar pay for managers and other key employees.

The channel linking digital innovation to the distribution of income we discuss herein is different and stems from digital innovations' impacts on market structures. It does not relate to how capital and labor complement or substitute for digital innovation. Winner-take-all market structures affect the distribution of income in two ways. First, market concentration results in higher market rents. This affects the distribution of income due to important differences in the negotiation power of different claimants to these rents, including investors, top executives, and different workers. Second, higher market risk as generated by more creative destruction results in higher compensation for risk takers (owners, investors, and executives). The specific implications for different input factors and the evidence are discussed below.

9.6.2   Higher Returns to Capital Invested in the Digital Economy

Winner-take-all market conditions have resulted in higher returns to the capital affecting the distribution of income as capital ownership is concentrated among the highest income groups (Atkinson 2015). The returns to capital invested in digital innovation increase because the market rents are mainly captured by the residual claimants, who are the investors and managers, while employees' wages are largely fixed in the labor market. "Efficiency wage" mechanisms ensure that some of the rent goes to employees. Rents are not necessarily "excessive"—that is, higher than required—from an incentive/efficiency perspective. Investors require a risk premium to invest, as market risk is higher with more creative destruction.

An indicative piece of evidence of more rents for investors and owners is that over the past decades, corporate profits have increased while interest rates have decreased (figure 9.13). If there were no rents, then corporate profits would follow the path of interest rates, as these reflect the returns to capital in the economy. Barkai (2016) also documents a substantial increase in the profit share of US businesses over the past 30 years. Recent work by de Loecker and Eeckhout (2017) also shows that markups and market power increased since the 1980s.

As pointed out by Kornai (2016), anecdotal evidence from the Forbes 400 richest individuals includes a number of key actors of digital innovation: Bill Gates (Microsoft), Larry Ellison (Oracle), Michael Bloomberg (Bloomberg), Mark Zuckerberg (Facebook), Larry Page and Sergey Brin (Google), and Jeffrey Bezos (Amazon).

The evolution of top income share has been a capital-driven phenomenon

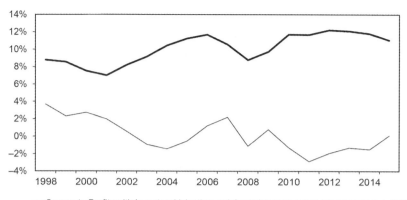

━━ Corporate Profits with Inventory Valuation and Capital Consumption Adjustments over GDI
── 1-Year Real US Treasury Rate

Fig. 9.13   Corporate profits and real interest rates (in percentages) for 1985–2015

Source: Based on data on corporate profits and the GDI from the Bureau of Economic Analysis, Bureau of Labor Statistics published May 27, 2016. Data on the one-year real US Treasury rate are taken from the US Treasury (http://www.multpl.com/1-year-treasury-rate/table) using the CPI for the United States from the OECD Main Economic Indicators database.

since the late 1990s (Piketty, Saez, and Zucman 2016). Data for 2000–2014 show that growth of average income per adult owed mostly to growth in capital income, which grew by 2.2 percent per year, while labor income grew by 0.1 percent per year.

Investigating the relationship between profits and the top 1 percent income, figure 9.14 shows the evolution of median and average profits of US stock-market-traded firms for 1992–2013 and pretax income for the top 1 percent and the middle 40 percent. Figure 9.15 shows a strong positive correlation between the growth rates of the top 1 percent income and profit: 0.48 (for the median) and 0.51 (for the average). By contrast, correlation between the middle 40 percent income and profits is lower (of 0.12 for the median and of 0.24 for the average). This suggests that the evolution of profits influences income inequality, as it benefits the top 1 percent but not others.

Bas, Paunov, and Rodriguez-Montemayor (2017) show that markets characterized by higher concentration and volatility (to proxy for risk) are associated with higher profits (column 1 of table 9.1). Market volatility benefits profit more than wages but less than executive pay (columns 2 and 3 of table 9.1). These results are obtained for the following specification:

$$(1) \qquad \Pi_{ijt} = \alpha + \beta_{herf} * Sh\_Top5_{jt-1} + \beta_{vol} * Volatility_{jt-1} + \Gamma * X_{ijt} + \Lambda$$

$$* J_{jt} + \tau_{st} + \lambda_i + \lambda_t + \varepsilon_{ijt},$$

where Π_{ijt} stands for the log profits as well as the profit-to-wage and profit-to-executive-pay ratios. *Sh_Top5* and *Volatility*, respectively, refer to the

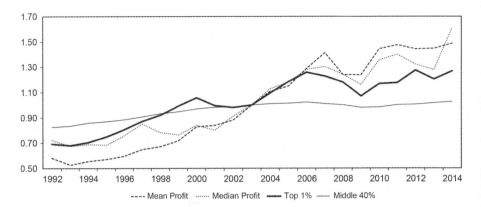

Fig. 9.14   Evolution of profits of publicly traded US-based firms and the US pretax income of the top 1 percent and middle 40 percent, 1992–2014 (2003 = 1)

Note: Profit data are computed using data for publicly traded firms in all industry and service sectors with the exception of the mining, quarrying, and oil and gas extraction sector (NAICS 21), excluding in this way the influence of the price of natural resources on the trend, and NAICS sectors 55–92.

Source: Bas, Paunov, and Rodriguez-Montemayor (2017), based on Compustat for profits, and Piketty, Saez, and Zucman (2016) for pretax income of the top 1 percent and middle 40 percent.

share of the top 5 percent of firms and the standard deviation of firms' stock market valuations for industry *j* at time *t* – 1. The specification includes time trends across industry sectors (τ_{st}) to control for sector-specific time trends that may affect executive pay and correlate with changing market dynamics. The authors also include firm fixed effects (λ_i) and year fixed effects (λ_t) to isolate any time-invariant unobservable differences in pay across industries, firms, and executives and year-specific shocks to executive pay from our estimates. J_{jt} is a vector of industry controls that includes industry size and capital intensity. X_{ijt} is a vector of firm observable characteristics varying over time that includes firm size, profit margins, and revenue.

9.6.3   The Declining Return to Labor

A corollary of higher returns to capital is the decreasing share of labor in value added in many OECD countries over the past three decades (figure 9.16). Official statistics from the US Bureau of Labor Statistics show a decline of the share of labor in the United States from 64 percent—a value that stayed constant from the immediate post–Second World War period—to 58 percent from the mid-1980s onward (Elsby, Hobijn, and Şahin 2013).[4] Official statistics may underestimate the decrease in the labor share because

---

4. Karabarbounis and Neiman (2014) also show that the share of corporate gross value added paid to labor declined by 5 percentage points for 59 economies over 1975–2012. Using industry-level data, Alvarez-Cuadrado, Van Long, and Poschke (2014) find that the income share from labor has declined in all but 3 of a set of 16 industrialized economies over the same period.

A. Average

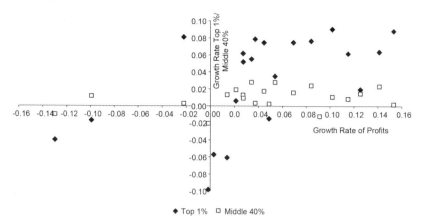

B. Median

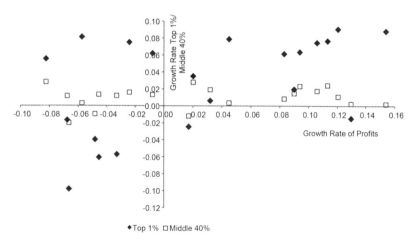

Fig. 9.15   Correlation of annual growth rates of profits and the average top 1 percent and middle 40 percent of the US pretax incomes, 1992–2014

Source: Bas, Paunov, and Rodriguez-Montemayor (2017), based on data on corporate profits from Compustat, and Piketty, Saez, and Zucman (2016) for pretax income of the top 1 percent and middle 40 percent. Growth rates are computed on real income and profits, applying the same deflator as described in Piketty, Saez, and Zucman (2016).

intangibles are not adequately accounted for in capital. Corrado, Hulten, and Sichel (2009) show that the USD 1 trillion increase in GDP (in 1999) arising from addition of intangible investment to GDP results in an equal increase in gross domestic income (GDI), all of which accrued to the owners of capital, consequently decreasing the share of labor income.

Several pieces of evidence point to a role of digital innovation in account-

Table 9.1   Impacts of market dynamics on profits

Dependent variables:	Profits$_{ft}$ (1)	Profit to wage ratio$_{ft}$ (2)	Profit to executive pay ratio$_{ft}$ (3)
Concentration $(s, t-1)$	0.181*	0.202	−0.253
	(0.103)	(0.150)	(0.222)
Volatility $(s, t-1)$	0.024	0.118***	−0.102***
	(0.018)	(0.031)	(0.036)
Firm controls	Yes	Yes	Yes
Industry controls	Yes	Yes	Yes
Industry-time trend	Yes	Yes	Yes
Firm fixed effects	Yes	Yes	Yes
Year fixed effects	Yes	Yes	Yes
Observations	44,570	10,039	9,584
R^2	0.95	0.86	0.76

Source: Bas, Paunov, and Rodriguez-Montemayor (2017) based on ExecuComp and Compustat for 1992–2013.

Notes: Market concentration is measured using the share of the top 5 percent of firms in total industry sales while market volatility is measured as the average annual standard deviation of firms' stock market value at the 6-digit NAICS industry level. See Bas, Paunov, and Rodriguez-Montemayor (2017) for a description of the other variables used in this estimation. Robust standards errors corrected for clustering at the 6-digit-industry-year level are reported in parentheses. *** $p < .01$, ** $p < .05$, * $p < .1$.

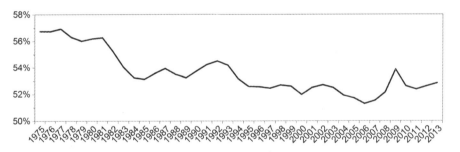

Fig. 9.16   Labor share in value added for the OECD-21 in percentages, 1975–2013
Source: OECD National Accounts Database.
Note: The figure shows statistics for the following 21 OECD countries with available data: Australia, Austria, Belgium, Denmark, Finland, France, Germany, Greece, Ireland, Italy, Japan, Luxembourg, Mexico, the Netherlands, Norway, Portugal, Republic of Korea, Spain, Sweden, the United Kingdom, and the United States.

ing for those changes. First, figure 9.17 shows that the labor share in the United States decreased significantly in the more R&D-intensive sectors but not in the least R&D-intensive sectors. Also, Koh, Santaeulàlia-Llopis, and Zheng (2015) show that the lowering of the labor share in the United States over the past three decades stems mainly from an increase in the income share of knowledge capital—that is, IPR and software and not physical capital. Related evidence comes from Karabarbounis and Neiman (2014), who

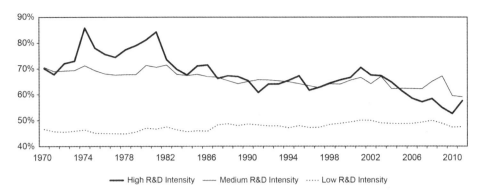

Fig. 9.17 Labor share of industry value added in the United States by sectoral R&D intensity in percentages, 1971–2011

Source: OECD STAN Database.

Note: Labor share of income is measured as labor costs (compensation of employees) over value added. Sectors are assigned to R&D intensity categories following OECD "OECD Taxonomy of Economic Activities Based on R&D Intensity," OECD Science, Technology and Industry Working Papers, No. 2016/04. (Paris OECD, 2016). The "medium R&D intensity sectors" category combines the medium-high-, medium-, and medium-low-intensity sectors.

find that countries and industries experiencing larger declines in the relative price of investment—a development mainly due to IT investments—had larger declines in labor shares.

Second, table 9.2 provides regression results for 27 OECD countries over 1995–2007 that show more direct evidence on the effects of innovation, following the methodology first proposed by Rajan and Zingales (1998). In our context, we compare the trends in labor share of income, concentration, and firms' mobility between industries that are relatively more and less dependent on R&D investments as a function of country level innovation, controlling for both industry- and country-year effects. The advantage of this approach is that it avoids cross-country comparison (which is more subject to endogeneity concerns deriving from omitted variables biases). The estimated regression is as follows:

$$(2) \quad Y_{cjt} = \beta_0 + \beta_1(Patenting_{ct} * Patent \ Int_j) + \beta_2(Graduates_{ct} * Skill \ Int_j)$$

$$+ \beta_3(Capital_{ct} * Capital \ Int_j) + \beta_4(Finance_{ct} * Intang \ Int_j)$$

$$+ \beta_5(Trade_{ct} * Transport_j) + \beta_6(Union \ Density_{ct} * Low \ Skilled \ Share_j)$$

$$+ \beta_7(GDP_{ct} * K \ Int_j) + u_{cj} + \eta_{ct} + \varepsilon_{cjt}$$

where Y_{cjt} is the labor share and β_1 is our coefficient of interest, indicating the effect of innovation—proxied for by patenting at country level and interacted with industry patent intensity—on the labor share. We also test for the effects of other factors that may be correlated with innovation and affect

Table 9.2   **Evidence on the impacts of innovation on the labor share from industry data for 1995–2011 across 27 OECD countries**

Dependent variable	Industry labor compensation over value added				
	(1)	(2)	(3)	(4)	(5)
Patents$_c$ * Patent intensity$_{ind}$	−0.054*	−0.056*	−0.068**	−0.058**	−0.064**
	(0.032)	(0.030)	(0.028)	(0.028)	(0.027)
Graduates$_c$ * Skill intensity$_{ind}$		−0.202*	−0.201*	−0.183*	−0.184*
		(0.115)	(0.116)	(0.110)	(0.106)
Capital$_c$ * Capital intensity$_{ind}$		0.038	0.068	0.043	0.009
		(0.421)	(0.419)	(0.423)	(0.430)
Finance$_c$ * Intangible assets$_{ind}$		−0.336**	−0.349**	−0.336**	−0.324**
		(0.145)	(0.143)	(0.145)	(0.145)
Trade$_c$ * Transport equipment$_{ind}$			0.196*	0.178	0.128
			(0.115)	(0.112)	(0.113)
Union Density$_c$ * Low-skill intensity$_{ind}$				0.007*	0.008*
				(0.004)	(0.004)
GDP$_c$ * Capital intensity$_{ind}$					0.393
					(0.317)
Country-year fixed effects	Yes	Yes	Yes	Yes	Yes
Industry-year fixed effects	Yes	Yes	Yes	Yes	Yes
Observations	4,070	4,070	4,070	4,070	4,070
R^2	0.25	0.26	0.26	0.27	0.27

Source: Regressions based on data from the OECD MSTI and STAN databases.

Notes: Regressions use data for 16 manufacturing industries in 27 countries and over a period of 17 years between 1995 and 2011. Both dependent and independent country-level variables are in logarithms. Industry-level exposure variables are normalized. As a consequence, coefficients are interpretable as difference in the elasticity of the dependent variable, to changes in the country-level variables, between industries with maximum exposure and industries with minimum exposure. Therefore, the coefficient on Patents$_{ct}$ * Patent intensity$_{ind}$ in column (5) reads as follows: the difference in the elasticity of the labor share to an increase in country-level innovation (Patents), in industries with the highest patent intensity (1) compared to industries with the lowest patent intensity (0), is −0.064. For instance, if patenting doubled (increase by 100 percent), then the labor share in industries with high patent intensity would decrease by 6.4 percent more than in industries with low patent intensity. The identification is based on the hypothesis that industries that use patents more intensively have a lower labor share than industries that rely relatively less on patents. The data appendix provides definition of variables included. Robust standards errors are reported in parentheses. *** $p < .01$, ** $p < .05$, * $p < .1$.

the labor share. This includes controls of the availability of human capital, finance, and capital, as well as the importance of labor unions and trade. We also add country GDP as well as country-year and industry-year fixed effects to account for and control for other country and industry factors and their evolution over the period analyzed. The data appendix provides details of the variables we use.

Our findings show a negative relation between labor shares and patenting performance, even as the effects of finance, skills, capital, labor unions, trade, and GDP are controlled for. We also find a negative effect of a more skilled labor force on the labor share. This may also be related to labor-replacing effects of technological change. The evidence is coherent with evidence by Bassanini and Manfredi (2012), who find for industries across 25 OECD countries over the 1980–2007 period that 80 percent of intra-industry labor-share contraction can be attributed to total factor productivity growth and capital deepening.

Third, other evidence that supports our model on the effects of winner-take-all markets on the decrease in the labor share includes recent evidence by Barkai (2016) and Autor et al. (2017). Barkai (2016) finds that the decline in the labor share is due to an increase in markups, thus confirming the link between the labor share and rent sharing. Autor et al. (2017) show across different datasets for the United States and other countries that the fall in the labor market share is strongest in industries with stronger market concentration and that market concentration is stronger in more technology-intensive industries.

Digital innovation is of course not the only cause behind the decreasing labor share and higher rewards to capital. Other factors have contributed as well, including the weakening of unions (as also shown in our results in table 9.1). Also, decreasing labor returns do not automatically translate into higher rewards to capital invested in digital innovation. Some of the gap may be related to higher depreciation rates: modern forms of capital, such as computers, software, and other communication technologies, depreciate much faster than equipment of the past. Computer R&D has an estimated depreciation rate of 40 percent (Li and Hall 2016). Moreover, capital includes, aside from intangible assets, real estate, tangible capital, and capital stocks of the government sector. Bonnet et al. (2014), for instance, shows evidence of higher returns to real estate.

Finally, several measurement issues need to be addressed to adequately measure the labor share, especially as digital innovation rises in importance. This includes accounting for the contribution of intangibles to income. The gap between income accounts that take intangibles into account and those that do not widens (Corrado et al. 2009). In addition, Elsby, Hobijn, and Şahin (2013) show that the methods used to impute the labor and capital income earned by entrepreneurs, sole proprietors, and unincorporated businesses influenced the changing labor shares reported by the US Bureau of Labor Statistics. The downward trend, however, remains even if self-employment is not taken into account (Karabarbounis and Neiman 2014). The gross labor share may also be much higher than the net labor share once tax deductions are taken into account. Bridgman (2014) finds, however, that adjustments to taxes are modest for most countries, including the United States.

9.6.4   Higher Returns to Executives

Growing risk has increased the impact of managers' decisions on profits. Under stable market conditions, decisions made by managers make little dif-

Table 9.3   Share of executive compensation in net sales over 1992–2014, on average and by percentile

Sector	10th	50th	90th	Average
IT-related services	0.3%	2.0%	16.9%	6.4%
Innovation-intensive manufacturing	0.3%	1.7%	13.4%	5.4%
Finance and insurance	0.2%	1.5%	7.7%	3.5%
IT-related manufacturing	0.3%	1.3%	6.7%	2.8%
Extractive industries	0.1%	1.1%	7.6%	2.8%
Non-IT-related services	0.1%	0.5%	2.8%	1.3%
Noninnovative manufacturing	0.2%	0.6%	2.3%	1.2%
Retail and wholesale trade	0.1%	0.4%	2.0%	1.0%
Transportation	0.1%	0.4%	1.6%	0.7%

Source: Bas, Paunov, and Rodriguez-Montemayor (2017) based on ExecuComp and Compustat.
Notes: Further detail on the categorization of industries is provided in the data appendix.

ference, as market shares have some inertia and the quality of decisions can be averaged over time. In winner-take-all markets, a manager's decision that is just marginally better or worse than that of competitors can result in large gains or alternatively large losses. The mechanism operates as described by Rosen (1981) when characterizing the earnings of the most successful athletes and entertainers ("superstars"), which exceed by far the predictions of conventional models. Evidence on the rewards of executives relative to firms' net sales shows striking differences in rewards for the top 90th percentile in a few key sectors of activity: IT-related services, innovation-intensive manufacturing, and IT-related manufacturing (table 9.3). Top managers in finance and insurance and extractive industries also receive high pay; this evidence points to the role of other factors such as the financialization of the economy in explaining changes in the distribution of income.

In addition, top managers' activity is subject to information asymmetry: it is difficult to monitor their actual capacity and effort, especially where only marginal differences might make a big difference in the outcome and where market risk is high. Competition between firms to attract the best managers has consequently increased, giving top managers the ability to negotiate favorable compensation packages. For those reasons, top managers have been able to capture part of the higher rent and have seen their average pay—particularly nonwage compensation—rise much faster than other employees who have less influence on firms' performance. There is the more intensive use of high-powered incentives such as stocks and stock options that give executives a share in the company's profits, boosting the pay for the winners and, in theory, punishing losers (Lerner and Wulf 2007; Hall and Liebman 1998; Murphy 1998). More than three quarters of executive pay in 2014 were due to nonwage compensations—up from slightly more than

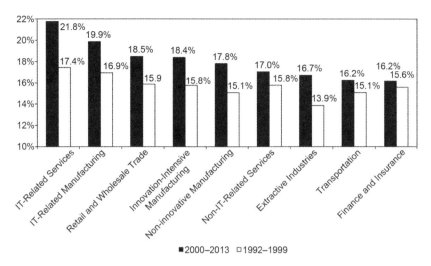

Fig. 9.18   Annual turnover rate of leading executives by sector of activity, for 1993–2013

Source: Bas, Paunov, and Rodriguez-Montemayor (2017), based on ExecuComp.
Note: Further detail on the categorization of industries is provided in the data appendix.

half in 1992. It is also these shares rather than the salary per se that explain the higher reward to top deciles during the period of the dot-com bubble.

Moreover, as is the case for investors, important nonwage compensation means that managers share in the market risks and consequently may claim higher risk compensation. One piece of evidence on risks for managers is their turnover rate. Checking the rates across sectors of activity, we find indeed that it is larger for IT and innovation-intensive activities. Over 2000–2013, top executives in IT-related services have the highest exit rate, with more than 1 in 5 leaving their position (this number may also partly reflect executives leaving for other firms as part of "poaching of the best"; figure 9.18). IT-related manufacturing is the second highest. The rate has increased relative to other sectors compared to 1993–99.

Digital innovation has evolved at the same time as top managers have seen their rewards increase, also in IT-intensive sectors. In the United States, the CEO-to-worker compensation ratio was 29.0 to 1 in 1978, grew to 122.6 to 1 in 1995, and was 272.9 to 1 in 2012 (Mishel and Sabadish 2013). An estimated 40 percent of the top 0.1 percent in the United States are managers in nonfinancial industries (Bakija et al. 2010 as quoted in CEA 2016). Top managers in sectors where digital innovation is important receive returns that are higher than expected from their industries' share in total sales (table 9.4). Executives in the IT-related services industries represented nearly one in five of the top 1 percent of executives in 2000–2014, a similar share to executives

Table 9.4   **Distribution of the top 1 percent of executives across sectors of activity**

	2000–2014		1992–99	
	Share of the top 1%	Industry share in sales	Share of the top 1%	Industry share in sales
Finance and insurance	24.9%	19.3%	26.5%	13.3%
IT-related services	24.1%	11.3%	21.4%	9.8%
IT-related manufacturing	12.4%	7.6%	9.8%	7.9%
Retail and wholesale trade	8.9%	13.0%	8.6%	13.7%
Innovation-intensive manufacturing	8.7%	7.1%	7.5%	7.9%
Extractive industries	7.4%	14.5%	3.5%	13.3%
Non-innovative manufacturing	6.9%	8.9%	9.5%	13.6%
Non-IT-related services	4.0%	7.9%	7.3%	8.5%
Transportation	2.7%	10.4%	5.9%	11.9%

Source: Bas, Paunov, and Rodriguez-Montemayor (2017) based on ExecuComp and Compustat.
Notes: Further detail on the categorization of industries is provided in the data appendix.

in finance and insurance. IT-related manufacturing is in third rank in terms of the share of top executives, above its rank in industry sales. Other sectors represent higher shares in sales than of top 1 percent executives.

Bas, Paunov, and Rodriguez-Montemayor (2017) show that winner-take-all market characteristics—that is, markets that are characterized by higher industry market concentration and market volatility (to proxy for risk)—are associated with higher pay of the top executive of US-based traded companies. Their evidence is based on the following specification:

$$(3) \quad Pay_{ifjt} = \alpha + \beta_{herf} * Sh\_Top5_{jt-1} + \beta_{vol} * Volatility_{jt-1} + \Gamma * X_{fjt} + K * Z_{ifjt}$$
$$+ \Lambda * J_{jt} + \tau_{st} + \lambda_{if} + \lambda_t + \varepsilon_{ifjt},$$

where *Pay* stands for executive *i*'s pay of firm *f* in industry *j* at time *t*. Z_{eijt} is a vector of executive-specific controls and includes the age of the executive, their tenure in the firm, and whether they are about to leave the firm (as pay may differ prior to executives' departure). Other variables are as specified for equation (1), described above.

Columns (1) and (2) of table 9.5 show a positive association between market concentration, volatility, and executive pay at both executive and firm levels. Specifically CEOs—that is managers who decide on firms' strategies (column 3)—receive higher pay on these markets. It is not the fixed-wage component but the share that varies with firm performance that is higher on more concentrated and volatility markets (column 4). This finding points to the role of risk compensation in executive pay. The effects of market concentration on executive pay are also consistent with that of Gabaix, Landier,

Table 9.5   **The impacts of market concentration and volatility on top executive compensation in the United States, 1992–2013**

Dependent variables:	Executive pay$_{ift}$ (1)	Executive pay share$_{ft}$ (2)	Executive pay$_{ift}$ CEOs vs. others (3)	Executive wage pay$_{ift}$ (4)
Concentration ($s, t - 1$)	0.474***	0.006***		−0.067
	(0.165)	(0.001)		(0.099)
Volatility ($s, t - 1$)	0.103***	0.026***		−0.006
	(0.021)	(0.007)		(0.012)
Concentration ($s, t - 1$) × CEOs			0.650**	
			(0.262)	
Concentration ($s, t - 1$) × Other executives			0.335	
			(0.255)	
Volatility ($s, t - 1$) × CEOs			0.121***	
			(0.023)	
Volatility ($s, t - 1$) × Other executives			0.091***	
			(0.022)	
P-Value of the Difference in Coefficients for Concentration			0.00	
P-Value of the Difference in Coefficients for Volatility			0.07	
Firm controls	Yes	Yes	Yes	Yes
Executive controls	Yes	No	Yes	Yes
Industry controls	Yes	Yes	Yes	Yes
Executive-firm fixed effects	Yes	No	Yes	Yes
Firm fixed effects	No	Yes	No	No
Year fixed effects	Yes	Yes	Yes	Yes
Observations	42,407	8,608	42,407	42,407
R^2	0.79	0.47	0.79	0.76

Source: Bas, Paunov, and Rodriguez-Montemayor (2017) based on ExecuComp and Compustat.

Notes: Market concentration is measured using the share of the top 5 percent of firms in total industry sales while market volatility is measured as the average annual standard deviation of firms' stock market value at the 6-digit NAICS industry level. Robust standards errors corrected for clustering at the 6-digit NAICS-year level are reported in parentheses. See Bas, Paunov, and Rodriguez-Montemayor (2017) for a description of the variables used in this estimation. Robust standards errors corrected for clustering at the 6-digit-industry-year level are reported in parentheses. *** $p < .01$, ** $p < .05$, * $p < .1$.

and Sauvagnat (2014), who show that CEOs in larger-sized firms get more pay. Although not identical, firm size and market power are correlated.

The evidence reported associates executive pay to winner-take-all market characteristics of their own industry. The rent-sharing effects should apply with regards to executives' own industry because higher pay arises from the profits generated in executives' own industry and executives' ability to negotiate shares in profits in their company. This would not be affected by market dynamics in other sectors than executives' own because rents are not transferable.

However, developments across the economy at large are also relevant to executive pay because executives may have transferable skills that can be applied in other markets. This means that the market characteristics in one sector may influence the pay in another. This is well illustrated by the Heckscher-Ohlin model that can obtain very different outcomes compared to a single-industry model (see Haskel et al. 2012). This regards executive pay compensation given in winner-take-all markets as skills that complement capital in the digital innovation economy. These effects are not adequately captured if the focus is only on developments in executives' own industry. The role of such effects is consistent with the finding in Bas, Paunov, and Rodriguez-Montemayor (2017) of strong significant effects of market dynamics across the larger industry in which executives operate. However, the effects are no longer significant if industry characteristics are also included in those regressions, suggesting that effects of market dynamics operate at the specific industry level. Evidence from the 20-year panel of executives of ExecuComp also shows that few executives switch to other industries.

Interestingly, during the "dot-com bubble" of 1999–2000, a period during which the stock market value of IT companies skyrocketed, these companies increased rewards to their executives (figure 9.19A). During the period, the total compensation of the highest-paid group increased substantially more than that of other groups. Other industries did not experience similar trends (figure 9.19B).

The trend in executive pay over 1992–2013 closely mimics the evolution of the income of the top 1 percent, similar to the evidence shown in figure 9.14 for profits. The correlation between growth rates of the top 1 percent income and executive pay is high: 0.63 (for the median) and 0.70 (for the mean). The correlation between the growth rates of the middle 40 percent and executive pay is slightly lower for both the median (0.47) and the mean (0.60; figure 9.20). This evidence suggests that executive pay influences income inequality as profits do. The stronger correlation of average compared to median executive pay suggests that the dispersion of executive pay is also related to income inequality.

Finally, evidence on the wealthiest 400 Americans is also consistent with the "superstar" explanation: Kaplan and Rauh (2013) find that in 2011 compared to 1982, the richest individuals were less likely to have grown up wealthy but had a university education and succeeded in industries— technology, finance, and mass retail—where digital innovation has driven growth. Andersson et al. (2009) show that the firms operating in the US software sector with high potential upside gains to innovation pay "star" workers, notably programmers, more than firms that operate less innovation-intensive industries.

9.6.5   Labor Compensation

Digital innovation may also be expected to increase the rewards to those employees that play a critical role in securing rents of winning firms. Emerg-

A. IT-related services and manufacturing

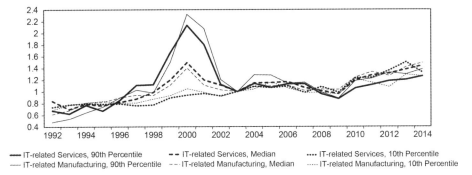

━━ IT-related Services, 90th Percentile   ― ― IT-related Services, Median   ···· IT-related Services, 10th Percentile
─── IT-related Manufacturing, 90th Percentile   ─ ─ IT-related Manufacturing, Median   ····· IT-related Manufacturing, 10th Percentile

B. Other industries (excluding IT-related manufacturing and services)

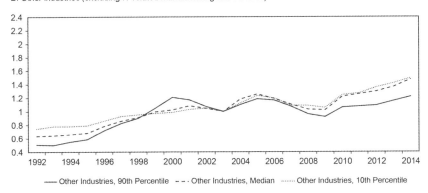

─── Other Industries, 90th Percentile   ─ ─ ─ Other Industries, Median   ········ Other Industries, 10th Percentile

Fig. 9.19   Trends in executive income by income decile for 1992–2014 (2003 = 1)
Source: Bas, Paunov, and Rodriguez-Rodriguez-Montemayor (2017), based on Compustat.
Note: Further detail on the categorization of industries is provided in the data appendix.

ing microevidence shows rent sharing with workers. Song et al. (2015), for instance, find that over 1978–2012, inequality in US labor earnings increased across firms, within industries and US states, which is suggestive of rent sharing with employees. Evidence from the United Kingdom suggests these rents are shared with more skilled workers; Mueller, Simintzi, and Ouimet (2015) find that in this country, wage differentials between high-skilled and either medium- or low-skilled jobs increase with firm size, while differentials between medium- or low-skilled jobs are either invariant to firm size or (if anything) slightly decreasing. They also identify a link between wage inequality and the average number of employees of the largest firms in Australia, Austria, Belgium, Canada, Denmark, Finland, France, Germany, Greece, Italy, the Netherlands, Spain, Sweden, the United Kingdom, and the United States over 1981–2010. Card, Heining, and Kline (2013) also find that increasing heterogeneity across firms explains over 60 percent of the growth in wage inequality across occupations and industries in West

A. Average

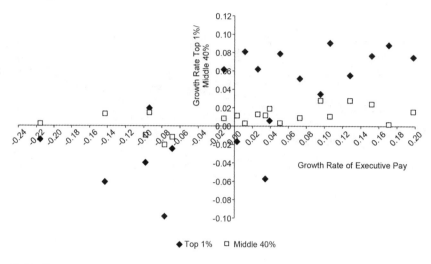

♦ Top 1%   □ Middle 40%

B. Median

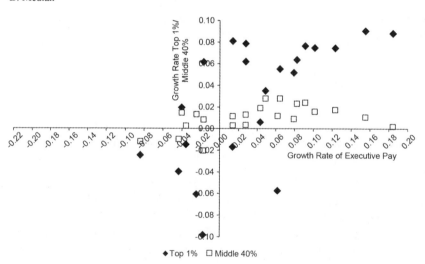

♦ Top 1%   □ Middle 40%

Fig. 9.20   Correlation of annual growth rates of executive pay and the average top 1 percent and middle 40 percent of the US pretax incomes, 1992–2014

Source: Bas, Paunov, and Rodriguez-Montemayor (2017), based on data on executive pay from ExecuComp and Piketty, Saez, and Zucman (2016) for pretax income of the top 1 percent and middle 40 percent. Growth rates are computed using deflated income and executive pay, applying the same deflator as described in Piketty, Saez, and Zucman (2016).

Germany over 1985–2009. The increased wage differential between highly skilled workers and others as reflected in those studies is not likely to be related to skill-biased technological change, as it depends on the size of the employer, and there is little reason why technical trends would differ across differently sized firms. An explanation in terms of rent sharing is more plausible, as rents may differ across firms.

Evidence provided by Bas, Paunov, and Rodriguez-Montemayor (2017) on publicly traded firms in the United States that report on wage payments shows no association of firms' wage pay and average wages in more concentrated and volatile markets, which is different from the findings on effects on executive pay and profits (tables 9.1 and 9.5).

The negotiation power of most workers, however, is weaker for a number of reasons. First, labor market pressure, which tends to equal the price of similar labor across firms, is stronger for employees than for managers. It is more difficult to replace managers than a number of workers. Second, another factor that reduces labor's share in rents is that information asymmetries regarding capacity and effort that allow negotiating higher pay are often less prominent for employees than for managers. Third, IT-enabled outsourcing and more temporary work arrangements weaken workers' connections to winning firms, increasing the competitive pressure on employees (Goldschmidt and Schmieder 2015). From 2005 to 2015, virtually all job creation in the United States was related to alternative work arrangements, defined as temporary help agency workers, on-call workers, contract workers, and independent contractors or freelancers (Katz and Krueger 2016). Goldschmidt and Schmieder (2015) show that reducing rent sharing was one of the motivations for German firms to outsource noncore activities, such as food, cleaning, security, and logistics services starting in the early 1990s.

9.6.6   Opportunities for Social Mobility

Inequality indicators capture the relative position of individuals at any point in time; an important question these indicators do not address is whether individuals in lower income categories have the opportunity to move upward (Jones and Kim 2014). In many countries, higher inequalities are, however, associated with lower upward social mobility (as described by the so-called Great Gatsby curve). Chetty et al. (2014), for instance, find that a child born in the 1980s to parents in the bottom 20 percent of the income distribution has only a 7.5 percent chance of moving to the top 20 percent.

Social mobility is connected to creative destruction, as this mechanism triggers a change in market winners (and losers), affecting respective incomes as new winners move up the distribution (while new losers move down). With digital innovation's impacts on the incidence and role of creative destruction, social mobility may increase in the digital innovation economy.

There is some evidence connecting social mobility and innovation: anecdotal evidence from the Forbes 400 list of the richest Americans shows that between 1982 and 2001 (as digital innovation was progressively taking off), the share of individuals who were not wealthy prior to their business success compared to that of individuals who inherited their wealth (an indicator of cross-generational social mobility) increased. However, having professional skills is a critical precondition for success: the share of people with a college education rose in the list from 77 percent in 1982 to 87 percent in 2011 (Kaplan and Rauh 2013). Recent empirical work also suggests that social mobility increases with innovation: Aghion et al. (2015) shows that US states with more innovation-led growth had higher upward social mobility over the 1995–2010 period.

9.7   An Open Research Agenda

This chapter puts forward an understudied mechanism that links digital innovation to changing market structures and, consequently, impacts on the distribution of income. It provides initial evidence pointing to the importance of this mechanism. Further evidence is important to improve our understanding of the issues and channels involved. The following areas in particular are critical.

First, the changes brought by digital innovation require continued efforts to measure the phenomenon of software-based innovations and relevant intangible investments. With continued technological progress, developing the right types of indicators is by nature a moving target that requires continued adaptation. While a decade ago indicators on computer and internet access were suitable for analysis, at present such an indicator is at best of weak interest given widespread adoption and the further development of digital innovations. It is important to know more about digital innovations across firms, industries, and countries over time to trace systematically the effects of digital innovation on market dynamics. Such evidence is particularly important to explore the wider impacts of digital innovation beyond the sectors most closely associated with the digital economy, such as software and hardware producers, search engines, and online portals. Evidence on digital innovation and intangible investments at sector and firm levels are also important.

Second, the impacts of digital innovations on market dynamics in the United States and other countries require further attention. An analysis of economic census data would allow testing of the extent of changes and in what contexts they arise. Recent work by Autor et al. (2017) and de Loecker and Eeckhout (2017) provides first evidence on the evolution of market concentration. Analyses of risk would also be important. Analyses need to address a number of conceptual challenges; accounting for "redefining" the industry associated with particular businesses is increasingly important as the digital economy changes markets. For instance, IT firms' investments in automated cars points to the company's role as competitor in a number of markets. Moreover, the absence of monetary transactions in two-sided markets such as online search engines also requires thinking about what measures of market concentration to use in addition to traditional sales-based measures.

Third, there is the large agenda on impacts of winner-take-all markets on the incomes of different groups in society and on social mobility. Matched employer-employee data allow documenting, beyond executives and investors, which workers benefit from rent sharing and which are excluded. Such data also allow an understanding of whether digital innovation creates opportunities for social mobility and, if so, how. Documenting the evidence of countries can allow an understanding of whether country-specific contexts, including differences in opportunities provided for social mobility, affect how winner-take-all markets impact the distribution of income.

Fourth, further analyses aimed at assessing the relative importance of the new channel linking innovation to the distribution of income outlined in this chapter compared to others (financialization, globalization, skill-biased technological progress, etc.) would also be an important development.

Appendix A
The Impact of Reduced Costs of Innovation on the Sequencing and Versioning of Innovation

The effects of reduced costs of innovation on the rate of innovation in the context of digital innovations can be accounted for in a simple two-period framework.

In the basic, one-period setting, the total cost of a product is

$$C = R + F + d*V,$$

where R is the investment in research (fixed cost), F is the fixed cost for producing and marketing the product (setting up a factory or retooling, setting up or reorienting a commercial network, etc.), d is the variable unit cost, and V is the volume of sales.

The turnover is

$$S = p*V,$$

where p is the unit price.

A firm will decide to engage in the research investment leading to the product if and only if the (expectancy of) profit is positive—that is, the (expected) turnover exceeds the (expected) cost:

$$\text{Condition 1: } S > C \Leftrightarrow V > (R + F)/(p—d) = V°.$$

There is a minimum volume of expected sales $V°$ below which the company will not engage in innovation.

Digital innovation reduces the fixed cost of producing, marketing, and distributing the product, and the variable unit costs approach zero. According to Condition 1, $V°$ is decreasing in F and in d, meaning that the lower fixed cost of production and marketing, or a lower variable unit cost, makes it profitable for a firm to innovate with a lower expected volume of sales. This implies that digital innovation reduces the threshold for triggering spending in innovation, resulting in more innovations.

The impact of digital innovation on the cost of innovation also makes it more rewarding for a firm to split its innovations into smaller parts and market those new products rather than launch more advanced new products (cumulating several rounds of innovation) at longer time intervals. This can be described by defining two periods of production.

Assuming that the research, production, and sale can be sequenced in two periods if the firm decides to, the firm can produce and sell a "partial version," or a "smaller innovation" version, of the final good. Across two periods, 1 and 2, the costs and turnover equations are as follows:[5]

$$C1 = R/2 + F + d*V1$$

$$C2 = R/2 + F + d*V2$$

$$S1 = p*V1$$

$$S2 = p*V2$$

The supplementary cost for the firm generated by sequencing its innovation is due to further production and marketing fixed costs that are incurred every time the firm issues a new product, independently of the degree of novelty and the volume of sales of the product.

By accessing the market earlier, the firm can increase total sales by stealing customers from competitors. This is reflected in the assumption that $V1 + V2 = V + V' > V$.

The condition for the firm to divide its innovation in two smaller innovations is that profit should be higher when it does so (it should also be positive, Condition 1):

Condition 2: $(S1 + S2) - (C1 + C2) > S - C ? F < (p - d)V'$

This condition is all the easier to satisfy with low F and d. This is exactly what happens with digital innovation. F is lower due to digital distribution,

---

5. We ignore discounting of period 2 because (i) the difference between the two periods is often a question of months and because (ii) interest rates have been very low for a decade. Introducing discounting would also not provide additional insights into the main mechanism we illustrate.

and d is even zero for digital products. Therefore, digital innovation tends to accelerate the pace of innovations and increase versioning by making it beneficial to split innovations over time into smaller marketable pieces. In addition, in a winner-take-all context, small innovations, with only a marginal advantage over competition, might be enough to gain all the market: this reinforces the impact of the reduction in cost on the incentive to put innovations of a small size to market rapidly.

Appendix B
Information on Data Used

9.B1   Industry Categories Used in Tables 9.3 and 9.4 and Figures 9.18 and 9.19

The SIC two-digit industries of all firms in ExecuComp and Compustat are categorized into the following groups:

- *Extractive industries* include Metal Mining (10); Coal Mining (12); Oil and Gas Extraction (13); Mining and Quarrying of Nonmetallic Minerals (14); and Petroleum Refining and Related Industries (29).
- *Construction* includes Construction—General Contractors and Operative Builders (15); Heavy Construction, Except Building Construction, Contractor (16); and Construction—Special Trade Contractors (17).
- *IT-related manufacturing* includes Industrial and Commercial Machinery and Computer Equipment (35) and Electronic and Other Electrical Equipment and Components (36).
- *Innovation-intensive manufacturing* includes Chemicals and Allied Products (28) and Measuring, Photographic, Medical, and Optical Goods, and Clocks (38).
- *Noninnovative manufacturing* includes Food and Kindred Products (20); Tobacco Products (21); Textile Mills Products (22); Apparel, Finished Products from Fabrics and Similar Materials (23); Lumber and Wood Products, Except Furniture (24); Furniture and Fixtures (25); Paper and Allied Products (26); Printing, Publishing and Allied Industries (27); Rubber and Miscellaneous Plastic Products (30); Leather and Leather Products (31); Stone, Clay, Glass, and Concrete Products (32); Primary Metal Industries (33); Fabricated Metal Products (34); and Miscellaneous Manufacturing Industries (39).
- *IT-related services* include Business Services (73); Communication (48); and Engineering, Accounting, Research, and Management Services (87).

- *Finance and insurance* includes Depository Institutions (60); Nondepository Credit Institutions (61); Security and Commodity Brokers, Dealers, Exchanges and Services (62); Insurance Carriers (63); Insurance Agents, Brokers and Service (64); and Holding and Other Investment Offices (67).
- *Retail and wholesale trade* includes Wholesale Trade—Durable Goods (50); Wholesale Trade—Nondurable Goods (51); Building Materials, Hardware, Garden Supplies and Mobile Homes (52); General Merchandise Stores (53); Food Stores (54); Automotive Dealers and Gasoline Service Stations (55); Apparel and Accessory Stores (56); Home Furniture, Furnishings and Equipment Stores (57); Eating and Drinking Places (58); and Miscellaneous Retail (59).
- *Transportation* includes Railroad Transportation (40); Local and Suburban Transit and Interurban Highway Transportation (41); Motor Freight Transportation (42); Water Transportation (44); Transportation by Air (45); Transportation Services (47); and Transportation Equipment (37).
- *Non-IT-related services* include Electric, Gas and Sanitary Services (49); Real Estate (65); Hotels, Rooming Houses, Camps, and Other Lodging Places (70); Personal Services (72); Automotive Repair, Services and Parking (75), Motion Pictures (78), Amusement and Recreation Services (79); Health Services (80); and Educational Services (82).

9.B2   Data on the Distribution of Income in Figures 9.2 and 9.3

Data on the top 1 percent income share (before taxes) are taken from the World Top Incomes Database, http://topincomes.g-mond.parisschool ofeconomics.eu/ (accessed July 15, 2015).

The following adjustments are undertaken to deal with missing values:

- For figure 9.2, missing values of the top 1 percent income share (before taxes) have been replaced by the year in parentheses for the indicated year: Germany: 1987 (1986), 1988 (1989), 1990 (1989), 1991 (1992), 1993 (1992), 1994 (1995), 1996 (1995), 1997 (1998), 1999(1998), 2000 (2001), 2009 (2008); Italy: 1996 (1995), 1997 (1998); Netherlands: 1987 (1985), 1988 (1989); Switzerland: 1988 (1987), 1990 (1989), 1992 (1991), 1994 (1993); United Kingdom: 2008(2007). The data series of the top 1 percent income share used for each country (and period) are as it follows: Australia: Main series: 1976–2010; Canada: Main series: 1986–2000; Longitudinal Administrative Data: 2001–2010; Denmark: Adults: 1986–2010; France: Main series: 1976–2012; Germany: Main series: 1976–2008; Ireland: Main series: 1986–2009; Italy: Main series: 1976–2009; Japan: Main series: 1986–2010; Netherlands: Main series: 1986–2012; New Zealand: Adults: 1986–2012; Norway: Main series:

1986–2011; Sweden: Main series: 1986–2013; Switzerland: Main series: 1986–2010; United Kingdom: Married couples and single adults: 1986–1989; Adults: 1990–2012; United States: Main series: 1986–2014.

- For figure 9.3, missing values of the top 1 percent income share (before taxes) have been replaced by the year in parentheses for the indicated year: Finland: 2010 (2009); Germany: 1981 (1980), 2010 (2008); Indonesia: 1981 (1982); Ireland: 2010 (2009); Italy: 2010 (2009); Malaysia: 1981 (1983). The data series on the top 1 percent income share used for each country (and period) are the following: Australia: Main series: 1981 and 2010; Canada: Longitudinal Administrative Data: 2010; Main series: 1981; Denmark: Adults: 1981 and 2010; France: Main series: 1981 and 2010; Germany: Main series: 1981 and 2010; Ireland: Main series: 1981 and 2010; Italy: Main series: 1981 and 2010; Japan: Main series: 1981 and 2010; Malaysia: Main series: 1981 and 2010; Netherlands: Main series: 1981 and 2010; New Zealand: Adults: 1981 and 2010; Norway: Main series: 1981 and 2010; Singapore: Main series: 1981 and 2010; South Africa: Adults: 2010; Married couples and single adults: 1981; Spain: Main series: 1981 and 2010; Sweden: Main series: 1981 and 2010; Switzerland: Main series: 1981 and 2010; United Kingdom: Adults: 2010; Married couples and single adults: 1981; United States: Main series: 1981 and 2010.

9.B3   Industry- and Country-Level Data Used for Labor Share Regressions Reported in Table 9.2

Regression results reported in table 9.2 combine several OECD industry and country data, including the OECD database for Structural Analysis (STAN) and the Main Science and Technology Indicators (MSTI). The data are complemented with data from EU KLEMS, the OECD National Accounts database, and the World Bank Enterprise Surveys. The variables are defined in table 9.A2 jointly with their sources.

The estimating sample combines data for the following 27 countries: Australia, Austria, Belgium, Canada, Czech Republic, Estonia, Finland, France, Germany, Greece, Hungary, Iceland, Ireland, Italy, Luxembourg, Mexico, the Netherlands, New Zealand, Poland, Portugal, Korea, Slovak Republic, Slovenia, Spain, Sweden, the United Kingdom, and the United States.

The industries covered include the following 15 industries at three- and two-digit ISIC Rev. 4 level as defined in the OECD STAN database: basic metals, construction, electrical equipment, food products, beverages and tobacco, motor vehicles, trailers and semitrailers, machinery and equipment n.e.c., other nonmetallic mineral products, paper and paper products, printing and reproduction of recorded materials, rubber and plastic products,

Table 9.A1   Characteristics of the estimating sample for regression results of table 9.5

	Number of observations	Percentage share
Number of executives	7,812	
Number of firms	1,106	
Sector of activity		
Oil and gas extraction	3,008	7.1%
Chemicals and allied products	4,151	9.8%
Petroleum refining and related industries	114	0.3%
Industrial and commercial machinery and computer equipment	930	2.2%
Electronic, other electrical equipment and components	6,150	14.5%
Measuring, photographic, medical, optical goods, and clocks	3,297	7.8%
Furniture and fixtures	73	0.2%
Industry	17,723	41.8%
Communications	955	2.3%
Electric, gas, and sanitary services	2,111	5.0%
Food stores, eating and drinking places, miscellaneous retail	757	1.8%
Depository institutions	5,115	12.1%
Insurance carriers	3,382	8.0%
Holding and other investment offices	3,194	7.5%
Business services	9,170	21.6%
Services	24,684	58.2%
Time period		
1992–95	3,478	8.2%
1996–99	5,315	12.5%
2000–2003	6,154	14.5%
2004–7	10,226	24.1%
2008–11	11,809	27.8%
2012–13	5,425	12.8%

textiles, transport equipment, transportation and storage, wholesale and retail trade, and wood and products of wood and cork.

9.B4   Executive Pay Measures Used in Tables 9.3, 9.4, and 9.5 and Figures 9.19 and 9.20

Data on executive pay refer to total executive compensation (including salary, bonuses, and other annual rewards), except for results reported in column (4) of table 9.5 that refer to executives' salary only. Table 9.A1 describes the estimating sample used in regressions presented in table 9.5. More detail is provided in Bas, Paunov, and Rodriguez-Montemayor (2017).

Table 9.A2   Industry and country-level data used for results

Variables	Description	Source
Dependent variable		
Labor share	Industry labor compensation over industry value added	OECD STAN
Country-level variables		
GDP	Gross domestic product	OECD National Accounts
Patents	Ratio of triadic patent families to GDP	OECD MSTI
Graduates	Ratio of the number of tertiary educated people to GDP	OECD MSTI
Capital	GFCF as percentage of GDP	OECD National Accounts
Finance	Share of finance sector in national value added	OECD STAN
Trade	Ratio of industry import and exports to GDP	OECD National Accounts
Union density	Percentage of workers members of trade unions	OECD and J. Visser, ICTWSS database
Industry-level variables		
Patent intensity	Percentage of firms holding at least one patent	World Bank Enterprise Surveys across 50,013 firm observations from 117 countries for 2006–2011
Intangible assets	Share of intangible capital over total capital (US period average)	EU KLEMS
(Low) skill intensity	Industry share of highly (less) skilled workers (US period average)	EU KLEMS
Capital intensity	Industry ratio of capital stock over value added (US period average)	OECD STAN
Transport equipment	Transport equipment capital as ratio of total capital	EU KLEMS
R&D intensity	Ratio of industry R&D expenditure in value added	OECD (2016), "OECD Taxonomy of Economic Activities Based on R&D Intensity," OECD Science, Technology and Industry Working Papers, No. 2016/04.

References

Acemoglu, D., and P. Restrepo. 2016. "The Race between Machine and Man: Implications of Technology for Growth, Factor Shares and Employment." NBER Working Paper No. 22252. Cambridge, MA: National Bureau of Economic Research.

Aghion, P., U. Akcigit, A. Bergeaud, R. Blundell, and D. Hémous. 2015. "Innovation and Top Income Inequality." NBER Working Paper No. 21247. Cambridge, MA: National Bureau of Economic Research.

Aghion, P., U. Akcigit, A. Hyytinen, and O. Toivanen. 2016. "Living the 'American Dream' in Finland: The Social Mobility of Inventors." Unpublished manuscript.

Alvarez-Cuadrado, F., N. Van Long, and M. Poschke. 2014. "Capital Labor Substitution, Structural Change, and the Labor Income Share." *CIRANO-Scientific Publications* 2014s-02.

Andersson, F., M. Freedman, J. Haltiwanger, J. Lane, and K. Shaw. 2009. "Reaching for the Stars: Who Pays for Talent in Innovative Industries?" *Economic Journal* 119 (538): F308–F332.

Atkinson, Anthony B. 2015. *Inequality: What Can Be Done?* Cambridge, MA: Harvard University Press.

Autor, D., and D. Dorn. 2013. "The Growth of Low-Skill Service Jobs and the Polarization of the US Labor Market." *American Economic Review* 103 (5): 1553–97.

Autor, D., D. Dorn, L. F. Katz, C. Patterson, and J. Van Reenen. 2017. "Concentrating on the Fall of the Labor Share." NBER Working Paper No. 23108. Cambridge, MA: National Bureau of Economic Research.

Barkai, S. 2016. "Declining Labor and Capital Shares." Stigler Center for the Study of the Economy and the State New Working Paper Series (2), University of Chicago.

Bas, M., C. Paunov, and E. Rodriguez-Montemayor. 2017. "Superstar Rewards in Winner-Take-All Markets." Unpublished mimeo.

Bassanini, A., and T. Manfredi. 2012. "Capital's Grabbing Hand? A Cross-country/Cross-Industry Analysis of the Decline of the Labor Share." OECD Social, Employment and Migration Working Papers, No. 133. Paris: OECD.

Bonnet, O., P. H. Bono, G. Chapelle, and E. Wasmer. 2014. "Does Housing Capital Contribute to Inequality? A Comment on Thomas Piketty's *Capital in the 21st Century*." Sciences Po Economics Discussion Papers 7:12.

Branstetter, L., M. Drev, and N. Kwon. 2015. "Get with the Program: Software-Driven Innovation in Traditional Manufacturing." NBER Working Paper No. 21752. Cambridge, MA: National Bureau of Economic Research.

Bridgman, B. 2014. "Is Labor's Loss Capital's Gain? Gross versus Net Labor Shares." US Bureau of Economic Analysis, unpublished mimeo.

Brynjolfsson, E., A. McAfee, M. Sorell, and F. Zhu. 2007. "Scale without Mass: Business Process Replication and Industry Dynamics." Harvard Business School Technology and Operations Mgt. Unit Research Paper, No. 07-016.

Card, D., J. Heining, and P. Kline. 2013. "Workplace Heterogeneity and the Rise of West German Wage Inequality." *Quarterly Journal of Economics* 128 (3): 967–1015.

Chetty, R. et al. 2014. "Where Is the Land of Opportunity? The Geography of Intergenerational Mobility in the United States." *Quarterly Journal of Economics* 129:1553–1623.

Cincera, M., and R. Veugelers. 2013. "Young Leading Innovators and the EU's R&D Intensity Gap." *Economics of Innovation and New Technology* 22 (2): 177–98.

Cochrane, J. H. 2005. "The Risk and Return of Venture Capital." *Journal of Financial Economics* 75 (1): 3–52.

Corrado, C., C. Hulten, and D. Sichel. 2005. "Measuring Capital and Technology: An Expanded Framework." In *Measuring Capital in the New Economy*, edited by Carol Corrado, John Haltiwanger, and Daniel Sichel, 11–46. NBER Studies in Income and Wealth 65. Chicago: University of Chicago Press.

Corrado, C., C. Hulten, and D. Sichel. 2009. "Intangible Capital and US Economic Growth." *Review of Income and Wealth* 55 (3): 661–85.

Council of Economic Advisors (CEA). 2016. Economic Report of the President, Transmitted to the Congress in February 2016.

Damodaran, A. 2015. "Betas by Sector (US)." http://pages.stern.nyu.edu/~adamodar /New_Home_Page/datafile/Betas.html.

Decker, R., J. Haltiwanger, R. Jarmin, and J. Miranda. 2014. "The Role of Entrepreneurship in US Job Creation and Economic Dynamism." *Journal of Economic Perspectives* 28 (3): 3–24.

De Loecker, J., and J. Eeckhout. 2017. "The Rise of Market Power and the Macroeconomic Implications." NBER Working Paper No. 23687. Cambridge, MA: National Bureau of Economic Research.

The Economist. 2016. "The Rise of the Superstars." September 15, 2016, https://www .economist.com/special-report/2016/09/15/the-rise-of-the-superstars.

Elsby, M. W., B. Hobijn, and A. Şahin. 2013. "The Decline of the US Labor Share." *Brookings Papers on Economic Activity* 2:1–63.

Faurel, L., Q. Li, D. M. Shanthikumar, and S. H. Teoh. 2015. "CEO Incentives and Product Development Innovation: Insights from Trademarks." Paul Merage School of Business, University of California, Irvine. Unpublished mimeo.

Forbes. 2015. "The Most Profitable Industries in 2015." September 23, 2015, https:// www.forbes.com/sites/liyanchen/2015/09/23/the-most-profitable-industries-in -2015/.

Forbes, K. 2000. "A Reassessment of the Relationship between Inequality and Growth." *American Economic Review* 90:869–87.

Furman, J., and P. Orszag. 2015. "A Firm-Level Perspective on the Role of Rents in the Rise in Inequality." Presentation at "A Just Society," Centennial Event in Honor of Joseph Stiglitz, Columbia University, October 15.

Gabaix, X., and A. Landier. 2008. "Why Has CEO Pay Increased So Much?" *Quarterly Journal of Economics* 123 (1): 49–100.

Gabaix, X., A. Landier, and J. Sauvagnat. 2014. "CEO Pay and Firm Size: An Update after the Crisis." *Economic Journal* 124 (574): F40–F59.

Goldschmidt, D., and J. F. Schmieder. 2015. "The Rise of Domestic Outsourcing and the Evolution of the German Wage Structure." NBER Working Paper No. 21366. Cambridge, MA: National Bureau of Economic Research.

Goos, M., and A. Manning. 2007. "Lousy and Lovely Jobs: The Rising Polarization of Work in Britain." *Review of Economics and Statistics* 89 (1): 118–33.

Hall, B., and J. Liebman. 1998. "Are CEOs Really Paid like Bureaucrats?" *Quarterly Journal of Economics* 113:653–91.

Harhoff, D., F. M. Scherer, and K. Vopel. 2003. "Exploring the Tail of Patented Invention Value Distributions." In *Economics, Law and Intellectual Property*, edited by Ove Granstrand, 279–309. New York: Springer.

Haskel, J., R. Z. Lawrence, E. E. Leamer, and M. J. Slaughter. 2012. "Globalization and US Wages: Modifying Classic Theory to Explain Recent Facts." *Journal of Economic Perspectives* 26 (2): 119–39.

Haskel, J., and S. Westlake. 2017. "Intangibles and the Rise of Inequality." In *Capitalism without Capital: The Rise of the Intangible Economy*, 118–43. Princeton, NJ: Princeton University Press.

Jones, C. I., and J. Kim. 2014. "A Schumpeterian Model of Income Inequality." NBER Working Paper No. 20637. Cambridge, MA: National Bureau of Economic Research.

Kaplan, S., and J. Rauh. 2013. "It's the Market: The Broad-Based Rise in the Return to Top Talent." *Journal of Economic Perspectives* 27 (3): 35–55.

Karabarbounis, L., and B. Neiman. 2014. "The Global Decline of the Labor Share." *Quarterly Journal of Economics* 129 (1): 61–103.

Katz, L., and A. Krueger. 2016. "The Rise and Nature of Alternative Work Arrangements in the United States, 1995–2015." Unpublished mimeo.

Koh, D., R. Santaeulàlia-Llopis, and Y. Zheng. 2015. "Labor Share Decline and Intellectual Property Products Capital." Unpublished manuscript.

Koller, T., M. Goedhart, and D. Wessels. 2015. *Valuation: Measuring and Managing the Value of Companies.* New York: Wiley.

Kornai, J. 2016. "So What Is Capital in the Twenty-First Century? Some Notes on Piketty's Book." *Capitalism and Society* 11 (1): article 2.

Lerner, J., and J. Wulf. 2007. "Innovation and Incentives: Evidence from Corporate R&D." *Review of Economics and Statistics* 89 (4): 634–44.

Li, W. C., and B. H. Hall. 2016. "Depreciation of Business R&D Capital." NBER Working Paper No. 22473. Cambridge, MA: National Bureau of Economic Research.

Michaels, G., A. Natraj, and J. Van Reenen. 2014. "Has ICT Polarized Skill Demand? Evidence from Eleven Countries over Twenty-Five Years." *Review of Economics and Statistics* 96 (1): 60–77.

Mishel, L., and N. Sabadish. 2013. "CEO Pay in 2012 Was Extraordinarily High Relative to Typical Workers and Other High Earners." *Economic Policy Institute (EPI) Issue Brief*, no. 367, June 26.

Mueller, H., E. Simintzi, and P. Ouimet. 2015. "Wage Inequality and Firm Growth." LIS Working Paper, No. 632. March.

Murphy, K. 1998. "Executive Compensation." In *Handbook of Labor Economics*, edited by O. Ashenfelter and D. Card, 3:2485–2563. North Holland: Elsevier.

Nakamura, Leonard Isamu. 2001. "What Is the US Gross Investment in Intangibles? (At Least) One Trillion Dollars a Year!" Economic Research Division, Federal Reserve Bank of Philadelphia.

OECD. 2015a. *All on Board: Making Inclusive Growth Happen.* Paris: OECD.

OECD. 2015b. *OECD Science, Technology and Industry Scoreboard 2015: Innovation for Growth and Society.* Paris: OECD.

Paunov, Caroline, and Valentina Rollo. 2016. "Has the Internet Fostered Inclusive Innovation in the Developing World?" *World Development* 78:587–609.

Piketty, T., E. Saez, and G. Zucman. 2016. "Distributional National Accounts: Methods and Estimates for the United States." NBER Working Paper No. 22945. Cambridge, MA: National Bureau of Economic Research.

Rajan, Raghuram, and Luigi Zingales. 1998. "Financial Development and Growth." *American Economic Review* 88:559–86.

Rosen, S. 1981. "The Economics of Superstars." *American Economic Review* 71 (5): 845–58.

Schumpeter, J. 1911. *The Theory of Economic Development.* New Brunswick: Transaction.

Song, J., D. J. Price, F. Guvenen, N. Bloom, and T. von Wachter. 2015. "Firming Up Inequality." NBER Working Paper No. 21199. Cambridge, MA: National Bureau of Economic Research.

Varian, H. 2003. "The Economics of Information Technology." Revised version of the Raffaele Mattioli Lecture, delivered at Bocconi University, Milano, Italy, on November 15–16, 2001, and the Sorbonne on March 6, 2003.

IV

Improving Current
Measurement Frameworks

10

Factor Incomes in Global Value Chains
The Role of Intangibles

Wen Chen, Bart Los, and Marcel P. Timmer

10.1 Introduction

The long-run decline in the income share of labor in GDP since the 1980s is one of the most debated macroeconomic trends in recent years. Various studies have documented that the trend is widely shared across industries and countries. While it has been particularly strong in the United States, it has also been observed for other advanced countries and, perhaps surprisingly, also for various emerging and poor countries.[1] Recent research zooms in on potential drivers. Barkai (2017) and Karabarbounis and Neiman (2018) document a large increase in so-called factorless income in the United

Wen Chen is research fellow at the Institute of New Structural Economics at Peking University.

Bart Los is professor of the economics of technological progress and structural change at the University of Groningen.

Marcel P. Timmer is director of the Groningen Growth and Development Centre, and professor of economic growth and development at the University of Groningen.

We would like to thank participants at the NBER Conference on Research in Income and Wealth (CRIW) conference Measuring and Accounting for Innovation in the 21st Century, Washington, March 2017, at the IARIW conference, Copenhagen August 2018 as well as at the World Intellectual Property Organisation (WIPO) experts' meeting in Geneva, March 2017, for stimulating discussion, in particular (without implicating) Carol Corrado, John Fernald, Carsten Fink and Sacha Wunsch-Vincent. The authors have been consulting for the WIPO in 2017. The views expressed are those of the authors, and not (necessarily) of the WIPO. Financial support from the Dutch Science Foundation (NWO) for Marcel Timmer is gratefully acknowledged (grant number 453-14-012). For acknowledgments, sources of research support, and disclosure of the authors' material financial relationships, if any, please see https://www.nber.org/books-and-chapters/measuring-and-accounting-innovation-21st-century/factor-incomes-global-value-chains-role-intangibles.

1. See Elsby, Hobijn, and Şahin 2013; Karabarbounis and Neiman 2014; Rognlie 2015; Barkai 2017, and Dao et al. 2017.

States: a residual that remains after subtracting payments to labor and cost of capital from GDP. Karabarbounis and Neiman (2018) argue that it can be alternatively interpreted as economic profits arising from firms' pricing power, as income that accrues to forms of capital that are unmeasured in current national accounts statistics, or as a wedge between imputed rental rates for assets and the rate that firms perceive when making the investment. They argue that it is likely a combination of the three, concluding that the latter is most promising in explaining long-term trends in US GDP income shares.

So far, the discussion on factor incomes has been about shares in GDP of single countries. This chapter argues for the need for a multicountry approach in better understanding the drivers of increasing "factorless income." In today's world, goods are typically produced and distributed in intricate networks with multiple stages of production and extensive shipping of intermediate goods, services, and information. We refer to this as global value chain (GVC) production.[2] So-called factoryless goods producers like Apple provide an iconic example: they sell and organize the production of manufacturing goods without being engaged in the actual fabrication process (Bernard and Fort 2015; Fontagné and Harrison 2017). They capture a major part of the value as compensation for provision of software and designs, market knowledge, intellectual property, systems integration, and cost management, as well as a strong brand name. These assets are key in the coordination of the GVC and in the creation of value. Yet we have no way to directly infer the income that accrues to these "intangibles" due to their nonphysical nature such that their use cannot be attributed to a geographic location. In contrast, tangible assets (such as machinery) and labor have a physical presence, and their use is recorded in the national account statistics of the countries where they are located. A further complication is the fact that GVC production opens up the possibility for profit-shifting of multinational enterprises across countries.[3] More generally, increased cross-border sharing of intangibles is undermining the very notion of country-level factor incomes and GDP. This problem of income attribution is not new and has been discussed in the context of the system of national accounts for quite some time. The 26 percent jump in Irish GDP in 2015 also brought this "statistical problem" to public light and scrutiny.[4] Guvenen et al. (2017) find that US multinationals have increasingly shifted income from intellec-

---

2. See UNECE (2015) for examples of various types of global production arrangements.

3. Through profit shifting, including transfer pricing and other tax strategies, transnational companies can allocate the largest share of their profits to subsidiaries (Dischinger, Knoll, and Riedel 2014). A firm might not be fully free to do so, as it is bound by cost-pricing rules. Yet, in practice, profit shifting is abundant, involving complex IP arrangements, and this practice is not restricted to affiliated firms only; see Neubig and Wunsch-Vincent (2017). Tørsløv, Wier, and Zucman (2018) estimate that close to 40 percent of multinational profits are shifted to tax havens globally each year.

4. See Halpin (2016). UNECE (2015) and Landefeld (2015) report on the discussions in (inter)national statistical organizations.

tual property rights to foreign jurisdictions with lower taxes, suggesting an understatement of the labor share decline in US GDP.

The presence of GVC production suggests that there is a need to complement conventional factor income studies (at the country-industry level) by study of global value chains (that cross borders). Factor income analysis in GVCs will not be affected by the attribution problem and offers a unique opportunity to track the payments to intangible assets. This chapter is the first to provide such a study at the macroeconomic level.[5] To fix ideas, consider a firm selling shoes using local labor L and tangible capital K. This requires two activities: fabrication and marketing. Both activities require firm-specific knowledge B (e.g., market intelligence on consumers' preferences for particular types of shoes). Next suppose the fabrication stage is offshored to country 2. In this case the (vertically integrated) production function is $Y = F(K_1, L_1, K_2, L_2, B)$. To infer payments to B, we calculate residual profits in the chain as the sales of a good minus the payments to tangible factor inputs needed in any stage of production:

$$rB = pY - \Sigma_n w_n L_n - \Sigma_n r_n K_n,$$

with w_n the wage rate and r_n the rental rate of tangible capital used in country n. pY is the output value of the final good. rB is measured as the residual after subtracting the sum of payments to labor L and to tangibles K across all countries involved in production. We will refer to this residual as payment for intangible assets in the GVC.

It should be noted that, given the residual approach, we measure the combined income to all intangible assets used in a chain and do not attempt to measure the stock of intangibles and their rates of return separately. In their seminal work, Corrado, Hulten, and Sichel (2005, 2009) showed how stock estimates for certain types of intangibles that are currently not treated as investment in the national accounts (such as market research, advertising, training, and organizational capital) could be derived. This requires data on intangibles' investments as well as additional information on their depreciation rates and asset prices. Corrado et al. (2013) provide an updated analysis expanding measurement to a large set of countries. Yet the industry detail currently provided is too aggregate for our purposes. At this stage we therefore remain agnostic about the type of intangibles, their separate stocks, and returns. This is left for future research. Our main aim is to establish the overall importance of payments to intangibles compared to tangible assets and labor.

---

5. Studying factor incomes in GVCs has a much longer history in case study research going back at least to Gereffi (1994); see Kaplinsky (2000) for an overview. Studies in that tradition are typically more qualitative and analyze how interactions between buyers and sellers in the chain are governed and coordinated. In a seminal case study, Dedrick, Kraemer, and Linden (2010) apply the residual income approach to the value of an Apple iPod, using technical "teardown" reports to trace inputs. They find that Apple retains up to half of the iPod value.

The rest of the chapter is organized as follows. In section 10.2, we outline our GVC accounting methodology. The main measurement challenge is the fact that GVCs are not directly observable in the data and need to be inferred from information on the linkages between the various stages of production. We will build upon the approach to measuring value added in global production networks as introduced by Los, Timmer, and de Vries (2015). They showed how one can derive the value-added contributions of country-industries in a given GVC. This allows for a decomposition of the ex-factory value of a final product into the value added in each stage of production. We use information from so-called global input-output tables that contain (value) data on intermediate products that flow across industries as well as across countries. These are published in the World Input-Output Database (WIOD; see Timmer et al. 2015). This is combined with information on factor incomes in each stage, as discussed in section 10.3. We collected additional information from national accounts statistics on industry-level wages and investment in tangible assets in a wide set of countries. We built capital stocks using the perpetual inventory method and imputed the income payments to tangible capital by multiplying with a standard Hall-Jorgenson type of rental rate. Crucially, we use an ex-ante rate of return such that a residual remains.

Throughout the chapter, we will study factor income distribution in the global production of manufacturing goods. Worldwide consumption of manufactured goods (at purchasers' prices) makes up about a quarter of world GDP (in 2000). This includes value that is added in manufacturing industries as well as nonmanufacturing, such as in transport, communication, finance, and other business services, and also raw materials production. These indirect contributions will be explicitly accounted for by using information on input-output linkages across sectors. Section 10.4 provides main results on trends in factor incomes in GVCs over the period 2000–14 (the beginning and end points of the analysis are dictated by data availability in the WIOD 2016 release). Our main finding is that the share of intangibles in the value of final goods has increased, in particular in the period 2000–2007. Its share is generally (much) higher than the tangible capital income share. This is found at the aggregate as well as for more detailed manufacturing product groups. Nevertheless, there is clear heterogeneity in the pace of the increase. For some nondurable products, such as textiles or food, the intangible share in GVCs increased only marginally. In contrast, the share increased rapidly in durable goods' GVCs, such as machinery and electronic equipment products. We provide suggestive evidence that this variation is linked to variation in the speed of international production fragmentation. Taking the results together, one could consider the 2000s as an exceptional period in which global manufacturing firms benefited from reduced labor costs through offshoring while capitalizing on existing firm-specific intangibles, such as brand names, at little marginal cost. Section 10.5 provides a discussion of the robustness of the main results, concluding that the current system of national accounts is likely to still miss out on a large range of intangible assets, confirming Corrado, Hulten, and Sichel (2005). Section 10.6 offers concluding remarks. The measurement framework puts high demand on the data, and our results should thus be seen as indicative only. This study is explorative and mainly aimed at stimulating further thinking about the interrelatedness of factor incomes across industries and countries.

10.2 Accounting for Factor Incomes in Global Value Chains: Method

In this section, we outline our empirical method to slice up incomes in GVCs. The basic aim is to decompose the value of a final good into worldwide factor incomes. By representing the global economy in an input-output account in the tradition of Leontief, we can use his famous insight to map consumption value of products to value added in industries.[6] We first outline our basic accounting framework and intuition (section 10.2.1). Next, we outline how we trace value added in production stages of the GVC, building upon the method of Los, Timmer, and de Vries (2015; section 10.2.2). We extend this approach by including the distribution stage (section 10.2.3). This stage is ignored in all previous input-output based studies. Yet by overlooking distribution, one might miss out on up to half of incomes generated in GVCs. This is particularly the case for nondurable goods, where retailers capture a major part of the value in delivery from producer to consumer, as shown in section 10.4. This way we are also much more likely to fully capture intangible income in the production of goods, particularly in the case of factory-less goods producers (FGPs). In the current US statistical system FGPs might be classified in wholesaling, and their output is recorded as a wholesale margin rather than as manufacturing sales. See also contributions in Fontagné and Harrison (2017) on this topic.

10.2.1 Preliminary Notation and Intuition

We illustrate our empirical approach in figure 10.1. We distinguish three sets of activities in a global value chain. These are activities in

- the distribution of the final product from factory to consumer (D). This includes transportation, warehousing and retailing activities.

---

6. This approach of mapping final demand to value added is also used in related settings by Johnson and Noguera (2012), Valentinyi and Herrendorf (2008), and Herrendorf, Rogerson, and Valentinyi (2013). It should be noted that this type of analysis does not depend on, or presume, the production process being linear ("chain"). It is equally valid in any network configuration that can be described by individual stages of production that are linked through trade. To stick with commonly used terms, we refer to all fragmented production processes as "chains," despite the linear connotation of this term.

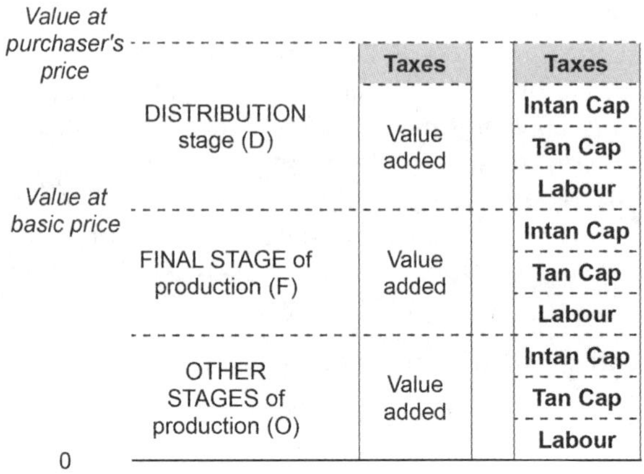

Value at purchaser's price		Taxes	Taxes	
	DISTRIBUTION stage (D)	Value added	Intan Cap	
			Tan Cap	
Value at basic price			Labour	
	FINAL STAGE of production (F)	Value added	Intan Cap	
			Tan Cap	
			Labour	
	OTHER STAGES of production (O)	Value added	Intan Cap	
			Tan Cap	
0			Labour	

Fig. 10.1   Decomposition of factor incomes in global value chains

- the final stage of factory production (F). This can be thought of as a low-value-added activity such as assembly, packaging, or testing but might also involve high-value-added activities such as placing an engine in a car body.
- all other stages of production (O). This might include the manufacturing of parts and components as well as business services (e.g., legal advice, finance, or consulting) and raw material production (e.g., mining and agriculture).

The sum of value added across the production stages makes up the value of the product at basic (ex-factory) prices. When one adds the value added in the distribution stage plus (net) taxes payed by the final consumer, one arrives at the value of a final product at purchasers' prices (see first pillar in figure 10.1). Subsequently, we decompose the value added in each stage into income payments to labor and tangible and intangible assets (second pillar in figure 10.1). Income to labor and tangible assets can be tracked in the data, and we define income to intangible assets residually.

The three activity sets (D, F, and O) are mutually exclusive and together cover all activities that contribute to the value of the final product. More formally, let p be the consumer (purchaser's) price of a good (adjusted for net product taxes), Y the quantity consumed, and V_x value added in stage x. Then we can state the following accounting identity:

$$(1) \qquad\qquad pY \equiv V_D + V_F + V_O.$$

In each activity, factor inputs are being used, and we will distinguish between labor (L), tangible capital (K), and intangible capital (B) inputs. Using this notation, we can write the production function of the final good as

$$(2) \qquad Y = f(B_D, K_D, L_D; \qquad B_F, K_F, L_F; \qquad B_O, K_O, L_O)$$

$$\text{DISTRIBUTION} \quad \text{FINAL STAGES} \quad \text{OTHER STAGES}.$$

The corresponding cost equation is given by multiplying the factor quantities with their respective prices:

$$(3) \qquad pY = \sum_{x \in F,O,D} (r_x^B B_x) + \sum_{x \in F,O,D} (r_x^K K_x) + \sum_{x \in F,O,D} (w_x L_x),$$

$$\text{INTAN CAPITAL} \quad \text{TAN CAPITAL} \quad \text{LABOR}$$

with w the wage rate and r the rental price for capital. This is our basic decomposition of the output value of a final product into three elements: the income to intangible capital, to tangible capital, and to labor. Some of these variables are observable in the data, while others need to be imputed.

In brief, V_x, $w_x L_x$, and K_x can be observed for each stage, r_x^K will be imputed based on an ex-ante rate of return, and $r_x^B B_x$ will be derived residually in each stage as $V_x - r_x^K K_x - w_x L_x$ (see section 10.3 for more explanation). Our main variable of interest will be the income share of intangibles in the GVC:

$$(4) \qquad \frac{\sum_{x \in F,O,D} (r_x^B B_x)}{pY},$$

to be compared with similarly derived shares for tangible capital and labor. The three shares add to one by construction.

10.2.2   Factor Incomes in Production Stages

Stages in GVCs can be inferred from information on the linkages between the various stages of production. A GVC is defined for a country-industry where the final stage of production is taking place—for example, the GVC of cars finalized in the German transport equipment manufacturing industry. We use information from so-called global input-output tables that contain (value) data on intermediate products that flow across industries as well as across countries. An example is the delivery of inputs from the steel industry in China to the automobile industry in Japan. More formally, our decomposition method builds upon the approach outlined in Los, Timmer, and de Vries (2015). It is a multicountry extension of the method suggested by Leontief (1936).

Leontief started from the fundamental input-output identity, which states that all products produced must be either consumed or used as intermediate input in production. This is written as $\mathbf{q} = \mathbf{Aq} + \mathbf{c}$, in which $\mathbf{q}$ denotes a vector of industry-level gross outputs and $\mathbf{c}$ is a vector with final consumption levels for the outputs of each of the industries. Both vectors contain SN elements, in which N stands for the number of countries and S for the number of industries in each country. $\mathbf{A}$ denotes the $SN\mathrm{x}SN$ matrix with input coefficients that describe how many intermediates are needed from any country-industry to produce a unit of output. The identity can be rewritten as $q = (I - A)^{-1}c$, in which I represents an identity matrix. The matrix $(I - A)^{-1}$ is famously known as the Leontief inverse. It can be used to derive output that is generated in all stages of the production process of one unit of a specific final product. To see this, let z be an SN column vector with a one for the element representing, say, iPhones assembled in China, and all other elements are zero. Then Az is the vector of intermediate inputs, both Chinese and foreign, that are assembled, such as the hard-disk drive, battery, and processors. But these intermediates need to be produced as well, and A^2z indicates the intermediate inputs needed to produce Az. This continues until the mining and drilling of basic materials such as metal ore, sand, and oil required to start the production process. Summing up across all stages, one derives the gross output levels for all SN country-industries generated in the production of iPhones by $(I - A)^{-1}z$, since the summation over all rounds converges to this expression.[7]

To find the value added by a particular factor—for example, labor—we additionally need wages paid per unit of output represented in an $SNxSN$ diagonal matrix H. The elements in this matrix are country- and industry-specific: one element contains the wages paid per dollar of output in the Chinese electronics industry, for example. To find the income of all labor that is directly and indirectly involved in the production of z, we multiply H by the total gross output value in all stages of production given above such that

(5) $L = H(I - A)^{-1}z.$

A typical element in the SN vector L indicates the wages of labor employed in country i and industry j in the production of z. A similar procedure can be followed to find the incomes of tangible and intangible capital with a suitable chosen requirement matrix (see next section on data). Following the logic of Leontief's insight, the sum over incomes by all factors in all countries that are involved in the production of this good will equal the output value of that product at basic prices. Thus we have measures for production stages F and O in decomposition equation (3).

10.2.3   Factor Incomes in the Distribution Stage

The Leontief method can be applied to decompose value added in various stages of *production*. It remains silent on the value added in *distribution* of the final product to the consumer, however. This is due to the nature of the data used: the distribution sector is represented in input-output tables as a so-called margin industry. This means that the goods bought by the distribution sectors (to be resold) are not treated as intermediate inputs. The gross output of the distribution sector is measured in terms of the

---

7. This is under empirically mild conditions. See Miller and Blair (2009) for a good starting point on input-output analysis.

"margin"—that is, the value of goods sold minus the acquisition value of those goods. Accordingly, we define the value added in the distribution stage by a margin-to-sales ratio (m) such that

$$(6) \qquad\qquad V_D \equiv m(pY).$$

We use the factor shares in the wholesale and retailing industries to derive the factor requirements in the distribution stage.

10.3   Data Sources

For our empirical analysis, we use three types of data: world input-output tables, information on distribution margins, and data on factor incomes of industries. The input-output tables and data on labor compensation and value added are derived from the WIOD 2016 release and have been extensively described in Timmer et al. (2015). Important to note here is that the WIOD contains data on 56 industries (of which 19 are manufacturing) in 43 countries and a rest-of-the-world region such that all value added in GVCs is accounted for. In this section, we provide more information on two new pieces of empirical information that are needed additionally: the income shares of tangible (and intangible) capital and data on distribution margins.

10.3.1   Capital Income Shares at the Country-Industry Level

Gross value added (V) and labor compensation (wL) can be derived from national accounts statistics (with appropriate adjustment for the income of the self-employed), and this information is taken from the WIOD. As in Karabarbounis and Neiman (2018), we impute the income to tangible assets and derive intangible income as the residual for each industry i as

$$(7) \qquad\qquad r_i^B B_i \equiv VA_i - w_i L_i - r_i^K K_i.$$

Tangible asset income for industry i is derived through multiplying tangible capital stock K_i with an (ex-ante) rental price r_i^K. According to neoclassical theory, the rental price (user cost) of capital consists of four elements: depreciation, capital taxes (net of subsidies), (expected) capital gains, and a (net) nominal rate of return (Hall and Jorgenson 1967). For want of data, we abstain from capital taxes in our empirical analysis. The rental price is then given by

$$(8) \qquad\qquad r_i^K = (\delta_i^K + \rho_i^K) p_i^I,$$

with the depreciation rate δ_i^K, the real (net) rate of return ρ_i^K and the tangible investment price p_i^I. The rate of return is ex ante such that a residual remains in (7), which is the income for intangible capital. The rate of return reflects the opportunity cost of capital in the market. We set it to 4 percent for all tangible assets, following long-standing practice (at least before the financial crisis in 2007). We show in additional robustness analysis that using time-varying rates based on government bond yields, or another alternative instead, will have no significant impact on our main results (reported in section 10.5).

Our definition of tangible capital assets follows the tangible asset boundary in the System of National Accounts (SNA) 2008, including buildings, machinery, transport equipment, information technology assets, communication technology assets, and other tangible assets. Country-industry tangible asset stocks are derived from the EU KLEMS database December 2016 release (Jäger 2016) for Australia, Japan, and the United States and 12 major European countries (Austria, Czech Republic, Denmark, Finland, France, Germany, Italy, the Netherlands, Slovenia, Spain, Sweden, and the United Kingdom). For the other countries, we only have stocks by industry but not by asset type. These countries are mostly reporting under the rules of SNA93, which means that the industry-level asset stocks may include some intangible assets—most notably software. They typically constitute a small share, though, as most countries still reporting in SNA93 are poor. Geometric depreciation rates for detailed asset types are taken from EU KLEMS. These rates take into account the differences in the composition of capital assets both across countries and industries as well as over time. We carefully distinguish between various data environments across countries. The appendix in Chen et al. (2017) provides elaborate discussion on a country-by-country basis.

10.3.2 Value Added in Distribution Stage

To measure the value that is added in the distribution stage, we need to have information on the margin-to-sales ratios for final manufacturing goods (m). We derive this from the ratio of output valued at basic and at purchaser's prices. The purchaser's price consists of the basic price plus trade and transport margins in the handling of the product and any (net) product taxes. Put otherwise, the margin is the difference between the price paid by the consumer and the price received by the producer. Margins are calculated from information on final expenditures at purchaser's and basic prices as given in national supply and use tables. This data can be found for most countries in the WIOD (under the heading of national supply-use tables). For China, Japan, and the US, only data at producer prices is given in the WIOD, however. We complemented this with data from detailed retail and wholesale sector censuses. We adjust purchaser's prices for (net) taxes on the products, as these are paid for by the consumer to the government and do not constitute payment for factor inputs in any stage of production.

10.4   Main Results

In this section, we will present our main findings on the factor income shares in global value chains of manufactured goods. As background, it is useful to note that consumption of manufactured goods (at purchasers' prices) makes up about 27.9 percent of world GDP (in 2000, derived from the WIOD). This high number might be surprising given that gross value added in the manufacturing sectors, aggregated across all countries in the world, is only 18.4 percent of world GDP. This is because consumption value of manufactured goods also includes value added from primary goods and services sectors (including distribution).[8] We will map the consumption value of final manufactured goods into income generated for labor and capital in all countries that contributed to production and distribution of these goods. We will do this for 19 detailed manufacturing product groups and also present aggregate results.

The production processes of goods have been fragmenting across borders with major impetuses from the North American Free Trade Agreement (NAFTA) in the early 1990s and China's accession to the World Trade Organization (WTO) in 2001. Previous work on manufactured goods, reported in Timmer et al. (2014), found that the share of labor income in final output was declining over the period from 1995 to 2007. Surprisingly, this was the case not only in those stages carried out in advanced countries but also in stages carried out in less-advanced regions. The former was expected given that offshored stages are typically labor intensive, but the latter finding was not. This highlighted the increased importance of capital in production, as its income share increased in virtually all GVCs. Timmer et al. (2014) hypothesized that this was related to the increased importance of intangibles. With our new data, we are in the position to test this hypothesis, distinguishing between tangible and intangible incomes. We can also investigate trends in the period after 2007.

10.4.1   Finding 1: Declining Share of Labor Income in GVCs

The GVC decomposition results, aggregated across all manufacturing goods, are given in table 10.1. It shows the income shares for labor and tangible and intangible capital as defined in equation (4). Figure 10.2 charts the cumulative changes in factor income shares with the year 2000 as base. We find a strongly increasing capital share and a concomitantly declining trend in the share of labor. The labor share dropped from 56.4 percent in 2000 to 51.8 percent in 2007. This resonates well with previous findings (Timmer et al. 2014).[9] It stabilized afterward: in 2014, the share was 51.2 percent. We conclude that the declining trend in labor share did not continue after

---

8. And not all manufacturing value added ends up in final manufacturing goods (e.g., when used in production of final services). See Herrendorf, Rogerson, and Valentinyi (2013) for results from a similar exercise mapping consumption to sectoral value added for the US economy.

9. The 2014 study used a previous version of the WIOD (the 2013 release) and did not include distribution activities but only production stages (F and O)—that is, it decomposed output at basic prices. Our extension to output at purchaser's prices did not appear to have a major impact on factor income distribution.

Table 10.1   **Factor income shares in GVCs of manufacturing goods (%-share)**

	Labor		Tangible capital		Intangible capital	
	Share (%)	Change	Share (%)	Change	Share (%)	Change
2000	56.4		15.8		27.8	
2001	56.2	−0.2	16.1	0.3	27.7	−0.1
2002	55.1	−1.1	16.2	0.1	28.7	1.0
2003	54.6	−0.5	16.3	0.1	29.1	0.4
2004	53.5	−1.1	16.3	0.0	30.2	1.1
2005	52.7	−0.8	16.2	−0.1	31.2	1.0
2006	52.1	−0.6	16.1	−0.1	31.8	0.6
2007	51.8	−0.3	16.3	0.2	31.9	0.1
2008	51.8	0.0	16.8	0.5	31.4	−0.5
2009	52.2	0.4	17.6	0.8	30.2	−1.2
2010	50.5	−1.7	17.8	0.2	31.7	1.5
2011	50.6	0.1	17.6	−0.2	31.8	0.1
2012	51.0	0.4	17.7	0.1	31.3	−0.5
2013	51.1	0.1	17.8	0.1	31.1	−0.2
2014	51.2	0.1	18.1	0.3	30.7	−0.4

Notes: Share of factor income in worldwide output of final manufacturing products valued at purchaser's prices, before product tax (in percentages). Labor income includes all costs of employing labor, including self-employed income. Tangible capital income includes gross returns to tangible assets based on a 4 per cent real (net) rate of return. Intangible capital income is calculated as a residual (gross value added minus labor and tangible capital income). Own calculations based on the WIOD 2016, extended with data on tangible capital stocks and distribution margins as described section 10.3.

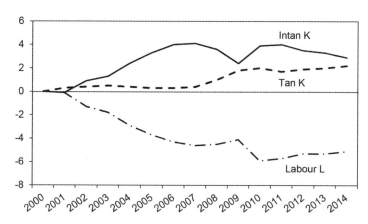

Fig. 10.2   Cumulative percentage point change in factor income shares (2000 base)
Note: See table 10.1.

2007 but also did not reverse. This is suggesting that the decline was not a temporary phase in some kind of business-cycle pattern.

10.4.2   Finding 2: Increasing Share of Intangible Income Share up to 2007 but Not After

A novel finding of this study is that the increasing share of capital after 2000 is mainly due to increasing incomes to intangibles. The income share of tangible capital grew only slowly, from 15.8 percent in 2000 to 16.3 percent in 2007. The low volatility of the tangible share is partly by virtue of its measurement: it is based on a stock estimate multiplied by an ex-ante rental rate, and both variables move only slowly over time. The decline in the labor share was thus mainly mirrored by an increase in the intangible share, which is measured as a residual after subtracting labor and tangible capital incomes. Its share jumped from 27.8 percent in 2000 to 31.9 percent in 2007. This increase was not sustained, however, and even reversed in 2011, declining to 30.7 percent in 2014.

10.4.3   Finding 3: Income Share of Intangible Assets in GVCs Is (Much) Higher Than That of Tangible Assets

Another interesting, and perhaps most surprising, finding is the high income share of intangibles relative to tangible assets. For all manufacturing goods combined, intangible income was 27.8 percent of final output value in 2000 relative to only 15.8 percent for tangible assets, so about 1.8 times as high (table 10.1).[10] The ratio reached a peak in 2007 at 2.0 and gradually declined again to 1.7 in 2014. Similarly high ratios are found for more detailed product groups. In table 10.2, we provide an overview of the factor income shares in 2014 for 12 major manufacturing product groups.

Factor income shares are informative on the factor intensity of production. Traditionally, products are classified as labor or capital intensive depending on the factor intensity of production in the parent industry. With production fragmentation, this classification is less straightforward as factor intensities of all contributing industries need to be considered. The intangible income share is shown to be more than double the tangible share for pharmaceuticals, chemical products, and oil-refining products (see last column in table 10.2). The high ratio for petroleum products is likely related to the importance of brand names, tightly controlled distribution systems, and restricted resource access generating supranormal profits that end up in our

---

10. In related research, Karabarbounis and Neiman (2018) find what they call the "factorless" income share to be 15 percent of value added in the 2000s in the US private business sector. This is the share that is not attributable to labor or measured capital stocks, using the asset boundary of the SNA 2008 (thus including IPP). Factorless income is found to be larger than measured capital income. In a different exercise, Bhandari and McGrattan (2018) also find a high ratio of intangible to total assets: their estimate of what they call "sweat equity" (firm-specific intangibles) is close to the estimate of marketable fixed assets used in production by private businesses.

Table 10.2   Factor income shares in GVCs (%-share), major product groups, 2014

Final product group name	ISIC rev. 4 code	Labor share	Tangible capital share	Intangible capital share	Ratio of intangible to tangible
Petroleum products	19	37.9	20.0	42.1	2.1
Chemical products	20	44.9	17.5	37.5	2.1
Pharmaceuticals	21	48.8	16.5	34.7	2.1
Food products	10t12	52.6	16.4	31.0	1.9
Furniture and other	31t32	53.7	16.3	30.1	1.8
Textiles and apparel	13t15	52.4	17.7	29.9	1.7
Electronic products	26	50.0	18.6	31.3	1.7
Motor vehicles	29	51.3	19.0	29.7	1.6
Electrical equipment	27	50.6	20.0	29.5	1.5
Nonelec. machinery	28	53.9	18.8	27.2	1.4
Other transport equipment	30	55.2	18.5	26.3	1.4
Fabricated metal products	25	55.2	20.8	24.0	1.2
All manufacturing products		51.2	18.1	30.7	1.7

Notes: See table 10.1. Twelve major manufacturing product groups, ranked by ratio of intangible to tangible income share (last column).

residual intangible measure. Pharmaceuticals are known to be highly R&D and patent intensive, which is reflected in the high intangible to tangible income ratio. Perhaps more surprising is the finding that the ratio is also high for textiles and apparel and "other" manufacturing products, which includes, among others, furniture and toys. These products are mainly produced in extensive international supply networks, and value-added generation relies on chain orchestration as well as strong marketing and branding of the products. The ratio between intangible and tangible incomes is lower, but still well above one, for electrical equipment (not including electronics), nonelectrical machinery, and other transport equipment. Their production is characterized by large tangible investments with high minimum efficient scales. The ratio is lowest for metal industries that are characterized by heavy reliance on tangible assets in the form of large-scale smelters and metal processing plants. The ranking of product groups is rather stable of time (not shown).

What type of intangible assets might be responsible for the large income share found in GVCs? One might suspect that intellectual property plays a major role. In the 2008 System of National Accounts (SNA08), investment in intellectual property products (IPP) is tracked. This includes computer software and databases, research and development, mineral exploration, and artistic originals. Thus we can carry out a simple back-of-the-envelope exercise to impute the income accruing to IPP, using information on IPP capital stocks (from national accounts statistics, as reported in EU KLEMS), and proxy the rental price by the IPP depreciation rate (taken as 30 percent) plus

Table 10.3   Income shares for intangible capital in global value chains (percent of final output)

Final product group name	ISIC rev. 4 code	2000	2007	2014	Change 2000–2007	Change 2007–2014	Change 2000–2014
Elec. machinery	27	24.3	31.6	29.5	7.3	−2.1	5.1
Chemicals	20	32.4	36.5	37.5	4.1	1.0	5.1
Vehicles	29	24.8	29.9	29.7	5.1	−0.2	5.0
Metal products	25	19.3	25.6	24.0	6.3	−1.6	4.7
Nonelec. mach.	28	23.3	30.1	27.2	6.8	−2.8	4.0
Electronics	26	28.2	33.8	31.3	5.6	−2.4	3.2
Other transport eq.	30	23.4	29.4	26.3	6.0	−3.1	2.9
Furn. and other	31t32	28.0	30.5	30.1	2.5	−0.4	2.1
Oil products	19	40.5	47.0	42.1	6.5	−4.9	1.6
Food	10t12	29.8	31.1	31.0	1.3	−0.1	1.2
Textiles	13t15	28.7	31.1	29.9	2.4	−1.2	1.2
Pharmaceuticals	21	34.8	37.7	34.7	3.0	−3.1	−0.1
All products		27.8	31.9	30.7	4.1	−1.2	2.9

Notes: Share of intangibles in the final output value of manufacturing products (%). Product groups ranked by change during 2000−2014 (last column).

a real (net) rate of return of 4 percent, as we did for tangible assets.[11] Doing so, we find that the income share to IPP in manufacturing GVCs would amount to 2.4 percent in 2000, hovering between 2.2 and 2.7 percent during the period 2000–2014. It thus can explain only a minor part of the intangible income share that stood at 27.8 percent in 2000. We conclude that there must be a major set of intangible assets that is still outside the asset boundary currently covered in the SNA08. This reinforces the findings of Corrado, Hulten, and Sichel (2005, 2009) and Corrado et al. (2013). They provide estimates for market research, advertising, training, and organizational capital that are currently not treated as investment in the national accounts. Yet the industry detail currently provided is too aggregate to be used for analysis of GVCs of manufacturing products. "Aggregate manufacturing" is the lowest level of industry detail for which data are given.[12] This is a fruitful avenue for future research.

10.4.4   Finding 4: Increase in Intangible Income Is Driven by International Production Fragmentation

In table 10.3 we provide an overview of the changes in intangible income shares for 12 manufacturing product groups. They are ranked according to the change over the 2000–2014 period. There is clear heterogeneity. For some products, such as pharmaceuticals, textiles, and food, the intangible

11. Not all countries have implemented the SNA08, however (most notably China, India, and Japan), so we are not able to carry out a full exercise, but it seems plausible that the majority of IPP is in Europe and the United States.

12. See http://www.intaninvest.net/ for a database covering a large set of countries.

share barely increased over the whole period 2000–2014. An initial increase up to 2008 was almost nullified in the period after. In contrast, the share increased over 2000–2014 by 4.0 percentage points or more in electrical machinery, chemicals, vehicles, metal products, and nonelectrical machinery. For some of these product groups, the intangible income shares increased strongly until 2008, followed by a moderate decline afterward. Yet the share continued to increase in the production of chemicals and barely declined in the production of vehicles.

The variation in intangible income shares across products invites further investigation into possible drivers. One possible hypothesis centers around the speed of international production fragmentation. The period from the mid-1990s until 2008 is characterized by a strong process of fragmentation across borders, sped up by the opening up of China and its joining the WTO in 2001. Yet the impact varied across product groups (Timmer et al. 2016). International fragmentation was, for example, high in the production of electronics (including computers), electrical machinery, and metal products in the 2000s. But production of textiles and furniture was already quite fragmented before 2000. Other products are arguably less susceptible to international fragmentation trends, such as food manufacturing (which has strong domestic supply links for intermediate inputs) and pharmaceuticals manufacturing. To test this hypothesis more formally, we combine our estimates of intangible income shares with information on international fragmentation of production processes. Timmer et al. (2016) provide a new measure that tracks all imports made along the production chain and argue that this is a good indicator for international production fragmentation. In figure 10.3 we plot the change in this indicator for our 19 manufacturing product groups against the change in the share of intangible income in those GVCs from table 10.3 for the period 2000–2008. We find that there is a clear positive correlation (0.52), which fits our conjecture. Yet unexplained variation is still high, and further investigation into the drivers of intangible income shares is warranted.

10.4.5   Finding 5: Increasing Importance of Intangibles in Upstream Production Stages

So far, we have reported on income for factors aggregated over all stages and remained agnostic about the division across stages. Yet our methodology allows one to also track in which stage of the GVC the returns to intangibles are recorded using a straightforward disaggregation of equation (4) by stage: distribution stage, final stage of production, and other upstream stages of production. Results are reported in table 10.4. We find that in 2014 about one quarter of the intangibles income is accounted for in the distribution stage. One quarter is accounted for in the final production stage and about half in other upstream production stages. There is a clear shift away from intangible income recorded in the final production stage (minus 4.2

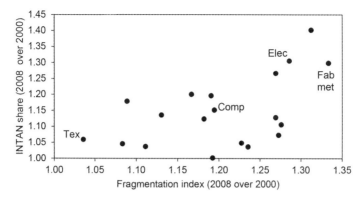

Fig. 10.3   Intangible income shares and international production fragmentation

Notes: Fragmentation index from Timmer et al. (2016) based on all imports made along the production chain (2008 as ratio of 2000 level). Intangible income share in 2008 as ratio of level in 2000. Observations for 19 manufacturing product groups. Observations for textiles (tex), electrical machinery (elec), electronics and computers (comp), and fabricated metal products (fab met) are indicated.

percentage points over the period 2000–2014) to the other production stages (plus 5.5 percentage points). This shift mainly occurred before the crisis of 2008. This finding is consistent with a story of offshoring of final production stages (such as assembly, testing, and packaging) from advanced to low-wage economies such that the incomes in this stage decline rapidly compared to the other stages that remained.

Interestingly, the aggregate trend is not shared across all product groups, which might be related to the type of governance in the chain. Gereffi (1999) proposes a distinction between what he refers to as buyer-driven and producer-driven GVCs. GVCs are governed by so-called lead firms that have a large share of control over the activities that take place in the chain. The lead firm in a buyer-driven chain is typically a large retail chain or a branded merchandiser and often has little or no goods-production capacity. The lead firm in a producer-driven chain is a manufacturer that derives bargaining power from superior technological and production know-how.[13] We find that for buyer-driven GVCs like textiles, furniture, toys, and other manufacturing, the returns to intangibles are mostly realized in the distribution stage (up to 50 percent; see table 10.4). In contrast, in producer-driven GVCs like vehicles, fabricated metal, and other transport equipment, intangible returns are mostly realized in the upstream production stages (up to 60 percent). All

13. Most GVCs are governed in complex ways and combine elements of both governance modes. Governance modes are not necessarily product-group specific. An electronic gadget can be produced in a chain driven by an international retailer (e.g., in the case of a generic nonbranded product) or in a producer-driven chain (e.g., in the case of a high-end branded product).

Table 10.4   Share of stages in intangible capital income (in %)

Final product group name	Code	Distribution stage			Final production stage			Other (upstream) production stages		
		2000	2014	Change	2000	2014	Change	2000	2014	Change
Furn. and oth.	31t32	48.3	50.0	1.7	23.1	18.8	−4.3	28.7	31.3	2.6
Textiles	13t15	44.1	50.6	6.5	21.6	14.9	−6.7	34.3	34.5	0.2
Food	10t12	30.6	29.8	−0.8	36.9	30.1	−6.7	32.5	40.1	7.6
Chemicals	20	25.8	23.5	−2.2	35.7	35.9	0.3	38.6	40.5	2.0
Nonel. mach.	28	25.2	23.6	−1.6	26.3	24.4	−1.9	48.5	52.0	3.5
Metal	25	23.2	17.4	−5.7	20.7	20.4	−0.3	56.1	62.1	6.0
Vehicles	29	22.7	16.3	−6.5	26.4	29.3	2.9	50.9	54.4	3.5
Pharma	21	22.1	19.9	−2.1	48.6	46.1	−2.5	29.3	34.0	4.7
Elec. mach.	27	19.7	23.3	3.6	28.1	21.8	−6.3	52.2	54.9	2.7
Oth. trans.	30	17.7	15.2	−2.6	30.5	24.8	−5.7	51.7	60.0	8.3
Electronics	26	17.6	20.7	3.0	38.6	34.9	−3.6	43.8	44.4	0.6
Oil	19	16.8	12.7	−4.1	26.0	20.9	−5.2	57.2	66.5	9.3
All products		28.3	27.0	−1.3	30.8	26.6	−4.2	40.9	46.4	5.5

Notes: Intangible capital income in each stage of GVC, as share in total income for intangibles across all stages, see table 10.1 for sources.

products share the trend of a declining share of the final production stage in intangible income, with the notable exception of vehicle production.

10.4.6   Interpretation

So far, we have interpreted the residual income share in GVCs of goods as payments to intangible assets. Other interpretations are possible. For example, Barkai (2017) suggests that the increase in the residual in US GDP is related to a decline in competition.[14] In our view, competition and the buildup of intangible assets are interrelated. More specifically, we prefer to think of the global market for manufacturing goods in the following way. Final goods are supplied by large firms that organize production in vertically integrated processes spanning across borders. The market structure for final goods is monopolistic competition: each firm supplies a differentiated good and is able to charge a price higher than average costs.[15] A firm derives monopoly power from investment in intangible assets that are specific to the firm. Conceptually, they differ from other factor inputs because, by and

14. Karabarbounis and Neiman (2018) contend that the residual, which they dub "factorless income," also contains a possible wedge between imputed rental rates for assets and the rate that firms perceive when making the investment. In the robustness section that follows, we show that this wedge needs to be extremely large in order to explain away the residual.

15. Romalis (2004) provides a many-country version of a Heckscher-Ohlin model with a continuum of (final) goods produced under monopolistic competition and with transport costs. Mark ups might of course also be the result of a natural monopoly or government regulation. This situation is less likely to be relevant for manufacturing goods that are heavily traded worldwide (with the exception of petroleum products).

large, companies cannot freely order or hire them in markets. Instead, these assets are produced, and used, in-house: they are not reported in balance sheets and not tracked as investment in national accounts statistics. Viewed this way, intangible capital is the firm-specific "yeast" that creates value from hired labor and purchased assets. The residual that remains can thus be interpreted as income to own-account intangibles.

The "yeast" perspective on residual income has old antecedents harking back at least to Prescott and Visscher (1980). See Cummins (2005) for further analysis on firm-level data. It is also related to the concept of sweat equity, defined as the time that business owners spend in building up firm-specific intangibles; see Bhandari and McGrattan (2018) for recent work. They emphasize the importance of organizational capital that is typically built at own-account and not (adequately) picked up as investment in national account statistics. In the appendix, we show through a capitalization-of-intangibles exercise as in Corrado, Hulten, and Sichel (2005) that residual income in a GVC is equal to the income for own-account intangibles when (part of the) workers are assumed to build up firm-specific capital. Under a "steady-state" assumption such that the creation of intangibles in each period is equal to depreciation, the intangible income is shown to be a *net* measure. So in terms of disposable incomes (Bridgman 2018; Rognlie 2015), intangible earnings might be even larger relative to tangible earnings, as the latter is inclusive of depreciation. Yet this is only under the steady-state assumption, which cannot be verified through direct observation.

Taking our findings together, we argue that the 2000s was a unique period in the global economy where supranormal returns to tangibles were (temporarily) captured based on firm-specific intangible assets that went largely unrecorded in national account statistics. Our results support a story in which global manufacturing firms benefitted from increased opportunities for offshoring. Changes in the global economic environment in the early 2000s—in particular China's accession to the WTO and developments in information and communications technology (ICT)—made it profitable to develop extensive global production and distribution networks. Multinational firms built up firm-specific coordination systems, benefitting from increased opportunities for offshoring of labor-intensive activities to low-wage locations. The income accruing to labor in the GVC declined due to wage cost savings. This matches our finding that incomes in final production stages (such as assembly, testing, and packaging) declined rapidly compared to upstream production stages. If the production requirements (and prices) for tangible capital remain unaltered, the share of intangibles must go up by virtue of its definition as a residual.[16] In addition, the growth in purchasing power in the global economy (such as growing consumer demand in

---

16. This is true only under the assumption that factor substitution possibilities between labor and capital are limited. See Reijnders, Timmer, and Ye (2016) for an econometric analysis of factor substitution and technical change in global value chains. They find wage elasticities to be well below one.

China) might have benefitted incumbent multinational firms that were able to capitalize on existing intangibles such as brand names and distribution systems at little marginal cost. Apparently, this process was interrupted by the financial crisis in 2007, likely related to subsequent heightened uncertainty on future global demand.

10.5 Discussion of Robustness of Main Findings

How robust are our main findings presented in section 10.4? Gross value added and the income payments to labor are recorded in the national accounts. The payments to tangible assets are imputed based on asset stocks and a rental price that includes a chosen rate of return. The higher this rate is set, the higher the tangible income will be and the lower the intangible income, which is measured residually. Setting the real (net) rate of return to tangible assets is not straightforward: from theory it depends on the opportunity cost of capital in the market as well as the expected inflation. It was set at 4 percent in our analysis so far, but alternative choices can be defended as well.

To have an idea about the sensitivity of results, one might ask what rate of return to *tangibles* would exhaust all nonlabor income such that no residual remains. The physical-capital-to-output ratio was about 1.3 (that is, the value of the tangible asset stock relative to final output) in 2000. It follows that the real (net) rate of return to physical capital needs to be as high as 25 percent to exhaust final output, clearly well outside the boundary of plausible rates. For example, Barkai (2017, figure 1) shows that debt costs in the United States, set to the yield on Moody's AAA bond portfolio, declined from about 7 percent in 2000 to 5 percent in 2014. He calculated expected capital inflation as a three-year moving average of realized capital inflation and found it to oscillate around 2 percent. This suggests a small but steady decline in the real rate of return from 5 percent to 3 percent over our period of analysis (2000–2014). Rognlie (2015) took the ten-year Treasury bond yield, subtracting the lagged five-year rate of change of the GDP deflator as a proxy for inflation expectations. This real rate was about 4 percent in 2000, gradually declining to just above 0 percent in 2014. These alternative estimates are relatively close to our chosen 4 percent, so our findings on relative levels of tangible and intangible income appear robust. Moreover, the findings of a *declining* rate of return over the period considered suggests that, if anything, we are *under*estimating the importance of intangibles in later years. For example, using a 0 percent real rate of return instead of 4 percent would indicate that in 2014 the tangible income share was only about 12 percent and the intangible share more than 36 percent: a ratio of 3 rather than barely 2 as we reported. These results suggest that using plausible time-varying instead of a constant real (net) rate of return to tangible assets is strengthening our conclusions on the increased importance of intangibles in manufacturing GVCs.

Yet one might argue that we nevertheless overestimate intangible incomes, as we are using gross value-added statistics that are measured according to the SNA08. Gross value added is defined in the SNA as the value of output less the value of intermediate consumption. In the SNA08, expenditures on IPP are treated as capital formation, not intermediate consumption.[17] This increases the value added but not the *tangible* capital stock. Thus if we take value-added statistics recorded in SNA08, gross value added might be overestimated for our purposes, and so will our intangible income measure through its residual nature.[18] To have an upper-limit estimation of the bias, we assume that all IPP is bought in the market and recorded at cost.[19] Costs of IPP can be proxied by multiplying IPP stocks with the sum of the IPP depreciation rate (taken as 30 percent) plus a real (net) rate of return of 4 percent (as we did before). Doing so, we find that value added (and hence intangible income) in the GVC is overestimated within a range of 2.2 to 2.7 percent during the period 2000–2014. This shows that our main results on the relative levels and growth rates of intangible income are robust to this data issue.

A potentially more serious issue is the asset boundary of tangible capital. We follow the convention of the SNA08 and include fixed assets (such as machinery, equipment, and buildings) but not land and inventories. Yet both land and inventories tie up capital, and their use entails an opportunity cost. Estimating stocks of inventory and land is fraught with difficulties, however. The SNA tracks changes in inventories but not necessarily their value. Land is even more problematic, as land improvement expenditures do fall within the SNA asset boundary—in particular when they are tied with (improved) buildings or infrastructure. The US Bureau of Labor Statistics tries to take into account these assets when constructing their multifactor productivity statistics along the lines of Jorgenson (1995). They find for the manufacturing sector that capital compensation for inventories and land adds about a quarter to the income of the tangible assets covered in the SNA. This can go up to 65 percent in retail and even 100 percent in the wholesaling sector due to the important role of inventories in these sectors.[20] Yet these numbers are based on calculations that use an *ex-post* rate of return, which

17. IPP covers R&D, computer software and databases, mineral exploration, and entertainment and artistic originals. See Koh, Santaeulalia-Llopis, and Zheng (2016) for more information on treatment of IPP by the US Bureau of Economic Analysis (BEA).

18. For countries that still publish national accounts according to SNA93, these imputations will be only small, including an imputation for own-account software at best. More discussion of this overestimation can be found in Chen et al. (2017).

19. This is clearly an extreme assumption, as a major part of IPP is own-account and not purchased. In the United States, the share of purchased is about two-third and own-account is about one-third, while it is 50-50 in the United Kingdom (from additional info in national account statistics).

20. The data are taken from *Bureau of Labor Statistics*, Office of Productivity and Technology, Division of Major Sector Productivity, published on line March 21, 2018, at http://www.bls.gov/mfp/.

exhausts value added, rather than an ex-ante rate as required. As such, the reported incomes also contain all income by assets that are not covered in the analysis. Corrado, Hulten, and Sichel (2005) argued forcefully that many intangibles are still outside the SNA asset boundary, echoed in our finding of a large residual income. In that case, the ex-post rate of return will be overestimated and likewise the rental price of land and inventories— more so because their depreciation rates are zero by nature. We conclude that the capital compensation numbers for income to land and inventories as in the Bureau of Labor Statistics data are not suitable for our purposes. This does highlight, however, that more information on these asset types—in particular, on their stocks—is desirable.

A particular caveat is needed for our findings on intangible incomes in each stage (finding 5). For a proper interpretation of the results, one should realize that what is measured here is the stage where the intangible income is recorded. This does not necessarily imply that the income is also captured by the firms that operate in that stage. For example, compare a situation in which Apple charges the iPhone assembler for its intellectual property with a situation in which it does not. The ex-factory price of the iPhone would be higher in the former case and the measured return to the intangibles consequently lower in the distribution stage. But the measured return to intangibles would be higher in one of the earlier stages of production, as it would include a payment for use of Apple's intangibles. The division of intangible incomes across stages is thus sensitive to accounting practices by lead firms, as discussed in the introduction. Results that are based on aggregating across all stages (which underlie findings 1 to 4) are not sensitive to these shifts.

As a final remark, it should be clear that the validity of all the findings relies heavily on the quality of the database used. Data can, and needs to, be improved in many dimensions. For example, the WIOD is a prototype database developed mainly to provide proof of concept, and it is up to the statistical community to bring international input-output tables into the realm of official statistics. For example, one currently has to rely on the assumption that all firms in a country-industry have a similar production structure, because firm-level data matching national input-output tables are largely lacking. If different types of firms—in particular, exporters and nonexporters—have different production technologies and input sourcing structures (i.e., exporters import larger shares of inputs), more detailed data might reveal an (unknown) bias in the results presented here.[21] From the perspective of measuring intangibles' returns, one of the biggest challenges is in the concept and measurement of trade in services (Houseman and Mandel 2015). Fortunately, there are important developments in the international

---

21. The development work done by the Organisation for Economic Co-operation and Development (OECD) is certainly a step in the right direction; see http://oe.cd/tiva for more information.

statistical community. Recently, the United Nations Economic Commission for Europe (UNECE) published its *Guide to Measuring Global Production* (UNECE 2015). Building on this are new initiatives, most notably the initiative toward a *System of Extended International and Global Accounts (SEIGA)*. In the short run, this would involve mixing existing establishment and enterprise data (in extended supply and use tables) as well as expanding survey information on value-added chains and firm characteristics. In the longer term, this would entail common business registers across countries, increased data reconciliation and linking, and new data collections on value chains beyond counterparty transactions (Landefeld 2015).

10.6   Concluding Remarks

Recent studies document a decline in the share of labor and a simultaneous increase in the share of residual ("factorless") income in national GDP. We argue that study of factor incomes in GVCs is needed to better understand this residual. This is the first chapter to do so. We show how to measure income of all tangible factor inputs (capital and labor) in a GVC. We define intangible capital income residually by subtracting the payments for tangible factors (capital and labor) from the value of the final product. Importantly, these factors are identified in all stages of production (final and upstream stages) as well as in the distribution stage. This is important, as a large share of value might be added in the delivery of the good to the final consumer rather than in the production stages.

We focus on GVCs of manufactured goods and find a declining labor income share over the period 2000–2014 and a concomitant increase in the capital income share. Our main finding is that this increase in capital income in GVCs is mostly due to the increase in income for intangible rather than tangible assets. This is found at the aggregate as well as for more detailed manufacturing product groups. Yet we also find clear heterogeneity: for some nondurable products, the intangible share increased only slightly, contracting later on. In contrast, the share increased rapidly in durable goods (such as machinery and equipment products). We provide suggestive evidence that this variation is positively linked to variation in the speed of international production fragmentation. Taken together, our results suggest that the 2000s should be seen as an exceptional period in the global economy during which multinational firms benefitted from reduced labor costs through offshoring while capitalizing on existing firm-specific intangibles, such as brand names, at little marginal cost.

We discussed robustness of these results to issues like missing information on land and inventories, value added imputations for some intangibles in the SNA08, and choice for (ex-ante) rate of return to tangible assets. We argued that the level of intangible income might be *over*estimated, but the trend over time is likely to be *under*estimated, if anything. In any case, there is a robust large residual income in GVCs that can be attributed neither to tangible assets nor to the wider asset class considered in the SNA08 (which includes intellectual property products). We reinforce the claim made by Corrado, Hulten, and Sichel (2005) that national account statistics are missing out on a sizeable set of intangible assets. Our conjecture is that most of these are own-account. To bring this hypothesis to the data, one would need information on investment in assets that are (or can be) purchased in the market, to be distinguished from "own-account" investment that is firm specific. Unfortunately, investment statistics from the national accounts typically do not separate own-account and market-mediated investment flows, although company balance sheets might provide information (Peters and Taylor 2017). Hopefully this type of information will be systematically collected and separately reported in future national account statistics. We also emphasized that the measurement framework puts high demand on the data, and our results should thus be seen as indicative rather than definitive.

The main aim of this study was to stimulate further thinking about the interrelatedness of factor incomes across industries and countries. We showed that it mattered in an accounting sense, as the use of intangibles is blurring the attribution of incomes to particular geographical locations and industries in national accounts statistics. In addition, it invites further investigation of the role of governance in global value chains. Gereffi (1994, 1999) highlighted the crucial role of multinational lead firms in the generation and division of value in the chain. In particular, the importance of internationally operating retailers highlights the need to consider the distribution stage alongside production stages that are the traditional confines of empirical GVC studies based on input-output tables. Further research is also needed to identify various types of intangibles and their investment flows, prices, and depreciation rates in macrowork following Corrado, Hulten, and Sichel (2005, 2009) and Corrado et al. (2013) as well as firm-level research, such as in Peters and Taylor (2017). At the minimum, we hope to have convinced the reader that a deeper understanding of global value chains is needed before our measurement systems will adequately capture the importance of intangibles, and their incomes, in today's global economy.

Appendix

Linking "Factorless" Income to Intangible Assets: An Accounting Model

In this appendix, we will outline a simple accounting model that points to a straightforward interpretation of the factorless (residual) income measure in GVCs as reported on in the main text. We will show how, under steady-state conditions, this residual can be interpreted as net income payment to intangible assets. We analyze the case in which the intangible is produced by the firm for own account (i.e., in house). To do so, we follow the capital accounting approach to intangibles as pioneered in Corrado, Hulten, and Sichel (2005).

To fix ideas, we use the example of a multinational firm that sells goods but does not produce them. This firm imports a good—say, shoes—from an affiliate and sells them (at a premium) under its brand name. The firm only employs marketing staff that work on branding. We model the production function of this firm as $Y(L^B,S)$, with Y sales of shoes, L^B number of workers, and S imports of shoes. Let p denote prices, with superscripts indicating the output or input to which it refers.[22] Gross profit of the firm in the distribution stage, π^B, is then given by

$$(A1) \qquad \pi^B = p^Y Y - w^B L^B - p^S S.$$

π^B can be observed in the data, yet how should it be interpreted? The brand name is created with a view of generating profits over a longer time period and hence should be considered as a capital input as argued by Corrado, Hulten, and Sichel (2005). In their capitalization approach, the firm is using an intangible asset input—namely, the intangible capital stock B (for "brand"). This stock is generated by the usual accumulation of investments,

$$(A2) \qquad B_{t+1} = (1 - \delta^B)B_t + I_t^B,$$

where δ^B is its depreciation rate and I_t^B the investment flow. The firm is producing the brand using its own workers (producing for own account in the jargon of the System of National Accounts). Viewed this way, nominal output of the firm should now also include the value of the assets created—namely, $p^B I^B$ with p^B as the investment price. Factor input costs go up as well: by $r^B B$ with r^B as its user cost, as the brand stock is used. As in the main text, we simplify and write the user cost as

$$(A3) \qquad r^B = (\rho^B + \delta^B)p^B,$$

where ρ^B is the (net) real rate of return to intangible capital. This rate is pinned down by the requirement that the sum of all factor incomes exhausts output, as we now have included all factors of production. Put otherwise, ρ^B is determined using an *ex-post* endogenous rate of return such that

$$(A4) \qquad p^Y Y + p^B I^B = w^B L^B + r^B B + p^S S.$$

It is obvious, but important, to see that the measured returns to intangibles depend crucially on the price the firm is paying for the imported shoes. Suppose the shoes are produced by an affiliated firm, opening up the possi-

---

22. We only use the time subscript in cases where its omission might generate confusion. Otherwise, it will be suppressed for expositional simplicity.

bility for profit shifting. In that case, returns to intangibles cannot be identified by studying the last stage only. The solution is to consider the profits in the two stages together.

To see this, we also model the fabrication stage (F) of shoes. Assume shoes are fabricated with labor (L^F) and tangible capital (K^F)—say, machines. We can then write

(A5) $$\pi^F = p^S S - w^F L^F - r^F K^F,$$

where π^F is the residual profit measure after subtracting the cost of tangible inputs from gross output in the fabrication stage. The particular division of the profits in the selling and fabrication stages will depend on the price of the shoes, which is an endogenous variable to be set by the lead firm for accounting purposes. However, the overall profit in the chain, $(\pi^R + \pi^F)$ is independent of this choice. It equals sales minus the cost of tangible inputs in the integrated production process. Combining (A5) and (A1), we derive

(A6) $$(\pi^B + \pi^F) = p^Y Y - (w^B L^B + w^F L^F) - r^F K^F.$$

Equation (A6) shows how $(\pi^B + \pi^F)$ can be measured in the data. The method to do so is outlined in the main text. How can we interpret it? Using (A4) and (A5), we have

(A7) $$(\pi^B + \pi^F) = r^B B - p^B I^B.$$

The left-hand side is observable in the data, but none of the right-hand side variables are. In practice, many alternative combinations of r^B, B, p^B, and I^B are possible that satisfy the accounting restrictions set by the observable data. To simplify, let us consider two extreme cases. First, suppose a start-up firm produced the intangible but is not producing and selling shoes yet. In that case, $w^B L^B = p^B I^B$ and $r^B B = 0$. Alternatively, when the firm stops to produce its intangible but continues selling, it can be said to "exhaust" its brand name. In that case, $(\pi^B + \pi^F) = r^B B$ as $p^B I^B = 0$. An intermediate situation is when the firm is in a steady state such that in each period depreciation of the intangible is equal to new investment:

(A8) $$\delta^B p^B B = p^B I^B.$$

Substituting (A8) in (A7) and using (A3), we find that in this case,

(A9) $$(\pi^B + \pi^F) = \rho^B p^B B.$$

Under a steady-state assumption, the observable profit in the GVC is measuring the returns to intangible assets, net of depreciation. It is thus a net income measure.

A number of characteristics of this measure need to be noted. First, ρ^B is an *ex-post* rate of return. It is calculated to exhaust output minus tangible costs such that all value added is allocated to factors of production. This ex-post rate contains a "normal" rate of return to capital, $\bar{\rho}$, which is the opportunity cost of the invested capital. This rate is by definition similar to the rate for tangible capital assets. Any returns above this can be referred to as "supranormal" such that the rate of return for intangibles can be split into normal returns and supranormal returns: $\rho^B = (\rho^B - \bar{\rho}) + \bar{\rho}$. There are many reasons why the rate of return to intangibles might be different from the rate of return to tangible capital. Beyond the standard business risk, it may include additional compensation for its unusual risk profile (Hanson, Heaton, and Li 2005). Second, for simplicity, we abstained from tax and capital gain considerations in the discussion above as in our empirical work reported on in the main text. This is not to say that they are unimportant; they are simply unknown, and further work is needed in this direction. Third, equation (A9) shows that intangible income measured by $(\pi^B + \pi^F)$ can increase because of an increase in its rate of return, ρ^B, or because of an increase in the nominal stock, $p^B B$. Without quantifying the stock, we are not able to distinguish between the two. More generally, the firm might not be in a "steady state," driving a wedge between depreciation and new investment. This wedge will also be absorbed in $(\pi^B + \pi^F)$. Without further information on intangible depreciation, prices, and quantities (δ^B, I^B, and p^B), we will not be able to separate changes in stocks and in rates of return. Corrado, Hulten, and Sichel (2005, 2009) and Corrado et al. (2013) provide stock estimates for intangible assets that are currently not treated as investment in the national accounts. This is a fruitful avenue for future research.

References

Bhandari, A., and E. R. McGrattan. 2018. "Sweat Equity in US Private Business." NBER Working Paper No. 24520. Cambridge, MA: National Bureau of Economic Research.

Barkai, S. 2017. "Declining Labor and Capital Shares." Job market paper, University of Chicago.

Bernard, Andrew B., and Teresa C. Fort. 2015. "Factoryless Goods Producing Firms." *American Economic Review* 105 (5): 518–23.

Bridgman, Benjamin. 2018. "Is Labor's Loss Capital's Gain? Gross versus Net Labor Shares." *Macroeconomic Dynamics* 22 (8): 2070–78.

Chen, W., R. Gouma, B. Los, and M. P. Timmer. 2017. "Measuring the Income to Intangibles in Goods Production: A Global Value Chain Approach." *WIPO Economic Research Working Papers*.

Corrado, Carol, Jonathan Haskel, Cecilia Jona-Lasinio, and Massimiliano Iommi. 2013. "Innovation and Intangible Investment in Europe, Japan, and the United States." *Oxford Review of Economic Policy* 29 (2): 261–86.

Corrado, Carol, Charles Hulten, and Daniel Sichel. 2005. "Measuring Capital and Technology: An Expanded Framework." In *Measuring Capital in the New*

Economy, edited by Carol Corrado, John Haltiwanger, and Daniel Sichel, 11–46. NBER Studies in Income and Wealth 65. Chicago: University of Chicago Press.

Corrado, Carol, Charles Hulten, and Daniel Sichel. 2009. "Intangible Capital and US Economic Growth." *Review of Income and Wealth* 55 (3): 661–85.

Cummins, Jason G. 2005. "A New Approach to the Valuation of Intangible Capital." In *Measuring Capital in the New Economy*, edited by Carol Corrado, John Haltiwanger, and Daniel Sichel, 47–72. NBER Studies in Income and Wealth 65. Chicago: University of Chicago Press.

Dao, Mai, Mitali Das, Zsoka Koczan, and Weicheng Lian. 2017. "Why Is Labor Receiving a Smaller Share of Global Income? Theory and Empirical Evidence." IMF Working Paper.

Dedrick, J., K. L. Kraemer, and G. Linden. 2010. "Who Profits from Innovation in Global Value Chains? A Study of the iPod and Notebook PCs." *Industrial and Corporate Change* 19:81–116.

Dischinger, M., B. Knoll, and N. Riedel. 2014. "The Role of Headquarters in Multinational Profit Shifting Strategies." *International Tax and Public Finance* 21:248–71.

Elsby, Mike, Bart Hobijn, and Aysegul Sahin. 2013. "The Decline of the U.S. Labor Share." *Brookings Papers on Economic Activity*, Fall, 1–42.

Fontagné, Lionel, and Ann Harrison, editors. 2017. *The Factory-Free Economy. Outsourcing, Servitization, and the Future of Industry*. Oxford: Oxford University Press.

Gereffi, G. 1994. "The Organisation of Buyer-Driven Global Commodity Chains: How U.S. Retailers Shape Overseas Production Networks." In *Commodity Chains and Global Capitalism*, edited by G. Gereffi and M. Korzeniewicz, 95–122. Westport, CT: Praeger.

Gereffi, G. 1999. "International Trade and Industrial Upgrading in the Apparel Commodity Chain." *Journal of International Economics* 48:37–70.

Guvenen, Fatih, Raymond J. Mataloni Jr., Dylan G. Rassier, and Kim J. Ruhl. 2017. "Offshore Profit Shifting and Domestic Productivity Measurement." NBER Working Paper No. 23324. Cambridge, MA: National Bureau of Economic Research.

Hall, R., and D. Jorgenson. 1967. "Tax Policy and Investment Behavior." *American Economic Review* 57 (3): 391–414.

Halpin, P. 2016. "Irish 2015 GDP Growth Raised to 26 Percent on Asset Reclassification." Reuters, July 12, 2016. https://www.reuters.com/article/uk-ireland -economy/irish-2015-gdp-growth-raised-to-26-percent-on-asset-reclassification -idUKKCN0ZS0ZC.

Hanson, L. P., J. C. Heaton, and N. Li. 2005. "Intangible Risk." In *Measuring Capital in the New Economy*, edited by Carol Corrado, John Haltiwanger, and Daniel Sichel, 111–52. NBER Studies in Income and Wealth 65. Chicago: University of Chicago Press.

Herrendorf, Berthold, Richard Rogerson, and Akos Valentinyi. 2013. "Two Perspectives on Preferences and Structural Transformation." *American Economic Review* 103 (7): 2752–89.

Jäger, Kirsten. 2016. EU KLEMS Growth and Productivity Accounts 2016 release— Description of Methodology and General Notes, December. http://www.euklems .net/TCB/2016/Metholology_EU%20KLEMS_2016.pdf.

Johnson, Robert, and Guillermo Noguera. 2012. "Accounting for Intermediates: Production Sharing and Trade in Value Added." *Journal of International Economics* 86 (2): 224–36.

Jorgenson, Dale W. 1995. *Productivity, Vol. 1: Postwar U.S. Economic Growth*. Cambridge, MA: MIT Press.

Houseman, S. N., and M. Mandel, eds. 2015. *Measuring Globalization: Better Trade Statistics for Better Policy*. Kalamazoo: W. E. Upjohn Institute for Employment Research.

Kaplinsky, Raphael. 2000. "Globalisation and Unequalisation: What Can Be Learned from Value Chain Analysis?" *Journal of Development Studies* 37 (2): 117–46.

Karabarbounis, L., and B. Neiman. 2014. "The Global Decline of the Labor Share." *Quarterly Journal of Economics* 129 (1): 61–103.

Karabarbounis, L., and B. Neiman. 2018. "Accounting for Factorless Income." *NBER Macroeconomics Annual 2018*, vol. 33, edited by Martin Eichenbaum and Jonathan Parker, 167–228. Chicago: University of Chicago Press.

Koh, D., R. Santaeulàlia-Llopis, and Y. Zheng. 2016. "Labor Share Decline and Intellectual Property Products Capital." University of Arkansas Working Paper.

Landefeld, J. Steven. 2015. *Handbook for a System of Extended International and Global Accounts (SEIGA). Overview of Major Issues*. Draft for United Nations Statistical Division.

Leontief, W. 1936. "Quantitative Input and Output Relations in the Economic System of the United States." *Review of Economic and Statistics* 18:105–25.

Los, B., M. P. Timmer, and G. J. de Vries. 2015. "How Global Are Global Value Chains? A New Approach to Measure International Fragmentation." *Journal of Regional Science* 55:66–92.

Miller, R. E., and P. D. Blair. 2009. *Input-Output Analysis: Foundations and Extensions*. Cambridge: Cambridge University Press.

Neubig, T. S., and S. Wunsch-Vincent. 2017. "A Missing Link in the Analysis of Global Value Chains. Cross-border Flows of Intangible Assets and Related Measurement Implications." *WIPO Economic Research Working Papers* No. 37.

Peters, R. H., and L. A. Taylor. 2017. "Intangible Capital and the Investment-q Relation." *Journal of Financial Economics* 123 (2): 251–72.

Prescott, E. C., and M. Visscher. 1980. "Organization Capital." *Journal of Political Economy* 88:446–61.

Reijnders, L. S. M., M. P. Timmer, and X. Ye. 2016. "Offshoring, Biased Technical Change and Labour Demand: New Evidence from Global Value Chains." *GGDC Research Memorandum No. 164*. University of Groningen.

Rognlie, Matthew. 2015. "Deciphering the Fall and Rise in the Net Capital Share." *Brookings Papers on Economic Activity* 46 (1): 1–69.

Romalis, John. 2004. "Factor Proportions and the Structure of Commodity Trade." *American Economic Review* 94 (1): 67–97.

Timmer, M. P., E. Dietzenbacher, B. Los, R. Stehrer, and G. J. de Vries. 2015. "An Illustrated User Guide to the World Input-Output Database: The Case of Global Automotive Production." *Review of International Economics* 23:575–605.

Timmer, M. P., A. A. Erumban, B. Los, R. Stehrer, and G. J. de Vries. 2014. "Slicing Up Global Value Chains." *Journal of Economic Perspectives* 28:99–118.

Timmer, M. P., B. Los, R. Stehrer, and G. J. de Vries. 2016. "An Anatomy of the Global Trade Slowdown based on the WIOD 2016 Release." *GGDC Research Memorandum No. 162*. University of Groningen.

Tørsløv, T. R., L. S. Wier, and G. Zucman. 2018. "The Missing Profits of Nations." NBER Working Paper No. 24701. Cambridge, MA: National Bureau of Economic Research.

United Nations Economic Commission for Europe (UNECE). 2015. *Guide to Measuring Global Production*. Prepared by the Task Force on Global Production. Geneva: UNECE.

Valentinyi, Akos, and Berthold Herrendorf. 2008. "Measuring Factor Income Shares at the Sector Level." *Review of Economic Dynamics* 11 (4): 820–35.

11

Measuring Moore's Law
Evidence from Price, Cost, and Quality Indexes

Kenneth Flamm

"Moore's law" in the semiconductor manufacturing industry is used to describe the predictable historical evolution of a single manufacturing technology platform ("silicon CMOS") that has been continuously reducing the costs of fabricating electronic circuits since the mid-1960s.[1] Some features of its future evolution were first correctly predicted by Gordon E. Moore (then at Fairchild Semiconductor) in 1965, and Moore's law became an industry synonym for continuous, periodic reduction in both size and cost for electronic circuit elements.

Technological innovation for this manufacturing platform was coordinated and synchronized across a variety of different engineering fields,

Kenneth Flamm is professor and Dean Rusk Chair in the LBJ School of Public Affairs at the University of Texas at Austin.

I am most grateful to Anjum Khurshid, Kevin Williams, Caroline Alexander, Pablo Cruzat, Javier Beverinotti, Manuel Chavez, Changgui Dong, and Miha Vindis for their excellent research assistance over the years this data was collected and maintained, and to financial support from the Kauffman Foundation and the National Science Foundation. This research is based in part upon work supported by the National Science Foundation under Grant No. 0830389. I would also like to thank Ana Aizcorbe, David Byrne, Carol Corrado, Stephen Oliner, James Prieger, Marshall Reinsdorf, Steve Sawyer, Dan Sichel, Neil Thompson, participants in the Conference on Research in Income and Wealth (CRIW) conference Measuring and Accounting for Innovation in the 21st Century and the International Monetary Fund (IMF) Fifth Statistical Forum, "Measuring the Digital Economy," and two anonymous referees, for their many useful comments on earlier versions of this chapter. Supplemental appendix tables referred to in the text are available online at https://www.nber.org/data-appendix/c13897/appendix.pdf. For acknowledgments, sources of research support, and disclosure of the author's material financial relationships, if any, please see https://www.nber.org/books-and-chapters/measuring -and-accounting-innovation-21st-century/measuring-moores-law-evidence-price-cost-and -quality-indexes.

1. Complementary metal oxide semiconductor (CMOS) is the most widely used "flavor" of semiconductor technology used to manufacture an integrated circuit (IC).

including materials, optical systems, ultraclean precision manufacturing, factory automation, electronic circuit design and simulation, and improved computer software for computational modeling in all of these fields. It was a self-reinforcing dynamical process, since the largest market for the semiconductor manufacturing industry's products has always been the computer industry.[2] Cheaper computing hardware meant cheaper modeling and engineering to further reduce the costs of the semiconductors manufactured for use in future computers. New public-private institutions and organizations were developed to coordinate the simultaneous arrival of the very heterogeneous technological building blocks required for this increasingly complex semiconductor manufacturing technology platform.

The result was an industrial dynamic that, since the mid-1960s, had effectively worked as a "virtual shrinking machine" for electronic circuits. On a regular basis, new "technology nodes" delivered 30 percent reductions in the size of the smallest dimension ("critical feature size," F) that could be reliably manufactured on a silicon wafer. This implied a 50 percent reduction in the area occupied by the smallest manufacturable electronic circuit feature (F^2) and a doubling in density—the number of circuit elements (e.g., transistors) per area of silicon in a chip.

Section 11.1 of this chapter develops some stylized economic facts, reviewing why this progression in manufacturing technology delivered a 20 to 30 percent annual decline in the cost of manufacturing a transistor, on average, as long as it continued. It constructs a simple economic framework that explains how improvements in manufacturing technology, which resulted in feature size reductions, created manufacturing cost reductions for all types of electronic circuits.

Section 11.2 reviews other economically significant benefits (in addition to increased density and lower cost per circuit element) that would be associated with smaller feature sizes. Some of those characteristics would be expected to have significant economic value, and historical trends for these characteristics are reviewed. Chip speed, in particular, would have major impacts on computer performance. Econometric analysis of software benchmark data provided in this section of the chapter shows that rates of performance improvement in microprocessors fell off dramatically in the new millennium, a retreat from very high rates of increase measured in the late 1990s. Lower manufacturing costs alone pose no special challenges for price and innovation measurement, but these other benefits do, and they motivate quality adjustment methods when semiconductor product prices are measured.

Section 11.3 analyzes empirical evidence of recent changes to the his-

---

2. This defines the computer industry expansively, to include the computer systems embedded in the smart electronic systems and mobile devices whose sales have grown most rapidly in recent decades.

torical Moore's law trajectory and finds corroborating evidence for a slowdown of Moore's law in prices for the highest-volume products: memory chips, custom chip designs outsourced to dedicated contract manufacturers (foundries), and Intel microprocessors. In this section, in addition to reviewing price indexes available in the public literature, I construct a new, high-frequency hedonic price index for Intel desktop microprocessors utilizing very detailed chip characteristics. I use a variety of data sources, including both Intel list prices and retail processor transaction prices. My results are consistent with the other public data I review and support the notion of a marked slowdown in Moore's law–driven price declines over the last decade.

Section 11.4 reviews evidence to the contrary, which relates primarily to Intel microprocessors. It analyzes Intel's own publicly released information on the topic, discusses economic reasons why Intel microprocessor prices might behave differently from prices for other types of semiconductor chips, and reviews other published studies, one of which came to the opposite conclusion: that quality-adjusted price decline for Intel processors continued at unchanged high rates in recent years. After investigating a variety of forms of evidence in detail, I conclude that the finding of an unchanged rate of price decline for Intel microprocessors is most likely an artifact of omitted variables in the estimated econometric model.

Section 11.5 dives into Intel microprocessors in even greater depth and tests the computer architecture textbook view of how a small set of specific chip characteristics affects performance of microprocessors in executing programs. I outline a simple structural model of microprocessor computing performance and then estimate that model empirically. Simple econometric models, using only a small set of explanatory chip characteristics, explain 99 percent of variance across processor models in performance on different, commonly used CPU performance benchmarks. However, the impact of different chip characteristics on performance varies quite dramatically across benchmarks.

The economic implication is that these characteristics, which determine benchmark scores, should clearly be included in any hedonic price equation. Most of these chip characteristics would also be expected to affect chip production cost and therefore have an independent rationale for inclusion in a hedonic price equation. It may seem reasonable to assume that a scalar, fixed-weight average of different benchmark scores for a chip perfectly captures the impact of changing chip characteristics on computer performance and therefore on user demand (though this is a very strong assumption given substantial heterogeneity and change over time in the mix of computer applications relevant to different computer market segments). But even if it were true that some fixed weighted average of benchmark scores was a perfect measure of changes in chip performance relevant to demand shifts, inclusion of this variable would not eliminate the need to also include cost-shifting product characteristics as additional controls in a hedonic model of market equilibrium chip prices. This argument is actually illustrated by a simulation created to depict the impact of perfect collinearity among chip characteristics on hedonic price coefficients in section 11.3.

A sixth and final section of the chapter points to some economically important conclusions that can be drawn from this evidence. Available empirical evidence, on balance, suggests that Moore's law–related historical declines in chip manufacturing cost have clearly been greatly attenuated over the last decade, resulting in much more slowly declining quality-adjusted chip prices. If we accept earlier economic research showing a strong link between technological innovation in semiconductors and IT and productivity growth across the broader economy, then a slowdown in semiconductor manufacturing innovation, inducing slower quality-adjusted price declines for both chips and IT utilizing those chips, will affect measures of productivity growth in industrialized economies. Finally, the winding down of Moore's law means that much of the continuing hardware cost decline driving ever more intensive use of IT across the economy over the last 50 years will no longer hold and that computing costs—including energy use per computation, the principal variable cost—will decline much more slowly in the future than was true in the past. Improvement in software, rather than dramatically cheapening hardware, may well emerge as the main focus for IT innovation over the next 50 years.

11.1   Stylized Facts about Semiconductor Manufacturing Innovation

In 1965, five years after the integrated circuit's invention, Gordon E. Moore (who would shortly move on to cofound Intel) predicted that the number of transistors (circuit elements) on a single chip would double every year.[3] Later modifications of that early prediction—Moore's law—became shorthand for semiconductor manufacturing innovation.

Moore's prediction requires other assumptions in order to create economically meaningful connections to the information age's key economic variable: the cost (or price) of electronic functionality on a chip (embodied in the 20th century's supreme electronic invention, the transistor).[4] Chip fabrication requires coordinating multiple technologies, combined in very complex manufacturing processes.

The pacing technology has been the photolithographic process used to pattern chips. From the 1970s through the mid-1990s, a new "technology node"—a new generation of photolithographic and related equipment and materials required for successful use—was introduced roughly every three years or so. Starting in the mid-1970s, this three-year cycle coincided with the time interval between introductions of next-generation DRAM computer

3. G. Moore (1965).
4. Jorgenson (2001); Flamm (2003, 2004); Aizcorbe, Flamm, and Khurshid (2007).

memory chips, storing four times the bits in the previous-generation chip.[5] This observed 18-month "doubling period" became a new de facto "revised" Moore's law.[6]

The close early fit of DRAM product development cycles with leading-edge chip manufacturing technology introductions was no coincidence. DRAMs at that time were the highest-volume standardized commodity chip product manufactured, and a rapidly expanding computer market drove leading-edge chip manufacturing technology development. Moore's prediction morphed into an informal—and later, formal—technology coordination mechanism (the International Technology Roadmap for Semiconductors, or ITRS) for the entire global semiconductor industry—equipment and material producers, chip makers, and their customers.

Relationships between Moore's law and fabrication cost[7] trends for integrated circuits can be described by the following identity, giving cost per circuit element (e.g., transistor):

$$(1) \quad \frac{\$}{\text{element}} = \frac{\dfrac{\$\text{processing cost}}{\text{area "yielded" good silicon chips}}}{\dfrac{\text{elements}}{\text{chip}}} \times \frac{\text{silicon wafer area}}{\text{chip}}.$$

Moore's original "law" described only the denominator—a prediction that elements per chip would quadruple every two years. Back in 1965, Moore hadn't originally anticipated rapid future advances in technology nodes. Acknowledging that an integrated circuit (IC) containing 65,000 elements was implied by 1975, Moore wrote, "I believe that such a large circuit can be built on a single wafer. With the dimensional tolerances already being employed . . . 65,000 components need occupy only about one-fourth a square inch."[8]

Rewriting this more concisely without relying on Moore's prediction about numbers of elements per chip (therefore eliminating the need for assumptions about chip size) yields

$$(2) \quad \frac{\$}{\text{element}} = \frac{\$\text{processing cost}}{\text{area "yielded" silicon}} \times \frac{\text{silicon area}}{\text{element}},$$

5. DRAM (dynamic random access memory) was invented in 1968 by Robert Dennard at IBM and first commercialized by Moore's newly founded company, Intel, in 1970. DRAM chips are the most common type of IC used for "main" memory storage in modern computer systems and, until the early 21st century, were the type of IC semiconductor chip produced in the highest production volume. DRAMs are a type of "volatile" memory chip—information stored on the chip in binary (0,1) form disappears when electrical power is turned off.

6. A decade later, Moore himself revised his prediction to a doubling every two years. G. Moore (1975), 11–13.

7. Analysis of fabrication costs, which account for most of chip costs, ignores assembly, packaging, and testing.

8. G. Moore (1965). The largest wafer sizes in use then were comparable in diameter to a modern minipizza appetizer.

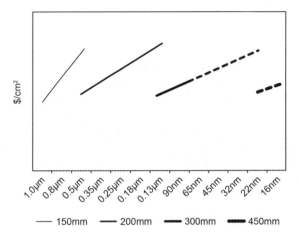

Fig. 11.1   Wafer size conversions offset Intel's increased wafer-processing cost
Source: Holt (2005).

which depends directly on the defining characteristic of a new technology node, the smallest patternable feature size, as reflected in chip area per transistor. This "Moore's law" variant came into use in the semiconductor industry as a way of analyzing the economic impact of new technology nodes. New technology nodes increased the density of transistors fabricated in a given area of silicon in a readily predictable way. Time between new nodes— and a new node's impact on wafer-processing costs—jointly determined decline rates in transistor fabrication cost.

Through 1995, new technology nodes were introduced at roughly three-year intervals. Each new node reduced the smallest planar dimension ("critical feature size," F) in circuit elements by 30 percent, implying 50 percent smaller silicon areas (F^2) per circuit element.

Completing the economic story, the cost per silicon wafer area processed, averaged over long periods, increased only slowly.[9] At new technology nodes, processing cost per silicon wafer area indeed increased. But episodically, larger wafer sizes were introduced, sharply reducing processing costs per area. The net effect was nearly constant long-run costs with only slight increases. Figure 11.1, presented in 2005 by Intel's chief manufacturing technologist, shows new wafer sizes "resetting" wafer-processing costs. Significantly, larger diameter wafer sizes (450mm) were expected at the 22 nanometer (nm) node. However, 450mm wafers were not introduced as Intel adopted 22nm technology in 2012 and had not been introduced by 2020, and even future introduction now seems highly uncertain. The most recent wafer

9. Over 1983–98, wafer-processing cost/cm² silicon increased 5.5 percent annually. Cunningham et al. (2000), 5. This estimate relates to total silicon area processed (including defective chips). Since defect-free chips' share of total processed area increased historically (chip fabrication yields increased), wafer-processing cost per good silicon area rose even more slowly, approximating constancy.

size "reset," adoption of 300mm diameter wafers, occurred at the 130nm technology node, around 2002.

Using these stylized trends—wafer-processing cost per area of silicon roughly constant and silicon area per circuit element halved, with new technology nodes introduced every three years—equation (2) above predicts that every three years, the cost of producing a transistor would fall by 50 percent, a 21 percent compound annual decline rate.

In reality, leading-edge computer chips—like DRAM memory (the primary product originally produced at Intel after Moore and others founded that company, which immediately became the largest-volume product in the semiconductor industry and the primary product driving Intel's initial growth)—dropped in price substantially faster than 20 percent pre-1985. The steeper decline rate in part reflected further increases in density due to circuit design improvements (e.g., reduction in memory cell footprint),[10] 3D interconnect layers enabling tighter packing of circuit elements,[11] and gradual introduction of 3D into physical designs of transistors and other circuit elements.[12] In addition, operating characteristics of a given circuit design—in particular, switching speed and power requirements—improved with new manufacturing technology and made additional contributions to quality-adjusted price. Finally, smaller and cheaper transistors made it economical to add ever greater electronic functionality to chips, and more and more of a complete electronic system was progressively integrated onto a single chip, which greatly improved system reliability.[13]

In the mid-1990s, the semiconductor manufacturing industry arrived at a significant technological inflection point.[14] New technology nodes began

10. Flamm (2010), figure 2, documents a 62 percent decline in minimum memory bit cell footprint between 1995 and 2004.
11. Anticipated by Moore back in 1965: "no space wasted for interconnection . . . using multilayer metallization patterns separated by dielectric films." G. Moore (1965).
12. Recent examples of 3D transistor structures include RCAT (recessed cell array transistor) and FinFET (fin field effect transistor) structures; 3D capacitor designs have been used in DRAM since the late 1990s.
13. Electrical interconnections between components have historically been the most frequent point of failure in electronic systems.
14. Industry road maps originally dated this transition to two-year node rollouts to 1995; post-2004 road maps revised that date to 1998. Aizcorbe, Oliner, and Sichel (2008) have persuasively argued that the turning point was closer to the mid-1990s than late in the decade.
The mid-1990s were also a technological inflection point for Intel's manufacturing capabilities. Intel had exited the DRAM business in 1985, which previously had been driving its leading-edge manufacturing technology development, and refocused its R&D on logic circuit design (Burgelman 1994, 32–46). As a consequence, by the late 1980s, Intel manufacturing capability was trailing well behind the leading edge of the manufacturing technology it had once pioneered.
In order to catch up, Intel began adopting new nodes every two years, even as the rest of the industry continued at the historical three-year pace. Comparing launch dates for Intel processors at new technology nodes with initial use of those nodes by DRAM makers, Intel was two years behind in 1989 (at 1000nm); three years behind in 1991 (800nm); and one year behind in 1995 (350nm). Intel caught up with the DRAM makers in 1997, at 250nm, and remained on a roughly two-year cycle through 2014. Author's calculations based on Intel (2008), IC Knowledge (2004), and http://ark.intel.com.

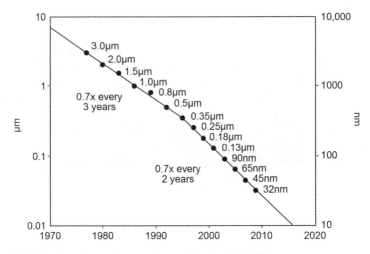

Fig. 11.2   Feature size scaling as observed by Intel in 2005
Source: Holt (2005).

arriving at two-year intervals, replacing three-year cycles. (Intel's perception of this trend, as of 2005, is documented in figure 11.2.) The origins of this change lie in the early 1990s, when the US SEMATECH R&D consortium sponsored a road map coordination mechanism in pursuit of an acceleration in the introduction of new manufacturing technology, intended to benefit the competitiveness of US chip producers. By the mid-1990s, with the increasing reliance of semiconductor manufacturing on a global industrial supply chain, the American national road map evolved into the International Technology Roadmap for Semiconductors (ITRS).[15] Explicitly coordinating the simultaneous development of the many complex technologies required to enable a new manufacturing technology node every two years apparently succeeded in raising the tempo of semiconductor manufacturing innovation for over a decade.[16]

Using equation (2) but adopting shorter two-year cycles for new technology nodes implies rates of annual decline in transistor costs accelerating to almost 30 percent. In short, if the historic pattern of 2- to 3-year technology node introductions, combined with a long-run trend of wafer-processing costs increasing very slowly, were to have continued indefinitely, a minimum floor of perhaps a 20 to 30 percent annual decline in quality-adjusted costs for manufacturing electronic circuits would be predicted due solely to these "Moore's law" fabrication cost reductions. On average, over long periods, the denser, "shrunken" version of the same chip design fabricated a year

15. Flamm (2009); Spencer and Seidel (2004).
16. The last (incomplete) official road map prepared by ITRS was released in 2012. Intel and others reportedly withdrew from ITRS around this time.

earlier would be expected to cost 20 to 30 percent less to manufacture purely because of the improved manufacturing technology.

It now appears that this two-year cycle for technology nodes definitively ended in 2014 with deployment of the 14nm node. The most historically prominent adopter of leading-edge chip manufacturing technology, Intel, currently projects a delayed introduction of its next 10nm processor products to no earlier than late 2019.[17] This means that the time between introductions of new technology nodes now is approaching *five* years for Intel, a dramatic change from its two-year cadence through 2014.[18]

At Intel, the post-1995 two-year technology development cycle had been explicitly incorporated into marketing efforts and was dubbed the Intel "tick-tock" development model in 2007.[19] Every two years, there would be a new technology node introduced ("tick"), with the existing microprocessor computer architecture ported to the new node (effectively, "die shrinks" using the new process), followed by an improved architecture fabricated with the same technology the following year ("tock"). The death of the "tick-tock" model was officially acknowledged by Intel in its 2016 annual report.[20]

Intel publicly disclosed a version of equation (2) to its shareholders in 2015, purged of sensitive cost numbers by indexing all variables to equal one at the 130nm technology node—the technology node at which the transition to a larger wafer size occurred.[21] The 2015 Intel decomposition of manufacturing cost per transistor, using equation (2), is shown as figure 11.3 and in table 11.1. Generally, Intel's average silicon area per transistor did not decline by the predicted 50 percent between technology nodes, primarily because of the increasing complexity of interconnections in processor designs.[22] If accurate, these numbers indicate that the average chip area per transistor shrank by 38 percent at each new node from 130nm through 22nm.[23] Nor did Intel's wafer-processing costs stay constant over the post-130nm period as a whole, since the adoption of 450mm wafers, and the subsequent cost reset, never happened at 22nm as had been predicted back in 2005. However, as long as the average area per transistor declined at

17. See Moammer (2017).

18. Intel chip manufacturing competitor TMC was said in early 2017 to be manufacturing a "10nm" node in volume for Apple (see Merritt 2017), but it is widely believed in the industry that its current technology is physically equivalent to a half-node advancement over the previous-generation Intel technology node. See https://www.semiwiki.com/forum/f293/intel-tsmc-samsung-10nm-update-8565.html; Pirzada (2016); Rogoway (2018); Cutress and Shilov (2018).

19. See Intel (2017).

20. Intel (2016), 14.

21. Intel actually produced microprocessors in volume on both 200mm (8″) and 300mm (12″) wafers using its 130nm manufacturing process technology. See Natrajan et al. (2002), 16–17.

22. See Flamm (2017), 34, for a more detailed explanation.

23. Absolute constancy in reported decline rates for average area per transistor over five generations of new Intel manufacturing technology is puzzling, suggesting long-run trend-based estimates rather than actual averages computed from empirical manufacturing data.

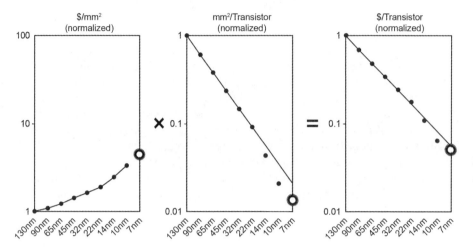

Fig. 11.3   Intel 2015 version of equation (2)
Source: Holt (2015).

Table 11.1   Decomposing Intel transistor cost declines into wafer cost and transistor size changes

Year Intel 1st shipped product at new tech node	Tech node (nm)	Wafer processing cost ($/mm²) ×	Silicon area (mm² /transistor) =	$ cost/ transistor	Compound annual percentage change		
					Wafer processing cost ($/mm²)	Silicon area (mm²/ transistor)	$ Cost/ transistor
2002	130	1	1	1			
2004	90	1.09	0.62	0.68	5%	−21%	−18%
2006	65	1.24	0.38	0.47	7%	−21%	−16%
2008	45	1.43	0.24	0.34	7%	−21%	−15%
2010	32	1.64	0.15	0.24	7%	−21%	−16%
2012	22	1.93	0.09	0.18	8%	−21%	−14%
2014	14	2.49	0.04	0.11	14%	−31%	−22%

Source: Holt (2015), slide 6, graph digitized using WebPlotDigitizer. Year node introduced from ark.intel.com.

faster rates than processing costs per area increased, transistor costs would continue to decline. Intel's cost-per-transistor estimates are revisited below.

How would reductions in production cost translate into price declines? One very simple way to think about it would be in terms of a "pass-through rate," defined as dP/dC (incremental change in price per incremental change in production cost). The pass-through rate for an industry-wide decline in marginal cost is equal to 1 in a perfectly competitive industry with constant returns to scale but can exceed or fall short of 1 in imperfectly competitive industries. Assuming the perfectly competitive case as a benchmark for long-run pass-through in "relatively competitive" semiconductor product markets, this would then imply an expectation of 20 percent to 30 percent annual declines in price due solely to Moore's law.

Historically, most semiconductor chip production ultimately seems to have migrated to more advanced technology nodes.[24] Other kinds of innovations in semiconductor manufacturing, or innovations in the design and functionality going into electronic circuits, might be expected to stimulate even greater rates of quality-adjusted price declines. Thus the 20 percent to 30 percent annual decline in manufacturing cost associated with Moore's law could be interpreted as a floor on the quality-adjusted price declines in the most competitive segments of the semiconductor market.

11.2   Other Benefits from "Moore's Law" Manufacturing Innovation

Impressive declines in transistor manufacturing cost accompanying denser chips with smaller feature sizes at more advanced technology nodes measure only a part of the economic benefits of the Moore's law innovation dynamic. With smaller transistor sizes also came faster switching times and lower power requirements.[25] The complementary benefits of speed and power improvements were highly significant for chip consumers (like computer makers) and their customers.

This was particularly true for chip makers manufacturing microprocessors. Existing computer architectures running at faster speeds run existing software faster and enable more data processing in any given time. Until 2004, computer processor clock rates increased rapidly, as did performance of computers incorporating these faster microprocessors. Figure 11.4 shows clock rates for Intel desktop microprocessors in computers tested on industry standard benchmark programs over the last 20 years as well as benchmark scores for these computers. As clock rates increased, so did performance.[26] Cheaper processors were also faster, stimulating increased demand for new computers in offices, homes, and workplaces.

The logarithmic scale used in figure 11.4 obscures a fairly dramatic slowdown in improvement in CPU performance after the millennium. Table 11.2 shows compound annual growth rates in performance over time of Intel desk-

24. At SEMATECH, the US semiconductor industry consortium (with which the author worked as a consultant in the first decade of the 2000s), the planning rule of thumb was that a fab would be a candidate for an upgrade to a new technology node no more than twice over its lifetime and then would be shut down as uneconomic.

25. The underlying theory ("Dennard scaling") suggested that a 30 percent reduction in transistor length and a 50 percent reduction in transistor area would be accompanied by a 30 percent reduction in delay (40 percent increase in clock frequency) and a 50 percent reduction in power. Esmaeilzadeh et al. (2013), 95.

26. For given software and computer architecture, time required for programs to execute is inversely proportional to processor clock rate, assuming data transfer does not constrain performance. Lower rates of performance improvement after 2004, as processor clock rates plateaued, were obvious to computer designers. See Fuller and Millett (2011), chap. 2; Hennessey and Patterson (2012), chap. 1.

A. Log(Processor Speed)

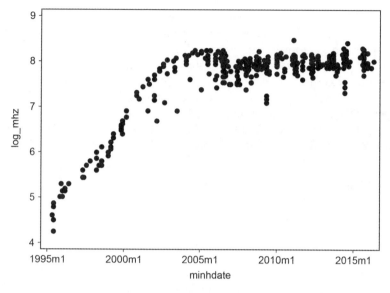

B. Log(Performance)

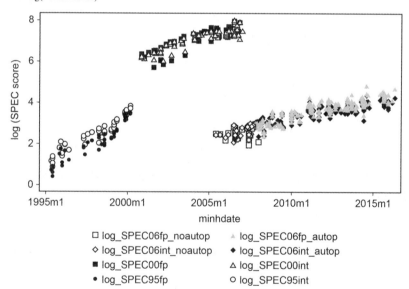

□ log_SPEC06fp_noautop	▲ log_SPEC06fp_autop
◇ log_SPEC06int_noautop	◆ log_SPEC06int_autop
■ log_SPEC00fp	△ log_SPEC00int
● log_SPEC95fp	○ log_SPEC95int

Fig. 11.4   Processor clock rate and performance for Intel desktop processors running SPEC CPU benchmarks, by first availability date of tested hardware

Source: Author's analysis of SPEC submissions, SPEC.org. Performance scores for 1995, 2000, and 2006 SPEC benchmarks have different values for same processor, and different vintage benchmark scores are not directly comparable. "minhdate" is date on which first SPEC benchmark for computer system with that processor is run. "log_SPECyyxx" is log of median SPEC year yy benchmark xx score, by processor model. SPEC06xx results include separate scores with compiler autoparallelization turned on (autop) and off (noautop) for same model, when reported.

Table 11.2   **Annual growth in processor performance improvement over different time periods and benchmarks**

SPEC CPU benchmark	Coeff. CAGR	Robust SE
1995m5–2000m3		
int95	.583	.018
fp95	.640	.023
int95_rate	.624	.027
fp95_rate	.723	.033
2000m11–2004m11		
int2000	.330	.017
fp2000	.343	.024
int2000_rate	.470	.051
fp2000_rate	.399	.035
2005m2–2007m1		
int2000	.322	.016
fp2000	.337	.022
int2000_rate	.465	.048
fp2000_rate	.399	.033
2005m6–2012m11		
int2006	.171	.007
fp2006	.247	.008
int2006_rate	.247	.013
fp2006_rate	.254	.010
2013m1–2016m5		
int2006	.169	.006
fp2006	.241	.007
int2006_rate	.242	.012
fp2006_rate	.248	.009

Source: Author analysis of SPEC benchmark performance of Intel desktop processors.

top processors on standard CPU benchmark software (the Standard Performance Evaluation Corporation [SPEC] benchmarks; see appendix 11.A1).

Three different versions of the SPEC CPU test suite were released— one around 1995, one in 2000, and the most recent in 2006. Each suite contains a selection of "integer" application tests (e.g., programming and code processing, artificial intelligence, discrete-event simulation and optimization, gene sequence search, video compression) and a set of "floating point" math-intensive application tests (e.g., solution of systems modeling problems in physics, fluid dynamics, chemistry, and biology; finite element analysis; linear programming; ray tracing, weather prediction; speech recognition). These test suites are designed to test single-process (programming task) performance on a CPU.[27]

27. The overall benchmark score is calculated as a geometric mean of scores on the individual programs within the benchmark.

In addition, so-called rate versions of these test suites, which run multiple versions of the single-process benchmarks simultaneously on a single CPU, are available. The "rate" benchmarks are intended to show how the CPU would perform as a server running multiple independent jobs or, alternatively, running an "embarrassingly parallel" programming problem—a task that could be divided up into multiple software processes not requiring any communication or coordination between processes.[28]

Changes in trends over time in the SPEC benchmark performance scores for Intel desktop processors are quite dramatic.[29] Over the 1995–2000 period, integer computing performance increased by about 58 percent annually and floating point performance by 64 percent. The suite was revised in 2000, and from the end of 2000 through 2004, both integer and floating-point performance improvement rates were almost halved, to an increase of about 33 percent to 34 percent per year.[30] Finally, over the most recent time period, after the 2006 revision of the SPEC benchmarks, from 2005 through 2016, annual performance gains were reduced substantially again, to rates of 17 percent (integer) and 25 percent (floating point) annual improvement.[31]

11.3   An End to Moore's Law?

Unfortunately, the golden age of more rapidly cheapening transistors (which were also faster and drew less power) that began in the late 1990s did not survive unchallenged past the new millennium.

2004: The End of Faster. The first casualty was the "faster thrown in for free," along with smaller, cheaper, and greener. Around 2003–4, higher clock rates stalled (see figure 11.4), as disproportionately greater power was required to run processors reliably at ever higher frequencies. With tinier transistors drawing higher power in denser chips, dissipating heat generated by higher power density became impossible without expensive cooling systems. (The highest processor speed shipped by Intel until very recently was 4 GHz; IBM's fastest z-series mainframe CPU, with advanced cooling, hit 5.5 GHz in 2012, but subsequent CPUs ran at lower frequencies.[32]) Intel and others abandoned architectures reliant on frequency scaling to achieve

28. Unfortunately, there is no SPEC rule about how many instances of the single benchmark programs should be run for the rate benchmarks on a multicore CPU. It could be as many as the number of cores in the CPU or twice that number (the number of threads that can be run simultaneously on a CPU with additional processor hardware supporting symmetric multithreading—a feature called hyperthreading by Intel) or some number of instances less than either of those bounds.

29. Pillai analyzed the apparent slowdown in microprocessor quality improvement (as measured by software benchmarks) from 2001 to 2008. See Pillai (2013), figure 1.

30. There was a statistically significant—but substantively insignificant—additional decline of under a percent per year after 2004 through 2007.

31. There was another statistically significant, but substantively insignificant, decline by a fraction of a percent in performance improvement rates after 2012.

32. Raley (2015), 23.

better processor performance after 2004. Clock rates in subsequent processor architectures actually fell, and processing more instructions per clock tick became the focus for improved computing performance.

Two-year node introductions continued to produce smaller and cheaper transistors, though. Ever-cheaper transistors were utilized to create more CPUs—"cores"—per chip, thus processing more instructions per clock at lower clock frequencies. This new "multicore" strategy's weakness was that application software required "parallelization" to run on multiple cores simultaneously, and software applications vary greatly in the extent to which they can be easily parallelized. Further, improving software was more costly than simply adopting the cheaper hardware delivered by new technology nodes: quality-adjusted prices for software historically have fallen much more slowly than quality-adjusted prices for processors.[33]

The difficulty and cost of parallelization of software is an economic factor limiting utilization of cheap multicore CPUs on hard-to-parallelize applications.[34] In addition, a fundamental result in computer architecture (Amdahl's law) maintains that if there is any part of a computation that cannot be parallelized, then there will be diminishing returns to adding more processors to the task—and in many applications, decreasing returns are noticeable fairly quickly. One widely used computer architecture textbook summarized the challenges in utilizing multicore processors: "Given the slow progress on parallel software in the past 30-plus years, it is likely that exploiting thread-level parallelism broadly will remain challenging for years to come."[35]

2012: The End of Rapid Cost Declines? Until roughly 2012, transistor fabrication costs continued falling at rapid rates. At the 22/20nm technology node, which went into volume production around 2012 (at Intel), continuing cost declines began to look uncertain. Figure 11.5 shows contract chip maker GlobalFoundries' 2015 transistor manufacturing costs at recent technology nodes.[36]

Numerous fabless chip design companies, which outsource chip production to contract manufacturing "foundries," began to publicly complain that transistor manufacturing costs had actually *increased* at the 20/22nm node.[37]

---

33. Economic studies of mass-market, high-volume packaged software prices have typically found quality adjusted rates of annual price decline in the 6 percent to 20 percent range. See, e.g., Gandal (1994); Oliner and Sichel (1994); White et al. (2005); Copeland (2013); and Prudhomme and Yu (2005).

34. The opposite—software problems easily divided up across processors and run with little or no interprocessor communication or management required—is described in the computer engineering literature as "embarrassingly parallel."

35. Hennessey and Patterson (2012), 411.

36. Like table 11.1, this figure probably does not include R&D costs.

37. Fabless chipmakers Nvidia, AMD, Qualcomm, and Broadcom all publicly complained about a slowdown or even halt to historical decline rates in their manufacturing costs at foundries. Shuler (2015), Or-Bach (2012) (2014), Hruska (2012), Lawson (2013), Qualcomm (2014), Jones (2014, 2015).

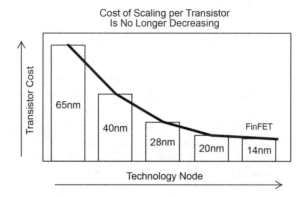

Fig. 11.5   GlobalFoundries' transistor manufacturing cost at recent technology nodes
Source: McCann (2015).

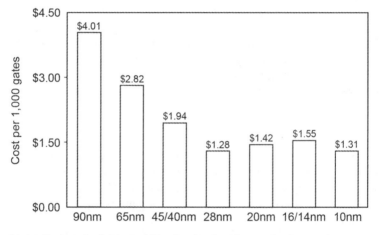

Fig. 11.6   Cost per logic gate, with projection for 10nm technology node
Source: Jones (2015).

(Fabless companies accounted for 25 percent of world semiconductor sales in 2015; foundries, which also build outsourced designs for semiconductor companies with fabs, had a 32 percent share of global production capacity.[38]) Charts like figure 11.6, showing increased costs at sub-28nm technology nodes, were frequently published between 2012 and 2016. Figure 11.6 is not inconsistent with figure 11.5, since figure 11.6 likely includes the fab-

38. Foundry share calculations based on Yinug (2016), Rosso (2016), IC Insights (2016). Charts like figure 11.6 should be viewed cautiously, as underlying assumptions about products, volumes, and costs are rarely spelled out in published sources.

less customer's nonrecurring fixed costs for designing a chip and making a set of photolithographic masks used in fabrication, while figure 11.5—the foundry's processing costs—would not.[39] These fixed costs have grown exponentially at recent technology nodes and create enormous economies of scale.[40] Some foundries have publicly acknowledged that recent technology nodes now deliver higher density or performance at the expense of higher cost per transistor.[41]

Because of these trends, fabless graphics chip specialists Nvidia and AMD actually skipped the 20/22nm technology node, waiting a high-tech eternity—five years—after launch of 28nm graphics processors in 2011 to move to a new technology node (14/16nm) for their 2016 products.

2018: "Dark Silicon" and Limits on Green? The microprocessor industry's response to the end of frequency scaling was to use ever-cheaper transistors to build more cores on a chip. Though limited by software advances in parallelizing different kinds of applications, this strategy at first seemed effective. More recently, continued future improvement of CPU performance on even easy-to-parallelize applications has been questioned.

As transistors get very small, power requirements to switch these transistors are not reduced at the same rate as transistor size. The "green," lower-power benefit of smaller transistors diminishes. Furthermore, as the power density of chips increases, heat dissipation becomes an issue. Thus the heat problem that blocked further frequency scaling returns in a new guise and prevents the increasing numbers of smaller cores squeezed into a multicore chip from simultaneously operating at a chip's fastest feasible clock rate.

The fraction of a chip's cores that must be powered off at all times in order for a chip to operate within thermal limits, dubbed "dark silicon" by researchers modeling the problem, had been projected to grow as large as 50 percent by 2018.[42] Indeed, current PC users are already seeing their multicore machines "throttling" with attempts to use all cores for intensive computations at the highest clock rates, hitting thermal limits and then either falling back to lower clock rates or idling cores. Continued reductions in power requirements are still feasible but no longer are a free benefit of Moore's law—they now come at the cost of reduced speed and additional on-chip circuitry needed to turn off power to unused portions of a processor chip.

---

39. Historically, a set of 10 to 30 different photomasks was typically employed in manufacturing a chip design. For a low- to moderate-volume product, acquisition of a mask set is effectively a fixed cost.

40. Brown and Linden (2009), chap. 3. McCann (2015) cites a Gartner study showing design costs for an advanced system chip design rising from under $30 million at the 90nm node in 2004, to $170 million at 32/28nm in 2010, to $270 million at the 16/14nm node in 2014.

41. Samsung's director of foundry marketing said, "The cost per transistor has increased in 14nm FinFETs and will continue to do so" (Lipsky 2015). "GlobalFoundries believes the 10nm node will be a disappointing repeat of 20nm, so it will skip directly to a 7nm FinFET node that offers better density and performance compared with 14nm" (Kanter 2016).

42. Esmaeilzadeh et al. (2013), 93–94.

2021+: An End to Smaller in Conventional Silicon? Even some manufacturing technologists from Intel now believe that the Moore's law cadence of technology nodes, with ever-smaller feature sizes in conventional silicon, will end sometime in the next five years. Intel's Bill Holt put it in these terms recently: "Intel doesn't yet know which new chip technology it will adopt, even though it will have to come into service in four or five years. He did point to two possible candidates: devices known as tunneling transistors and a technology called spintronics. Both would require big changes in how chips are designed and manufactured, and would likely be used alongside silicon transistors."[43]

11.3.1   Can We See a Slowing Down of Moore's Law Cost Declines in Price Statistics?

If Moore's law has slowed or even stopped, we would expect to see it in economic metrics, like prices and manufacturing costs.[44]

11.3.1.1   Prices

An obvious place to look is in the price statistics for computer memory chips, which remained the mass-volume semiconductor product par excellence through the end of the 20th century. DRAMs were later superseded by flash memory as the technology driver for new memory manufacturing technology. After the millennium, new technology nodes were first adopted in flash memory chips before DRAMs; flash had become the highest-volume commodity chip by sales around 2012.[45]

Table 11.3 shows changes in price indexes for high-volume memory chips. The DRAM "composite" index is a matched-model, chain-weighted price index based on consulting firm Dataquest's quarterly average global sales price for different density (bits per chip) DRAM components available in the market over the years 1974–1999.[46] These data have no longer been available in recent years.

In the mid-1980s, Korean producers Samsung and Hynix entered the DRAM business and, along with US producer Micron Technology, now account for the vast bulk of current DRAM sales.[47] The Bank of Korea's export price index (based on dollar-basis contracts) and the Bank of Korea's

43. Bourzac (2016).

44. A very useful bibliography of prior matched-model and hedonic studies of semiconductor prices may be found in Aizcorbe (2014), 107–8.

45. See IC Insights (2012).

46. The data prior to 1990 are the same data used in Flamm (1995), figure 5-2. From 1990 on, the data are taken from Aizcorbe (2002).

47. Taiwanese firms entered the DRAM market in force in the early 1990s but have since largely exited, as have all Japanese producers (US producer Micron acquired Japanese DRAM fab facilities). The last remaining European producer (Qimonda) filed for bankruptcy in early 2009. By 2011, the top three producers (Samsung, Hynix, and Micron) accounted for between 80 percent and 90 percent of global sales. See Competition Commission of Singapore (2013).

Table 11.3   Price indexes for memory chips

	Compound annual decline rate, quarterly price indexes					
	Flamm-Aizcorbe DRAM composite	Bank of Korea, DRAM export, $ contract price index	Bank of Korea, Flash export, $ contract price index	Bank of Korea, DRAM producer price index, converted to $ at current market rate	Bank of Korea, Flash memory producer price index, converted to $ at current market rate	Bank of Japan, Chain-Wtd MOS Memory Producer Price Index, Converted to $ at Current Market Rate
1974:1–1980:1	−45.51					
1980:1–1985:1	−43.45					
1985:1–1990:1	−24.74					
1990:1–1995:1	−17.40	−10.81				
1995:1–1999:4	−46.37	−44.28		−33.26		
1999:4–2005:1*		−28.94	−31.28	−31.76		−24.04
2005:1–2011:4		−37.94	−26.92	−30.65	−29.28	−28.79
2011:4–2016:4		2.33	−12.70	−1.42	−5.76	−13.57

Source: Author's calculations from sources described in text.

*Bank of Korea Flash export price index and Bank of Japan MOS memory PPI are for 2001:1–2005:1.

producer price index (PPI, converted to a dollar basis using quarterly average exchange rates) for DRAM and flash memory chips are available.[48]

Finally, since 2000, the Bank of Japan has published a chain-weighted "MOS memory PPI" with weights that are updated annually. This index is likely to be predominantly a mix of DRAM and flash memory, tilting more toward flash in recent years. Generally, except for the period from 1985 to 1995, when a string of trade disputes (between the United States and Europe and Japanese, Korean, and Taiwanese memory chip producers) had significant impacts on global chip prices;[49] prices for DRAMs and flash fell at average rates exceeding 20 percent to 30 percent annually.

It is notable that rates of decline in memory chip prices in the last five years generally have been half or less of their historical decline rates over the previous decades. Korean price indexes (which track the majority of the DRAM manufactured and sold) have basically been flat for the last five years. US memory chip manufacturer Micron (like other flash memory manufacturers) is no longer planning to invest in new technology nodes beyond 16nm in its leading-edge flash memory production. Instead, a new device design built vertically (3D NAND[50]) using existing manufacturing process technology is more cost effective than the continued planar scaling of components at new technology nodes described by the Moore's law dynamic.[51] In DRAM, the mantra that "technology-driven growth slows due to scaling limits" ("scaling limits" being industry jargon for a slowing or ending of Moore's law manufacturing cost reductions) had become a staple in Micron's investor conferences.[52]

Another "commodity-like" price in the semiconductor industry in recent years has been the cost that chip design houses face in having their chips

48. These are not well documented but are believed to be fixed-weight Laspeyres indexes, with weights updated every five years, that have been spliced together (2010 is the current base year). The export indexes are actually measured in dollars, while the Korean won-denominated and Japanese yen-denominated producer price indexes have been converted to dollars at current exchange rates. As a practical matter, except for a brief period during the 1980s when export controls related to the US-Japan Semiconductor Trade Agreement were put in place, DRAM prices historically and through the present have been set and quoted in dollars in a highly integrated global market. See Flamm (1993), 163–64, 167–68. Flamm (1995), chapter 5, analyzes empirical evidence that regional price differentials in DRAM briefly appeared and then disappeared when restrictive trade policies were applied and then removed in the 1980s. With minuscule transport costs relative to product value, zero tariff costs globally for most countries (under the Information Technology Agreement, concluded in 1996 and bound into the WTO), and a large number of active global distributor/broker arbitrageurs, the global DRAM market has always been the poster child for the relevance of a "law of one price."

49. See Flamm (1995).

50. Since the early 21st century, the highest-volume semiconductor chips produced have been so-called flash memory chips, and in particular flash memory using Not-AND (NAND) logic (a type of logic circuit) to store binary data. Flash memory is a nonvolatile storage medium—information stored on the chip is maintained after electric power is turned off.

51. Micron 2015 Winter Analyst Conference (2015).

52. Micron's Raymond James Institutional Investor Conference (2016); Micron Analyst Conference (February, 2017).

Table 11.4   **A quality-adjusted price index for fabricated "foundry" wafers**

	Annual index	% rate of change
2004	100	
2005	83.90	−16.10
2006	74.76	−10.89
2007	65.94	−11.80
2008	57.89	−12.20
2009	52.95	−8.53
2010	48.67	−8.09

Source: Byrne, Kovak, and Michaels (2017).

manufactured on their behalf at so-called foundries. The outsourced manufacturing of semiconductors designed at "fabless" semiconductor companies at foundries accounted for about 25 percent of world semiconductor sales in 2015. Foundries, which also build outsourced designs for semiconductor companies with fabs, held 32 percent of global production capacity in that year.[53]

A recent study of quality-adjusted fabricated wafer prices (the form in which manufactured chips are sold to the semiconductor design houses that have outsourced their production) by Byrne, Kovak, and Michaels (2017) portrays a slowing decline in fabricated wafer prices prior to 2012. (See table 11.4.) While the pattern seems consistent with a slowing down of Moore's law prior to 2012, this study unfortunately ends with data from 2010 and thus cannot be used as a check against the claims of the most vocal US fabless designers (see above) that the prices they pay for having their transistors manufactured in foundries were no longer declining significantly at new technology nodes post-2012.

Price Indexes for Intel Processors. Since their invention in the 1970s, microprocessor sales have grown rapidly and since the 1980s have constituted another huge market segment. Official government statistics show a tremendous slowdown in the rate at which microprocessor prices have been falling after the millennium as well as a significant attenuation in the rate at which prices of the desktop and laptop PCs that make use of these processors have declined. The US Producer Price Indexes for microprocessors show annual (January-to-January) changes in microprocessor prices steadily falling from 60 percent to 70 percent peak rates during the "golden age" of the late 1990s and early 2000s to a low of about 1 percent annual decline for the year ending in January 2015. (The Bureau of Labor Statistics stopped reporting its PPI for microprocessors in April 2015, apparently because of confidentiality concerns.) A parallel fall in price declines for laptop and desktop computers seems also to have occurred, from peak annual decline

53. Foundry share calculations based on Yinug (2016), Rosso (2016), and IC Insights (2016).

Table 11.5   Annualized decline rates for microprocessors per the BLS

	Microprocessors (including microcontrollers)		
	Commodity price		Producer price
	Index (discontinued)	Index (current)	Index
1995:1–1999:4	−50.0		−50.5
1999:4–2004:4	−48.6		−49.2
1999:4–2005:1			−47.8
2005:1–2007:4			−37.7
2007:4–2011:4		−10.8	−10.8
2011:4–2015:1		−3.0	−3.0

Author's calculation. Middle month for quarter used, except December 2007 used for 2007:4.

rates of 40 percent in the late 1990s to rates mainly in the 10 percent to 20 percent range in the last few years.

Table 11.5 shows compound annual decline rates in the PPI for microprocessors (including microcontrollers) as constructed by the Bureau of Labor Statistics (BLS), along with similarly defined indexes for the commodity "microprocessors." Annual decline rates slow from a rate near 50 percent in the late 1990s and the first half decade of the new millennium, to a little over 10 percent in the second half of that first decade, to about 3 percent annually in recent years. This too is consistent with a substantial slowing down in the impact of Moore's law manufacturing technology innovation.

The Bureau of Labor Statistics had historically been somewhat opaque about its methodology in constructing its microprocessor price series (there is no published methodology describing precisely how these numbers were constructed).[54] It is believed that these were matched-model indexes based on some weighted selection of products appearing on Intel list price sheets (the same data source I utilize below),[55] but this is not entirely certain. There is also some evidence that the BLS may have experimented with several different methodologies for measuring its microprocessor price indexes over the 1995–2014 periods[56] before ceasing publication of the index for confidentiality reasons in 2015.

54. Ironically, the BLS is now much more open about the details of how it constructs the current (unpublished) microprocessor price index than it was about some previous (published) versions. See Sawyer and So (2017).
55. Based on a brief conversation with BLS officials, Cambridge, MA, July 2014. See also Sawyer and So (2017).
56. The BLS website showed three different "commodity" price indexes (as opposed to its single microprocessor producer price index) for microprocessors over this period. The most recent microprocessor "commodity" price index is based in December 2007 but is only reported monthly from September 2009 through 2015. There are also two discontinued microprocessor commodity price indexes, one based in December 2004 and running through June 2005 and another based in December 2000 and running from 1995 through December 2004. One might speculate that the BLS changed its methodology for measuring microprocessor prices three times during this period.

As an alternative to the BLS measure, I have previously constructed alternative price indexes for Intel desktop microprocessors, tracing the contours of change over time in microprocessor prices using a unique, highly detailed dataset I have collected over the last two decades.[57] Since the mid-1990s, Intel has periodically published, or posted on the web, current list prices for its microprocessor product line in 1,000-unit trays. These list prices are available at a very disaggregated level of detail—distinguishing between similar models manufactured with different packaging, for example—and were typically updated every four to eight weeks, though price updates have sometimes come at much shorter or longer intervals.[58] By combining these detailed prices with detailed attributes of different processor models, it is possible to construct a very rich dataset relating processor prices to processor characteristics, over time.

This permits the construction of both "matched-model" price indexes, the traditional means by which government statistical agencies measure industrial prices, and so-called hedonic price indexes, which relate processor prices to processor characteristics. It is now well understood in the price index literature that there is a close relationship between matched-model indexes and hedonic price indexes.

The Intel dataset permits measuring differences in processor characteristics down to individual models of processors, controlling for such things as processor speed, clock multiplier, bus speed, differing amounts of level 1 (L1), level 2 (L2), and level 3 (L3) cache memory, architectural changes, and particular new processor features and instructions. The latter have become particularly important recently—beginning in mid-2004, Intel dropped processor clock speed as the principle characteristic used to differentiate processors in its marketing and introduced more complex "processor model number" systems that distinguish between very small and arguably minor differences between processors that proliferated at more recent product introductions.

For comparison purposes, I begin by constructing a matched-model price index for Intel desktop processors. Since I do not have sales or shipment data at the individual processor model level, I weight each observed model equally by taking the geometric mean of price relatives for adjoining periods in which the models are observed.[59] A price index based on the simple geometric mean of individual product price relatives (dubbed the Jevons price index) is chained across pairs of adjacent time periods and depicted in figure 11.8. It has the same qualitative behavior as the official government producer

57. See Flamm (2007).

58. My data initially (over the 1995–98 period) made use of compilations of these data collected by others and posted on the web; since 1998–99, most of these data were collected and archived directly from the Intel website.

59. Since there occasionally were multiple price sheets issued within a single month, I have averaged prices by model by month. Since Intel did not issue new price sheets monthly, "adjoining time periods" means temporally adjacent observations.

price index for microprocessors, falling at rates exceeding 60 percent in the late 1990s and slowing to a decline rate under 10 percent since 2009.

This geometric mean matched-model index actually falls a little more slowly than the official US microprocessor PPI, which may be attributable to the fact that the geometric mean index weights all models equally, while the PPI probably uses a subset of the data, with some weighting scheme for models drawn (and replaced periodically) from subsets of processor types. The PPI also uses fixed weights from some base period to weight these price changes, while my Jevons index chains adjoining paired comparisons of models and therefore implicitly allows weights given to different models over pairs of adjoining time periods to evolve over time.

I have also constructed a hedonic price index, using an econometric model that utilizes more of the information available in my sample of Intel list prices. The basic hedonic price model I estimated statistically was

$(H0)$ lprice_{it} = constant + d_t + $b_a \text{arch\_d}_i$ + $b_p * \text{lproc}_i$ + $b_m \text{lmaxmhz}_i$

$\qquad$ + $b_w \text{lbw}_i$ + $b_{co} \text{lcores}_i$ + $b_h \text{ht}_i$ + $b_{ca} \text{lcache}_i$ + $b_g \text{int\_graph}_i$ +

$\qquad$ $b_{tdp} \text{ltdp}_i$ + $b_{64} \text{em64t}_i$ + $b_{st} \text{eist}_i$ + $b_v \text{vt}_i$ + u_{it},

with the following covariates for chip model i, period t:

- d_t, a time dummy indicator variable for the later period in a pair of adjacent time periods
- arch_d_i, architecture dummy for Intel chip architecture (e.g., Haswell, Coppermine, Ivy Bridge)
- lproc_i, log of base processor clock rate
- lmaxmhz, log of maximum clock rate if processor has turbo mode, = lproc if not
- lbw_i, log of memory bandwidth (8 × memory bus clock rate if older front-side bus architecture or max memory bandwidth if reported in Intel Ark database)
- lcores_i, log of number of physical cores on chip
- ht_i, hyperthreading (additional virtual core per physical chip core) hardware support, binary indicator variable
- lcache_i, log of maximum cache memory for highest level cache on processor
- int_graph_i, binary indicator variable for integrated graphics, 1 if on chip graphics
- ltdp_i, log of thermal design power (watts), rating of chip
- em64t_i, binary indicator dummy for Intel 64-bit memory architecture
- eist_i, binary indicator dummy for enhanced Intel speedstep technology (dynamic frequency scaling and power reduction) feature
- vt_i, binary indicator dummy for hardware virtualization support, 1 if virtualization hardware support
- and u_{it}, a statistical disturbance term for chip model i, time period t

Choice of Characteristics. Choice of characteristics was primarily based on a review of the computer architecture literature (discussed below). The most widely used textbook in that literature holds that computer instruction processing performance is based primarily on the *processor architecture* (which determines how many software instructions can be executed per processor clock cycle: IPC, or instructions per clock) and the computer's *clock rate.* Since the mid-2000s, desktop PC processors have further boosted performance by incorporating a *turbo* mode, increasing clock rate to some maximum above the chip's baseline frequency for short periods of time. Frequently, software performance can also depend on its on-chip *(cache) memory size* and on the sustained speed at which a computer can transfer data from its off-chip, secondary memory—its *maximum memory bandwidth.* Over the last decade, additional processor units (cores) have been added to desktop computer processors, and if software can be parallelized and run simultaneously on multiple *cores,* this too will improve performance. In addition, adding hardware support for "virtual cores," so that a hardware processor core can be time-shared simultaneously by two instruction-processing threads, can speed things up—Intel's version of this feature is called *hyperthreading.* Several other features—hardware support for *virtualization* and a *64-bit memory architecture*—can improve computer performance on particular applications, particularly when desktop processors are used in servers. Basic *graphics* are now integrated onto many processor chips, sparing the end user the need to purchase a costly discrete graphics card, which should also affect demand for a processor by consumers. Finally, power consumption is probably the major variable cost of computing (and drives use of relatively expensive cooling systems needed to dissipate heat from high-powered processors). Low thermal design power (TDP) in desktop processors is considered beneficial for this reason,[60] and processor makers like Intel have also developed hardware support for power-saving features in the chip's micro architecture (Intel's proprietary version—enhanced Intel Speedstep—is abbreviated EIST).

Note that maximum memory bandwidth, cache sizes, number of cores, and even TDP typically take on only a handful of discrete values in any two-period estimation sample interval and are often perfectly collinear with binary indicators for processor architecture, 64-bit support, hardware virtualization, and integrated graphics. In addition, as I show below, performance on different SPEC processor benchmark suites is nearly perfectly predicted by a linear combination of a subset of five of these processor characteristics (chip architecture, clock rate, number cores, hyperthreading, turbo mode).

The regression coefficients (weights) on each of these characteristics, however, vary substantially by software benchmark type. Since the mix of software programs run on computers has evolved substantially over time

60. In addition, low power consumption has the additional very important benefit of producing longer battery life in a laptop computer, irrelevant for a battery-less desktop computer processor.

(these changes have led SPEC to periodically revise its various benchmarks), using the underlying characteristics determining processor benchmark performance (rather than a particular benchmark score) seems the more flexible way to accommodate the impact of changes over time in market demand for different types of software applications running on computers.

The very same characteristics that one might expect to affect processor demand would also be expected to affect processor cost on the supply side. Faster chips supporting the highest clock rates are culled from larger numbers of chips fabricated in batches of wafers through extensive testing (a process dubbed "binning" within the industry). Slower- and faster-running chips are sorted into higher and lower performance bins and sold as distinct chip models. Processors with defects in circuitry in their memory caches and feature circuits also have their defective circuitry fused off electronically and are then sold as lower performance chips (with less memory and fewer features). Redundant circuits can be added to a chip design (at a cost, by increasing chip die area) to yield larger shares of chips on a wafer with functioning features. Every desirable feature of a processor also has some incremental cost incurred in order to increase the number of chips produced with that functioning feature—either through a bigger and therefore more costly chip footprint on a silicon wafer (driven by redundant circuitry needed to fix defects) or through the larger numbers of wafers that must be processed in order to get the desired target numbers of chips with functional features and characteristics.

Computer architectures also affect processor cost, as well as performance, since numbers of transistors on a chip, and therefore chip manufacturing cost, are directly related to the chip's architecture. In addition, since at least the early 2000s, Intel has marked the introduction of new manufacturing technology nodes by rolling out improved chip architectural designs when introducing the new node. So manufacturing technology nodes and chip architectural family will be perfectly collinear in a statistical analysis of Intel prices and costs.

In short, the chip characteristics in this hedonic regression would be expected to affect both computing performance and power consumption, as well as processor cost, and are relevant to both the demand and supply cost sides of the market. For that reason, even if a single, perfectly accurate measure of average processor computing performance (a "market average" benchmark based on the relative mix of software applications run by final computer end users in computing service markets at that particular moment in time) existed, changing in perfect lockstep with the changing mix of applications run by different end users,[61] changes in processor character-

61. It is worth noting that the SPEC benchmarks report an unweighted geometric mean of performance in a variety of applications and that these fixed (equal) weights remain fixed over long periods of time (since 2006, as of October 2018) for the SPEC benchmark composite scores.

istics would have additional impacts on price working through processor manufacturing cost and therefore need to be accounted for separately in the estimated hedonic price equation.

One potentially important pitfall in using large numbers of characteristics in a hedonic equation is that many of these characteristics are likely to be perfectly collinear with others. This is a real-world problem. For example, all the chips developed with a new architecture design may, at least initially, have a common size for their highest-level cache, may all have a 64-bit architecture, or may all have hyperthreading. Most regression software will drop perfectly collinear characteristics automatically, and the coefficients of the other covariates (the ones with which the dropped characteristics are perfectly collinear) will include the effects of the dropped covariates in their estimated values.

This can make interpretation of signs and values of hedonic characteristics problematic and liable to big jumps in value (and coefficient interpretation) in different estimation periods, depending on which characteristics are perfectly collinear and which characteristics are dropped (often automatically) by the statistical software. It also may appear at first glance to look like undesirable "coefficient instability."

However, as long as the key variable of substantive interest (the last period time dummy variable in a regression model spanning two adjacent time periods, the coefficient of which is used to construct a hedonic price index) is not perfectly collinear with the other included characteristics variables, there is no difficulty in interpreting the coefficient of the time dummy variable. Fortunately, it is straightforward to check that this is the case by simply running an auxiliary linear regression of the time dummy on all other explanatory covariates and verifying that it is not perfectly predicted by other regression covariates.

Perfect Collinearity in a Simple Hedonic Simulation. The problem of perfect collinearity—and its effects—is very real in my sample of Intel microprocessors. In every single pair of adjacent time periods, multiple characteristics are dropped as perfectly collinear by statistical software. The problems this can create in interpreting regression results are easily illustrated in a simple simulation model.

Consider a simplified, stylized processor market over two adjacent time periods. Suppose that half of manufacturing capacity is used to fabricate a baseline processor architecture (arch_dummy = 0) and half is dedicated to a different architectural alternative (arch_dummy = 1). Suppose that initially, half of fabricated chips from both architectures can run at a clock rate of 1,000, and half at 1,500. All chips manufactured run 500 faster in the later period (i.e., half at 1,500, half at 2,000; think of this as the result of manufacturing process improvement). Substantively, this means there will be a positive correlation between a binary time period indicator variable (first_period = 0, last_period = 1) and processor clock rates.

Let us also suppose that the only thing all processor buyers care about is processing speed on a single, common software application (so we are ignoring the problem of heterogeneity in demand—i.e., which benchmark to run). Further, let's assume that this single measure of speed (software processing performance) relevant to users is perfectly determined by a simple linear function of three processor characteristics:

$$speed = clock\_rate + 500*arch\_dummy + 200*turbo$$

(where "turbo" is a binary indicator for a functioning turbo speedup feature that is enabled in half of the chips produced for each architecture and clock combination).

Each unique combination of architecture, clock rate, and turbo capability under these assumptions can be thought of as a distinct "processor model."[62] With this setup, there are 12 distinct microprocessor models (2 processor architectures × 3 clock rates × 2 turbo values) sold over two periods. Half the models are sold in both periods (the ones running at 1,500), and half are sold only in the beginning or end periods (the models running at the 1,000 and 2,000 clock rates, respectively).[63]

Unit manufacturing cost for the chip is assumed to be given by

$$cost = 50 + 2 * clock\_rate + 2000 * turbo + 500 * arch\_dummy - 10$$
$$* end\_period.$$

End-period manufacturing costs decline by $10 for any constant quality "computer model," simulating a uniform $10 drop in manufacturing cost, given any set of fixed model characteristics, over time.

In the spirit of Pakes (2003), we write out an extremely simple hedonic price reduced-form equation:

$$price = 600 + 2 * speed + cost + random disturbance term,$$

with the first two terms on the right-hand side of the equation reflecting the further assumption that expected markup over incremental unit cost, reflecting user demand, is a linear function of speed alone. After substituting for unit cost (which we typically cannot observe in available data), this gives us a "hedonic price equation" as a function only of observable processor characteristics:

62. I draw a sample of 10 million observations, using pseudorandom draws from independent uniform distributions, to create a simulated population of processor "models," uniformly and independently distributed over architecture, clock rate and turbo feature. Another set of independent, pseudorandom draws from a uniform distribution create a mean zero disturbance term added into the realized sales price on the left-hand side of the hedonic price equation.

63. Because clock rates increase over time, a binary indicator variable for the end period is positively correlated with clock rate but uncorrelated with either architecture or the turbo feature (which are independently and randomly assigned to wafers/chips prior to fabrication).

$$(H1) \; price = 650 + 2 * speed + 2 * clock\_rate + 2000 \; turbo$$

$$+ \; 500 * arch\_dummy - 10 * end\_period$$

$$+ \; random \; disturbance \; term.$$

The disturbance term in the simulation is drawn from a zero-mean uniform distribution. The assumed across-the-board $10 end-period average reduction in manufacturing cost, conditional on fixed processor characteristics, induces a $10 decline over time in quality-adjusted (constant characteristic) mean price across all computer models (since markup by assumption depends only on speed, in turn a function of the other processor characteristics we are conditioning on).

Most importantly, we cannot actually estimate (H1), because speed, architecture, frequency, and turbo characteristics, as a group, are perfectly collinear with one another (since speed is a linear function of arch dummy, clock rate, and turbo). Since these three chip characteristics exactly determine speed, any three of these four variables exactly determines the value of the fourth. If we were to substitute for speed as a function of its three determinants and so drop it from the hedonic price equation, we get

$$(H2) \; price = 650 + 4 * clock\_rate + 1500 * arch\_dummy$$

$$+ \; 2400 * turbo - 10 * end\_period.$$

If we substitute for turbo in terms of the other three variables, we get

$$(H3) \; price = 650 + 12 * speed - 8 * clock\_rate - 4500 * arch\_dummy - 10$$

$$* \; end\_period.$$

If we substitute for clock_rate in terms of the other three characteristics, we get

$$(H4) \; price = 650 + 4 * speed - 500 * arch\_dummy + 1600 * turbo - 10$$

$$* \; end\_period.$$

And substituting for architecture, we get

$$(H5) \; price = 650 + 3 * speed + clock\_rate + 1800 * turbo - 10$$

$$* \; end\_period.$$

Table 11.6 summarizes a simple simulation demonstrating that with a large simulated sample (10 million observations), a regression model with any of the four above specifications (H2–H5) recovers the above parameters correctly.[64] A key point of substantial practical relevance is that *all four of*

---

64. Appendix 11.A2 contains the short Stata program giving these simulation results.

Table 11.6   Simulation of perfectly collinear characteristics in hedonic price equation

	(drop speed) p	(drop turbo) p	(drop clock) p	(drop arch) p	(speed only) p
time	−10.22***	−10.22***	−10.22***	−10.22***	−75.24***
	(0.258)	(0.258)	(0.258)	(0.258)	(0.677)
clock_rate	4.000***	−7.999***		1.000***	
	(0.000365)	(0.000983)		(0.000517)	
architecture_dummy	1,500.0***	−4,499.8***	−500.1***		
	(0.183)	(0.492)	(0.258)		
turbo dummy	2,399.9***		1,599.9***	1,799.9***	
	(0.183)		(0.197)	(0.197)	
speed		12.00***	4.000***	3.000***	4.130***
		(0.000913)	(0.000365)	(0.000365)	(0.000762)
constant	650.0***	650.0***	650.0***	650.0***	992.5***
	(0.492)	(0.492)	(0.492)	(0.492)	(1.281)
N	10,000,000	10,000,000	10,000,000	10,000,000	10,000,000
R^2	0.980	0.980	0.980	0.980	0.808

Notes: Standard errors in parentheses. * $p < .05$, ** $p < .01$, *** $p < .001$. Stata code for this simulation in appendix 11.A2.

these estimable specifications are correct and produce exactly the same esti-mate for the coefficient of the time dummy variable, the parameter of greatest substantive interest. But the coefficients of the perfectly collinear charac-teristics need to be interpreted differently in each case as the joint effects of that characteristic plus the effects of the dropped, perfectly collinear characteristic. In fact, there are wild swings in coefficient values (from 12 to 3 for speed and from 1,600 to 2,400 for turbo) and even sign (from 1,500 to –4,500 for arch_dummy) as different candidates from the set of perfectly collinear variables get dropped from the estimated regression specification.

This is important because with large numbers of characteristics in a hedonic regression, particularly with binary dummies, or nominally con-tinuous covariates that in any given time frame take on only a fixed number of discrete values, perfect collinearity among characteristics is very com-mon. Covariates are typically dropped from the regression automatically by the econometric software. If this is happening and different subsets of the perfectly collinear covariates are used in two different time periods, then wild variation in coefficient estimates, rather than representing worrisome instability in (nonperfectly collinear) explanatory covariates selected and used in the estimated regression, should be anticipated.

A second, even more important point is that estimated coefficients for vari-ables that are not in the set of perfectly collinear variables are not affected by which of the perfectly collinear variables is dropped. In this simulation, for example, the estimated effect of the time dummy—the variable of greatest substantive interest, since its coefficient would be used to estimate a hedonic price index—does not change in value at all as the excluded perfectly collinear variable changes. It is likely to be relatively rare and fairly obvious when a time dummy variable is perfectly collinear with other covariates. In any event, it is easy to verify that the time dummy variable is not perfectly collinear with other included variables by simply running auxiliary regressions of the time dummy against all other explanatory variables, both those included and those dropped as perfectly collinear.

Finally, there is an important specification issue illustrated by this simulation. If one uses speed as one of the explanatory covariates, it is also important to include the full, nonperfectly collinear subset of relevant characteristics affecting cost, even if speed entirely captures the impact of these characteristics from the user demand side. Table 11.6 demonstrates that when only speed and time are used as explanatory variables (last column in the table), bias from the omitted characteristics greatly confounds the coefficient estimate for the time dummy variable, incorrectly magnifying the drop of quality-adjusted price by a factor of 7.5! I return to this point below.

A Hedonic Price Index for Intel Desktop Processors. Model (H0) above was run for each of 162 pairs of adjacent months in which I collected Intel's desktop processor list prices.[65] The first set of adjacent list prices is for January and February 1996. The last pair of adjacent price sheets is for June and July 2014.[66] Overall, R^2 was uniformly high and was not driven primarily by the inclusion of the architectural dummy variables—these were treated as fixed effects, and I also report a "within" R^2 (after demeaning all variables by their group mean), which is also quite high. (See appendix tables 11.A4 and 11.A6.)

The time dummy variables in the above regression were then exponentiated and used to construct price index relatives for adjacent time period

65. The list prices refer to per-chip prices for processors packaged in quantity 1,000 trays sold to original equipment manufacturers (OEMs). By adjacent month, I mean a month and the next month in which an updated list price was published. For example, if Intel issued a price sheet in January, March, April, August, and November of a year, there would be four adjacent month pairs: January–March, March–April, April–August, and August–November. Roughly three-fourths of the monthly observation pairs were a month apart; the next most frequent value observed was two months; the largest time gap between adjacent price lists observed was four months. A hedonic model excluding TDP produced useful estimates for price relatives over 162 adjacent pairs of months. Results for a model with TDP are shown in the appendix tables based on an initial period ending in October 1998, but the problem of a large share of observations lacking a TDP measure does not really fade away until the pair of adjacent months ending in January 2000.

66. The number of processors in early years was very small and characteristics extremely collinear; numbers of processor prices (with TDP) in adjacent month pairs more than double from under 15 to over 30 in late 1999, and estimated price relatives after that date are probably much more reliable. See appendix table 11.A4 and 11.A6 for details on numbers of observations in different adjacent month samples. Entry and exit of architecture and indicator variables from estimation period to period have been color coded in this table. After the first nonzero observation for an indicator variable occurs, blanks indicate the variable was dropped as perfectly collinear. In no case was the time dummy variable perfectly collinear with other covariates; this was checked with auxiliary regressions.

pairs.[67] The resulting price index relatives were then used to chain link these period-to-period indexes into a longer chained price index, shown in appendix table 11.A3.

In addition, I report the values of other coefficients in the hedonic regression in appendix tables 11.A5 and 11.A7, which show how large qualitative jumps in coefficient values from estimation period to period often occur as nonzero values for new characteristics, indicators, or architecture variables that enter and exit the sample, due to perfect collinearity. But there is often perfect collinearity even when there is no new architecture or indicator entering or exiting the sample—this may be seen in the many blank coefficient estimates that appear when architecture or other indicators, or even continuous covariates (which often take on only a handful of discrete values in any single estimation period), are dropped due to perfect collinearity.

The processor architecture family variables are treated as fixed effects and not reported. There were anywhere from one to seven such architecture fixed effects, depending on the pairs of adjacent months used for estimation of the hedonic equation.

Note that nominal power consumption for a processor (TDP, thermal design power) was simply unavailable for most Intel processors released prior to late 1999. I therefore estimated two versions of a hedonic index: one with TDP as a characteristic and one without. TDP is statistically significant when it is used, and therefore the hedonic price index including TDP is the preferred index from 2000 onward (the small numbers of observations with TDP reported prior to late 1999 make these pre-2000 estimates less reliable). I have linked the post-2000 index with TDP to the pre-2000 index without TDP and show this in the final column of table 11.A1 as a composite "best effort" index. The TDP-inclusive and -exclusive indexes are virtually identical from 2000 through January 2005, departing significantly from one another only afterward. Prior to 2000, the earlier the time period, the more limited the available data and the less reliable the resulting estimate.

Figure 11.7 visualizes some of the estimation model summary statistics from appendix table 11.A6 for the TDP variant of the price index (which is also the "composite" index over the period from 2000 onward). The upper panel shows an overall R^2 that across estimation periods averaged .96 and ranged from .91 to .99 from 2000 onward. "Within" R^2 (explained variance after demeaning all variables by architecture fixed effects group means) averaged .92 and ranged from .74 to .99. The lower panel, using a logarithmic

---

67. One-half of the coefficient's squared standard error was added to the exponentiated coefficient to produce an unbiased estimate of the price relative (the exponentiated coefficient's value). See the sources cited in Triplett (2006, 54n41) for details on the rationale for the correction. Sergio Correia's reghdfe Stata command was used to estimate the hedonic regressions, because it removes noninformative singleton observations for dummy variables from the regression, because it provides detailed reports on perfectly collinear variables, and because it also calculates a "within" R^2—that is, an explained variance of the dependent variable after demeaning all variables within fixed effect groups (in this case, the processor architecture indicator variables were treated as fixed effects).

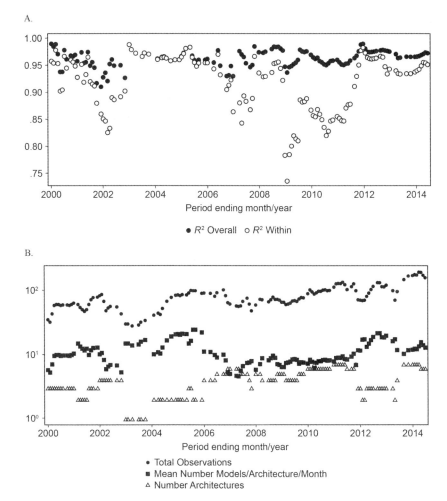

Fig. 11.7   Summary statistics for hedonic regressions
Source: Appendix table 10.A6.

scale, shows that anywhere from one to seven processor architectures were being listed for sale as Intel desktop processors during two-month adjacent estimation periods over this time frame. The number of observations used in the individual hedonic regressions after 1999 ranged from 28 to 190, averaging 82. The average number of processor models per architecture per month listed for sale during the post-1999 period ranged from 4.7 to 24.5, indicative of significant historical changes to Intel's product differentiation strategies in marketing desktop processors over time.

Some important substantive points are supported by figure 11.7. First, there is substantial variation over time in how important the processor design (architecture) dummy variables are in accounting for price variation. While the overall explained variation in price in these hedonic regressions remained uniformly high, within relatively narrow bounds (.91 to .99) throughout the sample period, the role of architectural dummies varied greatly over different subperiods. "Within" R^2 measures how much of the variation in price around architecture-specific means is explained by other covariates. The "within" R^2 coincides exactly with "overall" R^2 in the special case of their being only one "architecture" fixed effect (i.e., a single common constant intercept). The difference between overall and within R^2 can therefore be interpreted qualitatively as a measure of how important controlling for the multiple intercept levels (the processor architecture fixed effects) is in a hedonic model explaining price variation.

Figure 11.7 shows that, at times, a substantial share of overall explained variation (as much as a difference of .10 to .20 between overall R^2 and within R^2) was accounted for by the processor architecture effects prior to 2003 and from late 2006 through 2012. Processor architecture effects from 2013 onward are more modest contributors to explaining price variation, but not nil.

As is suggested visually by figure 11.7, within R^2 (measuring the role of nonarchitectural characteristics in explaining price variation) has a negative and statistically significant correlation with the number of different desktop processor architectures present on Intel price sheets.[68] Not surprisingly, perhaps, it appears that processor architectural variation is more important in explaining price during periods when Intel marketed a larger variety of processor architectural designs and less important in periods with less architectural variation. Indeed, the two measures of R^2 are virtually identical from 2003 through 2005, the heyday of the Pentium 4 series and its "Netburst" design, when only one or two design families accounted for all Intel desktop processors listed on its price sheets (compared with four architectures in 2002 and as many as seven architectures in late 2006).

Figure 11.8 visualizes the hedonic price indexes produced using these models. A dramatic slowing of declines in quality-adjusted price from 2004 through 2006 is quite apparent, followed by a temporary resumption of a somewhat faster rate of decline after 2006 and then another marked slowdown from 2010 onward.[69]

68. For the TDP-inclusive hedonic specification for adjacent periods ending after December 2000, the correlation coefficient between within R-squared and number of processor architecture dummies used is –.53. I reject the hypothesis that it is equal to zero (p-value is .0000).

69. It is not coincidental that in 2004, the Pentium 4's architecture hit its clock rate ceiling and power dissipation reached maximum limits compatible with inexpensive air cooling systems. The rollout of Intel's next-generation response—the Conroe architecture (two cores on a single die at a much lower clock rate but with more instructions per clock processed)—happened in mid-2006. To many industry observers, Intel appeared to be lagging behind its effectively duopolist rival AMD, architecturally, in the early 2000s. AMD was first to market with a 64-bit architecture and, later, the first single die dual core chip. (AMD had brought its Athlon X2 processor out in 2005, a full year before Intel's Core 2 Duo [Conroe architecture] chips.) For empirical evidence on AMD's technological challenge to Intel in the early 2000s, see Nosko (2011), Pakes (2017), and European Commission (2009).

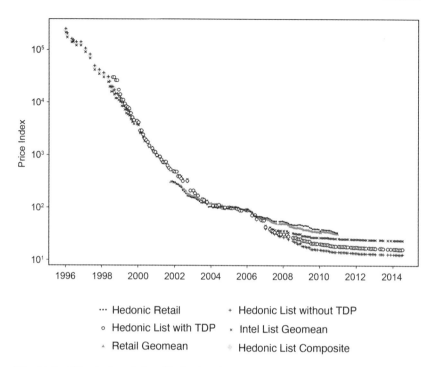

Fig. 11.8   Matched-model and hedonic price indexes for Intel desktop processors, January 2005 = 100

The first four columns in table 11.7 compare my estimated hedonic and matched-model price indexes and the BLS PPIs. As expected,[70] the matched-model geometric mean (Jevons) index price declines are mostly very close to the hedonic indexes but generally decline more slowly than those measured by the hedonic price index based on the same dataset. My estimates over comparable earlier time periods are quite similar to the matched-model indexes of Aizcorbe, Corrado, and Doms (2003) and to the US producer price indexes. Prior to 2004, my Jevons matched-model (geometric mean) index and the PPI move quite closely, while my hedonic indexes show a modestly higher rate of decline, as expected. The hedonic price indexes based on Intel list prices with and without TDP are virtually identical over the period beginning in 2000 through the beginning of 2005.

From 2004 through 2006, both my Jevons and hedonic price indexes decline much more slowly than the PPIs, while from 2006 through 2009, my Jevons and hedonic indexes fall at rates a little faster than the PPI. From 2009 to 2010, the Jevons and hedonic bracket the PPI. Finally, from 2010

70. Since if there were no entering or exiting processor models (all sampled processor models were observed in both time periods) and all hedonic coefficients were the same in the two adjacent periods (assumed by the time dummy method), the time dummy hedonic price index would be equal to the Jevons price index. See De Haan (2010), equation (23), and Triplett (2006), 55.

Table 11.7   Annualized compound rates of change in microprocessor price indexes

	Intel OEM list prices			Intel retail		BLS
	Hedonic w/TDP	Hedonic w/o TDP	Jevons matched model	Hedonic	Jevons matched model	Microproc PPI
1998m9−2001m12	−71.5%	−66.2%	−64.0%			−56.8%
2001m12−2004m4	−49.6%	−49.6%	−48.9%	−40.2%	−35.5%	−47.1%
2004m4−2006m1	−9.6%	−10.1%	−10.7%	−4.6%	−11.1%	−25.2%
2006m1−2009m1	−35.4%	−40.3%	−31.5%	−19.9%	−24.2%	−29.0%
2009m1−2010m11	−13.3%	−13.5%	−6.2%	−15.9%	−11.3%	−10.7%
2010m11−2014m7	−3.5%	−2.9%	−2.3%			−4.2%

Source: Author's dataset and calculations, except Microprocessor PPI, from BLS. See appendix table 11.A3.

through 2014, my hedonic indexes fall more slowly than the PPI, but all decline rates are in the low single digits. These are not the only hedonic price indexes for Intel processors available over this time span, and below I discuss alternative estimates that others have constructed.

Using almost the exact same hedonic regression model,[71] I also estimated a hedonic index using weekly data on retail internet pricing for desktop processor models that I had collected over the same time span. The data came from a now-defunct website (sharkyextreme.com) that published the minimum weekly price quoted by a selection of national US internet retailers over the period from the end of 2001 through the end of 2010. Similarly, I calculated a Jevons index based only on matched models in adjacent periods. These prices are a relatively limited subset of the much larger set of list prices for all Intel desktop processors and presumably are more representative of lower-end models most popular in the retail marketplace. Generally, the pattern over time is similar (steepest declines over 2001–4 and 2006–9 and slower declines over 2004–6 and 2009–10).

One interesting observation that emerges from these results is that except for the period from 2006 through the end of 2007, all the Intel list price indexes, including both hedonic and geometric mean matched-model (Jevons) indexes, move together in a fairly tight formation. This can be seen by comparing the original index (with January 2005 = 100) to rebased indexes with January 2010 = 100. (See figure 11.9.) This is consistent with 2006–7 being a highly atypical period, with many more older, exiting models (from now obsolete Pentium 4–branded architecture families) and new

71. With one additional characteristic—a binary "OEM" indicator variable, indicating whether the product sold by the retailer came in a "boxed" retail package with heatsink and fan or it came in "OEM" packaging without a fan, heat sink, and retail box. Monthly average prices were calculated from published weekly reports. The published weekly price was the reported minimum in a sample of larger internet component retailers.

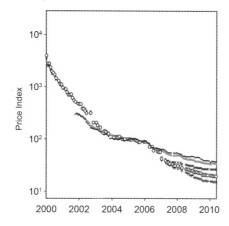

A. January 2005 = 100

··· Hedonic Retail   + Hedonic List without TDP
o Hedonic List with TDP   × Intel List Geomean
▲ Retail Geomean   Hedonic List Composite

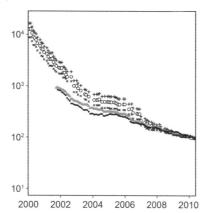

B. January 2010 = 100

··· Hedonic Retail   + Hedonic List without TDP
o Hedonic List with TDP   × Intel List Geomean
▲ Retail Geomean   Hedonic List Composite

Fig. 11.9 Jevons (geometric mean) and hedonic price indexes with alternative base periods

entering models (from its new Core 2 Duo–branded architecture families) than has generally been the case for Intel historically, before or after this period. The change in Intel's product design strategies from 2006 through 2007, in responding to AMD's earlier technological challenge, has been commented upon by researchers[72] and appears to have had impacts that are visible in these price indexes.

Although there are substantial differences in the magnitude of declines across different time periods and data sources, all the various price indexes I have constructed concur in showing substantially higher rates of decline in desktop microprocessor price prior to 2004, a stop-and-start pattern after 2004, and a dramatically lower rate of decline after 2010.

Taken at face value, this creates a puzzle. Even if the rate of innovation had slowed in particular for microprocessors, if the underlying innovation in semiconductor manufacturing technology had continued at the late 1990s pace (i.e., a new technology node every two years and roughly constant wafer-processing costs in the long run), then manufacturing costs would continue to decline at a 30 percent annual rate, and the recent rates of decline in processor price just measured fall well short of that mark. Either the rate of innovation in semiconductor manufacturing must also have declined, or the declining manufacturing costs are no longer being passed along to consumers to the same extent, or both. The semiconductor industry and engineering consensus seems to be that the pace of innovation derived from continuing feature-size scaling in semiconductor manufacturing has slowed markedly. I next examine what other direct evidence is available.

11.3.1.2   Costs

Evidence on Manufacturing Costs. Microprocessors are a semiconductor product sold in truly large volumes. The overwhelmingly dominant player in this market, Intel, released a slide in a presentation to its stockholders in 2012 that supports the narrative of a slowing down in Moore's law cost declines (table 11.8). The figures from Intel's 2012 Investor Meeting seem to show accelerating cost declines in the late 1990s and rapid declines near a 30 percent annual rate around the millennium, followed by substantially slower declines in cost per transistor after the 45nm technology node (introduced at the end of 2007). As discussed previously, the transition to use of

---

72. "Note that in June 2006 there was intense competition for high performance chips with AMD selling the highest priced product at just over $1000. Seven chips sold at prices between $1000 and $600, and another five between $600 and $400. July 2006 saw the introduction of the Core 2 Duo and Fig. 2 shows that by October 2006; (i) AMD no longer markets any high performance chips (their highest price chip in October is just over two hundred dollars), and (ii) there are no chips offered between $1000 and $600 dollars and only two between $600 and $400 dollars. Shortly thereafter Intel replaces the non-Core 2 Duo chips with Core 2 Duo's.

"Nosko goes on to explain how the returns from the research that went into the Core 2 Duo came primarily from the markups Intel was able to earn as a result of emptying out the space of middle priced chips and dominating the high priced end of the spectrum." From Pakes (2017), 251–54; see also Nosko (2011), 8–9.

Table 11.8   **Annualized decline rates for Intel transistor manufacturing cost, 2012**

		Transistor cost index, 90nm = 100 Otellini 2012 Wafer size		Percent transistor cost decline rate between nodes Otellini 2012 Wafer size		Compound annual decline rate Otellini 2012 Wafer size	
Intro date	Tech node	200mm	300mm	200mm	300mm	200mm	300mm
1995q2	350	1,575.35					
1997q3	250	1,033.14		−34.4		−17.1	
1999q2	180	616.10		−40.4		−22.8	
2001q1	130	311.09		−49.5		−32.3	
2004q1	90		100.00		−67.9		−31.5
2006q1	65		48.87		−51.1		−30.1
2007q4	45		27.54		−43.6		−27.9
2010q1	32		17.69		−35.8		−17.9
2012q2	22		11.23		−36.5		−18.3

Source: Otellini (2012), digitized using WebPlotDigitizer. Intro dates: 130nm and up from http://www.intel.com/pressroom/kits/quickreffam.htm. < 130nm from ark.intel.com.

a larger wafer size after the 130nm technology node was accompanied by a particularly large reduction in transistor cost at the next node, using the larger-size wafers.

11.3.1.3   Other Economic Evidence

Depreciation Rates for Semiconductor R&D. Another innovation metric in semiconductors is the depreciation rate for corporate investments in semiconductor R&D. As the rate of innovation increases (decreases), the stock of knowledge created by R&D should be depreciating more rapidly (less rapidly). One recent economic study estimates R&D depreciation rates in a number of high-tech sectors, including semiconductors. The authors conclude that "the depreciation rate of the semiconductor industry shows a clear declining trend after 2000 in both datasets, albeit imprecisely measured."[73] This is consistent with a slowing rate of innovation.

Semiconductor Fab Lives. Faster (slower) technological change in semiconductor manufacturing should presumably shorten (lengthen) fab lifetimes. There are no recent studies of economic depreciation rates for semiconductor plants and equipment, but the anecdotal evidence on the 200mm fab capacity "reawakening" (detailed below) strongly suggests that fab lives have increased, consistent with a slowing rate of innovation in semiconductor manufacturing.

In August 2018, GlobalFoundries (one of four remaining firms that had committed to the development of leading-edge logic manufacturing pro-

73. Li and Hall (2015), 13.

cess technology) announced that it was abandoning its effort to move to its next targeted technology node (7nm) and would stick instead with its current-generation technology: "'The lion's share of our customers . . . have no plans for' 7nm chips. Industry-wide demand for the 14/16 node was half the volume of 28nm, and 7nm demand may be half the level of the 14/16nm node, Caulfield said. 'When we look out to 2022, two-thirds of the foundry market will be in nodes at 12nm and above, so it's not like we are conceding a big part of this market,' he added."[74] This left only three remaining semi-conductor manufacturing firms (Samsung, Intel, and TSMC) developing sub-10nm manufacturing technology going forward into 2019.

A slowing pace of innovation in semiconductor manufacturing was even undeniable at Intel. Intel had introduced its 14nm technology node back in 2014 but ran into difficulties bringing its next-generation 10nm technology to market. In August 2018, Intel acknowledged that it was now delaying volume manufacturing of 10nm technology products until late 2019, over five years after its last technology node (i.e., almost triple its previous two-year "tick-tock" cadence between new technology nodes) and almost three years after its initial projection (see table 11.9 below).[75]

Personal Computer Replacement Cycles. One reason for businesses and consumers replacing computers more frequently (less frequently) is if the rate of innovation in key components in computers, like microproces-sors, increases (decreases), so performance improvements associated with replacement are more (less) economically compelling. While published stud-ies of PC replacement cycles are scarce, Intel monitors replacement cycles for PCs, a major market for its desktop processors. In 2016, Intel CEO Brian Krzanich noted that PC replacement cycles had extended from four years, the previous average, to five or six years, the current average.[76] This, again, is consistent with a slower rate of innovation.

11.4 Is Moore's Law Still Alive? Intel's Perspective in Microprocessors

The most significant evidence against any current slowdown in semicon-ductor manufacturing cost reduction from Moore's law had come from Intel. Fairly recent Intel statements about its manufacturing costs had been the primary factual evidence within the semiconductor manufacturing commu-nity countering the proposition that Moore's law is ending. Unfortunately, Intel had not been consistent in the data it had presented publicly on this issue. Since late 2017, Intel appears to have refrained from releasing any new public information on its manufacturing costs.

The problem with Intel's previous statements is illustrated by figure 11.10

74. Merritt (2018); see also S. Moore (2018).
75. Rogoway (2018); see also Cutress and Shilov (2018).
76. Krzanich (2016).

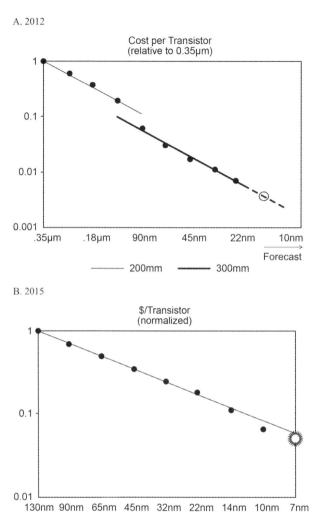

Fig. 11.10   Intel transistor manufacturing costs, 2012 vs. 2015 versions
Source: Otellini (2012); Holt (2015); Intel.

and table 11.9, which contrast two exhibits on manufacturing costs per transistor that Intel had presented at its annual investor meetings—one in 2012 (by then-CEO Paul Otellini) and one in 2015 (by its top manufacturing executive, Bill Holt; see figure 11.2). Some version of the bottom pane in figure 11.10 had been the primary factual evidence in Intel's assertions that Moore's law continues at its historical pace. The graphics in figure 11.10 have been digitized[77] and recorded in table 11.9, then rebased to 100 at the 90nm

77. Using http://arohatgi.info/WebPlotDigitizer/.

Table 11.9   Comparison of Intel cost per transistor at various technology nodes, 2015 vs. 2012

Intro date	Tech node	Transistor cost index, 90nm = 100			Percent transistor cost decline rate between nodes			Compound annual decline rate between nodes		
		Otellini 2012		Holt 2015	Otellini 2012		Holt 2015	Otellini 2012		Holt 2015
		Wafer size			Wafer size			Wafer size		
		200mm	300mm	300mm?	200mm	300mm	300mm?	200mm	300mm	300mm?
1995q2	350	1,575.35								
1997q3	250	1,033.14			-34.4			-17.1		
1999q2	180	616.10			-40.4			-22.8		
2001q1	130	311.09		146.93	-49.5			-32.3		
2004q1	90		100.00	100.00		-67.9	-31.9		-31.5	-12.0
2006q1	65		48.87	71.26		-51.1	-28.7		-30.1	-15.6
2007q4	45		27.54	50.30		-43.6	-29.4		-27.9	-18.1
2010q1	32		17.69	35.64		-35.8	-29.1		-17.9	-14.2
2012q2	22		11.23	26.03		-36.5	-26.9		-18.3	-13.0
2014q3	14			16.13			-38.0			-19.2
2017q4?	Intel 2015 10nm estimate			9.46			-41.4			-21.1
2019q4?	Intel actual 10nm			9.46			-41.4			-9.7

Notes: "300mm?" assumed by author, based on Intel using both 200mm and 300mm wafers with its 130nm tech node. Natarajan et al. (2002). "2017q4?" assumes 2015 Intel forecast of 3 years to next tech node intro date, for 10nm, and 2015 projections of transistor cost decline. "2019q4?" estimated cost decline rate uses Holt (2015) projections of 10nm transistor cost declines at 10nm, but with actual 10nm ship date. Intro dates: 130nm and up from http://www.intel .com/pressroom/kits/quickreffam.htm. < 130nm from ark.intel.com.

technology node. Compound annual decline rates have been calculated in this table using quarterly introduction dates for the first processors manufactured by Intel at that technology node.

The figures presented by Intel to shareholders in 2012 seem to show rapid declines in the 30 percent range around the millennium, then substantially slower declines in cost per transistor after the 45nm technology node (i.e., after 2007). In contrast, a more recent presentation by Intel in 2015 restates the more distant history to show very much slower declines in cost per transistor at earlier technology nodes. Intel has a stock disclaimer that numbers it presents are subject to revision, but in this case the revisions to the historical record are quite dramatic.

The 2015 graphic substantially revises what in the semiconductor industry would be considered the distant historical past (i.e., five technology nodes back from the 22nm node that was in production at the time the earlier 2012 presentation was given). Intel's most recent version of its history now shows transistor costs declining at 12 percent to 18 percent annual rates after the millennium rather than the 30 percent annual declines it showed to its investors in 2012. Its transistor cost decline rate accelerates, rather than slowing further, at the most recent couple of technology nodes.

It now seems likely that one important reason for Intel's restatement of its historical cost declines in 2015 was a definitional change in technical information made public by Intel. Instead of reporting transistor density (transistors per die area) based on actual die area and the number of transistors processed on an actual microprocessor die (which allows one to calculate an actual average of transistors fabricated per die area), Intel apparently began using an entirely theoretical measure of area per designed transistor that appears not to take into account the increasingly relaxed (from design rules) layout of transistors in actual die designs, imposed in part by the need to allow for additional area between transistors needed to fabricate increasingly complex interconnections.[78] (For die designs released prior to 2010, Intel had previously disclosed both actual die size and the number of transistors processed on the die for many of its chip models.)

Most interestingly, assume Intel's 2015 forecast of 10nm transistor manufacturing costs was correct and simply postpone its use in shipped processors from 2017 by an additional two years (2019 was the actual ship date for Intel's first commercial 10nm processors). This delay slows the annual decline rate for its transistor manufacturing costs from 21 percent to 9.7 per-

---

78. See Flamm (2017, 34) for a brief explanation of this issue. Intel's latest redefinition of its publicly disclosed "transistor density metric" is entirely theoretical: .6 × (transistors in a NAND logic cell / area of a NAND logic gate) + .4 × (transistors in a complex scan logic flip-flop cell / area of complex scan logic flip-flop cell) = # transistors/mm². Such a definition does not allow for the practical effects of relaxation (from theoretical design rules) in actual cell layout needed, for example, to accommodate metal interconnections between logic cells. On Intel's new transistor density definition, see Bohr (2017).

cent and implies a marked attenuation of Moore's law–driven cost declines, consistent with the other evidence discussed previously.

11.4.1   An Intel Exception?

Interpreting the recent economic history of Moore's law, how can Intel's description of accelerating declines in manufacturing cost per transistor (as recently as September 2017[79]) be consistent with reports from other chip manufacturers, and their customers, of stagnating cost declines or even cost increases? Increasingly important scale economies provide one plausible and coherent explanation.

Scale economies at the company level are obvious. The cost of a production scale semiconductor fab has increased dramatically at recent technology nodes, and only the very largest chip IDMs (integrated device manufacturers) can depend on their internal demand to justify a fab investment. Intel made this case quite accurately at its 2012 Investor Meeting, predicting that only Samsung, TSMC, and itself would have the production volumes required to economically justify investment in leading-edge fab technology for logic chips by 2016.[80] (Intel overlooked GlobalFoundries, which, by acquiring IBM's semiconductor business in 2015, substantially increased its scale.)[81] Both TSMC and GlobalFoundries are "pure" foundries and achieve their volumes entirely by aggregating the demands of external chip design customers.

Many US-based semiconductor companies have exited chip manufacturing (e.g., AMD, IBM) or stopped investing in leading-edge fabrication while continuing to operate older fabs (Texas Instruments pioneered this so-called fab-lite strategy). Other "pure play" US foundries (e.g., TowerJazz, On Semiconductor) operate mature foundry fabs that remain cost effective for lower volume chips. Long-established American chip companies, such as Motorola, National Semiconductor, and Freescale, disappeared in the course of mergers or acquisitions that continue to reshape the industry.

This consolidation in leading-edge IC fabrication is global. In Europe, there are no manufacturers currently investing in leading-edge technology.[82] In Asia, there are arguably only Toshiba in Japan, Samsung and Hynix in Korea, and foundry TSMC in Taiwan. Firm-level scale economies explain

79. See Smith (2017), slide 6, "Is Moore's Law Dead? No!" Interestingly, since September 2017, Intel has not—to the best of my knowledge—published a claim that its manufacturing cost per transistor continues to decline at rates exceeding previous historical decline rates or is even falling at new technology nodes.

80. Krzanich (2012), slide 19.

81. What constitutes leading-edge technology in memory chips is somewhat more nebulous, and several large memory specialist IDMs (Hynix, Toshiba, Micron) might also arguably be categorized as being near the leading edge. Global Foundries has since announced that it is dropping out of future development of new manufacturing technology nodes.

82. The last remaining leading-edge chipmaker headquartered in Europe, ST Microelectronics, announced in 2015 that it will be relying on foundries for future advance manufacturing needs.

why fewer firms can afford leading-edge fabs but can't explain why Intel's cost per transistor would have declined much faster than that at other producers still investing in leading-edge fabs, particularly the foundries. It's possible that Intel has unique, proprietary technological advantages. A more mundane explanation is that product-level scale economies drive these differences.

In particular, there has been an exponential increase in the costs of the ever more-complex photomasks needed to pattern wafers using lithography tools—a set of masks cost $450,000 to $700,000 back in 2001, at 130nm, compared with a wafer production cost of $2,500 to $4,000 per wafer.[83] At 14nm (updating wafer-production costs using Intel costs in table 11.9 implies 150 percent increases), wafer production cost would be $6,225 to $9,960. By contrast, costs for a mask set at 14nm are estimated to run from $10 million to $18 million, a 22- to 40-fold multiple of 130nm mask costs![27] Lithography cost models suggest that with 5,000 wafers exposed per photomask set (a relatively high-volume product at recent technology nodes), mask costs per unit of output will exceed both average equipment capital cost and average depreciation cost. With smaller production runs for a product, photomask costs become the overwhelmingly dominant element of silicon wafer–processing cost at leading-edge technology nodes.[84]

Intel, with the largest production runs in the industry (perhaps 300 to 400 million processors in 2014[85]), has huge volumes of wafers to amortize the cost of its masks and is certainly benefitting from significant economies of scale. A single Intel processor design (and mask set) is the basis for scores of different processor models sold to computer makers. Processor features, on-board memory sizes, processor speeds, and numbers of functioning cores can be enabled or disabled in the final stages of chip manufacture, and manufacturing process parameters can even be altered to shift the mix of functioning parts in desired ways.[86]

For Intel, this creates average manufacturing costs per chip that are vastly smaller than costs for fabless competitors running much smaller product volumes using the same technology node at foundries. Foundries recoup those much higher per-unit mask costs through one-time charges or through high finished wafer prices charged to its fabless designer-customers. The customer

---

83. Both 130nm mask and wafer cost estimates were presented by an engineer in Intel's in-house Mask Operation unit (Yang 2001). Mask set cost estimates at 14nm are taken from Black (2013), slide 6.

84. Lattard (2014), slide 6.

85. Based on the fact that Intel publicly revealed that it had shipped 100 million processors a quarter, a record-setting event, in the third quarter of 2014. Intel (2014), 1.

86. When chips are tested after manufacture, the speed, power consumption, and functioning memory and feature characteristics are used to "bin" the processor into one of many different part numbers. As process yields improve over time with experience, new part numbers with faster speeds or lower power consumption are introduced. VanWagoner (2014) is a concise discussion by a former Intel manufacturing engineer of how a large variety of processor models are manufactured from a single unique processor design.

directly bears the much higher design costs per unit if the latest technology node is chosen for the product.

Exponentially growing design and mask costs at leading-edge nodes now make older technology nodes economically attractive for lower-volume products. Higher variable wafer-processing costs per transistor at older nodes are more than offset by much lower fixed design and photomask costs.

Such scale-driven cost disadvantages are increasingly pushing low-volume chip production to older chip-making technology running in depreciated fabs. This is reshaping the economics of chip production, extending the economic lives of aging fabs. Older 200mm wafer fab capacity is now growing rapidly, forecast to expand almost 20 percent by 2020![87]

Historically, this is unprecedented. The additional 200mm capacity coming into service cannot use more-advanced process technologies designed for 300mm wafer-processing equipment. Much lower fixed design and photomask costs with older technology are the primary factor making it economically attractive to fabricate low-volume products. As inexpensive computing penetrates into everyday appliances, "Internet of Things" chip designers are generating low-volume foundry orders for chip designs tailored to market niches, filling these old fabs with chip orders that don't require the greatest possible density.

Is Intel an exceptional case in the semiconductor industry? Is its portrait of recently accelerating manufacturing cost declines reflected in the actual behavior of its product prices? The problem is, Intel does not disclose data on its product pricing to either the public or government statistical agencies, so analysis of what an economist would call a quality-adjusted price is quite difficult.

Alternative Hedonic Price Indexes for Microprocessors. Apart from Intel's pre-2018 declarations of optimism, a second piece of evidence arguing against a slowdown in Moore's law is a study by Byrne, Oliner, and Sichel (2018), which also utilizes the same list price data from Intel (that I used) in making its argument. Using only the first four quarters of prices for recently introduced models, they run an annual time dummy hedonic price model over adjoining pairs of years and find quality-adjusted prices declining at the same rate in 2000–4 as in 2009–13, at about a 42 percent annual rate of decline, and an even more impressive 46 percent decline over 2004–9.[88] This is higher than any of the rates shown for 2004–9 and very much higher than the decline rates post-2009 in table 11.7.

The key differences between my hedonic price indexes and the Byrne, Oliner, and Sichel (2018) hedonic price indexes are that (1) Byrne, Oliner, and Sichel use only a subset of the desktop processors for which their chosen software benchmark scores are available (vs. all desktop processors listed on

Intel's current price sheets); (2) Byrne, Oliner, and Sichel include quarterly average list prices for individual processors only during the first four quarters after their introduction onto the market (vs. using all available monthly average list prices); and (3) Byrne, Oliner, and Sichel use only a single processor characteristic (geometric mean of benchmark software performance scores[89]) in their hedonic model (vs. using a much larger set of processor characteristics that I argue is likely to be relevant to both demand and unit cost).

Sample Selection: SPEC Benchmark vs. No SPEC Available. Byrne, Oliner, and Sichel (2018) acknowledge that there are some differences between chips that have benchmark (SPEC) scores available and chips without (SPEC scores are primarily used to compare processor performance in servers and technical computing workstations, which generally use higher-end processors than the consumer market).[90] They report that a matched-model price index using only the SPEC chips generally falls faster than an index using the non-SPEC chips in all time periods. They also report that their matched-model indexes produce a qualitative pattern in price declines over time that is very similar to what is shown in table 11.7 for all Intel desktop processors. Thus these results suggest that the restriction of the price sample to higher-performance processors with SPEC scores may bias estimates of quality-adjusted price declines toward higher rates of price decline but is not responsible for the very different qualitative behavior over time (relatively constant vs. dramatic reductions in rates of decline after 2004).

First Four Quarters Only vs. All Prices. Byrne, Oliner, and Sichel (2018) observe that individual Intel processor list prices very rarely change over time on price sheets after 2011, in contrast to the prior decade. They identify two scenarios they believe may explain this. In one scenario, "Intel offers progressively larger [but unobserved] discounts to selected purchasers as models age,"[91] producing a measurement error for older processors but not recently introduced models. This would complicate estimation of hedonic price indexes using list price data. "The introduction period index would be unbiased even if there are unobserved discounts at the time of introduction provided that these discounts do not vary systematically over time or across models,"[92] while an index using all periods would presumably be biased.

Alternatively, they argue that even if the posted list prices are actual transactional prices, the older chips must be getting progressively more expensive in quality-adjusted terms if their nominal prices do not change, so relative demand for these models must be falling: "By focusing on prices [only]

---

89. They take the geometric mean of processor performance on industry consortium SPEC's benchmark scores on single program integer and floating-point software test suites. Their procedure for splicing the two or three distinct sets of benchmarks used over their sample period (SPEC2000 and SPEC2006, and possibly SPEC95) over their 2000–2013 sample period is not explicitly described. See figure 11.4 above for evidence that both levels and slopes of these benchmarks change over time when they are compared.

90. Byrne, Oliner, and Sichel (2018), table 2.

91. Byrne, Oliner, and Sichel (2018), 690.

92. Ibid.

at the beginning of each model's life cycle, a regression that applies equal weights to all observations avoids over-weighting models whose quantities have dropped off."[93] These arguments are used to justify using only prices observed during the first four quarters after a model's introduction, discarding the majority of their sample of Intel list prices.

However, in a recent study, Sawyer and So (2017) replicate the substance of the Byrne, Oliner, and Sichel (2018) results over the period after 2009 in a sample utilizing only "early" (first four quarters after introduction) Intel list prices.[94] However, when processor characteristics are added to SPEC scores as explanatory covariates, Sawyer and So show that standard statistical tests decisively reject the exclusion of processor characteristics from a hedonic price equation that also includes SPEC scores.[95] When these other processor characteristics are not excluded, estimates of recent decline rates for quality-adjusted processor prices over time are dramatically smaller than those estimated by Byrne, Oliner, and Sichel.[96] We can reasonably conclude that it is the restriction of hedonic characteristics to benchmark scores only, and not the restriction to early prices, that is producing the pattern of unremittingly high price declines found in Byrne, Oliner, and Sichel over the post-2004 time period.

Sawyer and So (2017) also note that Intel processors are typically sold in their largest volumes only after the first four quarters in which they are available for sale.[97] Intel's own economic expert made this point in its antitrust case before the European Commission, noting that processor production begins with a "ramp-up" phase that "begins with low volumes and typically lasts three to five quarters."[98] Therefore, using price data for a processor only during the first four quarters following its introduction likely would place relatively high weights on products actually being sold in relatively low volumes compared to other products.

It seems reasonable to suggest that this may be a real-world example of omitted variable bias, akin to that created in the last column of the perfect collinearity simulation in table 11.6. However, Byrne, Oliner, and Sichel (2018) articulate some real concerns about use of Intel list price data to measure processor pricing trends. They note "a sharp change over the course of the 2000s in the life-cycle properties of Intel's posted prices . . . In the early period prices fell steeply over a model's life cycle. However, by 2011–2012, price paths are flat or nearly so, with only a few instances of sizable price declines."[99] These observations are spot on.

Figure 11.11 shows the fraction of incumbent (i.e., omitting newly intro-

93. Ibid.
94. Sawyer and So (2017), 8.
95. Ibid., 11.
96. Ibid., 10.
97. Ibid., 14–15.
98. European Commission (2009), 326.
99. Byrne, Oliner, and Sichel (2018), 687.

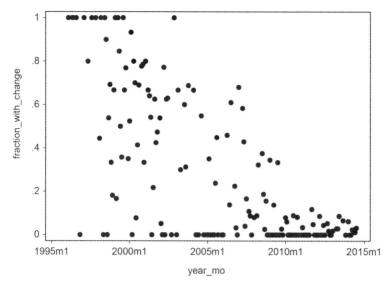

Fig. 11.11   Fraction of Intel desktop processor prices changing from one price list to the next

Source: Author's tabulation from Intel list price dataset.

duced products) desktop processor prices that changed from one list price sheet to the next one issued, from 1998 through mid-2014. Through mid-2014, it is evident that Intel's propensity to alter list prices on existing processors diminished over time, though it never entirely stopped adjusting list prices on its existing product line through mid-2014. In 2008 and 2009, for example, there were price sheets on which anywhere from 35 percent to 40 percent of already introduced desktop processor prices changed from the previous sheet.[100] Since 2014, however, existing processor prices rarely if ever change from one price sheet to the next.

Indeed, if one had to choose a date based on this chart for a climacteric in Intel pricing practices, 2010—the year after its antitrust cases were settled—would seem a promising choice. That year also apparently coincides with the beginning of a determined campaign by Intel to raise its profit margins, an effort that seems to have had some success (aided at that point by a greatly diminished competitive threat from its historical rival, AMD; see figure 11.12). Raising its average sales prices (ASP) was a key element of this strategy. (See figure 11.13.)

In earlier versions of their research, Byrne, Oliner, and Sichel (2018) focused on the evident change in Intel pricing strategies during the first decade of

---

100. Byrne, Oliner, and Sichel (2018), figure 4, show a similar set of patterns over time in the share of Intel desktop processors with a list price decline within four quarters of introduction.

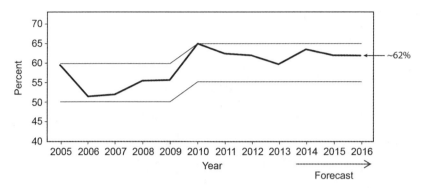

Fig. 11.12   Intel's post-2010 gross margin elevation objective
Source: Smith (2015).

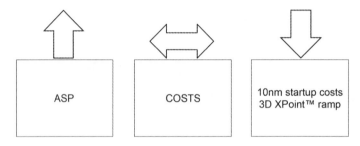

Fig. 11.13   Intel's 2015 explanation to its shareholders for success in maintaining high profit margins
Source: Smith (2015).

the 2000s as the motivation for restricting their Intel prices to "early" initial processor prices.[101] Their hypothesis, that Intel may have changed its pricing strategy during the first decade of the new millennium, actually seems quite plausible given that the European Commission launched a major antitrust case against Intel over its processor price discounting practices during the 2002–6 period, culminating in a preliminary decision against Intel in 2007 and a final decision in 2009.[102] A related private US antitrust case by AMD was filed and then settled in 2009.

The Byrne, Oliner, and Sichel (2018) scenario of "progressively larger discounts to selected purchasers as models age" is difficult to test, since no

101. In the earlier 2017 Federal Reserve working paper version of their study, BOS speculated that "it is possible that Intel actually changed its life-cycle pricing strategy to extract more revenue from older models, with the posted prices reflecting this change." Byrne, Oliner, and Sichel (2017), 8.

102. See European Commission (2009). The same antitrust concerns also resulted in government antitrust actions in Japan and Korea and by the US Federal Trade Commission. Acting on an appeal by Intel, the European Court of Justice sent the EU case back to a lower court for further consideration in 2017, so this seems destined to be litigated for years to come.

data on Intel transaction prices for its wholesale sales to large buyers are publicly available. We do know that evidence produced in the EU antitrust investigation seems to show that even the newest chips sold to large original equipment manufacturer (OEM) customers were heavily discounted from list prices prior to 2006, at times with conditional exclusivity rebates that were not publicly reported by Intel or its customers.[103]

However, there is one public source of Intel transactional price data that is real and observed and does not require any assumptions about unobserved behavior. Retail prices in the electronics industry are linked to wholesale prices, directly and indirectly. Most directly, the very largest retailers can purchase boxed processors directly from Intel or, like smaller retailers, from distributors. (Approximately 20 percent of Intel processors in recent years, by volume, were sold directly as boxed processors, primarily to small computer makers and electronic retailers.[104]) Computer OEMs, electronics system manufacturers, and electronic parts distributors who purchase processors directly from Intel can resell excess inventories to other distributors, resellers, and retailers, and these actually show up on the retail market labeled as "OEM package" (vs. "Retail Box" packaging).

Both boxed and OEM-packaged processors are sold by retailers, distributors, and brokers with a price that is advertised publicly and is directly observable in the marketplace. (The retail data used in constructing my matched-model price index include both OEM and retail-packaged chips sold by internet retailers.) The retail data used in table 11.7 also seem to clearly point to a deceleration in microprocessor price declines after 2004.

It seems reasonable to presume that retail transaction prices (which are observable in the market), at least in the long run, should have some stable stochastic relationship to wholesale producer transactional prices. Indeed, at least one previous study found such linkages between OEM contract transactional prices and retail prices for high-volume chips sold in the semiconductor industry.[105]

There are market-driven economic reasons behind this linkage. Both

103. See European Commission (2009). See also SEC v. Dell Inc. et al. Complaint (US Securities and Exchange Commission 2010), which asserts that unreported exclusivity rebates given by Intel to Dell had climbed to about three-fourths of Dell's operating income by 2006.

104. "Although it sells microprocessors directly to the largest computer manufacturers, such as Dell, Hewlett Packard, and Lenovo, its Channel Supply Demand Operations (CSDO) organization is responsible for satisfying the branded boxed CPU demands of Intel's vast customer network of distributors, resellers, dealers, and local integrators. Intel's boxed processor shipment volume represents approximately 20 percent of its total CPU shipments . . . Processors ship from CW1 to one of four CW2 'boxing' sites, which kit the processors with cooling solutions (e.g., fan, heat sink) and place them in retail boxes and distribution containers. Such boxing sites are typically subcontracted companies that ship the boxed products to nearby Intel CW3 finished-goods warehouses where they are used to fulfill customer orders. Channel customers range in size and need; they are mostly low-volume computer manufacturers and electronics retailers" (Wieland et al. 2012).

105. See Flamm (1993) for a study documenting linkages between retail prices and OEM contract prices for DRAM memory chips.

semiconductor manufacturers and their OEM customers sell their excess inventories of chips to brokers and distributors during industry downturns, pushing small buyer spot prices down in distributor and retail sales channels as excess OEM inventories of chips are absorbed in those sales channels. In tight markets, conversely, when semiconductor manufacturers are capacity constrained, wholesale contract prices to large OEMs rise. To meet surging demand, OEMs may even try to purchase additional volumes of chips, beyond the volumes negotiated in contracts with chip manufacturers, in retail and distribution markets. As both large OEMs and smaller buyers compete fiercely over the remaining unallocated output, upward pressure on retail and distributor prices is felt. In short, both direct and indirect linkages between small buyer (retail and distributor) markets and large buyer (contracts with OEMs) markets, as well as arbitrage across distribution channels, would lead an economist to expect to observe a structural relationship between observed retail processor prices and unobserved large OEM wholesale prices.

In a still earlier version of their research, Byrne, Oliner, and Sichel (2015) had speculated that the change in Intel pricing behavior (resulting in a systematic change in the relationship between Intel list prices and unobserved OEM contract prices) may have occurred after 2006.[106] This is actually an interesting and plausible choice of dates for a change in Intel pricing behavior, since it coincides approximately with the end of the exclusivity rebates that had been the subject of the government and private antitrust actions mentioned earlier. There is also a significant drop in the maximum fraction of Intel list prices changing between adjacent price sheets evident after 2006 visible in figure 11.11 (the last occasions on which 60 percent of prices for existing processors were changed at the end of 2006 and early 2007). If there was a structural shift in Intel pricing practices that caused list prices to diverge more sharply from actual transactional prices after 2006, we might then also expect to see a change in the relationship between movements in observed transactional prices in the retail market and Intel list prices after 2006. This is testable using observational data.

I explored the possibility that there was some detectable change in the relationship between Intel list (posted wholesale) prices and observed retail prices after 2006 by constructing a panel of monthly observations on average retail price and posted list price covering 163 distinct Intel desktop processor models sold by internet retailers over the years 2000 through 2010.[107] I allow for model fixed effects (which permits a particular low-end Celeron model, for example, to be related to Intel list price with a different retail margin

106. "By 2006, this pattern had completely changed; the posted price of a specific model tended to remain constant, even after a new, higher performance model became available at a similar price" (Byrne, Oliner, and Sichel 2016, 9).
107. This is the same sharkyextreme.com data I previously used to construct Jevons and hedonic retail price indexes.

Table 11.10   **Fixed effects model of log retail price for Intel desktop processors**

	(Full model) lp_ret	(Constrained model) lp_ret
Log Intel Tray Price	0.763***	0.768***
	(15.37)	(17.93)
OEM dummy	−0.0497***	−0.0496***
	(−6.70)	(−6.77)
Age	−0.00676***	−0.00582***
	(−3.70)	(−4.91)
After2006 dummy	0.0204	
	(0.13)	
After2006 × age	0.00162	
	(0.83)	
After2006 × log Intel Tray Price	−0.0108	
	(−0.39)	
Constant	1.347***	1.303***
	(4.87)	(5.55)
N	1,580	1,580
R^2	0.987	0.987
Adj. R^2	0.986	0.986

Notes: *t* statistics in parentheses. * $p <.05$, ** $p < .01$, *** $p <.001$.

than a high-end Core i7 model). The model that I estimated specified the log of retail price as

$$\ln(R_{it}) = a_i + b \ln(I_{it}) + c \, Age_{it} + d \, OEM + e \, After2006 + f \, After2006$$
$$\times \ln(I_{it}) + g \, After2006 \times Age_{it} + u_{it},$$

with R_{it} as an observation on average retail price for model i in month t; I_{it} as the average posted Intel list price in a month in which list price had been posted at least once; Age_{it} as the number of elapsed months since the month the model's price had been first posted on a published Intel price sheet; After2006 as a binary indicator variable with value of 1 in 2006 and thereafter and 0 before; OEM as a binary indicator for whether the product sold was the retail boxed version or the bare chip in OEM packaging; and u_{it} as a random disturbance term. If post-2006 transaction prices reflect age discounts from Intel list prices that pre-2006 prices did not, we would expect to find a statistically significant shift coefficient on the interaction of After2006 with Age.

Table 11.10 shows the results of estimating this model.[108] The After2006 shift variable and all of its interactions, including interactions with processor model Age, are close to zero and statistically insignificant individually

108. Robust standard errors clustered on processor models are shown in figure 11.8.

and jointly.[109] The relatively flatter trajectories over time for Intel list prices after 2006 are mirrored in the behavior of flatter retail price trajectories for the same chips.

Therefore, based on the only evidence on actual transaction prices that is publicly available—that is, advertised retail prices from internet-based vendors—there is no evidence of some structural change occurring after 2006 in the relationship between observed Intel list prices and observed retail market prices. Of course, this does not directly prove that there was no change in the relationship between Intel list prices and (unobserved) discounted OEM contract prices for processors, but it certainly weighs against it.

Figure 11.11 and our earlier discussion suggests that 2010–11 is another candidate time period in which to search for a shift in Intel pricing practices. Unfortunately, the retail data analyzed in table 11.10 do not extend past this date.

SPEC scores vs. chip characteristics. As previously remarked, Sawyer and So (2017) have shown that the Byrne, Oliner, and Sichel (2018) results showing no slowdown in quality-adjusted Intel processor price declines since 2000 are not the result of using only "early" Intel list prices but instead are driven primarily by use of SPEC benchmark scores as the sole characteristic in a hedonic model in lieu of a more extensive set of chip characteristics.

The use of SPEC scores instead of actual chip characteristics is based on the argument that direct performance measures are easier to get right than relevant chip characteristics. But this argument overlooks three fundamental reasons why chip characteristics should still be included in a hedonic price equation.

First, there is a computer architecture literature that tells us that benchmark scores of a CPU on any given task should be well explained by a small set of chip characteristics, including numbers of cores and threads, computer architectural design, chip clock rate, and on-chip memory cache sizes. This literature actually identifies the chip characteristics that are relevant and even uses them to model computer CPU performance out of sample.[110] As I next show, scores on various SPEC processor benchmarks are almost perfectly predicted by a linear function of the small set of chip characteristics that the computer design literature predicts are its determinants.

Second, economics tells us that the characteristics that belong in a hedonic price equation are there because they are relevant to user demand and that they have an additional effect on price if they alter supplier marginal cost.[111]

---

109. The Wald F(3,162) test statistic for the joint hypothesis that all After2006 terms were zero was .8 and the p-value .49.

110. Hennessey and Patterson (2003), in the third edition of their classic computer architecture textbook (59–60) do exactly this to compare the Pentium III with a Pentium 4 operating at the same clock rate.

111. Pakes (2003, 1581, equation 3) notes that the hedonic price function can be interpreted as the sum of the expected marginal cost, conditional on characteristics, and expected markup (derived from the demand function), conditional on characteristics. The key point is that the product characteristics are arguments in the separate cost and demand function terms in the hedonic price equation.

At best, software benchmark scores might correctly serve as a perfect summary measure of quality perceived by users on the demand side. But there is no reason, technological or economic, why a measure of chip performance relevant to demand should also perfectly capture the separate effects of underlying characteristics that determine performance on chip cost. Omitting variation in processor characteristics that affects chip cost will induce omitted variable bias in the hedonic coefficient estimates if the omitted characteristics' effects on cost are correlated (but not perfectly collinear) with the included benchmark scores.

That is, assume for the sake of argument that the mix of user demands for various types of computer applications was fixed over time and that processor performance on this fixed-weight mix of computer applications was correctly captured in some SPEC benchmark. Even with the heroic assumption that this aggregated benchmark correctly captured everything relevant to chip quality on the demand side (and it is clear it does not[112]), there is no plausible technological or economic reason why variations across chip models in marginal production costs related to chip characteristics that determine benchmark scores should be perfectly mirrored by variation in SPEC benchmark scores.

Indeed, the computer architecture literature teaches us that a variety of chip characteristics can affect performance and that, therefore, the same SPEC score can potentially be produced with diverse, nonunique combinations of numbers of cores, threads, cache memory, clock frequency, and so on. In fact, if we look at actual SPEC scores, multiple distinct chip models can produce approximately the same score. But variation in each of these chips' characteristics—cores, threads, on-chip memory, and clock frequencies—may have very different impacts on production cost for the processor compared with impact on SPEC scores.

Third, if benchmark scores are determined by chip characteristics, using chip characteristics directly in the hedonic equation—instead of, or in addition to, a single benchmark score—effectively allows coefficients in the hedonic equation to change to mirror changes in the average mix of tasks run by computer users over time. Use of a single benchmark or fixed-weight index of benchmarks effectively assumes the mix of tasks relevant to performance for users is fixed over time.[113]

112. Since power draw minimization, graphics, and hardware virtualization capabilities clearly are desirable to large subsets of computer users yet will have no direct impact on SPEC scores if missing or disabled in a processor.

113. That is, assume we have two benchmarks, b1 and b2, and two processor characteristics, c1 and c2. Assume b1 = a1 c1 + a2 c2, while b2 = e1 c1 + e2 c2. Assume users in the aggregate run b1 applications 50 percent of the time and b2 applications the other 50 percent. Then we can represent performance on the "average market workload" with a performance index that looks like .5 b1 + .5 b2, or equivalently, .5 (a1 c1 + a2 c2) + .5 (e1 c1 + e2 c2) = [.5 (a1+e1)] c1 + [.5 (a2 + e2)] c2. That is, the benchmark index is equal to a simple linear function of the two characteristics. Now if the weights of b1 and b2 change to 25 percent and 75 percent on the new "market workload," workload performance will be incorrectly captured by the original performance index (50 percent weights) even if scaled by some arbitrary constant. However,

For all these reasons, use of the SPEC score as the sole characteristic in a hedonic price equation is not a highly plausible economic assumption. In addition, because SPEC scores are only available for the subset of Intel desktop processors used by OEMs in servers, the use of SPEC scores in a desktop processor hedonic price regression will considerably reduce sample size compared with statistical models using chip characteristics but not SPEC scores. In the Intel list price data, the number of Intel desktop processors with SPEC scores available for analysis is a fraction of all Intel desktop processors with list prices available in any time period. When using other publicly available retail or distributor desktop processor price data, an even larger fraction of the available data may not have SPEC scores available.[114]

To support this point, I next demonstrate that SPEC processor benchmark scores are almost perfectly predicted by a small number of underlying chip characteristics and provide little or no additional information. In making this claim, I note that I make use of a set of processor microarchitecture dummy variables in the set of chip characteristics used. Neither Sawyer and So nor Byrne, Oliner, and Sichel (2018) use processor architecture dummy variables (which I have shown make an important contribution to the explanatory power of a hedonic price model) in the set of characteristics they employ when estimating a chip characteristic–based hedonic model. It is quite possible that adding a software benchmark score to a set of chip characteristics that excludes the architectural dummies has the effect of capturing much of the effect of these dummy variables in the hedonic price model.

The role of different chip characteristics on different SPEC benchmarks, however, varies greatly across different types of SPEC benchmarks, which argues for direct use of the underlying characteristics in a hedonic equation. It is an argument for letting the data decide what the correct weights on processor characteristics in a hedonic price equation are rather than adopting the implicit weights embedded within a time-invariant weighted average benchmark score.

11.5   Chip Characteristics and Computer Performance: Building Blocks for a Hedonic Analysis

By forcing us to focus on the relationship between performance of microprocessors on representative software benchmarks—which all agree should

---

performance on "market workload" is still correctly captured by a linear function of the two underlying chip characteristics (though the coefficients of the characteristics in this function change). The specification that is linear in the underlying characteristics is simply more flexible in representing shifts in demand.

114. This is because the selection of processors commonly sold to consumers for use in desktop PCs may include relatively fewer desktop processors used in servers (the ones that would have SPEC scores available).

be an important determinant of chip demand—and chip characteristics, Byrne, Oliner, and Sichel (2018) have done us a great service in providing focus for a discussion of what chip characteristics should be used when estimating a hedonic price equation for microprocessors.

The theoretical computer architecture literature makes use of a *processor performance equation* to predict processor performance. Effectively, this relationship models the execution time a computer processing unit takes to perform some given software benchmark program (i.e., a given sequence of programming instructions) as the product of two parameters: average clock ticks per instruction and the seconds per clock tick in the processor's clock.[115] Since a processor performance benchmark score is proportional to the inverse of time required to run a benchmark program on a particular computer processor, we can invert the processor performance equation and then have

$$\text{Performance} \sim \text{IPC} \times \text{clock rate},$$

where IPC is processed instructions per clock tick, clock rate is measured in ticks per second, and the performance index basically compares benchmark instructions executed per unit time across processors. Indeed, given a particular computer architecture, computer engineers simply scale measured performance linearly by clock rate in order to model the approximate impact of raising clock rate on processor performance.[116]

IPC will depend on both the design (architecture) of the computer processor and the particular mix of instructions being executed in the benchmark software. The specified clock rate of a processor model is typically fixed after testing, at the end of the chip fabrication process.[117] "Binning" during testing of finished chips creates different speed grade bins, which are subsequently sold as different processor models to computer manufacturers and other consumers. The effective, yielded mix of nondefective, more-valuable fast processors and less-valuable slow processors on a fabricated wafer containing hundreds or thousands of these processors is a determinant of processor manufacturing costs.

Speed is not the only chip processor characteristic affected by random fabrication process variation. There may also be random manufacturing variation affecting the voltage needed to run the chip properly, varying from die to die on the same wafer. Chips that require less power to perform cor-

---

115. See Hennessey and Patterson (2012), section 1.9, 48–52.

116. Hennessey and Patterson (2003), in the third edition of their classic computer architecture textbook (59–60), do exactly this to compare Pentium III performance with a Pentium 4 operating at the same clock rate.

117. Random variation in a highly complex semiconductor manufacturing process leads to a distribution of functional chips by the maximum clock rate at which they can successfully execute some test suite. A "fast" processor can operate at a higher-than-average clock frequency, while a "slow" processor can only operate correctly at a slower-than-average clock rate.

rectly may be identified through testing and sold as low-power models of the processor.[118]

Microprocessor chips generally have on-chip caches of fast local memory that can also affect the execution time for given software. The portion of on-chip cache memory that is defect-free and therefore usable by the chip can also vary with the incidence of manufacturing defects during the fabrication process, and testing then leads to additional binning of finished chips by usable, functional cache memory.

Similarly, particular sections of chip circuitry associated with some advanced features of the chip may not be fully functional due to random processing defects. In order to maximize revenue from all usable products yielded from a finished silicon wafer, a complex system of testing "bins" based on speed, memory, power requirements, and working feature functionality is used to define distinct processor models sold as different chips to final consumers. Indeed, chips are generally designed with some redundant circuitry and electrical "fusing" options intended to maximize saleable product, and revenues, from a processed wafer with dies that may not be perfect. A dozen processor models may be derived from a single, artfully designed die manufactured in the thousands on a single wafer.[119]

At Intel, microprocessor designs are identified with a "microarchitecture," which historically is associated with a publicly available codename. (For example, the processor microarchitecture launched by Intel in October 2017 was given the codename "Coffee Lake."[120]) Prior to 2010, Intel also made public information on its processors' die sizes and the number of transistors on the die processed in its manufacture. Based on this information (which is no longer publicly released), it appears that the many dozens of microprocessor models for each of its microarchitectures were based on somewhere between one and three basic die designs.[121] That is, the dozens of different processor models corresponding to a single microarchitecture product family were manufactured from just one to three basic chip designs fabricated on silicon wafers.

---

118. And processing of the wafer can be optimized to produce relatively more chips requiring less power.

119. The design of a chip will segment the circuitry into functional blocks that can be disabled electronically (e.g., with programmable "fuses") during the manufacture and testing process. Some redundant circuitry is typically made part of the design, to maximize yield of usable parts after test. A more capable chip can generally be made less capable by disabling portions of its circuitry at the final stages of manufacture. This may be done deliberately by manufacturers to create additional supplies of lower-end chips when customer demand for lower-end parts exceeds the portion of output physically binned into low-end chip models on the basis of test results.

120. Cranz (2017).

121. Prior to 2010, Intel publicly released the exact die area and number of "processing transistors" used in manufacturing most of its microprocessor models. All processors with exactly the same microarchitecture, die area, and numbers of processing transistors can be assumed to be derived from a single die design. Analysis of this data shows anywhere from one to three unique microarchitecture / die size / processing transistor combinations were being used to produce many dozens of processor models.

It is straightforward to analyze the relationship between SPEC scores and microprocessor characteristics. Table 11.10 shows the results from estimating a linear regression model explaining log SPEC scores with a set of explanatory variables suggested by the computer engineering literature: a full set of microarchitecture dummy variables (since IPC is going to depend on computer microarchitecture), log of the base processor clock rate, a dummy variable indicating a "turbo" feature is enabled on the chip (the highest clock rate achievable by a single core on the chip will differ from the base processor clock rate if this feature is available), log of on-chip memory cache size,[122] log of the number of physical processor cores on the chip, and a dummy variable indicating that multithreaded "virtual" logical cores are available on a chip.[123] In addition, a binary indicator variable for use of "autoparallelization" in compiling the SPEC benchmark software code is included, since that can enable a speedup on multicore processors or on processors with multithreading.[124]

A simple log linear regression model that explains SPEC benchmark performance as a function of six processor characteristics (and a full set of 29 to 31 dummy variables for different Intel x86 processor microarchitectures) accounts for a remarkable 97 percent to 98 percent of the variation in SPEC2006 benchmark scores for thousands of computer models using Intel x86 processors over the 2005–17 period (table 11.11). Note that this regression utilizes all Intel x86 desktop, server, and mobile processors in the SPEC2006 database and, further, that it is estimated using every different individual computer making use of an included processor as the underlying set of observations used in estimating the model.

That is, variation in chipsets, motherboards, configured memory, and other components in the computer systems from different manufacturers making use of any particular chip model, which is reflected in the residual, accounted for no more than 2 percent to 4 percent of observed variation in SPEC scores. This analysis utilizes individual tested computer system data—that is, on average there are four to five different computer systems using a specific processor model.

We can alternatively calculate a median or mean score across all computer systems utilizing each processor chip model to more closely resemble the Byrne, Oliner, and Sichel (2018) procedure for deriving a single SPEC score for each chip model. Using that as the basis for our SPEC2006 performance

122. Actually, I am using the size of the "last level cache," since microprocessors can have a hierarchy of successively larger (and slower) caches onboard.
123. Hyperthreading is Intel's name for multithreading capability, additional circuitry added to the processor that creates two logical (or "virtual") processors that can access every physical core. One logical processor can begin processing the next instruction while the other logical processor is actually executing an instruction in a core, thus allowing a form of chip-level parallelism that can speed up performance when a computer program spawns multiple threads.
124. Indeed, after a short number of months at the beginning of the SPEC2006 suite in 2006, almost all the single-process SPEC benchmark scores have autoparallelization turned on.

Table 11.11   **Log of SPEC 2006 benchmark as function of processor characteristics**

Dependent variable is log of	Six characteristics model			
	SPECf06	SPECi06	SPECfr06	SPECir06
Log base processor speed	0.196***	0.115**	0.383***	0.429***
	(0.0401)	(0.0396)	(0.0590)	(0.0746)
Log cache memory size	0.0965**	0.0861***	0.140**	0.109***
	(0.0283)	(0.0232)	(0.0442)	(0.0208)
Log number physical cores	0.157***	0.0385	0.642***	0.826***
	(0.0284)	(0.0285)	(0.0357)	(0.0249)
Hyperthreading dummy	0.0644**	0.0318**	0.132***	0.201***
	(0.0179)	(0.0111)	(0.0169)	(0.0130)
Log max speed w/turbo	0.514***	0.722***	0.101	0.328***
	(0.0651)	(0.0560)	(0.103)	(0.0747)
Autoparallelization dummy	0.0649*	0.00310	0.0107	−0.0134
	(0.0262)	(0.0534)	(0.0211)	(0.0362)
Microarchitecture dummies	Y	Y	Y	Y
Observations	1,160	1,190	2,207	2,417
R^2	0.966	0.960	0.982	0.974
N_clusters	31	31	29	30
R^2 within	0.687	0.697	0.896	0.893

Cluster robust standard errors in parentheses, clustered on Intel microarchitecture.
* $p < .05$, ** $p < .01$, *** $p < .001$
Log base processor speed is processor base clock rate
Log of max speed is log of maximum clock rate if turbo mode available
Log cache memory is log of amount of last level cache memory on processor chip
Autoparallelization dummy =1 if feature enabled in compiler when SPEC software was compiled

regression model, we get an even higher R^2, of about .99[125] (table 11.12). It is clear that computer architecture dummies and five processor characteristics together essentially perfectly predict SPEC benchmark scores.

Two points are significant. First, the coefficients of (weights assigned to) different processor characteristics in determining SPEC scores are very different for different SPEC benchmarks. The clear implication is that different processor characteristics can have very different effects on performance for different types of workloads. A flexible hedonic price model, reflecting a changing distribution of chip consumers across distinct types of workloads, would best let the empirical data decide the weights users place on particular characteristics rather than aggregating the characteristics into a single benchmark score with the time-invariant weights implicitly used to perform the aggregation into a performance metric.

125. I drop all chips shown as underclocked or overclocked by computer system maker (having reported clock rate more than 10Mz slower or faster than the Intel-specified base clock rate) and ignore autoparallelization in calculating medians or means in table 11.12. Table 11.12 reports results using logs of medians; using logs of means would give almost identical results.

Table 11.12   **Log of median SPEC 2006 benchmark as function of processor characteristics**

	Five characteristics model			
Dependent variable is log of median computer system score for particular processor model	SPECf06	SPECi06	SPECfr06	SPECir06
Log base processor speed	0.279***	0.156***	0.507***	0.460***
	(0.0347)	(0.0338)	(0.0767)	(0.0565)
Log cache memory size	0.0783**	0.0575**	0.155**	0.122***
	(0.0259)	(0.0194)	(0.0531)	(0.0184)
Log number physical cores	0.190***	0.0697*	0.644***	0.810***
	(0.0254)	(0.0274)	(0.0513)	(0.0167)
Hyperthreading dummy	0.0721***	0.0371***	0.134***	0.211***
	(0.0133)	(0.00727)	(0.0132)	(0.00788)
Log max speed w/turbo	0.421***	0.677***	−0.0109	0.286***
	(0.0716)	(0.0526)	(0.105)	(0.0575)
Microarchitecture dummies	Y	Y	Y	Y
Observations	331	340	449	454
R^2	0.988	0.985	0.990	0.994
N_clusters	30	30	28	28
R^2_within	0.843	0.853	0.941	0.975

Notes: Cluster robust standard errors in parentheses, clustered on Intel microarchitecture.
* $p < .05$, ** $p < .01$, *** $p < .001$

Second, these characteristics also will affect cost. Every distinct Intel microarchitecture is manufactured using a single fabrication technology node, so in addition to representing the processor's design architecture, the microarchitecture dummies also capture variation in microprocessor manufacturing cost that is induced by variation in chip microarchitectures and manufacturing technology. As previously described, different quality grades (measured by processor clock rates, amounts of on-chip cache memory, and chip features) produced by testing and binning are also associated with cost differences. Coefficients on these characteristics in a hedonic reduced-form price equation should be regarded as reflecting both demand and cost effects.

Finally, in addition to the chip characteristics determining SPEC performance, there is a small set of additional chip characteristics that we would certainly want to include in a hedonic price equation for microprocessors. Power dissipated by a chip determines whether expensive cooling solutions are required, shifting demand for that processor; power requirements are also important (for battery life) in mobile applications. Electricity use, the principle variable cost of computing, will vary with power consumed. Further, power dissipation varies with random manufacturing process variations, so the power rating of a chip is also going to be related to chip cost. Whether or not a graphics processor is integrated into the microprocessor will also affect both demand and cost for that chip. Support for hardware virtualization will have no practical effect on processor performance on SPEC benchmarks but is a valuable feature for business customers wishing to increase server efficiency by running numerous "virtual machines" on their servers simultaneously.

In conclusion, we should remember that SPEC scores are maintained by organizations that sell servers, processors used in servers, and the largest server customers, so a SPEC-selected sample will be skewed toward the models of chips that perform best as server processors. The SPEC performance regressions in tables 11.11 and 11.12 would then seem to tell us that desktop and server performance should be modeled separately, with different weights placed on different chip characteristics.

This suggests a natural segmentation of microprocessors for purposes of price measurement. A desktop segment oriented toward single software program application performance, a mobile (laptop and tablet) segment tilted toward both performance and low power, and a server segment with a greater emphasis on performance on embarrassingly parallel workloads (servers running a mix of uncoordinated applications with performance more like the SPEC "rate" benchmarks). In terms of finding public data useful in estimating a hedonic price equation, retail/distribution prices will be most readily observable and useful in estimating desktop microprocessor prices. Retail data will be much more limited and less useful for mobile processors and even more limited, and therefore least useful, for hedonic measurement of server processor prices.

The absence of a reliable source of producer transactional data for microprocessors, for use in government price indexes, is a serious and increasingly formidable barrier to measuring prices and innovation correctly in the semiconductor industry.

11.6   Conclusion

There is considerable evidence that semiconductor manufacturing innovation has historically been responsible for perhaps a 20 percent to 30 percent annual decline in the cost of manufacturing transistors on a chip. One would expect that this predictable cost decline would be transformed into a similar price decline in a competitive industry, at least in the long run, and therefore that a decline of this magnitude would serve as a floor on the long-run trajectory of semiconductor prices for high-volume semiconductor products. Innovations in the architecture and designs being manufactured on the chip, new kinds of chip designs, and superior performance characteristics of existing designs fabricated using more-advanced fabrication technology would be additional factors explaining even higher long run rates of decline in quality-adjusted semiconductor prices.

Historically, most high-volume semiconductor applications ultimately migrated to more-advanced manufacturing technology nodes, pulled there by the simple economics of continuing declines in cost using more-advanced fabrication technology. This migration pressure now seems to have lessened, in part the result of rapidly escalating fixed costs that must be sunk into the design of new chips using the most-advanced manufacturing technology and in part due to an apparent slackening in the rate of cost decline at the technological frontier of semiconductor manufacturing.

The available empirical evidence, on balance, suggests that Moore's law–related historical declines in chip manufacturing cost have clearly been attenuated over the last decade. For chips where market price data are collected, decline rates in chip prices over time seem to have greatly diminished. The evidence for exceptionality in Intel microprocessor price declines is shaky, indicative primarily of the increasingly poor quality of publicly available processor price data, changing Intel policies on public release of meaningful list prices for its older processors, and likely, omitted variables in hedonic price models using Intel list price data.

A substantial economic literature has connected faster innovation in semiconductor manufacturing to rapidly improving price performance for semiconductors, to larger price declines for information technology, to increased uptake of IT across the economy, and to higher rates of labor productivity growth. If correct, this implies that a slowdown in semiconductor manufacturing innovation and attenuation of price declines in both chips and IT may play an important role in current stagnation in labor productivity growth.

Finally, it is now almost an article of faith in high-tech industry that an expanding cloud of computing and machine intelligence is in the process of transforming our economy and society. Much of this faith is built on projection into the future based on past experience with increasingly powerful and pervasive computing capabilities that both cost less and use less energy year after year. The winding down of Moore's law means that the technological scaling that drove these historical declines and implicitly underlies the most optimistic assumptions about the spread of ubiquitous computing in the future may no longer hold. Both cost and energy use now seem more likely to increase in lockstep with the scale of cloud computing in the future. Unless there are continuing, significant improvements in software technology, computing costs—and energy use per computation—are unlikely to decline, or even stay constant as computing capacity increases, as was true in the past. Investments in entirely new technologies will be needed, as will a renaissance of creativity and innovation in software. Software, the neglected sibling living in the shadow cast by Moore's law—and dramatically cheapening hardware—for the last 50 years, must increasingly shoulder the burden of delivering comparable economic benefits from continuing technological innovation in information technology.

References

Aizcorbe, A. 2014. *A Practical Guide to Price Index and Hedonic Techniques.* Oxford: Oxford University Press.

Aizcorbe, A. 2002. "Why Are Semiconductor Prices Falling So Fast? Industry Estimates And Implications For Productivity Measurement." Finance and Economics Discussion Series 2002-20, Board of Governors of the Federal Reserve System.

Aizcorbe, A., C. Corrado, and M. Doms. 2003. "When Do Matched-Model and Hedonic Techniques Yield Similar Price Measures?" Federal Reserve Board of San Francisco Working Paper 2003-14.

Aizcorbe, A., K. Flamm, and A. Khurshid. 2007. "The Role of Semiconductor Inputs in IT Hardware Price Decline: Computers versus Communications." In *Hard-to-Measure Goods and Services: Essays in Honor of Zvi Griliches,* edited by E. Berndt and C. Hulten, 351–81. Chicago: University of Chicago Press.

Aizcorbe, A., S. D. Oliner, and D. E. Sichel. 2008. "Shifting Trends in Semiconductor Prices and the Pace of Technological Progress." *Business Economics* 43 (3): 23–39.

Black, R. 2013. "Rambus, Bring Invention to Market." July. http://www.iesaonline .org/downloads/IDC_Presentation_to_IESA_Thought_Leadership_Forum .pdf.

Bohr, M. 2017. "Moore's Law Leadership." Intel Newsroom, March 2017. https:// newsroom.intel.com/newsroom/wp-content/uploads/sites/11/2017/03/Mark -Bohr-2017-Moores-Law.pdf.

Bourzac, K. 2016. "Intel: Chips Will Have to Sacrifice Speed Gains for Energy Savings." *MIT Technology Review,* February. https://www.technologyreview.com/s /600716/intel-chips-will-have-tosacrifice-speed-gains-for-energy-savings/.

Brown, C., and G. Linden. 2009. *Chips and Change, How Crisis Reshapes the Semiconductor Industry.* Cambridge, MA: MIT Press.

Burgelman, R. 1994. "Fading Memories: A Process Theory of Strategic Business Exit in Dynamic Environments." *Administrative Science Quarterly* 39 (1): 24–56.

Byrne, D., B. Kovak, and R. Michaels. 2017. "Quality-Adjusted Price Measurement: A New Approach with Evidence from Semiconductors." *Review of Economics and Statistics* 99 (2): 330–42.

Byrne, D., S. Oliner, and D. Sichel. 2015. "How Fast Are Semiconductor Prices Falling?" AEI Economic Policy Working Paper 2014-06, revised Nov. 2015. https:// www.aei.org/wp-content/uploads/2015/03/Byrne_Oliner_Sichel_Nov-16-2015 .pdf.

Byrne, D., S. Oliner, and D. Sichel. 2017. "How Fast Are Semiconductor Prices Falling?" Finance and Economics Discussion Series 2017-005. Washington, DC: Board of Governors of the Federal Reserve System. https://www.federalreserve .gov/econresdata/feds/2017/files/2017005pap.pdf.

Byrne, D., S. Oliner, and D. Sichel. 2018. "How Fast Are Semiconductor Prices Falling?" *Review of Income and Wealth* 64 (3): 679–702.

Competition Commission of Singapore. 2013. "Grounds of Decision Issued by the Competition Commission of Singapore in Relation to the Notification for Decision of the Proposed Acquisition by Micron Technology Inc. of Elpida Memory Inc. Pursuant to Section 57 of the Competition Act." Case number CCS 400/009/12.

Copeland, A. 2013. "Seasonality, Consumer Heterogeneity and Price Indexes: The Case of Prepackaged Software." *Journal of Productivity Analysis* 39 (1): 47–59.

Cranz, A. 2017. "Intel's Latest Coffee Lake Processors Are Fast as Hell." Gizmodo, October 5, 2017. https://gizmodo.com/intels-latest-coffee-lake-processors-are -fast-as-hell-1819129322.

Cunningham, C., et al. 2000. "Silicon Productivity Trends." International Sematech SEMATECH Tech. Transfer #00013875A-ENG, 29 Feb.

Cutress, I., and A. Shilov. 2018. "Intel Server Roadmap: 14nm Cooper Lake in 2019, 10nm Ice Lake in 2020." August 8. https://www.anandtech.com/show/13194/intel -shows-xeon-2018-2019-roadmap-cooper-lakesp-and-ice-lakesp-confirmed.

Dieseldorff, C. 2016. "Watch out for 200mm Fabs!" October 19. http://www.semi .org/en/watch-out-200mm-fabs-fab-outlook-2020-0.

De Haan, J. 2010. "Hedonic Price Indexes: A Comparison of Imputation, Time Dummy and 'Re-pricing' Methods." *Jahrbucher fur Nationalokonomie und Statistik* 230 (6): 772–91.

Esmaeilzadeh, H. E., et al. 2013. "Power Challenges May End the Multicore Era." *Communications of the ACM* 56 (2): 93–102.

European Commission. 2009. *Non-Confidential Version of the Commission Decision of 13 May 2009, Case COMP/37.990 Intel.* May.

Flamm, K. 1993. "Measurement of DRAM Prices: Technology and Market Structure." In *Price Measurements and Their Uses*, edited by M. Foss, M. Manser, and A. Young, 157–206. NBER Studies in Income and Wealth 57. Chicago: University of Chicago Press.

Flamm, K. 1995. *Mismanaged Trade? Strategic Policy in the Semiconductor Industry.* Washington, DC: Brookings Institution.

Flamm, K. 2003. "Moore's Law and the Economics of Semiconductor Price Trends." *International Journal of Technology, Policy and Management* 3 (2): 127–41.

Flamm, K. 2004. "Moore's Law and the Economics of Semiconductor Price Trends." National Research Council, *Productivity and Cyclicality in Semiconductors: Trends, Implications, and Questions: Report of a Symposium.* Washington, DC: National Academies Press.

Flamm, K. 2007. "The Microeconomics of Microprocessor Innovation." Presented at Productivity Workshop, NBER Summer Institute 2007, Cambridge, MA, July. http://conference.nber.org/confer/2007/si2007/PRB/flamm.pdf.

Flamm, K. 2009. "Economic Impacts of International R&D Coordination: SEMATECH and the International Technology Roadmap." In *21st Century Innovation Systems for Japan and the United States: Lessons from a Decade of Change: Report of a Symposium*, edited by K. Flamm and S. Nagaoka. Washington, DC: National Academies Press.

Flamm, K. 2010. "The Impact of DRAM Design Innovation on Manufacturing Profitability." *Future Fab International* 35, November.

Flamm, K. 2017. "Has Moore's Law Been Repealed? An Economist's Perspective." *Computing in Science and Engineering* 19 (2): 29–40.

Fuller, S., and L. Millett, eds. 2011. *The Future of Computer Performance: Game Over or Next Level.* Washington, DC: National Academies Press.

Gandal, N. 1994. "Hedonic Price Indexes for Spreadsheets and an Empirical Test for Network Externalities." *RAND Journal of Economics* 25 (1): 160–70.

Hennessy, J., and D. Patterson. 2003. *Computer Architecture: A Quantitative Approach*, 3rd ed. Cambridge, MA: Morgan Kaufmann.

Hennessey, J., and D. Patterson. 2012. *Computer Architecture: A Quantitative Approach*, 5th ed. Cambridge, MA: Morgan Kaufmann.

Holt, B. 2005. "Facing the Hot Chip Challenge (Again)." Presented at Hot Chips 17. http://www.hotchips.org/wp-content/uploads/hc_archives/hc17/2_Mon/HC17 .Keynote/HC17.Keynote1.pdf.

Holt, B. 2015. "Advancing Moore's Law." Presented at Intel Investor Meeting, Santa Clara. http://files.shareholder.com/downloads/INTC/0x0x862743/F8C3E42B -7DA9-4611-BB51-90BED3AA34CD/2015_InvestorMeeting_Bill_Holt_WEB2 .pdf.

Howse, B., and R. Smith. 2015. "Tick Tock on the Rocks: Intel Delays 10nm, Adds 3rd Gen 14nm Core Product 'Kaby Lake.'" Anandtech, July. http://www.anand tech.com/show/9447/intel-10nm-and-kaby-lake.

Hruska, J. 2012. "Nvidia Deeply Unhappy with TSMC, Claims 20nm Essentially Worthless." Posted March. http://www.extremetech.com/computing/123529 -nvidia-deeply-unhappy-with-tsmc-claims-22nm-essentially-worthless.

IC Insights. 2012. "Total Flash Memory Market Will Surpass DRAM for First Time in 2012." December 19, 2012. http://www.icinsights.com/news/bulletins/Total -Flash-Memory-Market-Will-Surpass-DRAM-For-First-Time-In-2012/.

IC Insights. 2016. "Global Wafer Capacity 2016–20 Product Brochure." http://www .icinsights.com/data/reports/4/0/brochure.pdf?parm=1454865474.

IC Knowledge. 2004. "DRAM Trends." https://web.archive.org/web/20041210172733 /http://www.icknowledge.com/trends/dram.html.

Intel. 2007. "Intel Demonstrates Industry's First 32nm Chip and Next-Generation Nehalem Microprocessor Architecture." Press release, September. http://www .intel.com/pressroom/archive/releases/2007/20070918corp_a.htm.

Intel. 2014. "Intel Reports Record Quarterly Revenue of $14.6 Billion." News Release. http://files.shareholder.com/downloads/INTC/2751719461x0x786397 /D4904F61-2F5F-48CC-82E2-21A4D0C49583/Earnings_Release_Q3_2014 _final.pdf.

Intel. 2016. 2015 Intel Annual Report. https://s21.q4cdn.com/600692695/files/doc _financials/2015/annual/2015_Intel_Annual_Report_web.pdf.

Jones, H. 2014. "Why Migration to 20nm Bulk CMOS and 16/14nm FinFETS Is Not Best Approach for Semiconductor Industry." Los Gatos, CA: International Business Strategies, January, p. 1.

Jones, H. 2015. "10nm Chips Promise Lower Costs." EE Times, June 15. http://www .eetimes.com/author.asp?section_id=36&doc_id=1326864.

Jorgenson, D. 2001. "Information Technology and the US Economy." American Economic Review 91 (1): 1–32.

Kanter, D. 2016. "GlobalFoundries Offers 7nm Roadmap." http://www.linleygroup .com/newsletters/newsletter_detail.php?num=5592.

Krzanich, B. 2012. "Big or Small . . . It's All about the Details." Presentation at Intel Investor Meeting. http://www.cnx-software.com/pdf/Intel_2012/2012_Intel _Investor_Meeting_Krzanich.pdf.

Krzanich, B. 2016. "Intel Corporation's (INTC) CEO, Brian Krzanich Presents at Sanford C Bernstein Strategic Decisions Conference 2016 - Brokers Conference Transcript." June 1. http://seekingalpha.com/article/3979164-intel-corporations -intc-ceo-brian-krzanich-presents-sanford-cbernstein-strategic-decisions?part =single.

Lattard, L. 2014. "Mask Less Lithography for Volume Manufacturing." SEMICON Europa. http://semieurope.omnibooksonline.com/2014/semicon_europa/SEMI CON_TechARENA_presentations/TechARENA1/Lithography/02_Ludovic %20Lattard,%20Cea-Leti.pdf.

Lawson, S. 2013. "The Moore's Law Blowout Sale Is Ending, Broadcom's CTO Says." PC World, December 5. http://www.pcworld.com/article/2069740/the -moores-law-blowout-sale-is-ending-broadcoms-cto-says.html.

Li, W., and B. Hall. 2015. "Depreciation of Business R&D Capital." Working paper, November. https://eml.berkeley.edu/~bhhall/papers/LiHall16_bus_rnd _depreciation.pdf.

Lipsky, J. 2015. "Samsung Describes Road to 14nm." EE Times, April 16. http:// www.eetimes.com/document.asp?doc_id=1326369.

McCann, D. 2015. "Silicon Interconnect, Packaging and Test Challenges from a

Foundry Viewpoint." June. http://www.swtest.org/swtw_library/2015proc/PDF
/SWTW2015_Keynote_McCann_GlobalFoundries.pdf.

Merritt, R. 2017. "TSMC, Samsung Diverge at 7nm." EE Times, February 8, 2017.
http://www.eetimes.com/document.asp?doc_id=1331324.

Merritt, R. 2018. "GlobalFoundries Halts 7nm Work." *EE Times*, August 28. https://
www.eetimes.com/document.asp?doc_id=1333637.

Moammer, K. 2017. "Intel Delays 10nm Cannon Lake CPUs to End of 2018."
Wccftech, September 20, 2017. http://wccftech.com/intel-delays-10nm-cannon
-lake-cpus-end-2018/.

Moore, G. 1965. "Cramming More Components onto Integrated Circuits." *Electronics* 38 (8): 114–17. Reprinted in 1998 in *Proceedings of the IEEE* 86 (1):
82–85.

Moore, G. 1975. "Progress in Digital Integrated Electronics." *Technical Digest. International Electron Devices Meeting*, 11–13.

Moore, S. 2018. "GlobalFoundries Halts 7-Nanometer Chip Development." *IEEE
Spectrum*, August 28. https://spectrum.ieee.org/nanoclast/semiconductors
/devices/globalfoundries-halts-7nm-chip-development.

Natarajan, S., et al. 2002. "Process Development and Manufacturing of High-
performance Microprocessors on 300mm Wafers." *Intel Technology Journal* 6
(2), May.

Nosko, C. 2011. "Competition and Quality Choice in the CPU Market." Harvard
University, June.

Oliner, S., and D. Sichel. 1994. "Computers and Output Growth Revisited: How Big
Is the Puzzle?" *Brookings Papers on Economic Activity* 25 (2): 273–334.

Or-Bach, Z. 2012. "Is the Cost Reduction Associated with IC Scaling Over?" *EE
Times*, July 16.

Otellini, P. 2012. "Investor Meeting 2012." Presentation to Intel Investor Meeting,
Santa Clara, CA.

Pakes, A. 2003. "A Reconsideration of Hedonic Price Indexes with an Application
to PCs." *American Economic Review* 93 (5): 1578–96.

Pakes, A. 2017. "Empirical Tools and Competition Analysis: Past Progress and Current Problems." *International Journal of Industrial Organization* 53(C).

Pillai, U. 2013. "A Model of Technological Progress in the Microprocessor Industry."
Journal of Industrial Economics 61 (4): 877–912.

Pirzada, U. 2016. "Exclusive: Is Intel Really Starting to Lose Its Process Lead? 7nm
Node Slated for Release in 2022." Wccftech, September 10, 2016. http://wccftech
.com/intel-losing-process-lead-analysis-7nm-2022/.

Prudhomme, M., and K. Yu. 2005. "A Price Index for Computer Software Using
Scanner Data." *Canadian Journal of Economics* 38 (3): 999–1017.

Qualcomm. 2014. "Qualcomm Snapdragon Integrated Fabless Manufacturing." January 2014, 4. https://www.qualcomm.com/documents/qualcomm-snapdragon
-integrated-fabless-manufacturing.

Raley, T. 2015. "IBM z13 Overview and Related Tidbits." Presentation, March.
https://www.ibm.com/developerworks/community/wikis/form/anonymous/api
/wiki/33d270cb-c060-40f6-99f3-956c3cb452a3/page/a3b86697-49c1-4be0-b247
-805276033049/attachment/f49e69a1-fb8d-4710-a23e-0318bbf76e83/media/IBM
%20z13%20Overview%20for%20DFW%20System%20z%20User%20Group
_2015Mar.pdf.

Rogoway, M. 2018. "Intel Splits Up Manufacturing Group amid Production Delays."
The Oregonian, October 17. https://www.oregonlive.com/silicon-forest/index.ssf
/2018/10/intel_manufacturing_vp_sohail.html.

Rosso, D. 2016. "Global Semiconductor Sales Top $335 Billion in 2015." February. http://www.semiconductors.org/news/2016/02/01/global_sales_report_2015/global_semiconductor_sales_top_335_billion_in_2015/.

Sawyer, S., and A. So. 2017. "A New Approach for Quality Adjusting PPI Microprocessors." Presented at NBER Summer Institute, July 18. http://www.nber.org/conf_papers/f97472/f97472.pdf.

Shuler, K. 2015. "Moore's Law Is Dead: Long Live SoC Designers." February. http://www.design-reuse.com/articles/36150/moore-s-law-is-dead-long-live-soc-designers.html.

Smith, S. 2015. "Investor Meeting 2015 Santa Clara." Presentation to Intel Investor Meeting, Santa Clara, CA.

Smith, S. 2017. "Strategy Overview." Presented at Intel Technology and Manufacturing Day China, September 19. https://newsroom.intel.com/newsroom/wp-content/uploads/sites/11/2017/09/stacy-smith-on-milestones-in-intels-process-technology-roadmap.pdf.

Spencer, W., and T. Seidel. 2004. "International Technology Roadmaps: The US Semiconductor Experience." National Research Council, *Productivity and Cyclicality in Semiconductors: Trends, Implications, and Questions: Report of a Symposium*. Washington, DC: National Academies Press.

Triplett, J. 2006. *Handbook on Hedonic Indexes and Quality Adjustments in Price Indexes*. Paris: OECD.

US Securities and Exchange Commission. 2010. *SEC v. Dell Inc. et al. Complaint*. https://www.sec.gov/litigation/complaints/2010/comp21599.pdf.

VanWagoner, J. 2014. "How Does Intel Design and Produce So Many Models of CPUs?" https://www.quora.com/How-does-Intel-design-and-produce-so-many-models-of-CPUs.

White, A. J., et al. 2005. "Hedonic Price Indexes for Personal Computer Operating Systems and Productivity Suites." *Annales d'economie et de Statistique* 79/80: 787–807.

Wieland, B., P. Mastrantonio, S. P. Willems, and K. G. Kempf. 2012. "Optimizing Inventory Levels Within Intel's Channel Supply Demand Operations." *Interfaces* 42 (6): 517–18.

Yang, C. 2001. "Challenges of Mask Cost and Cycle Time." October. http://www.sematech.org/meetings/archives/litho/mask/20011001/K_Mask_cost_Intel.pdf.

Yinug, F. 2016. "Made in America: The Facts about Semiconductor Design." June. http://www.semiconductors.org/clientuploads/Industry%20Statistics/White%20Pape%20Profile%20on%20the%20U.S.%20Semiconductor%20Design%20Industry%20-%20061016%20-%20Final.pdf.

12
Accounting for Innovations in Consumer Digital Services
IT Still Matters

David Byrne and Carol Corrado

12.1 Introduction

Capturing the impact of innovations in consumer content delivery in conventional well-being measures—for example, GDP—presents significant challenges. It also seemingly requires a new approach because the manifestation of these innovations in consumer welfare (e.g., time spent consuming high-quality content via networked IT devices) does not involve a market transaction at the time of consumption, which is where price collectors/estimators look to pick up new goods as they appear. Figure 12.1 shows that innovations in consumer content delivery have been very rapid since the turn of this century, suggesting their impacts may be missed in existing GDP; indeed, they are clustered in the mid-2000s when the slowdown in trend GDP growth emerged. Is it possible that the substitution of uncounted, so-called

David Byrne is a principal economist at the Board of Governors of the Federal Reserve System.

Carol Corrado is distinguished principal research fellow in economics at the Conference Board and a senior policy scholar at the Center for Business and Public Policy, McDonough School of Business, Georgetown University.

This chapter was prepared for the NBER Conference on Research in Income and Wealth (CRIW) conference Measuring Innovation in the 21st Century. Besides feedback at the conference, we have benefited from presentations of this chapter at the 5th IMF Statistical Forum in Washington, DC (November 2017), the ESCoE Measurement Conference in London (May 2018) and the fifth World KLEMS Conference in Cambridge, Massachusetts (June 2018). We received no financial support for this chapter. The views expressed in this chapter are those of the authors and do not necessarily reflect those of the Board of Governors or other members of its staff. For acknowledgments, sources of research support, and disclosure of the authors' material financial relationships, if any, please see https://www.nber.org/books-and-chapters/measuring -and-accounting-innovation-21st-century/accounting-innovations-consumer-digital-services -it-still-matters.

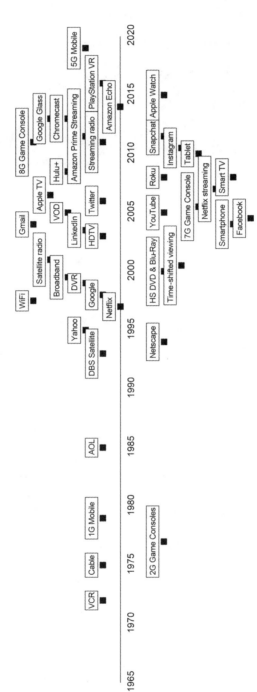

Fig. 12.1 Timeline of innovations in consumer content delivery

Source: Authors' adaption and extension of information in *Total Audience Report*, Nielsen, December 3, 2014, http://www.nielsen.com/us/en/insights /reports/2014/the-total-audience-report.html.

free goods for purchased counterparts is a culprit in this much-discussed slowdown?

This chapter adapts a not-so-new approach—capitalization of consumer digital goods—to address this question, but the standard approach is augmented by an accounting for how IT devices and subscription network access services are used and consumed.[1] To understand why a use-adjusted version of an "old" approach is both (a) needed and (b) up to the task of capturing 21st-century innovations, consider first that it is consumer-owned devices with advanced processing technology—computers, powerful smartphones, smart TVs, and video game consoles—that enable the consumption of high-quality content in many homes (and elsewhere), and these services currently are uncounted in national accounts (though their paid-for predecessors often were). Consider next that the spread of broadband since 2000 and the rise of social media since 2004 suggest that the use of services that enable the delivery of content to consumers has risen dramatically (see figure 12.2). The rise in use of network services implies greater consumption volume (for a given number of subscriptions) because subscription costs do not fully depend on use rates. All told, we translate the problem of capturing the innovations shown in figure 12.1—including what Brynjolfsson and Saunders (2009) call "free goods"—into a quest for comprehensive measurement of (a) consumer services derived from IT device use and (b) consumer network service volumes in constant-quality terms; (a) involves an imputation to GDP for the missing services and (b) involves creating a new price index for the paid-for services.

Because consumers' IT capital use is inextricably tied to households' utilization of public broadband, wireless, and cable networks (including their take-up of over-the-top [OTT] media and personal cloud services), its imputation must be linked to paid-for services. In other words, home services and paid-for services exhibit demand complementarity,[2] and a joint analysis of these two types of consumer digital services is required. This aspect of the approach to capitalization of consumer digital capital is novel with this chapter. A related literature addresses the measurement of "free goods" using alternative methods and very different frameworks (Nakamura, Samuels, and Soloveichik 2016; Nakamura, Soloveichik, and Samuels 2018; Brynjolfsson, Collis, and Eggers 2019; Brynjolfsson et al. 2020). We compare our findings to these works later in this chapter.

The road map of this chapter is as follows. Section 12.2 sets out our framework for thinking about how the standard framework for capitalizing consumer digital goods needs to be adjusted to take into account the dramatic

---

1. The standard approach refers to the productivity literature that capitalizes consumer durables, originally due to Christensen and Jorgenson (1969, 1973); see also Jorgenson and Landefeld (2006). The US national accounts do *not* capitalize consumer durables in headline GDP.

2. Thanks to Shane Greenstein for suggesting this interpretation.

A. Broadband Use

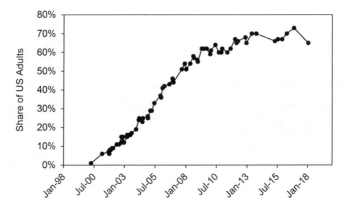

B. Social Media Use

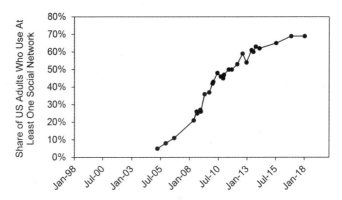

C. Mobile Device Use

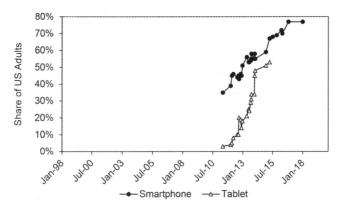

Fig. 12.2   Consumer digital capital use
Source: Pew Center for the Internet.

increase in household digital asset use shown in figure 12.2. Then we review the relationship between device use rates and the volume of services that deliver content over networks, which forms the basis for the quality-adjusted price index for network access services developed in this chapter. Section 12.4 summarizes our empirical findings in terms of impacts on real GDP and consumer surplus. Section 12.5 concludes.

Our new estimates imply that accounting for innovations in consumer content delivery matters: the innovations boost consumer surplus by nearly $1,920 (2017 dollars) per connected user per year for the full period of this study (1987 to 2017) and contribute 0.6 percentage point to US real GDP growth during the last 10 (2007 to 2017). All told, our more complete accounting of innovations is (conservatively) estimated to have moderated the post-2007 US real GDP growth slowdown by 0.3 percentage point per year. Because some of this GDP kick comes from an imputation (akin to the imputation for services from owner-occupied housing), the measured slowdown in business productivity growth is shaved by somewhat less, about 0.2 percentage point per year.

12.2   Framework: Demand Complementarity

Digital device services and network access services work together to deliver consumer content. This section illustrates how their demand complementarity can be exploited to capture and account for quality change in consumer digital services.

12.2.1   Definitions

Because consumer digital services reflect both households' use of digital devices and households' take-up of network access services, the value of total consumer digital (T) services, $P^{S_T}S_T$, is expressed as the sum of two components:

$$(1) \qquad P^{S_T}S_T = P^{S_T^H}S_T^H + P^{S_T^\beta}S_T^B.$$

The components are nonmarket (or "home") and market (or "paid-for") services, respectively, where superscripts on the component digital services volume indexes (the Ss) denote location of the capital used to deliver each type service—that is, business sector (B) or household sector (H).

Home services, $P^{S_T^H}S_T^H$, are generated via households' use of IT goods purposed for accessing digital networks.[3] Paid-for services, $P^{S_T^\beta}S_T^B$, are derived from subscriptions to networks—for example, payments for internet access, cellular access, and so on. Where are the seemingly "free" services provided by Google, Facebook, and other apps? Our answer is that they are embod-

---

3. IT goods used without network access produce uncounted services as well, such as personal computers used to work on local files. This use is outside the scope of our analysis.

ied in *both* nonmarket and market services in this framework. The demand for consumer IT capital is a derived demand induced by the availability of search engines, social networks, and so forth that push users to purchase higher quality equipment for, for example, streaming YouTube and Netflix videos. The intensity of use of network access services is increased because the "free" services require that data—pictures, videos, and search results—need to be delivered from the cloud for configuration and display by browsers and/or apps on the home device. It is tempting to associate the capture of "free goods" as solved by the imputation for home services that we propose in this chapter, but the derived demand dynamic underscores that it is equally important to use quality-adjusted price statistics for the purchased parts of content-delivery systems, as improvements in quality are also seemingly "free."

Quality change is reflected in the price indexes of both components of equation (1). It stems from (a) the quality of the equipment used to access content via networks (e.g., the storage capacity of smartphones), (b) the quality of network services (e.g., download and upload speeds of broadband service, channel variety in video service), and (c) the use intensity of the combined content delivery system (i.e., the equipment plus the access service). After controlling for the quality of systems (equipment-cum-access services) at the time of their purchase, the change in system use intensity reflects changes in the system's performance—that is, change in the marginal product of its combined net capital stocks (just as ex-post private capital income reflects changes in the return to capital). Not much of (b) and none of (c) is in existing GDP, and while (a) is included to a significant degree, we improve its capture in this chapter.

Network use intensity reflects how consumers use their IT devices and is revealed by the take-up of paid-for network access services. Denoting network use intensity by λ and letting N be the number of users on the network (i.e., consumer accounts from the perspective of the service provider), then average network use intensity is defined as

$$(2) \qquad\qquad \lambda = \frac{S_T^B}{N},$$

where S_T^B is the volume of paid-for access services consumed, per equation (1). λ and N are most easily understood from a producer perspective—that is, λ is an *intensive* per-customer use margin and N is an *extensive* margin whose increases reflect customer growth—for example, for broadband providers, the number of "customers" N is households with broadband subscriptions. For cellular service providers, N is individuals with cellular phone subscriptions.[4]

---

4. Although households have other modes of network service (e.g., cable, OTT) and all such services are considered in our empirical analysis, for simplicity, the discussion in this section considers N as the number of subscriptions to a single service—that is, connected households.

There are other, largely demographically driven dimensions of use—for example, the number of users per household and the age of users, as this feeds into hours of use per connection. Note that per equation (2), these distinctions in margins of use are implicit in λ to the extent they are not counted in N.

12.2.2   Home Services

Our starting point is the Christensen and Jorgenson (1969, 1973) framework, based on Jorgenson (1963), for imputing service flows from capitalized consumer durables. Letting K_T^H denote the net stock of digital goods held by consumers and $P^{K_T^H}$ the per-period rental price for use of a unit of those stocks, then the value of their capital services $P^{K_T^H} K_T^H$ in the standard formulation would be given by

$$(3) \qquad P^{K_T^H} K_T^H = (\bar{\rho} + \delta_T^H) P^{I_T^H} K_T^H,$$

where $\bar{\rho}$ is an ex-ante real household discount rate, δ_T^H is a depreciation rate for household IT stocks, and $P^{I_T^H}$ is a quality-adjusted asset price index for new investments in those stocks.

Nominal home services for consumer digital goods, the $P^{S_T^H} S_T^H$ term in equation (1), does not correspond to equation (3) because (3) is essentially a capacity flow; that is, (3) does not reflect actual consumption.[5] Demand complementarity suggests that incorporating the "connected" IT use dynamic implied by figure 12.2 is necessary to capture the actual consumption of digital content over networks in $P^{S_T^H} S_T^H$.

The IT device use dynamic is specific to each device type, which implies we need to define a use rate ψ_a for each asset type a—for example, for computers, mobile phones, TVs, and so on. We thus have the following:

$$(4) \qquad \psi_a = \left(\frac{Dev_a}{D^*} \right),$$

where Dev_a is the number of hours per day the device type a is used to connect to networks and D^* is the potential number of hours per day any device can be used.

We can then define an "effective" stock of network access equipment and software, K_T^{eH}, that accounts for how the *use* of a given stock of network access equipment and software expands, in which case the value of nonmarket consumer digital services in equation (1) is given by

$$(5a) \qquad P^{S_T^H} S_T^H = P^{K_T^H} K_T^{eH}$$

---

5. Private-industry capital income is generally understood to include a utilization effect when the rate of return is calculated on an ex-post basis as in Jorgenson and Griliches (1967). When consumer durables are capitalized, service flows are imputed using an ex-ante return as in (3), and therefore a utilization effect is not "automatically" present. See Hulten (2009) for a discussion.

(5b) $= \psi \cdot P^{K^H_T} K^H_T,$

where ψ reflects the appropriately weighted aggregate of the individual ψ_as. A related issue is that some consumer digital capital goods are not used for the consumption of content over networks (e.g., digital cameras), suggesting it is necessary to identify a relevant group of IT devices—call this network access equipment (NAE)—for generating the relevant capital services flows. The relevant IT products comprising NAE stocks will be identified in measurements; we thus proceed with the assumption that only NAE products are included in the capital measures subscripted by T.

Consider next how to measure the implicit volume of services, whose value is given by (5b). Log differentiation of equations (5b) and (3), holding $\bar{\rho}$ and δ^H_T constant, suggests that the growth of nominal free services $P^{S^H}_T + S^H_T$ is equal to $P^{K^H}_T + K^{eH}_T$. This in turn implies that $P^{S^H}_T = P^{I^H}_T$ and that growth of real services S^H_T equals the growth of the effective stock K^{eH}_T, or

(6a) $\dot{S}^H_T = \dot{K}^{eH}_T$

(6b) $= \dot{K}^H_T + \dot{\psi}.$

12.2.3   Paid-for Services

Digital access services are typically sold as subscriptions, where households pay a monthly fee for a "plan" in return for access to a range of services—for example, broadband, smartphone, cable TV, or subscription video on demand. Each plan has a fixed set of characteristics—download speed, upload speed, number/availability of videos or video channels, and so on—for the services involved. Plan heterogeneity by service type and service type characteristics is ignored (for now) for ease of exposition.

Producers offer digital access service plans at prices $P^{O\beta}_T$. Offer prices are subscription contract prices set at the outset of the period, and the average price each customer pays is expressed as

(7) $\bar{P}^{O\beta}_T = \dfrac{P^{O\beta}_T O^B_T}{N},$

where $P^{O\beta}_T O^B_T$ are producer revenues from consumer sales of N plans. Nominal consumer payments, $P^{S\beta}_T S^B_T$ of equation (1), equals this producer sales revenue. We assume that producers' capacity is constrained in the short run (the period of the contract) and, after accounting for the usual issues regarding peak load planning, that producers set offer prices based on a preferred rate of capacity utilization determined by anticipated average customer usage, λ^a.

These assumptions imply that O^β_T is a planned quantity of delivered services and not necessarily equal to S^β_T, the actual quantity of services consumed by users—unless, of course, actual usage λ is perfectly anticipated (i.e., $\lambda^a = \lambda$). It follows that the offer price index $P^{O\beta}_T$ does not necessarily equal the consumption price index $P^{S_T^\beta}$ of equation (1). Let u be an index of actual capacity utilization, where $u = 1$ denotes the situation where $\lambda^a = \lambda$. We then have $\lambda = \lambda^a u$, in which case the relationship between real services consumption and real services offered and between consumption prices and offer prices is given by

(8) $$S_T^B = O_T^B u.$$

(9) $$P^{S_T^\beta} = \frac{P^{O_T^\beta}}{u}.$$

Equation (9) states that the consumption price index $P^{S_T^\beta}$ is a utilization-adjusted contract price.

Equations (8) and (9) are not very helpful for conventional, timely price measurement (as in a monthly Consumer Price Index [CPI]) because producers' preferred utilization rate u is not readily observed. However, substitution of (8) into (9) reveals that the consumption price may be alternatively written as

(10) $$P^{S_T^\beta} = \frac{P^{O_T^\beta} O_T^B}{S_T^B},$$

which suggests that consumption prices for access services may be obtained by dividing producer revenue by a relevant, consistently defined volume measure—that is, ideally, $S_T^B \equiv \text{VOL}$, where VOL is such a measure.

What might that volume measure be? We know that total consumption increases along with the number of users and/or hours of use, but these are very coarse indicators that do not capture consumption intensity or service quality. An ideal measure would capture consumers' use in terms of the potential performance of communication networks and where utilized performance is a comprehensive measure capable of being consistently defined in the face of rapid technical change (e.g., Internet Protocol [IP] data traffic measured as optimally compressed megabytes/petabytes per year)—that is, that

(11) $$S_B^T \equiv \text{VOL} = IP.$$

A range of services are delivered over networks, and dataflows/IP traffic may not always be a relevant indicator of quality, but for internet access services via computers of mobile phones, IP traffic would appear to be a solid choice (e.g., see Abdirahman et al. 2017). For video services, quality is not so simple; cross-country studies have found that the quality dimension for video services is captured by a range of controls, including the number of channels (HD and standard) and availability of premium channels and 4K display resolution (Corrado and Ukhaneva 2016, 2019; Díaz-Pinés and Fanfalone 2015).

12.2.4   Use Intensity, λ

With real services captured by a performance measure, the changes in network and device intensity of use, $\dot{\lambda}$, can be shown to reflect the difference between changes in the average price paid by users for a plan and the price index for access services—that is, it reflects changes in the quality of services consumed. To see this, log differentiate (2):

(12) $$\dot{\lambda} = \dot{S}_T^B - \dot{N}.$$

After adding and subtracting the nominal change in paid services, $P^{O_B^B}O_T^B$, and combining terms, we obtain

(13) $$\dot{\lambda} = \left(\frac{P^{O_B^B}O_T^B}{N} \right) - \left(\frac{P^{O_B^B}O_T^B}{S_T^B} \right).$$

Substitution of (7) and (10) for the first and second terms yields

(14) $$\dot{\lambda} = \bar{P}^{O_B^B}_T - P^{S_B^B}_T.$$

In equation (13), the change in use intensity $\dot{\lambda}$ reflects the difference between the rate of change in a per-user price and a unit volume price or, per equation (14), the difference between the rate of change in the price index for access services and the rate of change in the average price per plan—that is, quality change.

Statistical agencies generate price indexes in terms of offer prices $P^{O_B^B}$, not consumption prices $P^{S_B^B}$. Consider now the relationship between $\dot{\lambda}$ and the quality change in official price indexes for network access service (based on offer prices)—for example, quality change that might be captured using hedonic techniques that account for improvements in speeds and other capabilities in subscription telecom service plans.[6] Note first that the change in the offer price index, $P^{O_B^B}$, also can be decomposed into the rate of change in the quality of offered plans, $\dot{v}$, and the rate of change in the average price per plan, $\bar{P}^{O_B^B}$—that is, $P^{O_B^B} = \bar{P}^{O_B^B} - \dot{v}$. Next, from log differentiation of (9), after subtracting the result from (14) and combining terms, the relationship between $\dot{v}$ and $\dot{\lambda}$ is readily shown as

(15) $$\dot{\lambda} = \dot{v} + \dot{u},$$

which says that the quality change in real network access services consumption is equal to the quality change in offered plans (at offered prices) plus the unanticipated change in network service provider utilization.

12.2.5   Network Utilization, u

Consider now how one might measure u. We do not need to measure u to measure prices for consumer digital services, but knowing u helps us

---

6. As done, e.g., at the BLS (see Williams 2008).

interpret and analyze them. For example, knowing the direction of change in u helps us understand how little change in measured quality change in contract prices (v) might coexist with notable declines in consumption prices for network access services ($P^{S\beta}$); per equation (15), this situation occurs when there are notable increases in both household use intensity (λ) and network utilization (u).[7]

As previously indicated, private industry capital income is generally understood to include a utilization effect, and previous work has considered how to extract a measure of network capital utilization from productivity data for internet service providers, or ISPs (Corrado 2011; Corrado and Jäger 2014; see also Corrado and van Ark 2016). The basic idea in these works is that when an ex-ante approach is used to determine an industry's return, a utilization factor can be calculated so as to exhaust observed capital income, provided that the industry's aggregate net stock of capital is not particularly sensitive to composition differences in asset use—that is, it acts more or less as a single capital good (Berndt and Fuss 1986; Hulten 1986). This is arguably the case for network services providers in the United States, whose capital stock is a physical network whose parts largely operate as a single good. Employing this assumption, Corrado (2011) found a substantial difference between the US ISP industry's ex-post calculated nominal rate of return and the market interest rates typically used in ex-ante productivity analysis; the difference was able to be interpreted as network utilization.

The network services–providing industry's ex-post gross return is defined as

$$(16) \qquad \Phi^{ISP} = (r^{ISP} + \delta^{ISP} - \pi^{ISP}),$$

where r^{ISP} is an ex-post nominal net return determined residually (e.g., as in Jorgenson and Griliches 1967) given depreciation δ^{ISP} and revaluation of the industry's capital stock π^{ISP}. Now define the industry's *ex-ante* gross return as

$$(17) \qquad \bar{\Phi}^{ISP} = (\bar{r} + \delta^{ISP} - \pi^{ISP}),$$

where $\bar{r}$ is an ex-ante nominal rate of interest. Let u^{ISP} be the industry's capital utilization rate. As shown in appendix section 12.A1, this utilization rate is given by

$$(18) \qquad u^{ISP} = \frac{\Phi^{ISP}}{\bar{\Phi}^{ISP}},$$

which suggests that the underlying relationship between the ex-post and ex-ante net rate of return—that is, r versus $\bar{r}$—for an industry or sector is an indicator of its capital utilization.[8]

---

7. On the other hand, quality-adjusted contract prices are likely mismeasured when there is little change in u in the face of increases in household use intensity.

8. In models that introduce imperfect competition in an otherwise standard neoclassical growth framework (e.g., Rotemberg and Woodford 1995), utilization is absorbed in a more

12.2.6   Summary

To summarize, changes in the quantities and prices of consumer digital services as set out in equation (1) are as follows:

(19a) $$\dot{S}_T^H = \dot{K}_T^H + \psi$$

(19b) $$\dot{P}^{S_T^H} = \dot{P}_T^{IH}$$

(19c) $$\dot{S}_T^B = \dot{V}ol$$

(19d) $$\dot{P}^{S_T^B} = \dot{\bar{P}}_T^{OB} - \lambda.$$

where λ and ψ were defined above and $P_T^{I^H}$ is a quality-adjusted asset price index for network access equipment.

12.3   Measurement

This section summarizes how the prices and quantities of the previous section are measured and presents some key results. We begin with the new network access services price index, describing how this index may be built using alternative volume measures. We then present results for λ and for our calculations of utilization from the business side, $\dot{u}$. A second subsection sets out how our consumer digital capital stocks, their connectivity use rates, and digital capital services are obtained.

12.3.1   Access Prices, Household Use Intensity, and Network Utilization

We calculate a price index for four types of IT services provided to households by the business sector (cable, internet, mobile, and video streaming services) by dividing nominal spending for each service type (j) by a measure that reflects the quality-adjusted time spent using the service—that is, an appropriate VOL for each j. The quality-adjusted price indexes by service type are aggregated to create an overall access price index that, when used to deflate total spending on access services, captures real access services consumption.

For exposition and analysis, we consider price indexes constructed using four alternative measures of quantity: the number of households subscribed to the service, the number of individual users, time spent on the service, and time spent adjusted for quality (our ultimate measure). The four alternative price and volume concepts will be indexed by k. Thus four alternative price indexes for each service type are calculated by dividing revenue for the service type by the four alternative volume measures, yielding prices paid per household ($k = H$), per individual ($k = I$), per unit of time ($k = D$), and per unit of constant-quality time ($k = Q$)—that is, we have $P_H^{S_j^B}$, $P_I^{S_j^B}$, $P_D^{S_j^B}$, and

---

general inefficiency wedge capturing, among other things, the ability of firms to maintain a price markup.

$P_Q^{S\beta}$ for each service type j. (*Note:* D is the notation used for time—i.e., as in hours per day).

The alternative price indexes are calculated as follows: Let $(P^{O\beta}O_T^{\beta})_j$ be payments for service type j within total payments $P^{O\beta}O_T^{\beta}$. The price change for price index concept k covering all J types of services is then

(20) $$\Delta ln P_k^{S\beta} = \sum_{j=1}^{J} \bar{w}_j \Delta ln \left(\frac{P^{O\beta}O_T^{\beta}}{VOL_k} \right)_j \qquad \text{where} \quad k = H, I, D, Q,$$

$\bar{w}_j$ is a Divisia payments share for digital access service type j, and $VOL_{k,j}$ is service type j's volume measure corresponding to price index concept k. In terms of the framework set out in section 12.2, we thus have the following:

(21) $$\Delta \ln P^{S\beta} = \Delta \ln P_Q^S$$

(22) $$\dot{\lambda} = -(\Delta \ln P_Q^{S\beta} - \Delta \ln P_H^{S\beta}).$$

Note that the suite of indexes constructed along margins of use enables changes in the quality-adjusted price index to be decomposed into contributions from I, T, and Q—that is, into contributions from growth in individuals per household using the service, time spent on the service per individual user, and the quality of an hour of use of the service, respectively. Appendix section 12.A2 documents the data sources for each price concept for each access service price index, including reporting the time series for prices by access service type and aggregate prices for each alternative measure of volume. Note that the contract price $P^{O\beta}$, the price observed by the consumer, is not needed for the calculations (or analysis) in this chapter.[9]

The aggregate quality-adjusted price index for access service corresponding to equation (21), shown as the dashed line in figure 12.3, falls 12.4 percent per year over the full period of this study. Household use intensity, $\dot{\lambda}$ per equation (22) and the solid line in the figure, increases 13.9 percent at an annual rate. Figure 12.3 also shows a price index for network access services constructed using components of the Bureau of Economic Analysis (BEA) personal consumption expenditures (PCE) price index and our per household price index (i.e., the average price per household, $P_H^{S\beta}$). Note first that our new access services price index (the gray line) falls much faster than the implicit price index in existing GDP (the black line); the growth implications of this finding will be reviewed in the next section of this chapter. Note

9. Depending on the contract arrangement, the price observed by the consumer may correspond to any of the four price concepts we consider. For example, if a consumer pays a cable company a fixed amount to keep the household connected each onth, $P^{O\beta}$ equals $P_H^{S\beta}$. If a consumer pays an internet provider a fixed amount to have unlimited access each month, $P^{O\beta}$ equals $P_I^{S\beta}$. If the consumer has a prepaid plan for a certain number of hours of talk time on a feature phone, $P^{O\beta}$ equals $P_D^{S\beta}$. And if the consumer has a contract for smartphone use based on data traffic consumed, $P^{O\beta}$ equals P_Q^X. This information is not needed to construct our price indexes, even though these details are required for official prices based on contract arrangements.

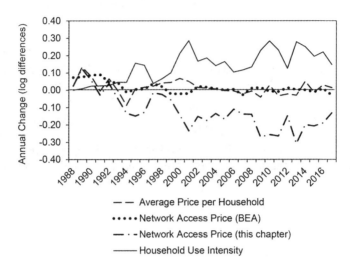

Fig. 12.3 Network access services price change and use intensity

second that changes in the BEA price index hovers about changes in our per-household price from about 2000 on; if the BEA index accurately represents changes in contract prices, the result implies that there is very little quality change in measured offer prices from 2000 to 2017—that is, $\dot{v}$ has shown essentially no change since 2000.

Results for the overall price index by subperiods are plotted in panel (a) of figure 12.4; spending shares for its subcomponents by type are shown in panel (b) of the figure. As may be seen, the decline in the quality-adjusted network access price index accelerates over time, first as internet service accounts for a rising share of spending (1997 to 2007) and then as smartphone access becomes more important (2007 to 2017).

The trends in the aggregate network access price index also reflect large differences in the contributions by access mode, shown in figure 12.5. Contributions to the overall volume price change by each intensity margin (i.e., volume measure) show the following. First, there is little difference between changes in per-individual-user prices relative to per-household prices; as a result, only the contribution of changes in the price per household shows in figure 12.4. Second, quality change contributes significantly to the overall decline in network access prices in most subperiods. Third, consumers' increase in time connected provides a substantial additional kick from 1997 to 2012; time connected is especially important in driving price change for mobile and subscription video-on-demand (SVOD) services.

Finally, given that both usage trends and technological change are major drivers of the drops in our network access price index, we calculate values for producer network utilization u in light of the fact that figure 12.3 sug-

A. Contributions to Price Change by Volume Measure

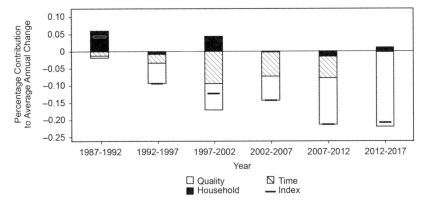

B. Shares of Spending by Mode of Network Access

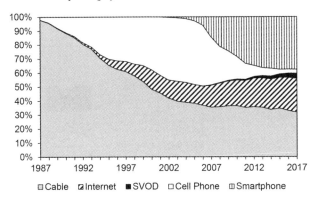

Fig. 12.4   **Network access services price index**

gested there was very little (measured) quality change in official access prices since 2000. As previously discussed, λ will reflect trends in consumer usage as well as technological improvements in content delivery systems measured on the basis of contract prices. Our calculation of u is detailed in appendix section 12.A1, and figure 12.6 shows the result, which covers the period from 2000 to 2016. While the utilization measure bounces about year by year, it rises more than 4.5 percent per year, on balance. This pattern is interesting for several reasons, but before we offer our interpretation, note that the measure in figure 12.6 pertains to the entire telecommunications and broadcasting industry—that is, it includes commercial and enterprise customers and thus does not solely reflect the interaction between the demand and supply of consumer content delivery services as defined in this chapter. That said, per equation (15), the rather sharp rise in u supports our decomposition showing that a significant fraction of the large divergence between ν and λ

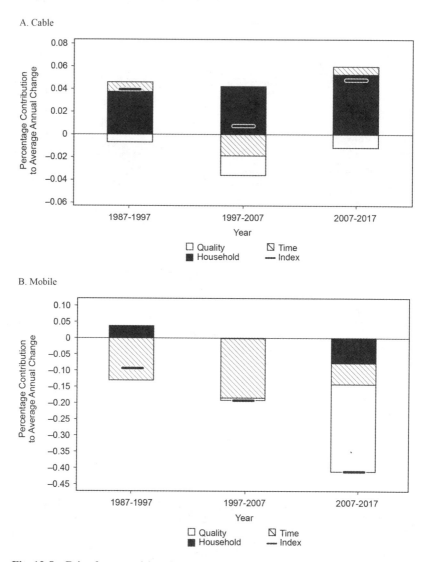

A. Cable

B. Mobile

Fig. 12.5   **Price decompositions by mode of network access**

after 2000 reflects increases in use rates. In terms of the model of section 12.2, λ consistently exceeded λ^e and lowered the effective price paid by each consumer (holding per-plan quality constant).[10]

10. Seen from another perspective, the rise in *u* reflects strengthening industry profitability and pricing power. On a per-household basis, changes in households' average prices actually *decelerated* (or fell) after 2002 relative to earlier experience (see again figure 12.4), suggesting that the rise in relative profitability reflected a prolonged positive demand shock—that is, consistent with a situation in which λ consistently exceeded λ^e.

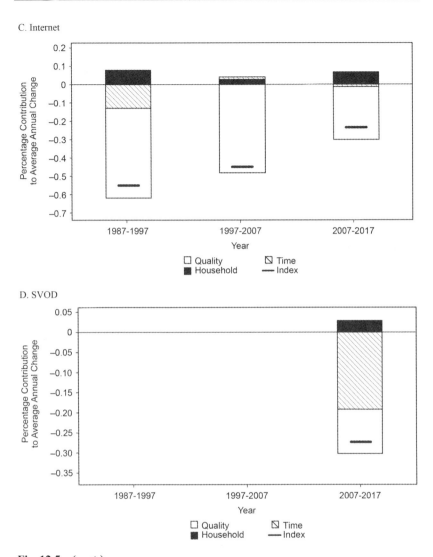

Fig. 12.5   (cont.)

12.3.2   Digital Net Stocks, Capital Services, and Asset Prices

In this section, we set out our measures of consumer digital services based on "connected" IT capital stocks. Table 12.1, column (1), lists the 14 product classes of durable goods considered to be consumer durable digital (or IT) goods. This list ranges from TVs, to computers and software, to cell phones.[11] Consumer spending for most of these products may be developed

---

11. Game consoles, which have embodied massive innovation in the period of this study, are not included for lack of data.

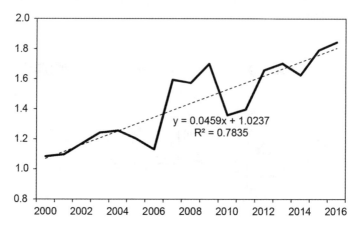

Fig. 12.6   Implied network utilization

Table 12.1   PCE durable digital goods

Product class (1)	Depreciation group[a] (2)	NAE group[b] (3)
1. Televisions	A	Y
2. Cameras	B	N
3. Other photographic equipment	A	N
4. Other video equipment	A	N
5. Audio equipment	A	N
6. Recording media	A	N
7. Computers	B	Y
8. Data storage equipment	B	Y
9. Monitors	B	Y
10. Computer peripherals	B	Y
11. Miscellaneous office equipment	A	N
12. Software and accessories	B	Y
13. Cell phones	B	Y
14. Other telephone and communications equipment	A	N

[a]A = nine-year service life, B = five-year service life.
[b]NAE = network access equipment.

from underlying detail in the US National Income and Product Accounts (NIPAs); indeed, the first 12 product classes shown in the table directly correspond to categories of digital goods reported in the annual PCE bridge table.[12] For the analysis in this chapter, estimates of the retail value of consumer cell phone purchases are developed from industry sources; see

12. BEA's annual PCE bridge table begins in 1998 and does not extend through the most recent NIPA year. Nine categories of PCE spending on digital goods are reported on NIPA table 2.4.5U, however, and these data are used to develop the more detailed, bridge table–based series from 1970 to 1997 and for the year 2017.

appendix section 12.A3 for further details on how this series and the other telephone equipment series are estimated.

In terms of service lives, the products are grouped into two categories: those with a nine-year service life (A) and those with a five-year service life (B). These groupings are indicated in column (2) of the table and are a (slight) simplification of the service life categories used by the BEA in their fixed asset accounts.[13] To compute net stocks, we follow the BEA and Hulten and Wykoff (1981a, b) and use a declining-balance rate of 1.65 for these goods, which implies geometric rates of depreciation of 0.1833 and 0.3300 for groups A and B, respectively. An end-of-year (EOY) net stock of each product class a in table 12.1 is calculated using the perpetual inventory method with geometric depreciation, again following the BEA (see page M-7 in US Department of Commerce, Bureau of Economic Analysis 2003):

$$(23) \qquad K_{a,EOY}^{H} = I_{a,t}^{H}\left(1 - \frac{\delta_a^H}{2}\right) + (1 - \delta_a^H)K_{a,EOY-1}^{H},$$

where $I_{a,t}^{H}$ is annual real investment for each asset class a in year t.

The analysis of demand complementary of payments for digital access services with the use of device stocks pertains to NAE stocks only—that is, it pertains to only the equipment used for cable TV, subscription video, and internet or mobile network access. Column (3) of the table is an indicator of whether the asset class a is included in these stocks—that is, whether the equipment is included in K_T^H and requires an estimate of its use intensity $\psi a = DDva/D^*$ per equation (4). These equipment-use intensities allow us to identify the stock of IT capital that yields unpriced services $P^{SH} S_T^H$ per equation (5b).

There are three types of equipment that require estimates of their use intensity: televisions, computers, and cell phones. Our estimates begin with our time-based estimates of average household time spent using each access service, panel (a) of figure 12.7. We then measure the share of households with at least one of each device and the number of devices in use conditional on the household having such a device (panels b and c). The total number of hours households spend on each device is calculated from these elements, which also requires allocating time spent on accessing each digital service to the capital used for the access. The result expressed as the share of the day each device type is in use (ψ_a) is shown in panel (d). Additional details and data sources for this calculation are spelled out in appendix section 12.A4.

To calculate $P^{SH} S_T^H$, we proceed as follows: The nominal value of the *capacity* flow of services from each consumer digital asset is calculated via equation (3) with the gross ex-ante rental rate formed using the 10-year constant-maturity government bond rate, the relevant depreciation rate as

---

13. Compared to BEA's methods, the major simplification we make is to use geometric depreciation for computers.

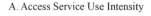

A. Access Service Use Intensity

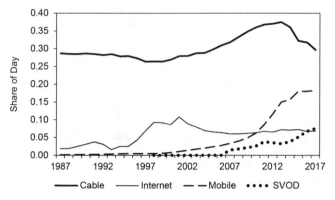

B. Device Penetration

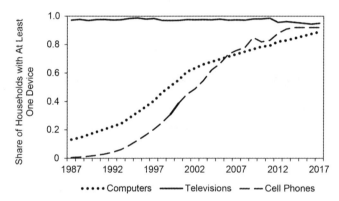

Fig. 12.7   Time-based equipment use intensity

described above, and actual price change for each asset type.[14] Then we (a) sum over all asset types to obtain an estimate of consumer capital services based on total digital goods stocks and (b) sum over the asset types included in network access equipment to obtain the subcomponent for services from total NAE stocks. Finally, we (c) adjust the *capacity* of NAE services for the extensive margin (i.e., we apply our estimates of ψ_a) to obtain *actual* capital services generated via households' use of IT goods purposed for accessing digital networks—that is, capital services from the effective NAE stocks. The results of (a), (b), and (c) are shown in figure 12.8, plotted relative to GDP adjusted to include them.

Our estimate of home-generated digital services relative to GDP, the dashed-dotted line in figure 12.8, rises steadily over the 30 years shown in the figure, reflecting both the increase in relative importance of NAE stocks in

14. In the implementation of (3), midperiod stocks computed from EOY stocks are used.

C. Device Multiplicity

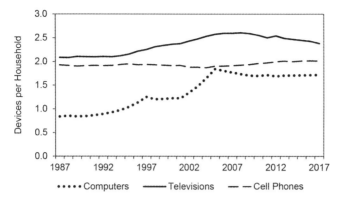

D. Device Use Intensity (ψ_a)

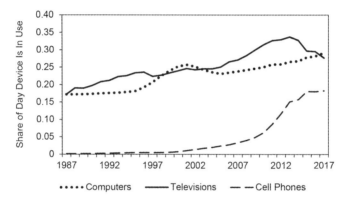

Fig. 12.7 **(cont.)**

all digital stocks (the dashed line versus the thin solid line) and the increased portion of NAE stocks connected to networks (the dashed-dotted versus dashed lines) that reflects the increase in ψ. The ratio of $P^{S^H_T} S^H_T$ relative to GDP stood at 1.04 percent of GDP in 2017, up from 0.48 percent 10 years earlier. This trajectory is roughly similar to estimates of free services prepared using a very different approach (the black dots in the figure).[15]

The real investment used to develop net stock estimates via equation (23) is calculated by deflating nominal spending on each product class using asset price indexes based on the sources documented in the appendix. These prices are research indexes largely adapted from prior work (Byrne and Corrado 2015a, 2015b, 2017a, 2017b; Byrne 2015). In new moves, we incorporate

15. Nakamura, Soloveichik, and Samuels (2018) estimate the costs of producing both professionally created and user-generated consumer content. The black open dots in the figure are their estimates for the digital component of their professionally created free content plus their estimate of the value of user-generated free content.

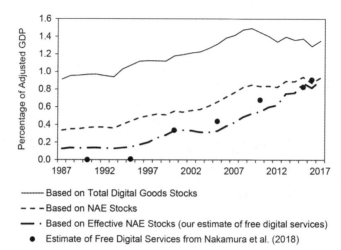

Fig. 12.8   Consumer digital capital services, nominal estimates from 1987 to 2017

two quality-adjusted price indexes from Statistics Japan and exploit work by Copeland (2013) on consumer game software in combination with results from the BLS producer price index for game software. Our price index for the 14 consumer digital goods listed in table 12.1 falls 11.7 percent per year from 2007 to 2017, 2.6 percentage points faster than its official counterpart (based on published PCE prices); see appendix section 12.A3 for further details.

The implicit deflator for consumer digital assets depends on the weighting of the components in the effective NAE aggregate. Figure 12.9 shows the annual price for total NAE stocks versus effective NAE stocks. As may be seen, the weighting of the underlying components produces very similar results for effective NAE stocks versus a simple aggregate of those stocks. Our price index for home services, P^{SH}_t, is the Jorgensonian rental price index for effective NAE stocks (the solid line in the figure), which is driven by the appropriately weighted asset price (the dotted line). The effective NAE rental price fell 12.5 percent per year over the full period of our study and dropped 17.2 percent from 2007 to 2017.

12.3.3   Summary

Our new estimates of digital services consumption consist of two components: a paid-for network access services component and an imputed connected IT capital services component. The price index for network access services was reviewed in section 12.3.1. To obtain real spending, we deflate nominal figures from the national accounts published by Bureau of Economic Analysis, incorporating some additional detail as explained in appendix section 12.A2.

The imputed component was reviewed in section 12.3.2. The new nominal spending measure was developed as a capital services flow derived from the

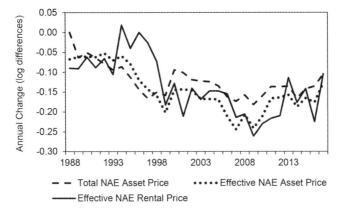

Fig. 12.9   **Consumer digital asset prices, annual price change from 1988 to 2017**
Source: Elaboration of price indexes developed for this chapter.

effective NAE stocks shown in figure 12.8. The price deflator is then the corresponding rental price, displayed in figure 12.9.

12.4   Results and Implications

This section reports the new real digital services consumption measures and discusses their implications for real GDP and consumer surplus.

12.4.1   GDP

Our results for GDP are summarized in table 12.2. These results are calculated under the conservative assumption that overall real GDP is unaffected by differences in the PCE IT goods investment price indexes developed in this chapter and official prices used in GDP because these goods are primarily imported (whether for "effective" investment or all IT goods spending); recall too that we are unable to include the rapid quality change in game consoles in our price indexes.

The key takeaways from table 12.2 are, first, as shown on line 2, column (1), real services from use of connected digital systems grow very strongly, averaging 26.2 percent per year for the full period of the study. Second, our new results for real access services (line 4) are also very strong; as shown in column (5), real growth averaged nearly 34 percent per year during the Great Recession and its immediate aftermath (i.e., from 2007 to 2012). Third, this chapter's approach to accounting for innovation in consumer digital services shows that it is possible to "see" digitalization in GDP. If our methods were to be incorporated in the national accounts of the United States, the contribution of consumer digital services (both components) to real GDP growth would average 0.57 percentage points from 2007 to 2017 (line 7, column 4), and annual real GDP growth would be 0.46 percentage points per year higher (line 7a, column 4).

Table 12.2   Changes in consumer digital services, 1987 to 2017

Percent change, annual rate	1987 to 2017 (1)	1987 to 1997 (2)	1997 to 2007 (3)	2007 to 2017 (4)	2007 to 2012 (5)	2012 to 2017 (6)
Capital services:						
1. Nominal	11.9	10.9	13.6	11.2	10.5	11.9
2. Real	**26.2**	18.1	29.5	31.2	33.7	28.8
Access services:						
3. Nominal	11.5	15.1	13.3	6.2	7.7	4.7
4. Real	26.2	18.1	29.5	31.2	**33.7**	28.8
Memos:						
Effective NAE investment:						
5. Nominal	12.2	10.5	15.6	10.5	11.2	9.8
6. Real	27.9	19.4	37.8	32.4	35.6	29.3
Contribution to GDP[a,b]						
7. Consumer digital services	0.33	0.09	0.30	0.57	0.57	0.59
7a. Net of existing	0.25	0.05	0.17	**0.46**	0.38	0.54
8. Capital services	0.09	0.02	0.06	0.17	0.15	0.19
9. Access services[b]	0.24	0.07	0.24	0.40	0.40	0.40
9a. Net of existing	0.16	0.03	0.11	0.29	0.23	0.34

[a]Percentage points.

[b]GDP contributions are calculated assuming that differences between PCE digital goods investments and their price indexes and their official counterparts have no impact on existing GDP because they are largely imported.

The GDP impacts shown in table 12.2 are substantial. As reported and analyzed elsewhere (Byrne and Corrado 2020), the inclusion of our price index for paid-for digital access services in the national accounts consumer/ PCE price measures also are substantial.

With regard to changes in the trend rate of real GDP growth, the impact of using our framework for measuring consumer digital services boosts the rate of real GDP growth from 2007 to 2017 relative to 10 years earlier (1997 to 2007) by 0.29 percentage point (line 7a, column 4 less column 3)—a notable acceleration. Both the GDP boundary expansion (adding imputed real digital capital services) and the adoption of a quality-adjusted consumption price index for network access services contribute to this acceleration, with about 60 percent stemming from the net contribution of the new access services price index (0.16 percentage point). The latter contribution also boosts business productivity growth; as with services from owner-occupied housing, the imputation for self-generated digital capital services is not factored into conventional measures of productivity change.

12.4.2   Consumer Surplus

The consumer surplus stemming from innovations in consumer content delivery can be calculated using an index number approach if the quality-adjusted price indexes used in the analysis fully capture the benefits of the changes in question. Assuming our price indexes are up to the task, we compute consumer surplus as the macroeconomic gain from the relevant continuing commodities following Diewert and Fox (2017) as

$$(24) \qquad .5(\Delta \Pi^{S^H_T} \Delta S^H_T) + .5(\Delta \Pi^{S^B_T} \Delta S^B_T) + .5(\Delta \Pi^{I^{eH}_T} \Delta I^{eH}_T),$$

where Δ is a long difference and the $\Delta \Pi$s are changes in the relative prices—that is,

$$(25) \qquad \Pi^{S^H_T} = \frac{P^{S^H_T}}{P^{PCE}} \;\;, \;\; \Pi^{S^B_T} = \frac{P^{S^B_T}}{P^{PCE}} \;\; \text{and} \;\; \Pi^{I^{eH}_T} = \frac{P^{I^{eH}_T}}{P^{PCE}},$$

where P^{PCE} is the overall price index for consumer spending.

In the textbook exposition of consumer surplus, the price drop from the Hicksian reservation price to the transaction price of the new good or service is the welfare gain stemming from the innovation in question. To capture this gain, benefits of an innovation can be quantified by estimating demand elasticities or parameters of utility functions—for example, as in Petrin (2002) or Greenwood and Kopecky (2013). Many individual innovations are relevant to this study, however, and eschewing a parametric approach and estimating consumer surplus using long differences applied to our annual quality-adjusted price (and quantity) indexes via (24) should well approximate the relevant gain. Recall that these indexes are built from annual and quarterly information (prices, revenues, characteristics) on detailed components of each product/service. They are designed to incorporate the serial innovations we wish to capture despite the fact that, strictly speaking, Hicksian reservation prices for each innovation are not estimated. But even for significant innovations, such as the iPhone relative to the smartphones that preceded it, the omission of an initial reservation price in the quarter before introduction has a negligible impact on GDP (in the introductory quarter) and on long differences calculated from an otherwise accurate time series of quality-adjusted price change. This is mainly because the revenue weight on the unobserved initial price drop for a new good is usually very small (half of the revenue in the initial period), which greatly diminishes the impact of the missing initial price change.[16]

The results of computing (24) are presented in table 12.3. Changes from the beginning of our sample (1987, arguably also the beginning of the internet) to the beginning of social media and mobile broadband (taken as 2004) are assessed, as are changes from this point to 2017, the last year of our estimates. As may be seen on row 1, the consumer surplus due to innovations in

---

16. To see this, we continue with the iPhone example. Total iPhone revenue in the quarter of its introduction in 2007:Q4 was $8 million according to Apple's financials, or $32 million at an annual rate. GDP was $14,452 billion in 2007. One-half of the revenue gain from the iPhone in its introductory quarter at an annual rate was then $0.11 \times 10{-}5$ relative to GDP. Consider now, as a thought experiment, that the change from the reservation price to the actual price of the iPhone in the quarter of introduction was a ginormous $-1,000$ percent. Price change for GDP is essentially unaffected.

Table 12.3   Consumer surplus from innovations in content delivery systems

	1987 to 2004 (1)	2004 to 2017 (2)
Surplus, in billions of 2017 dollars		
1. Digital goods and services, total	892	5,841
2. Capital investment	262	1,287
3. Capital services	311	2,301
4. Access services	319	2,254
Surplus, in thousands of $ per user[a]		
5. Digital goods and services, total	27,320	30,294
6. Capital investment	8,031	6,672
7. Capital services	9,510	11,933
8. Access services	9,779	11,689
Annual surplus per user		
9. Digital goods and services, total	1,607	2,330
10. Capital investment	472	513
11. Capital services	559	918
12. Access services	575	889

Notes: All figures are in 2017 dollars.

[a]The per-user figure is obtained by dividing the results on rows 1 to 4 by the average number of connected users during the period indicated.

digital content delivery from 1987 to 2004 (18 years) was nearly $900 billion in 2017 dollars (column 1) and $5.8 trillion over the next 14 years (column 2). These are substantial amounts. On a per-user basis, rows 5 through 8, the gain hovered at or slightly below $30,000 (in 2017 dollars). While these numbers seem very large (implying a per-user gain in economic welfare of more than $2,000 per year, on average, during the latter period), they are in the same neighborhood as estimates of consumer surplus obtained by Brynjolfsson, Collis, and Eggers (2019) using massive online choice experiments. The sum of their median willingness-to-pay estimates for the items included in their surveys (search engines, email, maps, video, e-commerce, social media, messaging, and music) was $32,232 in 2017 (Brynjolfsson, Collis, and Eggers 2019, table 7, sum of items in column 2).

We compare our long difference estimates with the single-point-in-time survey results of Brynjolfsson, Collis, and Eggers (2019) based on a conjecture that respondents in their massive online experiments are thinking about what they would have to pay to "return" to life before social media, smartphones, and mobile broadband. Brynjolfsson, Collis, and Eggers (2019) also report median willingness-to-pay estimates for a survey conducted in 2016, and these values sum to $26,150, expressed in 2017 dollars.[17] Using (24) with a long difference from 2004 to 2016 (i.e., dropping the last year and dividing by a slightly lower number for the average number of users) yields an estimate of the consumer surplus of $24,676 per user—again in the same ballpark.

17. The simple sum of their figures is $25,697.

12.5 Conclusion

The household is an important locus of the digital revolution and one of its most visible since smartphones and social media became widespread. Entertainment, communication, and work from home have been supercharged by advances in hardware, software, and communication. Hardware innovation has proceeded at an especially blistering pace as the major household platforms—smartphones, tablets, televisions, gaming consoles, and all the apps that run on them—have become extraordinarily powerful (and cheap) and as datacenter innovation (i.e., the cloud) has charged ahead in the background. And faster communication speeds—both wireline and wireless—have been essential; for example, nearly one-third of all IP traffic in 2016 was accounted for by Netflix alone, a usage volume not possible one or two years earlier.

The highly visible innovations in consumer content delivery raise the question of whether existing national accounts are missing consequential growth in output and income associated with content delivered to consumers via their use of digital platforms. The changing production border for digital content delivery suggests that GDP (as well as other macroeconomic measures, such as PCE prices) needs to account for the substitution away from market-based digital services consumption. How and whether to address distortion to the production boundary created by the substitution between market and household activity is an old issue in national accounting, an issue that is often dismissed as second-order except for the case of owner-occupied housing.

We believe the digitization of consumer content delivery presents a first-order distortion to the production boundary of national accounts—and that an imputation for the omitted services from connected IT capital needs to be made to avoid imparting a bias to GDP. The case for imputing services from owner-occupied housing is based on the size of the omitted services and the importance of accounting for them in international comparisons. The case for imputing services from connected IT capital is based on the astonishingly fast relative growth of the omitted services in both real and nominal terms. As shown in the analysis of the contribution of business IT goods and services to real GDP growth set out in Byrne and Corrado (2017b), even as the extensive aspects (e.g., hours per day) driving consumer digital services growth run their course, access services and services from connected IT capital will continue to provide an extra kick to real GDP growth due to their declining relative price.

All told, we estimate that consumer welfare due to growth in digital content consumption has been enhanced to the tune of $2,330 per connected user per year from 2004 to 2017 (2017 dollars). And when the demand complementarity framework set out in this chapter is incorporated into existing GDP, we find that real consumer digital services contribute nearly .6 percentage points per year to US economic growth from 2007 to 2017, about 1/4 percent per year faster than its contribution from 1997 to 2007.

Appendixes

12.A1   Network Utilization

This appendix provides a derivation of equation (18) in the main text—that is, we set out how to extract a measure of network capital utilization from productivity data and document the calculations reported in section 12.3.1.

12.A1.1   Derivation

What follows is based on the framework set out for analyzing communication networks and network externalities in Corrado (2011), in which it is assumed there are no markups due to imperfect competition or other inefficiency wedges; see also Corrado and Jäger (2014) and Corrado and van Ark (2016).

In sources-of-growth accounting, the contribution of private capital is expressed in terms of the services it provides. Let the value of the relevant private stocks be denoted as $P^I K$, where the price of each unit of capital P^I is the investment price and the real stock K is a quantity obtained via the standard perpetual inventory model. In our application, the value $P^I K$ represents the replacement value of network service provider capital in terms of its capacity to deliver digital services (i.e., including in this application, the value of the "originals" for the content the provider can disseminate). The value $P^K K$ represents the service flow provided by that capital.

The price P^K is an unobserved rental equivalence price that is related to the investment price by the user cost formula, $P^K = P^I(r + \delta - \pi)$, where r is an after-tax *ex-post* rate of return, δ the depreciation rate used in the perpetual inventory calculation, π is capital gains, and T is the Hall-Jorgenson tax term. The rental equivalence price is simplified by defining the gross return $\Phi = (r + \delta - \pi)T$ so that when capital services $P^K K$ are equated with observed capital income via the residual calculation of an *ex-post* after-tax rate of return r, we have

(A1)   observed capital income $= P^I K * \Phi$.

When capital services are computed on the basis of an *ex-ante* financial rate of return $\bar{r}$, the value for capital income of network providers must be expressed differently. Defining the *ex-ante* gross return $\bar{\Phi} = (\bar{r} + \delta - \pi)T$ accordingly, network provider capital income is expressed as

(A2)   observed capital income $= P^I K u^{ISP} * \bar{\Phi}$,

where u^{ISP} is network capital utilization and, via Berndt and Fuss (1986), capital utilization u^{ISP} (rather than r) exhausts capital income.

Equating expressions (A1) and (A2),

$$P^I K * \Phi = P^I K u^{ISP} * \bar{\Phi},$$

and solving for u^{ISP} yields

(A3) $$u^{ISP} = \frac{\Phi}{\overline{\Phi}}.$$

This equation states that under the conditions set out in Berndt and Fuss (1986), the relationship between the *ex-post* and *ex-ante* gross rate of return for an industry or sector reflects its capital utilization.

12.A1.2   Calculations

The implied network utilization calculating according to equation (A3), where r in the definition of Φ is calculated following Jorgenson and Griliches (1967) as the ex-post return for the combined Motion Picture, Sound Recording, Telecommunications, and Broadcasting industries (North American Industry Classification System [NAICS] 512,515,517) and where $\overline{r}$ in the definition of $\overline{\Phi}$, is set to Moody's AAA corporate bond rate.

The ex-post net return and the δ and π components of Φ and $\overline{\Phi}$ were calculated by the authors for the combined sector using data from BEA's industry accounts (accessed October 2018). The results for u are shown in text figure 12.6.

12.A2   Access Service Prices and Consumption

To calculate a price index for each of the network access services provided by the business sector—cable, internet, mobile, and subscription video streaming—we begin with nominal spending and divide by a measure of aggregate time spent using the service adjusted for quality. These individual price indexes are aggregated to create an overall access price index used to deflate nominal spending on access services and produce a measure of consumption.

For exposition and analysis, we also consider price indexes constructed using four alternative measures of quantity: the number of households subscribed to the service, the number of individual users, time spent on the service, and time spent adjusted for quality (our preferred measure for deflation). Thus four alternative indexes are calculated for each of the four services by dividing revenue by each of the alternative measures of quantity, yielding prices paid per household, per individual, per unit of time, and per unit of constant-quality time: P_H, P_I, P_D, and P_Q.

Data sources and calculation methods for service prices are summarized in table 12.A1.

12.A2.1   Nominal Spending

For nominal spending, we use figures from the national accounts published by the Bureau of Economic Analysis, table 2.4.5U, "Personal Consumption Expenditures by Type of Product." In the cases of mobile access and video on demand, we developed additional detail as explained below.

Table 12.A1   Sources and methods for access service prices

	Revenue	Households	Users	Time units	Quality units
Cable	BEA NIPA table 2.4.5U., line 215: "Cable, satellite, and other live television services"	1987–88: *Statistical Abstracts of the United States* (citing *Census of Housing*). 1989–2015: FCC reports, "Status of Competition in Markets for the Delivery of Video Programming" (citing SNL Kagan reports), various years. 2016–17: Extrapolated based on reports from available companies (AT&T, Verizon, Chartered, Comcast, DIRECTV, DISH).	1987–present: Number of subscribing households times number of residents at least two years old per TV household reported by Nielsen.	Average hours by age group (2–11, 12–17, 18+) reported by Nielsen, weighted by population age distribution from US Census.	1987–present: Hours weighted by (natural log of) number of channels per system reported by FCC.
Internet	BEA NIPA table 2.4.5U., line 285: "Internet access"	Broadband: 1999–2017: FCC report, "Internet Access Services," various years. Dial-up: 1987–2000: Company financial reports and press reports, extrapolated. 2001–9: FCC report, "Internet Access Services," various years. 2010–17: AOL reports through 2014, extrapolated to 2017.	1987–97: Extrapolated using 1998–2008 growth rate. 1998–present: Prevalence of home internet use for adults and for population younger than 18 from *Current Population Survey* supplement, times population by age from US Census.	1987–91: Judgmental extrapolation using 50 percent growth rate. 1992–2008: Hours per user from *Statistical Abstract of the United States* (reporting data from VSS Consulting). 2009–10: Log-linear interpolation. 2011–18: Hours per user reported by Nielsen.	1987–89: Extrapolation using 1990–1993 growth rate. 1990–93: Volume extrapolated using global fixed internet traffic. 1994–2004: Volume extrapolated using overall fixed internet data traffic (North America) from Cisco. 2005–17: Volume of consumer fixed internet data traffic (North America) from Cisco.
Feature Phone	BEA NIPA table 2.4.5U., line 281: "Cellular telephone services" allocated according to weighted feature/smartphone user mix (Assume smartphone contracts are 4 times as expensive as feature phone contracts.)	US households times individual feature phone penetration share.	1987–2004: *Statistical Abstracts of the United States* (citing Consumer Telecom Industry Association). 2005–18: Share of adults who own cell phone less share who own smartphone (Pew Research Center) times population greater than 15 years old (US Census).	1987–1992: Extrapolated using 1993–98 growth rate. 1993–2014: Talk time per subscriber from FCC reports, various years (citing CTIA), smoothed. 2015–17: Average talk time, 2010–14.	Hours of talk time (no quality change).

Smart-phone	BEA NIPA table 2.4.5U, line 281: "Cellular telephone services" allocated according to weighted feature/smartphone user mix. (Assume smartphone contracts are 4 times as expensive as feature phone contracts.)	US households times individual smartphone penetration share.		2005–10: Extrapolated using 5 percent growth rate. 2011–17: Average time spent on smartphone from press reports (citing eMarketer), smoothed.	Cisco-reported mobile IP traffic.
Netflix	2007–2011: Revenue per member extrapolated backward using 2012–2013 growth rate times reported paying members (members reported for 2009–2011, extrapolated for 2007–2008). 2012–17: Company annual reports.	Company reports supplemented by press reports and extrapolated.	Number of households times average household size reported in population census.	Data use divided by data rate per time unit using North American fixed internet protocol traffic reported in Cisco VNI Forecast, various years times share of traffic for each provider reported by Sandvine, times average data rate based on HD/SD shares derived from Cisco VNI Forecast.	Raw viewing hours multiplied by high-definition video share, scaled by (natural log of) number of titles available by service scaled as one movie = two TV episodes, one TV season = 15 TV episodes. (FCC reports, news sources.)
Amazon	(Introduced in 2011) 2011–17: Standard subscription price (press reports) times number of viewers (eMarketer) times 0.4 (eMarketer assumes 2.5 viewers per subscription).	Company reports supplemented by press reports and extrapolated.	Number of households times average household size reported in population census.	Data use divided by data rate per time unit using North American fixed internet protocol traffic reported in Cisco VNI Forecast, various years times share of traffic for each provider reported by Sandvine, times average data rate based on HD/SD shares derived from Cisco VNI Forecast.	Raw viewing hours multiplied by high-definition video share, scaled by (natural log of) number of titles available by service scaled as one movie = two TV episodes, one TV season = 15 TV episodes. (FCC reports, news sources.)
Hulu	(Introduced in 2010). Number of subscribers (2012–17 from press reports, extrapolated to 2010) times standard subscription price.	Company reports supplemented by press reports and extrapolated.	Number of households times average household size reported in population census.	Data use divided by data rate per time unit using North American fixed internet protocol traffic reported in Cisco VNI Forecast, various years times share of traffic for each provider reported by Sandvine, times average data rate based on HD/SD shares derived from Cisco VNI Forecast.	Raw viewing hours multiplied by high-definition video share, scaled by (natural log of) number of titles available by service scaled as one movie = two TV episodes, one TV season = 15 TV episodes. (FCC reports, news sources.)

Cable. Spending is taken from table line 215, "Cable, satellite, and other live television services." We use "cable" as shorthand for spending in this category, which includes spending on the services of multichannel video programming distributors (MVPDs) of all kinds, including (in addition to cable television) programming provided via telecommunications service provider, direct broadcast satellite, home satellite dish, wireless cable, master antenna, and open video systems.

Internet. Spending is taken from table line 285, "Internet access." Spending on internet services includes access via "dial-up" service and access via broadband, whether obtained through a telecommunications service provider, a cable system, or a satellite system. We extrapolate a spending figure for 1987 using the growth rate of internet households.

Mobile. Spending is taken from table line 281, "Cellular telephone services." Mobile services spending includes access to broadband via smartphone as well as access to conventional features such as voice and text using a smartphone or feature phone. We split nominal access spending between smartphone service and feature phone service, for which we construct distinct quantity measures, using the number of subscribers of each type (derived as explained below) and a judgmental assumption that the price paid for a smartphone contract is four times the price paid for a feature phone contract. (At the time of writing, a casual review of prices on the worldwide web showed basic plans with no data were $10–15 per month and common smartphone plans were $40–60 per month.)

Video. Total video spending is taken from table line 220, "Video streaming and rental."[18] We focus on SVOD, which we use as an indicator for the broader category, due to data limitations.[19] In particular, we construct estimates of revenue for the three most prominent SVOD providers—Netflix, Amazon Prime, and Hulu—based on company financial reports and press reports. Netflix reports revenue per subscription beginning in 2012, which we extrapolate back to 2007 using the modest 2012–13 growth rate. Revenue per subscription for Amazon Prime and Hulu are assumed to be their standard charges ($7.99 per month for Hulu and $79 per year for Amazon Prime through 2013 and $99 per year afterward). These figures are multiplied by the number of households for each service estimated as described below.

12.A2.2   Households

Cable. Periodic reports from the Federal Communications Commission (FCC), "Status of Competition in Markets for the Delivery of Video Programming," provide household subscription figures for 1990 to 2015, citing

18. BEA also provides revenue for "Audio streaming and radio services (including satellite radio)." We did not develop a price index for this category.

19. In addition to SVOD, video streaming and rental as defined in the NIPAs encompasses one-off video on demand, such as sports events, and rental of DVDs, for which we do not have data.

reports by consulting firm SNL Kagan. Earlier years were collected from *Statistical Abstracts of the United States*, which reports figures from *Census of Housing*. Figures for 2016 and 2017 were extrapolated using available reports from cable, telecom, and satellite service companies (Chartered, Comcast, AT&T, Verizon, DIRECTV, and DISH).

Internet. Periodic reports from the FCC, "Internet Access Services: Status," provide household figures for broadband access for 1999–2016 and dial-up access for 2001–9. Prior to 1999, we assume all access was via dial-up service. Dial-up service figures for years not covered by FCC reports were available from financial reports and press reports for America Online, Compuserve, Prodigy, Microsoft Network, AT&T Worldnet, and Genie. The company series were judgmentally extrapolated to the year of introduction for each service. Dial-up subscribers from 2010 onward were extrapolated using figures from America Online (AOL) through 2014 and the 2011–14 rate of AOL subscription decline for 2015–17.

Mobile. We do not have data on the number of households with cell phone service. We assume the share of households with service equals the share of individuals in the adult population with service.

Video. Netflix reports the number of paying members beginning in 2009, which we extrapolate back to 2007 using the 2009–10 growth rate. Hulu and Amazon Prime subscribers are collected from press reports, which typically cite estimates from eMarketer. Because eMarketer figures estimate the number of active users using an assumption of 2.5 users per subscribing household, we multiply these reported user figures by 0.4 to estimate the number of households, assuming one subscription per household.

12.A2.3   Individuals

Cable. We scale cable household figures using the number of residents at least two years of age per TV household reported by Nielsen for 1985, 1990, 1995, 2000, 2005, and 2010, interpolated and extrapolated.

Internet. In 1998, 2000, 2001, 2003, 2007, 2009–13, 2015, and 2017, the *Current Population Survey* supplemental survey on computer and internet use provided estimates of the share of people living in a household with an internet connection and the share of individuals going online at home. We use this information to construct a time series for the share of people who use the internet at home for 1998–2017 for adults and children separately. We extrapolate these shares back to 1987 using the growth rate for 1998–2009. These shares are applied to the average composition by age of US households to derive the total number of home internet users by year.

Mobile. The number of cell phone users (smartphone and feature phone collectively) is taken from Consumer Telecommunications Industry Association (CTIA) estimates as reported in *Statistical Abstracts of the United States* for 1987–2004. Estimates for 2005–17 are from population shares reported by the Pew Research Center (Pew) times the US population. Pew also provides separate estimates for smartphone users, which are subtracted from total cell phone users to get (solely) feature phone users.

Video. For each SVOD service, the number of users is estimated by multiplying the number of households by the average household size reported by the US Census for the year. That is, we assume all household members make use of the service.

12.A2.4   Time Use

Cable The Nielsen Corporation (Nielsen) provides time spent per day on live and time-shifted television by age group (2–11 years old, 12–17 years old, at least 18 years old) beginning in 1992, which we extrapolate to 1987 using the value for 1992. We weight these figures by the US Census–reported share of the population at least 2 years old for each age group to get an average number of hours per day for residents of households with cable access, which we multiply by total users to get total hours.

Internet. Hours spent using the internet for 1992–2008 were taken from *Statistical Abstracts of the United States*, various years, reporting estimates published by Veronis, Suhler, Stevenson (VSS). For 2011–17, Nielsen reports of time spent accessing the internet on a computer were used. Estimates for 2009–10 were interpolated, and for 1987–91 a growth rate of 50 percent per year was assumed, yielding a trivial level for 1987 in order to match a report from VSS that hours were negligible prior to 1987.

Mobile. Our measure of time use for feature phones is talk time. Minutes of talking is calculated as a three-year centered moving average of estimates taken from FCC reports, citing CTIA surveys for 1993–2014 and extrapolated. For smartphones, we use a three-year centered moving average of estimates from eMarketer available for 2011–17 of average time spent per day with smartphones for US adults, which we extrapolate back to 2005.

Video. To calculate hours spent on each SVOD service, we first estimate the data used in streaming using the share of internet traffic for each service reported by Sandvine, Inc. multiplied by the quantity of fixed internet traffic for the North American consumer market reported by Cisco's Visual Networking Index (VNI) reports. Sandvine reports are available annually from 2010 to 2014 and for 2016; the shares for 2014 are linearly interpolated, and the share for each service for 2017 is set equal to its 2016 value. Then we divide by the number of bytes required to stream an hour of video to get the number of hours. The estimate of bytes per hour used is a weighted average of the number of bytes used for standard-definition and high-definition video streaming, where the share is estimated using VNI reports. In particular, VNI provides a high-definition share for SVOD of 0.59 for 2014. This estimate is extrapolated to 2010 using the growth reported in VNI for the high-definition share of global managed IP video-on-demand traffic. The share is extrapolated further back to 2007 using a 5 percent growth rate and forward to 2017 using the VNI forecast published in 2014, the last VNI vintage where Cisco provided data on the subject.

12.A2.5   Quality-Adjusted Hours

Cable. To account for the increase in quality associated with the programming choices available to viewers, we scale hours by the average number of channels per cable system reported by the FCC. We use a natural log transformation, assuming, for example, that the additional quality obtained going from 100 to 200 channels equals the increase in quality obtained going from 10 to 20 channels.

Internet. Our indicator for quality of internet service is the VNI estimate of IP traffic for consumer fixed internet use for North America. We use North American traffic in the absence of information on the US share, essentially assuming that the US share of North American traffic is unchanged over time. Direct measures of the indicator are available for 2005–16, along with a forecast for 2017 from the latest VNI reports, various years. We extrapolate back to 1994 using overall fixed internet traffic estimates for North America and back to 1990 using global fixed internet traffic from VNI reports. For 1987–89, we use the 1990–93 growth rate.

Mobile. We assume the quality of talk time is unchanged over time, so no quality adjustment is necessary for feature phones. For smartphones, we use the volume (petabytes) of consumer mobile IP traffic per month for the North American market reported by VNI for 2005–17, extrapolated to 2002 using the average growth rate for 2005–8.

Video. Our quality-adjusted series is raw hours of viewing time scaled by a library quality indicator and multiplied by high-definition video share. Our indicator for the quality of SVOD service is the natural log of the size of the video library for each service measured in the number of equivalent feature films available for streaming. FCC reports in 2013 and 2016 provide data on the number of films and the number of TV seasons available on each service. Estimates from the press were found for 2010 and 2018. Netflix press releases provide data for 2007 and 2008. Missing years are interpolated. We reweight TV seasons using the judgmental assumption that two episodes of a television show are equivalent to one feature film and TV seasons have 15 episodes. The high-definition share adjustment employed to calculate hours of viewing time above is reversed to produce the quality-adjusted hours indicator, implying that the quality of high-definition viewing is 1.67 times the quality of standard-definition viewing, corresponding to the ratio of data transmission required for each type, 5 megabits per second and 3 megabits per second, respectively.

12.A2.5.1   Price Indexes

Table 12.A2 shows the quality-adjusted price index for each access service and price indexes for each concept of quantity. Our aggregate quality-

Table 12.A2 Price indexes for access services

Year	Quality-adjusted price index for cable	Quality-adjusted price index for internet	Quality-adjusted price index for mobile	Quality-adjusted price index for video	Aggregate Service price by household	Aggregate service price index by user	Aggregate service price index by hour	Quality
1987	62.40	2,158,866.63	1,691.56	ND	62.74	62.60	171.95	492.25
1988	63.61	1,630,616.32	2,076.07	ND	64.29	64.49	177.27	504.31
1989	72.05	1,590,688.49	2,366.66	ND	73.47	74.10	201.91	571.27
1990	77.42	1,476,658.56	2,206.42	ND	79.68	80.72	215.08	605.28
1991	77.17	1,476,658.56	1,791.89	ND	79.35	80.18	209.93	588.03
1992	82.59	1,125,952.15	1,634.17	ND	84.69	85.44	219.88	611.09
1993	83.96	608,383.33	1,256.09	ND	84.48	85.00	211.99	582.35
1994	77.40	594,355.07	934.09	ND	77.39	77.53	187.02	509.98
1995	77.75	116,043.76	745.84	ND	78.01	77.81	178.29	439.39
1996	83.07	18,465.35	725.84	ND	79.33	79.38	181.38	386.76
1997	92.62	8,883.37	664.56	ND	81.19	81.07	183.51	381.03
1998	98.15	5,389.04	628.31	ND	84.62	84.55	183.93	371.65
1999	103.06	3,869.68	542.59	ND	88.44	88.49	183.37	351.24
2000	108.05	1,973.82	436.65	ND	94.71	94.87	177.46	304.20
2001	105.71	880.03	327.16	ND	99.63	100.01	154.95	240.57
2002	104.80	491.32	277.21	ND	101.17	102.73	145.78	206.70
2003	102.06	311.61	221.78	ND	102.36	103.98	134.44	173.59

2004	106.52	185.71	187.51	ND	103.01	104.72	128.90	151.64
2005	103.10	115.31	155.39	ND	102.73	103.39	116.75	128.21
2006	99.13	114.93	127.98	ND	102.20	102.59	108.33	114.85
2007	100.00	100.00	100.00	100.00	100.00	100.00	100.00	100.00
2008	103.51	81.92	78.07	62.65	99.44	99.45	94.48	86.94
2009	104.86	51.17	51.43	47.85	95.47	95.35	84.74	66.34
2010	107.61	36.55	32.69	36.60	98.17	97.45	81.33	51.36
2011	105.70	27.51	20.91	17.93	94.99	94.89	73.15	39.44
2012	112.03	26.50	14.51	14.81	92.85	91.48	66.96	33.99
2013	113.01	24.77	7.25	13.20	90.13	89.76	60.96	24.97
2014	120.32	23.46	4.43	12.68	94.85	94.26	63.92	20.45
2015	145.81	16.03	2.85	9.00	93.70	92.50	64.61	16.63
2016	150.56	11.47	2.14	6.59	96.56	95.31	68.10	13.75
2017	161.95	9.65	1.61	6.56	98.01	96.93	70.10	12.05
Growth rate								
1987–2017	3.2%	−41.1%	−23.2%	ND	1.5%	1.5%	−3.0%	−12.4%
1987–1997	3.9%	−54.9%	−9.3%	ND	2.6%	2.6%	0.7%	−2.6%
1997–2007	0.8%	−44.9%	−18.9%	ND	2.1%	2.1%	−6.1%	−13.4%
2007–2017	4.8%	−23.4%	−41.3%	−27.2%	−0.2%	−0.3%	−3.6%	−21.2%

Source: Authors' calculations.

adjusted price index for access service, shown in the right-most column, falls 12.4 percent per year, on average, over the full period of this study. The price index decline accelerates over time, first as internet service accounts for a rising share of spending in the 1997–2007 period and then as mobile and video on demand access become more important in the 2007–17 period. (Decomposition of growth in the final index into contributions from each margin is discussed in the chapter.)

12.A3   Consumer IT Durable Prices and (Household) Investment

Data sources and methods used for constructing nominal consumer durable spending and price indexes used for deflation are summarized in table 12.A3.

12.A3.1   Nominal Spending

Nominal spending estimates were based on detailed personal consumption expenditures reported by the BEA. In particular, detailed annual-frequency estimates of spending by product type were allocated to the more detailed categories used in the chapter based on the 2007 input-output tables. (The quinquennial "benchmark" input-output table from 2007 provides not only detailed product spending information but also commodity codes corresponding to the primary products of the industries of the North American Industry Classification System [NAICS].) For example, the annual-frequency estimates of PCE detailed spending include a category for "video, audio, photographic, and information processing equipment" with further detail provided for eight commodity codes, including "computer and electronic products." The 2007 input-output table provides the six-digit industry of origin of the products within this category, allowing one to distinguish among personal computers, computer monitors, televisions, and so forth.

In the case of cellular phones and digital cameras, outside sources were used. Although these categories can be derived using the method described, their share of expenditure has changed rapidly since 2007, rendering the allocation process inaccurate. Expenditures on other products that share the relevant higher-level categories are offset proportionally to accommodate the rising spending on cell phones and the rise and subsequent rapid fall in spending on digital cameras.

Cell Phones. We use an estimate of cellular phone spending in the US consumer market provided by IDC, Inc., rather than estimates reported in the NIPA PCE detail tables for several reasons. Cellular phone equipment spending is not reported separately, appearing instead as part of a broader category, "telephone and related communication equipment." And as noted in Aizcorbe, Byrne, and Sichel (2019), this broader NIPA spending line does not account for the substantial portion of the relevant acquisition of consumer stocks of cell phones that takes place in conjunction with the purchase of cellular phone services. In contrast, the estimates for IDC

Table 12.A3   Sources and methods for consumer capital spending and prices

Audio-Visual and Communications Equipment	Spending	Prices
Televisions	BEA PCE detail. (see note)	PCE price index for televisions, BEA (employing BLS CPI).
Digital Cameras	Unit sales, Americas market, Camera and Imaging Products Association, times average price from press reports, extrapolated and interpolated. 2007 BEA IO Bridge Table detail for US spending used to estimate US share of Americas market.	CPI for cameras, Statistics Japan.
Photographic Equipment excluding Digital Cameras	BEA PCE detail for photographic equipment less estimate of digital camera sales.	PCE price index for photographic equipment, BEA (employing BLS CPI).
Other Video Equipment	BEA PCE detail for video equipment less spending on televisions and computer monitors.	CPI for video cameras, Statistics Japan, extrapolated for 1987–1989 using price index for digital cameras.
Audio Equipment	BEA PCE detail. (see note)	PCE price index for audio equipment, BEA (employing BLS CPI).
Recording Media	BEA PCE detail. (see note)	PCE price index for recording media, BEA (employing BLS CPI for video discs and other media).
Mobile Phones	1987–1994: Byrne and Corrado (2017) stock-flow model adjusted for consumer market. 1995–2006: Gartner wholesale value times 50 percent retail markup times 0.7 consumer share. 2007–2008: IDC total market times 0.7 consumer share. 2009–2017: IDC consumer market units by model times price for unit without contract commitment.	1987–2010: Spending price index for mobile phones, Byrne and Corrado (2017). 2011–17: Consumer price index for mobile phones, Aizcorbe, Byrne, and Sichel (2019).
Telephone Equipment excluding Mobile Phones	Byrne and Corrado (2017) adjusted for consumer market.	Spending price index for telephones, Byrne and Corrado (2017), updated by FRB.

(continued)

Table 12.A3   (cont.)

Audio-Visual and Communications Equipment	Spending	Prices
Information Processing Equipment		
Computers	BEA PCE detail. (see note)	Spending price index for personal computers, Byrne and Corrado (2017), extrapolated for 2015–17 using BEA PCE price index for computers and peripherals adjusted for average difference with Byrne-Corrado index for 2009–14 period.
Data Storage Equipment	BEA PCE detail. (see note)	Spending price index for data storage equipment, Byrne (2015), updated by FRB.
Monitors	Proportional to spending on personal computers based on Gartner research on typical system configuration.	PCE price index for televisions, BEA (employing BLS CPI).
Peripherals	BEA PCE detail. (see note)	Spending price index for peripherals, Byrne and Corrado (2017), extrapolated for 2015–17 using BEA PCE price index for computers and peripherals adjusted for average difference with Byrne-Corrado index for 2009–14 period.
Other Information Processing Equipment	BEA PCE detail. (see note)	PCE price index for calculators, typewriters, and other information processing equipment, BEA.
Software and accessories	BEA PCE detail. (see note)	Gaming software 1987–97: PCE price index for computer software and accessories, BEA. 1998–2017: Producer price index for game software publishing, BLS, 1998–2017 adjusted for average difference with Copeland (2013) for 1998–2004 period. Other software Consumer price index for prepackaged software, Byrne and Corrado (2017) extrapolated for 2015–17 using 2012–17 average growth rate.

Notes: BEA is US Bureau of Economic Analysis; BLS is US Bureau of Labor Statistics; FRB is Federal Reserve Board of Governors. Spending for categories with "BEA PCE detail" designation was estimated using BEA annual PCE spending by type of product, NIPA table 2.4.5. further allocated using 2007 benchmark Input-Output detail.

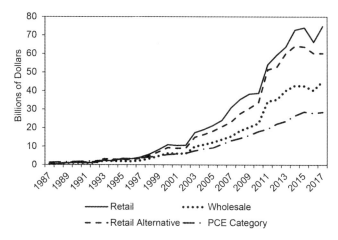

Fig. 12.A1   Estimates of US consumer cell phone spending
Source: IDC Inc. (retail); authors' calculations (wholesale, retail alternative); Bureau of Economic Analysis (PCE category).

impute a value for cell phones acquired as part of a service contract using the price a consumer would pay for the phone if acquired without a contract commitment. The IDC estimates thus provide a consistent estimate of the retail value of all phones acquired over time, which serves the purpose of measuring the household capital stock. As shown in figure 12.A1, the IDC estimate of consumer cell phone expenditures is substantially higher than the NIPA estimate for the category containing cell phones. To corroborate the IDC estimate, we constructed an alternative estimate using US sales at wholesale prices provided by Gartner through 2007, extrapolated by cell phone imports, which dominate the US market reported by the International Trade Commission, and inflated by 50 percent, a rough estimate of the retail margin in the cell phone market. This coarse indicator, shown by the dashed line, is quite close to the IDC estimate.

Digital Cameras. Unit sales of digital cameras for the Americas market provided by the Camera and Digital Products Association are scaled by an average price series constructed by interpolating between estimates reported in the press (falling from roughly $4,000 in 1987 to roughly $200 in 2007 and remaining stable since then). A US share of total Americas spending is constructed using the relevant line from the benchmark input-output tables for 2007 for consumer spending on digital cameras, which yields a share of approximately 48 percent, which we assume is constant in our period of study.

12.A3.2   Price Indexes

For equipment prices, we use either official estimates or substitutes drawn from the authors' research and, in some cases, other national statistical agencies. Aggregate prices for three broad categories are shown in table 12.A4: audiovisual equipment (televisions, digital cameras, photographic equip-

Table 12.A4   Price indexes for ICT durable equipment categories

Year	Audio-visual equipment	Information processing equipment	Communications equipment
1987	100.00	100.00	100.00
1988	94.22	82.49	89.59
1989	89.16	70.55	79.71
1990	85.96	62.40	69.95
1991	84.09	49.99	53.31
1992	82.26	37.52	45.58
1993	79.57	27.80	38.36
1994	76.29	22.48	31.04
1995	71.91	17.07	28.61
1996	67.83	12.52	23.10
1997	64.14	8.62	19.07
1998	61.25	6.04	15.26
1999	58.38	4.08	11.83
2000	55.54	3.40	10.51
2001	52.69	2.91	8.00
2002	48.43	2.53	6.43
2003	44.48	2.12	5.30
2004	40.84	1.80	4.57
2005	36.71	1.42	3.97
2006	32.29	1.06	3.37
2007	27.34	0.82	2.92
2008	23.88	0.62	2.51
2009	19.66	0.48	2.16
2010	16.26	0.41	1.85
2011	13.96	0.34	1.68
2012	12.03	0.30	1.45
2013	10.54	0.25	1.25
2014	9.20	0.22	0.95
2015	8.25	0.19	0.78
2016	7.36	0.16	0.63
2017	6.72	0.14	0.54
Growth rate			
1987–2017	−9.0%	−21.8%	−17.4%
1987–97	−4.4%	−24.5%	−16.6%
1997–2007	−8.5%	−23.6%	−18.8%
2007–17	−14.0%	−17.4%	−16.9%

Source: Authors' calculations.

ment excluding digital cameras, other video equipment, audio equipment, and recording media), information-processing equipment (personal computers, data storage equipment, monitors, and peripherals), and communications equipment (cellular phones and telephone equipment excluding cellular phones).

Televisions. We use the BEA PCE deflator for televisions, which corresponds to the Bureau of Labor Statistics (BLS) CPI for televisions.

Digital Cameras. We use the CPI for cameras from Statistics Japan.

Photographic Equipment excluding Digital Cameras. We use the BEA PCE deflator for photographic equipment, which corresponds to the BLS CPI for photographic equipment.

Other Video Equipment. We use the CPI for video cameras from Statistics Japan, available from 1990 forward, extrapolated backward using the Japanese CPI for cameras.

Audio Equipment. We use the BEA PCE deflator for audio equipment, which corresponds to the BLS CPI for audio equipment.

Recording Media. We use the BEA PCE deflator for recording media, which corresponds to the BLS CPI for video discs and other media.

Personal Computers. We use the price index from Byrne and Corrado (2017a) for personal computers through 2014, extrapolated by the BEA PCE price for computers and peripherals augmented by the average difference between the growth rate of the BEA price index and the growth rate of the Byrne-Corrado price index for the 2009–14 period.

Data Storage Equipment. We use the price index published by the Federal Reserve Board for computer storage equipment, which extends the price index developed in Byrne (2015).

Monitors. We use the BEA PCE deflator for televisions, which corresponds to the BLS CPI for televisions.

Computer Peripherals. We use the price index from Byrne and Corrado (2017a) for peripherals through 2014, extrapolated by the BEA PCE price for computers and peripherals augmented by the average difference between the growth rate of the BEA price index and the growth rate of the Byrne-Corrado price index for the 2009–14 period.

Other Information-Processing Equipment. We use the BEA PCE deflator for calculators, typewriters, and other information-processing equipment.

Software and Accessories. We use the price index for prepackaged software from Byrne and Corrado (2017a) for nongame PCE software, extrapolated for 2015–17 using the five-year average growth rate. For gaming PCE software, we use the BLS producer price index (PPI) for game software publishing, available for 1998–2009 and 2014–17, adjusted for the average difference between the PPI and Copeland (2013) over the 1998–2004 period. The 2010–13 period is interpolated using the average growth rate in our index for the 2005–29 period. For the 1987–1997 period, we use the BEA PCE price index for computer software and accessories.

Cell Phones. We use the Byrne and Corrado (2015a) price index for cell phones for the 1987–2010 period and the Aizcorbe, Byrne, and Sichel (2019) index for 2010–17.

Telephone Equipment excluding Cellular Phones. We use the Byrne and Corrado (2017a) price index for telephones for the 1987–2014 period as extended and published by the Federal Reserve Board through 2017.

12.A4   IT Equipment Use Intensity

We construct measures of use intensity for each type of capital employed to connect to the access services discussed in the chapter. These include personal computers and related capital (monitors, software, and data storage equipment), televisions, and cell phones. These use-intensity measures allow us to identify the effect on IT capital services from users spending a greater share of their time on digital access services and consequently the imprint that free and purchased services have on consumption.

Mechanically, constructing use intensity for a particular type of capital requires allocating time spent on accessing each digital service to the capital used for the access. For example, use intensity for personal computers is proportional to the share of household time spent accessing fixed internet services plus the portion of time spent using SVOD when viewing programming through the computer. Likewise, television use intensity is affected by cable access and by a portion of SVOD viewing time as well. Using the ratio of aggregate time spent on each access service to the number of each type of capital held by households, we construct intensity measures as the share of the working day a given PC, TV, or cell phone is in use.

The sources for the elements in our calculation of ψ are as follows.

Service Adoption. The adoption of access services by household is derived from the household figures calculated in the previous section and was shown in figure 12.7a. Subscription video on demand penetration has also risen briskly since appearing in 2007. The share of households with at least one of the major services reached 60 percent in 2017. Time spent on each service is allocated by device as discussed below.

Computers. Estimates of households with a personal computer are provided by the US Census Bureau for 1984, 1989, and 1993 and roughly annually from 1989 forward in collaboration with the supplemental survey published by the *Current Population Survey*. The number of PCs per household is based on periodic reports from the *Residential Electricity Consumption Survey* published by the *Energy Information Agency*. As was shown by the black line in figure 12.7b, internet access among computer households was roughly 20 percent as of 1990 and was over 90 percent by 2007. The number of PCs per computer-holding households nearly doubled (figure 12.7c). Dividing the total number of hours on the computer by the number of devices, we find that the share of the working day the average PC was in use for accessing the internet or SVOD rose from 18 percent in 1987 to roughly 29 percent in 2017 (figure 12.7d).[20]

Televisions. Estimates of households with a television are provided by *Statistical Abstracts of the United States*, citing figures from *Census of Housing*.

---

20. Note that time spent using the computer for other purposes, which averaged about 2.5 hours per day, is not included in this figure.

As was shown by the dashed lines in figure 12.7, nearly all households had a television at the beginning of our period of study, and this share remained above 90 percent as of 2017. The number of televisions per household is based on periodic reports from the *Residential Electricity Consumption Survey* published by the *Energy Information Agency*. Televisions per TV-using household moved up from roughly 2 to roughly 2.5 by 2005 and has eased down a touch since then. Dividing the total number of hours by the number of TVs in use yields a share of the day that peaked in 2013 at roughly a third and has moved down noticeably since then. The use intensity of PCs and TVs was roughly equal in 2017.

Cell Phones. Mobile phones (whether feature phones or smartphones) are assumed to be present whenever individuals have service, so the issue of adoption of the service conditional on the presence of the equipment does not arise. However, figure 12.7 showed that mobile phone adoption rose rapidly from 2007 to 2015 and advanced more slowly since then; cell phone adoption overall has stabilized at 90 percent. As noted above, we use individual adoption rates as proxies for the household adoption rate in the case of cell phones. The share of households with mobile phone service rose rapidly from essentially zero at the beginning of our period of study to over 90 percent as of 2013 and was stable through 2017. The number of hours of use shot up with the advent of widespread smartphone use, and the share of the working day phones are in use shot up as well and stood at 18 percent as of 2018.

References

Abdirahman, M., D. Coyle, R. Heys, and W. Stewart. 2017. "A Comparison of Approaches to Deflating Telecoms Services Output." Technical Report Discussion Paper 2017-04, ESCoE and ONS.

Aizcorbe, A., D. M. Byrne, and D. E. Sichel. 2019. "Getting Smart about Phones: New Price Indexes and the Allocation of Spending between Devices and Services Plans in Personal Consumption Expenditures." NBER Working Paper No. 25645. Cambridge, MA: National Bureau of Economic Research.

Berndt, E. R., and M. A. Fuss. 1986. "Productivity Measurement with Adjustments for Variations in Capacity Utilization and Other Forms of Temporary Equilibrium." *Journal of Econometrics* 33 (1): 7–29.

Brynjolfsson, E., A. Collis, W. E. Diewert, F. Eggers, and K. J. Fox. 2020. "Measuring the Impact of Free Goods on Real Household Consumption." *AEA Papers and Proceedings* 110 (May): 25–30.

Brynjolfsson, E., A. Collis, and F. Eggers. 2019. "Using Massive Online Choice Experiments to Measure Changes in Well-Being." *Proceedings of the National Academy of Sciences* 116 (15): 7250–5.

Brynjolfsson, E., and A. Saunders. 2009. *Wired for Innovation: How Information Technology Is Reshaping the Economy*. Cambridge, MA: MIT Press.

Byrne, D. M. 2015. "Prices for Data Storage Equipment and the State of IT Innovation." FEDS Notes, July 15. Washington, DC: Federal Reserve Board.

Byrne, D. M., and C. A. Corrado. 2015a. "Prices for Communications Equipment: Rewriting the Record." Finance and Economics Discussion Series 2015-069, September. Washington, DC: Board of Governors of the Federal Reserve System.

Byrne, D. M., and C. A. Corrado. 2015b. "Recent Trends in Communications Equipment Prices." FEDS Notes, September 29. Washington, DC: Federal Reserve Board.

Byrne, D. M., and C. A. Corrado. 2017a. "ICT Asset Prices: Marshalling Evidence into New Measures." Finance and Economics Discussion Series 2017-016, February. Washington, DC: Board of Governors of the Federal Reserve System.

Byrne, D. M., and C. A. Corrado. 2017b. "ICT Services and Their Prices: What Do They Tell Us about Productivity and Technology?" *International Productivity Monitor* (33): 150–81.

Byrne, D. M., and C. A. Corrado. 2020. "The Increasing Deflationary Influence of Consumer Digital Services." *Economics Letters*, forthcoming.

Christensen, L. R., and D. W. Jorgenson. 1969. "The Measurement of US Real Capital Input, 1929–1967." *Review of Income and Wealth* 15 (4): 293–320.

Christensen, L. R., and D. W. Jorgenson. 1973. "Measuring Economic Performance in the Private Sector." In *The Measurement of Economic and Social Performance*, edited by M. Moss, 233–351. NBER Studies in Income and Wealth 38. New York: National Bureau of Economic Research.

Copeland, A. 2013. "Seasonality, Consumer Heterogeneity and Price Indexes: The Case of Prepackaged Software." *Journal of Productivity Analysis* 39 (1):47–59.

Corrado, C. 2011. "Communication Capital, Metcalfe's Law, and US Productivity Growth." Economics Program Working Paper 11-01. New York: Conference Board, Inc. http://papers.ssrn.com/sol3/papers.cfm?abstract_id=2117784.

Corrado, C., and K. Jäger. 2014. "Communication Networks, ICT, and Productivity Growth in Europe." Economics Program Working Paper 14-04. New York: Conference Board, Inc.

Corrado, C., and O. Ukhaneva. 2016. "Hedonic Prices for Fixed Broadband Services: Estimation across OECD Countries." Technical report. OECD/STI Working Paper.

Corrado, C., and O. Ukhaneva. 2019. "Hedonic Price Measures for Fixed Broadband Services: Estimation across OECD Countries, Phase II." Technical report. OECD/DSTI/CDEP Report to CISP and MADE, revised.

Corrado, C. A., and B. van Ark. 2016. "The Internet and Productivity." In *Handbook on the Economics of the Internet*, edited by J. M. Bauer and M. Latzer, 120–45. Northampton, MA: Edward Elgar.

Díaz-Pinés, A., and A. G. Fanfalone. 2015. "The Role of Triple- and Quadruple-play Bundles: Hedonic Price Analysis and Industry Performance in France, the United Kingdom, and the United States." Paper presented at 43rd Research Conference on Communications, Information and Internet Policy, George Mason University School of Law, Arlington, VA.

Diewert, W. E., and K. Fox. 2017. "The Digital Economy, GDP and Consumer Welfare." Paper presented at the CRIW workshop, NBER Summer Institute, Cambridge, MA, July 17–18.

Greenwood, J., and K. A. Kopecky. 2013. "Measuring the Welfare Gain from Personal Computers." *Economic Inquiry* 51 (1): 336–47.

Hulten, C. 1986. "Productivity Change, Capacity Utilization, and the Sources of Efficiency Growth." *Journal of Econometrics* 33:31–50.

Hulten, C. 2009. "Growth Accounting." NBER Working Paper No. 15341. Cambridge, MA: National Bureau of Economic Research.

Hulten, C. R., and F. C. Wykoff. 1981a. "The Estimation of Economic Depreciation Using Vintage Asset Prices." *Journal of Econometrics* 15:367–96.

Hulten, C. R., and F. C. Wykoff. 1981b. "The Measurement of Economic Depreciation." In *Depreciation, Inflation and the Taxation of Income from Capital*, edited by C. R. Hulten, 81–125. Washington, DC: Urban Institute.

Jorgenson, D. W. 1963. "Capital Theory and Investment Behavior." *American Economic Review* 53 (2): 247–59.

Jorgenson, D. W., and Z. Griliches. 1967. "The Explanation of Productivity Change." *Review of Economic Studies* 34 (3): 249–83.

Jorgenson, D. W., and J. S. Landefeld. 2006. "Blueprint for Expanded and Integrated US Accounts: Review, Assessment, and Next Steps." In *A New Architecture for the U.S. National Accounts*, edited by D. W. Jorgenson, J. S. Landefeld, and W. D. Nordhaus, 13–112. NBER Studies in Income and Wealth 66. Chicago: University of Chicago Press. http://www.nber.org/chapters/c0133.pdf.

Nakamura, L., J. Samuels, and R. Soloveichik. 2016. "Valuing 'Free' Media in GDP: An Experimental Approach." Technical report, Bureau of Economic Analysis.

Nakamura, L., R. Soloveichik, and J. Samuels. 2018. "'Free' Internet Content: Web 1.0, Web 2.0, and the Sources of Economic Growth." Technical Report Research Paper WP 18-17, Federal Reserve Bank of Philadelphia.

Petrin, A. 2002. "Quantifying the Benefits of New Products: The Case of the Minivan." *Journal of Political Economy* 110 (4): 705–29.

Rotemberg, J. J., and M. Woodford. 1995. "Dynamic General Equilibrium Models with Imperfectly Competitive Product Markets." In *Frontiers of Business Cycle Research*, edited by T. F. Cooley, 243–93. Princeton, NJ: Princeton University Press.

US Department of Commerce, Bureau of Economic Analysis. 2003. *Fixed Assets and Consumer Durables Goods in the United States, 1925–99*. Washington, DC: US Government Printing Office.

Williams, B. 2008. "A Hedonic Model for Internet Access Service in the Consumer Price Index." *Monthly Labor Review*, July, 33–48.

The Rise of Cloud Computing
Minding Your Ps, Qs, and Ks

David Byrne, Carol Corrado, and Daniel Sichel

13.1 Introduction

A transformation is underway that is revolutionizing the way computing services are provided to businesses, households, and the government. This new way of accessing computing services, typically referred to as "the cloud" or "cloud computing," represents the latest transition to a new computing platform—one in which computing is done on a network of off-site computing resources accessed through the internet.[1] As this chapter shows, the changes are extraordinary and likely will have important consequences for the structure of the economy, productivity growth, and economic measurement.

Yet because the advent of these services is relatively recent and because they largely are intermediate business inputs rather than final demand, their

David Byrne is a principal economist at the Board of Governors of the Federal Reserve System.

Carol Corrado is senior advisor and research director in economics at the Conference Board and a senior policy scholar at the Center for Business and Public Policy, McDonough School of Business, Georgetown University.

Daniel Sichel is professor of economics at Wellesley College and a research associate of the National Bureau of Economic Research.

We thank Victoria Angelova, Prianka Bhatia, and Liang Zhang for extraordinary research assistance. We extend a special acknowledgment to Liang Zhang for her excellent Wellesley College thesis that developed semiannual price indexes for Amazon Web Services' basic compute product. All views expressed in this chapter are those of the authors alone and should not be attributed to organizations with which they are affiliated. For acknowledgments, sources of research support, and disclosure of the authors' material financial relationships, if any, please see https://www.nber.org/books-and-chapters/measuring-and-accounting-innovation-21st-century/rise-cloud-computing-minding-your-ps-qs-and-ks.

1. The notion of technological change in computing as a platform shift was introduced by Bresnahan and Greenstein (1999), who analyzed the disruptive effects of the introduction of PC/client-server platform on the computer industry.

imprint on the economy is difficult to identify in official statistics. Byrne and Corrado (2017b) assessed the macroeconomic impact of the shift to cloud computing and concluded that the productivity-enhancing impacts of the shift to cloud computing were not yet particularly evident in macroeconomic data—even after taking major steps to improve the measurement of information and communications technology (ICT) asset prices (Byrne and Corrado 2017a) whose prices should be indicative of cloud services prices.[2]

This chapter, building on Byrne and Corrado's work, develops measures to quantify the service prices and quantities and the capital investment relevant for tracking the US cloud services industry—the Ps, Qs, and Ks of the title. Our basic finding is that prices for cloud services have fallen rapidly and that the use of the cloud has grown tremendously, as has investment in the related infrastructure of IT equipment and software.[3]

For our analysis of prices, we assembled a unique dataset with quarterly data on prices and characteristics for cloud services offered by the largest provider, Amazon Web Services (AWS), since the first quarter of 2009, when AWS began posting prices on the internet. The data cover AWS's basic compute, database, and storage products.[4]

For AWS's compute product, prices fell at an average rate of about 7 percent during 2009–16. Price declines were slower before 2014 and more rapid starting in the beginning of 2014. Interestingly, 2014 is the year when Microsoft and Google began posting prices for their cloud offerings on the internet. We suspect that AWS's large price declines were, in part, a response to that change in the competitive environment. For AWS's database product, prices fell at an average rate of more than 11 percent during 2010–16. Here too, prices fell relatively modestly until the beginning of 2014, after which they fell at an average rate of more than 22 percent through the end of 2016. AWS's storage product followed a similar pattern, with prices falling at an average annual rate of about 17 percent during 2009–16 and even faster declines starting in 2014. These price declines are quite rapid and highlight how rapid advances in digital *products* are showing through to prices of digital *services*.

The extremely rapid growth of capital expenditures by large providers of cloud services that we document raises a measurement puzzle. Why has investment in IT equipment in the National Income and Product Accounts (NIPAs) been so weak if large and important firms are rapidly expand-

---

2. Other first-order macroeconomic impacts of the shift to cloud computing include (1) a weakening in the demand for IT equipment for a given volume of ICT services, (2) a lowering of the cost of supplying a given volume of ICT services (e.g., power consumption costs), and (3) an increase in the productivity of software development.

3. After this chapter was written, Coyle and Nguyen (2018) developed a price index for AWS's compute product for the United Kingdom. Their paper also documents the rapid growth of cloud computing.

4. We also collected data for Microsoft's and Google's basic compute, storage, and database services. We intend to develop price indexes for those in future work.

ing their capital expenditures for this equipment? In part, this tension could reflect, as noted in Byrne and Corrado (2017b), higher utilization of this equipment at cloud providers than at individual businesses that had deployed this equipment previously. That higher utilization would imply less demand for IT equipment for a given demand for computing services. But there is another possibility: cloud providers appear to be designing and assembling IT equipment (on an own-account basis) that is not fully counted as IT investment in the NIPAs. We believe that this own-account investment should be included in the figures for business investment in IT, and we present some back-of-the-envelope numbers suggesting that this own-account investment is large. Our calculation suggests that if this own-account investment were included in business IT investment, then the growth rate of nominal investment in IT equipment during 2007–15 would have averaged a little more than 2 percentage points higher, and real GDP average annual growth would have been a touch higher as well.[5]

The chapter is organized as follows. Section 13.2 defines cloud computing and provides nomenclature for describing different cloud service products. This section also discusses the key technologies underlying cloud infrastructure. Section 13.3 describes our new price indexes for cloud computing services, including the data, methodology, and results. Section 13.4 uses several different metrics to demonstrate the exceptionally rapid growth of cloud computing and the associated infrastructure. We also highlight the puzzle described above concerning IT capital investment. Section 13.5 concludes.

13.2   What Is Cloud Computing?

Because cloud computing is so new and has not been studied extensively by economists, we begin with some basic definitions and nomenclature. In particular, we start with the definition developed by the National Institute of Standards and Technology (NIST) and generally affirmed in the literature (e.g., Kushida, Murray, and Zysman 2011), then discuss the range of cloud services available, and finally turn to a brief review of key technologies underlying the development of cloud computing.

13.2.1   The NIST Definition of Cloud Computing

A definition of cloud computing was created by NIST in November 2009 and, after consultations with many industry and government experts and stakeholders, published in final form in September 2011 (Mell and Grance 2011). Their definition remains relevant and makes more concrete and complete the brief definition given above. After noting that cloud computing is an evolving paradigm, NIST states, "Cloud computing is a model for enabling

---

5. The level of nominal GDP in 2015 would have been $117 billion higher if our estimate of own-account investment in IT equipment were included.

ubiquitous, convenient, on-demand network access to a shared pool of configurable computing resources that can be rapidly provisioned and released with minimal management effort of service provider interaction."

NIST describes the following types of clouds:

- *private cloud* (a cloud infrastructure provisioned for a single organization or specific community of organizations; it may exist on or off premises)[6]
- *public cloud* (a cloud infrastructure provisioned for open use by the public; it exists on the premises of the cloud provider)
- *hybrid cloud* (a combination of the above bound together by standardized or proprietary technology that enables data and application portability)

Finally, NIST provides a concise description of the infrastructure that underlies the cloud as "the collection of hardware and software that enables the five essential characteristics of cloud computing. The cloud infrastructure can be viewed as containing both a physical layer and an abstraction layer. The physical layer consists of the hardware resources that are necessary to support the cloud services being provided, and typically includes server, storage and network components. *The abstraction layer consists of the software deployed across the physical layer, which manifests the essential cloud characteristics.* Conceptually the abstraction layer sits above the physical layer" (italics added; Mell and Grance 2011, 2).

13.2.2   Cloud Products

The NIST cloud computing definition also includes a description of service models, or service offerings. In measurement nomenclature, these services correspond to "product types" or product classes. These product classes include

- infrastructure as a service (IaaS),
- platform as a service (PaaS), and
- software as a service (SaaS),

with each described more fully in the box. As discussed below and in the box, we would add "serverless" or function as a service (FaaS) to NIST's list.

This collection of product types often is referred to as the cloud "stack," and the earlier point about a layer of abstraction lying across the physical layer becomes important for understanding the relationship among these products. As one moves up the stack from IaaS to PaaS and so on, the level of abstraction increases in the sense that the final user can abstract from (or ignore) more and more of the underlying infrastructure. As highlighted by the italicized sentences in the box, for IaaS, the user still needs to think

---

6. The NIST "community cloud" deployment model is grouped with the "private cloud" model for ease of exposition.

Definitions of Cloud Service Products

IaaS (infrastructure as a service): Provides computer processing, storage, networks, and other fundamental computing resources, where the consumer can deploy and run arbitrary software, including operating systems as well as applications. *The consumer manages or controls some aspects of the underlying cloud infrastructure (such as operating systems, storage, and select network components) and deployed applications.*

PaaS (platform as a service): Provides ability to deploy consumer-created applications created using programming languages, libraries, services, and tools. *The consumer neither manages nor controls the underlying cloud infrastructure but has control over the deployed applications.*

Serverless, also known as FaaS (function as a service): Provides the capability of deploying functions (code) on a cloud infrastructure on a metered basis—only charging the user when the function is operating. *The consumer (who would be a software developer) neither manages nor controls the underlying cloud infrastructure and, in contrast to PaaS, does not control the computing program.* An API (application program interface) gateway controls all aspects of execution.

SaaS (software as a service): Provides the capability of running providers' applications on a cloud infrastructure. The applications are accessible from various client devices through either a thin-client interface (e.g., web browser) or a program interface. *The consumer neither manages nor controls the underlying cloud infrastructure, including network, servers, operating systems, storage, or even individual application capabilities, apart from limited user-specific application configuration settings.*

Sources: Authors' update of NIST service models. See also Mell and Grance (2011), Cohen (2017), and Avram (2016).

about operating systems, storage, and other computing resources. For PaaS, the final user needs to think only about the deployed application and can abstract from (or largely ignore) other aspects of the infrastructure.

Since the NIST definition was published, the industry has introduced a new layer of abstraction, called "serverless" or FaaS. At this level of abstraction, the final user only needs to think about functions or code that are to be performed, and the cloud services provider manages all other aspects of the infrastructure. Serverless can be regarded as sitting above PaaS in the NIST stack (as in the box), although it may also be regarded as a refined PaaS service.

As a final point about nomenclature for cloud service products, we connect this discussion to the state of computing precloud by noting the role of traditional data centers. By using a data center, the final user could abstract from the physical hosting environment, a lower level of abstraction than in any of the cloud services described in the box. The growth of cloud computing thus has its roots, at least in part, in the competitive advantage the cloud offers customers in terms of cost, flexibility, and scalability. At the same time, the growth and popularity of the technology also reflects how the layers of abstraction in its products (especially the distinction between PaaS and SaaS) serve distinct classes of customers. With abundant computing resources, value in the stack moves up toward applications and platform, and the lower infrastructure layers become commoditized (Kushida, Murray, and Zysman 2015).

Recent developments in the cloud that facilitate the work of software developers could be particularly significant and could, in time, have important macroeconomic consequences. As cloud vendors adapt technologies that enable them to develop products "higher up the stack" and offer services with greater abstractions, the work of software development is simplified. Thus although all classes of customers benefit from the move to greater abstraction in the technologies deployed, the benefits enjoyed by software product developers are especially significant (Cohen 2017). As a specific example, the movement to serverless services with Amazon's 2014 release of the Lambda computing platform has enabled developers to focus only on code and its rapid deployment. This has lowered costs of new software product development among providers of software products for final sale (via SaaS or regular licensing) as well as for applications developed for use within a developer's own firm (or custom-developed for use within a given firm).[7]

Thus far, we have barely discussed SaaS. In the usual nomenclature, SaaS products sit on the top of the stack. However, we believe that SaaS is best understood as a category of software product services (albeit complex) rather than cloud services per se. SaaS products are usually supplied with transactional metering—that is, not as a collection of elastically provisioned services per the NIST definition. Thus SaaS products may thus be equally regarded as software products sold via an online subscription business model—a business model whose use has grown in the digital economy.[8][9]

---

7. Managed services featured at Amazon's 2017 developers conference, for example, included tools for business to leverage sophisticated deep-learning models and data without having to deal with complex infrastructure issues (Murray 2017).

8. For further discussion of the role of business models in services provision, see OECD (2014), chapter 4, "The Digital Economy, New Business Models and Key Features."

9. As reported by Rackspace, a leading IaaS provider, "In recent years there has been a move by traditional software vendors to market solutions as Cloud Computing which are generally accepted to not fall within the definition of true Cloud Computing." Rackspace goes on to describe SaaS as "software delivered over the web," which is precisely our point. Technically, some SaaS products satisfy the NIST definition of cloud—for example, the Salesforce Cus-

Accordingly, the prices and quantities we study as cloud computing in the remainder of this chapter exclude SaaS products.

13.2.3   Cloud Technologies

The cloud platform relies on a suite of technologies—mainly virtualization, grid computing, and microservices architectures—but also everything that makes high-speed broadband possible. Arguably, IT history is at the point where the tagline Sun Microsystems coined in the early 1990s, "The Network Is the Computer," is finally right.[10] The network is no longer a mere bridge between autonomous nodes on independent missions and prone to choke points (as in provision of transport). The continuous increase in network capacity and a near disappearance of limitations that could choke traffic in an earlier era (hardline security policies, storage performance issues, last-mile WAN hindrances) are the foundation of this latest platform shift in computing.

Behind a virtual machine host on a network of today, computing resources—storage, memory, networking, and CPUs—are physically distributed and managed via processing queues. Long before enterprises began moving onto the cloud, mainframes and servers were virtualized, and an essential element of computing focused on the function of processing queues. With cloud computing, some resource queue end-points are moved offsite, and more than ever, computing resource acquisition and allocation becomes the central task of cloud providers. One can be far more technical about the transformation of computing as it has undergone virtualization and moved to a cloud platform, but it is hard to be more prosaic than the old Sun tagline.

Cloud vendors have made increasing use of virtualization and grid computing to elastically supply information-processing services since the advent of the millennium, with the growth in capacity especially rapid since 2006, when Amazon Web Services opened its doors. The virtualization technology that is the primary enabler of cloud computing has been in commercial use since the 1970s via IBM mainframes. Modern IBM mainframes (circa the System/390 introduced in 1990 and renamed *zSeries* in 2000) are exceptionally adept at handling large, diverse, and varying workloads and remain in use today, though they have lost much force in the large datacenter market with the rise in cloud computing (Byrne and Corrado 2017b). Grid computing is applying the resources of many computers in a network to a single problem at the same time; the technology was first used in 1989 to link supercomputers and thereafter grew and evolved along with the internet (De Roure et al. 2003).

"Containers" are another new cloud technology. Containers—a scalable

---

tomer Relationship Management (CRM) product—but many others, including other CRM products, do not. See https://support.rackspace.com/white-paper/understanding-the-cloud-computing-stack-saas-paas-iaas/ accessed February 25, 2017.

10. The Sun Microsystems tagline is attributed to John Gage (Reiss 1996). The discussion in this paragraph draws from Hubbard (2014).

form of virtualization technology—allow users to run and deploy applications without launching a new virtual machine for each application, increasing the speed of software application development, deployment, and scalability. In terms of enterprise applications outside of Silicon Valley, it is still early in the application of containers. Indeed, the technology generally was not widely understood outside cloud vendors until the release of open source LINUX formats (Docker 1.0) in March 2013. Docker transformed container technology to a product for enterprise use. The consultancy IDC estimated that in 2014, only 1 percent of enterprise applications were running on containers that could readily be scaled, but reportedly growth in Docker adoption has been very rapid since then.[11]

One final point of history connects this discussion to the earlier use of commercial time-sharing services. These services were an important part of the computing environment in its earliest days. There was a period of frantic growth (1955–65), after which the industry flourished for another 20 years due to a competitive advantage that "arose from the nonlinear relationship between total operating costs and performance—the larger the time-sharing system, the lower the per-user cost" (Campbell-Kelly and Garcia-Swartz 2008, 27). Commercial time-sharing services underwent a complete industrial boom-to-bust cycle— like typewriters and punched-card machines—after the advent of the PC.[12]

13.3   Prices of Cloud Computing Services

Outside of sporadic media reports and research by some private consultants, relatively little is known about the prices of cloud computing services. This chapter develops new price indexes for three basic products provided by one of the leading providers of cloud services.

13.3.1   Data

We collected prices on a quarterly basis from AWS, the earliest and largest provider. We collected prices from when AWS began posting prices on the internet, with the earliest prices from 2009. To collect historical prices, we used the Internet Archive (also known as the Wayback Machine) to pull posted prices from web pages as they appeared in prior periods. We collected prices for a compute product (renting virtual machines), a selection of database products that offer SQL as well as other database software, and a range of disk storage products.

11. See DataDog (2015). See also Elliot and Perry (2018).
12. According to Campbell-Kelly and Garcia-Swartz (2008), the market for time-sharing existed because it was the only means at that time of providing a personal computing experience at a reasonable cost. They also present econometric evidence showing that the growth of time-sharing services in its heyday slowed down the growth of mainframe computer shipments; see their online appendix.

Of course, the services for which we gathered prices are just a subset of the wide array of services available, and they are at the lower end of the "stack" of cloud products described above. In particular, we place the compute and storage products in the IaaS category, and we place the database products in PaaS. That said, these compute, database, and storage services are key foundational elements on which many of the services that are higher in the stack are based. Accordingly, we believe that the compute, database, and storage products considered in this chapter provide a very useful and broadly representative sample of available cloud services.

AWS has been the market leader and has posted prices on the internet since 2009. Microsoft began posting prices in early 2014, and Google began posting prices in late 2014. We believe that AWS is broadly representative of the market, though future work on prices of other providers is needed to confirm that.

We note one important limitation of our data. We obtained data on prices and product characteristics but not on quantities because cloud service providers do not make product-level sales information readily available. We also were unable to obtain private data on quantities.

13.3.2   Amazon Web Services (AWS)

AWS offers an amazing array of products. One common feature across all products is that customers choose among regions—that is, where the servers are located on which they are running applications and storing data. Currently, AWS offers four regions in the United States, including Virginia, California, Oregon, and Ohio. (Amazon also offers many regions outside the United States.) For this chapter, we collected prices for Virginia, California, and Oregon. (The Ohio region was only introduced in October 2016.) For an AWS customer, choosing a region that is geographically closer reduces latency, and some customers will store data in multiple regions for redundancy. Prices differ across regions, with prices in California generally higher than those in Virginia or Oregon. In general, the differences in prices across regions are in levels, while changes in prices tend to be very similar across regions.

Compute Product (EC2—Elastic Compute Cloud). Using this product amounts to renting a virtual machine (PC or server) from AWS, and this product is priced in terms of dollars per hour. In cloud computing nomenclature, the use of a virtual machine is known as an "instance," and AWS offers instances in a wide range of configurations. During the span of our data from 2009 to 2016, AWS offered 55 different configurations of virtual machines. Each configuration has specified characteristics in terms of the power of the processor, the amount of RAM, and the amount of disk space allocated. In addition, customers can choose between Linux and Windows operating systems. For every available configuration, we collected prices as well as characteristics, and we have a total of 4,079 observations for EC2 prices. The characteristics are important, and we will use them to construct hedonic price indexes.

AWS offers several different pricing schemes for instances. For EC2, we collected data for only "on-demand" instances, which can be purchased at any time with no commitment. AWS also offers "reserved" instances, for which a customer pays in advance for a set volume of instances whether or not the instances are used. Prices of reserved instances are lower than those of on-demand instances. In addition, AWS runs a spot market for instances. Customers can bid for instances at a price of the customers' choosing. The customer will receive the instances if they are available but will not receive them if some other customer offered to pay a higher price for available instances. Prices of spot instances also tend to be below those of on-demand instances. Finally, AWS offers quantity discounts to heavier users.

Tracking prices for all of these different types of instances was beyond the scope of this chapter. For the purpose of constructing price indexes, a key question is whether the price trends for on-demand instances differ in systematic ways from those of other types of instances. Our sense is that prices within these different pricing schemes tend to move together, but that remains an open question. That said, we suspect that *individual* customers experience price declines that are more rapid for a time than are the trends we estimate. In particular, as customers gain experience with AWS and migrate more applications to the cloud, we suspect that they increasingly shift toward reserved instances and avail themselves of quantity discounts. This shift toward lower-priced instances generates faster price declines during the shift than we estimate from tracking prices of on-demand instances. Of course, once a customer has finished the shift toward lower-priced instance types, the trend in prices experienced by that customer likely would be in line with the price trends that we estimate.

Our raw data for EC2 prices are plotted in figure 13.1. This figure plots AWS's posted prices for each instance type for the full time it is in the market, with a different line style capturing each different instance type. In the figure, we show separate plots for each region and operating system pair, with each column of graphs covering a region and each row covering an operating system. The graphs, plotted with a log scale, indicate that prices tend to follow downward step functions, with longish periods of no price change. It also is evident that AWS revamped its offering of instance types around the beginning of 2014, dropping most extant instance types and introducing new ones. Of course the graphs reflect no controls for characteristics or quality of the instances, and as shown below, it turns out that this revamping was associated with a large drop in quality-adjusted prices.

Database Product (RDS—Relational Database Service). Using this product amounts to renting database software along with a virtual machine (called an instance class) to run the software. It is priced in terms of dollars per hour. AWS offers several different database engines, including MySQL,

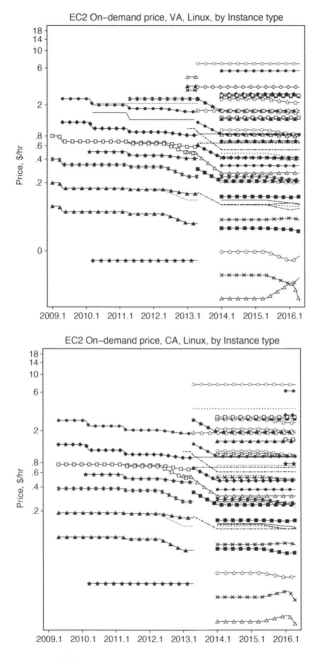

Fig. 13.1 Amazon EC2 posted prices by instance for each region and for Linux and Windows

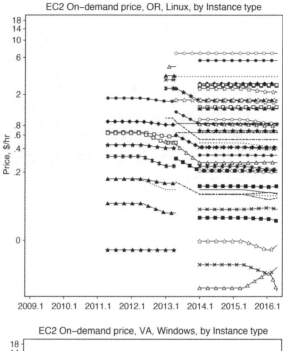

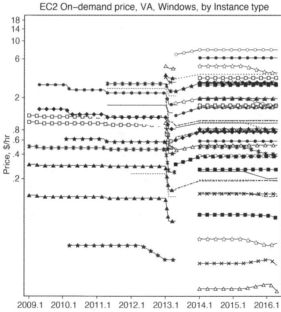

Fig. 13.1   (cont.)

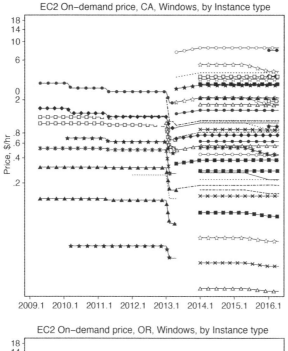

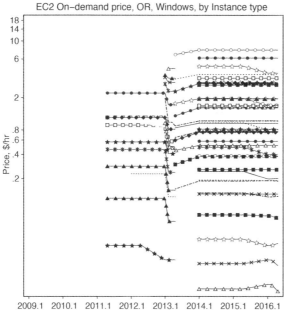

Fig. 13.1   (cont.)

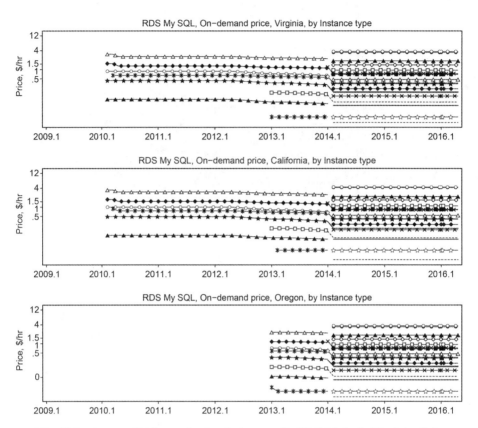

Fig. 13.2   Amazon RDS posted prices by instance for MySQL in the Virginia, California, and Oregon regions

SQL, SQL Standard, SQL Express, SQL Web, SQL Enterprise, PostgreSQL, Oracle, Aurora, and MariaDB. Some of these are open source, while others are proprietary and require a license. For those requiring a license, AWS offers instances for which customers use their own license as well as instances for which AWS provides the license (for a higher price). AWS also offers several different instance classes with differences in the CPU power of the virtual machine, the amount of RAM, network performance, and whether the instance class is optimized for input-output to storage. For every available configuration, we collected prices as well as characteristics for on-demand instances. (AWS also offers reserved instances for its database product.) In total, we have 5,340 observations on RDS prices.

Our raw data for a selection of RDS prices are plotted in figure 13.2. This figure plots AWS's posted prices for each RDS instance type for the MySQL database software for the Virginia, California, and Oregon regions. Because of the multiplicity of types of database software, it is not feasible to plot all our data in a single figure. That said, the data in this figure are broadly representative of those for other regions and database software. The graphs are plotted with a log scale and show the same overall pattern as the EC2 price plots. Prices tend to follow downward step functions, with longish periods of no price change. As with EC2, AWS revamped its offerings around the beginning of 2014, dropping most extant instance types and introducing new ones.

Storage Product (S3—Simple Storage Solution). Using this product amounts to renting hard disk space. It is priced in terms of dollars per terabyte (TB) per month.[13] The pricing scheme for S3 builds in volume discounts directly with pricing tiers. For example, customers pay one price for the first TB used, a lower price for the next 49 TB used, a still lower price for the next 50 TB used, and so on.[14] AWS also offers three different types of storage: "standard" allows immediate access to stored data; "infrequent" access is for longer-term storage, and data can be retrieved only with a delay; and "glacier" storage has an even longer delay for retrieval. As with other AWS products, customers can choose among regions. We collected prices for all pricing tiers, all three types of storage, and the Virginia, California, and Oregon regions. In total, we have 445 observations on S3 prices.

Our raw data for S3 prices are plotted in figure 13.3. This figure plots AWS's posted prices for each price tier for the full time it is in the market for each region and type of storage pair. (Each different price tier is represented by a different line style.) In the figure, each column is for a region, and each row is for a different type of storage (standard, infrequent, and glacier).

13.3.3   Results

The new quality-adjusted price indexes presented here for EC2 (compute) and RDS (database) are based on adjacent-quarter regressions. For S3 (storage), quality does not change appreciably because the product is just a TB of storage, so we rely on matched-model indexes.

To explain our rationale for using adjacent-quarter regressions, we first describe a dummy-variable hedonic specification:[15]

$$(1) \qquad \ln(P_{i,t}) = \alpha + \sum_k \beta_k X_{k,i,t} + \delta_t D_{i,t} + \varepsilon_{i,t},$$

where $P_{i,t}$ is the price of product i in period t, $X_{k,i,t}$ is the value of characteristic k for that product in period t (measured in logs or levels, as appropriate), $D_{i,t}$ is a time dummy variable (fixed effect) that equals 1 if the price i is observed in period t and 0 otherwise, and $\varepsilon_{i,t}$ is an error term.

A potential shortcoming of equation (1), highlighted by Pakes (2003) and

---

13. A terabyte of data is 1,014 gigabytes. The prefix *tera* is from the Greek word for monster.

14. The pricing tiers have changed over time. For example, early on, prices dropped after the first TB of data, while now pricing does not drop until after the first 50 TB of data. This change reflects the ongoing decline in the price of storage.

15. The language used here to describe adjacent-quarter regressions draws heavily from Byrne, Oliner, and Sichel (2018).

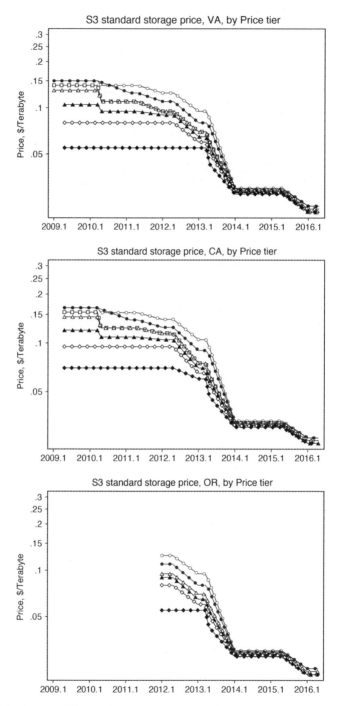

Fig. 13.3   Amazon S3 posted prices by price tier for each region and storage type

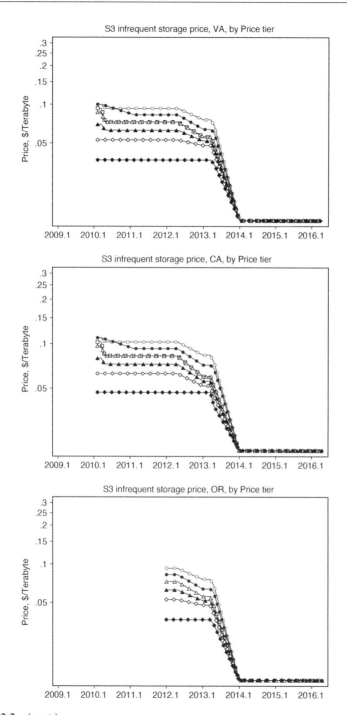

Fig. 13.3   (cont.)

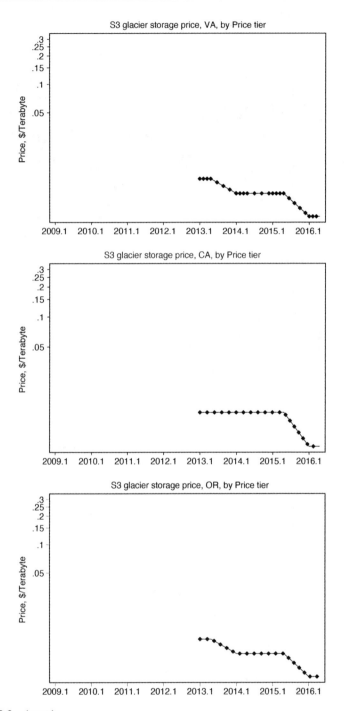

Fig. 13.3   (cont.)

Erickson and Pakes (2011), is that the coefficients on the characteristic are constrained to remain constant over the full sample period. Byrne, Oliner, and Sichel's (2018) study on microprocessors used adjacent-year regression; here, we follow their setup but use adjacent-quarter regressions.

To make things precise, we describe our adjacent-quarter procedure for EC2; the procedure for RDS is parallel. For EC2, we estimate the following regression for each two-quarter overlapping period:

$$(2) \qquad \ln(P_{i,t}) = \alpha + \sum_{k} \beta_k X_{k,i,t} + \delta D_{2t} + \varepsilon_{i,t},$$

where $P_{i,t}$ is the price of EC2 instance of type i in quarter t and $X_{k,i,t}$ is the kth characteristic of instance i in quarter t. The dummy variable D_{2t} equals 1 if the price observation is for the second quarter of the two-quarter overlapping period and 0 otherwise.

To construct a price index from these sequences of regressions, we spliced together the percent changes implied by the estimated coefficients on the D_{2t} variables. All the reported results are bias adjusted to account for the transformation from log prices to a nonlog price index.[16]

Because we do not have quantity data, the adjacent-quarter regressions are unweighted so that each observation receives an equal weight in the regression. This approach is an unfortunate limitation of not having quantity data.

EC2. For the adjacent-quarter regressions for EC2, the following characteristics entered as natural logs: *ECU* (AWS's designation of the power of the processor), *Mem* (the amount of memory in GB), and *Storage* (the amount of disk storage in GB).[17] The regressions also include the following fixed effects: *storSSD* (= 1 if the disk storage is solid state), *pltfrm* (= 1 if the processor is 64 bit; = 0 if the processor is 32 bit), *System* (= 1 if the system is Linux; = 0 for Windows), *inO* (= 1 if the price is for the Oregon region), and *inC* (= 1 if the price is for the California region).

Results of these regressions are summarized in table 13.1. Because of the number of adjacent-quarter regressions, the table summarizes the regression results, showing the minimum, maximum, and median values of coefficient estimates across the regressions.[18] In addition, of the 31 adjacent-quarter

---

16. Because the exponential function is nonlinear, the translation from the natural log of prices to price levels requires an adjustment in order to be unbiased. We apply the standard adjustment based on the estimated variance of the coefficient δ, as described in van Dalen and Bode (2004).

17. In later periods, AWS began charging separately for disk storage for some instances. For these observations, *Storage* is set equal to zero.

18. As is evident in the table (as well as in our adjacent-quarter estimates for other cloud services), some parameters exhibit considerable variation across the adjacent-quarter regressions. Running adjacent-year regressions likely would damp this variation. We chose not to consider adjacent-year regressions for two reasons. First, because prices of these services change infrequently and by large amounts and because new products are introduced infrequently, we wanted

Table 13.1   Amazon EC2 adjacent-quarter regressions, 2009:Q2–2016:Q4 (summary of coefficient estimates across all adjacent-quarter regressions)

	Minimum	Maximum	Median	Fraction significant at 5%	Fraction significant at 10%
D2	−0.329	0.031	0.0	2/31	2/31
ECU	−0.114	0.604	0.212	28/31	29/31
Mem	−0.739	0.85	0.630	31/31	31/31
Storage	−0.66	0.199	−0.067	30/31	31/31
StorSSD	−0.049	0.017	0.0	0/31	10/31
System	−0.444	0	−0.341	29/31	29/31
pltfrm	−0.477	2.103	0.0	10/31	10/31
inO	−0.025	0.038	0.0	0/31	0/31
inC	0.0	0.146	0.127	23/31	24/31
Constant	−5.939	−0.926	−4.616	31/31	31/31

Notes: D2 is the dummy variable for the second quarter of the adjacent-quarter regression. ECU, Mem, and Storage are in natural logs. ECU measures processor power, Mem is the amount of RAM, and Storage is the amount of disk storage. Other variables enter as fixed effects. StorSSD = 1 if solid state storage, System = 1 if operating system is Linux, pltfrm = 1 if the processor is 64 bit, inO = 1 if the region is Oregon, and inC = 1 if the region is California. The omitted categories are the Windows operating system in the Virginia region with magnetic hard drive disk storage and a 32-bit processor.

regressions, the table shows the fraction of the estimates for each coefficient that are significant at the 5 and 10 percent significance levels.

The coefficient on the dummy variable capturing quality-adjusted price change, D2, has a median value of zero, reflecting that prices are not changing in most quarters. The coefficient for the variable for processor power, ECU, generally is positive and highly significant, as prices are higher for instances providing more processor power. The same pattern holds for the memory variable, Mem. The variable for disk storage is almost always significant, though its sign often is negative. Among the fixed effects, solid-state disk storage, StorSSD, has relatively little effect on prices, while instances running with Linux, the System variable, are priced at a hefty discount to instances running with Windows (for which AWS would be paying a license fee). The coefficient on the fixed effect distinguishing between 32- and 64-bit processors (pltfrm) is quite variable across regressions and significant in about a third of the regressions. Prices in the Oregon region, captured by the inO variable, are little different from those in Virginia, while prices in the California region, the inC variable, typically are more than 10 percent higher than prices in Virginia.

Table 13.2 reports the price indexes generated by these regressions as well as the number of observations and adjusted-R^2 for each adjacent-quarter

---

to be able to isolate these periods of change. Second, our quarterly frequency coincides with that in the National Accounts.

Table 13.2   **Amazon EC2 (compute product) price index**

	Price index	Percent change (quarterly rate)	Number of observations	Adjusted R^2
2009: 1	100.00			
2009: 2	100.00	0.0	20	0.996
2009: 3	100.00	0.0	20	0.996
2009: 4	95.29	−4.7	38	0.91
2010: 1	95.29	0.0	56	0.927
2010: 2	95.29	0.0	60	0.926
2010: 3	91.27	−4.2	69	0.955
2010: 4	91.77	0.5	75	0.968
2011: 1	91.77	0.0	76	0.969
2011: 2	91.77	0.0	76	0.969
2011: 3	91.77	0.0	76	0.969
2011: 4	84.92	−7.5	98	0.967
2012: 1	87.71	3.3	126	0.961
2012: 2	88.68	1.1	132	0.96
2012: 3	88.68	0.0	132	0.963
2012: 4	88.68	0.0	132	0.963
2013: 1	82.37	−7.1	156	0.953
2013: 2	77.98	−5.3	182	0.949
2013: 3	77.98	0.0	184	0.974
2013: 4	77.95	0.0	242	0.974
2014: 1	56.15	−28.0	370	0.944
2014: 2	56.15	0.0	440	0.956
2014: 3	56.15	0.0	440	0.956
2014: 4	56.15	0.0	440	0.956
2015: 1	56.15	0.0	440	0.956
2015: 2	56.15	0.0	440	0.956
2015: 3	56.15	0.0	440	0.956
2015: 4	56.15	0.0	440	0.956
2016: 1	48.84	−13.0	518	0.938
2016: 2	48.84	0.0	596	0.936
2016: 3	48.72	−0.2	596	0.936
2016: 4	48.72	0.0	298	0.936
Memo: Avg. at annual rate				
2009:1−2016:4		−6.9		
2009:1−2013:4		−5.1		
2014:1−2016:4		−10.5		

Notes: Based on adjacent-quarter hedonic regression as described in the text. All estimates are bias adjusted to account for the translation from log price to a price index. The last two columns show the number of observations and adjusted R^2s from each of the adjacent-quarter regressions.

regression.[19] The adjusted-R^2s are quite high, indicating that the right-hand-side variables are capturing most of the sources of variation in prices. The price index is shown in the first column, and percent changes at *quarterly*

19. The price trends for EC2 are similar to those reported by Zhang (2016).

rates are reported in the second column. These figures highlight that prices do not change in most quarters. Price declines are large in some quarters, with the biggest drop in the first quarter of 2014, when AWS revamped its offerings of EC2 instances. Although not evident in the plots of posted prices in figure 13.1, the newly offered instances provided much higher quality at prices that were, on their face, roughly comparable to the posted prices of the old offerings of instances. Accordingly, the hedonic regressions identify a very large quality-adjusted price decline in that period.

All told, quality-adjusted prices for EC2 instances fall at an average *annual* rate of about 7 percent over the full sample. Interestingly, prices fell at an annual average rate of about 5 percent from the beginning of 2009 to the end of 2013. Then, in early 2014, just as Microsoft had entered the market to a sufficient degree that they were posting their cloud prices on the internet (and shortly before Google started doing the same), AWS began cutting prices more rapidly. That started with the big price drop in early 2014, and over the period from the start of 2014 to the end of 2016, EC2 prices fell at an average annual rate of 10.5 percent.

RDS. For the adjacent-quarter regressions for RDS, the following characteristics entered as natural logs: *Vcpu* (AWS's designation of the power of the processor) and *Memory* (the amount of memory in GB). The regressions also include the variable *IOPerformance*, which is a qualitative variable indicating whether the network performance is low, moderate, high, or very high. In addition, the regressions include the following fixed effects: *Provisioned IOPS optimized* (= 1 if instance is optimized for input to and output from storage), *inO* (= 1 if the price is for the Oregon region), and *inC* (= 1 if the price is for the California region), a set of fixed effects for each type of database software offered (the omitted category is SQL Standard).

Results of these regressions are summarized in table 13.3. As for the EC2 results, the table summarizes the regression results, showing the minimum, maximum, and median values of coefficient estimates across the regressions. In addition, of the 25 adjacent-quarter regressions, the table shows the fraction of the estimates for each coefficient that are significant at the 5 percent and 10 percent significance levels.

The coefficient on the dummy variable capturing quality-adjusted price change, *D2*, has a median value of zero, reflecting that prices are not changing in most quarters. The coefficient for the variable for processor power, *Vcpu*, generally is positive and relatively significant, as prices are higher for instances providing more processor power. The same pattern holds for the memory variable, *Memory*. The variable *IOPerformance* also is always positive and almost always significant. Among the fixed effects, the variable *Provisioned IOPS optimized* (indicating optimization of storage input/output) is always positive and significant. Just as for EC2, prices in the Oregon region, captured by the *inO* variable, are little different from those in Virginia, while prices in the California region, the *inC* variable, typically are more than 10

Table 13.3   **Amazon RDS adjacent-quarter regressions, 2010:Q3−2016:Q4**
                    (summary of coefficient estimates across all adjacent-quarter regressions)

	Minimum	Maximum	Median	Fraction significant at 5%	Fraction significant at 10%
D2	−0.53	0.01	0.00	5/25	5/25
Vcpu	−0.15	0.22	0.03	16/25	16/25
Memory	0.57	0.74	0.69	25/25	25/25
IOPerformance	0.04	0.35	0.25	24/25	24/25
Provisioned IOPS optimized	0.07	0.22	0.13	25/25	25/25
inC	0.09	0.12	0.11	25/25	25/25
inO	−0.01	0.01	0.00	0/25	0/25
Aurora	−1.31	0.00	0.00	5/25	5/25
MySQL	−1.44	0.00	−1.00	18/25	18/25
Oracle (own license)	−1.43	0.00	−1.00	17/25	17/25
Oracle (AWS provided license)	0.00	0.76	0.37	21/25	21/25
PostgreSQL	−1.38	0.00	0.00	12/25	12/25
SQL (own license)	−1.02	0.00	−0.67	18/25	18/25
SQL express	−1.37	0.00	−0.96	18/25	18/25
SQL web	−0.66	0.00	−0.60	18/25	18/25
MariaDB	−1.44	0.00	0.00	4/25	4/25
Constant	−3.10	−1.99	−2.87	25/25	25/25

Notes: No observations for 2015:Q4 were available in the web archive.

percent higher than prices in Virginia. Among the fixed effects for different database software, most are priced at significant discounts relative to SQL Standard. Oracle is the big exception; if AWS provides the license, Oracle is priced significantly above SQL Standard.

Table 13.4 reports the price indexes generated by these regressions. The adjusted R^2s are quite high, indicating again that the right-hand-side variables are capturing most of the sources of variation in prices. The price index is shown in the first column, and percent changes at quarterly rates are reported in the second column. As for EC2, these figures highlight that prices do not change in most quarters. Price declines are large in some quarters, with the biggest drop at the beginning of 2014, when AWS revamped its offerings.

All told, quality-adjusted prices for RDS instances fall at an average *annual* rate of more than 11 percent over the full sample. Over subperiods, the pattern is the same as that for EC2 prices. Prices fell at an annual average rate of about 3 percent from the beginning of 2009 to the end of 2013. Then, in early 2014, just as Microsoft had entered the market to a sufficient degree that they were posting their cloud prices on the internet, AWS began cutting prices more rapidly. That started with the big price drop in early 2014, and over the period from the start of 2014 to the end of 2016, RDS prices fell at an average annual rate of more than 22 percent.

Table 13.4   Amazon RDS (database product) price index, 2010:Q2–2016:Q4

	Price index	Percent change (quarterly rate)	Number of observations	Adjusted R^2
2010: 2	100.00			
2010: 3	100.00	0.0%	22	0.999
2010: 4	93.73	−6.3%	24	0.997
2011: 1	93.73	0.0%	24	1
2011: 2	93.73	0.0%	44	0.999
2011: 3	93.73	0.0%	64	0.999
2011: 4	93.73	0.0%	64	0.999
2012: 1	93.73	0.0%	64	0.999
2012: 2	93.73	0.0%	133	0.971
2012: 3	93.73	0.0%	202	0.967
2012: 4	93.73	0.0%	202	0.967
2013: 1	87.25	−6.9%	242	0.971
2013: 2	87.19	−0.1%	282	0.976
2013: 3	87.19	0.0%	282	0.976
2013: 4	87.19	0.0%	308	0.978
2014: 1	82.29	−5.6%	420	0.977
2014: 2	48.30	−41.3%	601	0.975
2014: 3	48.30	0.0%	696	0.981
2014: 4	48.30	0.0%	696	0.981
2015: 1	48.30	0.0%	696	0.981
2015: 2	48.30	0.0%	696	0.981
2015: 3	48.55	0.5%	712	0.981
2015: 4	48.55	0.0%		
2016: 1	38.38	−20.9%	1,183	0.983
2016: 2	38.20	−0.5%	1,218	0.985
2016: 3	38.20	0.0%	702	0.984
2016: 4	38.20	0.0%	606	0.983
Memo: Avg. at annual rate				
2010:2–2016:4		−11.6		
2010:2–2013:4		−3.3		
2014:1–2016:4		−22.6		

Notes: Based on adjacent-quarter hedonic regression as described in the text. All estimates are bias adjusted to account for the translation from log price to a price index. The last two columns show the number of observations and adjusted R^2s from the adjacent-quarter regressions. No observations are available for 2015:Q4; we assumed no price change in that quarter.

S3. As noted, quality does not change appreciably over time for S3, the AWS storage product. Accordingly, we construct matched-model indexes by tracking price changes over time for each price tier. Table 13.5 reports the resulting price indexes for each price tier. As for EC2 and RDS, these figures indicate that prices do not change in most quarters. Price declines are large in some quarters, with the biggest drop at the beginning of 2014, as AWS appeared to be responding to a competitive threat from Microsoft (and Google later in the year).

The bottom three lines of the table provide summary figures that are an

Table 13.5   **Amazon S3 (storage product) price indexes, standard storage, Virginia (percent change, quarterly rate)**

				Terabyte (TB) range			
	$s \leq 1$	$1 < s$ ≤ 50	$50 < s$ ≤ 100	$100 < s$ ≤ 500	$500 < s$ $\leq 1K$	$1K < x$ $\leq 5K$	$\geq 5K$
2009: 2	0.0	0.0	0.0	0.0			
2009: 3	0.0	0.0	0.0	0.0			
2009: 4	0.0	0.0	0.0	0.0			
2010: 1	0.0	0.0	0.0	0.0	0.0	0.0	0.0
2010: 2	0.0	0.0	0.0	0.0	0.0	0.0	0.0
2010: 3	0.0	0.0	0.0	0.0	0.0	0.0	0.0
2010: 4	−6.7	0.0	−21.4	−15.4	−9.5	0.0	0.0
2011: 1	0.0	0.0	0.0	0.0	0.0	0.0	0.0
2011: 2	0.0	−16.7	0.0	0.0	0.0	0.0	0.0
2011: 3	0.0	0.0	0.0	0.0	0.0	0.0	0.0
2011: 4	0.0	0.0	0.0	0.0	0.0	0.0	0.0
2012: 1	−10.7	−12.0	−13.6	−13.6	−5.3	0.0	0.0
2012: 2	0.0	0.0	0.0	0.0	0.0	0.0	0.0
2012: 3	0.0	0.0	0.0	0.0	0.0	0.0	0.0
2012: 4	0.0	0.0	0.0	0.0	0.0	0.0	0.0
2013: 1	−24.0	−27.3	−26.3	−26.3	−27.8	−25.0	0.0
2013: 2	0.0	0.0	0.0	0.0	0.0	0.0	0.0
2013: 3	0.0	0.0	0.0	0.0	0.0	0.0	0.0
2013: 4	−10.5	−6.2	−14.3	−14.3	−15.4	−15.0	−21.8
2014: 1	−64.7	−6.7	−51.7	−51.7	−48.2	−45.1	−36.0
2014: 2	0.0	0.0	0.0	0.0	0.0	0.0	0.0
2014: 3	0.0	0.0	0.0	0.0	0.0	0.0	0.0
2014: 4	0.0	0.0	0.0	0.0	0.0	0.0	0.0
2015: 1	0.0	0.0	0.0	0.0	0.0	0.0	0.0
2015: 2	0.0	0.0	0.0	0.0	0.0	0.0	0.0
2015: 3	0.0	0.0	0.0	0.0	0.0	0.0	0.0
2015: 4	0.0	0.0	0.0	0.0	0.0	0.0	0.0
2016: 1	−23.3	−22.0	−24.1	−24.1	−26.3	−25.0	−23.6
2016: 2	0.0	0.0	0.0	0.0	0.0	0.0	0.0
2016: 3	0.0	0.0	0.0	0.0	0.0	0.0	0.0
2016: 4	0.0	0.0	0.0	0.0	0.0	0.0	0.0
Memo: Avg. at annual rate							
2009:1−2016:4	−18.1	−18.7	−19.5	−18.8	−18.9	−15.7	−11.6
2009:1−2013:4	−10.9	−13.1	−15.9	−14.7	−14.5	−10.0	−5.5
2014:1−2016:4	−29.3	−27.6	−25.3	−25.3	−24.8	−23.4	−19.9
2009:1−2016:4 Average across all price tiers	−17.3						
2009:1−2013:4 Average across all price tiers	−12.1						
2014:1−2016:4 Average across all price tiers	−25.1						

Notes: Based on matched-model indexes for each price tier. AWS offered different sets of price tiers in different periods, so not all tiers have entries for every period.

unweighted average of price change across all the price tiers. All told, prices for S3 storage fall at an average *annual* rate of more than 17 percent over the full sample. Over subperiods, the pattern is the same as that for EC2 prices. Prices fell at an annual average rate of about 12 percent from the beginning of 2009 to the end of 2013. Then, in early 2014, just as Microsoft had entered the market to a sufficient degree that they were posting their cloud prices on the internet, AWS began cutting prices more rapidly. That started with the big price drop in early 2014, and over the period from the start of 2014 to the end of 2016, S3 prices fell at an average annual rate of about 25 percent.

13.4   How Big Is the Cloud?

Official revenue data for the cloud services industry and its main products according to nomenclature used in this chapter are not available. Nonetheless, a natural starting point is the Bureau of Economic Analysis (BEA) data on the closest intermediate-use category in the input-output account, 514 (Data Processing, Internet Publishing, and Other Information Services). This category includes data for North American Industry Classification System (NAICS) industry 518200 (Data Processing, Hosting, and Related Services), which subsumes much of the relevant core cloud services activity but includes other information services as well.[20] These data suggest the intensity of business use of purchased cloud services has been rising steadily (figure 13.4a). Because this category of spending is very coarse, it does not highlight the dynamism and explosive growth of cloud services, however. For example, the latest Census revenue data for Data Processing, Hosting, and Related Services (NAICS 518200) grew 8 percent and 10 percent in 2015 and 2016, respectively. While these rates of change are rapid relative to the overall economy, according to Amazon's company reports, AWS revenues grew 70 percent and 55 percent, respectively, in these calendar years.[21]

Using a broader definition of the cloud, Cisco Systems estimates that since emerging in the mid-2000s, the cloud model has rapidly dominated the data center market. Cloud data centers currently account for 90 percent of data center traffic and have accounted for essentially all growth since 2010 (figure 13.5). Indeed, traffic at cloud data centers rose at a 62 percent average annual rate between 2010 and 2016. This concept of cloud data centers, however, also does not correspond directly to the *purchased* services discussed in the previous paragraph for at least three reasons. First, it includes traffic

20. The structure of NAPCS (North American Product Classification System), introduced in 2017, usefully distinguishes among website hosting, data storage services, and so forth but does not distinguish between services provided by traditional data centers and those provided by cloud vendors. See the industry description at "North American Industry Classification System," US Census Bureau, https://www.census.gov/eos/www/naics/index.html, and the NAPCS structure at "North American Product Classification System," US Census Bureau, https://www.census.gov/eos/www/napcs/, both accessed March 5, 2017.

21. Data referred to in this paragraph were accessed September 10, 2018.

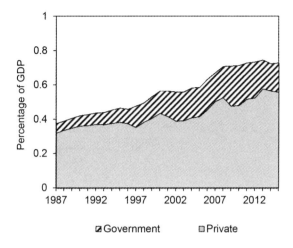

Fig. 13.4a   Intermediate uses of information services, 1987 to 2015

Note: Data processing, hosting, and other information services products, wherever produced (BEA IO product code 514, covering 2002 NAICS 5182, 51913).

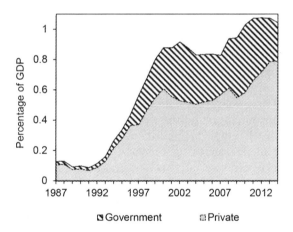

Fig. 13.4b   Intermediate uses of computer and network design services, 1987 to 2015

related to the massive core centers used for "free services"—for example, Google's centers for its Gmail service. Second, Cisco's measure of cloud activity includes traffic at dedicated centers designed but not owned by IT services companies (e.g., IBM Cloud Services). Payments for these services likely are included in the NAICS 541512 (Computer and Network Design Services) industry. Revenues in this industry have grown especially rapidly relative to GDP (figure 13.4b).

Third, the Cisco measures reflect the rise of the "edge" cloud, which has

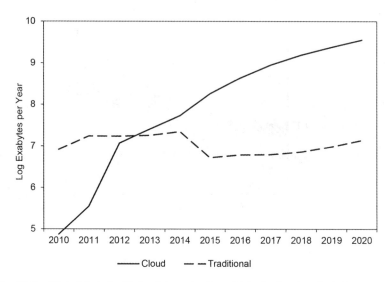

Fig. 13.5   Global data traffic by datacenter type, historical and projected, ratio scale

Source: Cisco Global Cloud Index, Forecast and Methodology, 2015–20 and earlier editions.

a restraining effect on both traffic and underlying business IT costs. A host of new technologies—including the Internet of Things (IoT), augmented and virtual reality, autonomous cars, drones, and smart cities—has led to an explosion in the volume of data that, given current bandwidth, cannot feasibly be transmitted to and from the cloud for processing in real time. Accordingly, this development has led businesses and governments to locate the processing and storage of their massive data collections locally or near the perimeter (i.e., near the "edge") of internet providers networks. Without going into details (but see AT&T 2017), edge computing streamlines the flow of data, transmitting only higher-value data (e.g., data from multiple IoT sources) to a shared central cloud center for further processing and analytic use.

Concurrently, capital expenditures at hyperscale cloud service providers have surged in recent years, rising at an annual rate of 21 percent during 2010 to 2015. Moreover, these expenditures now have reached roughly $50 billion per year, similar in magnitude to capital expenditures at telecom service providers (figure 13.6).[22]

Figure 13.7 shows the importance and rapid growth of the cloud from a different perspective: the share of the world's most powerful computers

22. Cisco classifies a data center operator as hyperscale if they have revenue of $1 billion in Iaas/Paas, $2 billion in SaaS, $4B from internet/search/social networking, or $8 billion from e-commerce / payment processing. Figure 13.6 includes the companies meeting this definition that provide cloud services.

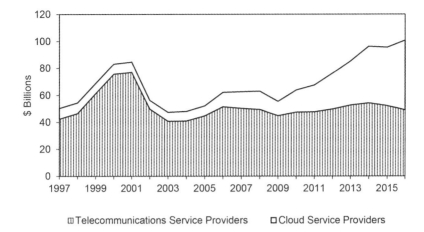

Fig. 13.6   US company capital expenditure   Selected IT service providers
Source: Authors' tabulation of company financial filings.
Note: Included cloud service providers meet Cisco definition of hyperscale. Included telecommunications service providers are AT&T, Verizon, Sprint, T-Mobile US, Century Link, and related companies.

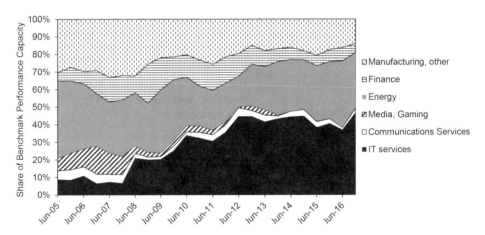

Fig. 13.7   Industrial supercomputer capacity by sector
Source: Top500.com, authors' calculations.

operated by IT service firms leapt from under 10 percent in 2006 to more than 40 percent in 2009 and has persisted at that level since.[23]

And tying back to the discussion of virtualization, IT consultancies com-

---

23. The IT services category is necessarily broader than cloud services because the descriptions of individual supercomputing sites vary in specificity. That being said, some sites are identified as Microsoft Azure and AWS.

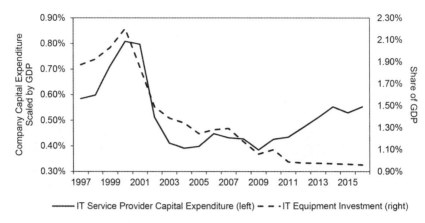

Fig. 13.8   Capital expenditure, selected US IT service providers and NIPA nominal IT equipment investment

Source: Bureau of Economic Analysis. Authors' tabulation of company financial reports.

Note: IT equipment investment includes communications equipment, computers, and peripherals. Included cloud service providers meet Cisco definition of hyperscale. Included telecommunications service providers include AT&T, Verizon, Sprint, T-Mobile US, Century Link, and related companies.

mented in 2008 that server virtualization had become the "killer app" for the business datacenter. Subsequently, IDC estimated that the number of virtual machines (VMs) per server in the United States—an indicator of the application workload of an enterprise server—advanced nearly 12 percent per year from 2007 to 2013 (Byrne and Corrado 2017b).

13.4.1   Where Has All This Investment Gone?

How well does this financial data align with official measures? Mapping company reports to official industry statistics is challenging. Companies providing cloud services provide a host of other IT services as well. Consequently, their establishments undoubtedly are classified to a variety of industries, most notably the industries in NAICS subsectors 511 (Publishing Industries, except Internet [includes Software]), 513 (Broadcasting and Telecommunications), and 519 (Other Information Services).

In light of this wave of investment by cloud service providers, the continuing shift away from IT equipment in business fixed investment in equipment and intangibles may be seen as puzzling. Figure 13.8 plots NIPA nominal IT investment and the capital expenditures figure for cloud service providers from figure 13.6 as shares of GDP. As shown, these two series tracked fairly closely from the mid-1990s through about 2009 as IT investment tailed off as a share of GDP. But after 2009, these series diverged sharply as capital expenditures surged while the series for NIPA IT investment remained sluggish. One possible explanation is the higher utilization that follows as firms outsource IT functions to the cloud. Such an increase in utilization could translate into weaker investment in the short run. Indeed, IDC Inc. reports that the nominal value of sales of servers to US firms fell at an annual average rate of 11 percent from 2004 to 2016, and the decline has accelerated since 2008.

That being said, we also consider another possibility: that cloud services firms have been building their own IT equipment, at least in part.[24] If so, then a portion of the capital expenditures reported above may be for components that have gone into IT equipment built on an own-account basis rather than for already-assembled IT equipment. Google, for example, is reported to have built both computing and network equipment from purchased components.[25] Consistent with this possibility, the "use tables" published by the US Bureau of Economic Analysis indicate that the output of the Computer and Electronics Manufacturing sector (NAICS 334) used by IT services sectors is substantial—$58.6 billion in 2015.[26] At the same time, the "make tables" indicate that these electronic intermediates are not made into final electronics sold by the IT services sector. This suggests that these components are used for own-account production of IT equipment used within the firms.

If this story is correct, this own-account investment should be (but we believe likely is not) counted in the NIPAs as business investment in IT equipment, albeit own-account investment. How much might this own-account investment add up to? For the sake of argument, we assume that the omitted investment value of the own-account production of final electronics is equal to the value of the electronic intermediates used.[27] With this valuation, the story for business investment in IT equipment changes markedly. As seen in figure 13.9, nominal IT equipment and software investment, including our estimate of own-account investment, would be $58 billion higher in 2015 than in the official estimates, amounting to 0.32 percent of GDP. For nominal investment in IT equipment, adding this own-account investment would boost the average annual growth rate during 2007–15 by roughly 2 percentage points compared with official estimates. For nominal GDP growth, including this own-account investment would add three basis points per year to the growth rate during this period.

13.5   Conclusion

We find that cloud computing has exploded. By available measures, the quantity of cloud activity has grown extremely rapidly, as has associated

24. A parallel presentation of own-account investment by cloud service providers appears in Byrne, Corrado, and Sichel (2017).

25. See *Wired* (2015).

26. We treat BEA categories 511, 512, 514, and 5415 as IT services. This group includes industry 518210 mentioned above (in category 514) as well as software publishing, telecom services, and computer design services.

27. We believe this assumption is conservative; although the details of data center server inputs are not available, Gartner Inc. reports that the market value of personal computers is roughly four times the value of electronic inputs.

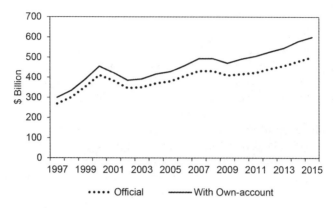

Fig. 13.9   IT equipment and software investment
Source: US Bureau of Economic Analysis, authors' calculations.

capital investment. At the same time, prices of basic cloud services have fallen rapidly since 2009, based on a unique dataset we assembled. However, because cloud is so new and so much of it is intermediate input, it is challenging to track in the statistical system, and the available data do not distinguish between cloud-based and traditional services, whether services are purchased or produced internally or generated at the "edge." We highlight one area where real GDP may be understated by a noticeable amount as a result of changes in the economy related to the rise of cloud computing.

References

AT&T Edge Cloud. 2017. AT&T Labs and AT&T Foundry, white paper. https://about.att.com/content/dam/innovationdocs/Edge_Compute_White_Paper%20FINAL2.pdf.
Avram, Abel. 2016. "FaaS, PaaS, and the Benefits of the Serverless Architecture." *InfoQ*, June 25, https://www.infoq.com/news/2016/06/faas-serverless-architecture.
Bresnahan, Timothy F., and Shane Greenstein. 1999. "Technological Competition and the Structure of the Computer Industry." *Journal of Industrial Economics* 47 (1): 1–40.
Byrne, David M., and Carol A. Corrado. 2017a. "Accounting for Innovation in Consumer Digital Services: Implications for Economic Growth and Consumer Welfare." Paper presented at the 5th IMF Statistical Forum, "Measuring the Digital Economy." IMF Headquarters, Washington, DC, November 16, 2015. http://www.imf.org/~/media/Files/Conferences/2017-stats-forum/carrado.ashx?la=en.
Byrne, David M., and Carol A. Corrado. 2017b. "ICT Prices and ICT Services: What Do They Tell Us about Productivity and Technology?" *International Productivity Monitor* 33 (Fall): 150–81.
Byrne, David M., Carol A. Corrado, and Daniel E. Sichel. 2017. "Own-Account IT Equipment Investment." FEDS Notes, October 4. Washington, DC: Federal Reserve Board. https://www.federalreserve.gov/econres/notes/feds-notes/own-account-it-equipment-investment-20171004.htm.

Byrne, David M., Stephen D. Oliner, and Daniel E. Sichel. 2018. "How Fast Are Semiconductor Prices Falling?" *Review of Income and Wealth* 64 (3): 679–702.

Campbell-Kelly, Martin, and Daniel D. Garcia-Swartz. 2008. "Economic Perspectives on the History of the Computer Time-Sharing Industry, 1965–1985." *IEEE Annals of the History of Computing* 30 (1): 16–36.

Cohen, Robert B. 2017. "Understanding the Next Production Revolution and its Relationship to Software Innovations." Mimeo, Economic Strategy Institute, January 22.

Coyle, Diane, and David Nguyen. 2018. "Cloud Computing and National Accounting." ESCoE Discussion Paper 2018-19, December.

DataDog. 2015. "8 Surprising Facts about Real Docker Adoption." October 2015, last updated June 2016, accessed February 25, 2017. https://www.datadoghq.com /docker-adoption/.

De Roure, David, Mark A. Baker, Nicholas R. Jennings, and Nigel R. Shadbolt. 2003. "The Evolution of the Grid." In *Grid Computing: Making the Global Infrastructure a Reality*, edited by F. Berman, G. C. Fox, and T. Hey, 65–100. Wiley Series in Communications Networking and Distributed Systems. Chichester: John Wiley.

Elliot, Stephen, and Randy Perry. 2018. "Adopting Multicloud: A Fact-Based Blueprint for Reducing Enterprise Business Risks." International Data Corporation White Paper, June.

Erickson, Tim, and Ariel Pakes. 2011. "An Experimental Component Index for the CPI: From Annual Computer Data to Monthly Data on Other Goods." *American Economic Review* 101 (August): 1707–38.

Hubbard, Patrick. 2014. "The Network in the Computer, Again." *Network Computing*, May 6. http://www.networkcomputing.com/cloud-infrastructure/network -computer-again/1827958867.

Kushida, Kenji E., Jonathan Murray, and John Zysman. 2011. "Diffusing the Cloud: Cloud Computing and Implications for Public Policy." *Journal of Industry, Competition and Trade* 11 (3): 209–37.

Kushida, Kenji E., Jonathan Murray, and John Zysman. 2015. "Cloud Computing: From Scarcity to Abundance." *Journal of Industry, Competition and Trade* 15 (1): 5–19.

Mell, Peter, and Timothy Grance. 2011. *The NIST Definition of Cloud Computing*. NIST Special Publication 800-145. http://nvlpubs.nist.gov/nistpubs/Legacy/SP/ nistspecialpublication800-145.pdf.

Murray, Jonathan. 2017. "The Third Wave." *Medium*, December 19. https://medium .com/@adamalthus/the-third-wave-b4ec5380079a.

OECD. 2014. *Addressing the Tax Challenges of the Digital Economy*. OECD/G20 Base Erosion and Profit Shifting Project. Paris: OECD.

Pakes, Ariel. 2003. "A Reconsideration of Hedonic Price Indexes with an Application to PCs." *American Economic Review* 93 (5): 1578–96.

Reiss, Spencer. 1996. "Power to the People." *Wired Magazine*, December 1. https:// www.wired.com/1996/12/esgage/.

van Dalen, Jan, and Ben Bode. 2004. "Estimation Bias in Quality-Adjusted Hedonic Price Indexes." Mimeo, Rotterdam School of Management. http://www.ipeer.ca /papers/vanDalenBodeOct.1,2004,SSHRC%20Paper17.pdf.

Wired. 2015. "Like Google and Facebook, Twitter Designs Its Own Servers." July 9, 2015. https://www.wired.com/2015/07/like-google-facebook-twitter-designs -computer-servers/.

Zhang, Liang. 2016. "Price Trends for Computing Services." Senior Thesis, Wellesley College, May.

BEA Deflators for Information and Communications Technology Goods and Services
Historical Analysis and Future Plans

Erich H. Strassner and David B. Wasshausen

14.1 Introduction

The Bureau of Economic Analysis (BEA) strives to ensure that the price indexes used to construct inflation-adjusted measures in the National Income and Product Accounts (NIPAs) and industry economic accounts (IEAs) accurately capture improvements in quality. The accuracy of BEA's featured measures, including inflation-adjusted (i.e., "real") GDP, consumer spending, and business investment, depends on this important goal. Moreover, it is often the high-profile, innovative goods and services that reflect rapidly changing technologies and notable improvements in quality that garner significant attention from the research community, further highlighting the need for accurate measures. These innovative goods and services are often the subject of important economic studies, including understanding their role in explaining changes in multifactor productivity (MFP).[1]

Erich H. Strassner is associate director for the national economic accounts at the US Bureau of Economic Analysis.

David B. Wasshausen is chief of the expenditure and income division at the US Bureau of Economic Analysis.

Michael Armah, Hussein Charara, Michelle Grier, and Greg Prunchak contributed to this chapter. Special thanks to Ana Aizcorbe for her helpful review and comments, as well as her ongoing efforts to improve Bureau of Economic Analysis (BEA) price deflators. The views expressed in this chapter are solely those of the authors and not necessarily those of the US Bureau of Economic Analysis or the Department of Commerce. For acknowledgments, sources of research support, and disclosure of the authors' material financial relationships, if any, please see https://www.nber.org/books-and-chapters/measuring-and-accounting-innovation-21st-century/bea-deflators-information-and-communications-technology-goods-and-services-historical-analyses-and.

1. Traditionally, the focus has been on ICT equipment, including Byrne and Corrado (2015), Byrne and Corrado (2017a), Byrne and Corrado (2017b), and Byrne, Oliner and Sichel (2017).

BEA has traditionally placed a high value on collaboratively developing and implementing quality-adjusted prices for innovative products, including information and communications technology (ICT) goods and services. This commitment began in the mid-1980s, when BEA first introduced quality-adjusted price indexes for computers and peripheral equipment that had been developed jointly by BEA and IBM. Quality-adjusted prices for semi-conductors were developed and implemented by BEA in the 1990s, followed by the introduction of hedonic, quality-adjusted prices for photocopying equipment developed by BEA in the early 2000s. Also in the early 2000s, BEA began devoting considerable resources to improving the price indexes for purchased custom software and software developed in-house.

With an aim toward facilitating and encouraging further price research, this chapter first provides a historical perspective and an analysis of BEA's ICT prices, including an overview of the sources and methods used to construct BEA's quality-adjusted prices. In the second part of the chapter, we discuss current work and future plans for continuing to ensure the accuracy of BEA's price indexes and corresponding inflation-adjusted measures. The appendix provides an update that assesses recent progress in price measurement as reflected in BEA's 15th comprehensive update of the NIPAs, released July 27, 2018.

14.2   Historical Overview of BEA's ICT Prices

BEA first introduced quality-adjusted price indexes for computers and peripheral equipment into the NIPAs with its eighth comprehensive update, released in December 1985. BEA worked with IBM in a joint effort to develop quality-adjusted price indexes for five types of computing equipment—computer processors, disk drives, printers, displays (terminals), and tape drives.[2] Hedonic methods were used to estimate coefficients (prices) for various characteristics (speed, memory, etc.). Composite price indexes were then constructed using both reported model prices and, for models not sold in the base year, model prices imputed from the characteristics' coefficients. The estimates of the computer deflators covered the period 1972–84, and the indexes were extended back to 1969 using information from other studies of computer prices. Prior to 1969, the deflator was held constant at the 1969 level.

During the 1987 NIPA annual update, a price index for personal computers (PCs) was introduced beginning with 1983. The PC price index was a chained matched-model price index based on IBM PC's, judgmentally

Another important area is software: see, for example, Abel, Berndt, and White (2003) on Microsoft's PC software products and Copeland (2013) on prepackaged software. Others have studied the associated services: Greenstein and McDevitt's (2012) work on broadband services, and Byrne, Corrado and Sichel's (2018) work on cloud computing services.

2. See Cartwright (1986), Cole et al. (1986), and Triplett (1986).

adjusted by BEA to take into account quality changes associated with the introduction of new models and to take into account models of other manufacturers.[3]

In 1991, the Bureau of Labor Statistics (BLS) began publishing quality-adjusted producer price indexes (PPIs) for computers. Soon after, BLS began publishing PPIs for peripheral equipment. As these PPIs became available, they replaced BEA's judgmental indicators and extrapolators for the quarterly NIPA computer price indexes. Eventually, PPIs also replaced BEA's annual quality-adjusted computer price indexes.[4]

In December 1991, BEA released its ninth comprehensive update of the NIPAs, and as part of it, several improvements in the price indexes for computers were incorporated. Among the most important of these improvements was the preparation of a separate price index for imports, which was used in the deflation of imported computers in private fixed investment and in imports of goods. The new index used import weights to combine separate indexes for imported mainframes, imported personal computers, imported printers, and domestic and imported direct access storage devices (DASD) and display terminals. The import price index for PCs was a Paasche chain-type matched-model price index, using prices and quantities from trade sources. The import price indexes for mainframes and printers were derived from existing BEA databases that were separated into imported and domestically produced models. The regression equations were modified to include a dummy variable, which took the value of 1 for imported models and the value of 0 for domestically produced models. Another significant improvement introduced during this revision was to develop separate regression equations and price indexes for four types of printers: serial impact, serial nonimpact, line-fully-formed, and page. In addition, the computer price indexes were extended back to 1959 based on indexes developed in several independent studies.[5]

In January 1996, BEA released its 10th comprehensive update of the NIPAs. With this release, BEA introduced quality-adjusted price indexes for memory and for microprocessor metal-oxide semiconductor integrated circuits (chips) beginning with 1981. The new quality-adjusted semiconductor price indexes were constructed by BEA using different methodologies for memory chips and for microprocessor chips. The price index for memory chips was quality adjusted using the price per bit of data storage capacity and the type of memory chip. Seven types of memory chips were weighted together to produce a summary price index for memory chips. The

3. See Cartwright and Smith (1988) and US Department of Commerce, Bureau of Economic Analysis (1987).

4. The PPIs for computers and peripheral equipment were typically superior to BEA's price indexes because they were available at a much greater frequency, reflected larger samples, and reflected more precise hedonic functions.

5. See Triplett (1989).

price index for microprocessor chips was quality adjusted using a "matched-model" approach. Most of the data used consisted of observed prices from major US manufacturers that BEA purchased from International Dataquest Corporation. Some price data were estimated using hedonic regressions that link chip prices to various performance characteristics.[6]

Also with this release, BEA replaced its previously featured fixed-weighted Laspeyres price measure with a Fisher chain-type price index. This resulted in a significant improvement by minimizing substitution bias not only in aggregate computer price indexes but also in aggregate quantity and price measures, such as gross domestic product and gross domestic purchases.[7] In accordance with the change in the featured measure, Fisher chain-type price indexes for detailed computer price indexes replaced traditional fixed-weighted measures wherever possible.

In October 1999, BEA released its 11th comprehensive update of the NIPAs. With this release, BEA modified the hedonic function used to impute laser printer prices and adopted the Fisher chain-type formula for estimating detailed printer price indexes. Moreover, a key feature of this update was the recognition of business and government expenditures for software as fixed investments. A major requirement of recognizing these expenditures as final demand included the need to develop quality-adjusted price indexes for prepackaged, custom, and "own-account" software.[8] Price indexes were developed for all three components, beginning with 1959, and reflected several different approaches, including hedonic modeling.[9]

In December 2003, BEA released its 12th comprehensive update of the NIPAs, and with this release, BEA introduced a new quality-adjusted price index for photocopying equipment. The new price began with 1992 and used a biennial hedonic regression model in which the natural logarithm of the price of a model of photocopying equipment was regressed on the following independent variables: the natural logarithm of the multicopy speed; quality-characteristic dummy variables for color, capability, multi-functionality, and capacity; and a time dummy variable that takes on the value 1 if the *ith* photocopy model was sold in the second year of the biennial regression datasets.[10]

With the 2003 update, BEA also incorporated an improved price index for investment in own-account and custom software. Previously, the price index for own-account and custom software was a pure input-cost index calculated from a weighted average of compensation rates for computer programmers

6. See Grimm (1998).
7. See Landefeld and Parker (1995).
8. Own-account software consists of in-house expenditures for new or significantly enhanced software created by business enterprises or government units for their own use.
9. See Parker and Grimm (2000).
10. See Moylan and Robinson (2003).

and systems analysts and the costs of intermediate inputs associated with their work; it assumed no changes in productivity. The improved price index was constructed as a weighted average of the percentage changes in the input-cost index (75 percent weight) and the BLS PPI for "prepackaged software applications sold separately" (25 percent weight), which did reflect changes in productivity.

Finally, also as part of the 2003 comprehensive update, BEA fully incorporated a Federal Reserve Board (FRB) price index for local area network equipment that more accurately captured quality improvements than the existing BEA price index. The improved FRB price was first adopted in the 2001 NIPA annual update and was incorporated back to 1992 with this update.[11]

In both the 13th and 14th comprehensive updates of the NIPAs—released in July 2009 and July 2013, respectively—little attention was focused on developing improved price indexes for ICT goods and services.[12] Looking forward and beginning with the 15th comprehensive update of the NIPAs to be released in July 2018, BEA is committed to reinvigorating its efforts to continually seek ways to explicitly improve prices for the types of innovative products that embrace rapidly changing technologies and drive economic growth.

14.3   Current Work and Future Plans

There is a renewed effort within BEA to more actively engage in the development and incorporation of improved price indexes for ICT goods and services, with an aim toward better measuring and accounting for innovation in national accounts statistics. As noted in a recent *Journal of Economic Perspectives* article, BEA has embarked on several initiatives with statistical agency partners as well as academic researchers to leverage alternative data sources to improve the measurement of high-tech goods and services prices.[13] As BEA prepares for its forthcoming comprehensive update of the national accounts, including both the NIPAs and the industry economic accounts (IEAs), there are three areas of focus with respect to improving price indexes: (1) software, (2) electromedical equipment, and (3) communications equipment (including cell phones). Each of these products experiences rapid rates of innovation and is associated with state-of-the-art technologies that present challenges when using standard matched-model techniques to construct quality-adjusted price indexes. In the remainder of

---

11. See Moulton, Seskin, and Sullivan (2001).
12. While price research related to ICT products waned a bit over this period, it is important to note that BEA continued to conduct important price research in other areas, including health care and research and development.
13. See Groshen et al. (2017).

this section, we will discuss plans and preliminary findings for each of these three ICT products, followed by a discussion of where BEA plans to focus next on price index improvement.

14.3.1 Software

Private fixed investment in software was over $350 billion in 2016 and accounts for about 15 percent of all private nonresidential fixed investment. BEA recognizes three types of software, and each presents its own unique set of measurement challenges: (1) prepackaged, (2) custom, and (3) own-account.

As part of the 2017 annual NIPA update, BEA improved the price index used to deflate fixed investment in prepackaged software, beginning with the first quarter of 2014.[14] The improved price index replaced the BLS PPI for "application software publishing" with the broader PPI for "software publishing, except games." The PPI for "software publishing, except games" captures movements in the prices of systems software publishing, which accounts for a large share of total investment spending on prepackaged software, as well as in the prices of application software publishing.[15] As part of the 2018 comprehensive update, BEA will incorporate this improved price index prior to 2014.

Constructing accurate, quality-adjusted price indexes for both custom and own-account software inherently presents challenges due to the very nature of these one-off products. The challenges are further compounded for pricing own-account software because there are no market transactions associated with this type of in-house production. Currently, both price indexes reflect a weighted average of the BEA prepackaged software price index and a BEA input-cost index that is based on BLS data on wage rates for computer programmers and systems analysts and on intermediate input costs associated with the production of software. BEA is actively pursuing data purchases and alternative methodologies that can be used to develop improved prices for these hard-to-measure products. Among them is a database that tracks prices, functionality, and quality of software projects. Here, the functionality is measured using an industry-accepted metric referred to as "function points," which can be used to compute a functional size measurement of a given software application. The database has over 8,000 observations spanning the years 2006–13. BEA is exploring several different techniques, including hedonic modeling, to estimate quality-adjusted prices for custom and own-account software using these data. Heterogeneity in price per function point across the database suggests that function points are not necessarily homogenous and that more does not necessarily mean

14. See McCulla, Khosa, and Ramey (2017).
15. This limitation in the producer price index for "application software publishing" and resultant bias in national accounts statistics was first raised by Byrne and Corrado (2017b).

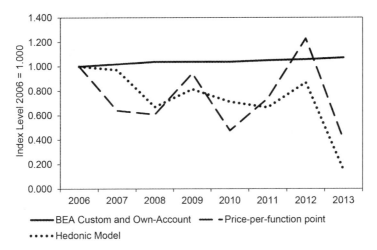

Fig. 14.1   Custom and own-account software price indexes

better. As part of this research, hedonic modeling is used to control for a variety of factors, including client size, client industry, computing platform, maturity of the firm, project type, and project size. Preliminary results indicate average rates of decline in the price index range from about 10 percent to 25 percent compared with the current price index, which shows an average rate of increase of about 1 percent over that same period. The notable range in average annual price declines and volatile behavior of the alternative prices speak to the challenge of estimating accurate price indexes for these products. Figure 14.1 presents the published BEA price index, a price-per-function point price index, and a price index derived using hedonic methods with control variables described above. The figure illustrates overall price trends as well as the volatile nature of these data.

The goal of this ongoing research is to develop an output-based price index or to discover new information that will better inform our current methodology. For example, we are also studying the possibility of introducing an explicit productivity adjustment to the input-cost index. The database described above also includes variables that track hours to complete each of the software projects, and these data may provide valuable insights to productivity trends for custom software development.

14.3.2   Electromedical Equipment

Private fixed investment in electromedical equipment was over $40 billion in 2016 and includes magnetic resonance imaging equipment, ultrasound scanning devices, and CT-scan machinery. These types of medical equipment embody rapid rates of product innovation, much like computers and semiconductors, that can present challenges when using standard matched-model techniques. BEA has completed some preliminary research for selected imaging equipment using data from ECRI, a nonprofit organization that collects data on hospital purchases of equipment. The ECRI database is rich and includes prices and attributes for all types of electromedical machinery. Preliminary results from this research suggest average annual rates of decline for selected electromedical equipment are about 10 percent.

14.3.3 Communications Equipment

In the 2010 NIPA annual update, BEA expanded its use of quality-adjusted price indexes from the FRB industrial production index program to deflate business purchases of three types of communication equipment: telephone switching equipment, carrier line equipment, and wireless networking equipment. (A fourth FRB price index was already being used to deflate data networking equipment.) Looking forward to the 2018 NIPA comprehensive update, including the 2012 Benchmark Input-Output accounts, BEA plans to better align its detailed communication equipment products with more current classifications that are consistent with the FRB's detailed price indexes. Moreover, BEA is currently collaborating with the FRB with an aim toward taking over the preparation of selected FRB communication equipment prices.

BEA is also conducting research on ways to improve its price index for smartphones. In collaboration with others, including researchers from the FRB, BEA completed a pilot study of iPhone prices for the years 2015–16. The pilot used data purchased from JD Power, and BEA has expanded the purchase to include historical data beginning with 2004. Smartphones clearly embody rapid rates of product innovation and are strong candidates for additional price research. Figure 14.2 illustrates the rapid rate of product innovation for selected smartphones since 2008.

14.3.4 What's Next?

As noted at the beginning of this section, there is a renewed effort within BEA to continually engage in the evaluation and development of improved price indexes, especially those for ICT goods and services. In addition to ongoing research for the aforementioned products, BEA is actively identifying priority sectors for exploratory research into the adequacy of current price measures. Several different criteria have guided BEA price research priorities, including the availability of data, the size of the sector, the likelihood of bias, and the extent of existing external research that would make BEA's work duplicative. Several products meet these criteria for BEA's near-term price research, including both wired and wireless telecommunications services, additional medical equipment (nonimaging), medical supplies (e.g., stents), cloud computing, and ride-sharing platform services.

An alternative approach BEA considers when setting its price research agenda is to target goods and services produced and used by "advanced" industries. The identification of "advanced" industries is somewhat subjec-

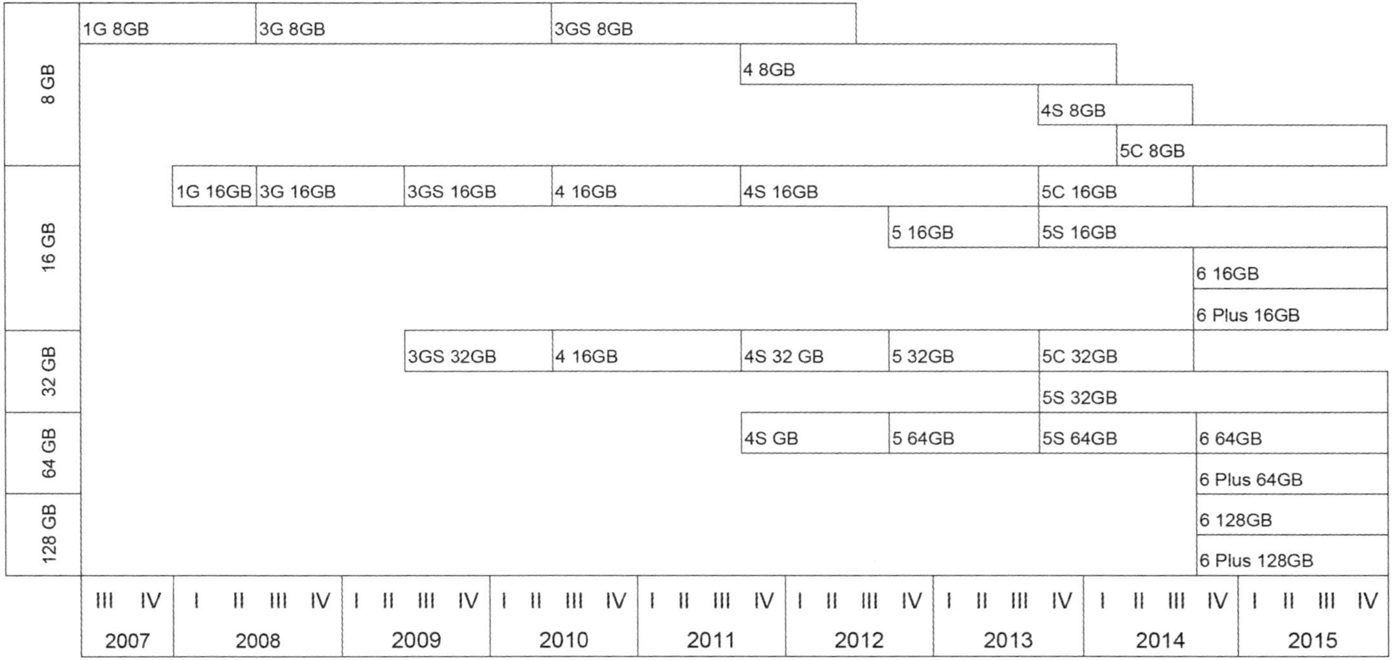
8 GB
1G 8GB
3G 8GB
3GS 8GB
4 8GB
4S 8GB
5C 8GB
16 GB
1G 16GB
3G 16GB
3GS 16GB
4 16GB
4S 16GB
5C 16GB
5 16GB
5S 16GB
6 16GB
6 Plus 16GB
32 GB
3GS 32GB
4 16GB
4S 32 GB
5 32GB
5C 32GB
5S 32GB
64 GB
4S GB
5 64GB
5S 64GB
6 64GB
6 Plus 64GB
128 GB
6 128GB
6 Plus 128GB
III IV I II III IV I II III IV I II III IV I II III IV I II III IV I II III IV I II III IV I II III IV
2007
2008
2009
2010
2011
2012
2013
2014
2015

Fig. 14.2 Apple iPhone launches
Source: Yadav (2014).

tive; however, there are metrics that are common across a number of studies. For example, a 2015 Brookings report examines an industry's R&D spending per worker as well as the share of workers in an industry whose occupations require a high degree of STEM (science, technology, engineering, and math) knowledge.[16]

While the definition of "advanced" industries may not be precise, the basic idea of focusing research on industries with relatively high R&D spending and STEM knowledge is to hone in on those industries that are more likely than others to be engaged in the production and/or usage of hard-to-measure, rapidly changing goods and services. It is important to emphasize that these industries need not solely be the producers of such goods and services to receive BEA attention but could also be users of such goods and services. This is an important qualification because a growing share of sophisticated goods and services is being imported and used by US industries, and the prices for these goods and services impact measured real imports and measured real value added at the industry level.[17]

The advent of smartphones and the rapidly changing technologies that underlie their production and usage illustrate this challenge. For example, the underlying research and development embodied in the iPhone is largely produced domestically, whereas the actual manufacturing of the iPhone occurs outside of the United States. As noted previously, BEA is conducting research on ways to improve its price index for smartphones, and any improvement in the price index for smartphones would necessarily be reflected in all relevant components of GDP, including fixed investment, personal consumption, and imports of goods. Under this alternative approach targeting "advanced" industries, additional attention may also be given to developing improved price indexes for the private fixed investment in the research and development devoted to the production of that smartphone. Finally, focusing on "advanced" industries identifies private-sector production of high-tech equipment that is purchased not only by the private sector but also by the government, including military aircraft, weapons, instruments, and communications equipment.

14.4 Conclusion

BEA has a rich history of developing quality-adjusted price indexes for various types of information and communications technology goods and services. Most, if not all, of these products embody the innovative spirit with which we strive to accurately measure in BEA's national accounts statistics. These products often present significant measurement challenges

---

16. See Muro et al. (2015).
17. See Samuels et al. (2015) for a discussion of how imports and import prices affect estimates of industry growth and productivity.

when using traditional approaches, especially when they are required to be produced at high frequencies. As Groshen et al. (2007) note, "The task of calculating price indexes and output in the 21st century, and doing so in a way that provide timely monthly data within budget constraints, is not for the rigid or the fainthearted."

BEA will continue to tackle these types of challenging products using a variety of source data and methods, including hedonic modeling, matched-model, and fixed-effect regressions. The required source data are often not sufficiently available at high monthly frequencies and instead may only be available annually. In these cases, BEA will first construct "best" annual price indexes and then force the higher-frequency monthly price indexes to conform with that "best" annual price index. While we recognize that this is not always feasible for all statistical programs, we believe these alternative approaches should be more widely considered.

Appendix
Results from the 2018 Comprehensive Update

On July 27, 2018, the BEA released the initial results of the 15th comprehensive update of the NIPA. The incorporation of improved price measures for ICT goods and services was an important feature of this comprehensive update, and in this appendix, we present those results and assess overall progress toward incorporating improved ICT deflators into BEA's national accounts statistics.

14.A1   Software

The BEA price index for prepackaged software was improved to reflect the use of a more appropriate PPI. This improvement was first introduced in the 2017 annual NIPA update beginning with 2014, and with this comprehensive update, that improvement has been carried back to 2007.[18] Over the period 2007–17, the revised BEA prepackaged software price index shows an average annual rate of decline of 3.6 percent compared with a decline of 2.6 percent in the previously published material. Figure 14.3 presents the revised and previously published price indexes for private fixed investment in prepackaged software.

The revised BEA price indexes for custom and own-account software reflect, for the first time, an explicit adjustment to account for changes in productivity to the input-cost index component. These price indexes con-

18. See McCulla, Khosa, and Ramey (2017).

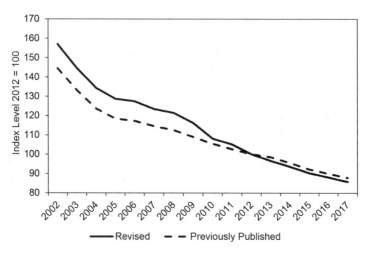

tinue to be estimated using a weighted average of the BEA prepackaged software price index and a BEA input-cost index that is based on BLS data on wage rates for computer programmers and systems analysts and on intermediate-input costs associated with the production of software. While the prepackaged software price reflects actual market prices and therefore captures changes in productivity, the input-cost index did not, and therefore BEA implemented an explicit productivity adjustment beginning with 1997. The adjustment reflects estimates for MFP for private nonfarm business published by the BLS as well as research conducted by BEA using reports from academic, commercial, and public sources. For 1997–2006, the trends in the BLS MFP for private nonfarm business were largely consistent with the trends derived by BEA using private data that included information on prices, functionality, size, and hours required to complete a given custom software project. Over this period, the productivity adjustment to the BEA input-cost index is about 1.5 percentage points per year. For 2007 forward, productivity trends for the creation of custom software derived by BEA showed slightly larger gains than the published BLS MFP for nonfarm private business. Deviations in trend between these two independent measures are neither surprising nor problematic because they are measuring different things. The productivity adjustment applied by BEA over this period reflects a judgmental combination of these two measures and was, on average, 0.8 percentage point. A combination of the internal BEA-derived custom-software productivity measure and the broader BLS MFP measure was chosen, reflecting the imprecise and conservative nature of this adjustment. Figure 14.4 presents the major components of the BEA input-cost index as well as the input-cost index with and without the productivity adjustment. The figure illustrates the overall effect of the adjustment as well as the fact that the adjustment is not applied to the components; rather, it is

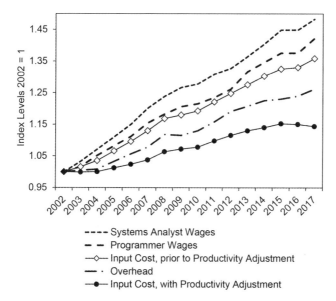

Fig. 14.4   BEA input-cost indexes for custom and own-account software

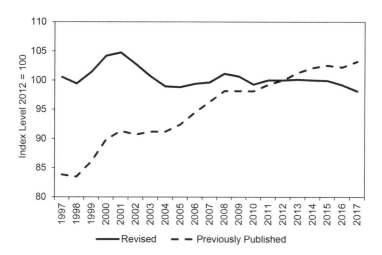

Fig. 14.5   Price indexes for private fixed investment in custom and own-account software

only applied to the aggregate input-cost index. Over the period 1997–2017, the revised BEA custom and own-account software price indexes show an average annual rate of decline of 0.1 percent compared with an increase of 1.0 percent in the previously published material. Figure 14.5 presents the revised and previously published price indexes for private fixed investment in custom and own-account software.

Although a significant amount of BEA resources were invested in developing a new, output-based price index for custom and own-account software, BEA was unable to produce a reliably stable price measure. While the available data included thousands of observations and dozens of valuable software characteristics, the resultant indexes were simply too volatile to trust. Dozens of models were tested, including pooled, biennial, and fixed-effects regressions. Some of these models yielded promising statistical results; however, more research and more data are required in order to develop accurate price indexes required for BEA's national accounts statistics.

14.A2   Electromedical Equipment

BEA introduced newly developed annual estimates of quality-adjusted price indexes for selected components of electromedical equipment, including magnetic resonance imaging equipment, ultrasound scanning devices, and CT-scan machinery. These types of medical equipment embody rapid rates of product innovation that can present challenges when using standard matched-model techniques. The new annual price indexes were developed using data from ECRI that included information on purchases of medical equipment by health care providers and were constructed using a (weighted) fixed-effects regressions model that yielded similar results to those derived using a matched-model approach. The estimated prices from the fixed-effects regressions were chosen over those from the matched model because the fixed-effect regressions were able to better handle some of the volatile transaction-level data and, as a result, were a bit smoother.[19]

These new price indexes better account for changes in product quality than the previously used price indexes, which were based on monthly PPIs and monthly international price indexes (IPIs). The improved price indexes were incorporated beginning with 2002 and are used to deflate annual private fixed investment and exports and imports of electromedical equipment. The previously used PPIs and IPIs will be used in conjunction with the newly developed annual indexes to estimate the higher-frequency quarterly prices. Over the period 2002–17, the revised BEA price index for private fixed investment in electromedical equipment decreases 4.7 percent at an average annual rate; the previously published price index decreased 0.4 percent. Figure 14.6 presents revised and previously published price indexes for private fixed investment in electromedical equipment.

14.A3   Communication Equipment

BEA price indexes for communication equipment were updated, reflecting the incorporation of the revised and newly available FRB communica-

---

19. Ana Aizcorbe, a senior researcher with BEA, developed these new and improved electromedical equipment price indexes. Additional details regarding these indexes will be published separately at a later date.

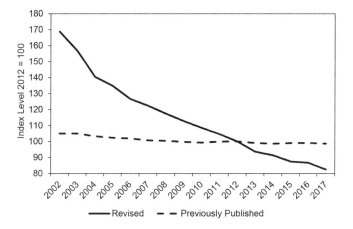

Fig. 14.6   Price indexes for private fixed investment in electromedical equipment

tion equipment price index.[20] In addition to the traditional communication equipment price indexes BEA uses from the FRB, a newly developed price index for smartphones was incorporated for the first time beginning with 2002. This newly available price index will be used to deflate consumer spending, private fixed investment, and imports of cellular phones. Previously, cellular phones were not separately deflated in any of these final demand categories and instead were deflated as part of aggregated series that included cellular telephones. These aggregated series were deflated using FRB prices, PPIs, IPIs, and consumer price indexes (CPIs) that implicitly included cellular phones. Beginning with January 2018, BLS introduced explicit quality adjustments for smartphones using hedonic modeling methods. Although a separate category for smartphones is not published as part of BLS's CPI program, these quality-adjusted prices for smartphones are reflected in the published CPI for "telephone hardware, calculators and other consumer information items." Within this category, cellular phones account for approximately half of the sample.[21] BEA plans to carefully study this improved CPI with an aim toward better understanding the underlying changes in the prices for smartphones.

In addition to incorporating revised and newly available FRB price indexes, the detailed commodity structure that underlies private fixed investment in communication equipment was updated to reflect benchmarking to BEA's 2012 Supply-Use tables, which in turn are based on newly incorporated detailed data from the 2012 Economic Census. Table 14.1 shows the

20. For details, see "Quality-Adjusted Price Indexes for Communications Equipment," June 1, 2018, Federal Reserve Board's Industrial Production and Capacity Utilization-G.17, https://www.federalreserve.gov/releases/g17/commequip_price_indexes.htm.

21. For more information, see the Consumer Price Index factsheet for telephone hardware, calculators, and other consumer information items on the BLS website (https://www.bls.gov/cpi/factsheets/telephone-hardware.htm).

Table 14.1   Private fixed investment in communications equipment

Line	Description	Deflation level[a]	2012 current-dollar investment level[b]	Old deflator description	New deflator description
1	Communication equipment		104,789		Blank indicates no change
2	Communications equipment—imports		56,239		
3	Telephone and telegraph wire and cable	x	319	BLS IPI for telecommunication equipment	
6	Television receivers	x	10,930	BLS IPI for home entertainment equipment	
7	Consumer high-fidelity components	x	817		
9	Telephone switching and switchboard equipment	x	868	FRB enterprise voice equipment	
10	Telephone and telegraph wire apparatus		3,175		
11	Data communication apparatus	x	232	FRB data networking equipment	
12	Other telephone and telegraph wire apparatus	x	2,943	FRB transmission equipment	
13	Communication equipment, ex. broadcast	x	36,291	FRB wireless networking equipment	Weighted composite of FRB cellular phones and FRB wireless networking equipment price indexes
14	*Radio station equipment*		*17,569*		
15	***Cellular handsets—cell phones***		***7,406***		
16	*Antenna systems, sold separately*		*260*		
17	*Other communication systems and equipment*		*2,328*		
18	*Wireless networking equipment*		*8,727*		
20	Broadcast-related equipment	x	2,700	BLS IPI for telecommunication equipment	
21	Intercommunication equipment	x	27		
22	Search, detection, and navigation equipment	x	1,113	BLS IPI for scientific and medical machinery	
23					
24	Communications equipment—domestic		48,550		
25	Other services on missiles + space vehicles	x	310	BLS PPI for civilian aircraft	
26	Telephone and telegraph wire and cable	x	2	BLS PPI for copper wire and cable	

30	Consumer high-fidelity components	x	10	BLS PPI for speakers and commercial sound equipment
32	Telephone switching and switchboard equipment	x	1,481	FRB enterprise voice equipment
33	Telephone and telegraph wire apparatus	x	4,194	FRB data networking equipment
34	Data communication apparatus	x	207	FRB transmission equipment
35	Other telephone and telegraph wire apparatus	x	3,987	
36	Force account, tel. equipment installation	x	7,155	BLS average weekly earnings of building equipment contractors
37	Industrial process design	x	5,774	BLS PPI for engineering services
39	Used communication equipment	x	54	BLS PPI for communications equipment mfg
40	Communication equipment, ex. broadcast	x	9,764	FRB wireless networking equipment
41	*Radio station equipment*		*1,979*	
42	***Cellular handsets—cell phones***		***375***	Weighted composite of FRB cellular phones and FRB wireless networking equipment price indexes
43	*Antenna systems, sold separately*		*467*	
44	*Other communication systems and equipment*		*4,622*	
45	*Wireless networking equipment*		*472*	
46	*Radio and TV broadcasting and wireless equipment, nsk*		*1,848*	
47	Broadcast-related equipment	x	2,290	BLS PPI for broadcast, studio, and related electronic equipment
48	Intercommunication equipment	x	1,040	BLS PPI for communications equipment mfg
49	Search, detection and navigation equipment	x	16,478	BLS PPI for search, detection, navigation, and guidance systems and equipment

Notes: PPI: Producer Price Index; IPI: Import Price Index; FRB: Federal Reserve Board; I-O: BEA Input-Output Accounts; BLS: Bureau of Labor Statistics. The values presented in this table are preliminary and subject to change.

a x indicates the level at which deflation occurs.

b BEA's benchmarked 2012 supply-use tables were not yet published at the time of this chapter's submission.

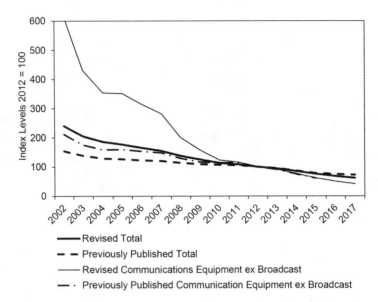

Fig. 14.7   **Price indexes for private fixed investment in communications equipment**

detailed commodity structure, including the nominal values that underlie the inflation-adjusted measures. Table 14.1 also presents descriptions of the detailed price indexes used to deflate communication equipment, including how the newly introduced smartphone price index was incorporated. Overall, private fixed investment in communication equipment was revised to $16.3 billion from $104.8 billion (table 14.1, line 1). The leading contributor to the upward revision was both imported and domestically produced "communication equipment ex. broadcast" (table 14.1, lines 13 and 40, respectively). Over the period 2002–15, the composite price index, including the new smartphone price index, used to deflate this category declines at an average annual rate of about 16 percent; the previously published corresponding price declined at an average annual rate of about 9 percent. Over the period 2002–17, the revised BEA price index for private fixed investment in communication equipment decreases 8.6 percent at an average annual rate; the previously published price index decreased 4.9 percent. Figure 14.7 presents revised and previously published price indexes for private fixed investment in communications equipment as well as the component "communication equipment ex. broadcast."

References

Abel, Jaison R., Ernst R. Berndt, and Alan G. White. 2003. "Price Indexes for Microsoft's Personal Computer Software Products." NBER Working Paper No. 9966. Cambridge, MA: National Bureau of Economic Research.

Byrne, David M., and Carol A. Corrado. 2015. "Prices for Communications Equipment: Rewriting the Record." Finance and Economics Discussion Series 2015-069. Washington, DC: Board of Governors of the Federal Reserve System.

Byrne, David M., and Carol A. Corrado. 2017a. "Accounting for Innovation in Consumer Digital Services: Impacts on GDP and Consumer Welfare." Paper presented at the NBER/CRIW conference Measuring and Accounting for Innovation in the 21st Century, Washington, DC, March 10–11.

Byrne, David M., and Carol A. Corrado. 2017b. "ICT Prices and ICT Services: What Do They Tell Us about Productivity and Technology?" Finance and Economics Discussion Series 2017-015. Washington, DC: Board of Governors of the Federal Reserve System. https://doi.org/10.17016/FEDS.2017.015.

Byrne, David M., Carol A. Corrado, and Daniel E. Sichel. 2018. "The Rise of Cloud Computing: Minding Your Ps, Qs and Ks." NBER Working Paper No. 25188. Cambridge, MA: National Bureau of Economic Research.

Byrne, David M., Stephen D. Oliner, and Daniel E. Sichel. 2017. "How Fast Are Semiconductor Prices Falling?" FEDS working paper 2017-005, January.

Cartwright, D. W. 1986. "Improved Deflation of Purchases of Computers." *Survey of Current Business*, March, 7–9.

Cartwright, D. W., and Scott D. Smith. 1988. "Deflators for Purchases of Computers in GNP: Revised and Extended Estimates, 1983–88." *Survey of Current Business*, November, 22–23.

Cole, R., Y. C. Chen, J. Barquin-Stolleman, E. Dulberger, N. Helvacian, and J. H. Hodge. 1986. "Quality-Adjusted Price Indexes for Computer Processors and Selected Peripheral Equipment." *Survey of Current Business*, January, 41–50.

Copeland, Adam. 2013. "Seasonality, Consumer Heterogeneity and Price Indexes: The Case of Prepackaged Software." *Journal of Productivity Analysis* 39 (1): 47–59.

Greenstein, Shane, and Ryan McDevitt. 2012. "Measuring the Broadband Bonus in 20 OECD Countries." OECD Digital Economy Papers No. 197, April. Paris: OECD.

Grimm, Bruce T. 1998. "Price Indexes for Selected Semiconductors, 1974–96." *Survey of Current Business*, February, 8–24.

Groshen, Erica L., Brian C. Moyer, Ana M. Aizcorbe, Ralph Bradley, and David M. Friedman. 2017. "How Government Statistics Adjust for Potential Biases from Quality Change and New Goods in an Age of Digital Technologies: A View from the Trenches." *Journal of Economic Perspectives* 31 (2): 187–210.

Landefeld, J. S., and Robert P. Parker. 1995. "Preview of the Comprehensive Revision of the National Income and Product Accounts: BEA's New Featured Measures of Output and Prices." *Survey of Current Business*, July, 31–38.

McCulla, Stephanie H., Vijay Khosa, and Kelly Ramey. 2017. "The 2017 Annual Update of the National Income and Product Accounts." *Survey of Current Business*, August, 1–32.

Moulton, Brent R., Eugene P. Seskin, and David F. Sullivan. 2001. "Annual Revision of the National Income and Product Accounts Annual Estimates." *Survey of Current Business*, August, 7–32.

Moylan, Carol E., and Brooks B. Robinson. 2003. "Preview of the 2003 Comprehensive Revision of the National Income and Product Accounts: Statistical Changes." *Survey of Current Business*, September, 17–32.

Muro, Mark, Jonathan Rothwell, Scott Andes, Kenan Fikri, and Siddharth Kulkarni. 2015. "America's Advanced Industries: What They Are, Where They Are, and Why They Matter." Brookings Report, February. https://www.brookings.edu/wp-content/uploads/2015/02/AdvancedIndustry_FinalFeb2lores-1.pdf.

Parker, Robert P., and Bruce T. Grimm. 2000. "Recognition of Business and Government Expenditures for Software as Investment: Methodology and Quantitative

Impacts, 1959–98." BEA paper, May. https://www.bea.gov/system/files/papers/P2000-2.pdf.

Samuels, Jon D., Thomas F. Howells III, Matthew Russell, and Erich H. Strassner. 2015. "Import Allocation across Industries, Import Prices across Countries, and Estimates of Industry Growth and Productivity." In *Measuring Globalization: Better Trade Statistics for Better Policy*. Vol. 1, *Biases to Price, Output, and Productivity Statistics from Trade*, edited by Susan N. Houseman and Michael Mandel, 251–92. Kalamazoo, MI: W. E. Upjohn Institute for Employment Research. https://doi.org/10.17848/9780880994903.vol1ch8.

Triplett, J. E. 1986. "Economic Interpretation of Hedonic Models." *Survey of Current Business*, January, 36–40.

Triplett, J. E. 1989. "Price and Technological Change in a Capital Good: A Survey of Research on Computers." In *Technology and Capital Formation*, edited by D. W. Jorgenson and R. Landau, 127–213. Cambridge, MA: MIT Press.

US Department of Commerce, Bureau of Economic Analysis. 1987. "The U.S. National Income and Product Accounts: Revised Estimates." *Survey of Current Business*, July, 15.

Yadav, S. 2014. "Apple iPhone 5S, 5C Still High in Demand Post iPhone 6 Launch." DazeInfoBriefs, October 7, 2014. https://dazeinfo.com/2014/10/07/apple-inc-aapl-iphone-5s-5c-price-offers-deals-iphone-6-market-us-uk/.

Contributors

Katharine G. Abraham
Department of Economics and Joint
  Program in Survey Methodology
University of Maryland
1218 LeFrak Hall
College Park, MD 20742

David Byrne
Federal Reserve Board
20th and Constitution Avenue, NW
Washington, DC 20551

Wen Chen
Institute of New Structural Economics
Peking University
Peking University Science Park 203
Haidian District
Beijing, China 100080

Wesley M. Cohen
The Fuqua School of Business
Duke University
Box 90120
Durham, NC 27708-0120

Carol Corrado
The Conference Board
845 Third Avenue
New York, NY 10022-6679

Emin M. Dinlersoz
Center for Economic Studies
US Census Bureau
4600 Silver Hill Road
Washington, DC 20233

Kenneth Flamm
Lyndon B. Johnson School of Public
  Affairs
SRH 3.227, P.O. Box Y
University of Texas
Austin, TX 78713-8925

Lucia Foster
Center for Economic Studies
US Census Bureau
4600 Silver Hill Road
Washington, DC 20233-6300

Nathan Goldschlag
Center for Economic Studies
US Census Bureau
4600 Silver Hill Road
Washington, DC 20233-6300

Cheryl Grim
Center for Economic Studies
US Census Bureau
4600 Silver Hill Road
Washington, DC 20233-6300

Dominique Guellec
Observatoire des Sciences et
   Techniques
2, rue Albert Einstein
75013 Paris France

John C. Haltiwanger
Department of Economics
University of Maryland
College Park, MD 20742

Jonathan Haskel
Imperial College Business School
Tanaka Building, Room 296
London SW7 2AZ United Kingdom

Charles Hulten
Department of Economics
University of Maryland
Room 3114, Tydings Hall
College Park, MD 20742

Ron Jarmin
US Census Bureau
4600 Silver Hill Road
Washington, DC 20233

Julia Lane
Wagner School of Public Service and
   CUSP
New York University
295 Lafayette Street
New York, NY 10012-9604

You-Na Lee
Lee Kuan Yew School of Public Policy
National University of Singapore
469C Bukit Timah Road
Singapore 259772

Bart Los
Faculty of Economics and Business
Groningen Growth and Development
   Centre
University of Groningen
9700 AV Groningen, The Netherlands

Javier Miranda
Economy-Wide Statistics Division
US Census Bureau
4600 Silver Hill Road
Washington, DC 20233

Pierre Mohnen
UNU-MERIT
Maastricht University
P.O. Box 616
6200 MD Maastricht, The Netherlands

Amanda Myers
US Patent and Trademark Office
600 Dulany Street
Alexandria, VA 22314

Leonard I. Nakamura
Economic Research
Federal Reserve Bank of Philadelphia
10 Independence Mall
Philadelphia, PA 19106-1574

Michael Polder
CBS/Statistics Netherlands
P.O. Box 24500
2490 HA The Hague, The Netherlands

Kristin Sandusky
Center for Economic Studies
US Census Bureau
4600 Silver Hill Road
Washington, DC 20233

Daniel Sichel
Department of Economics
Wellesley College
106 Central Street
Wellesley, MA 02481

James R. Spletzer
Center for Economic Studies
US Census Bureau
4600 Silver Hill Road
Washington, DC 20233

Erich H. Strassner
Bureau of Economic Analysis
4600 Silver Hill Road
Washington, DC 20233

Marcel P. Timmer
Faculty of Economics and Business
Groningen Growth and Development
   Centre
University of Groningen
9700 AV Groningen, The Netherlands

George van Leeuwen
CBS/Statistics Netherlands
P.O. Box 24500
2490 HA The Hague, The Netherlands

John P. Walsh
School of Public Policy
Georgia Institute of Technology
685 Cherry Street
Atlanta, GA 30332-0345

David B. Wasshausen
Bureau of Economic Analysis
4600 Silver Hill Road
Washington, DC 20233

Zoltan Wolf
Westat
1600 Research Boulevard
Rockville, MD 20850

Nikolas Zolas
Center for Economic Studies
US Census Bureau
4600 Silver Hill Road
Washington, DC 20233

Author Index

Note: Page numbers followed by "f" or "t" refer to figures or tables, respectively.

Abel, J. R., 42, 554n1
Aboal, D., 302
Abowd, J. M., 233, 234, 241
Abraham, K. G., 257, 259, 273, 282, 283, 289
Abramovitz, M., 38
Abrigo, M. R. M., 129n19
Acemoglu, D., 104, 123, 124, 125, 229, 232, 344
Adner, R., 148
Aghion, P., 328, 343, 360
Aguiar, L., 49
Aizcorbe, A., 406n4, 409n14, 420n44, 420n46, 437, 508, 513
Akcigit, U., 231
Allcott, H., 50
Alvarez-Cuadrado, F., 346n4
Amaya, A., 283
Anderson, M., 33n9
Andersson, F., 35
Andrews, D., 105, 105n4
Aoshima, Y., 149
Arora, A., 61, 62, 65, 144, 145, 151, 152n6, 155n13, 155t, 172, 173n23, 173t, 174, 178, 190
Athey, S., 303, 306
Atkinson, A. B., 344
Audretsch, D. B., 229, 231
Autor, D., 327, 344, 351, 360
Awano, G., 127

Baba, Y., 150
Baily, M. N., 105n2
Baird, M. D., 280
Bakija, J., 271, 353
Bania, N., 231
Barkai, S., 344, 351, 373, 373n1, 390, 392
Barker, K., 257
Baroncelli, E., 187, 188
Bartelsman, E. J., 105n2, 108, 302, 304, 316
Barth, E., 233
Bas, M., 341f, 345, 346f, 347f, 348f, 354, 354f, 355f, 356, 358f, 359, 366
Bassanini, A., 351
Behar, C. T., 299
Behrens, D. M., 62n2, 77, 141
Bei, X., 190
Bell, A., 70
Bell, M. A., 126n18
Bender, S., 229, 231
Bernard, A. B., 374
Berndt, E. R., 39, 42, 52, 481, 498, 554n1
Bhandari, A., 385n10, 391
Biagi, F., 301
Bils, M., 42, 46
Black, R., 447n83
Black, S. E., 232, 301
Blair, P. D., 380n7
Block, J., 189
Bloom, N., 107, 107nf6, 129, 229, 231, 233
Bode, B., 537n16

Bohr, M., 445n78
Bonnet, O., 351
Bosworth, B. P., 39, 39n11
Bosworth, D., 188
Bourzac, K., 420n43
Bowen, H. K., 150
Bracha, A., 282, 286
Branstetter, L., 332
Bresnahan, T. F., 148, 300, 301, 519n1
Bridgman, B., 351, 391
Brown, C., 419n40
Brown, J. D., 128, 288
Brown, L., 122
Brynjolfsson, E., 11, 49, 50, 299, 300, 301,
    334, 334f, 340, 340f, 473, 496
Burke, M. A., 282, 286
Byrne, D. M., 3n3, 11n5, 12, 42, 46, 105,
    105n4, 423, 448, 448n88, 449, 449n90,
    449n91, 449n92, 450, 450n93, 450n99,
    451, 451n100, 452, 452n101, 454,
    454n106, 456, 458, 459, 461, 491, 494,
    497, 508, 513, 520, 521, 525, 533n15, 537,
    548, 549n24, 553n1, 554n1, 558n15

Cabral, L., 219n34
Campbell, D., 105n2
Campbell-Kelly, M., 526, 526n12
Cappellari, L., 307, 317
Card, D., 357
Carlaw, K. I., 299
Caroli, E., 301
Cartwright, D. W., 554n2, 555n3
Castaldi, C., 189
Cerquera, D., 302
Chen, W., 301, 382, 393n18
Chen, Y., 49
Chetty, R., 359
Christensen, K., 257
Christensen, L. R., 473n1, 477
Clark, K. B., 152
Cohany, S. R., 279
Cohen, R. B., 523, 524
Cohen, W. M., 61, 62, 65, 142, 143n2, 144,
    145, 152, 153, 155t, 158, 172, 173n23,
    173t, 174, 177, 177n28, 177n29, 177n30,
    178, 190
Cole, R., 554n2
Collis, A., 50, 473, 496
Cooper, R. W., 108
Copeland, A., 417n33, 492, 554n1
Corrado, C. A., 3n3, 4, 12, 24, 24n4, 35, 36t,

40, 40n13, 42, 127, 128, 232, 301, 303,
    325, 331, 331f, 347, 351, 375, 377, 387,
    391, 396, 397, 399, 437, 479, 481, 491, 494,
    497, 498, 513, 520, 521, 525, 548, 549n24,
    553n1, 554n1, 558n15
Coyle, D., 20n1, 520n3
Cranz, A., 460n120
Crépon, B., 179, 301, 303
Crespi, G., 301
Criscuolo, C., 105, 105n4, 301
Cummins, J. G., 391
Cunningham, C., 122, 408n9
Cutler, D. M., 39, 52
Cutress, I., 411n18, 442n75

Dahlin, K. B., 62n2, 77, 141
Dao, M., 373n1
Dauda, S., 52
David, P., 148, 151
Davis, J., 233
Davis, S. J., 105n3, 196n18
Decker, R., 105, 105n3, 106, 106n5, 110,
    110n9, 111, 111n10, 112n11, 113n12,
    114n13, 118, 120, 120n14, 201n24, 229,
    343
Dedrick, J., 375n5
De Haan, J., 437n70
de Jong, J. P. J., 61, 64, 64n3, 64n4, 70,
    72n16
De Loecker, J., 344, 360
De Man, A.-P., 189
Deming, W. E., 62
De Rassenfosse, G., 144
De Roure, D., 525
de Vries, G. J., 376, 377, 379
Dey, M., 286
Díaz-Pinés, A., 479
Dieseldorff, C., 448n87, 448n88
Diewert, W. E., 4
Dinlersoz, E., 128, 218n33
Dischinger, M., 374n3
Dolfen, P., 49
Doms, M., 437
Doraszelski, U., 300
Dorn, D., 327, 344
Draca, M., 301
Dreisigmeyer, D., 71
Drev, M., 332
Dube, A., 259
Duguet, E., 179, 301, 303
Dunn, A., 52

Dunne, T., 105n3
Duranton, G., 232
Dynan, K., 3n3

Earle, J. S., 128, 288
Eberts, R. W., 231
Economides, N., 190n9, 218n33
Eeckhout, J., 344, 360
Eggers, F., 50, 473, 496
Elliot, S., 526n11
Elsby, M. W., 346, 351, 373n1
Engelstätter, B., 302
Erickson, T., 537
Ericson, R., 107
Esmaeilzadeh, H. E., 413n25, 419n42

Fairlie, R. W., 82
Fanfalone, A. G., 479
Farooqui, S., 302
Farrell, D., 289
Faurel, L., 341
Fernald, J. G., 46, 105n4
Fink, C., 187, 188
Flamm, K., 406n4, 409n10, 410n15, 411n22, 420n46, 422n48, 422n49, 425n57, 445n78, 453n105
Fleming, L., 147n5, 232
Flikkema, M., 189
Flowers, S., 61, 64, 64n4, 70, 72n16
Fogarty, M. S., 231
Fogel, R. W., 52
Fontagné, L., 374, 377
Forbes, K., 335, 343
Forman, C. C., 302
Fort, T., 259, 374
Foster, L., 3n2, 105n2, 108, 120n14, 122, 124, 125, 126, 127, 128, 212n32, 259, 287n19
Franke, N., 64
Freeman, R. B., 233
Fuller, S., 413n26
Furman, J., 326, 337, 337f
Fuss, M. A., 481, 498

Gabaix, X., 354
Gal, P. N., 105, 105n4
Gambardella, A., 151
Gandal, N., 417n33
Garcia-Swartz, D. D., 526, 526n12
Gereffi, G., 375n5, 389, 396
Gerstein, M., 122

Gertler, M. S., 232
Giuri, P., 145
Glaeser, E. L., 229, 231, 232
Goedhart, M., 337f
Goldschlag, N., 123, 200n23, 234
Goldschmidt, D., 259, 359
Gonzales-Brambila, C., 231
Goodridge, P., 127
Goolsbee, A., 49
Goos, M., 344
Gordon, R. J., 33, 105, 299
Gort, M., 7, 104, 105, 106, 109, 110, 112, 114, 116, 117, 118, 119, 121, 123, 125
Gourio, F., 184n2, 218n33
Graham, S. J. H., 67, 67n5, 93, 123, 124, 185, 188n6, 193, 194, 195, 195n17, 212n31, 225n43, 238
Grance, T., 521, 522
Greenhalgh, C., 187, 187n5, 188, 189
Greenstein, S., 46, 519, 554n1
Greenwood, J., 495
Greig, F., 289
Griliches, Z., 4, 20, 39, 105n2, 122, 123, 128, 144, 300, 477n5
Grim, C., 122, 128, 212n32
Grimm, B. T, 556n6, 556n9
Groshen, E. L., 41, 43, 45, 46, 51, 557n13
Groves, R. M., 282
Gu, F., 4
Guvenen, F., 374
Guzman, J., 231

Hall, A., 52
Hall, B., 301, 303, 316, 327, 352, 441n73
Hall, B. H., 71, 78, 144, 300, 301, 351
Hall, J., 289
Halpin, P., 374n4
Haltiwanger, J., 3n2, 105n2, 105n3, 108, 108n7, 110, 111, 111n10, 112n11, 115f, 120n14, 127, 128, 195, 196n18, 233, 234, 259
Hammond, L. A., 272
Hamoudi, A., 289
Hanson, L. P., 399
Harris, S. D., 259
Harrison, A., 374, 377
Hart, M., 229, 231
Haskel, J., 4, 127, 301, 327, 343, 344, 356
Hathaway, I., 112n11
Hausman, J., 42, 232
Hausman, N., 231

Hayakawa, K., 129n20
Heath, D., 190
Heaton, J. C., 399
Hecker, D. E., 110, 234
Heining, J., 357
Henderson, R. M., 152
Hennessey, J., 413n26, 417n35, 456n110, 459n115, 459n116
Herrendorf, B., 377n6, 383n8
Hill, P., 26n5
Hipple, S. F., 272
Hitt, L. M., 300, 301
Ho, M. S., 299
Hobijn, B., 346, 351, 373n1
Hollander, S., 143
Holt, B., 410f
Hopenhayn, H., 107, 108
Hortacsu, A., 219n34
Hottman, C. J., 108
Houseman, S. N., 260, 282, 286
Hruska, J., 417n37
Hsieh, C.-T., 108, 108n7, 109n8, 128
Hu, Y., 49
Hubbard, P., 525n10
Hulten, C. R., 4, 20, 21n2, 23, 24, 24n4, 29n7, 34n10, 35, 36t, 40, 40n13, 52, 53, 54, 105n2, 127, 128, 232, 301, 303, 325, 331, 331f, 347, 375, 377, 387, 391, 396, 397, 399, 477n5, 481, 489
Hurst, E. G., 108, 124, 126, 258
Hyatt, H. R., 260

Ichniowski, C., 233

Jackson, E., 259, 293
Jaffe, A. B., 71, 144
Jäger, K., 481, 498
Jarmin, R. S., 105n3, 110, 196n18
Jaumandreu, J., 300
Javorcik, B. S., 187, 188
Jenkins, S. P., 307, 317
Jensen, M. B., 151
Jensen, P. H., 188
Jeon, G. Y., 49
Johnson, R., 377n6
Jona-Lasinio, C., 301
Jones, B. F., 73
Jones, C. I., 359
Jones, H., 417
Jorgenson, D. W., 4, 299, 393, 406n4, 473n1, 477

Jovanovic, B., 104n1, 107, 109n8, 299, 314
Juda, A., 232
Jung, T., 144, 177

Kalton, G., 153n9, 154
Kanter, D., 419n41
Kantor, S., 232
Kaplan, E., 259, 360
Kaplan, S., 356
Kaplinsky, R., 375n5
Karabarbounis, L., 346n4, 348, 351, 373, 373n1, 374, 381, 385n10, 390n14
Katz, L. F., 258, 270, 280, 281n15, 286, 327, 359
Kehrig, M., 129
Keilbach, M. C., 229, 231
Kerr, S. P., 231
Kerr, W. R., 127, 229, 231, 232
Khosa, V., 558n14, 563n18
Khurshid, A., 406n4
Kim, J., 73, 359
Kim, K., 147
Kim, Y. M., 49
King, I. I. I. C., 232
Klein, G. J., 302
Kleis, L., 302
Klenow, P. J., 42, 49, 108, 108n7, 109n8, 128
Klepper, S., 7, 104, 105, 106, 109, 110, 112, 114, 116, 117, 118, 119, 121, 123, 125, 158
Klette, T., 104n1
Klevorick, A. K., 145
Kline, P., 357
Knoll, B., 374n3
Koh, D., 348
Koh, Y., 149
Koller, T., 337f
Kopecky, K. A., 495
Kornai, J., 344
Kortum, S., 104n1
Koustas, D., 289
Kovak, B., 423
Kraemer, K. L., 375n5
Kretschmer, T., 302, 303, 306
Krizan, C. J., 3n2, 120n14, 259
Krueger, A. B., 258, 259, 270, 280, 281n15, 286, 289, 327, 359
Krzanich, B., 442n76, 446n880
Kubota, T., 149
Kulick, R., 108, 108n7
Kushida, K. E., 521, 524
Kwon, N., 332

Lafontaine, F., 232
Lancaster, K. J., 6, 20, 26
Landefeld, J. S., 374n4, 395, 473n1, 556n7
Landes, W., 184n1, 184n2, 190n9, 218n33
Landier, A., 354
Lane, J. I., 230, 232, 233, 234, 235
Lattard, L., 447n84
Lawson, S., 417n37
Lazear, E. P., 229, 231, 233
Leberstein, S., 275
Lee, K. M., 288
Lee, Y.-N., 143, 144, 174, 175n24, 177
Lehmann, E. E., 229, 231
Lenihan, H., 229, 231
Lentz, R., 104n1
Leontief, W., 379
Lerner, J., 352
Lev, B., 4
Levin, R. C., 143n2, 144, 145, 153
Levinthal, D. A., 152
Lewbel, A., 304
Li, G.-C., 144
Li, N., 399
Li, W. C., 351, 441n73
Liebman, J., 327, 352
Linden, G., 375n5, 419n40
Lipsey, R., 299
Lipsky, J., 419n41
Lobo, J., 147n5
Lombarkdi, B., 287
Longland, M., 188
Looney, A., 259, 293
Los, B., 376, 377, 379
Lotti, F., 301, 303
Love, I., 129n19
Lowe, R. A., 231
Lucas, R. E., Jr., 107, 108
Lüthje, C., 63
Lynch, L. M., 232, 301

Mace, C., 190
Mairesse, J., 179, 300, 301, 303, 316
Manfredi, T., 351
Manning, A., 344
Mansfield, E., 143
Manyika, J., 282n17
Marschke, G., 73
Marshall, A., 149
Marx, M., 232
McAfee, A., 299
McCann, D., 419n40

McCulla, S. H., 558n14, 563n18
McDevitt, R., 46, 554n1
McGee, M., 281
McGowan, J. J., 49
McGrattan, E. R., 385n10, 391
McGuirk, H., 229, 231
Melitz, M., 108, 111, 119
Mell, P., 521, 522
Merritt, R., 442n74
Merton, R. K., 149
Michaels, G., 344, 423
Milgrom, P., 303
Miller, R. E., 380n7
Millet, L., 413n26
Millot, V., 188
Miranda, J., 82, 105n3, 110, 112n11, 123, 200n23, 234
Miravete, E., 302, 303, 304, 306
Mishel, L., 353
Moammer, K., 411n17
Mohnen, P., 300, 301, 304, 316
Moore, G., 406n3, 407n6, 407n8
Moore, S., 442n74
Mortensen, D. T., 104n1
Moses, K. E., 41
Moulton, B. R., 3n3, 41, 557n11
Moyland, C. E., 556n10
Mueller, H., 333, 357
Muro, M., 562n16
Murphy, K. M., 52, 352
Murray, J., 521, 524

Nagaoka, S., 144, 145, 174, 175n24
Nakamura, L., 20, 21n2, 29n7, 50, 54, 331, 473, 491n15
Nanda, R., 127
Natraj, A., 344
Natrajan, S., 411n21
Neiman, B., 346n4, 348, 351, 373, 373n1, 374, 381, 385n10, 390n14
Nelson, R. R., 144, 145, 153
Neubig, T. S., 374n3
Nevo, A., 46
Nguyen, D., 520n3
Niebel, T., 301
No, Y., 174, 175n24
Noguera, G., 377n6
Noll, R. G., 49
Nordhaus, W. D., 25
Norman, P., 124, 125, 126, 287n19
Nosko, C., 436n69, 440n72

Oliner, S., 11n5, 105, 409n14, 417n33, 448, 448n88, 449, 449n90, 449n91, 449n92, 450, 450n99, 451, 451n100, 452, 452n101, 454, 454n106, 456, 458, 459, 461, 533n15, 537, 549n24, 553n1
Ono, Y., 287
Or-Bach, Z., 417n37
Orszag, P., 326, 337, 337f
Ouimet, P., 333, 357

Pakes, A., 107, 436n69, 440n72, 456n111, 537
Parker, R. P., 556n7, 556n9
Patinkin, D., 22n3
Patterson, D., 413n26, 417n35, 456n110, 459n115, 459n116
Paunov, C., 339, 341f, 345, 346f, 347f, 348f, 354, 354f, 355f, 356, 358f, 359, 366
Pavitt, K., 123
Peck, M. J., 49
Pernías, J., 302, 303, 304, 306
Perrin, A., 33n9
Perry, R., 526n11
Peters, R. H., 396
Petrin, A., 105n2, 495
Peytcheva, E., 282
Pieri, F., 301
Piketty, T., 323, 324, 345, 346f, 347f, 358f
Pillai, U., 416n29
Pirzada, U., 411n18
Plewes, T., 122
Polanec, S., 119, 136
Polder, M., 301, 302
Polderr, 303
Polivka, A. E., 264, 279, 286
Pollard, M., 280
Ponzetto, G. A. M., 229, 231, 232
Poschke, M., 346n4
Posner, R., 184n1, 184n2, 190n9, 218n33
Prennushi, G., 233
Prescott, E. C., 391
Prudhomme, M., 417n33
Puga, D., 232
Pugsley, B., 108, 124, 126, 258

Quan, T. W., 49

Raley, T., 416n32
Ramey, K., 558n14, 563n18
Ramey, V. A., 52, 53
Ramnath, S., 259, 293
Rauh, J., 356, 360

Redding, S. J., 49, 108
Regev, H., 105n2
Reijnders, L. S. M., 391n16
Reinsdorf, M. B., 46, 105n4
Reiss, S., 525n10
Reiter, J., 105n2
Restrepo, P., 344
Restuccia, D., 108
Rhodes-Kropf, M., 127
Riedel, N., 374n3
Riley, R., 301
Roach, M., 142
Robb, A., 127
Roberts, J., 303
Roberts, M. J., 105n3
Robinson, B. B., 556n10
Robles, B., 281
Rodriguez-Montemayor, E., 341f, 345, 346f, 347f, 348f, 354, 354f, 355f, 356, 358f, 359, 366
Roehrig, C., 54n22
Rogers, M., 188, 189
Rogerson, R., 107, 108, 377n6, 383n8
Rognlie, M., 373n1, 391, 392
Rogoway, M., 411n18, 442n75
Rollo, V., 339
Romalis, J., 390n15
Romer, P. M., 232
Rosen, S., 325, 334, 351
Rosenberg, J., 19, 48
Rosenberg, N., 148, 151
Rosso, D., 418n38, 423n53
Rotemberg, J. J., 481n8
Rothwell, P. M., 52
Rousseau, P. L., 299, 314
Rudanko, L., 184n2, 218n33
Rybalka, M., 301, 303

Saam, M., 301
Sabadish, N., 353
Sadun, R., 301
Saez, E., 323, 324, 345, 346f, 347f, 358f
Şahin, A., 346, 351, 373n1
Samuels, J., 50, 473, 491n15, 562n17
Samuelson, L., 105n3
Sandner, P., 188, 189
Santaeulàlia-Llopis, R., 348
Saunders, A, 11, 300, 473
Sauvagnat, J., 355
Sawyer, S., 424n54, 424n55, 450, 450nn94–97

Scarpetta, S., 108
Schautschick, P., 187, 187n5
Schmidt, E., 19, 48
Schmieder, J. F., 259, 359
Schuh, S., 105n3
Schumpeter, J., 140, 325
Seidel, T., 410n15
Serrano, C. J., 62n1
Seskin, E. P., 557n11
Shah, S., 63, 64
Shane, S., 147n5
Shapiro, M. D., 41
Shaw, K. L., 229, 231, 232, 233
Sheiner, L., 3n3
Shilov, A., 411n18, 442n75
Shuler, K., 417n37
Sichel, D. E., 3n3, 4, 7n4, 11n5, 24,
    39n11, 40, 48, 105, 105n4, 127, 128,
    232, 301, 303, 325, 331, 347, 375, 377,
    387, 391, 396, 397, 399, 409n14, 417n33,
    448, 448n88, 449, 449nn90–92, 450,
    450n93, 450n99, 451, 451n100, 452,
    452n101, 454, 454n106, 456, 458, 459,
    461, 508, 513, 533n15, 537, 549n24,
    553n1, 554n1
Simintzi, E., 333, 357
Singh, J., 232
Slemrod, J., 271, 272
Smith, M. D., 49
Smith, S., 446n79
Smith, S. D., 555n3
So, A., 424n54, 424n55, 450
Soloveichik, R., 50, 473, 491n15
Solow, R. M., 21
Song, J., 327, 357
Spear, S., 150
Spencer, W., 410n15
Spiezia, V., 302
Spletzer, J. R., 263n1
Stern, S., 231, 303, 306
Stiroh, K. J., 299, 301
Strumsky, D., 147n5
Sullivan, D. F., 557n11
Svensson, R., 144
Syverson, C., 3n2, 46, 49, 104, 105, 108,
    108n7, 127, 128, 231, 300n1

Tacsir, E., 302
Tadelis, S., 219n35
Tambe, P., 231
Taylor, L. A., 396

Taylor, S. K., 259
Teece, D. J., 148, 150
Thompson, P., 143
Timmer, M. P., 376, 377, 379, 381, 383, 388,
    389f, 391n16
Topel, R. H., 52
Tørsløv, T. R., 374n3
Train, K., 307, 317
Trajtenberg, M., 71, 78, 144, 148
Triplett, J. E., 39, 39n11, 434n67, 437n70,
    554n2, 555n5
Turner, J. L., 46

Ukhaneva, O., 479

Vahter, P., 301
Valentinyi, A., 377n6, 383n8
van Ark, B., 481, 498
van Dalen, J., 537n16
van Leeuwen, G., 302, 304
Van Long, N., 346n4
Van Reenen, J., 301, 344
Van Wagoner, J., 447n86
van Zeebroeck, N., 302
Varian, H., 30, 49, 50, 330, 333
Vecchi, M., 301
Venturini, F., 301
Visscher, M., 391
von Hippel, E., 7n4, 48, 61, 63, 64, 64n4, 70,
    72n16, 150, 151

Waldfogel, J., 49
Wallis, G., 127
Walsh, J. P., 61, 62, 65, 143, 144, 145, 150,
    153, 155t, 172, 173n23, 173t, 174, 175n24,
    177, 178
Webster, E., 188
Weinstein, D. E., 49, 108
Wessels, D., 337f
Westlake, S., 4, 327, 344
Whalley, A., 232
White, A. G., 42, 554n1
White, A. J., 417n33
White, T. K., 105n2
Wier, L. S., 374n3
Wilcox, D. W., 41
Williams, B., 480n6
Williams, J. W., 46
Williams, K., 49
Woodford, M., 481n8
Wulf, J., 352

Wunsch-Vincent, S., 374n3
Wykoff, F. C., 489

Yang, C., 447n83
Ye, X., 391n16
Yinug, F., 418n38, 423n53
Yoon, J., 147
Yorukoglu, M., 218n33
Yu, K., 417n33

Zhang, L., 539n19
Zheng, Y., 348
Zimmerman, M. M., 150
Zolas, N., 122, 212n32, 232
Zucman, G., 323, 324, 345, 346f, 347f, 358f,
    374n3
Zysman, J., 521, 524

Subject Index

Note: Page numbers followed by "f" or "t" refer to figures or tables, respectively.

Abramovitz, Moses, 2–3
access services prices, 499–503; indexes, 505–8, 506–7t; sources and methods for, 500–501t
accounting, innovation and, 10
administrative data: capturing, for work arrangements, 265–67; household innovations and, 62; reconciling, with household survey data, 272–78
Amazon Web Services (AWS), 527–33

Bureau of Economic Analysis (BEA), 12, 553–54; current work of, 557–58; current work of–communications equipment, 560, 566–70; current work of–electromedical equipment, 559–60, 566; current work of–software, 558–59, 563–66; future work of, 560–62. *See also* information and communications technology (ICT)
Bureau of Labor Statistics (BLS), 555; measurement program, 42–45
business entry, 103
Business R&D and Innovation Survey (BRDIS), 140
Business Register (BR; US Census Bureau), 195, 230

capital, intangible, measurement problems of, 40

capital formation, 23–24
capitalization of consumer digital goods approach, 473
Census Bureau surveys, 3
chip processor characteristics, 459–60
cloud computing, 12, 519–21; definitions of products of, 523; National Institute of Standards and Technology (NIST) definition, 521–22; prices, 526–44; products of, 522–25; size of, 544–49
cloud technologies, 525–26
communications equipment: BEA's current work and, 556–70, 560; price indexes for private fixed investment in, 570t; private fixed investment in, 568–69t
communications technology, consumer choices and, 6
competition, market, innovation and, 170–72
complexity, innovation and, 150
computer architectures, 428
Conference on Research in Income and Wealth (CRIW), 1–2; papers delivered in, 5–12
consumer choices: communications technology and, 6; GDP measurement and, 20–21
consumer content delivery, 475; GDP impacts of innovations in, 11–12; time line, 471–73, 472f

consumer digital capital use, 473–75, 474f
consumer durable spending, sources and
    methods for, 509–10t
Consumer Price Index (CPI), 43–45
consumer welfare, improvement in, 20
consumption benefits, direct, GDP and,
    25–27
consumption technology, 20–21; expanded
    GDP and, 27–30, 28f; GDP and, 26f, 27f
Contingent Worker Supplement (CWS),
    279–81
Coyle, Diane, 6
CPI (Consumer Price Index), 43–45
creative destruction, 104–5; digital innova-
    tion and, 325–26; impacts of digital inno-
    vation on, 339–43; lower entry barriers
    and, 327–28; lower entry costs for digital
    innovation and, 339–43
CRIW (Conference on Research in Income
    and Wealth), 1–2; papers delivered in,
    5–12
CWS (Contingent Worker Supplement),
    279–81

"dark silicon," 419
data centers, 524
demand complementarity, framework
    for, 475–82; definitions, 475–77; home
    services, 477–78; measurement, 482–93;
    network utilization, 480–81, 498–99;
    paid-for-services, 478–79; results and
    implications, 493–96; use intensity, 480
demographics, patent data and, 97–99
Dennard, Robert, 407n5
digital capital use, consumer, 473–75, 474f
digital device services, 475
digital economy, returns to capital and,
    344–46
digital goods, rapid uptake of, 33–34
digital innovation: creative destruction and,
    325–26; defined, 323–24; effects of, on
    income distribution, 343–44; evolution of
    top incomes and, 324–25; global trends
    in income distribution and, 328–29;
    impacts of, on innovation, market entry,
    and creative destruction, 339–43; impacts
    of, on market structures and income dis-
    tribution, 324f; income distribution and,
    10; lower entry costs for, and creative
    destruction, 339–43; measuring GDP
    and, 19–21; rents and, 335–39; research
    agenda, 360–61; risks and, 340–41. See

also innovation; semiconductor manufac-
    turing innovation
digital nonrivalry (DNR), 324–25; growing
    importance of, 330–32; implications of,
    for market concentration in global mar-
    kets, 333–35; market concentration on
    global markets and, 333–35
digital revolution, GDP and, 6
distance. See implementation gaps, innova-
    tion and
distribution of income. See income distri-
    bution
DNR. See digital nonrivalry (DNR)
DRAM (dynamic random access memory),
    407, 407n5

education, 52–53
electromedical equipment, BEA's current
    work and, 559–60, 566
Enterprising and Informal Work Activities
    (EIWA), 281–82
entrepreneurial firms, 229. See also start-ups
entry costs, for digital innovations, and cre-
    ative destruction, 339–43
executive compensation, rise of, 351–56;
    compensation of, 351–56
expanded gross domestic product (EGDP),
    21; consumption technology and, 27–30,
    28f; estimation of, 32–35; future for mea-
    surement of, 53–55
experience, worker, and firm growth, 232–33

FaaS (function as a service), defined, 523
factor income distribution, 376
factorless income, 373–74
financial accounting, innovation and, 10
firm growth: university research training
    and, 232; workers with experience and,
    232–33
function as a service (FaaS), 523

GDI (gross domestic income), circular flow
    of, 21–23, 23f
germ theory, 33
gig economy, 9; alternative information
    sources on nonemployee work, 286–90;
    background, 257–61; historical data,
    267–72; improving household measures
    of nonemployee work, 278–86; reconcil-
    ing household survey and administrative
    estimates of, 272–78; typology of work
    arrangements in, 261–67

global input-output tables, 376
global value chain (GVC) production, 373–75; factor income analysis of, 375; function, 10–11; residual approach to, 375
global value chains (GVCs): data sources for methodology, 381–82; empirical methodology for accounting in, 377–81; results, 382–92; robustness of findings, 392–95
gross domestic income (GDI), circular flow of, 21–23, 22f
gross domestic product (GDP): adequacy of procedures to measure, in twenty-first century, 19–21; circular flow of, 21–23, 22f; consumer choice and measurement of, 20–21; consumption technology and, 27–30; definition of, 4–5; diagrammatic exposition of innovation and, 24–25, 25f; digital revolution and, 6; direct consumption benefits and, 25–27; expanded measure of (EGDP), 6
growth accounting, critique of, 37–40
GVC. See global value chain (GVC) production

health care, 51; innovation in, 51–52
home services, 477–78
household innovations: background, 63–65; characteristics of patenting firms and, 79–84; citation counts for, 74–77; data, 65–68; generality index of, 78–79; impact of, 73–74; inventor demographics and, 68–70; radical patents for, 77–78; team size and, 72–73; technology classes and, 70–72; transition to employer status, 84; use of administrative data for examining, 62; value of, 85–87
household innovations, patented: data sources for analyzing, 65–68; impacts of, 73–79; inventor demographics and, 68–70, 69t; studies of, 63–65; technology classes and, 70–72, 71t, 72t, 73t; types of business associated with, 79–87
household inventors, 62–63
households, private, as sources of innovation, 61–62
household survey data: capturing, for work arrangements, 265–67; improving, of nonemployee work, 278–86; reconciling, with administrative data, 272–78
Hulten, Charles, 6
human capital, 229–30; analysis, 244–51; baseline results of, for start-up outcomes,

246–51; formalization of model for, 244–45; framework for study, 233–88; literature linking survival and growth of start-ups to, 231–32; measures of, 230; measures used for examining, 234–35. See also start-ups
hyperthreading, 428

IaaS (infrastructure as a service), defined, 522, 523
ICT. See information and communications technology (ICT)
ILBD (Integrated Longitudinal Business Database), 91–92, 196–97
imitability, innovation and, 150–51
impacts, of quality household innovations, 73–79
implementation gaps, innovation and, 148–49; new attribute-based suggestions for, 176–77
import price indexes, for PCs, 555
income, factorless, 373–74
income distribution: digital innovation and, 10; effects of digital innovation and, 343–44; global trends in digital innovation and, 328–29; impacts of digital innovation on, 324f; rents from digital innovation and, 327
income inequalities, 323
Industrial Revolution, 32–33
industry economic accounts (IEAs), 553
information: current treatment of, in statistical system, 47–48; nature and value of, 46–47
information and communications technology (ICT), 9–10, 12, 299–300, 554; data used for model, 308–11; estimation results of model, 311–16; further research for, 316–17; literature on, 300–302; model for, 302–8; overview of prices of, 554–57; R&D and, 300–301. See also Bureau of Economic Analysis (BEA)
infrastructure as a service (IaaS), 523
innovation, 25f; complexity and, 150; current approaches to measurement of, 143–45; data survey design, 152–54; defined, 2, 140; descriptive design, 155–59; developing indirect indicator for recent, introduction to, 103–7; diagrammatic exposition of, and GDP, 24–25; direct measures of, 122–25; effects of, on market structures, 325; estimates of, on consumption side

innovation (*continued*)
    of economy, 40–46; estimation of, 32–35; features of, 146–51; illustrating utility of measuring characteristics of, 167–74; imitability and, 150–51; impacts of digital innovation on, 339–43; implementation gaps and, 148–49; indirect approach to, 104; intangible capital and, 127–28; linking entry and, 125–27; market competition and, 170–72; measure interpretation, 161–67; measurement challenges, 121–22; measuring, 2–3; measuring and tracking, 7–8; multidimensional perspective of, 145–46; private households as sources of, 61–62; process, 140–41, 141f; replicability, 150–51; start-ups and, 231; "sticky" knowledge and, 150–51; suggestions for new attribute-based measures of, 174–79; technological significance of, 146–47; total factor productivity approach, 2–4; trademarks and, 186; uniqueness and, 149–50; utility and, 147–48. *See also* digital innovation; household innovations; semiconductor manufacturing innovation
innovation measures, suggestions for new attribute-based, 174–79
innovation process, 140–41, 141f
innovation surveys. *See* surveys, innovation
instructions per clock (IPC) tick, 459
intangible capital, innovation and, 127–1128
Integrated Longitudinal Business Database (ILBD), 91–92, 196–97
Intel, perspective of Moore's law of, 442–58
intellectual property, market capitalization and, 4
internet: measurement literature on contribution to welfare of, 48–51
invention: defined, 140; outside sources of, and innovation-level indicators of value, 172–74
inventor demographics, patented household innovations and, 68–70, 69t, 71t, 72t
inventors. *See* household inventors

knowledge, "sticky," 150–51
knowledge assets, 8
knowledge-intensive markets, rents and, 335–39

labor: compensation, 356–59; declining return to, 346–51; from digital innovation and income distribution, 327

Lister, Joseph, 33
Longitudinal Business Database, Integrated (ILBD), 91–92
Longitudinal Business Database (LBD), 7, 8, 109–12, 195–97, 230
Longitudinal Employer Household Dynamics (LEHD) data set, 8
LPR (measures of labor productivity), 107–9

Maddison, Angus, 32
market capitalization, intellectual property and, 4
market entry, impacts of digital innovation on, 339–43
market structures: effects of innovation on, 325; impacts of digital innovation on, 324f
maximum memory bandwidth, 427
measurement, literature and internet's contribution to welfare, 48–51
medical revolution, 33
MFP (multifactor productivity), 553
Moore, Gordon E., 403
Moore's law, 11, 403–6; clock rates and, 416–17; "dark silicon," limits on green and, 419; depreciation rates semiconductor R&D and, 441; end of faster speeds and, 416–17; end of rapid cost declines and, 417–19; end to smaller and, 420; Intel's perspective of, 442–58; manufacturing costs and, 440–41; personal computer replacement cycles and, 442; prices and, 420–40; semiconductor fab lifetimes and, 441–42; semiconductor manufacturing innovation facts and, 406–13; transistors and, 417. *See also* semiconductor manufacturing innovation
multifactor productivity (MFP), 553

Nakamura, Leonard L., 6
National Income and Product Accounts (NIPAs), 1, 553, 555–56
National Institute of Standards and Technology (NIST), definition of cloud computing, 521–22
network access services, 475
network utilization, 480–81, 498–99
nonemployee work arrangements: alternative sources of information on, 286–90; historical data on, 267–72. *See also* gig economy

Oslo Manual, 2, 2n1, 3, 139
output growth, sources of, 35–37
output saving innovation: information and product quality change as sources of, 30–31

PaaS (platform as a service), defined, 522–23, 523
paid-for services, 478–79
parallelization of software, 417
patent data: demographics and, 97–99; innovative process and, 144–45
patents: firm-assigned, 67–68; household innovation, 65–68
PCs. *See* personal computers (PCs)
perfect collinearity, 428
personal computers (PCs): import price indexes for, 555; price index for, 554–55; producer price indexes (PPIs) for, 555
platform as a service (PaaS), 523
price measures, obtaining, 3
prices, quality adjusted, measures of, 11
processor architecture, 427
processor performance equation, 459
producer price index (PPIs), for PCs, 555
productivity dispersion, 103; conceptual/measurement challenges for, 121–31; empirical evidence, 112–21; high vs. low frequency dispersion, 128–31; sources of measured, review of, 107–9
productivity distribution, 105
productivity growth, 103, 112–21; conceptual/measurement challenges for, 121–31
product quality change, estimates of, 41–42

quality change, 31–32; product, estimates of, 41–42
quality measurement, bias in, 45–46
Quality of Worklife (QWL) supplement, 279

Rand-Princeton Contingent Work Survey (RPCWS), 280–81
R&D expenditures, innovative process and, 143–44
rents: digital innovation and, 335–39; from digital innovation and income distribution, 327; in global knowledge-intensive markets, 335–39
replicability: innovation and, 150–51; new attribute-based suggestions for, 177–78
residential income, "yeast" perspective on, 391

resource cost, 26–27
returns to capital, 337; digital economy and, 344–46
returns to labor, declining, 346–51
risks, digital innovation and, 340–41
RPCWS (Rand-Princeton Contingent Work Survey), 280–81

SaaS (software as a service), defined, 523, 524–25
schooling industry, 52–53
semiconductor manufacturing innovation: benefits from, 413–516; Moore's law and, 406–13. *See also* digital innovation; innovation; Moore's law
serverless, defined, 523
service sector, economic measurement and, 29
single manufacturing technology platform, 403
64-bit architecture, 427
social mobility opportunities, 359–60
software, BEA's current work and, 558–59, 563–66
software as a service (SaaS), 523
Startup Firm History File, 23–33, 230
start-ups, 229; basic facts about, 238–42; datasets on, 230; facts about human capital composition of, 242–44; framework for examining, 233; identifying/classifying, 233–34; innovations and, 231; outcomes for, 237–38, 242–44. *See also* human capital
start-up worker history file, 235–37, 236f
"sticky" knowledge, 150–51
Survey of Household Economics and Decisionmaking (SHED), 282
surveys, innovation, 145; descriptive statistics, 155–59, 155t, 156t, 157t; design, 153–54; measure construction for, 159–61; measure interpretation for, 161–67

TDP (thermal design power), 427, 434
team size, patented household innovations and, 66f, 72–73
technological significance, innovation, 146–47; new attribute-based suggestions for, 174–76
technology classes, patented household innovations and, 70–72, 100t
TFPQ (measures of technical efficiency), 107–9

TFPR (revenue measures of total factor productivity), 107–9
thermal design power (TDP), 427, 434
time cost, analysis of value and, 49
total factor productivity (TFP), 2–3; residual, as measure of ignorance, 38
Toyota Production System, 150
Trademark Case Files Dataset (TCFD), 8, 185, 193, 196–97; data construction, 219–26
trademarking, 8
trademarks: analysis of, 197–99; constructing new dataset for, 185; data used for study, 192–97; empirical analysis of, 184–85; firm characteristics filing for, 200–205; firm growth and, 206–12; firm innovation and, 186; firm intensity and, 205–6; innovation activity and, 212–17; literature on, 186–90; obstacle to empirical analysis of, 184–85; prior literature, 186–90; success of firms and, 185–86; theory and, 183–84, 190–92; trends in filings for, 199–200

uniqueness: innovation and, 149–50; replicability vs., 177–78
United States, income inequalities in, 323

United States Patent and Trademark Office (USPTO), 185. *See also* Trademark Case Files Dataset (TCFD)
USPTO patent data, 88–91
utility: augmenting, 21; innovation and, 147–48

value: innovation-level indicators of, and outside sources of invention, 172–74; time cost and analysis of, 49
value added, measuring, 3–4
virtualization, 427
von Hippel, Eric, 7

welfare: increases in, 33; measurement literature and internet's contribution to, 48–51
"winner-take-all" dynamics, 325–27
work arrangements, in gig economy: capturing, in household and administrative data, 265–67; characteristics of, 261–65; historical data on nonemployee, 267–72; typology, 261–67

"yeast" perspective, on residential income, 391

zero prices, 49–50